Lotus Notes 4.5 Administrator's Guide

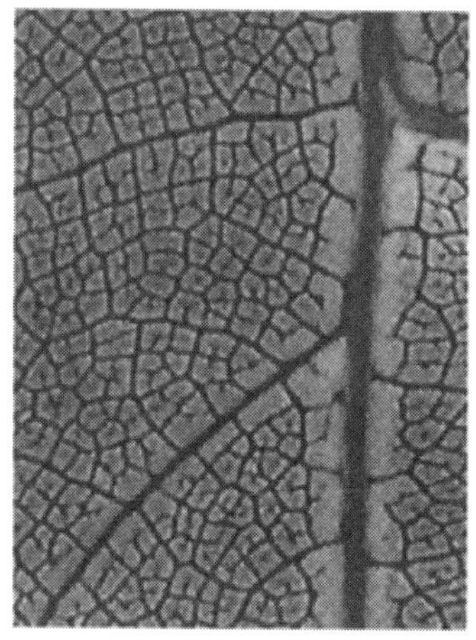

Lotus® Notes® 4.5 Administrator's Guide

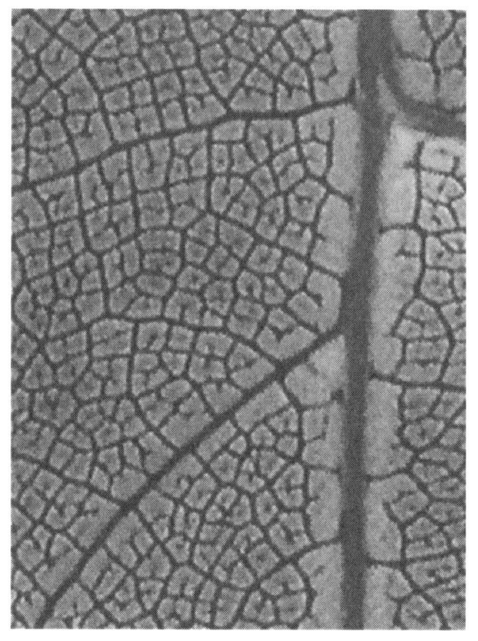

Bret Swedeen

San Francisco • Paris • Dusseldorf • Soest

Associate Publisher: Guy Hart-Davis
Acquisitions Manager: Kristine Plachy
Acquisitions & Developmental Editor: Neil Edde
Editor: Shelby Zimmerman
Technical Editors: Judith Miele, Chris Kirby
Book Designer: London Road Design
Graphic Illustrator: Inbar Berman
Electronic Publishing Specialist: Bill Gibson
Production Coordinator: Grey B. Magauran
Indexer: Matthew Spence
Cover Designer: Archer Design
Cover Illustrator/Photographer: FPG International

Screen reproductions produced with Collage Collage Complete.
Collage Complete is a trademark of Inner Media Inc.

Library of Congress Card Number: 97-65123
ISBN: 0-7821-1841-0

Manufactured in the United States of America

10 9 8 7 6 5 4 3 2

This book is dedicated to my wife, Suzanne. Thanks for the never ending support and for putting up with all the nonsense.

Acknowledgments

When I started writing this book I had no idea what I was in for. Initially I thought writing a book would be similar to writing an article for a magazine, except much longer. Wow, was I wrong! This book was more of an effort than I ever imagined. And between a full time job, a family with two daughters, the Extreme Summer Games on ESPN 2 followed by the Summer Olympics, a Presidential election, and the New England Patriots going to the Super Bowl it's amazing I ever got a single chapter finished. However, it did get done. And through all the difficulties (or at least perceived difficulties) several people were instrumental in helping this book finally come together, and now it's time to say thanks.

I would like to start by thanking Neil Edde for getting this project off the ground by saying, "Hey, do you want to write a book?" Thanks also to Shelby Zimmerman for her excellent job making me sound like I actually have a command of the English language. A big thank you to the technical editors, Judith Miele and Chris Kirby; and an extra thanks to Judy for her additional contributions.

I would also like to say thanks to the electronic publishing specialist, Bill Gibson, the production coordinator, Grey Magauran, the associate publisher, Guy Hart-Davis, and the indexer, Matthew Spence. These are the people who worked thanklessly behind the scenes. Although my direct contact with these people was limited, I owe them a tremendous amount of thanks nonetheless.

Aside from the people directly involved with the book, there were numerous people around me who provided support and encouragement along the way. Thanks to my wonderful wife and friend Suzanne, and my parents, Jim Murphy and Pankaj Srivastava.

Finally, special thanks to David Kodama from Advisor Publication for publishing my first article about Lotus Notes. Thanks David; I promise I'll start submitting articles now that I'm done with the book. I'd also like to thank Mac Rubel for answering my out-of-the-blue e-mail looking for advice about writing a book. Well Mac, I finally did it!

Contents at a Glance

Introduction		*xvii*
Chapter 1	An Introduction to Lotus Notes	1
Chapter 2	Notes Network Planning and Roll-Out	13
Chapter 3	Notes Release 3 to Release 4 Migration	43
Chapter 4	Notes Server Management	69
Chapter 5	User Management	123
Chapter 6	Database Management	165
Chapter 7	Notes Security	221
Chapter 8	Replication	267
Chapter 9	Notes Mail	323
Chapter 10	Notes Calendaring and Scheduling	371
Chapter 11	Notes Web Navigator	417
Chapter 12	The Notes Domino Server	451
Appendix A	Lotus Notes Certification	475
Appendix B	Notes Documents	487
Appendix C	Server Console Commands	497
Appendix D	The NOTES.INI File	507
Appendix E	Notes Add-On Products	551
Appendix F	Administrator's Resource Guide	559
Index		*569*

Table of Contents

Introduction *xvii*

Chapter 1 **An Introduction to Lotus Notes** **1**

The Elements of Notes 3
The Notes Client 3
The Notes Server 4
Notes Administration 5
What's New to Notes 4.5 7
Where Notes Is Heading 9
Where Notes Has Been 9
Summary 11

Chapter 2 **Notes Network Planning and Roll-Out** **13**

Defining the Business Purpose for Notes 15
Selecting the Notes Network Topology 17
The Importance of Topologies 22
Creating a Notes Standards Document 24
Selecting the Notes Server Platform 26
Available Server Platforms 26
UNIX (HP/UX, IBM AIX, Sun Solaris) 29
NotesBench 32
Selecting the Appropriate Notes Client Platform 34
Creating the Notes Roll-Out Plan 37
How Much Time Should You Allocate for the Roll-Out? 37
Who Will Build the Notes Infrastructure? 39
Who Will Get Notes First? 40
Who Will Train the End-User Community? 40
What Notes Feature Will This Roll-Out Focus On? 41
Who Will Support the Notes Infrastructure and End-Users? 41
Summary 42

Chapter 3 **Notes Release 3 to Release 4 Migration** **43**

Planning for Migration 44
- Evaluating the New Release 45
- Inventory the Current Environment 47
- Creating a Migration Team 47
- Creating a Test Environment 48
- Training the Technical Support Organization 49
- Creating the Migration Plan 50

Implementing Your Migration Plan 50
- Migration Rehearsal 51
- Server Migration 52
- End-User Training 57
- Workstation Migration 57
- Mail Migration 59
- Database and Application Migration 65

Post Migration Activities 66
- Migration Team Debriefing 66
- Updating Your Notes Standards Document 67

Summary 67

Chapter 4 **Notes Server Management** **69**

Installing Your First Server 70
- Advanced Server Setup Options 74
- Optional Server Setup Steps 77
- Starting the Notes Server 80

Creating Organizational Unit Certifiers 84

Installing Additional Servers 87
- Registering the New Server 87
- Installing the Server Software 90
- Setting Up the New Server 90

Server Disaster Planning 93
- Database Failure 93
- Hard Drive Crash 94
- Motherboard and Other Computer Card Failure 95
- External Power Failure 96

Notes Clusters 96
The Disaster Plan Document 97
Server Disaster Prevention 98
The Notes Log 98
Events Monitoring 101
Statistics Reporting 109
The Administration Process 112
The Agent Manager 118
Summary 121

Chapter 5 User Management 123

Creating Users 125
Registering Users One at a Time 125
Creating a User 127
Registering Several Users at Once 135
Setting Up a Notes Client 147
Installing the Notes Client Software 147
Other User Management Tasks 153
Renaming a User 153
Moving a User in the Hierarchical Naming Scheme 156
Moving a User's Mail Database to a New Server 159
Deleting a User from Your Notes Network 161
Summary 163

Chapter 6 Database Management 165

Rolling Out a New Database 166
Copying the New Database to a Notes Server 167
Setting the Maximum Database Size Limit 170
Setting the Access Control List 173
Replicating a Database to All Servers 176
Replicating the Design Template to All Servers 177
Distributing Encryption Keys 177
Creating a Mail-In Database Document 182
Including the New Database in the Database Catalog 183
Notify Users That There Is a New Database to Use 185

Maintaining Database Integrity 187
Creating and Maintaining Full Text Indexes 188
Updating a Database Design 195
Running a Database Analysis 199
Locating Missing Response Documents 205
Monitoring Database Activity 206
Managing Database Size 208
Moving Databases 209
Repairing Corrupted Databases 211
Troubleshooting Database Performance 215
Removing a Database 217
Summary 219

Chapter 7 Notes Security 221

Server Access 223
Validation and Authentication 224
Controlling Server Access 226
Execution Control List 232
Access Control List 239
The Access Control List Basics Section 242
The Access Control List Roles Section 244
The Access Control List Log Section 246
The Access Control List Advanced Section 247
Form, View, Folder, Section, and Field-Level Access Control 251
Form Access Control 251
View Access Control 254
Folder Access Control 256
Section Access Control 258
Field Access Control 258
Access Is Like a Filter 259
Quick Security Quiz 260
Access Roles for the Public Address Book 262
Notes Encryption 264
Summary 266

Chapter 8 Replication 267

How Replication Works 268
Replication between Servers 269
Replication between a Workstation and a Server 272
What Gets Replicated? 272
Planning for Replication 276
Determining Which Databases to Replicate 276
Replication Topology Options 277
Creating New Replica Copies 281
Replica Copies versus Regular Copies 283
Initiating Replication 285
Using Multiple Replicators 295
Controlling What Gets Replicated 298
The Access Control List and Replication 298
How the Access Control List Affects Replication 299
Determining What Gets Replicated 300
Replication Settings Scenarios 305
Monitoring Replication 307
Tools for Monitoring Replication 308
Establishing a Replication Monitoring Routine 312
Basic Replication Troubleshooting 313
When Replication Just Isn't Happening 313
Common Replication Error Messages 314
Personal Replication Experiences 315
Important NOTES.INI Replication Settings 318
Summary 321

Chapter 9 Notes Mail 323

The Fundamentals of Notes Mail 325
Notes Mail Components 325
How Notes Mail Gets Delivered 326
Setting Up Notes Mail 330
Notes Network Topology and Mail 331
The Server Connection Document 337

Mail Routing 339
Routing Mail within the Same Notes Named Network 339
Routing Mail between Different Notes Named Networks 340
Mail Routing between Adjacent Domains 346
Mail Routing between Non-Adjacent Domains 349
Connecting with Foreign Domains 354
Multi-Threaded Mail Routing 357
Controlling Mail Routing 358
Options to Prevent Mail Routing 359
Mail Routing and Priority Levels 360
Shared Mail 361
Enabling Shared Mail 361
Security Considerations for Shared Mail 362
Creating a New Shared Mail Database 363
Shared Mail Maintenance 364
When to Use Shared Mail 366
Troubleshooting Mail Problems 366
Running a Trace to Troubleshoot Mail Delivery Problems 367
Summary 370

Chapter 10 Notes Calendaring and Scheduling 371

How Calendaring and Scheduling Works 373
Making Sure Calendaring and Scheduling Is Running 374
Setting Up Calendaring and Scheduling 375
The Resource Reservations Database 375
Setting Up Users for Calendaring and Scheduling 379
The Calendar Profile 379
The Delegation Profile 384
Should You Train Users to Configure Their Own Profiles? 387
Basic Features of Calendaring and Scheduling 387
The Calendar View 387
To Do View 392
Meetings View 395
Using Calendaring and Scheduling 395
Navigating through the Calendar View 396

Responding to Meeting Notices 410
Not Responding to Meeting Notices 413
Troubleshooting 415
Summary 416

Chapter 11 Notes Web Navigator 417

The Server-Based Web Navigator 419
Web Navigator Setup in the Server Document 419
Specifying the Location of the InterNotes Server 423
The Web Server 424
Managing the Web Retriever Database 426
Setting the Access Control List for the Web Navigator Database 426
The Web Navigator Administration Document 427
The Workstation-Based Web Navigator 433
Creating the Personal Web Navigator 433
Internet Options 433
Editing the Location Document 438
Using the Personal Web Navigator 442
Using the Personal Web Navigator Database 442
Agents for the Workstation-Based Personal Web Navigator 446
Importing Bookmarks 448
Creating Web Tours 448
Troubleshooting 449
Summary 450

Chapter 12 The Notes Domino Server 451

Introduction to Domino 453
How Domino Works 453
Setting Up Domino 454
Selecting Your Domino Server 454
Basic Database ACL Settings 454
Configuring Domino 455
Running Domino 463
Multiple Web Sites with Domino 463

Domino Security 467
- Anonymous Access 468
- Registered Users 468
- Database Security 469
- Advanced Security with Secure Sockets Layer 469

Domino Activity Logging 472
- Setting Up Logging for Domino 472

Summary 474

Appendix A Lotus Notes Certification 475

Certified Lotus Professional Program 477
- Certification Options and Examinations 477
- Certification Preparation 480
- When You're Ready to Take the Exam 481
- The Benefits of Certification 482
- Recertification for Notes 3 Professionals 482
- Further Certification Information 485

Appendix B Notes Documents 487

- The Certifier Document 488
- The Connection Document 489
- The Domain Document 489
- The Group Document 490
- The Location Document 491
- The Mail-In Database Document 491
- The Person Document 492
- The Program Document 492
- The Resource Document 492
- The Server Document 493
- The Server Configuration Document 494
- The User Setup Profile Document 495

Appendix C Server Console Commands 497

Entering Server Console Commands from the Notes Client 498

Entering Server Console Commands at the Server Console 501

Appendix D **The NOTES.INI File** **507**

How to Edit the NOTES.INI File 508
Location of the NOTES.INI File 511
NOTES.INI Settings 511

Appendix E **Notes Add-On Products** **551**

ReCor Network-Based Training Solutions 552
Registration/Exchange 553
Remark! MessageCenter 554
Lotus Notes Fax Server 554
DocWatch 555
IntelliWatch 555
RemoteWare Essentials 556
V-Bridge NT for Notes 556
Open File Manager 557

Appendix F **Administrator's Resource Guide** **559**

Getting Help from Lotus 560
Information on the Web 561
The Notes List Server 562
Subscribing to the Notes List Server 563
Unsubscribing to the Notes List Server 563
Sending a Message to the Notes List Server 563
Other List Server Commands 564
Notes-Related Usenet Newsgroups 565
Notes Information on CompuServe 566
Notes-Specific Books 566
Notes-Specific Magazines 567

Index 569

Introduction

If you plan to administer a Notes network in the near future, you're probably wondering how to get started. The goal of this book is to help those new or semi-new Notes administrators get their start in the wonderful world of groupware à la Lotus Notes.

I don't claim to have all of the answers (God knows I wish I did). And this book is not the only book you'll ever need for successful Notes administration. However, for the first time Notes administrator, the essentials of Notes server setup and user creation are covered. For the more advanced Notes administrator, the finer points of replication, mail routing, calendaring and scheduling, and Domino are also covered. Regardless of your level of Notes experience, this book will certainly help you get started and provide greater insight into the primary aspects of Lotus Notes administration.

Who Should Read This Book?

If you're new to Notes administration but not new to computer systems administration in general, then this book is for you. If you've been doing Notes administration for awhile but still don't feel very comfortable doing what you do, this book is also for you.

To truly benefit from this book you should have a working knowledge of the following topics:

- Basic network connectivity
- What systems administrators are suppose to do

It also helps if you have some knowledge of NetWare, NT, OS/2, or UNIX but this is not required.

If what I've just listed has you scratching your head, you might not be ready for Notes administration or this book. Instead, you might want to explore some introductory books about computer networks before reading this book. If you have a basic working knowledge of the items presented and Notes administration is something you're involved in or want to get involved in, then you've come to the right place.

How This Book Is Organized

Everything presented in this book falls into one of two categories: how to get started with Lotus Notes or the components of Notes administration.

The fundamentals of how to get started with Notes are addressed in the first few chapters. These chapters provide an introduction to Lotus Notes, discuss how to set up your first Notes network, and cover migrating from Notes Release 3 to Notes Release 4.

Later chapters provide detailed coverage of the components of Notes administration. Among the topics addressed are the major aspects of Notes administration, starting with server management, user management, and registering and installing new users. There is also information about maintaining your Notes databases and the various aspects of Notes security, coverage on the elusive topic of replication, and a thorough presentation about one of the most used features of Notes that gives groupware its flexibility: Notes Mail. And finally, there is an introduction to the newest features of Notes: calendaring and scheduling, the Notes Web Navigator, and the exciting new feature, Domino.

The appendixes at the end of the book provide some useful information that can be divided into three categories: the next step for Notes administrators, administrative references, and additional resources for administrative tools and information.

If you're currently a Notes administrator and would like to take your administrative skills to the next level, consider getting involved with the Lotus Certified Lotus Professional (Lotus CLP) program. Details about this program are found in Appendix A. Before taking part in the Lotus CLP program, you should have a solid understanding of the important documents found in the Public Address Book (Appendix B), server console commands (Appendix C), and the various settings in the NOTES.INI file (Appendix D). Regardless of whether or not you pursue Lotus CLP status, you'll undoubtedly be interested in additional Notes administration tools (Appendix E) and other sources of Notes information (Appendix F).

Conventions Used in This Book

Throughout the book you'll encounter Notes, Tips, and Warnings. These highlight important points that a Notes administrator should or may need to know. A Note presents a point of interest or importance. A Tip is usually a better way to do something. And a Warning is something to watch out for.

Aside from the Notes, Tips, and Warnings, I've also added personal experiences and hypothetical scenarios whenever possible. These real life, personal experiences and hypothetical scenarios are intended to clarify a point or topic by placing it in a real-world context.

A Note from the Author

Lotus has recently changed the names of their products from Notes server and Notes client to Domino and Notes, respectively. The new names, while good from a marketing perspective, might be a bit confusing to anyone who has an awareness of Notes that dates back to before Release 4.5. Domino was originally introduced in 1996 as a Notes server task, and most people in the industry still think of Domino in that sense. Therefore, to avoid confusion between Domino the server task and Domino the new name for the Notes server I have used the original names: Notes server and Notes client. When you see the word Domino in this book, it is referring to the server task and not the Notes server as a whole.

No matter how the computer industry refers to Notes, Notes is still as great as it ever was and continues to get better and more exciting with each new release. I've been working with Notes and enjoying doing so since Release 2. I got my start with Notes by providing technical phone support to Notes administrators and developers. From there, my involvement with Notes took off like a rocket. I've done a tremendous amount of Notes administration, Notes consulting, and Notes development. Currently, I'm focused on what I like to call "proactive Notes consulting." I don't just tell people what to do and how to do it with Notes; I get right in there and do it with them. And when I'm not working with Notes, I'm writing about it in magazine articles for various industry magazines.

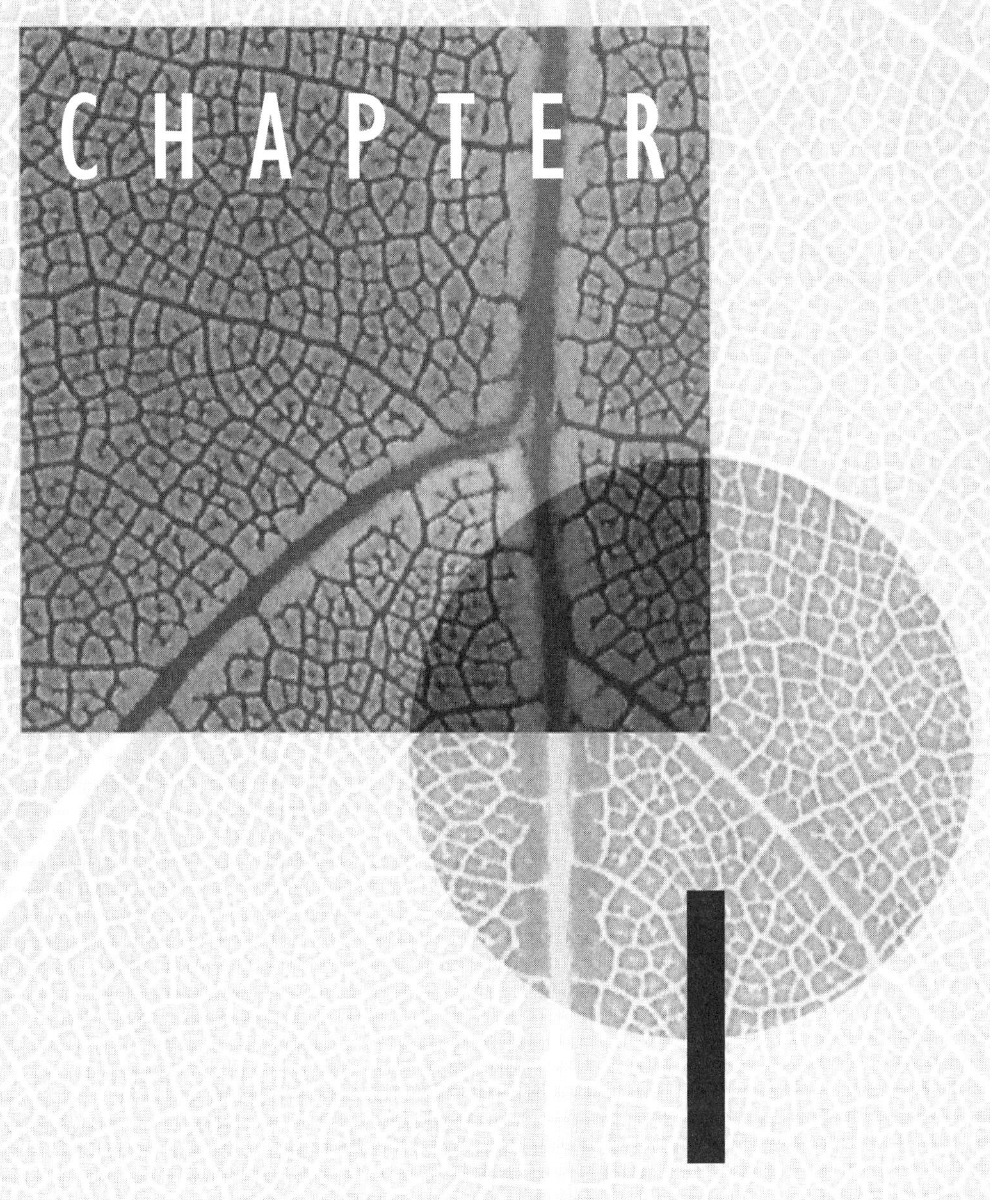

An Introduction to Lotus Notes

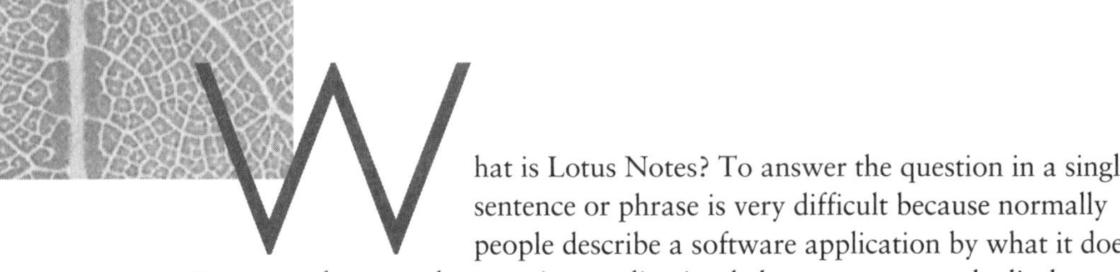

What is Lotus Notes? To answer the question in a single sentence or phrase is very difficult because normally people describe a software application by what it does. For example, a word processing application helps you create and edit documents such as interoffice memos or personal correspondence. A spreadsheet application helps make complicated calculations easy to perform and maintain, and is often used to create financial reports or organize and track budgets.

Although, Lotus Notes cannot be described completely in the same task-oriented manner, it is a good place to start. Notes has a number of built-in features that do perform certain tasks. Such features include e-mail (Chapter 9), group scheduling (Chapter 10), and a multi-user platform and versatile environment for custom application development. Each of these features is defined as follows:

- **E-mail:** Notes' built-in e-mail capabilities help people communicate quickly and can be used to extend the functionality of a simple database by making it "mail-enabled." For example, a new document entry in a Notes database can trigger one or more e-mail messages informing the appropriate people that a piece of information or a request has been added to a particular database. No longer do people need to communicate changes, requests, or new information through phone calls or interoffice memos.

- **Group Scheduling:** Another built-in feature is group scheduling. This feature works in conjunction with the built-in calendaring functionality and allows people to make more effective use of their time. With group scheduling, meetings no longer have to be manually coordinated. Now anyone can schedule a meeting and let Notes' Free Time search engine locate available resources and free time that works for everyone invited.

- **Custom Application Development:** The icing on the cake for Lotus Notes is its multi-user platform and environment for custom application development. Possible applications (sometimes also referred to as databases) include virtual discussion groups, where several topical discussions can happen simultaneously. A tracking application is another example of a common application developed using Notes. This type of application usually makes it easy for several different individuals to follow information that progresses through a series of statuses and states.

E-mail, group scheduling, and the multi-user platform and environment for custom application development are features of Lotus Notes that do help describe the product. However, if you understand Notes only for these features, then you're missing a lot of Notes' best capabilities. Notes combines all of the previously mentioned features into a single environment and places the usage emphasis on the group rather than on the individual.

Word processors and spreadsheet applications are intended for individual use. Notes, however, is aimed at group use. E-mail helps groups of people communicate more effectively. Group scheduling helps groups of people coordinate their time more effectively. And the custom application development environment helps developers build applications that help groups of people collaborate more effectively. In a nutshell, Notes enables groups to work together more effectively.

The Elements of Notes

Work more effectively by using group communication, coordination, and collaboration? To some people that may sound like a lot of marketing mumbo jumbo. The fact is that I often cringe when I hear myself explaining Notes in that manner, but the description, in my opinion, is an accurate explanation of the functional benefit of Notes. After all, Notes is not just a great software achievement; it's a flexible product aimed at delivering unique solutions to today's business problems. However, the marketing mumbo jumbo becomes easier to believe when you have a better understanding of the basic elements of Lotus Notes: The Notes client and the Notes server.

The Notes Client

The Notes client is a graphical front-end application through which users interact with the Notes environment, and Notes administrators administer that environment. Notes administrators are also often responsible for installing the Notes client at the desktop and therefore need an intimate understanding of the features and functionality of the client. Administrators will be expected to quickly and confidently troubleshoot connection and operational problems under the watchful eye of the end-user, as well as answer typical "how do I..." and "why can't I..." questions. If administrators appear as if they don't know what they are doing, it could result in a negative feeling about Notes on the part of the end-user.

Notes administrators: Make sure you take the time to play around with the Notes client and discover where things are and how things work. Don't just focus on the Notes server side of things because end-users usually don't appreciate that knowledge and would rather that you know how to quickly resolve a printing problem or something similar.

The Notes Server

The Notes server, on the other hand, makes up the core of the Notes environment by acting as a central repository for Notes applications and communications features.

Notes Applications

Notes applications can be something very simple such as a discussion database, or something as complex as an order entry/tracking application. Applications are stored on a Notes server and made available to individual users or groups of users. The availability of a particular database is controlled through the applications ACL (Access Control List).

Notes Communications

The communications controlled and managed by the Notes server are basic user connection support, the routing and delivery of electronic mail messages, and the dissemination of information through replication—which is a process of database synchronization. The Notes administrator must keep his or her finger on the pulse of Notes communications to ensure connectivity for users, reliable replication, and mail-routing between Notes servers. If the Notes communication breaks down and a Notes server becomes unreachable, either mail doesn't get delivered, or replication fails and databases become out of sync; then the perception in the user community is that the network is down, which can create some very unhappy users.

The Difference between Notes Servers and Operating Systems

One point of confusion that people often have with Lotus Notes is the server component of the product. People with networking backgrounds often think about servers as a self-supporting entity. A network server typically relies on nothing other than the physical hardware to do what it does. Network servers such as NetWare or NT manage every aspect of hardware interaction that a traditional computer operating system performs because these network servers are the actual operating system. The Notes server, however, is called a server but it is not a network operating system.

Notes relies on an operating system to provide hardware interaction and connection support over local area networks or remote dial-in. If you have any experience with database servers such as Microsoft SQL Server, then you know that even though Microsoft SQL Server is called a "server" and people log into it to use its resources, it still requires the NT operating system to run. Lotus Notes is much the same as a database server in that it requires an operating system to help perform its server functions.

Notes Administration

As a current (or soon to be current) Notes administrator, your primary concern is with the Notes server. Either by using the Notes client as an administrative interface, or by entering commands at the Notes server console (see the sidebar *The Notes Server Console*) and directly editing the NOTES.INI file, you'll be performing administrative tasks similar to those associated with other servers. Similar to a NetWare environment, you'll manage the following items:

- User accounts
- User and server groups
- Basic connectivity
- System backups
- Server maintenance and performance tuning

Unlike a NetWare or NT server environment, but much more like a database server environment, you'll also manage the databases on your servers, which entails using some of the following tools:

- FIXUP to repair corruption
- COMPACT to remove database white space
- UPDALL to update database indexes

The Notes Server Console

The Notes server console is accessible through a text-based window (see Figure 1.1) that resembles a DOS command prompt window—which you may be familiar with from Windows, Windows NT, or OS/2. Server activity is listed in this window and scrolls by as more activity occurs. As you view this box, you can watch users connect and disconnect, mail messages get transferred, and replications start and stop. All of the server activity is shown in this window and recorded in the server's Notes log (covered in Chapter 4). At the server console, you can type certain commands that initiate replication, show all server tasks, and show communication port status—just to name a few. (Appendix B provides a complete listing and description of all available console commands.) You also have the ability to type these very same commands through a remote server console interface available in the Notes client.

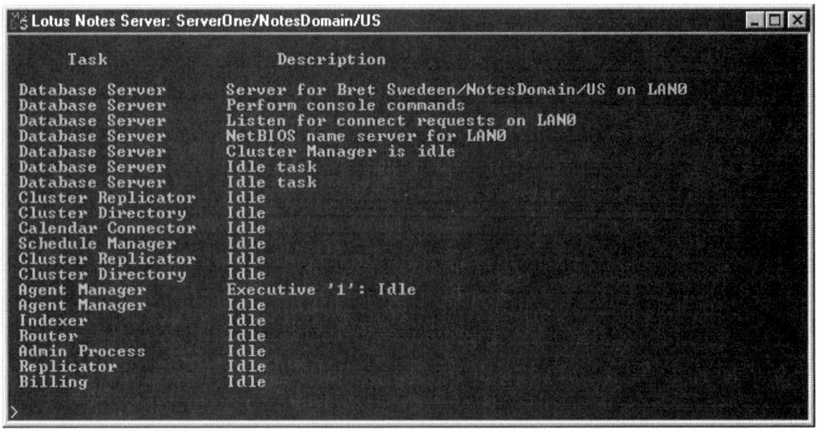

```
Lotus Notes Server: ServerOne/NotesDomain/US

     Task                    Description

Database Server         Server for Bret Swedeen/NotesDomain/US on LAN0
Database Server         Perform console commands
Database Server         Listen for connect requests on LAN0
Database Server         NetBIOS name server for LAN0
Database Server         Cluster Manager is idle
Database Server         Idle task
Database Server         Idle task
Cluster Replicator      Idle
Cluster Directory       Idle
Calendar Connector      Idle
Schedule Manager        Idle
Cluster Replicator      Idle
Cluster Directory       Idle
Agent Manager           Executive '1': Idle
Agent Manager           Idle
Indexer                 Idle
Router                  Idle
Admin Process           Idle
Replicator              Idle
Billing                 Idle
>
```

FIGURE 1.1
The Notes server console appears much like a command prompt window under Windows NT and OS/2.

Besides your database administrator role, you're also the e-mail administrator managing the Notes Mail environment and making sure that messages get delivered and foreign mail gateways or MTAs (Message Transfer Agents) keep running.

E-mail, database, and basic server management—is there more? Yes; you'll also maintain security by manipulating the Notes client's ECL (Execution Control List) to control what type of programs and files can run and exactly what those programs and files can do. You'll also control access to a database by setting access levels through the ACL (Access Control List). You'll grant or deny user and server access to your Notes server through the Server document in the Public Address Book. On top of all of this, you'll also have to possess intimate knowledge of the operating system on which your server runs, and be able to differentiate between a Notes server problem and an operating system problem.

As a Notes administrator, you'll more than likely be wearing more that one hat at a time. This multi-faceted position is what is confusing, and often frustrating, about Notes administration. There are Notes environments that have divided these responsibilities between several people, but those situations are typically for large organizations with a massive Notes installation. More often than not, because Notes is a single product, companies want a single administrator. However, despite the occasional moments of confusion and frustration, Notes is still a very exciting environment to administer.

Notes includes a wide assortment of technology. Because of the direct exposure to so many different areas of technology in one product, Notes administrators often have opportunities to move into other areas of technical focus and responsibility. For example, as you work with Notes you may begin to dabble in Notes development, which may lead to a full-time development position. You could also focus on Notes Mail and all of its capabilities, which may in turn lead to a position where you manage all electronic messaging in an organization. If you thought Notes administration would be boring, think again. Being responsible for a Notes network of nearly any size will keep you both on your toes and technically engaged.

What's New to Notes 4.5

What's new to Notes 4.5? Well, a lot more than one would think. The last release of Notes was 4.1*x*, which might lead you to believe that Release 4.5 is just a maintenance release. I'm sure there are some fixes, but Release 4.5 is primarily a significant feature release.

Here is a quick summary of what to expect in Release 4.5:

- **Message Transfer Agents (MTAs)**: cc:Mail MTA, SMTP MTA, and X.400 MTA are now included with the product.
- **Built-in calendaring and group scheduling**: combines the graphical user interface of Lotus Organizer with the powerful WAN scheduling expertise of PROFS.

- **Enhanced Web access for the Notes client**: provides client-side Web browsing without the requirement of a Notes server. It includes faster in-memory transfers, progressive rendering, and the ability to specify in which database, if any, to cache Internet documents.
- **Notes client presentation enhancements**: provide URL/search bar toggling, the ability to do "document-centric" launching, navigation from the preview pane, better background bitmaps and colors, and better HTML table support such as cell colors and border embossing.
- **Enhanced Notes client security**: provide supports SSL, Java applets, Netscape Plug-ins, and Helper apps.
- **Enhanced agents**: provides new agents such as a Web crawler, daily newspaper, Netscape cookie support, single-click for Doc-links and hyperlinks, as well as HTML authentication support for agents and LotusScript that need to go through a proxy server or interact with a secure Web site.
- **Domino**: HTTP Notes server task included with Notes 4.5. Domino exposes the Notes Object Store to Web clients and vice-versa.
- **NT integration**: logging onto your NT server will automatically log you onto your Notes server as well. Notes status and task commands can be recorded in the NT Event log. There is also the ability to synchronize the Notes Public Address Book with the NT user directory for centralized user management. And Notes 4.5 will also support Microsoft SMS for automated software installation.
- **Expanded security**: new Execution Control List, or ECL, looks at the contents of mail messages for destructive or suspicious executable programs.
- **Support for more concurrent users**: in Notes Release 3 the Notes server could only support somewhere between 120 and 150 concurrent users. In Release 4.*x* that number has reached well over 100 and the goal in 4.5 is for 2000 concurrent users.
- **Enhanced ActiveX support**: the addition of Notes Components is part of this enhancement.
- **Server clustering support**: you can now cluster from two to six Notes servers together, which increases redundancy, provides "fail over support," and allows for load balancing. This can also be done across platforms.

- **Enhanced templates and new templates:** features and functionality have been added into the current templates and new templates have been added.

These features are just some of the highlights of what is new in Notes Release 4.5. Nearly every aspect of Notes has been enhanced in one way or another.

Where Notes Is Heading

Regardless of how you got into Notes administration, you're probably concerned about the life span of this product. Everyone knows that technology is changing very rapidly. What is a highly marketable skill today may not be tomorrow. No one wants to invest a tremendous amount of time and effort in a product that is on its way out the door. So, where is Notes heading? Well, no one knows for sure, but to better understand where it might go, let's take a look at where it's been.

Where Notes Has Been

Notes reached its peak of popularity during Release 3 when it successfully created a new category of computer software called "groupware." Everyone was talking about this new area of computing and wanted a piece of the action. Developers wanted to develop applications with it and users wanted to use it. Business consultant types latched onto this new concept of groupware and took their failing business process re-engineering projects and claimed that groupware was the ultimate re-engineering solution. Clients bought into the idea, and before they knew it massive Notes roll-outs had begun. And then began the dark days of Lotus Notes.

The enormous Notes roll-outs began to fail miserably. The roll-outs took forever. Every time you turned around, Lotus had a new revision of Notes correcting yet another problem. The custom Notes applications that looked great on paper and performed well in small environments began to fall apart when rolled out to a large Notes environment. MIS (Management Information Systems) scrambled to make their Notes network more robust, but the cost to support the Notes infrastructure soared. More servers and support people were constantly needed. The ROI (return on investment) for Lotus Notes did not look good. People that led the Notes initiative labored to make the Notes investment work. Release 4 looked promising but most people were fearful of asking for more money to upgrade when the current investment was already being questioned.

Microsoft began to threaten Notes with Exchange. Most comparison reviews put Notes clearly ahead of Exchange, but everyone knows the best product doesn't always win. Microsoft has a reputation for being slow to start but delivering a solid product in the end. This reputation did more damage to the further spread of Notes than Exchange actually did.

Then, out of nowhere came the Internet and the World Wide Web explosion. Who would have thought that an open environment not controlled by any one company would have such a dramatic impact on the computer industry at large? Suddenly Notes' competition wasn't Microsoft Exchange, but rather this uncontrollable enigma called the World Wide Web.

The Web was an environment that everyone found intuitive. Information was everywhere and available with the simple point and click of a mouse. This new environment was a simpler way to communicate and share information than Notes was. How was Lotus to compete against this new opponent? Enter: the Lotus Notes InterNotes Web Publisher.

Notes may not be the best information navigation tool, but it certainly was a superior publishing environment. The Web was great, but the formatting language of HTML wasn't for everyone. People wanted to share their information on the Web but they didn't want to mark up everything with this funny little tagging language. The Lotus Notes InterNotes Web Publisher made it possible to publish a Notes database to a Web server. The database could then be viewed with browsers such as Netscape's Navigator and Mosaic.

Lotus had done it again! By figuring out early on that rather than being something to compete with, the Web was something to embrace, Lotus had the jump on its competitors. At a rapid pace, Lotus began to add more Web-oriented functionality into its Release 4 product. Along with the InterNotes Web Publisher, Lotus offered regular Web browsing through the familiar interface of Notes. Lotus has now taken this technology even further by adding Domino, which is a Notes server task that allows databases on a Notes server to be browsable through a regular Web browser. The Internet has arrived, and Notes Release 4 is Internet ready and aware.

What do all of these changes and Web-oriented enhancements mean to a Notes administrator? If you're guessing that it adds yet another dimension to Notes administration, you're absolutely correct. Notes administrators managing a Release 4 environment will have to understand all of the previously mentioned aspects of Notes and Web technology, such as HTTP and HTML, and be well versed in TCP/IP. Notes administration has gotten a little more complex, but these features have also brought another level of excitement and technical challenge to Notes administration.

Notes 4.5 with its Internet enhancements, performance improvement, and expanded programmability is hardly a product that is showing any signs of dying. Notes may have gone through a time where its future looked grim, but that time is far behind and the road ahead looks very promising. Current and potential Notes administrators fear not. Investing time and energy in learning the intricacies of Lotus Notes is not a waste of your time and effort. Even if the unheard of were to happen and Notes disappeared tomorrow, think of all of the technical exposures you would have had with just one product:

- The Internet
- Messaging technology
- Group calendaring and scheduling
- Programming in a client server environment
- A variety of network protocols
- Powerful network operating systems

No one can possibly say that working with Notes is a waste of time because it's a dead product. The product isn't dead! And as you can see, any time you spend with Notes is time well spent.

Summary

Lotus Notes is a difficult product to explain, but what it comes down to is that it's a product that helps groups communicate, coordinate, and collaborate more effectively. Products that enable this type of virtual group work environment are powerful products. The down side to having that much power is that it often means complexity. Notes can be complex at times, but it can also be very simple. The rewards for anyone willing to accept the complexities along with the simplicities are tremendous; Notes administrators will find technical excitement and challenge, and organizations will find new ways to work together more productively and effectively.

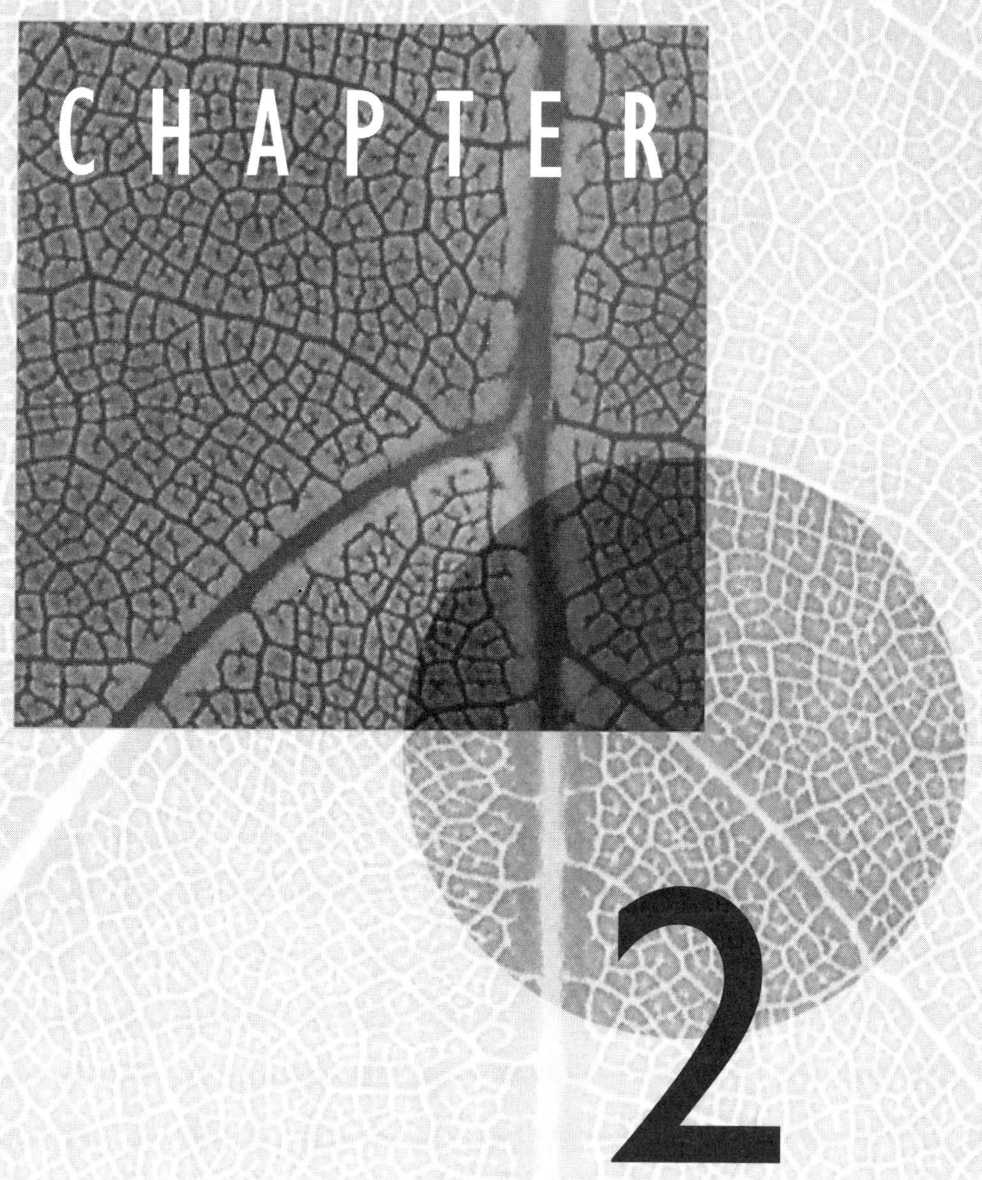

Notes Network Planning and Roll-Out

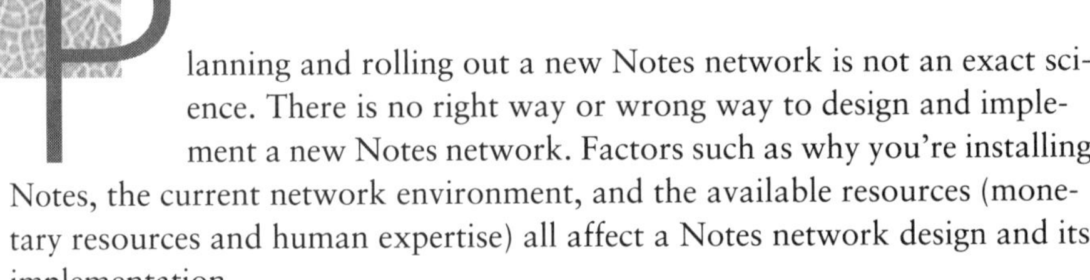

Planning and rolling out a new Notes network is not an exact science. There is no right way or wrong way to design and implement a new Notes network. Factors such as why you're installing Notes, the current network environment, and the available resources (monetary resources and human expertise) all affect a Notes network design and its implementation.

I've been an active participant in numerous Notes projects with a wide range of responsibilities. I've been the project manager responsible for the overall Notes network design and roll-out plan. And I've provided technical support well after the design has been implemented. I've seen a number of different Notes networks in various stages of implementation and as a result I've been able to see what works and what doesn't. Here is the general six-phase approach that I've come up with for planning and rolling out a successful Notes network.

1. Define the business purpose for which Notes is being used.
2. Select the Notes network topology.
3. Create a Notes standards document (discussed later in this chapter).
4. Select the Notes server platform.
5. Inventory the current desktop environment and select the appropriate Notes client platform.
6. Create the Notes roll-out plan and begin implementing it.

These phases are intentionally general so that they provide the greatest amount of flexibility, which is important because no two Notes networks are exactly the same. However, while the phases are general, they are focused enough to provide a reasonable guide to a successful Notes network.

Defining the Business Purpose for Notes

The single most important step in any new Notes network plan is to clearly identify the business purpose for Notes in your organization. This critical step seems so simple you would assume that it doesn't even need mentioning. However, it is amazing how many people start planning a new Notes network without even considering the business purpose.

The best way to determine the business purpose for Notes in your organization is to assemble a committee made up of those individuals interested in bringing Notes into the organization. These people should not only have an interest in Notes but also represent the various departments in your organization. If certain departments are not represented, consider drafting volunteers from the missing departments to help round out the committee. Once the committee is assembled, its first and only order of business is to answer the following two questions:

1. What does the company do?
2. How can Lotus Notes help the company do what it does better?

Although these questions appear simple, don't be fooled. You'll be amazed at how long people can agonize over these seemingly simple questions.

While some people are not fans of decision by committee, sometimes there is just no way around it.

Pick someone within the committee as the facilitator. This person should be a focused individual who is comfortable in front of a crowd and who has the ability to lead and control without dominating. Once the committee has hashed through the first question, you should be able to document it in a single paragraph. If it takes pages upon pages to answer the first question, either you haven't really answered it or your answer has too much detail and you need to try again.

Once everyone is satisfied with the first answer, move on to the next question. This second question is where you, the Notes administrator (or soon-to-be Notes administrator), play a very active role. You'll need to provide the technical reality for the answer to the second question. Undoubtedly, someone on this committee might have enough knowledge of Notes to make them dangerous, and you'll need to tactfully keep them in line. Be encouraging rather than discouraging, but don't let the dream of work flow nirvana get out of control.

An answer to the second question usually won't fit into a simple little paragraph like the first answer did. More than likely the answer will produce a list of things that Notes can make better within your company. An example of such a list is illustrated in the following business scenario.

Scenario #1: Lotus Notes Helps Acme Locators

Acme Locators is a company that focuses on locating niche products for other companies. They act as a broker for items in volume or in single units. They have a large database of manufacturers around the globe and can locate and arrange for the delivery of nearly anything you can imagine.

The company has fifty employees in one office. Half of those employees work directly in the office, while the other half is continually on the road meeting with clients and manufacturers. Workers on the road are constantly calling into the office to find out about the status of certain orders and the availability of certain items.

Acme Locators already has an accounting system they use to track debits and credits, which also ties into their product database. When a new product request comes, it is recorded in a very ad hoc manner. One person may simply record the request in a notebook while another person may record the request in a spreadsheet application or word processor. The request remains in this ad hoc state until the item requested is located and the customer agrees to buy it. At this point an invoice is created in the accounting system, which generates the appropriate forms for product acquisition, shipping, and billing. Until an order reaches this state there is no formal and consistent way to track the status of a request. If the person who took the order is out sick for a couple of days, the order sits idle and the customer has no way of knowing whether the item was located or not.

Acme Locators assembles its committee to determine the business purpose of Notes in their organization. The committee consists of two people from the inside sales force, two people from the field sales force, one person from operations, and one person from upper management. The committee meets and summarizes what Acme Locators does in the following manner:

"Acme Locators is in the business of locating niche products for other companies anywhere in the world. Acme Locators acts as a broker between manufacturer and customer, acquiring and delivering products in large volume or single units."

The committee then looks at its business processes and determines that Notes can help their organization in the following manner. It can:

- Provide a consistent way in which to take and track product requests.
- Provide a way for the field sales force to remotely place product requests without having to call an inside sales person.

The committee comes up with several other ways Notes can help the company. The facilitator records these ideas but gets the committee to agree that the most important benefits are the two previously described ideas. The committee stays focused and agrees that a new Notes network should only address these two ideas and that other ideas will be considered only after the most important needs are met.

Acme Locators has two real, meaningful ways Notes can help them do what they do better. These two ideas are used to create a simple document that explains why Lotus Notes is needed in the company and serve as a focus point for the next phases of Notes planning.

This step in planning a new Notes network may seem awkward for some people or organizations. Keep in mind, however, that the different phases of the planning process are flexible. You can adapt them to suit your unique situation.

For example, your company might have decided it needs an e-mail system or wants to migrate from their old system to a new one. A new e-mail system is a real business need and probably doesn't require a committee to reach that conclusion. In this case, you can skip the first phase of the planning process. You should, however, at the very least create a simple document that clearly states that Lotus Notes is being brought into the company as the new e-mail system. That document doesn't have to be long and drawn out because its only purpose is to serve as a point of focus for the rest of the planning phases.

Selecting the Notes Network Topology

With your business reasons for Notes clearly addressed and documented, you're ready to begin the next phase of the planning process: picking your Notes network topology.

There are a number of different ways to set up your Notes servers. However, no matter how you choose to set it up, it is likely to be based on one of the following four basic schemes:

- Hub and Spoke
- End-to-End
- Ring
- Mesh

You can easily mix and match these topologies to suit your needs. However, make sure that the selected topology supports your company's reason for using Notes.

Hub and Spoke

Hub and Spoke is the most popular and effective server topology. The Hub and Spoke scheme uses a central Notes server that schedules and initiates all communications with all other servers (known as spokes) in the organization. This topology is ideal for companies where Notes is a mission-critical piece of their information technology infrastructure. Hub and Spoke is very sizable. A single hub can service a couple of spokes (see Figure 2.1) or several hubs in a tiered design that services a high number of servers (see Figure 2.2). The total number of hubs and spokes can grow or shrink in accordance with a company's needs.

FIGURE 2.1

A single hub server controlling replication and mail routing with two other spoke servers

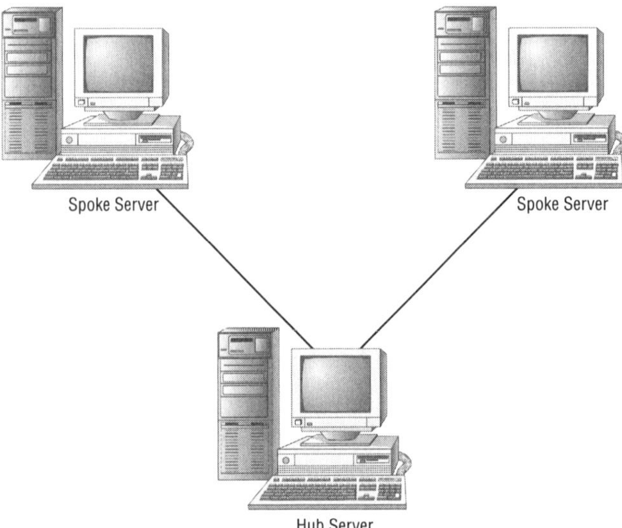

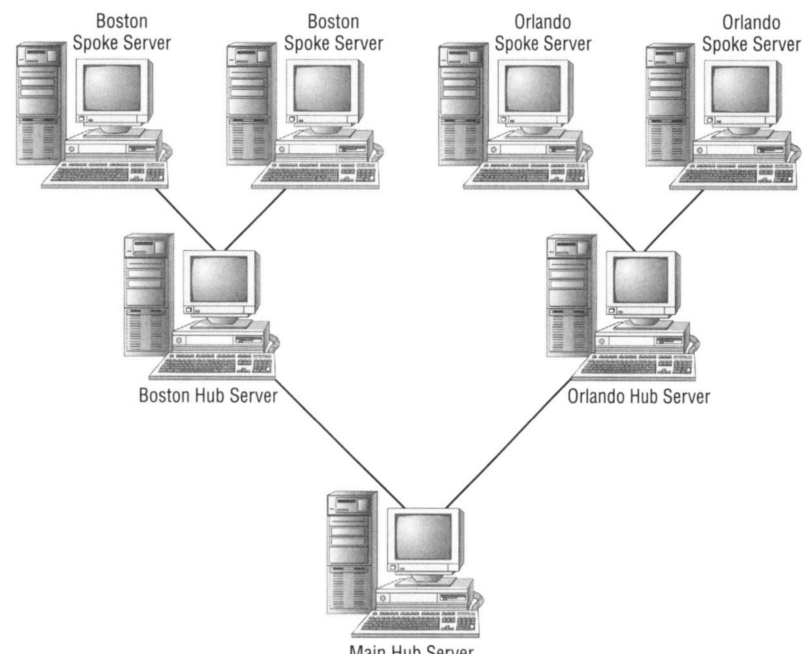

FIGURE 2.2
A single hub server servicing two other location-specific hub servers that in turn service two other servers

The Hub and Spoke model is also very useful in a heterogeneous network environment. For example, you might have a group of Macintosh computers communicating with AppleTalk, a group of PCs in a NetWare environment using IPX/SPX, and a group of UNIX machines using TCP/IP. A hub server could handle replication and mail-routing across these dissimilar environments (see Figure 2.3).

End-to-End

End-to-End, sometimes known as peer-to-peer, is a topology in which each server in a Notes environment communicates directly with the servers that it's connected to. This design works best in small Notes environments (see Figure 2.4).

This topology works well in small Notes environments where Notes is not a mission-critical piece of a larger information technology strategy. In such organizations, Notes might simply be a vehicle to host company-wide discussions and to disseminate policy manuals.

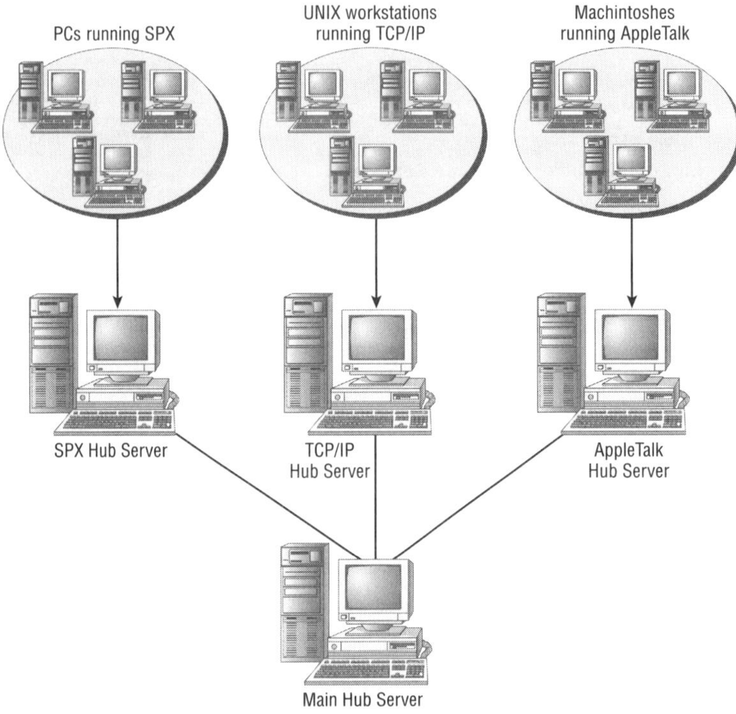

FIGURE 2.3

A single hub facilitates replication and mail-routing between dissimilar systems. The tiered Hub and Spoke topology shown here could also be replaced by a single hub servicing a variety of clients.

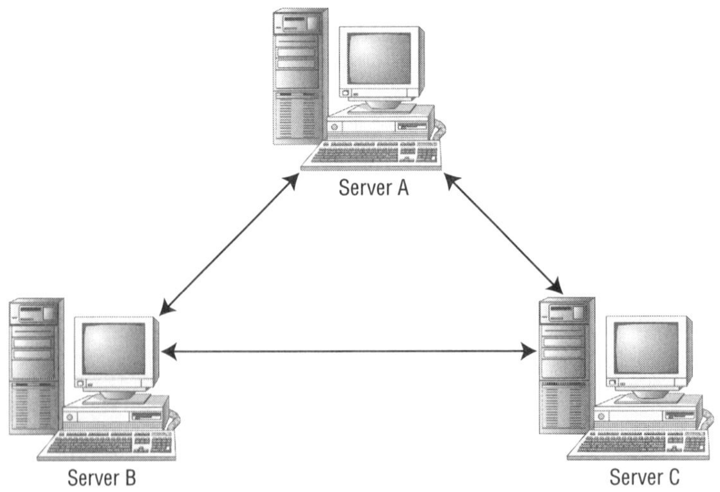

FIGURE 2.4

Three Notes servers in an End-to-End topology. Server A communicates directly with Servers B and C, and Server B communicates directly with Server C.

Ring

With the Ring topology, Server A communicates with Server B, and Server B communicates with Server C, and so on until the final server in the ring, Server x, communicates with Server A (see Figure 2.5). This scheme is useful when simplicity is required, timely updates are not necessary, and future growth is highly unlikely. Organizations with a very fixed use for Notes might select this topology because it is simple and easy to maintain.

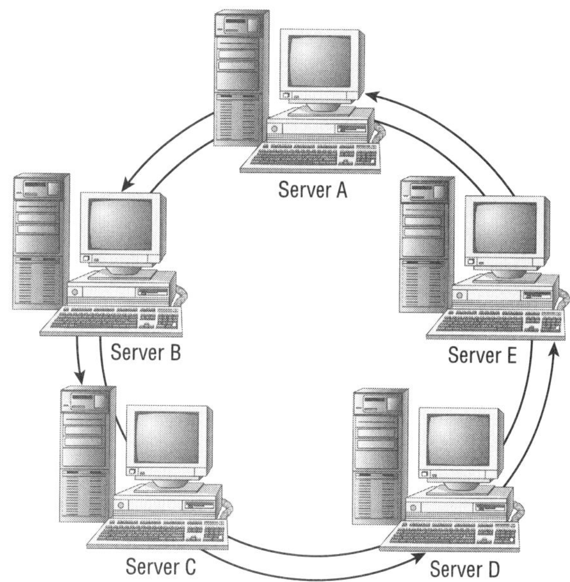

FIGURE 2.5

A simple five-server Ring topology. The arrows indicate the flow of communication.

Mesh

In a Mesh topology, every server communicates with every other server in the organization (see Figure 2.6). This is obviously not the best topology because it allows for seemingly random server-to-server communications, which can make mail routing and replication problems difficult to troubleshoot. It is often the case that this topology isn't planned; it just happens because every Notes server has its own administrator—none of whom communicate with each other.

However, in small Notes networks where every Notes administrator wants to be the captain of his or her own ship, the Mesh topology might be your only choice.

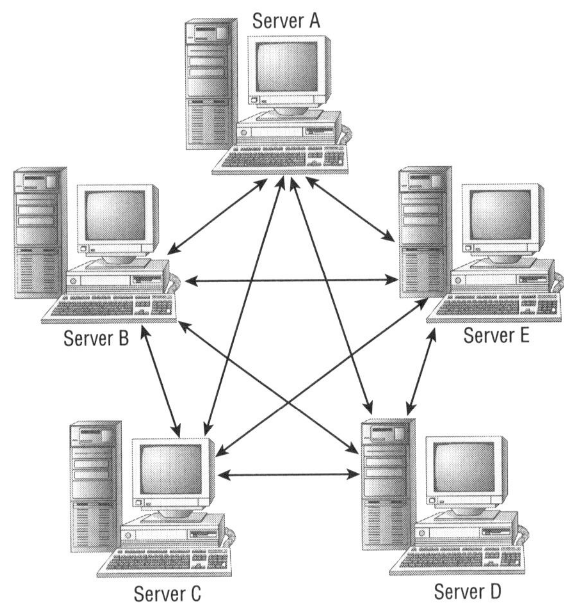

FIGURE 2.6
A Mesh topology can work, but it helps to promote chaos and disorganization.

If you have extra machines capable of running the Lotus Notes server software, you should build a simple Notes network and experiment with the different Notes network topologies.

The Importance of Topologies

Each of these topologies affects not only how you'll set up your servers, but also how replication and mail routing will work within your Notes network. Chapters 8 and 9 discuss replication and mail routing respectively and cover the various topologies in respect to how they work with replication and mail routing. It would be a good idea to skim through these chapters before settling on a definite server topology.

Scenario #2: A Notes Topology for Acme Widgets

Acme Widgets is a 200 worker company with two locations. One office is in Boston and one office is in Orlando. The number of workers is evenly split between the two offices.

Acme Widgets has decided to use Lotus Notes both as their e-mail system and as a support for a recently purchased sales force automation application that runs on Notes. Because Acme Widgets hopes for growth in the future they have decided to implement a Hub and Spoke topology, because it provides the most flexible growth path for the future.

One server is placed in the Boston office as the main hub server; it handles replication and mail routing between the spoke server in Boston and the spoke server in Orlando. The spoke servers handle all of the mail databases for the users at their respective locations. The main copy of the sales force automation application is on the hub server and replicas of this application are on each spoke server. Because the main Notes administrator is at this location, the Boston location also has a second spoke server which is set up to handle the SMTP Message Transfer Agent (MTA). Therefore, any message that is sent to the Internet from the Orlando office is first sent to the main hub server in Boston and then routed to the second spoke server for transmission to the Internet. Remote communications at Acme Widgets is provided through a remote network dial-up system which allows users to access Notes and the NetWare file server with a single call. The topology for Acme Widgets is illustrated in Figure 2.7.

You've got the Notes network topology all worked out. You've documented either in writing or with an illustration of your server layout the Notes server topology you've selected, and now you're ready to get started. Not so fast. There are still a few more things you should work out before you start building your production Notes environment. One such thing is creating a Notes standards document.

For experimental purposes, you can build a simple Notes network at any time during your Notes planning process. Keep in mind that this simple Notes network is just for testing and will be destroyed and rebuilt once you've completed the Notes planning process.

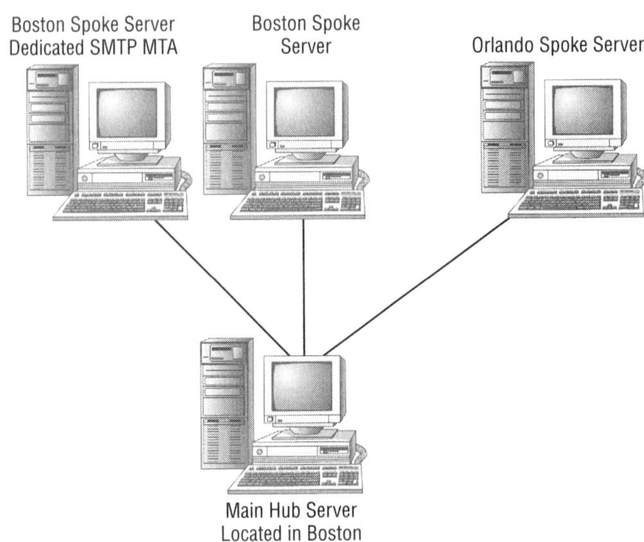

FIGURE 2.7 The Notes network topology for Acme Widgets

Creating a Notes Standards Document

The Notes network topology serves as the foundation on which to build your new Notes network; it also serves as the foundation for your Notes standards document. This document should start with three pieces of information that help facilitate the implementation and future growth of your Notes network:

- An illustration of the server layout graphically showing the selected Notes network topology.
- Guidelines for naming new users, servers, and groups.
- An illustration of your organizational hierarchy if you plan to use hierarchical naming (see the *Hierarchical Naming* sidebar).

As you become more experienced with Lotus Notes, you'll probably also add procedures to your Notes standards documentation for adding new users, creating new groups, and rolling out new Notes databases.

Why create a Notes standards document? The answer is simple. Creating a standards document clarifies exactly how naming conventions are handled within your organization and what they mean. The document also helps you plan for Notes network expansion. And the document helps demonstrate organizational hierarchy in those networks that choose to implement hierarchical naming.

For example, if you have several Notes administrators, the standards document helps them name and create users, servers, and groups consistently no matter which administrator is doing the creating. Users can also benefit from a standards document if naming conventions are designed so that a name includes information such as location, department, division, or even function.

In the beginning, the standards document doesn't have to be elaborate and lengthy. Three simple pages are all you need: one page for illustrating the server topology, another page defining naming conventions, and a final page for illustrating your organizational hierarchy.

Make sure to include examples of a user name, server name, and group name along with the naming definition to provide additional clarity.

Hierarchical Naming

Hierarchical naming is like a tree structure that reflects the actual layout of your organization. Sitting at the top of the tree is the organization name, which may be something like "Acme." Below that name are organizational units, which mirror logical units of the company, such as location, department, or division.

To implement the hierarchical naming scheme, create certifier IDs (see Chapter 4 for details). There are two types of certifier IDs: organizational and organizational unit. These certifiers are used when you register users, which stamps them with a hierarchical name that reflects their position within the company, or when you register servers.

Hierarchical names help ensure name uniqueness. Each user and server has a unique "common" name but shares certificates that allow them to communicate with other users and servers. For example, John Doe's hierarchical name, John Doe/Support/Boston/Acme, is easily differentiated from John Doe/Sales/Orlando/Acme; and because both users have the Acme certificate, both can communicate with each other.

> Hierarchical naming applied to servers can help indicate the department to which a particular server belongs. For example, an organization might contain a server named ServerOne/Service/Boston/Acme as well as a server named ServerTwo/Sales/Orlando/Acme. If you just looked at the names, ServerOne and ServerTwo, it wouldn't be clear whom these servers service or where these servers are located. However, the entire hierarchical name indicates that ServerOne is for the people in the service department in Boston. And ServerTwo is for the sales staff located in Orlando.

Selecting the Notes Server Platform

Without a doubt, Lotus Notes' multiple operating system support is one of its most attractive features. The beauty of multiple platform support is that any organization thinking about adding Lotus Notes to their environment can use an operating system that they already have.

Despite the multiple operating system support of Lotus Notes, everyone always wants to know if one operating system is better for Notes than another. I wish the answer came down to a simple list ranking the various operating systems from best to worst. Unfortunately, any such list would be extremely biased. Nevertheless, this section will attempt to provide a concise analysis of the operating systems that support Lotus Notes.

Available Server Platforms

If you've been using Notes since its inception, then you know that before the introduction of Lotus Notes Release 3, IBM OS/2 was the only operating system that could be used when setting up a Notes server. When Release 3 became available, Lotus began to offer other operating systems from which to choose. Now that Release 4.5 is in full swing, the tradition of multiple platform server support continues.

The big question is, which operating system should you use for your Notes network? Well, your first choice should always be the operating system you are already using in-house or already have expertise with unless, of course, you're completely dissatisfied with that system. If you're starting from scratch, your choices are wide open.

Windows 95

The Notes server for Windows 95 is really the same server you'd install for Windows NT. The 32-bit version of Notes server runs under Windows 95 and NT because they're both 32-bit operating systems. This dual compatibility was an unbelievable benefit to me in the first beta of Notes 4.5 because I could run it at home as well as on my laptop.

Despite the benefit, I don't recommend Windows 95 as a Notes server platform unless your Notes environment is very small, such as two to three users. Windows 95 is a 32-bit operating system, but it just isn't the industrial strength operating system you need to run a serious Notes server on top of. I do, however, like to use Windows 95 for what I call portable Notes environments. For example, I have Windows 95 on my laptop so I've set up a Notes server on this machine for demonstration purposes. I can take this Notes network with me wherever I go and it works great because it's not supporting any more than one or two users at a time.

Operating System Version: Windows 95

Processors Supported: Intel 486, Pentium

Required RAM: 16 MB minimum, 24 MB recommended

Required Hard Disk Space: 150 MB minimum, 300 MB or more recommended (It actually requires far less, but these recommendations assume you plan to have a few databases on it.)

Hard Disk Swap Space: 16 MB

Protocols Supported: SPX, NetBIOS/NetBEUI, TCP/IP, X.PC

The Pros Mobility! I have Windows 95 on one of my laptops at home because the laptop only has 24 MB of RAM and a 486 processor. With the 32-bit version of Notes, I can run both the client and server on my laptop, which allows me to take a full installation of Notes with me wherever I go. I'm not running a production system, so instability or poor performance is not a concern. This is a great way to take a mini-development environment with me wherever I go. It is also great for demonstrations or even situations where mini-ad hoc Notes networks are needed.

The Cons This is not the right choice for a production environment. I suppose I could go on and on about the negative aspects of a Notes server on Windows 95, but why bother? The point is simple. Windows 95 is a desktop operating system and not designed or intended to be used for mission-critical production servers.

NetWare NLM

When I first heard of the NetWare NLM version of Lotus Notes back during Release 3, I was very excited. The first performance reports looked very promising. Unfortunately, the potential was never completely realized. The old Release 3 NLM was fairly resource intensive and required 32 MB of RAM but preferred 64 MB. By today's standards 64 MB of RAM is not a lot of RAM. However, when the Release 3 NLM was released 64 MB of RAM was an enormous requirement.

NetWare's strength has always been its file and print service capabilities. Unfortunately, NetWare doesn't shine as bright when used as an application server. For that reason (plus the limited use in the industry of the Notes NLM) this platform makes somewhat of a poor choice. It does work, and some people swear by it. However, NetWare is not one of the platforms that I recommend.

The requirements for the Release 4 NLM are as follows:

Operating System Version: NetWare 3.12 and 4.*x*

Processors Supported: Intel 486, Pentium

Required RAM: 64 MB minimum, 96 MB recommended

Required Hard Disk Space: 300 MB minimum, 500 MB or more recommended

Hard Disk Swap Space: Not applicable

Protocols Supported: AppleTalk, IPX/SPX, TCP/IP, X.PC

The Pros NetWare NLM has always been known for its excellent exploitable fault tolerance. All of the third-party backup solutions and server monitoring tools available today can help build a very fault-tolerant Notes server.

The Cons I don't want to slam NetWare, but it always seems like every time you add something to your NetWare file server a new set of patches is required. If you don't apply the patches, things just don't work the way they are supposed to. This may be exaggerating a bit, but there are probably a lot of people right now who are nodding their heads in agreement.

UNIX (HP/UX, IBM AIX, Sun Solaris)

I love UNIX even though it can appear cryptic at times. UNIX comes in a variety of flavors, each of which is as powerful as the next. The down side to UNIX is that it usually comes with a steep price tag, and good UNIX people that want to work with Notes aren't easy to find. If you have UNIX in-house with experts that want to work with Notes, then UNIX is a great choice. Keep one thing in mind, however, some of the Notes server features aren't available on UNIX and probably never will be (for example, single password logon).

The various flavors of UNIX are great platforms for Notes if you already have the machines and the in-house expertise.

Operating System Version: AIX 4.1.3, HP-UX 10.01, Solaris 2.4

Processors Supported: RISC 6000 (for AIX), PA-RISC (for HP-UX), SPARC (for Solaris)

Required RAM: 64 MB minimum, 128 MB recommended

Required Hard Disk Space: 300 MB minimum, 500 MB or more recommended

Hard Disk Swap Space: 128 MB

Protocols Supported: SPX, SPX II (not available on AIX), TCP/IP, X.PC

The Pros

UNIX is a proven multi-threaded, multi-tasking environment and it has been the foundation for many client/server applications, so it makes sense that it is probably a solid platform for Notes. Plus, UNIX is a real workhorse of a platform. The UNIX platforms supported by Notes are all known to have some serious hardware. These machines can really cook, but all that performance comes at a price.

The Cons

Hardware is expensive. If you haven't priced an IBM, HP, or Sun UNIX system, go ahead and try it. You'll be quite surprised with how much more expensive it is than something like a Compaq Pentium-based server. Of course, I have also seen some very expensive Compaq servers. Cost is really just relative to what's in the machine.

IBM OS/2 Warp and Warp Server

It's made by IBM; they own Lotus; and it was the first platform for a Notes server. There is a tremendous amount of Notes and OS/2 expertise out there. And any Notes administrator that started with Notes release 2.0 has worked with a Notes server running on OS/2. The down side is that OS/2 is rumored to be getting the ax from IBM. However, the latest news claimed that the rumors were false.

Despite what the latest rumors might say about OS/2, I usually recommend sticking with it if you have it already (especially if you have in-house expertise with OS/2) because it is a solid operating system.

The grandfather of Notes' server platforms, OS/2 undoubtedly will be around for a long time. The system requirements for an OS/2 system are fairly modest and I've managed to run it on systems with resources well below the recommended configuration.

Operating System Version: OS/2 Warp, Warp Connect, Warp Server, and OS/2 2.11 SMP

Processors Supported: Intel 486, Pentium

Required RAM: 32 MB minimum, 48 MB recommended (The good-ole-days of Release 3 on OS/2 with as little as 8 MB are long gone.)

Required Hard Disk Space: 300 MB minimum, 500 MB or more recommended

Hard Disk Swap Space: 16 MB

Protocols Supported: AppleTalk, SPX, NetBIOS/NetBEUI, TCP/IP, VINES, X.PC, X.25 and SNA supported but sold separately

The Pros This operating system has a wealth of experience. Because it's been around since the beginning, experienced Notes people know this operating system fairly well. You shouldn't have any problem finding Notes people capable of managing the Notes environment as well as OS/2.

IBM owns it. Since IBM owns OS/2 and Lotus, the makers of Notes, support for and future enhancements of Notes on OS/2 will continue.

The Cons It seems to play second fiddle to Windows NT Server. Most of the new Notes server enhancements are coming out for Windows NT Server first. The same features can be added to Notes running on Warp Server, but often you have to wait. This drawback can be extremely frustrating, and it also makes it difficult to convince people to stick with Notes on OS/2.

Windows NT

I'm not a Microsoft bigot, but I pretend to be one at work—lest I die. Nevertheless, I do openly admit to really liking NT. I have heard that a considerable amount of Notes development is done on NT, which gives it a bit of an advantage. Most of the new Notes enhancements such as single-password logon are only available on NT at this time. Going with NT means you'll probably never have to wait for a new Notes feature—as you probably will if you go with one of the UNIX platforms.

The new star operating system for Lotus Notes has got to be Windows NT Server. Release 3 of Notes had a version for NT, but starting with Release 4.0 Notes on NT has really matured.

I've run Notes Release 4 on a variety of NT machines with different configurations. I've even gotten away with setting up Notes on an NT 3.51 machine with 20 MB of RAM and a meager 200 MB of hard drive space. I don't recommend this configuration, however, it can be done.

Operating System Version: Windows NT Server 3.51 and 4.0

Processors Supported: Intel 486, Pentium, and DEC Alpha

Required RAM: 48 MB minimum, 64 MB recommended (I've run it on as little as 20 MB and have supported small installations on 32 MB.)

Required Hard Disk Space: 300 MB minimum, 500 MB or more recommended (It actually requires far less, but these recommendations assume you plan to have a few databases on it.)

Hard Disk Swap Space: 64 MB

Protocols Supported: AppleTalk, SPX, SPX II, NetBIOS/NetBEUI, TCP/IP, VINES (not available on NT/Alpha combination), X.PC

The Pros It has tighter integration with the NT environment. If you're running an NT network, then you'll benefit greatly from this tight integration. Users can log into the NT environment and Notes environment at the same time (also known as single logon). Notes specific monitoring is now available in the process monitor. Messages sent to the Notes log can now be redirected to the NT Event Viewer. From one single location you can view both Notes and NT messages.

New Notes products seem to come out for NT first. And most of the new features available for Notes seem to be available for NT first. The InterNotes Web Publisher and Domino are two perfect examples.

Most NotesBench reports are from machines running NT. NotesBench is a product from Lotus that allows companies to perform a series of stress tests on a machine running Notes. The purpose of this product is to see how well the machine will perform. A lot of the guess work in hardware selection is removed with NotesBench. (NotesBench will be discussed further later in this chapter.)

The Cons NT and Notes experience is hard to find. Even though Notes on NT has been around since Release 3, it really didn't start becoming popular until Release 4. Therefore, people with both NT and Notes experience are difficult to find. This is the same problem as with UNIX and Notes. Fortunately, the lack of combined expertise won't be a problem for long.

Microsoft could pull a fast one. I've met countless people that firmly believe that Microsoft goes out of its way to undermine non-Microsoft products on its operating system. Whether this is true or not may really affect your decision to choose NT over something else.

Another potential drawback to Notes on NT is if you choose to install NT on an Alpha server machine from Digital Equipment Corporation (DEC). Microsoft does have a version of Windows NT compiled for the DEC Alpha chip that runs very well. However, try to buy a third-party utility such as an Open File Manager and you'll find very few options when compared to the NT/Intel combination.

NotesBench

I hope I've provided some helpful information for selecting a platform for Lotus Notes. I wish I could say definitively, "Pick this one. It's the best!" Unfortunately, I can't because there are often forces other than pure performance that need to be considered when picking your Notes platform. However, if you only want performance to drive your decision, then you should take a look at the reports generated by NotesBench from Lotus.

NotesBench is a performance testing tool created by Lotus to perform a series of tests on a Notes server running on various operating systems and hardware platforms. NotesBench is available to Lotus Premium Business Partners—specifically hardware vendors—who have completed a three day hands-on training session. With this tool, hardware vendors can perform Notes benchmarking and finally attempt to answer the long standing question, "Which server configuration is best?"

Lotus Premium Business Partners can make their benchmark information directly available to Notes customers to assist them during their platform selection, resource budgeting, and capacity planning. Lotus is quick to point out, however, that long term Notes planning should not be based entirely on benchmark information derived from NotesBench. Technological advances in hardware and software occur too frequently for benchmark statistics to remain valid for a long period of time.

Five specific areas of Notes server performance are targeted with NotesBench:

Replication Hub: In this test, a Notes server replicates changes to the Public Address Book and other databases with several spoke servers. The result for the replication hub is measured in the number of documents replicated per unit of time.

Mail Routing Hub: In a Notes network, a dedicated mail routing hub receives messages from other systems and routes or delivers these messages appropriately. The result for this test is measured in the number of messages routed or delivered per unit in time. Keep in mind that most Notes networks have hub servers that perform both replication and mail routing. If your hub servers perform these combined tasks, then you'll need to consider the Mail Routing Hub and Replication Hub test results together.

Server for Active Users: Most users in a Notes network use mail and a couple of simple databases. The amount of strain an average user places on a Notes server is typically low. This test attempts to return a metric for an average user which is the maximum number of users that can be supported before the average user response time becomes unacceptable.

Server for Power Users: This test considers a power user to be someone who sends large mail messages, adds documents to a database with attachments, performs full-text searches, and replicates changes from their local machine to the server. This test also returns a metric for an average user which is the maximum number of users that can be supported before the average user response time becomes unacceptable.

Idle Usage: This test provides an upper boundary on the number of idle sessions that a Notes server can support. This result is measured in the maximum number of user sessions that can concurrently exist.

The first two tests are the most valuable. These results should be able to help guide you in selecting which hardware and software to use for your Notes server. Let me stress, however, the word "guide." I'm not suggesting that NotesBench should make your decision for you, but rather it should help you focus your attention on a couple of hardware and software combinations that appear to work best.

NotesBench results can be found on various hardware vendor Web sites such as Compaq, IBM, and Digital Equipment Corporation. For a listing, go to www.lotus.com and search for NotesBench.

Selecting the Appropriate Notes Client Platform

The next thing to consider in your Notes plan is which Notes client you'll use. This decision isn't driven by which Notes client is the best, but rather which Notes client your current desktop environment can support (see Table 2.1).

TABLE 2.1 Hardware requirements for the Notes clients on different operating systems

Operating System	Hardware Requirements
Windows 3.1*x*	**Operating System Version**: Windows 3.1*x* (16–bit Windows client) **Processors Supported**: Intel 386 or higher **Required RAM**: 6 MB minimum, 8 MB recommended **Required Hard Disk Space**: 30 MB minimum, 40 MB recommended **Protocols Supported**: SPX, NetBIOS/NetBEUI, TCP/IP, VINES, X.PC
Macintosh	**Operating System Version**: System 7.1 or later **Processors Supported**: 680x0 PowerPC (requires System 7.5 or later) **Required RAM**: 12 MB minimum for 680x0, 16 MB minimum for PowerPC. 20 MB recommended for both **Required Hard Disk Space**: 30 MB minimum, 40 MB recommended **Protocols Supported**: AppleTalk, TCP/IP
Windows 95	**Operating System Version**: Windows 95 **Processors Supported**: Intel 386 or higher **Required RAM**: 8 MB minimum, 12 MB recommended **Required Hard Disk Space**: 30 MB minimum, 40 MB or more recommended **Protocols Supported**: SPX, NetBIOS/NetBEUI, TCP/IP, VINES, X.PC

TABLE 2.1 *(cont.)* Hardware requirements for the Notes clients on different operating systems (continued)

Operating System	Hardware Requirements
Windows NT	**Operating System Version**: Windows NT 3.51 and 4.0 **Processors Supported**: Intel 486, Pentium, and DEC Alpha **Required RAM**: 16 MB minimum, 20 MB or more recommended **Required Hard Disk Space**: 30 MB minimum, 40 MB or more recommended **Protocols Supported**: SPX, SPX II, NetBIOS/NetBEUI, TCP/IP, VINES, X.PC
AIX (UNIX)	**Operating System Version**: AIX 4.1.4 or 4.2 **Processors Supported**: PowerPC and Power2 **Required RAM**: 32 MB minimum, 64 MB recommended. **Required Hard Disk Space**: 90 MB minimum, 150 MB recommended **Protocols Supported**: IPX/SPX for AIX v2.1, AIX Connections v 4.1 (SPX II), TCP/IP, X.PC
HP/UX (UNIX)	**Operating System Version**: HP-UX 10.01 **Processors Supported**: HP 9000 Series **Required RAM**: 32 MB minimum, 64 MB recommended **Required Hard Disk Space**: 90 MB minimum, 150 MB recommended **Protocols Supported**: NetWare v3.12 for HP 9000 with SPX for 10.04 (SPX II), TCP/IP, X.PC
Solaris (UNIX)	**Operating System Version**: Sun Solaris 2.5, 2.51, or Intel edition 2.5 **Processors Supported**: Sparc and Intel **Required RAM**: 32 MB minimum, 64 MB recommended **Required Hard Disk Space**: 90 MB minimum, 150 MB recommended **Protocols Supported**: Connect/NW 2.0, TCP/IP, X.PC
OS/2 Warp	**Operating System Version**: Warp v. 3.0 and Warp Connect v. 3.0, Warp 4.0 **Processors Supported**: Intel 486 and Pentium **Required RAM**: 8 MB minimum, 12 MB recommended **Required Hard Disk Space**: 40 MB minimum, 50 MB recommended **Protocols Supported**: Banyan Vines, NetBIOS, TCP/IP, NetWare SPX

For example, you might install the Notes client on every Macintosh CX in your company only to find that these machines don't meet the minimum requirements to run Notes. In this case, you'll either have to upgrade these machines or bring in new machines capable of running Notes. Either way, the decision is not easy.

You need to start this part of your Notes plan by taking an inventory of all the machines in your company. This inventory needs to answer the following questions:

1. What is the current operating system?
2. How much RAM does it have?
3. How much available hard disk space does it have?
4. What is the CPU (486, Pentium, and so on)?
5. What network protocols is it running?
6. What kind of modem does it have (important only for mobile users)?

A simple spreadsheet using a column for each question and a row for each machine is an easy way to get started.

Once you've collected all of your information you'll need to compare your data to the minimum requirements for the Notes client on that machine's particular operating system. If all machines meet the required minimum, you're ready to move on. If, however, these machines are deficient, you'll have to decide whether to upgrade the hardware or replace the machine altogether. If the machine falls short in something as simple as hard disk space or RAM, then upgrading the hardware is probably the best option. If every aspect is lacking, however, think seriously about a new machine.

A serious lack of computing power on the desktop can easily side-track a Notes plan because it usually triggers a whole new project: desktop overhaul. Such a project involves the acquisition and installation of new desktop computers for everyone in the company. I'm sure you can imagine the effort involved in such a project. If this is your situation, I recommend you put your Notes plan on hold until you've finished the desktop upgrade project. Once that project is complete and stable, return to the Notes plan and pick up where you left off.

Creating the Notes Roll-Out Plan

Five out of the six phases are complete. You're almost done. Now it's time to create the actual Notes roll-out plan and begin implementation.

The roll-out plan itself needs to address the following questions:

- How much time should you allocate for the roll-out?
- Who will build the Notes infrastructure?
- How will Notes get installed at the desktop and who will get it first?
- Who will train the end-user community?
- What is the one Notes-centric feature that this roll-out will focus on?
- Who will support the Notes infrastructure and the end-users?

Each item appears very simple, but very serious planning needs to go into each item, otherwise your Notes roll-out might fail miserably.

How Much Time Should You Allocate for the Roll-Out?

Determining how much time to allocate for a Notes roll-out will vary from one installation to the next. Obviously small installations require less time than larger installations.

One way to determine the amount of required time is to break down the tasks into a series of steps:

1. Build the Notes network. This step involves the following tasks:
   - **A.** Installing servers
   - **B.** Configuring server-to-server connectivity
   - **C.** Confirming workstation-to-server connectivity
   - **D.** Installing and configuring any MTAs or other gateways, if any
   - **E.** Establishing a simple server backup and restore procedure
2. Train the users

3. Install Notes at the desktop. This step involves the following tasks:

   A. Register each user or the first group of users

   B. Create a set of installation instructions

   C. Begin installing the first user or group of users

The first server in a new Notes network is going to take the longest because from this server you will probably register subsequent servers and configure Server Connection documents. I usually estimate at least one week's time to get everything right on that first server. The actual software installation is quick and easy. Everything after the software installation, however, is what takes time.

After the first server is completely set up, additional servers shouldn't take as long unless you're configuring a very unique Notes network. I can usually install a new server in one to two hours. This estimate assumes a high speed Pentium processor and around 64 MB of RAM. If the server machine is brand new and still in its box and the operating system still needs installing, then of course more time is required. I usually estimate one to two hours for setting up the hardware and an additional two hours for installing the operating system. These time estimates are fairly generous because I try to build in some margin for error.

Estimating time for training users is totally unpredictable. The more focused the training, such as only teaching users how to use Notes Mail, the less time you'll need. I usually estimate a focused training session to last only one day and more complete Notes training to require an entire week.

Finally, estimate how long the Notes client software installation will take. The amount of time required for this, as you can already guess, is also difficult to predict. Machine speed, network traffic, and machine availability can all directly impact the time required to install the Notes client. A rough estimate, however, that I like to use is ten to fifteen Notes clients in a single day. This estimate assumes machines that have Pentium-based processors and meet all of the minimum hardware requirements: machine availability and no connectivity issues.

Take all of these estimates and arrange them into a task-oriented schedule laid out on a simple monthly calendar. Block the days or weeks for each task and clearly identify where each step begins and ends.

Who Will Build the Notes Infrastructure?

Once you've allocated time for the roll-out project and created a simple calendar schedule of tasks, you need to determine who will execute each task.

At this point in the project you'll build the Notes roll-out team. This team can be very small with only a couple of people doing everything, or very large with a dedicated group for each task. Whenever possible, I prefer to take a three team approach. This approach creates three task-specific teams that focus primarily on the task or role that they will assume when the roll-out is complete.

I start with the server administration team. This team is made up of the people who will assume the responsibility of Notes server administration after the roll-out is complete. Since these people will keep these machines running, they should be the ones who set them up in the first place. If these people have other responsibilities that require their time on a daily basis, try to rotate each individual through this team so that they all have a chance to do part of the infrastructure installation and configuration.

The next team is the desktop installation team. This team is made up of the people who normally do desktop support within an organization. Their participation in this team should help them perfect the skill of performing and troubleshooting Notes client installations.

The final team is the roll-out support team. This team is made up of people from the server installation team and desktop support team. The purpose of this team is to provide timely support for the new and growing Notes network so that acceptance of Notes in the company is quick and positive. Without this team, users that encounter a simple problem may become frustrated when there is no place to turn for help or the approach they take to acquire help is not effective. Users could wait anywhere from hours to days to receive an answer to a simple question such as, "How do I make a new folder for my mail?" Slow response to a question as simple as this one can have a very negative impact on user acceptance of Notes. Most users try to resist change in their computing environments because change usually means learning something new, which temporarily slows down their productivity. Users will often seize any opportunity to not use something new if they have the chance. Don't give them that chance. Be prepared with a responsive support team. After the roll-out is complete and Notes has taken hold, this group can be eliminated and Notes can be supported within your organization in the same manner you support all other desktop applications.

Each of these teams needs technically sharp people who are comfortable with supporting Notes and armed with solid troubleshooting skills. If Notes is new to the people in your organization who will make up these three teams, start sending them to training well before the official roll-out takes place.

Appendix A discusses Notes certification and lists the various courses and certification tests that an individual can take. I strongly recommend having your Notes support staff follow the certification path. If not for certification, at least for the official Notes classes related to certification, because these classes are excellent at teaching support personnel what they need to know about Notes to do their job.

Who Will Get Notes First?

After the support teams are created, you'll need to determine which users get Notes installed at their desktop first. This decision, unfortunately, is driven mostly by the internal politics within your organization. In an ideal roll-out plan, however, you'll want to schedule the installations by departments or divisions based on who needs Notes the most. After the decision is made, try to create an installation schedule and distribute it to the user community so everyone knows when Notes is coming.

When the installations begin, try to remain flexible and accommodate those users who need Notes before they are scheduled. However, be cautious and don't let your flexibility throw off your schedule.

Who Will Train the End-User Community?

Training is a critical piece of a successful roll-out. If no one knows how to use Notes, then no one will ever use the product. Training is also a great way for people to confirm what they know about something. Therefore, if at all possible, try to handle the training of users yourself. If staffing resources are limited, consider using an outside training company.

Once formal training is complete, that doesn't mean you'll never train users again. You'll need to have training available for new users and users that need a quick refresher from time to time. I suggest using a product from ReCor called NBT (Network Based Training) for Lotus Notes. This product provides topic-specific Notes lessons and can be configured for single user availability or network availability.

Details about ReCor's Network Based Training can be found in Appendix E.

What Notes Feature Will This Roll-Out Focus On?

Each company rolling out Notes has their own reason for doing so. Some want Notes for its e-mail capabilities. Others want Notes for its easy-to-customize application environment. And some want Notes for everything it has to offer.

Wanting to exploit every feature of Notes is an ideal use of Notes, but it also makes the focus of a Notes roll-out too broad. Rolling-out a product as powerful and flexible as Notes requires a certain amount of feature focus in the beginning or you'll run the chance of overwhelming your user community. New Notes users require time to get used to the environment before they are asked to do everything with Notes.

I like to focus my roll-outs on one functional feature of Lotus Notes so the user community gets slowly indoctrinated into the environment. This makes training easier to conduct; and it makes supporting Notes that much easier. As users become more comfortable with Notes, I roll-out out more of its functionality.

For example, I typically like to focus Notes roll-outs on Notes Mail. I focus on Notes Mail because it is the one thing that you don't have to beg users to use. People want to communicate, and they like to do so using e-mail. Start your roll-out focusing on Notes Mail and your Notes usage will take off from day one. As users become comfortable with Notes, roll out a couple of information databases, for example, news services. Once those databases are accepted, move on to custom Notes applications.

Who Will Support the Notes Infrastructure and End-Users?

Once the roll-out is complete, someone still has to support the Notes infrastructure and end-users. If you followed my three team roll-out approach, you already know who is going to provide ongoing Notes support. Even with the roll-out team approach, you probably want to know how many people you really need. Well, I wish I could provide a definite answer. Unfortunately, I can only give broad estimates. For large installations of ten servers or more and a couple thousand very active Notes users, you should consider dividing the responsibilities into the following categories:

- **Server administration:** One dedicated and one backup
- **Mail administration:** One dedicated and one backup
- **Database administration:** One working closely with the Notes developers (if any)
- **User support:** Two people per one thousand users

You can have one person manage two or more of these responsibilities in smaller installations (under ten servers and less than a thousand users), but don't leave one person handling all of these responsibilities even in very small installations. That person will eventually take a vacation or quit. Therefore, you'll need to have a backup.

Summary

Planning a new Notes network and rolling it out is not a process that is identical for everyone. There are, however, some general phases that you should try to move through as you plan and roll out Notes. Success is not guaranteed even if you follow every step, but success shouldn't be far away. Planning is the critical piece of a successful Notes network. If my guidelines don't particularly suit you, there are several other resources to turn to. Appendix F lists some of these resources. Even if you liked the guidelines presented in this chapter, I still recommend that you read other resources as well because you can never know too much about Notes network planning and roll-out.

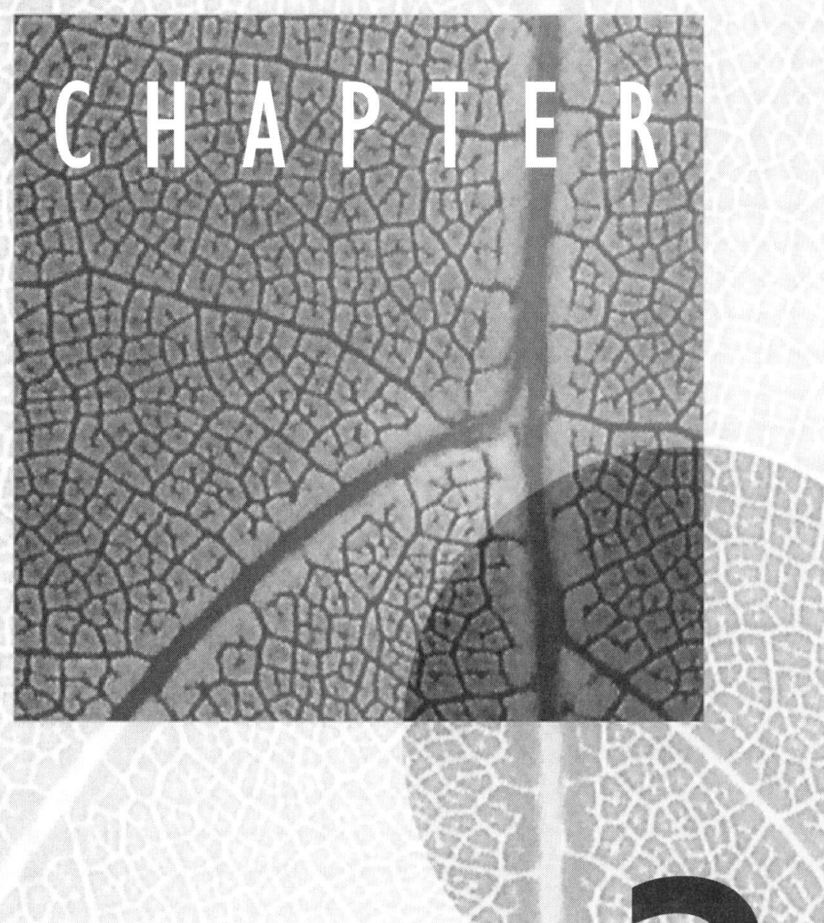

3

Notes Release 3 to Release 4 Migration

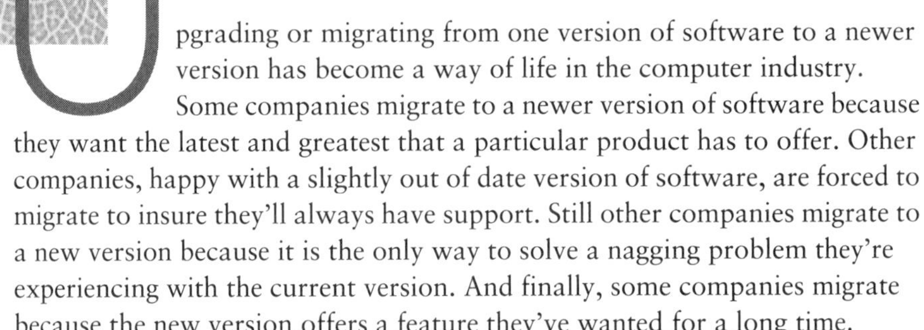

Upgrading or migrating from one version of software to a newer version has become a way of life in the computer industry. Some companies migrate to a newer version of software because they want the latest and greatest that a particular product has to offer. Other companies, happy with a slightly out of date version of software, are forced to migrate to insure they'll always have support. Still other companies migrate to a new version because it is the only way to solve a nagging problem they're experiencing with the current version. And finally, some companies migrate because the new version offers a feature they've wanted for a long time.

Depending on the software you're upgrading, the scope of the migration can be vast. With a product such as Lotus Notes, migration is a significant undertaking because it impacts much more than just computers. Notes migration directly affects the end-user, the support professional, and daily business operations. A failed migration can cause chaos beyond your wildest dreams, while a successful migration goes virtually unnoticed.

The phases you'll go through during a Notes migration are much the same as those for any other software product. You'll get started with migration planning and then move into implementing that plan. When the implementation is complete, you'll spend some time double-checking your work and updating your Notes standards documentation (provided you created such documentation when you installed your first Notes network). While the phases of migration are few, how these phases are carried out often makes the difference between a chaotic migration and a seamless change.

Planning for Migration

Migrating from one version of software to another, in some cases, is as simple as installing the new software. Little planning, if any, needs to happen. Often the sum total of planning for a migration is backing up your data and having a copy of the original software in case something goes wrong. You could, if you like to live dangerously, approach a Notes migration in the same manner, but doing so is strongly discouraged. A successful Notes migration from Release 3 to Release 4 requires a carefully documented migration plan to help keep everyone working together and hopefully avoid any problems.

Much the same as planning a new Notes installation, planning for a Notes migration is not an exact science. There is no absolute right way for migration because no two Notes environments are exactly the same. Despite the differences among Notes environments, I have found the following six-step approach very successful when creating a Notes migration plan:

1. Evaluate the new release.
2. Inventory the current environment.
3. Create a migration team.
4. Create a test environment.
5. Train the technical support organization.
6. Create the migration plan.

You won't have to complete each of the six steps to create a successful Notes migration plan. However, since each plan is dependent on your current Notes environment, you'll have to evaluate each step as it is presented in this chapter and make the final decision as to its relevance in your environment.

Evaluating the New Release

Even though I'm a firm believer that migration is inevitable whenever a new release of software comes out, that doesn't mean migration has to take place the minute a new release is available. With a product such as Lotus Notes a migration affects more than just one thing. Notes servers, each Notes server's clients, any Notes applications and databases, and Notes Mail (if used as the company's e-mail platform) are all directly affected during a migration. Because the scope of a Notes migration is large, the consequences, if poorly executed, can be severe. Therefore, you must carefully evaluate a new release of Notes to determine whether your organization is ready to upgrade its Notes environment or would do better to wait until a later date.

Start a new release evaluation by assembling a group of current Notes users from a variety of areas in your company. Invite a value added reseller (VAR), Notes consulting firm, or Lotus themselves to come in and give a presentation on the new release of Notes. Have them focus their presentation on topics that you think are important to your company, which might include some of the following:

- Major new features in the product
- Hardware and software requirements
- Estimated migration effort (time and expertise)
- Retraining requirements
- Estimated cost of migration (hardware upgrades, software acquisition, training, migration specialist, and so on)
- Case studies of successful migrations and how the new release is helping their business

After the presentation, allow the evaluation team some time to digest what they have just seen. Let a day or two pass and then gather the team together for a free form discussion on what they learned. The whole focus of the meeting is on two primary topics:

1. What is the state of the organization's current Notes environment? Good, bad, or ugly.
2. Does the new release have enough meaningful new features to justify the cost of migration?

If the current state of your Notes environment is ugly and the new release will correct the problem, then a migration makes sense. On the other hand, if your current Notes environment is ugly but the new release really won't correct the problem, then a migration can wait while you put your house in order.

Never attempt a migration and restructuring of your Notes infrastructure simultaneously. If problems occur, it'll be very difficult to determine if they are due to the infrastructure change or the new version of Notes.

Try to keep the focus of the evaluation meeting on the two previously mentioned points, but keep in mind that you may not come to a conclusion. More information about your current Notes environment may be necessary before reaching a final decision. This is where you need to be flexible with how you follow the stepped migration planning approach. Some steps will have to be skipped or left incomplete, while you move on to the next step in the migration planning process.

Inventory the Current Environment

Taking an inventory of your current Notes environment is the next step of migration planning. This step is either very easy or very time consuming. If you keep detailed information about each of the computers in your organization and detailed documentation about your Notes network, then this step is easy. If you don't have such information, this step is time consuming because you'll have to visit each computer that is part of your Notes environment and gather detailed information about those machines.

The goal during this step is to verify that all of the computers in your Notes network meet the minimum hardware and software requirements to run the new version of Notes (details of the hardware and software requirements can be found in Chapter 2). Therefore, the type of information you require are things such as the available hard disk space, total RAM, and current operating system. If all the computers in your current environment meet the minimum requirements, you can move on to the next step in your migration plan; otherwise, you'll have to upgrade or replace all of the deficient systems.

If the majority of your Notes environment fails to meet the minimum hardware and software requirements of Notes, be prepared to put the migration project on hold while you overhaul your current computer environment. Failing to upgrade your computer environment before implementing a Notes migration can result in a Notes environment that fails to work as it should.

Creating a Migration Team

Once the inventory of the current environment is complete and all computer upgrades, if any, are finished, then you can move on to creating the migration team. This team is divided into four focus areas:

- Server upgrade

- Workstation upgrade
- Application testing and conversion
- End-user training

Typically, each of these four focus areas will consist of the support professionals that are currently responsible for these areas. For example, the server upgrade team will consist of the current Notes administrators. The workstation upgrade team will consist of both Notes administrators and end-user support people. Application testing and conversion will be handled by the Notes developers that created the applications, or the Notes administrators if you don't have any in-house developers. And finally, the end-user training team should be whoever coordinates training in your organization with input from administrators, developers, and end-user support people.

If your Notes support infrastructure is not large enough to create four separate teams, consider making one team that tackles each area of focus as an individual topic for research, experimentation, and testing.

Once the four focus teams are created, they should get started by doing some research into their areas of responsibility. The Lotus Web site and Notes KnowledgeBase are good places to start; additional informational resources are listed in Appendix F.

Their research should focus on how to migrate, migration traps and pitfalls, and any available migration case studies. Once their research is complete, the information gathered should provide a basic outline for migration experimentation and testing. The overall goal is for your support organization to become comfortable with the new release of Notes and to learn what it takes to actually upgrade from one version to another.

Creating a Test Environment

To further assist your four focus teams with their research, experimentation, and testing, a Notes test environment is needed. Creating this test environment is a critical part of preparing the Notes support organization for what the teams are about to do. While some companies may not have the additional resources to allow for such a test environment, keep in mind that an average desktop computer with 32 MB of RAM and 1 GB of hard disk space is more than adequate for this temporary environment.

The test environment starts out as a place to practice installations, upgrades, and configurations. Initially, your Notes support people should have the freedom to build up and tear down the test environment as needed. At some point in time, however, everyone using the test environment should agree on stabilizing the environment and proceed to installing a simulation of their current Notes network.

By building a simulation of your current Notes network, the support professionals can begin to get a feeling for how migration will work on their production machines. From these experiments your Notes support people should begin to create their own set of migration steps for servers, workstations, and applications. Every aspect of Notes operation should be thoroughly tested in this controlled environment. Database access and usage, e-mail sending and receiving, and replication both between servers and from server to workstation are a few examples of what you should be testing to verify that migration will not damage your current Notes environment.

Training the Technical Support Organization

One of the most important steps in planning a Notes migration is training your support organization. This training includes server administration, Notes development, and end-user support. Although I maintain that migration planning should be a flexible process and that not all steps presented in this chapter need to be followed, training the support organization is one step you just can't skip. The reason training is required is simple: If your support organization doesn't fully understand the product they are migrating to, there is no possible way that the migration will be successful.

Therefore, get your support organization trained early in the migration planning process and make sure their training is complete and meaningful. Decide on a core requirement for relevant Notes knowledge such as Notes server administration, basic Notes development, and Notes user support. From this point, use your four focus groups to guide additional training. Even if one support professional appears very fluent in Notes Release 4, make sure you encourage that individual to take advantage of formalized training to reconfirm what they already know.

Avoid making knowledge assumptions about individuals. Just because someone talks the talk doesn't mean they can walk the walk.

Creating the Migration Plan

The final step in planning for a Notes migration is to create an actual migration document. This document attempts to assemble everything you know about Notes migration and have done in preparation for this project into a single cohesive schedule. This schedule serves as a map for the time and resources required to complete the following tasks:

1. Migration rehearsal
2. Server migration
3. End-user training
4. Workstation migration
5. Mail migration
6. Database and application migration

Once the migration plan is complete, you're ready to start implementing it.

Implementing Your Migration Plan

The next phase of migrating from Notes Release 3 to Release 4 is implementing your migration plan. During the final step of the first phase you should have created a migration document that outlines steps to follow during migration and a schedule for the project. During the implementation phase you will follow the six basic steps outlined in your migration documentation:

1. Migration rehearsal
2. Server migration
3. End-user training
4. Workstation migration
5. Mail migration
6. Database and application migration

As with other aspects of migration, these steps are not etched in stone and can be moved around, deferred to a later time, or skipped altogether depending on your unique Notes environment and needs.

Migration Rehearsal

Having experience with the actual steps involved in migration definitely helps to ensure that a migration is successful, but such experience is difficult to get. Either you've done a migration or you haven't. You can read all you want about migration, but all the reading in the world can't substitute for real hands-on experience. The only way to get such experience without really doing a migration is to conduct several migration rehearsals.

A Notes test environment is absolutely required for a migration rehearsal. The only possible substitution for a test environment is to back up your production servers, execute a migration on these servers, test the results, and then delete the migrated server and restore the original server from your backup. It's not the best way to rehearse a migration, but it's undoubtedly the closest you'll get to the real thing.

Assuming you have a test environment, you can start your rehearsal by configuring this environment to look just like the real thing. Servers will be configured to match their production counterparts as closely as possible. You can even take a backup from your production servers and restore the backup to servers in the simulated environment.

If you create the servers in your test environment from backup copies of the real thing, make sure you isolate these test servers on their own LAN to avoid confusion and conflicts.

The next step in your migration rehearsal is to work through the remaining migration tasks and schedule outlined in your document. Record the actual time it takes for each migration task and note any problems that occur during the rehearsal. When the rehearsal is complete, review any problems and try to determine why they occurred and come up with a solution. Review the time consumed by each task and make sure that your migration schedule is realistic. Repeat the rehearsal to verify that solutions to any problems work and reconfirm your previous task times.

Server Migration

The most critical machines to upgrade in your Notes environment are the Notes servers. These machines are the heart and sole of your Notes network and their upgrade should not be taken lightly. Extensive precautionary measures must be taken so you don't inadvertently render your Notes environment useless.

Upgrading a Notes server is much the same as installing a new one. The following steps detail the process of a Notes server upgrade:

1. Back up the entire Notes server machine. You may have to completely shut down the Notes server program in order to backup all of the Notes files. The Public Address Book (NAMES.NSF), for example, is always open, and unless your backup software can handle open files you'll have to shut down the Notes server program to close this file.
2. Verify that your Notes backup is valid and successful. As a cautionary measure you might want to create a second backup in case something happens to the first.
3. Create detailed instructions for restoring the tape backup in the event the migration is unsuccessful or problematic.
4. Start the migration by shutting down the Notes server program if it isn't already shut down.
5. Install the new version of Notes right over the existing version.
6. When the installation is complete, reboot the computer and make sure the Notes server doesn't automatically restart.

If you've customized any of the system templates, make sure you have backup copies of these templates. After the upgrade is complete you can copy these customizations into the new system templates.

Once the server is upgraded to the new version of Notes, you can proceed to upgrading your Public Address Book from the Release 3 format to the new Release 4 format.

Upgrading the Public Address Book

Once the Notes server is upgraded to the new version of Notes, you have to upgrade to the Public Address Book. The Public Address Book is a critical part of your Notes environment because it contains information about your Notes servers, users, groups, and connections between servers. Anything that defines your Notes environment is contained in the Public Address Book and without this essential database your Notes network doesn't function.

There are three main phases for upgrading the Public Address Book: Updating the database design, adding roles to the ACL, and enabling the delegation feature on all the documents in the database.

- **Update the database design:** The Public Address Book, the same as all Notes system databases, is based on a design template. Whenever a change is made to a design template and a database inherits its design from that template, the change won't appear in the database until the design is refreshed. Therefore, to completely upgrade your Notes environment you'll have to refresh the design on the Public Address Book. However, Notes will remind you about this requirement, as you will soon see.

- **Adding admin roles to the ACL:** Admin roles is a new feature for Notes Release 4 and eliminates the need to give Editor access to all Notes administrators. With admin roles you can assign all Notes administrators Author with Create access to the Public Address Book and selectively grant them specific roles. For example, you could grant one administrator the role of GroupCreator. This role enables that administrator to create new Group documents but does not allow them to create other documents in the Public Address Book.

- **Enable the delegation feature:** During this phase you'll enable the roles you've assigned to take affect by running a special delegation agent. If this agent hasn't been run for all the documents in the Public Address Book, then your role assignments won't work on the existing documents.

Updating the Public Address Book design is something you'll need to do on each server you upgrade. However, adding roles and the delegation feature only needs to be done on the first server upgraded. You can use replication to distribute roles and delegation to other servers after they're upgraded.

The following steps detail the process for completing the three phases of upgrading the Public Address Book to the new Release 4 version:

1. Before you begin make sure you have a valid backup of your entire server in the event of a problem.
2. If you've customized your company's Public Address Book, document the customizations or make a new copy of the database in a safe location and only copy the design.
3. Start the Notes workstation program on the first server or other server in the domain that is allowed to replicate design changes.
4. The program will start and Notes will ask whether you want to upgrade the Name and Address Book; select Yes.

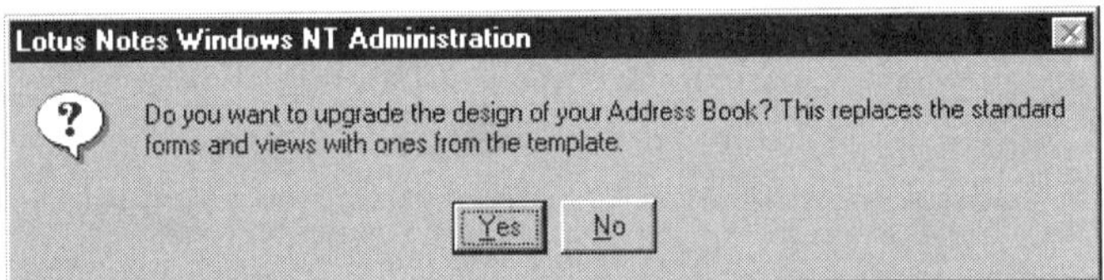

5. After the upgrade is complete, select the Public Address Book on the workspace.
6. Once the design for the Public Address Book is updated, select the Public Address Book and from the menu bar, select Actions ➢ Add Admin Roles to Access Control List. This menu selection launches a built-in agent that adds new roles to the Access Control List (ACL) in the Public Address Book (details about these new roles are available in Chapter 7).
7. When prompted, Click OK.
8. Once the new roles are added, you need to enable the delegation feature on all the documents in the Public Address Book. This task is accomplished with another built-in agent: Apply Delegation for All Selected Entries.
9. Open each view in the Public Address Book and select all of the documents in that view and then from the menu bar, select Actions ➢ Apply Delegation for All Selected Entries. This process could take some time depending on how many documents your Public Address Book contains.

10. If your migration upgrades all the servers in your Notes environment over a period of days, then you'll need to check the replication settings on the server you just upgraded and on all of the servers that will receive replication changes (see the sidebar *Replication Settings for the Public Address Book*).

Connection documents created in Release 3 are automatically assigned the Pull-Pull replication method. You can edit these connections and select another method. The possible methods of replication are discussed in Chapter 8.

After the Public Address Book is upgraded, you'll want to verify that all client connections and database access are still possible. Using a Notes client that has a previous version of Notes installed, connect to the upgraded server and try opening some databases and sending mail. If everything operates as it used to, you've successfully upgraded the Notes server, including its Public Address Book. Now you're ready to move on to end-user training and the workstation upgrades.

Replication Settings for the Public Address Book

The Public Address Book on the first server should have the following setting:

- In the Replication Settings dialog box (File ➢ Replication ➢ Settings) on the Send tab, deselect Do Not Send Changes in Database Title & Catalog Info to Other Replicas.

The Public Address Books on the servers that receive replication changes should have the following settings:

- In the Database properties box (File ➢ Database ➢ Properties) on the Design tab, select Inherit Design from Template and deselect Database Is a Template.
- In the Replication Settings dialog box on the Advanced tab, select the Forms, Views, Agents, and Access Control List options.
- In the Replication Settings dialog box on the Send tab, deselect Do Not Send Changes in Database Title & Catalog Info to Other Replicas.
- In the Access Control List (File ➢ Database ➢ Access Control), add the hub server as Manager.

After the Public Address Book upgrade is complete and you've tested connectivity to your upgraded server, you should consider updating the view indexes for the Public Address Book and converting the database file format to Release 4.*x*. These two additional steps, while not required, can help your server upgrade in two ways:

1. The view index format is updated the first time the server accesses the Public Address Book. If your Public Address Book contains several documents, view index format updates can take a long time and have a negative impact on server performance. You can specify a time for updating the view indexes to control when the server will take a performance hit, for example, late at night or over the weekend.
2. Converting the Public Address Book to Release 4 file format allows you to fully benefit from certain Release 4.5 features, such as field level replication.

The view index and database file formats are not replicated between Notes servers when you replicate the Public Address Book. Therefore, you'll have to update the view index and database file format on every server you upgrade.

Completing both of these optional steps is a fairly simple process. The combination of the COMPACT and UPDALL commands can update the view indexes and convert the file format with one command line entry:

1. At an operating system command prompt change to the Notes directory and type the command that corresponds to your Notes server operating system platform:
   - OS/2: **icompact names.nsf & iupdall names.nsf & notes server**
   - Windows: **ncompact names.nsf & nupdall names.nsf & notes server**
   - UNIX: **compact names.nsf;updall names.nsf;server**
   - Novell NetWare: **vcompact names.nsf & vupdall names.nsf & notes server**
2. Enter your password if prompted.
3. Repeat these steps on each server after the Public Address Book design changes replicate to other servers in your organization.

End-User Training

During the first phase of Notes migration I mentioned that training the support organization was a mandatory step. You couldn't expect a successful Notes migration without a support staff that fully understood the product they were migrating to. The same can be said about end-users. You can't expect a successful migration if the end-users don't know how to use the new product.

End-user training is less demanding than support staff training in that end-users don't need to understand every aspect of Notes like the support organization does. Notes administration and development training is completely unnecessary for end-users. What the users do need to know, however, is how to use this new product.

Since you're doing a migration versus an entirely new Notes installation, it is safe to assume that the user community has already been using Notes and won't need a thorough introduction to every aspect of the product. Most of your training can focus on the new features of Notes and what has changed since the last version. Lecture hall style training with follow up computer-based training supplements from companies such as ReCor (covered in Appendix E) are completely acceptable training approaches for a migration project. The only thing to keep in mind for end-user training is that you need to time it to coincide with their workstation upgrade.

The worst thing you can do when it comes to end-user training is to do it too early or too late. Training offered too early will probably be forgotten and have to be repeated for most users. On the other hand, training offered too late often covers material people have already learned the hard way.

Workstation Migration

Normally, a workstation migration is an administrative task and not a technical challenge. More time is spent on scheduling the migration than doing the actual work. And therefore, this step of the implementation phase is the most personal of them all.

You'll need to rely on whatever methods or processes you currently have in place to schedule a workstation migration. If you don't have any formalized upgrade procedures, you might want to consider one of the following suggestions:

- **At the desktop:** Visit each machine and manually execute the upgrade.

- **Over the network:** Install a copy of the Notes client to a read-only network drive and distribute installation instructions.
- **Using a third party installation product:** Products such as WinInstall and Microsoft's SMS help facilitate automating software installation so minimal instructions are required.

Whatever way you choose to upgrade your computers, make sure you plan for unique installations such as remote users.

Even though a workstation migration is mostly an administrative task, there are still a few steps you should follow for each upgrade. The following is a short check list for a workstation migration:

1. Make sure you have a copy of the previous version of Notes readily available.
2. Make a backup of the critical user files: USER.ID, NAMES.NSF, DESKTOP.DSK, NOTES.INI, and any custom databases or local mail databases that have been created.
3. Start the installation and install right over the previous copy of Notes.
4. Test the new installation:
   A. Access the server and use some of the databases.
   B. Open the user's mail and open, edit, and create a mail message.
   C. If the user also accesses the Notes server remotely, test that connection as well.
5. Stop and start Notes a few times and try the tests listed in step 4.
6. Try to cold and warm boot the computer; then restart Notes and use it as the final test.

If the computer passes all of the previously mentioned tests, the installation is a success. The starting and stopping of Notes as an installation test might seem excessive. However, these additional tests only take a few extra minutes and they give you the chance to catch any unexpected problems before the user encounters them.

Mail Migration

The Notes mail database inherits its design from a database template, which in Release 4 has been upgraded so that the new features such as folders are available in mail (MAIL4.NTF). In Release 4.5 there is yet another new mail template, MAIL45.NTF, which includes the calendaring and scheduling features. If your company is using Notes mail as its message platform, you'll need to upgrade the Notes mail database in one of two ways:

- Upgrade using the mail conversion utility (Convert server task).
- Upgrade using a Public Address Book form that automates both the workstation and mail upgrade.

Regardless of which method you choose to update your mail databases, the same tasks take place:

- The new mail template, MAIL45.NTF, is applied to each mail database.
- Mail categories become folders, subcategories become subfolders, categorized documents are added to the appropriate folder or subfolder, and uncategorized received documents are added to the Inbox.
- Notes adds StdR45Mail to the Inherit Design from Template setting in the Database Properties InfoBox if the mail database previously had a design template specified.

Folder and subfolder creation is not done when upgrading from Release 4.*x* to 4.5 because these folders and subfolders already exist.

The Mail Conversion Utility

The mail conversion utility is a server task that you launch from the server console and is most useful for upgrading several mail databases simultaneously. The following steps detail how to use this utility:

1. Make sure you upgraded the workstations and servers to Release 4.5 and have a valid tape backup of all mail databases about to be upgraded.
2. Inform the users who may have created custom forms, views, or agents (formally known as macros in Release 3) for their mail database to copy these items to a temporary database.

3. From the Notes server console, shut down the Mail Router to temporarily suspend mail delivery with the following command:

    tell router quit

4. Shutting down the Mail Router will cause mail messages to be stored in the server's MAIL.BOX file. When the Mail Router is reloaded, all pending messages will be delivered as intended.

5. Load the mail conversion utility according to the following syntax:

    load convert *<mail database> <current design> <new mail template>*

6. After the mail conversion utility completes the upgrade, restart the Mail Router with the following command:

    load router

7. Inform all users that they can copy previously created custom forms, views, and agents to the upgraded mail database.

Using the Convert server task is relatively simple. However, the syntax for loading the Convert task can be a bit tricky. Therefore, what follows is a description of the command's syntax and optional command line arguments indicated by brackets ([]):

> **load convert** [**-f**] [**-l**] [**-r**] [**-i**] [**-d**] [**-n**] [*drive:\directory*]*filename* [*oldtemplate newtemplate*]

- **-f:** Upgrades only the database names listed in a text file. Specify the text file to use for *filename*. The -f option can be specified before or after the text filename. This option cannot be used simultaneously with the -l option.
- **-l:** Creates a text file that contains a list of mail files on the server. To use this argument, you must upgrade the Public Address Book to the Release 4.5 design template. Specify a text filename to use when saving the mail file information for *filename* (any file extension is acceptable). The text file is created in the Notes data directory unless you include a drive letter and complete directory path when you specify the filename. If the filename already exists, the mail conversion utility warns you about the conflict and will not overwrite the file.
- **-r:** Searches the specified directory and all of its subdirectories.

- -i: Ignores the maximum folder limit. If you try to upgrade a database that has more than 200 categories or subcategories and you do not use the -i argument, the mail conversion utility does not upgrade the mail database. Do not attempt to use this argument unless the mail user's workstation has not been upgraded to Release 4.5 first.
- -d: Replaces the design template with the template you specify, but does not create folders or subfolders and does not add categorized documents to them.
- -n: Displays a list of databases that the Convert utility will attempt to upgrade. This option is a great way to ensure that the Convert utility will operate on only the databases you want upgraded.
- *Drive*: Specifies the drive letter on which the Notes databases or the text files exist. If no drive is specified, the Notes data directory is used as the root directory.
- *Directory*: Specifies the directory where the Notes databases or the text files exist. If you do not specify a drive, Notes uses the Notes data directory as the root directory to search for the databases or text files. For example, if you specify MAIL and your Notes data directory is located in D:\Notes\Data, the mail conversion utility looks for databases in the D:\Notes\Data\mail directory since it uses D:\Notes\Data as the root directory.
- *Filename*: Specifies the name of the databases to convert. Wildcards (*) are accepted to specify several databases.
- *Oldtemplate*: Specifies the name of the template or templates the databases are currently using and only upgrades those mail databases based on the *Oldtemplate*. Wildcards (*) are accepted to match more than one template name in the databases. If you use an asterisk (*), make sure the databases you specify are mail databases because the mail conversion utility upgrades the design of the databases to mail databases, regardless of whether they are actually mail databases.
- *Newtemplate*: Specifies the filename for the template you want the databases to use.

Do not attempt to upgrade a Release 3 mail database with the menu option File ➢ Database ➢ Replace Design. This approach does not convert categories to folders or subfolders as the conversion utilities do. If you have tried this approach, you can correct the mistake by opening the mail database and selecting View ➢ Design, selecting Folders, and deleting $Inbox. Then upgrade the database using the conversion utility.

Public Address Book Conversion Form

Upgrading mail databases using the Public Address Book form lets administrators upgrade Notes on workstations as well as upgrade mail databases. This upgrade method is useful when you need to control when workstation and mail upgrades occur.

The conversion form method allows Notes administrators to send a mail message with embedded buttons that enable quick and easy software and mail database upgrade. To use this process for mail database and workstation software upgrade, two essential items must be in place before you can begin:

1. A publicly accessible file server must have an installable copy of the Notes client software. You can put such a copy of Notes on a file server by selecting the Install on a File Server option during a standard Notes install.

2. Make sure Notes administrators are listed in the Public Address Book's Access Control List as having NetModifier, UserModifier, and at least Author with Create access rights.

Once both of these prerequisites are satisfied, you can begin the process of upgrading workstation software and converting mail databases:

1. From the Notes workspace, open the Public Address Book. Click System Databases and choose Address Book.

2. From the menu bar, select View ➢ Server ➢ Mail Users. The Send Upgrade Notifications button will appear on the Action bar.

3. Click the Send Upgrade Notifications button from the Action bar and an Upgrade Message document appears.

4. In the To field on the Upgrade Message document enter the names of the users you want to upgrade. You can also click the Address button on the Action bar and select users from the Address dialog box.

5. At the bottom of the Upgrade Message document there are two sections that enable you to specify additional information for the upgrade process. Start with the Notes Install Kit Paths section.

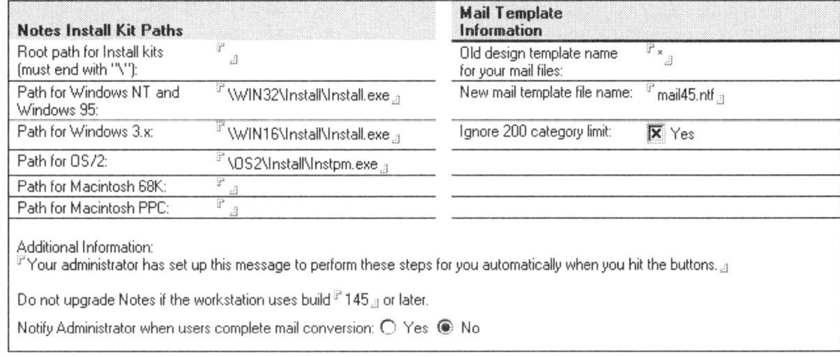

Notes Install Kit Paths		**Mail Template Information**	
Root path for Install kits (must end with "\"):		Old design template name for your mail files:	x
Path for Windows NT and Windows 95:	\WIN32\Install\Install.exe	New mail template file name:	mail45.ntf
Path for Windows 3.x:	\WIN16\Install\Install.exe	Ignore 200 category limit:	[X] Yes
Path for OS/2:	\OS2\Install\Instpm.exe		
Path for Macintosh 68K:			
Path for Macintosh PPC:			

Additional Information:
Your administrator has set up this message to perform these steps for you automatically when you hit the buttons.

Do not upgrade Notes if the workstation uses build 145 or later.

Notify Administrator when users complete mail conversion: ○ Yes ◉ No

- **Root path for Install kits:** This field allows you to specify the root for all of the install kits, for example, F:\Apps\Notes.

- **Path for Windows NT and Windows 95:** By default, this field is filled in, but you can change it if the location for these files is different than shown. This path assumes that the root precedes it.

- **Path for Windows 3.x:** By default, this field is filled in, but you can change it if the location for these files is different than shown. This path assumes that the root precedes it.

- **Path for OS/2:** By default, this field is filled in, but you can change it if the location for these files is different than shown. This path assumes that the root precedes it.

- **Path for Macintosh 68K:** By default, this field is blank. However, the function of this field is similar to the previous fields, which is the location, below the previously defined root, of the installable Notes Macintosh client software.

- **Path for Macintosh PPC:** By default, this field is blank. However, the function of this field is similar to the previous fields, which is the location, below the previously defined root, of the installable Notes Macintosh client software.

For both of the Path for Macintosh fields to work, the file server you are accessing must support Macintosh connectivity using a protocol such as AppleTalk.

6. The next section is where you specify Mail Template Information:
   - **Old design template name for your mail files:** Use this field to specify the name of the previous mail template. Entering a specific template name will limit the mail conversion to only the mail databases based on that specific template. All other templates will not be upgraded. If you want all mail templates upgraded, however, then enter * (asterisk) and Notes will upgrade all mail databases regardless of their current design template names.
   - **New mail template file name:** By default, this field lists the Notes 4.5 template (MAIL45.NTF). However, this field is editable in the event that you renamed the mail template or need to specify a different one.
   - **Ignore 200 category limit:** This field is used to convert mail databases that are based on a Release 3 template and contain more than 200 categories. If you are not upgrading a mail database based on a Release 3 template, or the user being upgraded doesn't care about converting categories over 200 to folders, then you can deselect this check box.
7. You can use the Additional Information field to communicate important upgrade information to the users being upgraded.
8. If you have some Notes 4.5 clients already installed you can choose to upgrade them if their build number is less than the one you specify in the Do Not Upgrade Notes If the Workstation Uses Build [*x*] or Later field.
9. If you want to receive a message indicating whether the upgrade process was completed successfully, select Yes in the Notify Administrator When Users Complete Mail Conversion field.

When the users finally receive the upgrade message, they will have the option to upgrade their workstation if they are not using the build specified or a later build than the one entered in step eight. To complete the workstation upgrade process and convert their mail database, they only need to follow the instructions shown in the mail message (see Figure 3.1).

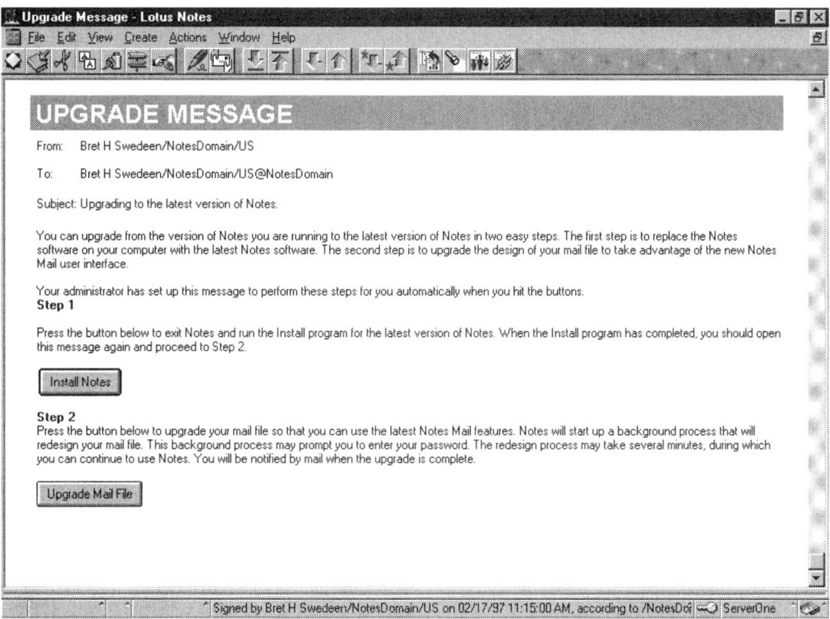

FIGURE 3.1 The Upgrade Message contains two buttons that facilitate the Notes upgrade process with simple instructions explaining the purpose of each button.

Both methods for upgrading a mail database, the conversion utility and the Public Address Book form, execute on all documents even if you create or modify them after you converted the database. Therefore, do not use either of these methods more than once on a mail database. Otherwise, if you've created private views or agents they'll be wiped out and you'll have to create them all over again.

Upgrading Replica Mail Databases

If users have replica mail databases on their local hard drives or on several servers, upgrade only their main mail databases and tell them to replicate the changes to the replicas. A user's main mail database is the database that the Mail Router delivers mail to on a server.

Database and Application Migration

Database and application migration is essentially a topic that affects Notes developers more than Notes administrators. This part of migration may go on well after the bulk of the migration is complete and your involvement as a

Notes administrator will probably be very limited. However, you should make yourself available and help the Notes developers whenever possible. You'll probably also want to set up a Notes server reserved for the developers. With a server of their own, the Notes developers can test their migrated applications in a controlled environment before putting them into production.

Post Migration Activities

Just because all the Notes servers, workstations, and applications are successfully migrated to the latest release doesn't mean the project is over. The migration team still needs to meet and review what they've done to double-check that the work started is complete. This meeting is also a great time to review the project, discuss what worked well and what went wrong, and evaluate changes to the Notes standards document.

Migration Team Debriefing

Large scale migrations such as Notes Release 3 to Notes Release 4 are not something you do every day. The magnitude of such a project requires great attention to detail. And therefore, time should be spent after the project double-checking the work done.

Because migration projects are so large, it is easy to overlook items that didn't directly affect the migration itself. One perfect example of something that can be overlooked is training new employees on the new release of Notes. There may have been a training program for the older version of Notes, but updating that material didn't seem necessary during a migration because training the current users was far more important at the time. Now that the migration is over, however, it is a good time to directly address such items and work on solutions.

Aside from double-checking your work, you should also conduct a project review session with the migration team. There is more to learn from a migration project than just technical knowledge. Migrations with the scope and importance of Notes Release 3 to Notes Release 4 allow people to learn about such things as technical research and planning, resource scheduling, and project management. Use this review meeting as a way to discuss what worked well, what failed, and ways to improve future migration projects.

Updating Your Notes Standards Document

The most tedious task of any migration project is updating the Notes standards document. Hopefully, when you first installed your Notes network you created such a document (Chapter 2 discusses what this document should contain). So, if this document does exist, take the time to update the Notes server topology, naming standards, and any documented procedures. Remember, this document is important to your Notes operation because it is a single, nonhuman point of reference used to guide the support and maintenance of your Notes network.

Summary

A Notes migration can run like a well-oiled machine if you just logically approach the task. Start with extensive migration planning. When the plan is complete, move on to the implementation phase. And when the implementation is done, don't forget to review your work, review the project, and update your Notes standards document.

Of the three phases of a migration project, the planning phase is the most critical. So many problems and so much confusion can be avoided with proper planning. Don't let anyone push you into the implementation phase if the planning phase is not complete. Implementing without a plan is like going on a trip to someplace you've never been without directions. More than likely you won't reach your destination.

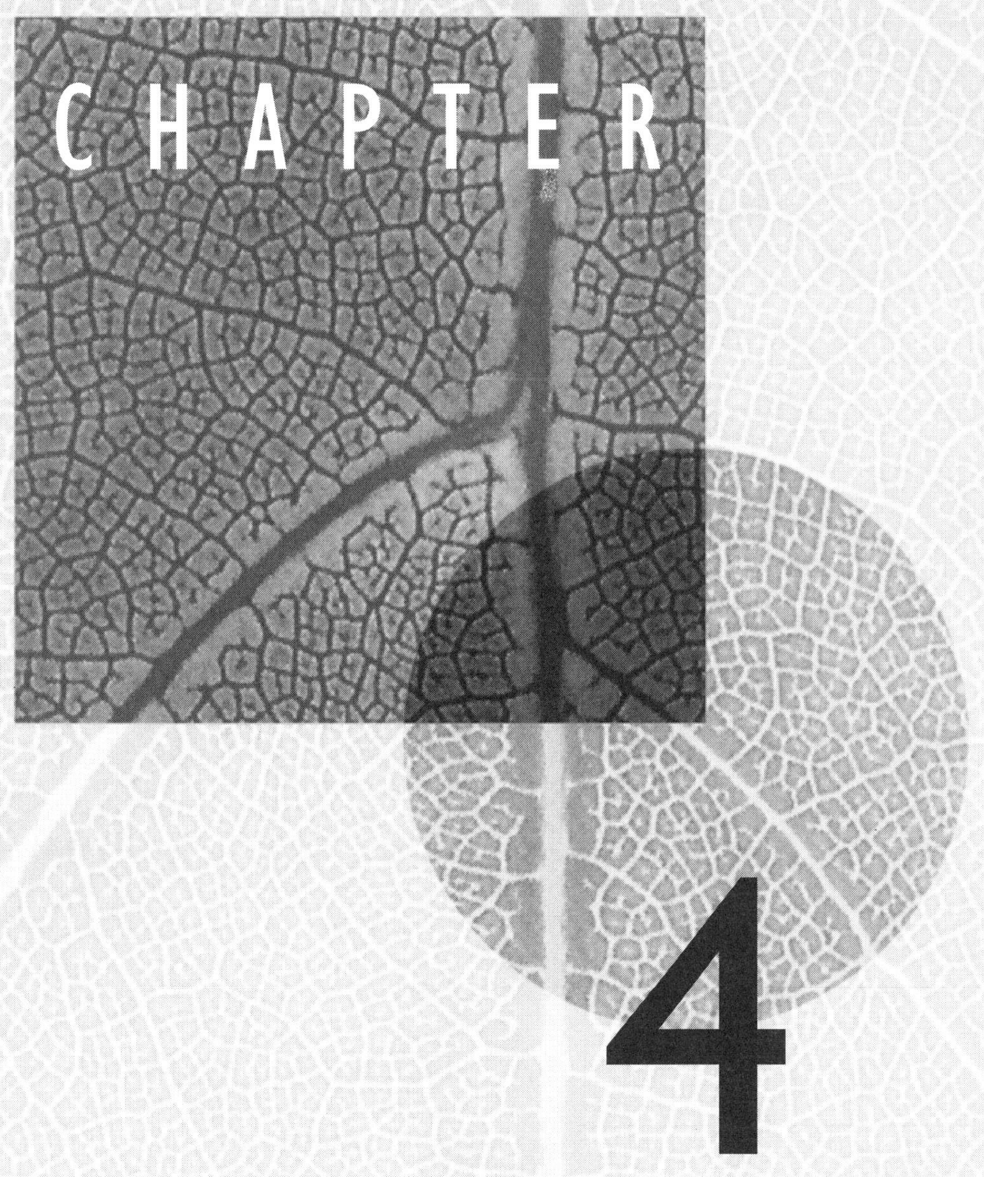

4

Notes Server Management

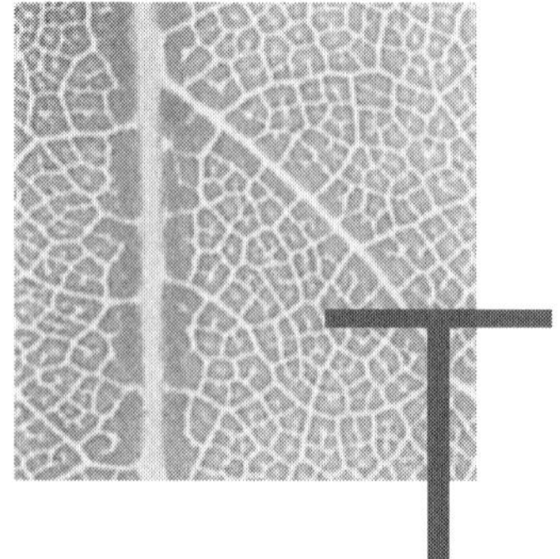

The Lotus Notes server is filled with exciting features and powerful capabilities. Many of these features and functions, such as electronic mail, calendaring and scheduling, and Web navigation are considered the responsibility of the Notes administrator. However, at the core of these features and capabilities is the Notes server itself. Without the Notes server these features and capabilities would not be possible. Therefore, as a Notes administrator it is your responsibility to keep your Notes server up and running.

Notes server management is a vast topic that encompasses a wide variety of routine activities and management tools. As a Notes administrator, you'll be installing servers, creating and certifying IDs, planning for disasters, and hopefully preventing disasters before they happen. You'll also get wrapped up in routine management tasks that can be made less mundane and less time consuming with the Administration Process management tool.

All of these routine activities and management tools are really only the tip of the iceberg when it comes to Notes server management. This chapter should give you a solid introduction to some of the things you'll be expected to do and know as a Notes administrator. However, what is presented here is by no means all that is involved in Notes server management. Each day of Notes server management presents new opportunities for learning, and some opportunities for frustration, as you will find out once you start managing your own network of Notes servers.

Installing Your First Server

The first Notes server you install in your Notes environment is the most important. From this first server comes your first organizational certifying certificate, which is used to create additional servers, other organizational unit certifiers, and new users.

The Notes server installation, much the same as the Notes client installation, is divided into two stages. The first stage copies the Notes software to your server machine according to settings you specify. Those settings include:

- Which directory to use for installation
- Installation type: Workstation, Server, or Custom

The second stage of the installation is when you actually set up your server. During this phase you will name your new server, assign an administrator, select a network protocol, and make other specifications. The following steps detail the server setup process:

1. After the server software is copied to your server machine, double-click the Lotus Notes Client 4 icon.
2. The Notes Server Setup dialog box appears. In this dialog box, specify whether this server installation is the first Lotus Notes server in your organization or an additional Lotus Notes server. By default, the first option is selected. Because this is your first Notes server, click OK.

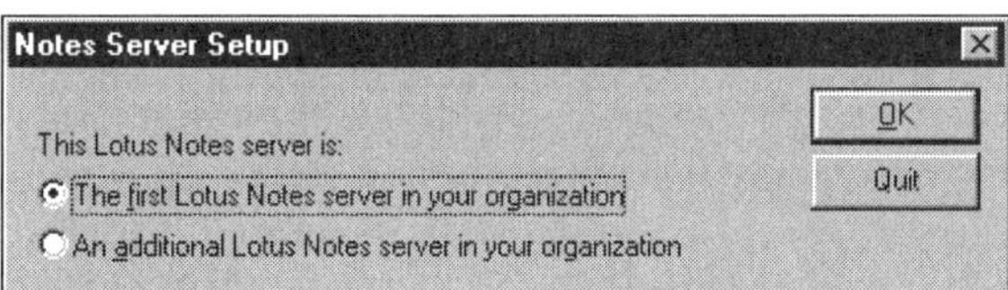

3. The First Server Setup dialog box appears, which includes several fields that help define the server being installed.

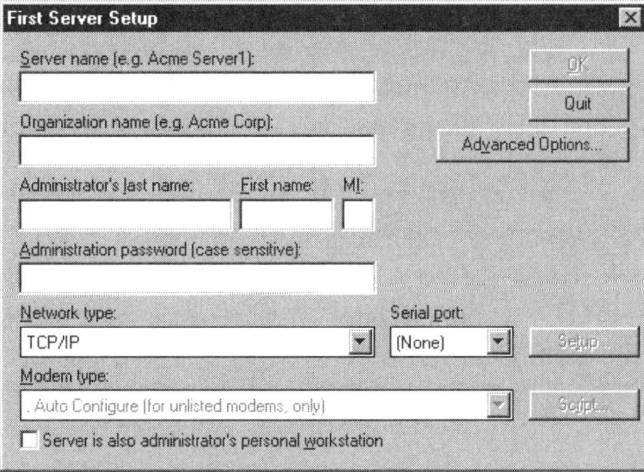

- **Server name**: Enter the name of your new server here (see the sidebar *Naming Guidelines* for more information).
- **Organization name**: Enter the name of your company or organization. The organization name entered during the first server installation becomes the domain name for your Notes network by default.
- **Administrator's last name**: Enter the last name for your first Notes administrator. I prefer to create a fictional administrator during this step which can later be used as a single administrator logon to share between several Notes administrators.
- **First name**: Enter the first name for your Notes administrator.
- **MI**: Enter the administrator's middle initial if one exists. Keep in mind that using a period after a middle initial can sometimes cause problems if you use the SMTP Message Transfer Agent (MTA).
- **Administrator's password**: A password is required. The password entered here is used for the administrator's ID and certifying ID created during this portion of the server setup. By default, you are required to enter a password of eight characters or more. Passwords are case sensitive and using a random alpha-numeric combination makes guessing a password more difficult than using a regular word.
- **Network type**: From a drop-down list, select the network protocol that will be used for this server. You can select from TCP/IP (the default setting), NetBIOS, SPX, Banyan Vines, or AppleTalk. You can also add more protocols later if this server will communicate with users and other servers with more than one network protocol.
- **Serial port**: If you don't select a Network Type, it's probably because you're selecting serial port communication. This drop-down list offers COM ports one through five to choose from.
- **Modem type**: If you selected a serial port for communication, then you'll have to select the type of modem connected to that port.
- **Server is also administrator's personal workstation**: If the Notes administrator is also going to use this Notes server as their personal workstation, check this option. However, if you plan to run one of the MTAs on this server, I recommend you don't use this machine as the administrator's personal workstation because it has been known to cause problems with the MTA.

4. After you've filled out the First Server Setup dialog box, press OK to complete the server setup or the Advanced button for more setup options.

Naming Guidelines

Chapter 2 addresses creating a Notes standards document that outlines guidelines for naming users, servers, and groups. If you have created such a document, refer to it as you install each server. Whether you have a Notes standards document or not, here are a few naming guidelines to keep in mind as you name each server:

- Server names can include one or more words (up to seventy-nine characters) and can consist of any characters except parentheses, at signs (@), slashes and backslashes (/ and \), equal signs (=), and plus signs (+). While spaces are permitted, they are not recommended.
- Choose a name you want to keep. Changing a server name involves recertifying the server ID and changing the name in the Server document, Group documents, ACLs, Connection documents, and the Person documents that use that server as their mail server.
- Avoid using spaces in server names. Spaces in a server name require that you enclose the server name in quotation marks when you use server console commands; and spaces have been known to cause problems when using the cc:Mail MTA.
- Replication and mail routing usually perform best when based on numeric rather than alphabetical order. For example, if the router has multiple choices for a routing path, Notes routes mail to the server 01Sales before routing to the server Support.
- A server name can contain up to seventy-nine characters, but in certain networks the first several characters must be unique in order for the network to identify the server:

  NetBIOS requires the first fifteen characters be unique.

  AppleTalk requires the first thirty-two characters be unique.

  SPX requires the first forty-seven characters be unique.

When you create your first organizational name remember that this name also becomes the default domain name. Here are a few things to keep in mind when creating domain and organizational names:

- Domain names should be a single word or string (up to thirty-one characters). Do not use periods (.) in a domain name because they are reserved characters.
- The organization name is the name of the Certifier ID and is appended to all user and server names. The name can be up to sixty-four characters.

Advanced Server Setup Options

If you select the Advanced button, the Advanced Server Setup Options dialog box appears (see Figure 4.1) and presents several additional options.

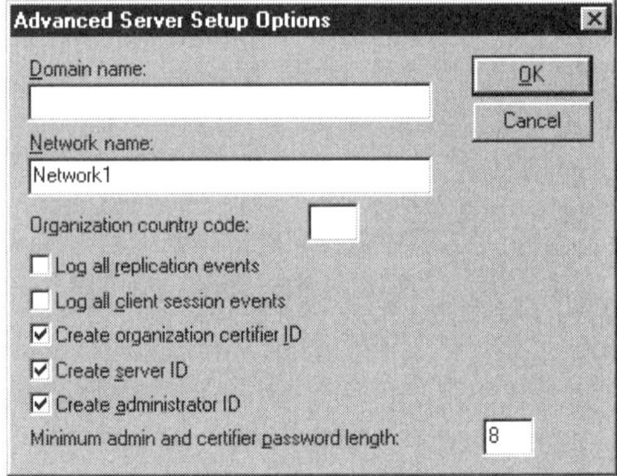

FIGURE 4.1

In the Advanced Server Setup Options dialog box you can specify additional settings for server setup. However, these additional settings are optional and may be configured at a later time.

- **Domain name:** If you want to override the use of the organizational name as the default domain name, you can specify a different domain name here (see the *Naming Guidelines* sidebar for domain name restrictions).
- **Network name:** By default, Network1 populates this field. You can change this default and specify a different Notes named network for the new server. A Notes named network identifies a group of servers that share a common protocol so they can communicate directly.

- **Organization country code:** If your company is using X.500 names and the people administering this naming convention approve the organization name for your Notes network, you can then specify a country code when you create an organization certifier ID. Country codes minimize the chance of naming conflicts as a result of another country having the same organization name as yours.
- **Log all replication events:** Place a check next to this option if you want all replication events recorded in the Notes Log. You can always change this option later through a NOTES.INI file setting.
- **Log all client session events:** Place a check next to this option if you want all client sessions recorded in the Notes Log. You can always change this option later through a NOTES.INI file setting.
- **Create organizational certifier ID:** By default, this option is selected. However, you can deselect this option and create the organizational certifier later through the Server Administration tool.
- **Create server ID:** By default, this option is selected. I recommend leaving the default for this field, as most people do, otherwise the first server ID won't be created.
- **Create administrator ID:** By default, this option is selected. However, you can deselect this option and create the administrator's user ID later using the Server Administration tool.
- **Minimum admin and certifier password length:** By default, this is set to eight. You can shorten or lengthen this setting to determine the minimum length that a password has to be.

Once all of the standard and any advanced options have been set, click OK to initiate the server setup process. During this process a number of activities take place:

- The new Notes domain for your Notes servers is created.
- The selected network protocols and serial ports are enabled.
- The Public Address Book for the new domain is created. The Install program uses the PUBNAMES.NTF template to create the Public Address Book. The address book is created in the same directory you previously chose for your server's data files and given the default name NAMES.NSF.

- The organization certifier ID for your organization is created. This ID file is saved to the same directory you previously chose for the server's data files and given the default name CERT.ID, which can be renamed for identification purposes.
- The Certifier document in the Public Address Book is created. This document describes the organization certifier.
- The server ID for the new server is created. This ID file is saved to the same directory you previously chose for the server's data files and given the default name SERVER.ID.
- The server ID is certified with the organization certifier ID.
- The Server document is created and added to the Public Address Book. This document describes the first server, based on information that you specify during setup.
- A Person document for the administrator is created and added to the Public Address Book.
- A user ID (USER.ID) and a password for the administrator are created and attached to the administrator's Person document in the Public Address Book.
- The administrator's user ID is certified with the organization certifier ID.
- The administrator's name and the server's name are added as managers in the Access Control List (ACL) of the Public Address Book.
- The server name is added to the LocalDomainServers group in the Public Address Book.
- The Notes Log for the server is created in the same directory you previously chose for the server's data files and given the default name LOG.NSF.
- The mail directory is created in the new server's data directory and a mail file for the administrator is created in that directory.

Once the setup process is complete you'll still have to select your server's time zone and determine if you want your server to observe daylight savings time. Once the zone selection is made, click OK in the Setup Complete dialog box and your new server is ready to go.

Optional Server Setup Steps

Once the server setup is complete, the Notes server is ready to start. There are, however, additional setup steps worth doing before you actually start your Notes server for the first time. For example, before I start a Notes server for the first time I like to specify an Administration Server for the Public Address Book, create a Certification Log database, and do a complete system backup.

Additional Public Address Book Settings

The Notes Administration Process (described later in this chapter) helps make routine administrative activities a little more automated than they normally are. However, to benefit from this additional level of automation, Notes requires that an Administration Server is specified for the Public Address Book. The following steps describe how to make this setting for the Public Address Book:

1. From the Notes client workspace, select the Public Address Book.
2. From the menu bar, choose File ➢ Database ➢ Access Control.
3. In the Access Control List dialog box, click the Advanced icon.
4. Under the Administration Server option, select Server and type in the name of your server.
5. Click OK.

Most database-specific menu bar commands can be quickly accessed by clicking a database icon once with the right mouse. A pop-up menu will appear which lists some of the most common commands.

Your Notes server will work as it should if an Administration Server isn't specified for the Public Address Book. However, when you start your Notes server, a message will appear in the server console reminding you that this setting hasn't been set.

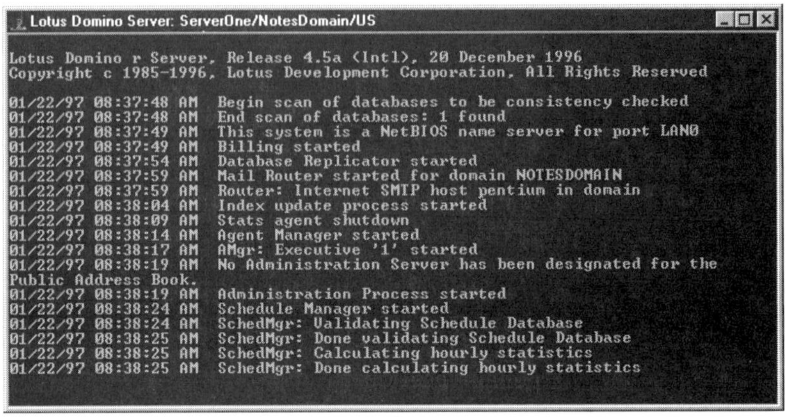

```
Lotus Domino Server: ServerOne/NotesDomain/US

Lotus Domino r Server, Release 4.5a (Intl), 20 December 1996
Copyright c 1985-1996, Lotus Development Corporation, All Rights Reserved

01/22/97 08:37:48 AM  Begin scan of databases to be consistency checked
01/22/97 08:37:48 AM  End scan of databases: 1 found
01/22/97 08:37:49 AM  This system is a NetBIOS name server for port LAN0
01/22/97 08:37:49 AM  Billing started
01/22/97 08:37:54 AM  Database Replicator started
01/22/97 08:37:59 AM  Mail Router started for domain NOTESDOMAIN
01/22/97 08:37:59 AM  Router: Internet SMTP host pentium in domain
01/22/97 08:38:04 AM  Index update process started
01/22/97 08:38:09 AM  Stats agent shutdown
01/22/97 08:38:14 AM  Agent Manager started
01/22/97 08:38:17 AM  AMgr: Executive '1' started
01/22/97 08:38:19 AM  No Administration Server has been designated for the
Public Address Book.
01/22/97 08:38:19 AM  Administration Process started
01/22/97 08:38:24 AM  Schedule Manager started
01/22/97 08:38:24 AM  SchedMgr: Validating Schedule Database
01/22/97 08:38:25 AM  SchedMgr: Done validating Schedule Database
01/22/97 08:38:25 AM  SchedMgr: Calculating hourly statistics
01/22/97 08:38:25 AM  SchedMgr: Done calculating hourly statistics
```

Create a Certification Log

The Certification Log (CERTLOG.NSF) is an important database if you plan to use the Administration Process (described in the *Administration Process* section later in this chapter) to rename, recertify, or upgrade users and servers. In order for the Certification Log to be most effective, this database should be created before you create any additional certifiers and register additional servers and users.

The Certification Log is specifically designed for administrative use, and contains the following information for each registered user and server:

- Name, license type, and ID number of the user or server
- Date of certification and expiration
- Name, license type, and ID number of the certifier ID used to create or recertify the ID

Even though the Certification Log has a certain purpose, it is still just a Notes database and can be opened and viewed the same as any other database, provided you have been granted access. However, unlike some administrative Notes databases, the Certification Log has to be created manually. The following steps describe the process of creating a Certification Log:

1. From the Notes client workspace choose File ➢ Database ➢ New.
2. Select the name of the server you're using to register users in the Server field.

3. In the Title field, give the new database a name, such as **Certification Log**.
4. For the file name, enter **CERTLOG.NSF**.
5. At the bottom of the dialog box, place a check mark next to Show Advanced Templates.
6. From the Templates box, select the Certification Log template and click OK.
7. After the database is created, add it to your Notes workspace.
8. Select the Certification Log and then choose File ➢ Database ➢ Access Control.
9. In the Access Control List dialog box, assign Editor access to all administrators, or to a single administration group, who will register users and servers and recertify IDs. The process is complete.

Notes requires a Certification Log to have the file name CERTLOG.NSF. Otherwise, the certification logging process won't work.

Backing Up the Notes Server

Because most backup software has difficulty backing up open files, before putting your Notes server into production is a great time to do a complete system backup. If you wait until after you've started your Notes server, critical files such as the Public Address Book (NAMES.NSF), the Notes Log (LOG.NSF), and any shared mail database (MAILOBJ.NSF) are open and will probably be skipped by the backup software. The only solution is to shut down the Notes server and run the backup again. To avoid such a situation, you might as well back up your system before starting the Notes server.

Backing up the server after installation is optional and your Notes server will work as expected if you decide to skip this step.

Starting the Notes Server

How you should start your Notes server after the installation is complete is a little different depending on which operating system you selected for your Notes server. I suggest you review the *Install Guide for Servers*, available online in the Doc directory on your Notes server, for a detailed explanation on starting and shutting down the Notes server for your particular operating system. However, if you don't have time to review the *Install Guide for Server* guide, the following sections can quickly get your Notes server up and running.

Starting a Windows NT-Based Notes Server

To start the Notes server under NT you have a couple of options. The following steps describe how to start and stop Notes from a program icon:

1. Locate the Notes server icon and double-click. The Notes server console opens up and the program begins.
2. To stop the Notes server after starting, type **Exit** or **Quit** at the command prompt in the Notes server console.

Be patient when shutting down a Notes server because it can take several seconds before the server responds to the Exit or Quit command.

If you prefer for the Notes server to start automatically each time NT starts, you can run the Notes server as an NT service. The steps listed below describe how to start and stop the Notes server as an NT service:

1. Open the NT Control Panel and double-click the Services icon. All current services, running or not, are listed.
2. Locate the Lotus Domino Server listing and select it.
3. Select the Startup button.
4. Set the Startup Type to Automatic.
5. Click the Close button and then restart the NT machine.
6. To shut down a Notes server running as an NT service, repeat steps one and two, then click the Stop button.

If the Lotus Domino Server service does not appear in the list of NT services, complete the following steps to add the Lotus Domino Server as an NT service:

1. Locate the MS-DOS Command Prompt icon and double-click:
   - In Windows NT 3.51, the MS-DOS Command Prompt icon is located in the Main program group.
   - In Windows NT 4.0, you can access the MS-DOS Command Prompt by selecting Start ➢ Programs ➢ MS-DOS Prompt from the Desktop bar.
2. At the C:\ prompt, type **cd \notes** and press Enter.
3. At the C:\NOTES prompt, type **ntsvinst -c** and press Enter.
4. Type **exit** and press Enter to close the command prompt window.

With Notes Release 4.5a for Windows NT, the file NTSVINST.EXE, used to add the Notes server program as a service, is not copied from the distribution CD to the program directory when the standard Server installation is selected. To avoid this problem, select the Custom installation and make sure all of the NT-specific options are selected.

After the previous steps are completed, "Lotus Domino Server" will appear in the list of NT services and you can use the steps described earlier to start the Notes service.

If you've installed Notes in a directory other than C:\NOTES, adjust the previous commands accordingly.

Starting an OS/2-Based Notes Server

Starting the Notes server installed on an OS/2 machine is similar to starting the server under NT. The following steps describe how to start and stop Notes from a program icon:

1. Locate the Notes server icon and double-click. The Notes server console opens up and the program begins.

2. To stop the Notes server after starting, type **Exit** or **Quit** at the command prompt in the Notes server console.

If you want the Notes server to start automatically when OS/2 starts, follow the steps listed below:

1. Locate the Notes server icon and drag it to the OS/2 startup group.
2. Shut down and restart OS/2 for your changes to take effect.

Starting a NetWare-Based Notes Server

Starting the Notes server installed on a NetWare file server doesn't afford you the luxury of double-clicking an icon as you can with Notes servers running on OS/2 and NT. The following steps describe how to start and stop Notes in the NetWare environment:

1. To start the server, you first have to gain access to the NetWare server console.
2. Once at the NetWare server console, type **load notessrv** at the system prompt and press Enter.
3. When you need to shut down the Notes server, repeat step one and then type **unload notessrv** at the system prompt and press Enter.

You can also use the Exit or Quit command at the NetWare server console to shut down the Notes server.

If you want the Notes server to automatically start whenever the NetWare server is started, you'll have to edit the NetWare AUTOEXEC.NCF file. The following steps describe how to edit this file:

1. To start, you have to gain access to the NetWare server console either directly or remotely.
2. Once at the NetWare server console, type **load install** at the system prompt and press Enter.
3. After the Install module loads, select one of the following options depending on your version of NetWare:
   - For NetWare 4.1 choose NCF File Options.
   - For NetWare 3.12 choose System Options.

4. From the Available System Options, choose Edit System AUTOEXEC.NCF File.
5. In the AUTOEXEC.NCF file, enter the following commands:
   - **load clib**
   - **load mathlib** (only if your machine has a math co-processor, otherwise enter **load mathlibc**)
   - **load tli**
   - **load ipxs**
   - **load spxs**
   - **load netdb**
   - **load notessrv**
6. If you want to add the Notes directory to the search path, enter **search add volumename:\directory**.

volumename and *directory* are the names that you specified for the Notes subdirectory during installation.

7. If you want to install the communications drivers, enter **load aiocomx**.
8. Save and close the AUTOEXEC.NCF file.
9. Restart your server in the following manner:
   - Type **down** and then type **exit** to exit to DOS.
   - Type **server** to restart the server.

Starting a UNIX-Based Notes Server

Even though there are three different flavors of UNIX supported by Notes, starting a Notes server based on any of these flavors is the same. The steps listed below describe this process:

1. From a UNIX window, or a UNIX command prompt, change to the user's home directory by typing **#cd <directory>/notesr4** and then pressing Enter (*<directory>* could be something similar to */home/bswedeen*).

2. Then type **#/opt/lotus/bin/server** and press Enter.

3. To shut down the Notes server, type **exit** or **quit** in the Notes server console and press Enter.

Setting up a UNIX-based Notes server to automatically start whenever the UNIX machine starts varies from one flavor of UNIX to the next. Refer to your UNIX documentation for instructions specific to your UNIX environment.

Creating Organizational Unit Certifiers

Creating organizational unit certifiers is an administrative task that can be done at any time. However, if you have a hierarchical naming scheme designed it makes sense to create the organizational unit certifiers before you install any additional servers or start creating users.

The process for creating an organizational unit certifier requires that you have access to the organizational certifier that was created during the first server setup. If you have that certifying ID, follow the steps listed below to start creating organizational unit certifiers:

1. From the menu bar of your Notes workspace, select File ➢ Tools ➢ Server Administration.

2. Click the Certifiers icon and select Register Organizational Unit from the pop-up menu.

3. The Register Organizational Unit Certifier dialog box appears and prompts you for the following information:

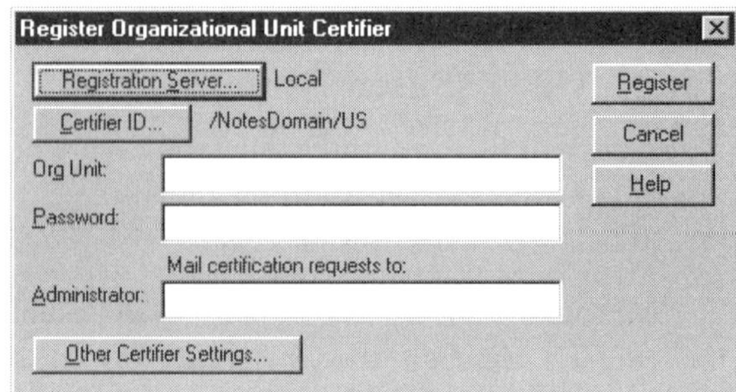

- **Registration Server:** This setting is for the server in which the certification processing is being done. Usually you select the server where the Certification Log database—created in the last section—is located.
- **Certifier ID:** This setting defaults to the last certifier used for certification, or the only certifier if only one. Click the button and you can navigate through drive letters and folders to specify a different certifier.
- **Org Unit:** This field is for the name of the organization unit that you want to create.
- **Password:** This field is for the password to associate with the certifier you are creating. If you don't want to add a password, you'll need to select Other Certifier Settings and set the minimum password length to zero.
- **Administrator:** The name listed in this field is the person that will receive requests for certification by this new certifier. Groups, instead of individual users, can also be used in this field.

4. Fill in the appropriate information in the Register Organizational Unit Certifier dialog box and click OK, or select Other Certifier Settings for additional options.

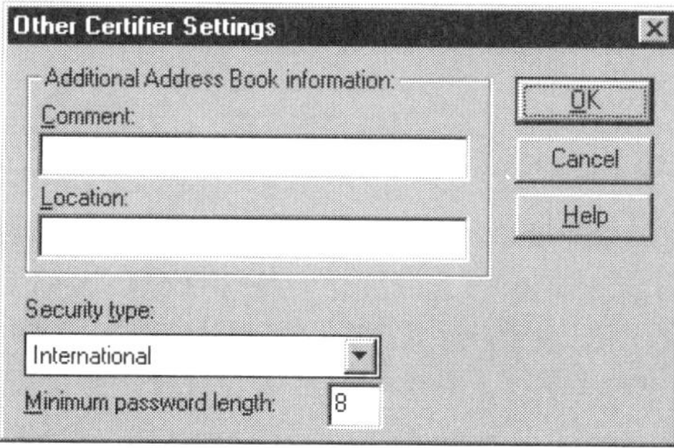

- **Comment:** Add comments in this field that help describe the purpose of this organizational certifier.
- **Location:** Add location-specific information in this field. You might consider describing which company location this certifier is used for.

- **Security Type**: From the drop-down list, select North American or International.
- **Minimum Password Length**: By default, this field is set to eight. You can set this field to zero if you don't want to add a password to the new certifier. However, because certifiers are very important and powerful to your Notes network, allowing you to create user ids that will in turn permit access to the server, passwords are highly recommended.

5. Once you've added any additional information, press OK and you'll return to the Other Certifier Settings dialog box.
6. If you're satisfied with all of the settings for the new organizational certifier, click OK.

Repeat the previous steps for each certifier required.

By default, Notes attempts to save the new ID file to drive A. If there is no diskette in that drive, an error will occur. To get past this error just select Abort and then Cancel in the next error message box. A dialog box will eventually appear letting you traverse the server's directory structure and save the file to the drive and directory you select.

Once the process is complete, a new certification ID file will be created and stored in the location you specified. Make sure you store the new certifier in a safe location.

I like to format a 3.5" diskette and build a directory structure that mirrors my organizational hierarchy. As I create new certifiers for my Notes network, I store these ID files in their respective directories on the diskette. After I've stored these files on disk, I make a backup copy of these diskettes and store them in a safe and secure off-site location (for example, in a safety deposit box).

Installing Additional Servers

More than likely, at some time you'll need to add additional Notes servers to your Notes network. In some respects, adding additional Notes servers is similar to the process you went through when you installed your first server. However, because additional servers are joining an existing domain you'll need to register each additional server in that domain. After the server is registered, however, install the software the same way you did for your first Notes server and perform a server setup similar to the one for setting up a Notes user.

Registering the New Server

1. From the menu, select File ➢ Tools ➢ Server Administration.

2. From the Administration screen, select the Servers icon and a pop-up menu appears.
3. From the pop-up menu, select Register Server.
4. If you have a valid Notes server license, answer Yes to the dialog box prompt. If you don't have a valid license, you can continue with the registration but don't forget to purchase a license immediately. Otherwise, you'll be in violation of software copyright laws.
5. When prompted, enter the password for your Certification ID and the Register Servers dialog box appears.

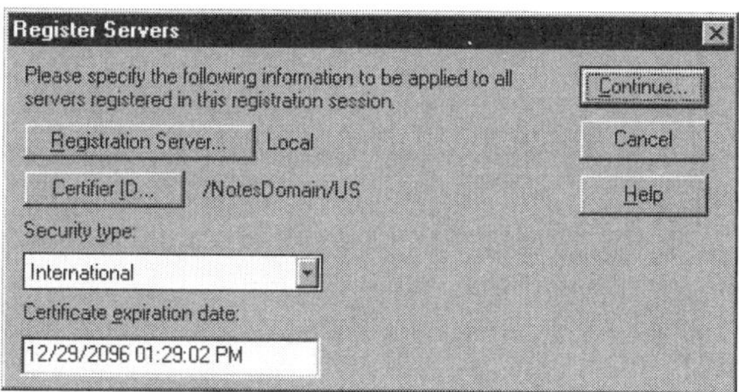

6. In the Register Servers dialog box the following information is required:

   - **Registration Server:** Click this button and select the registration server in your Notes network. If you have previously created a Certification Log database, choose the server where that database is located as your registration server.
   - **Certifier ID:** If you want to use a different certifier than the one currently specified, click this button and traverse through drives and directories to select the appropriate certifying ID.
   - **Security type:** From this drop-down list, select either International or North American.
   - **Certificate expiration date:** Accept the default expiration date shown or specify another one.

7. Once all of the previously described information is specified, click Continue and the Register Servers dialog box appears.

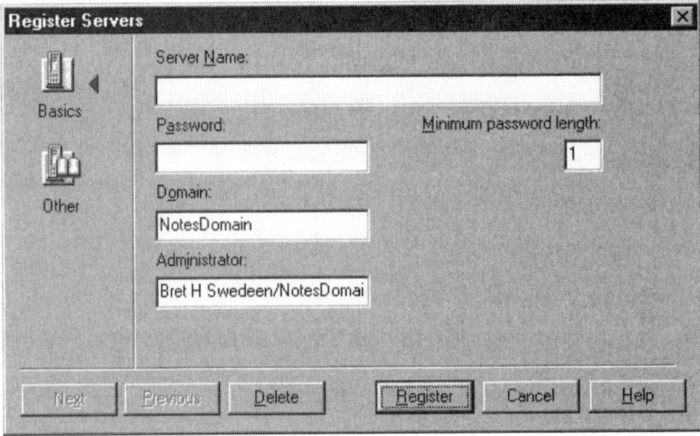

8. In the Basics section of the Register Servers dialog box, fill in the following fields:

   - **Server Name:** Use this field to name your new server. Refer to the *Naming Guidelines* sidebar earlier in this chapter and review the guidelines for naming Notes servers.
   - **Password:** Enter a password for the new SERVER.ID file in this field.

- **Minimum password length**: Set the minimum password length in this field. The default is eight characters, but I recommend you set this number to zero so you can clear the password later if you need to.
- **Domain:** Enter your Notes domain name here. This is filled in automatically with information available from the certification ID.
- **Administrator**: Enter the name of the Notes administrator in this field. By default, the administrator specified when you installed your first Notes server appears, but you can change this if necessary.

9. Once all of the information in the Basics section of the Register Servers dialog box is entered, click the Other icon.
10. In the Other section of the Register Servers dialog box, fill in the following fields:
    - **Server Title**: This field is optional. However, entering a title that describes this server's function is always helpful when there is more than one Notes administration.
    - **Network**: Enter the name of the Notes named network that you want this server to appear in.
    - **Local administrator**: If there is going to be a local administrator for this server, enter that name in this field.
    - **Store Server ID**: Decide whether you want to store the server ID in the Public Address Book or in a file on a disk. If you choose to store the ID on a disk, select the Set ID File button and specify the drive and directory you will use for the ID storage.
11. Once all of the new server information is entered, you can click the Next button to enter information for yet another server, or click the Register button to start the server registration process.

During the registration process, the new server ID is created and a Server document is added to the Public Address Book. After this process is complete, you're ready to install the server software.

Installing the Server Software

Installing the software for a new Notes server is exactly the same as installing the software on the first Notes server in your organization. During the installation, you'll basically make two important selections:

- Where to install the Notes server software (for example, the drive and directory).
- Which installation type—workstation, server, or custom.

Once the server software is installed, you're ready to start the Notes client, complete the installation process, and set up the new server.

Setting Up the New Server

The new Notes server has been registered in your Notes network. The Notes server software has been installed on the new server machine. Now you're ready to start the Notes client software and set up the new server according to what you previously specified when you registered the server. The following steps describe this final setup process:

1. Double-click the Notes Server icon.
2. The Notes Server Setup dialog box appears. In this dialog box, specify whether this server installation is the first Lotus Notes server in your organization or if it is an additional server.

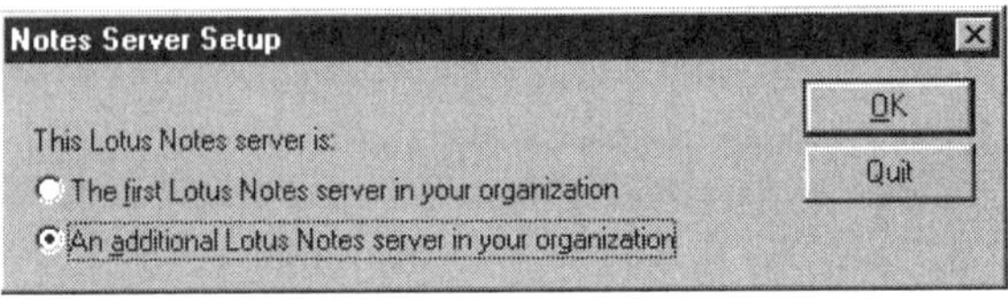

3. By default, the first Lotus Notes server option is selected. Because this is an additional Notes server, select the second option and click OK.
4. The Additional Server Setup dialog box appears.

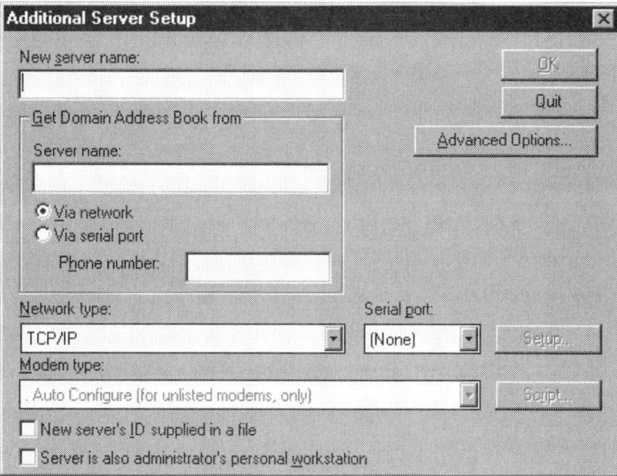

5. In the New Server Name field, enter the name of the new server exactly as you did when the server was registered, which includes the domain name.

6. In the Server Name field of the Get Domain Address Book From section, enter the name of the server that you used to register the new server.

7. Specify whether to connect to the registration server Via Network, or Via Serial Port.

8. If you are connecting to the registration server via the serial port, enter the server's phone number in the Phone Number field. Then select the Serial Port and Modem Type that this new server is using for serial port communications.

9. In the Network Type field, select the type of network protocol to use if you are connected to the registration server over the network.

10. In the final two options at the bottom of the dialog box, place a check mark next to one or both options as needed:

    - **New Server's ID Supplied in a File:** If you saved the server ID file to a disk when you registered the new server, you'll probably want to check this option.

- **Server Is Also Administrator's Personal Workstation:** You'll probably leave this option unchecked unless this server will actually be a personal workstation as well.

11. The Advanced Server Setup Options presents three Notes Log options, shown in Figure 4.2.
12. After you've finished with the Advanced Server Setup Options, click OK.
13. Click OK on the Additional Server Setup dialog box and the new server setup begins.
14. Before the setup process is complete, you'll need to select a time zone.
15. You can also check Observe Daylight Savings Time April-October if this server is located in a place where daylight savings is observed.
16. Finally, click OK when the Notes setup is complete.

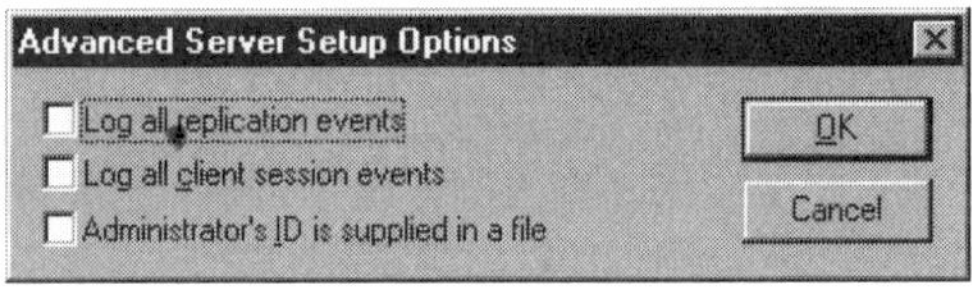

FIGURE 4.2

The Advanced Server Setup Options dialog box presents three additional options that pertain to what gets logged in the Notes Log. Place check marks next to options as needed.

With the new Notes server completely set up you won't need to create a certification, as was previously recommended. However, now is a good time to shut down your server and do a complete system backup before making it a full-time production server.

Server Disaster Planning

Keeping your Notes servers up and running is one of the Notes administrator's primary responsibilities. Unfortunately, no matter how much you know about Lotus Notes, a disastrous server failure is always possible. Being prepared for a possible disaster is very simple and can greatly reduce the mental anguish that a complete server failure can cause.

The first step in disaster preparation is admitting that a disaster is possible. If you simply don't believe that a disaster could ever happen to you, you'll never take the time to prepare for one. Be honest with yourself and acknowledge that a complete server failure is possible.

The next step in disaster preparation is creating a disaster plan. This plan is usually a document that can be added to your Notes standards document, if you created one, and made available to everyone within your MIS department. In this document you should outline the steps to take for each major disaster that could happen:

- Database failure
- Hard drive crash
- Motherboard or other computer card failure
- External power failure

These five kinds of disaster basically encompass nearly every possible problem you could encounter. For some of these problems you'll have limited options for getting your server back online quickly, while options for other problems will rely completely on your disaster plan for resolution.

Database Failure

Sometimes a database on one of your Notes servers will become so corrupted it is beyond repair, or accidentally deleted. These potential disasters are the easiest ones to prepare for, and there are a couple of possible solutions.

If you have several servers in your Notes network, you probably have the option of creating a new replicate copy of the problematic database from one of your existing servers. One way to ensure that you have the replication option as a solution is to dedicate one server in your Notes network as a "hot backup" server.

A hot backup server is a Notes server that doesn't directly support user connections. The primary purpose for this type of server is to have a fairly current replica copy of each database in your Notes environment. Other servers in the Notes network replicate with the hot backup server once or periodically throughout the day. When a database becomes corrupted or is deleted, a new replica copy can be created from the hot backup server.

The hub server in a Hub and Spoke Notes network topology is often considered a hot backup server. If you have implemented a Hub and Spoke topology in your Notes environment and the hub doesn't directly support any user connections, then you basically have a hot backup server. You should, however, double-check that your hub server has one copy of every Notes database in your environment.

If a hot backup server isn't available and you don't have any other Notes servers you can quickly replicate with, then you'll have to restore a copy of the problematic database from a tape backup. Of course, this solution assumes you have a fairly current tape backup.

If you don't have a tape backup dedicated to your Notes server, you should.

Hard Drive Crash

Computers don't have a lot of moving parts in them so they can usually last for a very long time (even though new technology keeps making them obsolete). The hard drive, however, is one of the few items in a computer that does have moving parts. Therefore, of all the parts to fail in a computer, hard drives usually top the list.

A graceful recovery from a complete hard drive failure is nearly impossible without a complete and current backup. You can back up a computer to a set of diskettes, another hard drive, or some type of optical disk. However, the number one choice for a backup device is a tape drive.

Tape devices range in price and backup capacity. You can purchase an inexpensive QIC type tape device that can back up a couple hundred megabytes, or you can select an expensive DLT tape device and back up anywhere between twenty to forty gigabytes. Regardless of which type of tape device you select, its value becomes immediately apparent the first time you use the device to recover from a complete hard drive crash.

To completely utilize a tape device, you'll need backup software. Most operating systems, such as Windows NT Server, come with their own backup utility. Unfortunately, the backup utility the operating system includes usually doesn't have the flexibility and speed that most third party backup solutions provide.

There are a number of software options on the market (too many to list here). Most of these third party solutions have fully functioning, but time-limited, evaluation copies available on the Internet. I suggest you download a couple of these evaluation copies and try them for yourself before settling on a specific solution.

Backing up open files such as the Public Name and Address Book (NAMES.NSF) and the shared mail database (MAILOBJ.NSF) is a critical part of a daily backup routine. Make sure the backup software you select has support for backing up these open files. One such product that works with Arcada Backup Exec from Seagate is Open File Manager from Saint Bernard. (Details about this product can be found in Appendix E.)

Having a tape device and backup software is not enough to ensure successful, reliable backups. Good administrative habits are also required. Take the time to establish a solid backup routine and document it so others know how to follow the routine in your absence. Don't forget to include instructions for restoring a backup. In addition, following a good backup schedule routine isn't enough. You still need to know how to restore a backup and have a process for routinely checking the integrity of your backup tapes. The last thing you want to have happen after a complete hard drive crash is to find out that your backups haven't run for the last week or the tapes you've been using are defective.

Motherboard and Other Computer Card Failure

Even though computer parts such as the motherboard, network card, and SCSI controller don't have moving parts they can still fail. Planning for this type of failure can be costly. However, if your Notes network is a mission-critical part of your company's information infrastructure, you'll need to have a solution for this type of problem. There are two approaches for preparing for this type of disaster:

- Keeping duplicate parts for everything in your Notes server.
- Having a server-critical care service contract with a network integrator.

Keeping a duplicate of every part in your server is an expensive option because basically it is the same as buying another server. The only difference is that this server just sits around and collects dust until a disaster happens.

A server-critical care service contract can also be expensive, but usually not as expensive as duplicate parts. Typically, these service offerings come from network integrators or value-added resellers. These contracts usually guarantee that a service technician will be on-site within a certain period of time. However, what you really want is your server guaranteed up and running within a certain period of time. Contracts that address this requirement are available, but come at a premium price.

General equipment warranties protect you financially but do little to protect you from excessive server down time.

External Power Failure

The last disaster you'll need to plan for is an external power outage. For most administrators of nearly any computer system, an uninterruptible power supply (UPS) is the solution for a loss of power. Unfortunately, a UPS, because it's basically just a large battery, only provides a temporary solution for a power outage. When the UPS loses its power, your server still goes down. Because there is no telling when power will be returned to a system after an outage, the UPS has to provide the functionality to gracefully shut down your server and prevent any further damage.

There are a number of UPS products on the market today, and most of them are designed to shut your server down gracefully when the power is lost. Some computer manufacturers, like Compaq and HP, sell UPS devices designed for their servers. There are also third party solutions from companies such as American Power Conversion (APC).

Notes Clusters

Wouldn't it be great if when a Notes server crashed for some reason, another server stepped in and took over? Fortunately, Notes 4.5 makes this dream possible with the use of Notes clusters.

A Notes cluster is a group of up to six Notes servers that are grouped together under one name and provide failover protection for mission-critical databases. Failover protection allows users to continue using a database when the server that the database is on goes down. In this case, requests made to this database are serviced by being redirected to other servers in the cluster.

Although Notes clusters is a fantastic feature, it is available only when you purchase the Lotus Notes Advanced Server license. Because of the special license requirement for this feature, Notes clusters will not be covered in this book at this time but further details can be found in the *Notes Administration Help Guide* from Lotus.

The Disaster Plan Document

There are other disasters you might want to consider depending on where your machines are located. Planning for disasters such as floods, earthquakes, or terrorist attacks may seem silly. However, these types of disasters are very real and worth planning for if your company depends on the Notes network for its daily operations (see the *Extreme Disaster Planning* sidebar). If you bring up the subject of planning for these types of disasters at a meeting and everyone laughs at you, just remind them of the Chicago floods from a few years back and the World Trade Center bombings. Those reminders should quickly bring a sober tone to the meeting.

Extreme Disaster Planning

A friend of mine used to work for a major investment firm that had offices in North America and Europe. When their European offices were caught in the middle of a terrorist attack, they were out of business for several days. They lost millions of dollars.

In order to prevent such a loss from happening again, they created a complete replica of their European office's data center on the other side of town. At the beginning of every day one person would take the backup tapes from the previous night's backup and restore them on the systems at the replica site. The two sites were as in sync as realistically possible and the company was ready for almost anything.

Keep in mind that while a double-site synchronization disaster plan worked for this financial company, this approach might not be appropriate for a company based in a state that is prone to earthquakes. A better solution might be to locate a data center double in another state entirely.

Once you have considered all of the potential disasters your Notes network might encounter, document your plan. The document should be short and to the point. A typical document would address the following issues:

- **Problem:** Clearly identify the problem here and try to rate its severity.
- **Solution:** Outline, in simple sentences, each step involved in the solution.
- **Contacts:** List the appropriate people to contact when such a problem occurs. List the people in order from first person to call to last resort.

You should also include any product warranties and service contracts in your disaster plan document. When disaster strikes, you shouldn't be scrambling to find critical information such as warranties, service contracts, and names of service technicians to contact.

Server Disaster Prevention

You might think that it makes more sense to be able to prevent disasters than to be prepared for one. This point of view is valid and there are many administrators that implement disaster prevention before disaster planning. Which way you choose to approach disasters is a personal decision. My rationale for planning before prevention is that if my prevention fails to catch a disaster, and I have no disaster plan, then I have no means for recovery from the disaster.

Lotus Notes provides three important tools to assist administrators with disaster prevention: The Notes Log (LOG.NSF), Events Monitoring, and Statistics Reporting. These tools used separately or together can reveal a tremendous amount of information about your Notes environment. However, the responsibility to act when the information provided from these tools indicates a pending problem still rests on the shoulders of the Notes administrator.

The Notes Log

The single most important diagnostic tool a Notes administrator has is the Notes Log (LOG.NSF). The Notes Log records server events, such as replications performed, mail routed, and databases used. By default, this log, which is actually a Notes database, is created for each server and workstation during installation.

As part of your daily administration activities, check the Log to look for potential server problems, missed scheduled replication events, mail routing errors, and modem problems. The Log has views that are arranged by function and categorize information by server, date, and time (see Figure 4.3).

FIGURE 4.3

A typical Notes Log with the Miscellaneous Events view selected

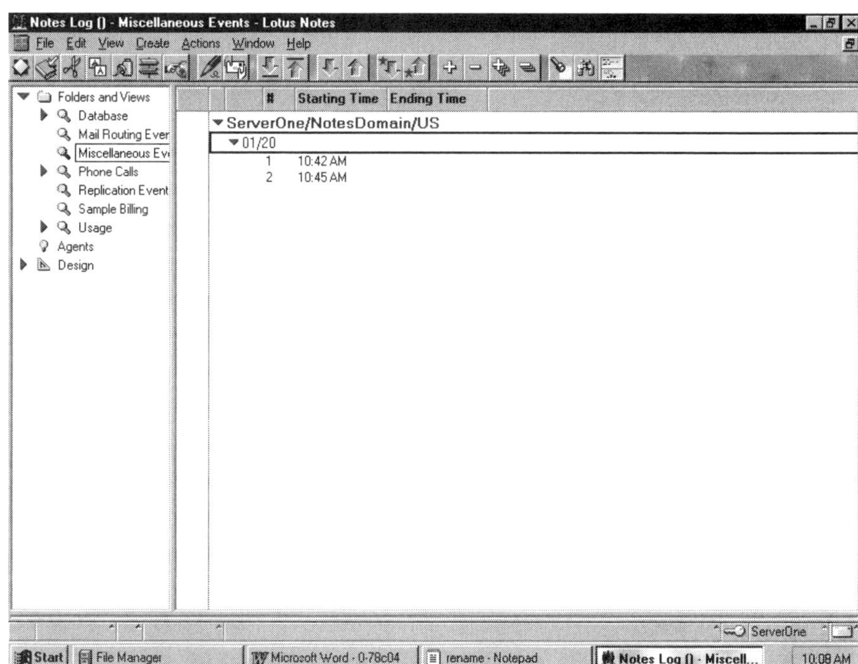

You can customize what information gets logged during the server setup process or through settings in the NOTES.INI file (see Appendix D for available options). However, even though what information gets logged is customizable, the Notes Log can still take a considerable amount of time to analyze. Fortunately, Notes provides the Log Analysis tool to facilitate analyzing a Notes Log. To access and use this tool, follow the steps listed below:

1. From the menu bar, select File ➢ Tools ➢ Server Administration and the Administration screen appears.

2. Select a server whose Notes Log you want to analyze from the Choose a Server to Administer list.

3. Select the Servers icon.

4. Select Log Analysis from the pop-up box and the Server Log Analysis dialog box appears.

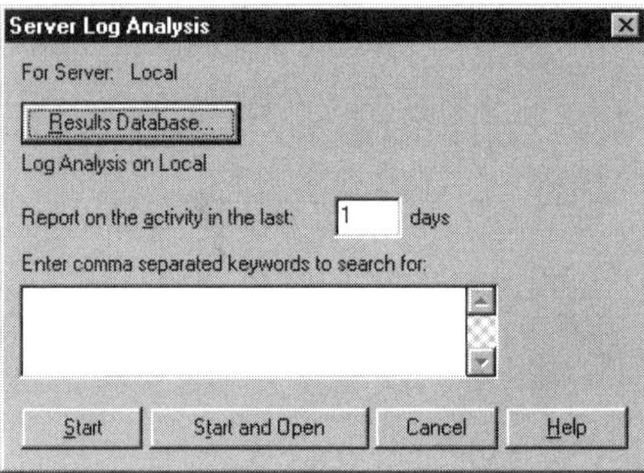

5. Specify an output database by selecting the Results Database button.

6. Select the server from the list presented for the Results database and the name of this database.

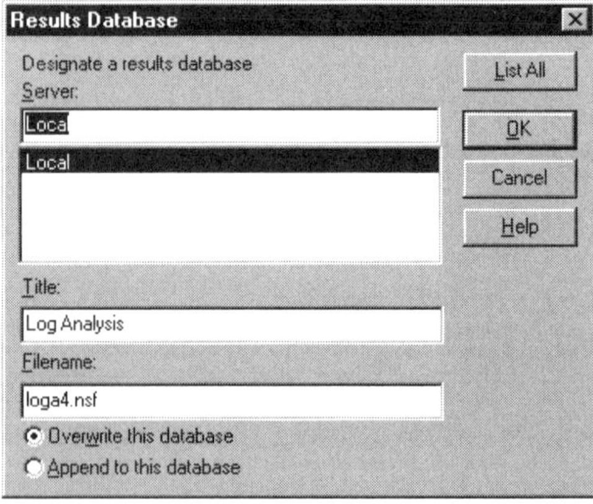

7. Decide whether you want to overwrite or append the analysis output to the Results database, then click OK to return to the Log Analysis dialog box.

8. Specify the last number of days to include in the analysis.

9. Separating each word with a comma, enter the words to search for during the analysis.

10. Click the Start button to start the analysis or click the Start Open button to start the analysis and open the Results Database when the analysis is complete (see Figure 4.4).

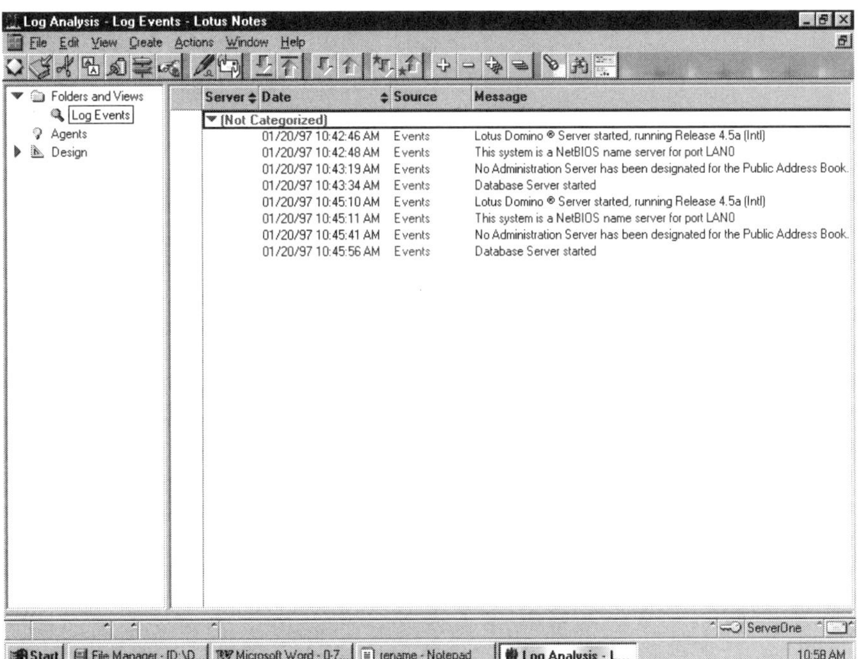

FIGURE 4.4

A sample analysis output from the Results Database

Experiment with the Log Analysis tool and search for such words as "error," "failed," and "cannot." The results of searching for these words will often reveal most system problems and help you to isolate potential problems.

Events Monitoring

Another important administration tool for disaster prevention is the Events Monitoring feature of Lotus Notes. This feature runs on the Notes server as a server task and collects much of the same information as the Notes Log. There are, however, significant differences between the Events Monitoring and the Notes Log which are defined in Table 4.1.

TABLE 4.1 The Notes Log versus Events Monitoring

The Notes Log	Events Monitoring
The Notes Log is always collecting information about server activity.	Events Monitoring is only working when the Event task is loaded, which, by default, is not done automatically.
The Notes Log collects information about nearly every server event.	Events Monitoring watches only those events that you specify using Event documents.
Information in the Notes Log must be manually analyzed to find errors and potential problems.	Events Monitoring allows you to set severity levels for certain events and thresholds which can trigger notification messages. These messages can be e-mailed to a person or a group, sent to a database, relayed to another server, sent to a server management program using an SNMP trap, or logged to the Windows NT Event Viewer in an NT environment.
Each server in your Notes network has its own Notes Log. You have to run a Log Analysis to pull together information from several logs into one central location.	Each server in your Notes network can run the Event task. However, all servers can report their event messages to the same server, which makes centralized management much easier.

The Notes Log and Events Monitoring clearly have their differences, and therefore one does not necessarily replace the other. Events Monitoring should be viewed as a more specialized, yet complementary, tool than the Notes Log.

Despite the specialized functionality of Events Monitoring, it still remains flexible and simple to configure. The process for getting Events Monitoring going in your Notes network consists of two simple steps:

1. Load the Event server task, which also creates the Statistics & Events database (EVENTS4.NSF), if it doesn't already exist.

2. Create an Event document for each type of event you want to monitor.

The Statistics & Events database is an important database because it is also used for Statistics Reporting (covered in the next section) with the Reporter task.

Loading the Events Server Task

The first step to get Events Monitoring set up in your environment is to load the Events server task. Starting this task is similar to starting all other server tasks. You can load the tasks directly from the server console, or indirectly through the Remote Console screen. Whichever method you choose to interface with the server console, the command you enter is the same: **load event**. The following steps detail how to execute this command directly from the server console:

1. Gain direct access to the server console.
2. Press Enter to make sure you have a server prompt.
3. At the prompt type **Load event** and press Enter.

Once the previous command is typed, the Event task loads and creates the Statistics & Events database (EVENTS4.NSF). An icon for this database can be added to your Notes workspace like any other Notes database using File ➢ Database ➢ Open.

The Event task is not one of the server tasks that automatically loads each time the server is started. Therefore, you'll have to edit the NOTES.INI file and add a parameter to the ServerTasks setting. The following steps walk you through this process:

1. Open the NOTES.INI file in a simple ASCII text editor.
2. Search for the ServerTasks setting.
3. Go to the end of the ServerTasks line and add a comma.
4. After the comma, type **Event**.
5. Save the file and restart your Notes server to make sure the changes have taken effect.

With the Event parameter added to the ServerTasks setting, the Event task will load automatically each time the server is started.

Whenever you add a new server task to a Notes server you should make sure you have enough available systems resources to support the new task. However, in the case of the Event task, the impact on server resources is minimal.

Creating the Events Monitoring Documents

Once the Statistics & Events database is created and the Event task is loaded, you can start to create Events documents. These documents determine which events you want to monitor, which include the following:

- Communications events
- Mail events
- Miscellaneous events
- Replication events
- Resource events that relate to system resources
- Security events
- Server events that relate to server conditions, such as tasks not executed or problems with the Server document in the Public Address Book
- Statistics which include statistic alarms set by you and generated by the Report server task
- Update events (related to Indexer)

To create an Event document, follow the steps listed below:

1. If the Statistics & Events database isn't on your Notes workspace, add the database icon. To do this, follow the steps listed below.

   A. Select File ➢ Database ➢ Open.

   B. Select the server where the database is located.

   C. Select the database and click the Add Icon button.

   D. Click the Done button.

2. Double-click the Statistics & Events database icon and open the database.

3. From the menu bar, select Create ➢ Monitors ➢ Events Monitor.

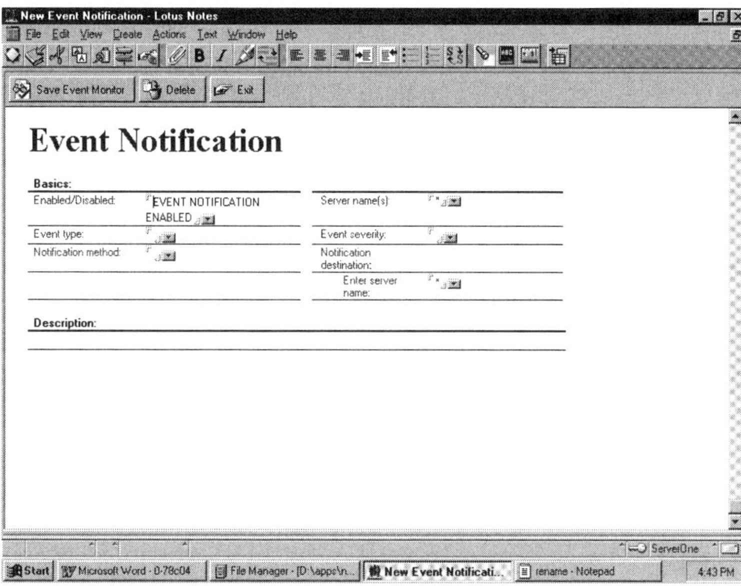

4. Accept the default setting for the Enabled/Disabled field.

5. In the Event Type field, click the arrow and select one of the following types to report:

   - **Comm/Net**: Modem or network communications events.
   - **Security**: ID files, servers, and database access events.
   - **Mail**: Mail routing events.
   - **Replication**: Replication events.
   - **Resource**: System resource events.
   - **Server**: Events related to the status of a particular server, which include server tasks not working or problems with the Server document in the Public Address Book.

- **Statistic:** Events that generate alarms that were set up in the Statistics Reporting database (covered in the next section, *Statistics Reporting*).
- **Misc:** Events that do not fall in the other categories.

6. In the Notification Method field, click the arrow and select one of the following methods:
   - **Mail:** This method allows you to send e-mail notifications to a user or group you specify in the Enter Mailing Address field.
   - **Log to a Database:** This method posts notifications in a database of your choosing. This method is useful if you have created a custom database for recording and assigning certain events.
   - **Relay to Other Server:** This method sends notifications to a server for central collection of event notifications. This method is useful when you have several servers recording events but want to view those events from a central location.
   - **SNMP Trap:** This method sends notifications to a server management program such as NotesView.
   - **Log to NT Event Viewer:** Logs all event messages in the NT Event Viewer, which is one of the Windows NT Server administration tools. This option is only available for Notes servers running on NT.
7. If you want all servers in your domain to report on the selected event type, keep the default asterisk (*) in the Server Name field. Otherwise, click the arrow and select a specific server or servers to report this event. You can also type the name of a server that is not displayed.
8. In the Event Severity field, click the arrow and select one or more of the following severity levels:
   - **Fatal:** Imminent system crash.
   - **Failure:** Severe failure that does not cause a system crash.
   - **Warning (high):** Loss of function requiring intervention.
   - **Warning (low):** Performance degradation.
   - **Normal:** Status messages.

- **All Severities:** All of the above messages. Be careful using this setting if you've selected e-mail as the notification method because you might end up getting more e-mail than you want.

9. Under the Notification Destination item, different fields appear depending on which Notification Method you selected previously. These different fields are described below:

   A. **Enter Mailing Address:** This field appears when you specify Mail as the Notification Method. Enter any Notes user or group name in this field. External mail addresses are also valid provided your Notes environment can resolve the destination for the address entered.

   B. **Enter Database Name:** This field appears when you specify Database as the Notification Method. A valid filename is required here and the server where the database is located is required in the On Server field.

   C. **Enter Server Name:** This field appears when you select Relay to Another Server of SNMP Trap as the Notification Method. A valid Notes server name is required in this field. (No additional Notification Destination fields appear when you select Log to NT Event Viewer as the Notification Method.)

10. Press F9 to automatically fill in a brief description of the event.

11. Click the Save Event Monitor button on the Action bar and click the Exit button to close the Event document.

12. Repeat steps 1 through 11 to monitor additional events.

The Event document might seem confusing the first time you create one because it's not very clear exactly what is being monitored. The key to understanding the Event document, however, is in the Event Type and Event Severity fields. The combination of these two fields determines exactly what gets monitored and when an event notification gets generated.

The Notes server generates event messages as certain activities take place. When the Event task is not running, the only place to view these messages is either on the Server Console screen or in the Notes Log. When the Event task is running, however, the Event documents you create tell the Event task which event types to watch for. If an event matches an Event Type specified in an Event document, the Event task takes notice and evaluates the severity of the event. If the severity for that event matches the severity specified in the Event document, an event notification message is generated and handled according to the specifications in the Event document. If, however, the severity of the event does not match the severity specified in the Event document, the event message is ignored.

For example, if I want to monitor situations when the mail router seriously fails, I would create an Event document and specify the Event Type as Mail and set the severity to Warning (High). An example of what this Event document might look like is shown in Figure 4.5.

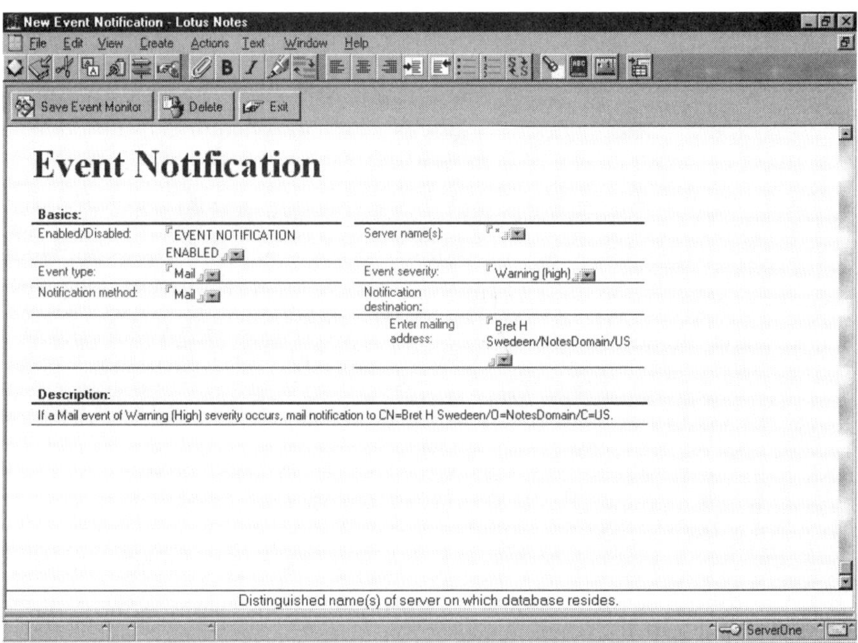

FIGURE 4.5 This Event document monitors for mail routing events that have failed and require intervention on any server.

Because you are trying to prevent disasters with the Events Monitoring feature of Lotus Notes, you'll probably want to monitor events that meet the severity level of Warning (Low). This severity level indicates a performance degradation, which gives you an opportunity to look into the problem before a loss of functionality occurs.

Statistics Reporting

The next useful administration tool for disaster prevention is the Statistics Reporting feature of Lotus Notes. This feature relies on the existence of the Statistics & Events database (EVENTS4.NSF) so it makes sense to configure Events Monitoring before setting up Statistics Reporting.

The Statistics Reporting feature of Lotus Notes uses the Report server task to gather server information and it stores that information in the default statistics database (STATREP.NSF) or a database of your own choosing. The gathered information can be viewed for analysis or used to trigger "alarms" when certain predefined thresholds are crossed. The type of information the server task can collect includes the following:

- System information, including information about sessions, disk and memory usage, server configuration, and server load.
- Mail information, including shared mail.
- Database and replication information.
- Communications information.
- Network information.
- Cluster information.

Setting Up Statistics Reporting

The steps required to get started with Statistics Reporting are much the same as the steps for Events Monitoring:

1. Load the Report server task, which also creates the Statistics & Events database (EVENTS4.NSF), if it doesn't already exist.
2. Configure Statistics and Reporting from the Server Administration screen.

If you've already set up Events Monitoring, then Statistics Reporting will use the same Statistics & Events database that was previously created.

Loading the Report Task

The first step to get Statistics Reporting set up in your environment is to load the Report server task. Starting this task is similar to steps described for loading the Event task. You can use the server console, as we did when loading the Event task, or you can use the remote server console as described in the steps shown below:

1. From the menu bar, select File ➢ Tools ➢ Server Administration.
2. When the Server Administration screen appears, choose the Console icon.
3. The Remote Server Console appears.
4. Select the server you want to load the Report task on.
5. In the Server Console Command field enter the command **Load Report.**
6. Press the Send button and watch the results in the Server Output window.

The Report task is the same as the Event task and does not automatically load each time the server is started. Therefore, you'll have to edit the NOTES.INI file and add a parameter to the ServerTasks setting. The following steps walk you through this process:

1. Open the NOTES.INI file in a simple ASCII text editor.
2. Search for the ServerTasks setting.
3. Go to the end of the ServerTasks line and add a comma.
4. After the comma add the word **Report**.
5. Save the file and restart your Notes server to make sure the changes have taken effect.

After the Report task is loaded and running, you'll need to configure the Statistics and Reporting feature to determine how, when, and where statistic reports are generated.

Configuring Statistics and Reporting

The Report task collects statistical information for analysis and file statistic reports along with regular statistic reports and alarms. This server task creates simple reports that show the averages, highs, and lows for reported statistics over a specified interval. File statistic reports generated by this server task show the size, replica ID, and percent of used space for each database and template on a server. If the used space in the database drops below seventy percent, a warning is posted in the Statistics database indicating that you should compact the database.

If you plan to use the Report task to report statistics, you must run it on each server from which you want to collect statistics. The steps listed below describe how to configure statistics reporting using the Report task:

1. From the menu bar, select File ➢ Tools ➢ Server Administration.
2. Click the System Databases icon and choose Configure Statistics Reporting from the pop-up menu.
3. Choose View ➢ Servers to Monitor.
4. Click Add Server and a new Server to Monitor document appears.
5. For the Server Name field, click the arrow and select a server, then click OK. Notes fills in the administrator, server title, and domain for the server.
6. In the Collection Interval field, specify how frequently the Reporter task should report statistics for the server specified.
7. If you want, you can add a description in the Server Description field. This description might include the server's hardware configuration or the server's purpose.
8. In the Report Method field, select one of the following two methods:
   - **Log to Database:** Selecting this option requires that you also specify the database name (usually STATREP.NSF) and server location for the database in the Enter Server Name and Database to Receive Reports fields respectively.

- **Mail-In Database:** Selecting this option automatically mails statistic reports to the mail-in database specified in the Mail-In Database Address to Receive Reports field.

9. For the Analysis Interval, select either Daily, Weekly, or Monthly. This setting will cause the Reporter task to create an analysis report at the specified interval. The report generated summarizes statistical highs, averages, and lows for the range of time indicated by the Analysis Interval.
10. Once the Server to Monitor document is complete, click the Save Server To Monitor button on the Action bar. Click the Exit button to close the document.
11. Repeat steps 4 through 10 to set up statistics reporting for additional servers.

If you don't want to run the Report task but still want to occasionally view statistics, you can type **Show Stat** at the server console for a quick statistical report. This command produces a considerable amount of information that normally scrolls off the screen. Therefore, you might want to run this command from the remote console and copy the response to a word processor for easier viewing.

The Administration Process

The Administration Process is new to Notes since Release 4.0 and is designed to help you perform routine administrative tasks. This new feature runs as a server task (adminp) and gets started, by default, automatically during the server startup process. For any server running the Administration Process server task, Notes also creates the Administration Requests database (ADMIN4.NSF). This database stores Administration Process requests and responses to each request posted to the database. Each Administration Requests database in a domain has the same replica ID and must replicate to all other servers in the domain that run the Administration Process. This enables, for example, one server to post a request and another to respond to it.

The Administration Process can be thought of as an assistant to a Notes administrator. You, the administrator, start a specific administrative task and the Administration Process completes it for you. Unfortunately, the Administration Process can't do every administrative task for you, but it can help with the following activities:

- Create mail files during setup.
- Upgrade users and servers to hierarchical naming.
- Rename users.
- Recertify users and servers.
- Delete users, servers, and groups.
- Add resources to and delete them from the Public Address Book when these actions are initiated in the Resource Reservations database.
- Set the Master Address Book field in the Public Address Book to enable directory assistance.
- Create replicas of multiple databases.
- Enable password checking during authentication.
- Add servers and remove servers to and from a cluster.
- Move databases from a cluster server.

To completely benefit from all that the Administration Process has to offer, the IDs in your organization must be hierarchical.

To get started with the Administration Process, you should first assign the Public Address Book an administration server (the steps to complete this task were described in the *Installing Your First Server* section of this chapter). Then assign individual databases an administration server in the same manner. Or, if you have to assign an administration server to several databases at once, you can use the Database Tools icon available on the Administration screen. To use this method of assignment follow the steps listed below:

1. From the menu bar, select File ➢ Tools ➢ Server Administration.

2. Click the Database Tools icon and the Tools to Manage Notes Database dialog box appears.
3. In the Server box, select the server storing databases for which you want to select an administration server.
4. In the Databases box, select each database you want to assign an administration server for.
5. In the Tool box, select Administration Server.
6. In the Administration Server box, select an administration server for the databases.
7. Decide whether or not you want the administration process to update names in Reader and Author fields, and make the appropriate selection.
8. When you've completed your selections, click the Update button.
9. Repeat steps 3 through 8 to specify another administration server for a different group of databases on the same server or a different server.

If a database has replica copies on another server, you only need to assign an administration server to one of the copies and let that assignment replicate to the remaining copies.

After an administration server has been assigned to a database, you'll need to configure Notes servers to work with the Administration Process.

1. If necessary, upgrade all servers to the current release of Notes.
2. Create a Certification Log (CERTLOG.NSF) if one doesn't already exist (detailed instructions are found in the *Installing Your First Server* section of this chapter).
3. Start the Notes client on the server that you want to be the administration server for the Public Address Book.
4. Open the local copy rather than the server copy of the Public Address Book.

5. Choose File ➢ Database ➢ Access Control, and make sure that an administration server is set for the Public Address Book (detailed instructions are found in the *Installing Your First Server* section of this chapter).

6. Start the Notes server you designated as the administration server for the Public Address Book.

7. Open the server rather than the local copy of the Administration Requests database (ADMIN4.NSF).

8. Choose File ➢ Database ➢ Access Control and make sure administrators who initiate Administration Process requests have the necessary access. For most requests, the Default access is sufficient.

After the Notes servers are set up with the Administration Process, monitor the Administration Requests database daily for requests requiring approval and for errors. Requests that might appear in the database are activities such as deleting or renaming a user, server, or group. While these activities still require an administrator to manually initiate them, the Administration Process helps with disseminating a deletion or renaming request throughout the entire Notes network. The following example of deleting a user should help clarify how the Administration Process helps this routine administrative activity:

1. Open the Public Address Book on a server rather than choosing Local.

2. Select the People view and select one or more Person documents.

3. Click Delete Person and click Yes when prompted to continue.

4. The three options shown below appear in a dialog box. Select one and click OK.

    - Delete Just the Mail File Specified in Person Record.

    - Delete Mail File Specified in Person Record and All Replicas.

    - Don't Delete the Mail File.

5. In the next dialog box, select one of the following options:

    - Yes immediately deletes all references to the person in this replica of the Public Address Book and posts a Delete in Access Control List request.

- No posts a Delete in Address Book request in the Administration Requests database and the Administration Process deletes references to the person in the Public Address Book and database ACLs according to the Interval setting for the Administration Process.

6. Next, delete the user's mail file in one of two ways:

    - If shared mail is used on the server, unlink the user's mail file and delete that file manually. (Chapter 9 describes how to unlink shared mail.)
    - If shared mail is not used on the server, have the Administration Process delete the user's mail file. Then examine the Approve File Deletion request in the Pending Administrators Approval View of the Administration Requests database. Open the pending request in edit mode, and click Approve File Deletion to request the Administration Process to delete the file.

7. Finally, deny the user access to all servers.

You can see from this example that while the administrator still executes the primary steps for deleting a user, the time consuming process of removing that user from all occurrences in the Public Address Book, and in some cases deleting the user's mail file, is handled by the Administration Process.

The Administration Process does its job according to settings in the Administration Process section of the Server document. Each setting controls the timing of specific types of requests (see Figure 4.6).

- **Maximum number of threads**: Under the heading Basics you can set how many threads the Administration Process can use. By default, this field is set to 3, which is adequate. However, if you use a multi-processor computer as your Notes server and you want to increase the performance of the Administration Process, you can increase this number.
- **Interval**: Under the heading Normal Request Settings, this field is used for setting an interval, in minutes, at which to complete requests that correspond to this setting, such as Rename Person in the Address Book and Rename in the Access Control List.
- **Execute once a day requests at**: Also in the Normal Request Settings section, this field allows you to specify a time of day to update Person documents in the Public Address Book.

FIGURE 4.6

The Server document contains an Administration Process section where process settings can be specified.

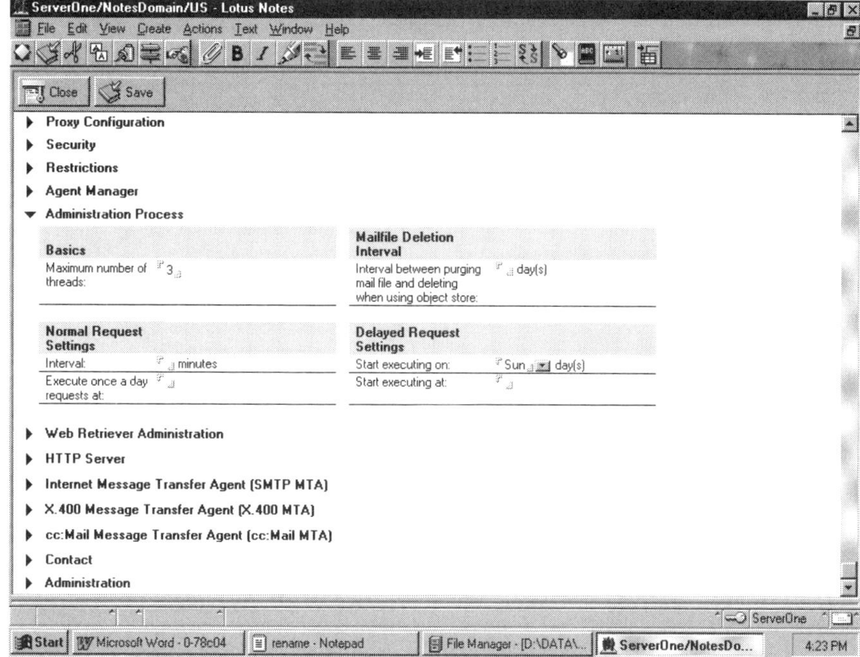

- **Interval between purging mail file and deleting used object store:** This field, found in the Mailfile Deletion Interval section, is for setting an interval of days that should elapse between when the Object Collect task runs against a mail file that uses shared mail and when the mail file is deleted (when you choose to delete mail files while deleting user names).
- **Start executing on:** In the Delayed Request Settings section, this field specifies a day, or days, of the week to carry out delayed requests.
- **Start executing at:** Also in the Delayed Request Settings section, this field is used to specify a time of the day to carry out delayed requests.

While letting the Administration Process do its work according to its schedule is the easiest way to work with this new feature of Notes, waiting for a particular time of day for a request to be processed may not always be possible. Fortunately, there is a way to manually kick-off the Administration Process and have pending requests processed. Table 4.2 lists a number of server console commands you can use to start the Administration Process according to what you need done.

TABLE 4.2 Adminp Server Console Commands

Console Command	Command Description
tell adminp process interval	This command processes all immediate requests and all requests that are usually processed according to the interval setting. You can also use the command **tell adminp process new**.
tell adminp process daily	This command processes all new and modified requests to update Person documents in the Public Address Book. You can also use the command **tell adminp process people**.
tell adminp process delayed	This command processes all requests that are usually carried out according to the Start Executing On and Start Executing At settings.
tell adminp process time	This command processes all new and modified Delete Unlinked Mail File Requests.
tell adminp process all	This command processes all types of new and modified requests except for Delete Unlinked Mail File Requests.

The Administration Process is a powerful tool to facilitate routine Notes administrator's tasks. Not every administrator will use all of the features of the Administration Process. Determine which features are most useful to you and refer to the online *Notes Administration Guide* for detailed "how-to" instructions.

The Agent Manager

In Notes Release 3 we had macros; now with Release 4 we have their replacement: agents. Agents allow Notes users to automate certain tasks in Notes. For example, an agent might automatically send a response to all incoming e-mail indicating that you are out of the office or away on vacation.

To allow users to leverage the power of agents, Notes provides a set of predefined agents. And if the predefined agents don't do the trick, the Notes Agent Builder is always available when users want to create their own agents using formulas or LotusScript.

There are basically two types of agents: Personal agents, which are used and created by users with at least Reader access to the database, and Public agents, which are created by a database designer for use by specified users.

Agents can sometimes have unexpected results when run. Therefore, as the Notes administrator, you'll want to have a certain level of control over who has the authority to execute agents on a specified server. And the Agent Manager is the administrative tool you'll use to control agents in your Notes environment.

Controlling the use of agents on a Notes server is done through the Agent Manager section of the Server document. The following steps describe how to limit agent access on a Notes server:

1. From the Notes client workspace, open the Public Address Book.
2. Select the Servers view.
3. Select the appropriate Server document and click the Edit Server button from the Action bar.
4. Open the Agent Manager section of the Server document.
5. Enter the appropriate information in the fields found in this section:
   - **Run personal agents:** Users listed in this field can run private agents that they create using the Agent Builder or formulas. Users still have to have at least Reader access to the database before they can create a personal agent.
   - **Run restricted LotusScript agents:** Users listed in this field have access to a limited set of LotusScript features to create agents. Tasks such as opening a network or local database, creating or deleting a database, using environment variables, using a disk-based log file, encrypting or signing, or file I/O are considered restricted.
   - **Run unrestricted LotusScript agents:** Users listed in this field can create agents using the full set of LotusScript features to manipulate databases and server resources. Populate this field with caution. Too much access can have a seriously negative impact on your Notes server.

- **Start time**: This field appears under both the daytime and nighttime headers and is used to control a start time for agents.
- **End time**: This field appears under both the daytime and nighttime headers and is used to control an end time for agents.
- **Max concurrent agents**: This field appears under both the daytime and nighttime headers and specifies how many agents can run at the same time. Only one agent can run on a database at one time, but agents can run on different databases on the same server concurrently. Increasing the number in this field means you're allocating more server resources to the Agent Manager, which takes away resources from other server processes such as replication and mail routing.
- **Max LotusScript execution time**: This field appears under both the daytime and nighttime headers and allows you to limit the amount of time an agent can run on a server. This allows further control over the allocation of server system resources.
- **Max % busy before delay**: This field appears under both the daytime and nighttime headers and specifies the amount of CPU polling time the Agent Manager can use before it initiates an automatic delay. Increasing the number in this field dedicates more server resources to the Agent Manager and decreases the resources available for other server processes.
- **Refresh agent cache**: This field determines how often the cached agents are refreshed.

6. After all of the settings are finished, save and exit the document.
7. Restart your Notes server for your changes to take effect.

When your Notes server restarts, the Agent Manager server task scrutinizes agents that attempt to run in the following manner:

1. The Agent Manager first validates the signature on the agent. If the signature is missing, the agent is not allowed to run.
2. The Server document in the Public Address Book is checked to determine whether the user is allowed to run restricted and/or unrestricted agents. API restrictions for agents are also checked at this time.

3. The agent begins execution according to the information gathered from the Server document.

If users or groups are allowed to run unrestricted agents, the agent has full access to the server's system and can manipulate system time, file I/O, and operating system commands.

Summary

The amount of hands-on Notes server management you'll do will depend largely on the importance of Notes in your company. In situations where Notes plays a small role in a company, setting up servers and doing regular backups is probably the most Notes server management you'll do. In other environments where Notes is a company's primary e-mail system and also hosts mission-critical applications, Notes server management includes everything in this chapter and more.

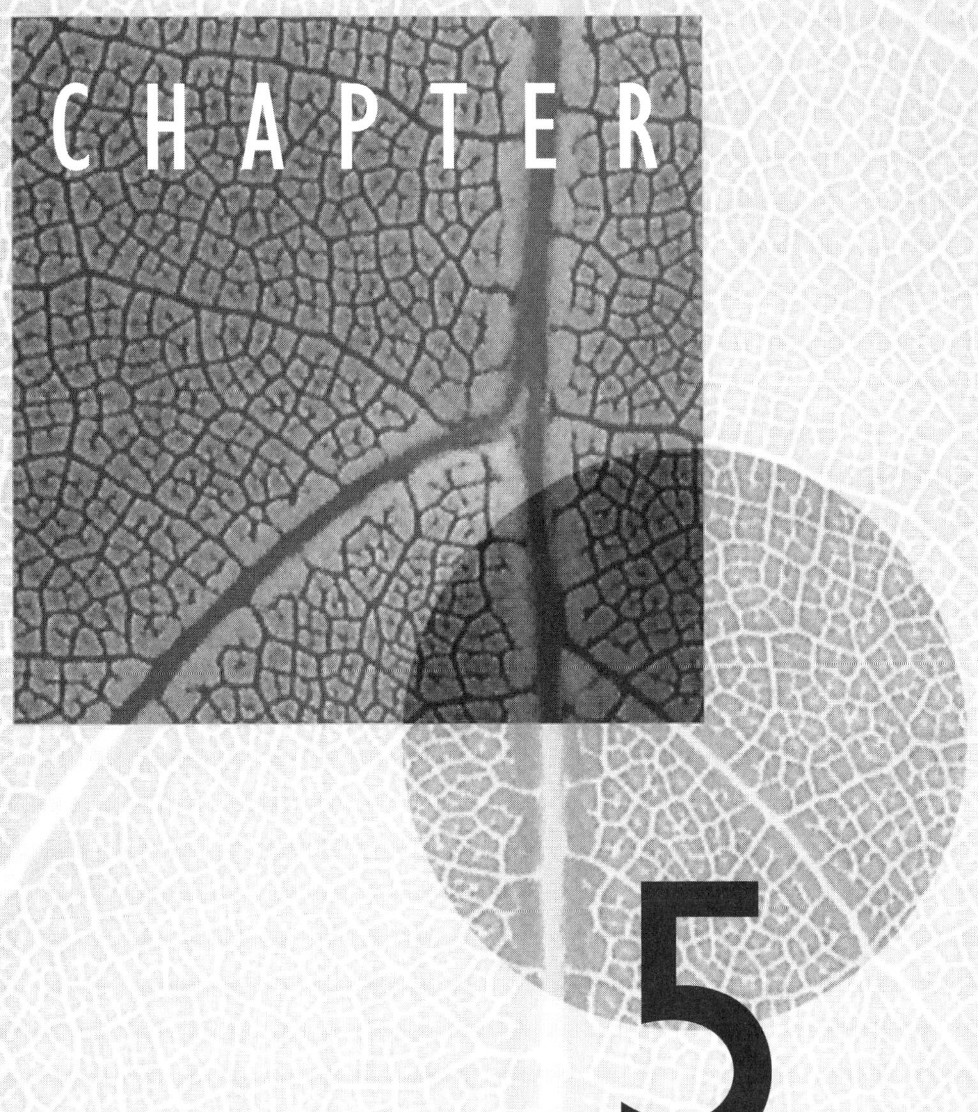

5

User Management

User management is probably one of the most dreaded responsibilities for a Notes administrator because it usually means tedious, boring tasks or more user interaction than an administrator has time for. Even though user management might not be as exciting as managing the Notes servers themselves, most of the tasks involved have been made considerably easier in Notes Release 4.5.

User management, in general, consists of creating users and connecting them to the network, renaming a user on occasion, relocating personal data files to a different server, and deleting users. In Notes, these same general user management tasks exist:

- New users are created (or registered, as Notes prefers to call it).
- Notes client software is installed and configured for your Notes network.
- Users are renamed as needed.
- Users are moved around in your organizational hierarchy, which is similar to NetWare 4.*x* Network Directory Services (NDS).
- Users' mail databases are moved from one server to another as needed.
- Users are deleted from the Notes network when they leave the organization.

As a Notes administrator, these are the basic user management functions you'll perform on a regular basis. Obviously, tasks such as creating new users and installing the client software is something you'll do mostly when your Notes network is new. However, new people are always being hired so you'll never stop doing this particular task entirely. Other tasks, such as renaming a user, you'll do infrequently. No matter how frequently or infrequently you do a particular task, it is your job as the Notes administrator to do it and do it well.

Creating Users

Creating new users in Notes is a very simple process. There are two possible ways to create them:

1. Register them individually.
2. Register them en masse using a simple informational text file.

Which way you choose to create your users depends largely on how many users you have and how much pre-existing information you have stored in some type of electronic format.

For example, if you have approximately fifty users and information about them doesn't exist in an electronic format, then you'll probably want to register each user individually. Perhaps you do have information about each user in an electronic format; you still might decide to register each user individually if you find repetitive typing easier than data manipulation. On the other hand, the user information might be contained in a spreadsheet making it easy to extract and insert just what you need. In that case, you'll probably want to create each user based on an informational text file that you create from your spreadsheet of user information. You'd also want to use an informational text file to create all of your users when you're registering massive numbers of users, say 500 or more, because you'll more than likely have their information contained in some type of electronic format.

Whichever method for creating users you choose, you'll have to know how to use them both. Creating users from an informational text file is usually only done when you first create your Notes network. After initial network setup and user roll-out, new users will probably only need to be added occasionally and not in large groups. I am making certain assumptions here, but I think it is a fairly safe assumption.

Registering Users One at a Time

The Notes client makes registering new users very simple. However, there are still a few things you need, and a few things you will need to know before you start.

You will need:

- **A valid Notes client license:** This is to make sure you're not violating any software copyright laws. Technically, you can use the same set of diskettes, or CD-ROM, for each client installation. However, you should have valid proof that you own a license for each copy of Notes installed.

- **Access to a certification ID**: You need a certification ID to stamp each user created. If you've created several certification IDs to support your organization's hierarchy, make sure you have physical access to these IDs and know their passwords before attempting to register them to users.

This is what you'll need to know:

- **User's name**: It seems obvious that you need to know the user's name. However, by user's name I also mean their name based on a naming convention that you have devised for your Notes network. This naming convention should be outlined in a Notes standards document, discussed in more detail in Chapter 2. A naming convention enforces consistency in how names appear in the Public Address Book and also defines how to handle duplicate names.
- **Registration server**: This server is the server that will do the actual registration, which is a fairly CPU-intensive operation. Because registering new users can place a heavy load on the CPU, I don't recommend a bulk registering of users on a mission-critical server during peak traffic.
- **Password**: You need to know if you plan to apply passwords to the user ID file. If you do plan to apply passwords at creation, how will you name them? How will you communicate that information to the user? Have you taught users how to change their passwords? And have you educated them on the importance of using passwords? If you don't plan to apply passwords at creation time, you'll need to know where you plan to store the ID files once you do create them.
- **Home server**: The home server is different from the registration server in that the home server is where the user's mail file is stored. The home server, or what I like to call the user's mail server, should have been addressed in the Notes standards document (covered in Chapter 2).

These pieces of information are just some of the basics you'll need to know before you create a user. There are other items that will come up, but for now the ones above are the bare essentials to get started.

Creating a User

Once you have all of the "needs" and "need to knows" together you're ready to get started creating a user.

Start by opening the server Administration window by selecting File ➢ Tools ➢ Server Administration (see Figure 5.1).

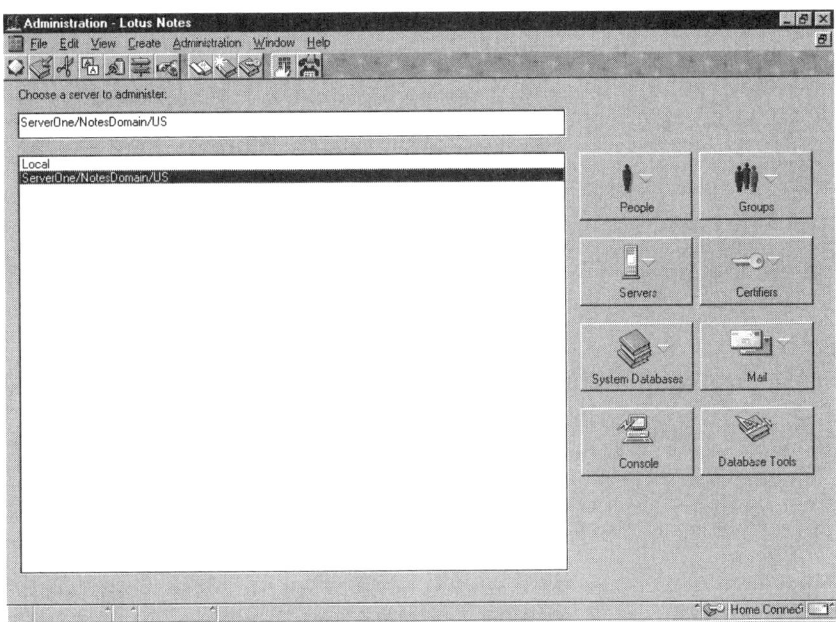

FIGURE 5.1 The server Administration window with its eight administrative tools lined up along the right side of the screen

Click the People button and select Register Person from the drop-down menu. A software license warning message will appear to make sure you have purchased a Notes client license.

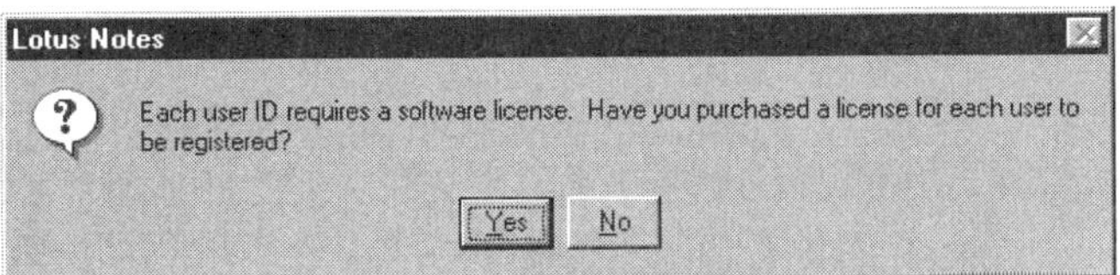

If you have a valid client license, click Yes. Otherwise click No and purchase another copy of Notes. After you click Yes in the warning box, the Register Person dialog box will appear (see Figure 5.2).

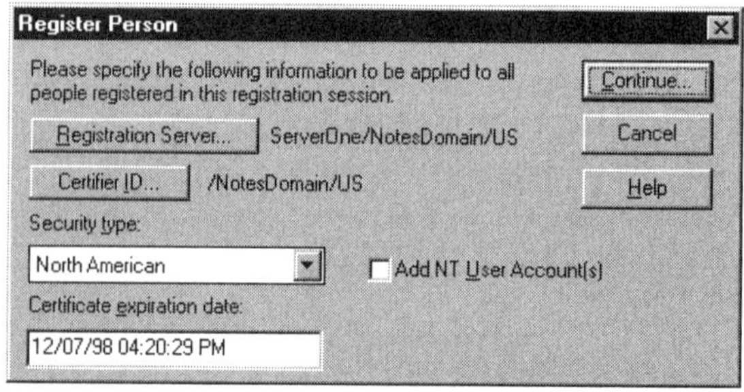

FIGURE 5.2
The Register Person dialog box requires you to make a few basic selections for the new user you are about to create.

In the Register Person dialog box, start by clicking the Registration Server button and selecting a server from the Registration Server drop-down menu of the Choose Registration Server dialog box. As previously mentioned, this server is the one that will actually process the registration. This server may not be the user's actual home server or mail server.

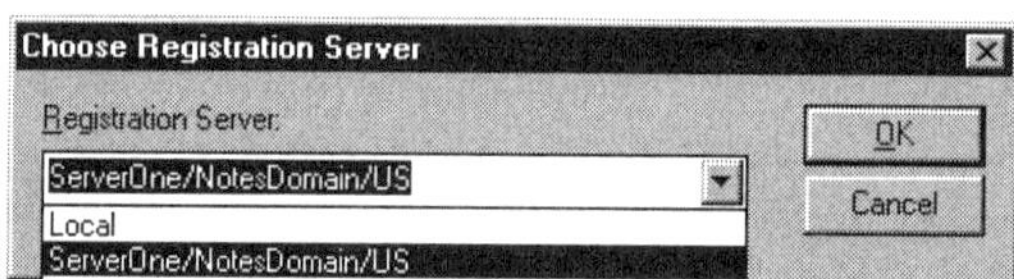

After you select a registration server, click the Certifier ID button and choose the certification ID that you will use to certify this new user in the Choose Certifier ID dialog box (see Figure 5.3). The last certifier ID that was used will be displayed by default.

FIGURE 5.3
Choose a certifier ID from the Choose Certifier ID dialog box.

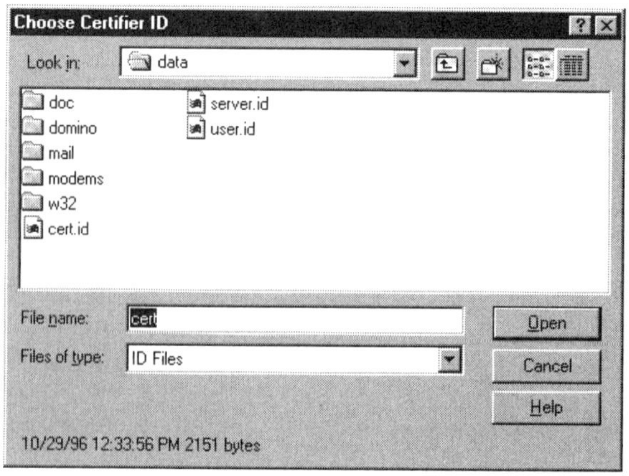

Certifier IDs are discussed in detail in Chapter 4.

The next step is to select a Security type. You have two choices for the security type: North American and international. The difference between these two security types is that the North American version uses a longer encryption key than the international version (see the *Why Is There a North American Security Type and an International Security Type?* sidebar).

Why Is There a North American Security Type and an International Security Type?

The United States government restricts Notes' encryption technology from being used outside of North America. For that reason, the international encryption key is shorter (and thought to be easier to crack).

The difference in length does cause an important capability problem that you need to keep in mind when designing an International Notes network. The different encryption key length means that anything encrypted using a North American key can only be decrypted by a North American key. On the other hand, anything encrypted using an International key can be decrypted using either International or North American keys. If your Notes network is an international environment, you'll have to keep this encryption limitation in mind or avoid the problem completely by just using the International security type for all users and servers.

The Certification expiration date is, by default, two years from the point of registration. The expiration length only determines how long an ID is valid before it must be recertified again, which is covered later in this chapter.

If your Notes server is on the Windows NT Server platform, you will have the option to create an NT account at the same time you register this Notes user. To utilize this feature simply click once in the box next to Add NT User Account(s).

Once everything is selected in the Register Person dialog box, press the Continue button and another Register Person dialog box with more options will appear. There are three additional sections for user registration indicated by the three icons on the left side of the dialog box (see Figure 5.4). The Basics section is the first section displayed.

FIGURE 5.4

After clicking the Continue button in the Register Person dialog box, another Register Person dialog box appears.

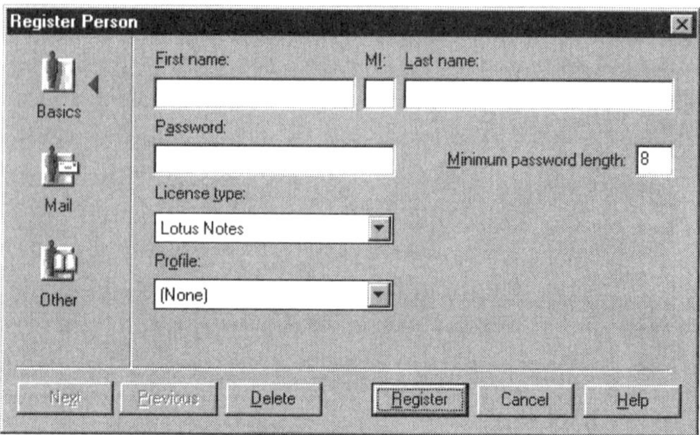

Continue in this dialog box by adding the new user's first name, middle initial, and last name. Press the Tab key to move from left to right between each field and Shift + Tab to move back from right to left.

If you're going to apply passwords when you register your users, enter the password in the Password field (see the *Password Restrictions and ID File Locations* sidebar).

Password Restrictions and ID File Locations

User ID files are stored in one of two locations (or in both): the Public Address Book and/or a diskette. The diskette can be either a local drive or a network drive, and in any directory on either drive. The actual location you want to use is set in the Other section of the Register Person dialog box and explained later in this section. If you choose to not apply passwords during user registration, you cannot store the ID in the Public Address Book without Notes complaining.

Next, set the Minimum Password Length. If you want, you can enter a password, but set the minimum length to 0 so users can clear it later if they want.

Now select the License Type. You have three choices: Lotus Notes, Lotus Notes Desktop, and Lotus Notes Mail. See the *Lotus Notes License Types* sidebar for details about these three license types.

The Lotus Notes License Types

There are three types of Notes workstation licenses: the Lotus Notes license, the Lotus Notes Desktop license, and the Lotus Notes Mail license. Which type of license you've selected determines which databases and templates you can use, and the extent to which they can perform design tasks and administrative tasks.

The Lotus Notes license is the original license type. It allows you to create new databases based on any of the supplied templates and to perform design tasks and administrative tasks. In a nutshell, this license has no restrictions. Make sure that, as an administrator, you install this version of the license on your personal workstation.

The Lotus Notes Desktop license allows you to create and use databases based on any of the supplied databases. The only restriction here is that you cannot perform design tasks or administrative tasks. This license is useful for most end-users. Be prepared, however, to get complaints from those users that are very computer literate and like to dabble in development.

The final license type is the Lotus Notes Mail license. This license is the most restrictive of all the license types, but is useful for environments that are using Notes primarily for its e-mail capabilities. Users with this license cannot perform design tasks or administrative tasks. Also, this license only allows use and creation of new databases based on the following templates: Discussion (R4), Document Library (R4), Lotus SmartSuite Library (R4), Microsoft Office Library (R4), Personal Journal (R4), Room Reservations (R4), Agent Log, Database Library, Mail (R4), Mail Router Mailbox, Notes Log, Personal Address Book, and the Web Navigator.

As an administrator, you'll need to be aware of the restrictions so that you can help developers make sure that the applications they develop can be used by all of your installed Notes clients.

The final step for the Basics section is to select a profile, if you have previously created one to use. Profiles allow you to quickly supply some useful information that will be entered into each Person document. User profiles are covered later in this chapter.

The next step is to fill out the mail information for this new user. Click on the Mail icon and the Mail section of the Register Person dialog box is displayed (see Figure 5.5).

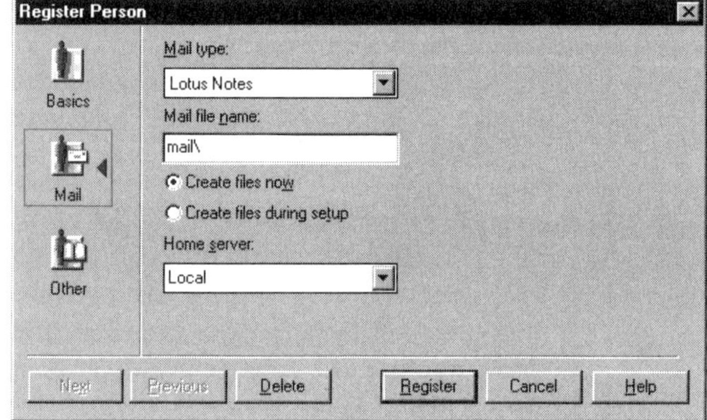

FIGURE 5.5
The Mail section of the Register Person dialog box allows you to set mail-specific user information.

The option you will need to set is the Mail type. By default, this field is set to Lotus Notes. Your other options are cc:Mail and VIM (Vendor Independent Messaging).

The next field is Mail File Name. By default this field is set to the first initial followed by the last name of the new user, but is restricted to the eight-character naming convention of DOS (even on non-DOS based servers).

Keep in mind that since the mail file name is based on a user's first initial followed by the first seven characters of their last name, duplicate file names are easy to come by. Notes will warn you if it is about to overwrite an existing mail file, so be prepared to rename this file or use your own custom mail file naming scheme. I like to use a combination of first initial, first four characters of the last name, and then an incrementing three digit number. Using such a scheme on my name creates a mail file named BSWED001.NSF.

The next choice to make is whether to create the mail file now or during user setup. I prefer to create the mail file while I'm in this screen so that I can troubleshoot problems, if any, alone and not in front of the user.

The final selection to make is the user's Home server, which is really their mail server. This is a useful option to set if you use more than one mail server at your location. By default this field is set to Local, but simply look through the drop-down list for other available servers.

Now it's time to move to the final section of the Register Person dialog box. Select the Other icon to display the Other section (see Figure 5.6).

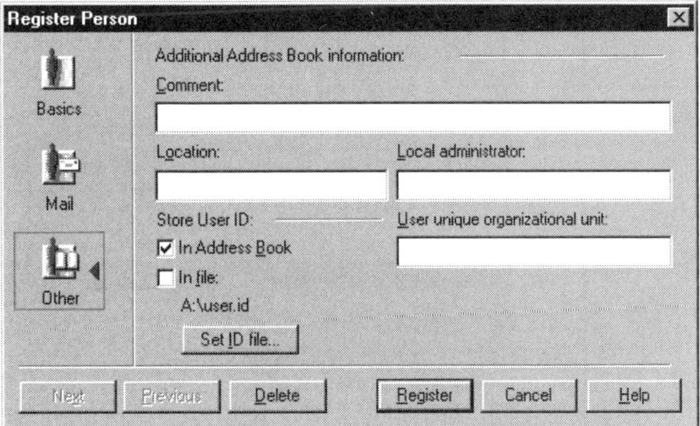

FIGURE 5.6

The Other section of the Register Person dialog box

The Comment, Location, and Local administrator fields are optional fields that you can fill with additional descriptive information.

Now you must choose whether to store the new USER.ID file in the Public Address Book or in a file. If you store the ID file in the Public Address Book, which is the default selection, you'll have to enter a password for this user in the Basics section of the Register Person dialog box. If you don't want to impose passwords on ID files, then you'll have to store these new ID files on disk. This disk, by default, is indicated as the A drive, but can be any drive and directory you have access to. Use the Set ID File button to select where you want the ID stored (see the *Setting the Storage Location for the ID File* sidebar for details).

The final field to set in the Other section of the Register Person dialog box is the User Unique Organizational Unit field. This field is optional but very useful because it allows you to create ad hoc organizational units to help avoid naming conflicts. For example, you can quickly add a Sr. or Jr. extension to someone's name using this field.

Setting the Storage Location for the ID File

Selecting the button to set the location for the ID file causes an error message to appear.

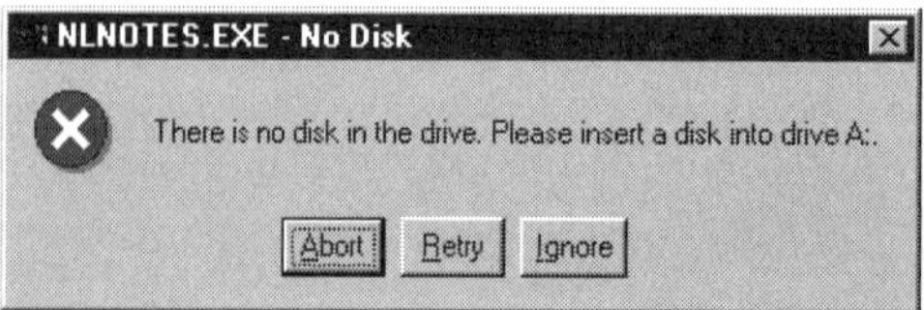
NLNOTES.EXE - No Disk
There is no disk in the drive. Please insert a disk into drive A:.
Abort
Retry
Ignore

The above message makes you think that your only location option is a diskette in the A drive. However, you have location options other than the A drive. To get past this error and select a location other than the A drive, click Ignore. But wait! There is yet another error message informing you that the A drive is not accessible.

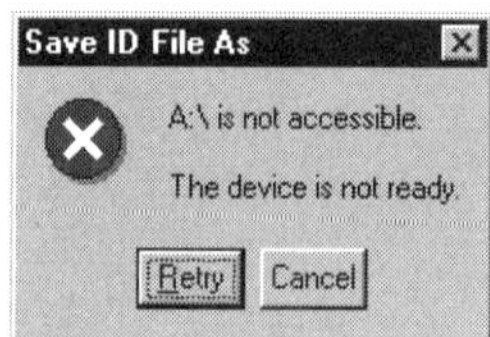
Save ID File As
A:\ is not accessible.
The device is not ready.
Retry
Cancel

Ignore this error by clicking the Cancel button. Finally, a dialog box appears that allows you to set an ID file location other than your A drive.

I'm not sure why these misleading errors occur, and they might not exist by the time you read this book. However, they existed in an NT version of Notes Release 4.1 and in the beta of Release 4.5, so be aware.

With the other appropriate fields set, click the Register button to begin the registration process. The status bar at the bottom of your Notes client workspace indicates the progress of the user registration. When the user is completely registered, a dialog box appears asking whether or not you want to register another user.

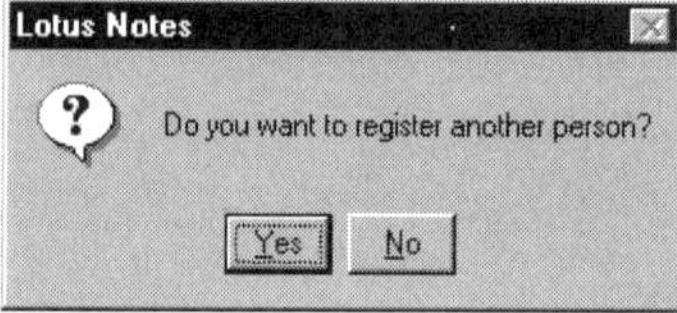
Lotus Notes
Do you want to register another person?
Yes
No

Throughout most of the user registration process you probably noticed that a Delete button was available. Selecting this button, when available, clears all of the entries you've made so far in the Register Person dialog box. This is not the method you would use to delete existing users. Deleting users is covered later in this chapter.

The registration process is repeated for each user you need to create. This process works well for a couple of users but becomes tedious for hundreds of users. Fortunately, Notes provides a process for registering several users at one time without having to navigate all of the registration screens and sections for each user. This process is described in the next section.

Registering Several Users at Once

Registering users from a file, or what I like to call "bulk user registration," is a simple process as long as you are prepared with the necessary information before you get started. As with registering a single user, you need to have and know a couple of things ahead of time.

You will need:

- **Valid Notes client license**: This is to make sure you're not violating any software copyright laws. Technically, you can use the same set of diskettes or CD-ROM for each client installation. However, you should have valid proof that you own a license for each copy of Notes you install.
- **Access to a certification ID**: You need a certification ID to stamp each user you create. If you've created several certification IDs to support your organization's hierarchy, make sure you have access to these ID files and know their passwords before using them to register a new user.
- **User information text file**: This simple text file contains all of the necessary user information to help automate the registration process. Each line of this file contains information for a single user and each item is semicolon delimited (This file will be discussed in further detail later in this section).

You will need to know:

- **User's name**: It seems obvious that you need to know the user's name. However, by user's name I also mean their name based on a naming convention that you have devised for your Notes network. This naming convention should be outlined in a Notes standards document, which is discussed in more detail in chapter 2. A naming convention enforces consistency in how names appear in the Public Address Book and also defines how to handle duplicate names.

- **Registration server:** This server is the server that will do the actual registration, which is a fairly CPU-intensive operation. Because registering new users can place a heavy load on the CPU, I don't recommend a bulk registering of users on a mission-critical server during peak traffic.
- **Password:** You need to know if you plan to apply passwords to the user ID file. If you do plan to apply passwords at creation, what will the passwords be? How will you communicate that information to the users? Have you taught users how to change their passwords? And have you educated them on the importance of using passwords? If you don't plan to apply passwords at creation time, you'll need to know where you plan to store the passwords once you decide to create them.
- **Home server:** The home server is different from the registration server in that the home server is where the user's mail file is stored. The home server, or what I like to call the user's mail server, should have been addressed in the Notes standards document (covered in Chapter 2).

Once you have everything you "need" and "need to know," you're ready to begin.

Creating the User Information File

The file used to register users in bulk is a simple ASCII text file. You can create this file using any word processor or text editor that allows you to save the file in ASCII format. Each line in the file contains information pertaining to a single user and each piece of information is separated using a semicolon in the following manner:

Lastname;Firstname;Middleinitial;organizationalunit;password;IDfiledirectory;IDfilename;homeservername;mailfiledirectory;mailfilename;location;comment;forwardingaddress;profilename;localadministrator <enter>

As you can see, there is a fair amount of information you can add for each user. Most of the informational items are self-explanatory. Nevertheless, here is a brief description of each item:

- **Lastname:** This is the user's last name.
- **Firstname:** This is the user's first name.
- **Middleinitial:** This is the user's middle initial. If you plan to use periods after the middle, you can also enter that here.
- **Organizationalunit:** If the user is part of a particular organization or organizational unit within your Notes hierarchy, you can enter that here. However, you will probably certify each user using the appropriate organizational certifier, so this informational item may not be required (more about this later in this section).
- **Password:** If you plan to apply passwords when you register each user, supply a password here.
- **IDfiledirectory:** This is the directory in which you plan to store the user ID files once they are created. If you plan to store ID files in the Public Address Book, leave this item blank.
- **IDfilename:** Enter the name of the ID file here. I strongly recommend that you supply this filename so that you avoid overwriting previously existing ID files.
- **Homeservername:** Enter the name of the user's home server, also known as their mail server.
- **Mailfiledirectory:** Enter the directory in which the mail file is to be stored once it is created. The default is the Mail directory under the Notes Data directory. If the default is acceptable, leave this field blank.
- **Mailfilename:** Enter the name for the personal mail file here. By default Notes will use the user's first initial followed by the first seven characters of his or her last name. I strongly recommend that you create your own custom naming scheme here to avoid duplicate filenames. (The previous section described one possible way to customize these filenames.)

- **Location:** This piece of information is optional, but it is provided for you to add user location information. You could enter physical or organizational location information or any other type of location information that you find useful.
- **Comment:** This item of information is optional, but it is provided for you to add additional useful comments.
- **Forwardingaddress:** If this user receives mail from a system other than Notes, and you have set up a mail gateway or Message Transfer Agent between that system and Notes, you can add a forwarding address here.
- **Profilename:** If you want to use a user profile, you can list that profile here.
- **Localadministrator:** This item allows you to specify the name of the Notes administrator responsible for this user. You can also use a group name instead of an individual user name if you want.

To help illustrate how this text file might appear with actual information I've provided a few examples.

Example #1: A Very Simple File The file shown below is for a bulk registration of users where middle initials, organization, passwords, mail file directory, location, comments, and forwarding addresses are not used. This sample also assumes the ID will be stored on a disk and not in the Public Address Book.

Swedeen;Bret;;;;C:\IDFILES;bswed001;ServerOne/NotesDomain;;bswed001;;;

Doe;John;;;;C:\IDFILES;jdoe001;ServerOne/NotesDomain;;jdoe001;;;

Smith;Jane;;;;C:\IDFILES;jsmit001;ServerOne/NotesDomain;;jsmit001;;;

To store the above sample IDs in the Public Address Book, you must add each entry's password in the appropriate location and leave its ID file directory blank.

Notice that anywhere I did not enter a piece of information I left the area blank but placed semicolons as delimiters. If I had left out the extra semicolons and created a file such as the one in the example shown below, my bulk registration would probably fail because the information I provided wouldn't line up with what Notes is expecting. For example, the sixth piece of information Notes is expecting is the ID file directory and in the example shown below I'm telling it what name to give the mail file. Notes will think that this intended filename is a directory, which Notes will be unable to find. My bulk registration will fail as a result.

Swedeen;Bret;C:\IDFILES;bswed001;ServerOne/NotesDomain;bswed001

Doe;John;C:\IDFILES;jdoe001;ServerOne/NotesDomain;jdoe001

Smith;Jane;C:\IDFILES;jsmit001;ServerOne/NotesDomain;jsmit001

Example #2: Accepting Some of the Defaults The example shown below doesn't specify an ID file directory or an ID filename because it plans to store these ID files in the Public Address Book. It also doesn't provide information for the home server, mail file directory, mail filename, location, or comments because it either plans to accept the defaults or doesn't want to include that information. This file does, however, include a forwarding address because these users receive their mail in cc:Mail, which already has the cc:Mail MTA configured in Notes.

Swedeen;Bret;H;Service;17u45;;;;;;;;Bret Swedeen @ CCMAIL

Doe;John;A;Sales;78j65;;;;;;;;John Doe @ CCMAIL

Smith;Jane;T;Accounting;98k65;;;;;;;;Jane Smith @ CCMAIL

Notice how I have included an organizational unit in this file. Once I create these users, these organizations are tagged onto the end of the organizational certifier that I use during registration whether I used the appropriate certifying ID or not.

Even though you can provide a fair amount of information in the registration file, most of it is not necessary because the bulk registration process prompts you for some of this information before you even get started.

Registering from a File

Once you have your user information file, make sure it is located in a directory you can access when you start to register users from a file. Then follow the steps below.

1. Start by opening the Server Administration window by selecting File ➢ Tools ➢ Server Administration.
2. Click the People button and a drop-down menu appears with three options: People View, Register Person, and Register From File.
3. Select Register From File and a software license warning message appears. If you have a valid client license, click Yes. Otherwise, click No and purchase another copy of Notes.

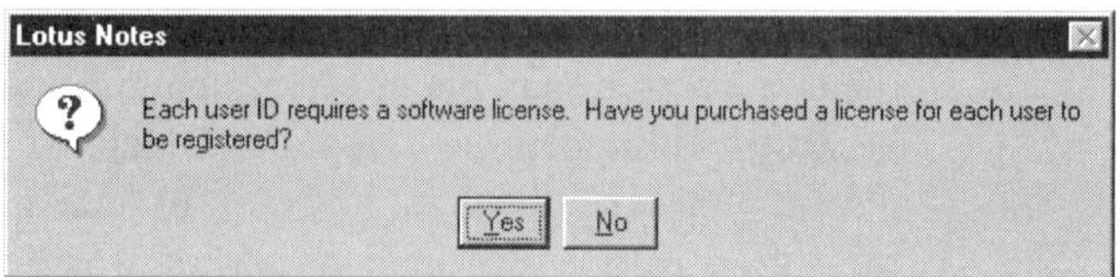

4. After clicking Yes in the warning box, the Register Person dialog box appears, just as it did when you registered a single user (see Figure 5.7).

FIGURE 5.7
The Register Person dialog box

5. Click the Registration Server button and select a server from the Choose Registration Server dialog box and drop-down list. Keep in mind that because you are registering several users at once, they will all use the server selected here. You cannot select different registration servers for different users in a file.

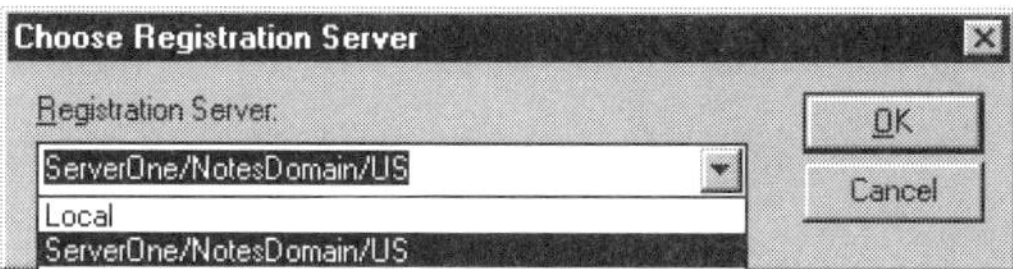

6. After you select a registration server, click the Certifier ID button and choose the certification ID that you will use to certify the users in this file. Enter the password for the certification ID when prompted. As with the registration server, only one certifier is used to register users from a file. If you need to use different certifiers for different users, you should create individual user information files that group users together and require the same certifier.

7. Next, select a security type from the Security Type drop-down list in the Register Person dialog box (your choice is North American or International; they differ in the length of their encryption key). Once again, the selection made here applies to all users contained in the user information file. As before, if you need to use different security types for different users, consider creating a separate file for just those users.

8. Once all of the initial selections are made, click the Continue button and the Choose Text File with Person Information dialog box will appear (see Figure 5.8).

9. Select the file that contains your user information and click Open. In the example below, I used a file called USERS.TXT.

   Swedeen;Suzanne;T;;;;sswed001;;;sswed001;;;

   Doe;John;K;;;;jdoe001;;;jdoe001;;;

   Doe;John;T;;;;jdoe002;;;jdoe002;;;

   Doe;Jon;W;;;;jdoe003;;;jdoe003;;;

   Smith;Jane;G;;;;jsmit001;;;jsmit001;;;

   Smittens;Jackie;G;;;;jsmit002;;;jsmit002;;;

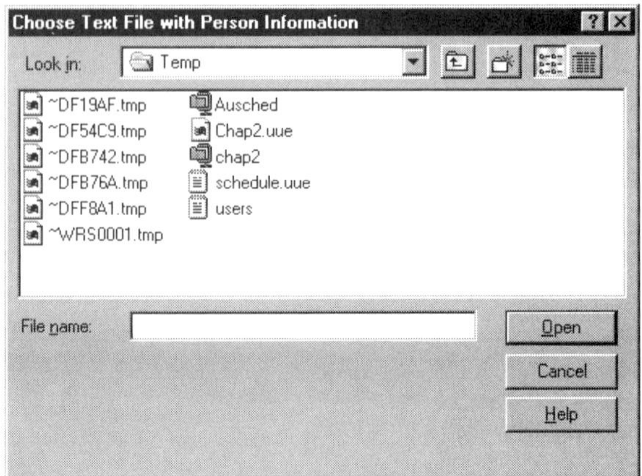

FIGURE 5.8

Traverse through your directory structure in the Choose Text File with Person Information dialog box and locate your user information text file.

Note how I've resolved duplicate names in my user information file and that I have left a considerable amount of information out of the file.

10. The Register Person from Text File dialog box appears. Note that it has fewer options than when you're registering users individually in the Register Person dialog box (see Figure 5.9).

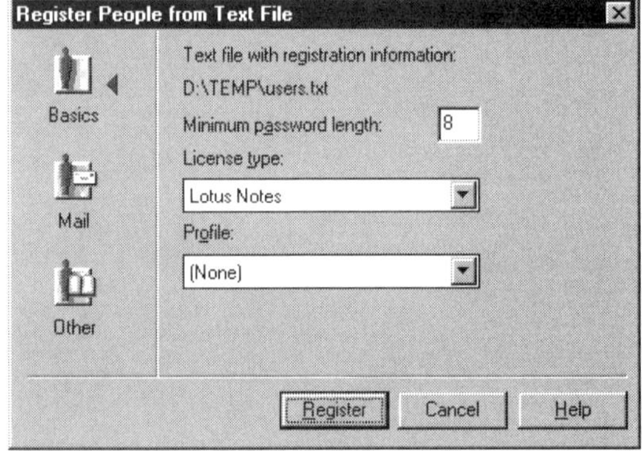

FIGURE 5.9

The Register Person from Text File dialog box has the same three sections that the Register Person dialog box has, but there are fewer options.

11. Next, set the minimum password length, choose the license type, and select the user profile (if any).

    A. The default password length is eight characters, but because I'm not storing my ID files in the Public Address Book, I don't need to supply a password. Therefore, I have to set the password length to zero.

    B. For the license type, three choices are available: Lotus Notes, Lotus Notes Desktop, and Lotus Notes Mail.

    C. Select the profile from the Profile drop-down list if you have previously created one. Otherwise, leave this field blank.

12. Click the Mail icon to go to the Mail section of the Register People from Text dialog box (see Figure 5.10).

FIGURE 5.10

The Mail section of the Register People from Text File dialog box

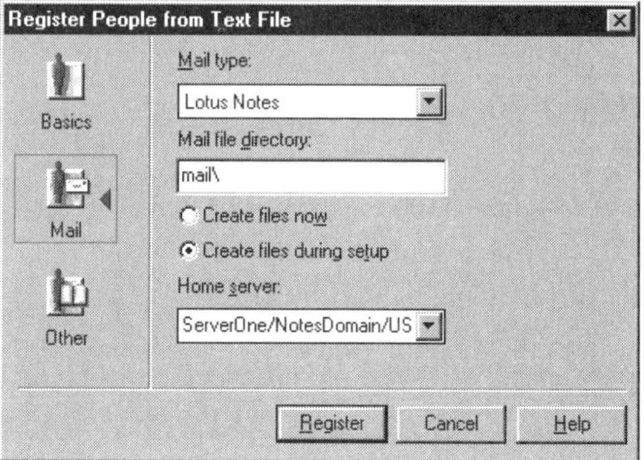

13. Select your Mail type: Lotus Notes, cc:Mail, or VIM (Vendor Independent Messaging), and specify your mail directory. Since I can set this directory here, I didn't include it in my user information text file.

14. Decide whether you want to create the mail files now or during user setup and select the corresponding option. I prefer to set up the mail files now so I could troubleshoot problems, if any, before I start to install and configure individual Notes workstations.

15. Now select the home server, also known as the mail server, from the Home Server drop-down list. This setting will be the same for each user defined in your user information text file. If you want these users to have different home servers, consider creating different user information text files based on these server groupings.

16. Click the Other icon to move to the Other section of the Register People from Text File dialog box (see Figure 5.11). The field Local Administrator is optional. If you want to add information about the local administrator to the user's Person document, here is where you would do it. Remember, this information is applied to all users created through the user information text file you selected for this bulk registration process.

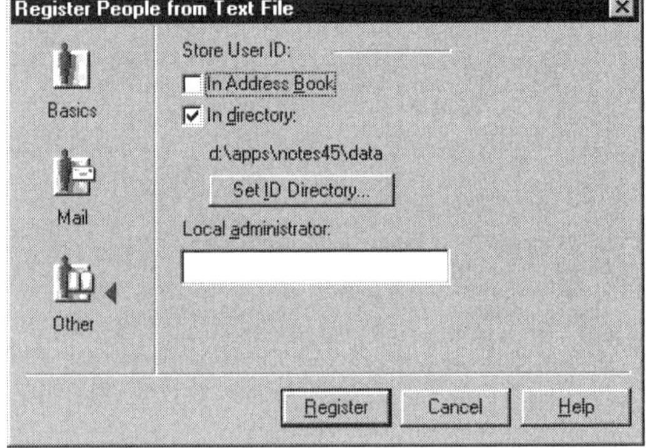

FIGURE 5.11
The Other section of the Register People from Text File dialog box

17. The final step in the Other section is to determine where to store your ID files. In the previous steps I've been making selections based on the idea that I plan to store IDs in a file. To do this, I click the Set ID Directory button shown back in Figure 5.11. I don't experience the same errors I did when I clicked this button for single user registration. Instead, the dialog box shown in Figure 5.12 appears.

18. In my example, I traverse to the NotesID directory I created under my Notes45 directory and click OK.

FIGURE 5.12

Choose the drive and directory where you want to store the user ID files in the Choose ID Files Directory dialog box.

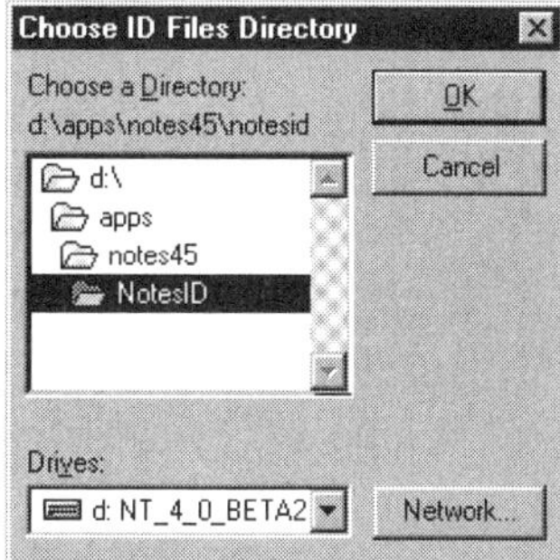

19. Finally, click the Register button and the process takes off. As each user is created, information about the status and progress of the registration process is displayed in the status bar of your Notes client. You can also view the progress from the server console.

When the process is complete, Notes informs you that it's done by displaying a dialog box indicating how many users were just registered.

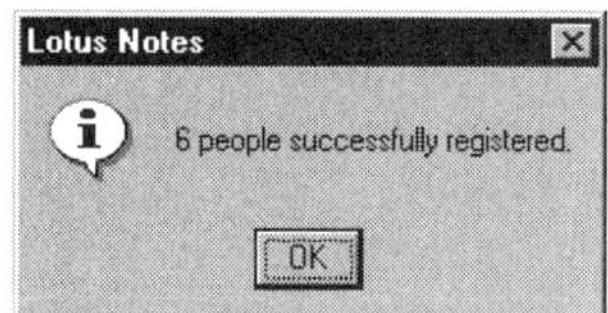

Now that you have finished registering users, you should check your results to make sure everything worked as expected. Below is a list of things you might want to verify before setting up users' individual workstations:

- Make sure that the ID files were created and stored in the proper location.
- Make sure the mail files were created in the Mail directory under the Notes Data directory.
- Make sure there is a Person document in the Public Address Book for each person.

To verify the existence of the ID files, use your graphical file manager to open drives and/or directories until you reach the one that should have the ID files. In my case, I use Windows NT Explorer to open the apps folder, then the Notes45 folder, and then the NotesID folder to see all of my ID files.

Next, verify the existence of the user mail files. Once again, I use Windows NT Explorer to open the apps folder, then the Notes45 folder, then the data folder, and finally the mail folder. Figure 5.13 shows all of the mail files created as I specified in my user information file.

FIGURE 5.13

The mail folder under the data folder displayed in Windows NT Explorer

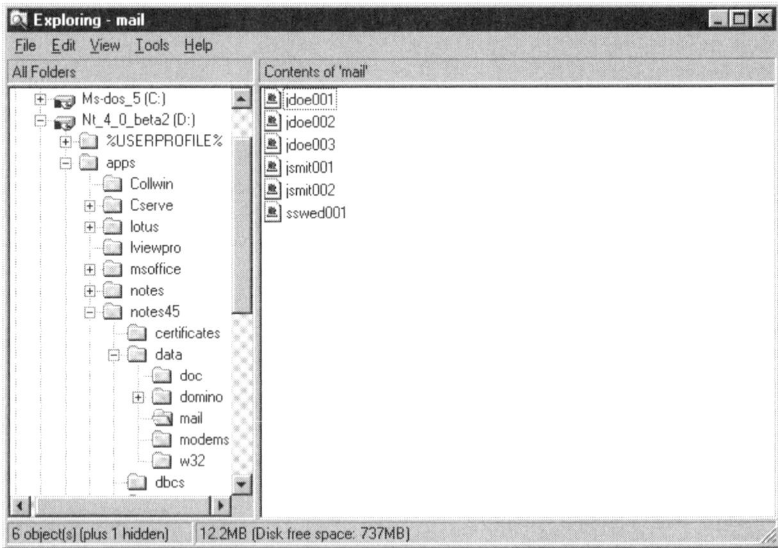

Finally, from the menu bar select File ➢ Tools ➢ Server Administration and then click the People button, select View People, and double-check that the Person documents were created (see Figure 5.14).

Once everything is present and accounted for, go ahead and either register more users from another file or start installing the Notes client software at each user's computer.

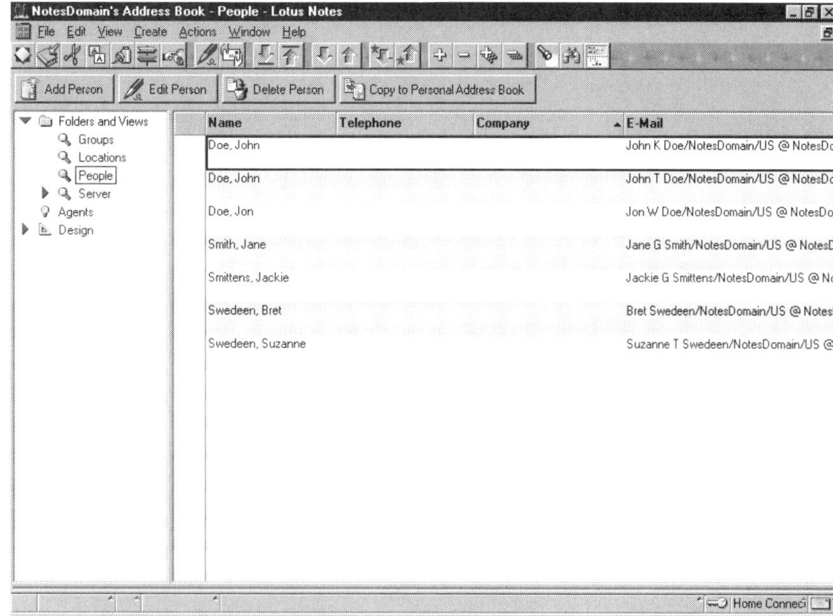

FIGURE 5.14
The People view from the Public Address Book shows all of the people registered in your Notes domain.

Setting Up a Notes Client

Registering new Notes users is only the first of two steps when it comes to completely setting up a new user. The second step is actually installing the Notes client software.

Installing the Notes client software and configuring the Notes client for a user is very simple. If you've seen it or done it before, go ahead and skip to the next section. For those of you who haven't installed a Notes client before, keep reading.

Installing the Notes Client Software

The first thing you'll have to do to get your new users rolling, other than registering them at the Notes server, is install the actual software at their workstation. This installation process is broken down into two phases:

1. Copying the files to the user's machine.
2. Configuring the user's copy of Notes to talk to your Notes network.

Installing the Notes software to the user's local machine can be done either using 3.5" diskettes (a very time consuming process) or a CD-ROM, or from a shared network drive that the Notes software has been installed to. The following steps summarize the process you'll go through during the first phase of installation.

1. To get the process going, insert the first diskette or CD-ROM, or change to the network drive that contains the shared installable copy of Notes, and start the setup program.

2. After Notes copies some files to the user's workstation hard drive, you are prompted to enter a name and company. Enter the appropriate information and click Next. Then click Yes in the Confirm Names dialog box to confirm that your name and company name are correct.

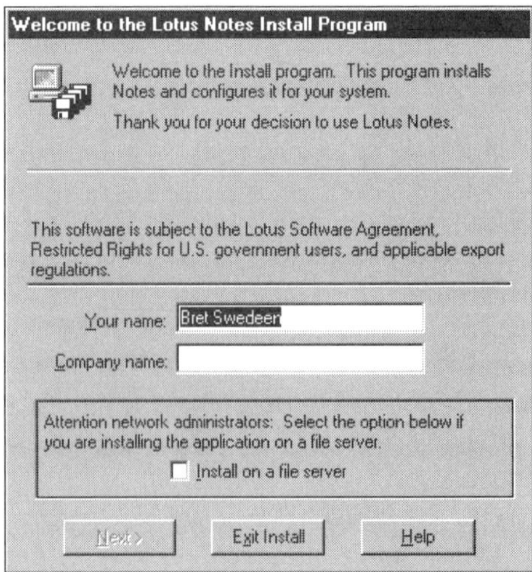

3. If there is a previous copy of Notes already on your system, Notes suggests that you install the new copy into the same directory.

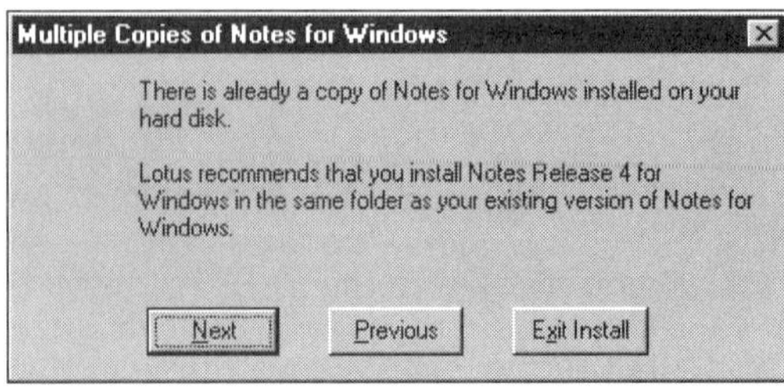

4. Notes displays the Install Options dialog box (see Figure 5.15) where you can choose between Standard Install, Server Install, and Customize Features - Manual Install. Since you are just installing a Notes client, select Standard Install. You could also select Customize Features - Manual Install and select or deselect certain items to install additional features such as online documents.

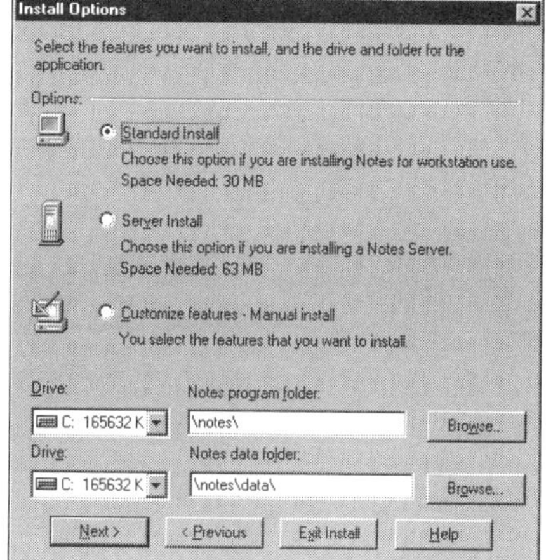

FIGURE 5.15

Select the installation type from the Install Options dialog box.

5. Notes then prompts you to select a program group to place the new icons into in the Select Program Group dialog box. Usually, the program group you will want to select is Lotus Applications, and therefore it is the default. For this example, accept the default.

6. In the Begin Copying Files dialog box, Notes asks for confirmation one last time before actually copying the files to your hard drive. Make sure there aren't any other programs running, then click Yes and the files will be copied.

This is your last chance to exit the installation process.

When all of the files have been copied to your machine, Notes congratulates you on your successful installation. You have just completed the first phase of the Notes installation process. Now you can begin to configure the new Notes client for your Notes network, which is described in the following steps.

1. Locate the Notes icon in the program group that it was installed in. If you accepted the default in the previous steps, that program group is Lotus Applications.
2. Double-click the Notes icon and start Notes.
3. Notes starts up and displays the Notes Workstation Setup dialog box (see Figure 5.16).

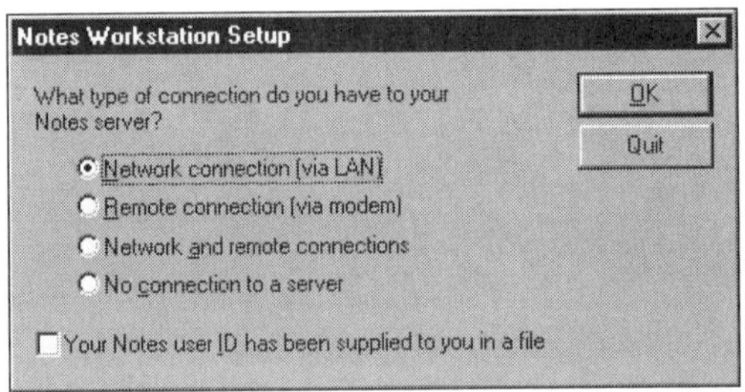

FIGURE 5.16

The Notes Workstation Setup dialog box is where you select the type of connection you have, and if your ID file has been supplied to you or if it's stored in the Public Address Book.

4. Select the connection type for the Notes client. The default is Network Connection Only, and in most cases this is the right type of connection. If, however, this installation is for a remote user, then you would select Remote Connection Only or perhaps Network and Remote Connections. The "No Connection" option means this installation of Notes does not connect to a Notes server.
5. If your ID has been supplied to the user in a file, select the Your Notes User ID Has Been Supplied to You in a File check box at the bottom of the dialog box. Otherwise, the default assumes that the ID is stored in the Public Address Book.
6. Click OK and the Network Workstation Setup dialog box appears. Type the user's name as it appears in the Public Address Book in the Your User Name field. Next, enter the user's home server, also known as the

mail server, in the Home Server Name field. Then, select the appropriate network type and click OK. Make sure you enter the correct information in this dialog box.

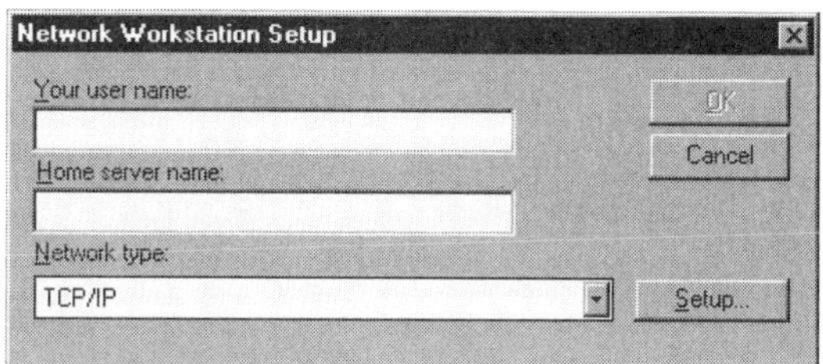

If you have problems connecting a client to your Notes network, it's probably because you entered the wrong information in the Network Workstation Setup dialog box.

The setup process will now begin. This usually takes a few minutes depending on the type of machine the client has, the speed of your Notes server, and how fast your network is overall. If, for whatever reason, the setup fails at this point, try it again and double-check all spelling and character case. If you're using hierarchical names, make sure you include them when you enter the user's name and home server. Also, if you have applied a password to the user ID file, you'll be prompted for that password after you enter the user name, home server name, and network type. When the setup is complete, you'll be prompted to select a time zone and then Notes will let you know that the setup is complete.

Adding More Icons to the Desktop

The first time you install a Notes client it populates the desktop for you with an icon for the user's mail database, Public Address Book, and Personal Address Book. If you'd like to automatically add more icons to the desktop, follow the steps listed below:

1. Perform the installation and manually add all of the icons to the desktop.

2. Copy the DESKTOP.DSK file created from this installation in the Notes data directory to a network accessible drive or floppy diskette.

   A. If you are installing Notes from a network copy, copy the DESKTOP.DSK file to that directory.

   B. If you are doing installations from floppy diskettes or a CD-ROM, then you'll have to manually copy the file to the Notes data directory after the first phase of the installation and then start the Notes setup program as described above.

Further customization of the Notes client installation is possible. However, doing so requires the use of third party applications such as WinInstall.

Quick Installation Tips

Notes client installation usually works. However, if it doesn't work, it is usually because of simple human error. Below is a quick list of things to check when you encounter client installation problems:

- Make sure you spelled every name correctly, including capitalization.
- Make sure the name you are typing in is presented as it appears in the Public Address Book.
- Include a user's and server's fully distinguished name if you're using hierarchical naming conventions.
- If the client can't find the server, make sure the client is connected to the LAN and can see and attach to other network-based servers to verify basic connectivity.
- If you're connecting using TCP/IP, open a command prompt window and type **ping name**, where "name" is the name of the Notes server you are trying to reach. If the server doesn't respond (the error would be "request timeout"), try using the ping command with the server's complete IP number instead. If the server responds, you need to either add the server name to your local DNS or create a local HOSTS file that resolves the name to an IP number.

- If you're connecting via SPX, go to the NetWare file server system console and type **Display Servers**, or go to the workstation and type **SLIST.** The Notes server you are trying to connect to should appear in the list of servers. If the server doesn't appear, it probably doesn't have the SAP agent or the service loaded.
- If you are connecting to a server via Banyan Vines, make sure that the server is listed as a PC-based service in the StreetTalk Directory.

Other User Management Tasks

As a Notes administrator you'll do a few user management tasks other than registering users and setting up the Notes client. Such tasks include:

- Renaming a user.
- Moving a user in the hierarchical naming scheme.
- Moving a user's mail database to a new server.
- Deleting a user when he or she leaves the company or no longer needs your Notes network.

Most of the tasks are made much easier in Notes Release 4.5 because of the Administration Process (described in Chapter 4). This new feature can make your administrative life a whole lot easier.

Renaming a User

At some time or another one of your users is going to need his or her name changed. Unfortunately, changing a name isn't just a matter of selecting the name from the Public Address Book and typing a new one. Because users are registered with a certification ID, renaming a user requires that you certify them again a valid certification ID. The following steps describe the renaming process:

1. Open the Public Address Book and switch to the People view to display all the registered people (see Figure 5.17).
2. Select the user you want to rename. In this example, I am renaming John K. Doe.

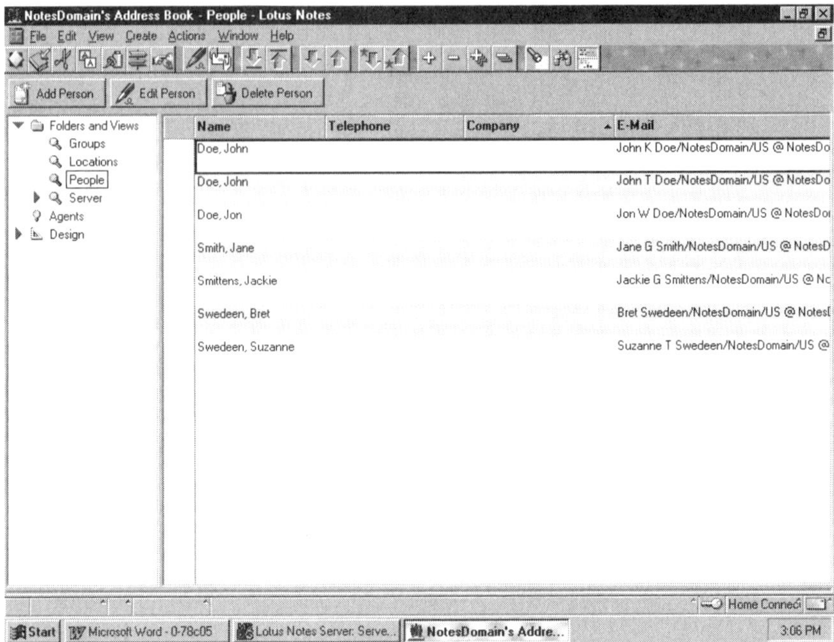

FIGURE 5.17

The People view displays all of the people you've registered.

3. From the menu bar, select Actions ➢ Rename Person and the Certify Selected Entries dialog box appears.

4. The Certify Selected Entries dialog box provides three actions you can execute on the selected Person document. For this example, click the Change Common Name button.

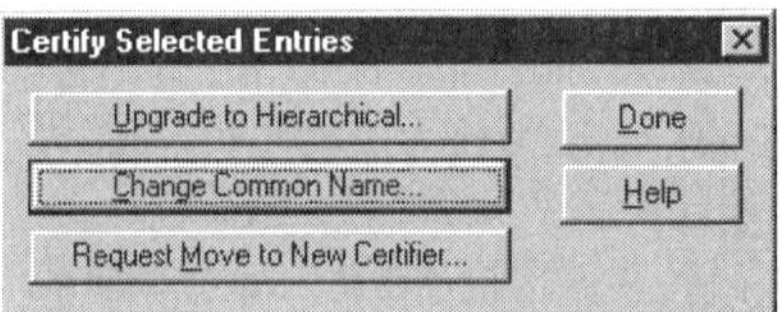

5. Choose the certification ID from the Choose Certifier ID dialog box and click OK.

6. A password dialog box appears and prompts you for a password. Enter the password for the selected certifier and click OK.

7. In the Rename Selected User dialog box either enter the certification expiration date or accept the default, which is two years from the date of renaming. Enter the new first name, new middle initial, and new last name. Then, in the New Qualifying Org. Unit (If Any) box enter the qualifying organizational unit, if any. (This field helps avoid naming conflicts.)

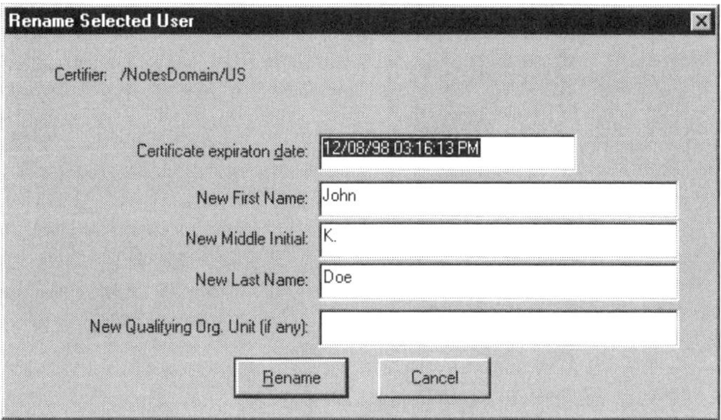

8. Click Rename.

When Notes completes the renaming process it reports its success, or failure, in a Lotus Notes dialog box and refers you to the Certifier Log for details.

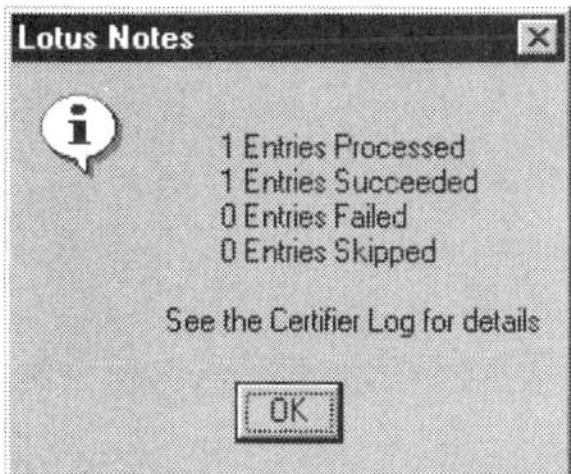

To rename a user using the previously described steps, a Certification Log must exist. This log is a database that you must create based on the supplied Certification Log database template.

At this point, the Administration Process takes over and changes the user's common name. When the process is complete, the new name is visible in the People view of the Public Address Book (see Figure 5.18).

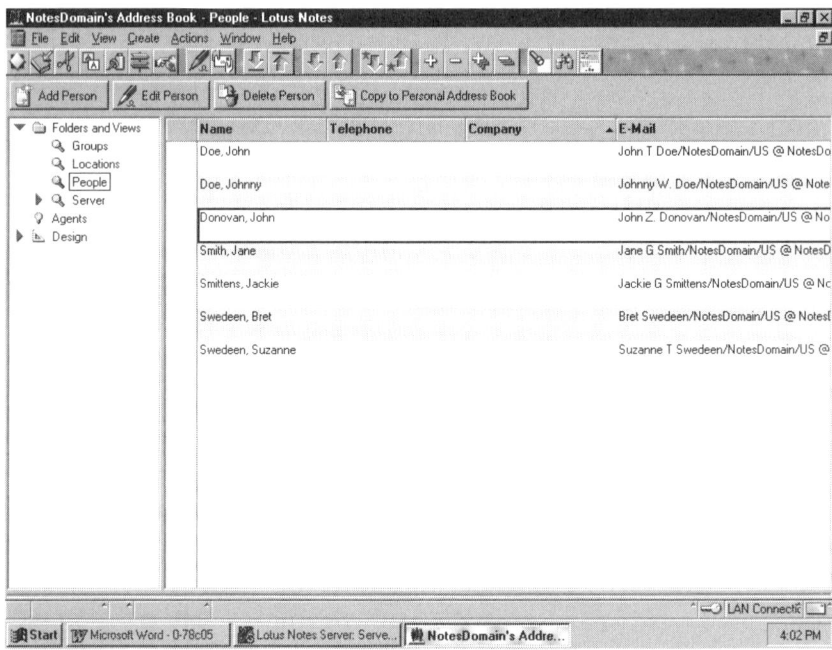

FIGURE 5.18
The People view shows John K. Doe renamed to John Z. Donovan.

John Z. Donovan's old name is still listed in his Person document (see Figure 5.19), which helps you keep track of who used to be who in your Notes network.

Moving a User in the Hierarchical Naming Scheme

Aside from renaming a user, you might also have to move them in your organizational hierarchy. For example, if a user is certified with the organizational unit certifier for the Sales organizational unit but has now taken position in the Service organizational unit, you should move that user to that part of the organization. The following steps describe the process for moving a user, Jane Bradybrook in this instance, from the hierarchical name Sales/NotesDomain/US to Service/NotesDomain/US.

1. Open the Public Address Book and switch to the People view.
2. Select Jane Bradybrook.
3. From the menu bar, select Actions ➢ Rename Person.

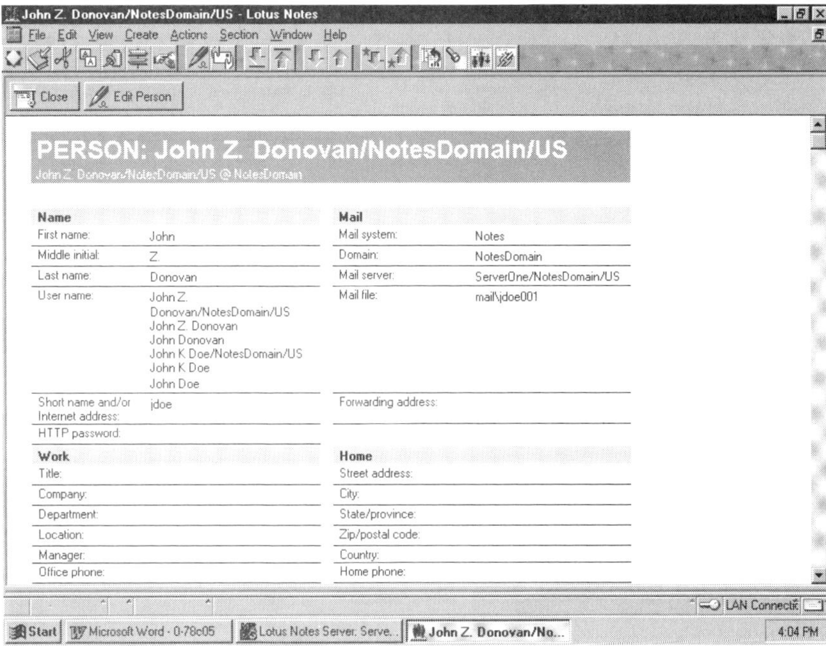

FIGURE 5.19

The Person document still has a record of John Z. Donovan's old name.

4. In the Certify Selected Entries dialog box appears, click the Request Move to New Certifier button.

5. Select the certifier previously used to register the user. In this example, select the Sales certifier.

6. Enter the password for this certifier, if prompted.

7. Enter the name of the certifier used for the organizational unit that you want to move the user to in the New Certifier box in the Request Move For Selected Entries dialog box. In this example, enter **/Service/Notes-Domain/US**.

8. Click the Submit Request button.

9. Notes reports whether the submitted request was a success or a failure.

10. Open the Administration Process database, choose View ➢ Name Move Requests, and select the name of the user that was just submitted to be moved. In this example, I have selected Jane Bradybrook (see Figure 5.20).

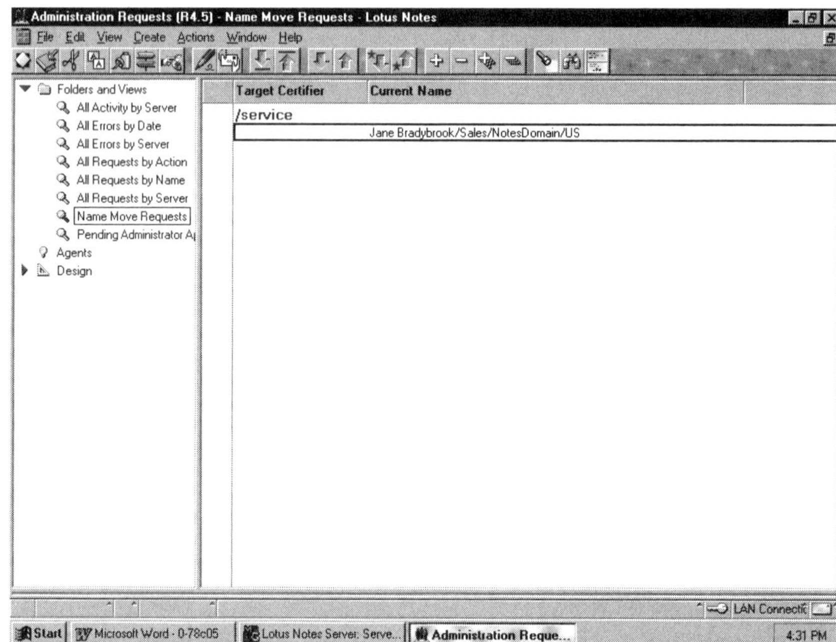

FIGURE 5.20

Jane Bradybrook is selected in the Name Move Request view in the Administration Process database.

11. From the menu bar, select Actions ➢ Complete Move for Selected Entries.
12. From the Choose Certifier ID dialog box, choose the certifier to which you want to move the user. In this example, I have selected the Service certifier (SERVICE.ID).
13. Enter the password, if prompted.
14. In the Complete Move for Selected Entries dialog box, enter a new certification expiration data, if desired. Also, add a new qualifying organizational unit to help avoid duplicate names.
15. Click the Certify button.
16. When the process is complete, Notes reports, once again, on its success or failure.
17. Check the Administration Process database to view the report in the Name Move Requests view (see Figure 5.21).

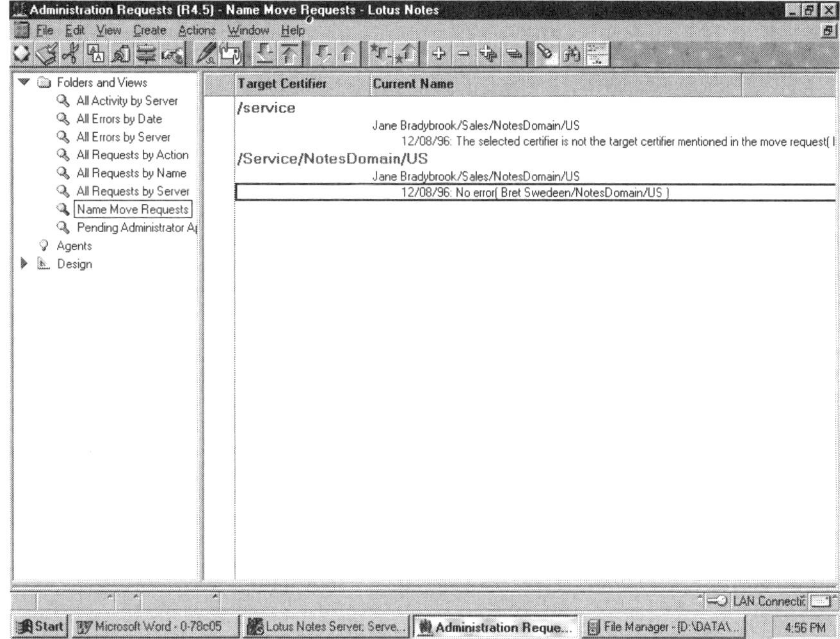

FIGURE 5.21 The Name Move Requests reports appear below the original request in the Name Move Requests view of the Administration Process database.

18. Double-click the report and you should see something similar to Figure 5.22.
19. Check the Public Address Book and view the user's Person document, which should reflect the change made.

Moving a User's Mail Database to a New Server

Because of a location change or because you need to reduce work load on a particular server, you may have to move a user's mail database from one server to another. The actual process is similar to copying a file from one location to another but requires one additional step to make the process complete. The following steps describe what you have to do to move a mail database from one server to another.

1. From the destination server choose File ➢ Database ➢ Open.

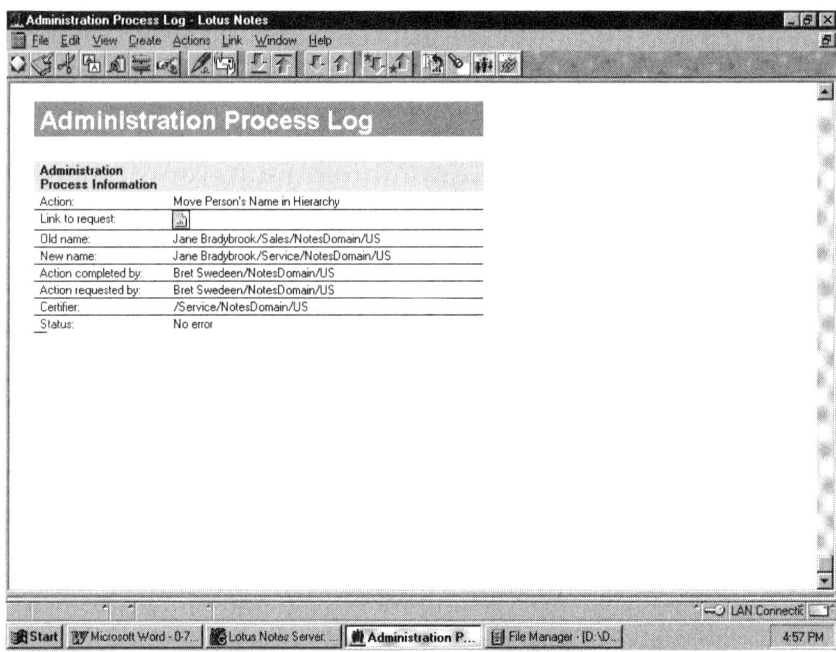

FIGURE 5.22
The Name Move Request Change report

2. From the Open Database dialog box (see Figure 5.23) select the server that currently contains the mail database and then open the mail directory.

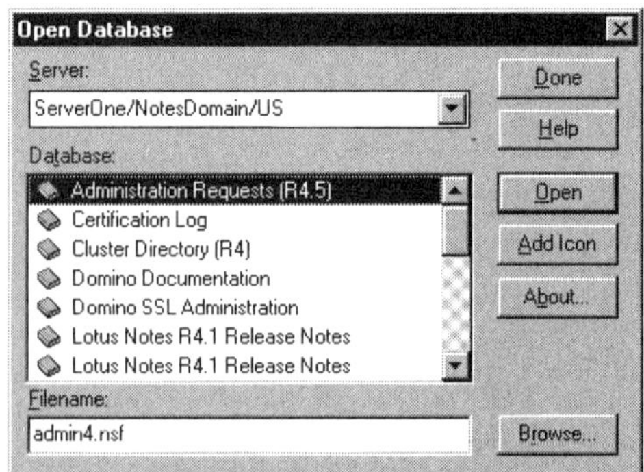

FIGURE 5.23
Select the appropriate server and then locate the mail database to be moved from the Open Database dialog box.

3. Locate the desired mail database and click the Add Icon button.
4. Once the database is added to your workspace, select it and then choose File ➢ Database ➢ New Copy.
5. In the Copy Database dialog box select the destination server, directory location, and mail filename.
6. Make sure that the Database Design and Documents option in the Copy section is checked, along with the Access Control List option. Once those settings are correct, click OK.
7. Once the database is copied, open the Public Address Book and switch to the People view.

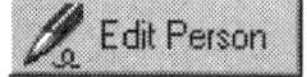

8. Select the Person document that corresponds to the mail database you just copied and click the Edit Person button on the Action bar.
9. With the Person document in edit mode, change the name of the server in the Mail server field of the Mail section to the name of the server that you moved the mail database to. Then save and close the document.

I recommend that you remove the old mail file from the original server and then force a Public Address Book replication throughout your domain at this point. Otherwise, this user could experience some mail delivery problems if the old mail database still exists and the Public Address Books are out of sync.

Deleting a User from Your Notes Network

When users leave the company or no longer need your Notes network, you'll need to delete them from your system. Follow the steps listed below to delete a user with the assistance of the Administration Process:

1. If the user's mail file is linked to a shared mail database, unlink it. Refer to the *Shared Mail Maintenance* section in Chapter 9 for detailed instructions on how to unlink a mail database.
2. Open the Public Address Book and choose the People view.

3. Select the user you want to delete and click the Delete Person button on the Action bar. Notes will reconfirm your request.

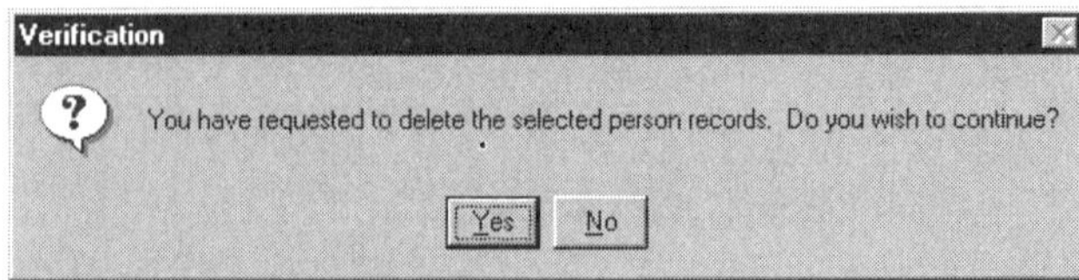

4. Click Yes in the Verification dialog box and you are presented with a few other user deletion options.

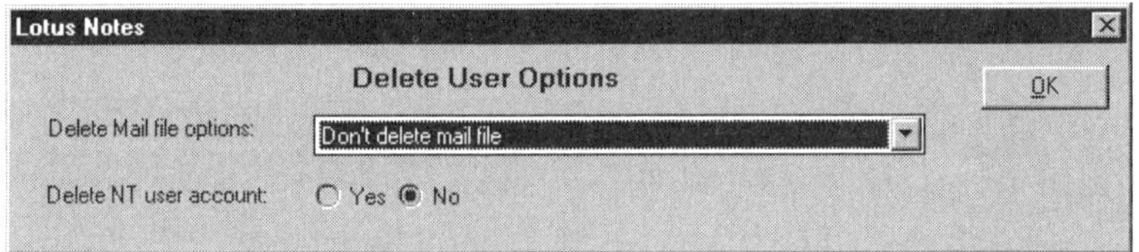

5. The Delete Mail File Options allows you to either not delete the mail database, delete the mail database specified in the Person document, or delete the mail database and all replica copies. Select the Delete Just the Mail File Specified in the Person Document option and click OK. (If you are running Notes server on Windows NT, you also have the option to delete the user's NT account as well. This option assumes the person actually has an NT account.)

6. Next, the Immediate or Via Administration Process? dialog box appears to verify whether it should execute your request immediately or let the Administration Process take care of it when it kicks off next time. Click Yes to immediately delete all references to the person in this replica of the Public Address Book and post a Delete in Access Control List request. If you select No, Notes will post a Delete in Address Book request to Administration Requests to have the Administration Process later delete the references of the person in the Public Name and Address book and in all ACLs.

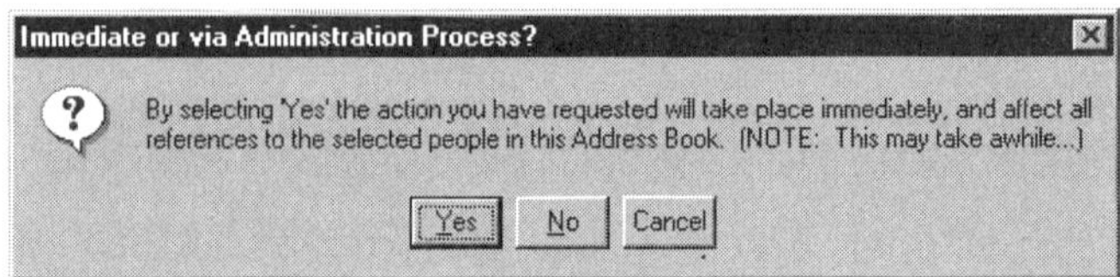

7. When the process is complete, Notes lets you know that it was successful.

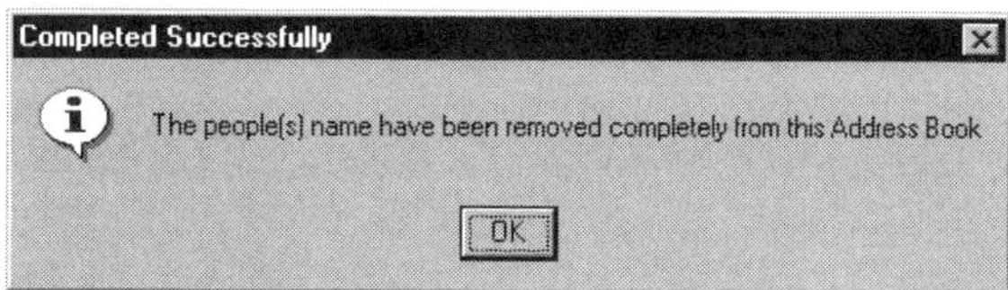

Completed Successfully
The people(s) name have been removed completely from this Address Book
OK

8. Complete the process by denying the deleted user access to all servers, which is usually done by adding them to your deny access group.

The user's mail database and all references to the user are now completely removed from the server.

To ensure that the person is completely incapable of accessing any servers in your Notes network, I recommend that you immediately force replication of the Public Address Book across all of your servers.

Summary

Basic user management in your Notes environment involves a couple of simple tasks:

- Registering users
- Installing the Notes client
- Renaming users
- Moving users in your organizational hierarchy
- Moving mail databases
- Deleting users

Some of these tasks, such as renaming and moving users in the organizational hierarchy, are made much easier with the Administration, while other tasks, such as installing the Notes client, still require a fair amount of human intervention. Regardless of what the task is, it is your job as the Notes administrator to make sure it gets done because if it weren't for the user community, there would be no Notes network to administer.

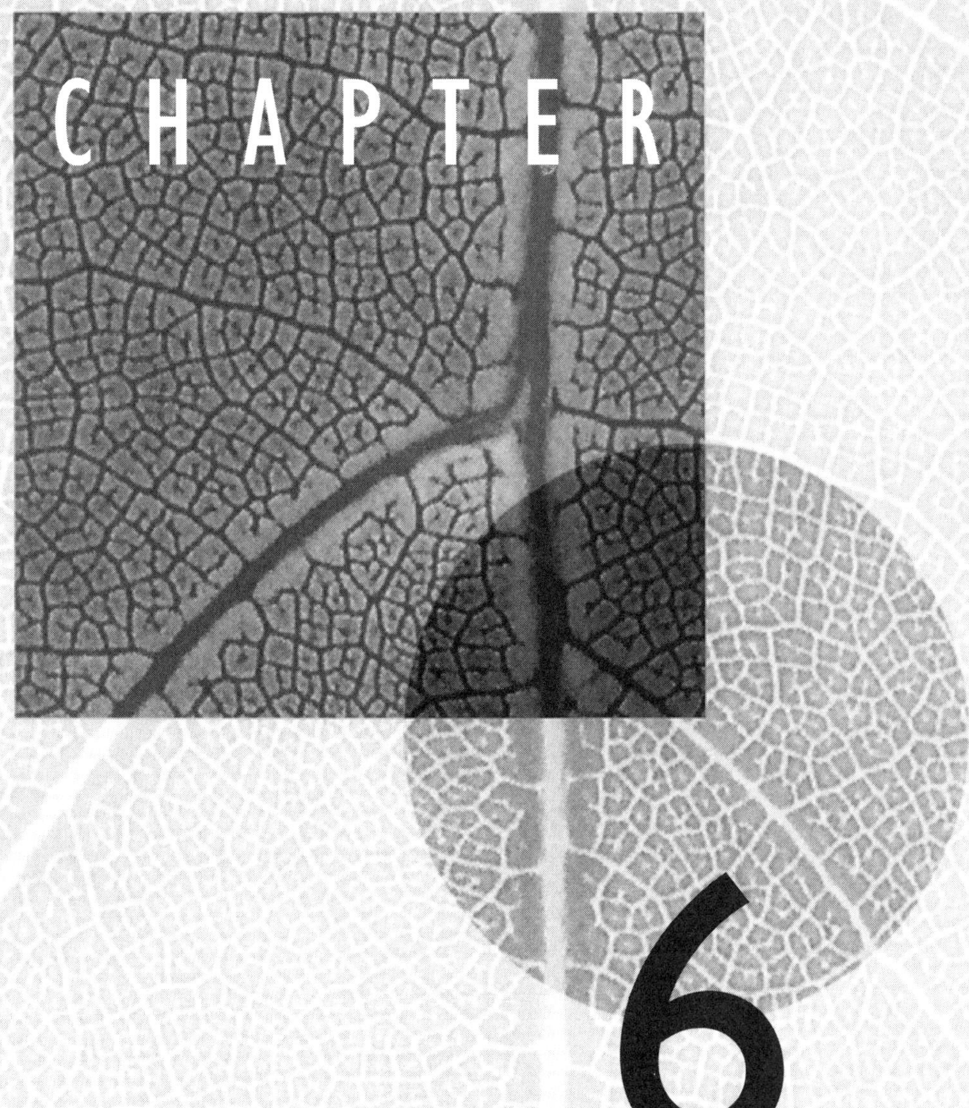

CHAPTER 6

Database Management

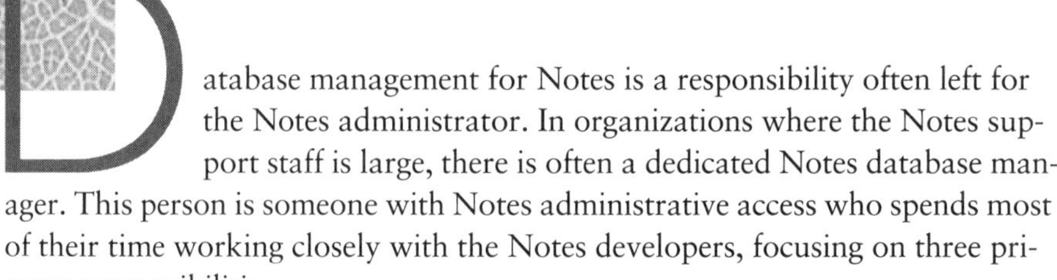

Database management for Notes is a responsibility often left for the Notes administrator. In organizations where the Notes support staff is large, there is often a dedicated Notes database manager. This person is someone with Notes administrative access who spends most of their time working closely with the Notes developers, focusing on three primary responsibilities:

- Rolling out new databases
- Maintaining the databases once they are rolled out
- Removing old obsolete databases

Rolling Out a New Database

From a Notes administrator's perspective, rolling out a new Notes database is a simple series of steps:

1. Copy the new database to a Notes server.
2. Set the maximum database size limit.
3. Set the ACL (Access Control List) to the developer's specifications.
4. Replicate the database to all servers specified by the developer.
5. Replicate the design template to all servers specified by the developer, if needed.
6. Distribute encryption keys, if any.
7. Create a Mail-In Database document, if needed.

8. Include a database in the Database Catalog (CATALOG.NSF) database, if needed.

9. Help notify users that there is a new database to use.

While these steps may seem trivial to a Notes administrator, the steps are a crucial part of a successful Notes database roll-out. If the Notes administrator doesn't thoughtfully execute each step, a number of simple but frustrating problems might occur. For instance:

- If the ACL is incorrectly set, users might not be able to gain access.
- If the database is replicated to the servers specified by the developer, then some users won't be able to access the database simply because it is not where they can get to it.
- If the database is a Mail-In database, and the administrator doesn't create a Mail-In Database document, then there is no way for the database to receive documents mailed to it.

These problems are easy to correct for a Notes administrator, but from the users' perspective these problems are very frustrating and may discourage them from using the database. Furthermore, a lack of database usage due to frustration is aggravating to the developers because they may feel that their new database failed due to reasons outside of their control.

Frustrated users and aggravated developers are easy to avoid if you don't trivialize your involvement when rolling out a new Notes database. Thoughtfully execute each step of a new database roll-out. Make sure you have a clear understanding of what the developers expect from you during the roll-out. And make sure the developers understand what you need from them to make the new database roll-out a success.

Copying the New Database to a Notes Server

More than likely, the new database ready for production will be located on a Notes server specifically used for Notes development. This server may be part of the production Notes domain or in a domain all by itself used specifically for development. If the server is part of your current Notes domain, you can replicate the new database to its final server destination by following these steps:

1. Select the database icon from the Notes workspace and then from the menu bar, select File Replication ➢ New Replica.

2. In the New Replica dialog box, specify the destination server and filename for the new database.

3. If you anticipate that this database will grow beyond the 1 GB default size limitation, click the Size Limit button and set a larger size limit.

4. After you've completed all of the appropriate fields, click the OK button (see Figure 6.1)

Details on how to set a database's maximum size limitation are in the following section, *Setting the Maximum Database Size Limit.*

FIGURE 6.1

The New Replica dialog box allows you to specify the destination server and filename for the new replica.

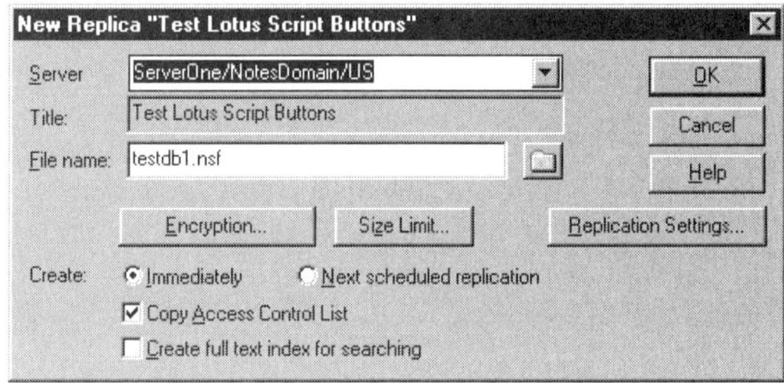

After replication is complete, a replica copy of the new database is available on the server you specified.

Other replication settings available in the New Replica dialog box are explained in Chapter 8.

Another option for moving the new database to its production location is to copy the database from one server to another. The advantage of copying the database as opposed to replicating it is that you can easily leave behind any data that the developers may have created for testing the new database.

1. From the menu bar, select File ➢ Database ➢ Open.

2. Select the server and database from the Open Database dialog box and click Add Icon.

3. Once the database icon is added to your desktop, click it once to select it.

4. From the menu bar, select File ➢ Database ➢ New Copy to display the Copy Database dialog box (see Figure 6.2).

5. Specify the destination server, database title, filename, and file directory for the new copy.

6. In the Copy area of the Copy Database dialog box, make sure that Database Design Only is selected.

7. If the developers already set up security for this database, make sure there is a check mark next to the Access Control List option.

8. If you anticipate that this database will grow beyond the 1 GB default size limitation, click the Size Limit button and set a larger size limit.

9. Click OK when you're ready to begin copying.

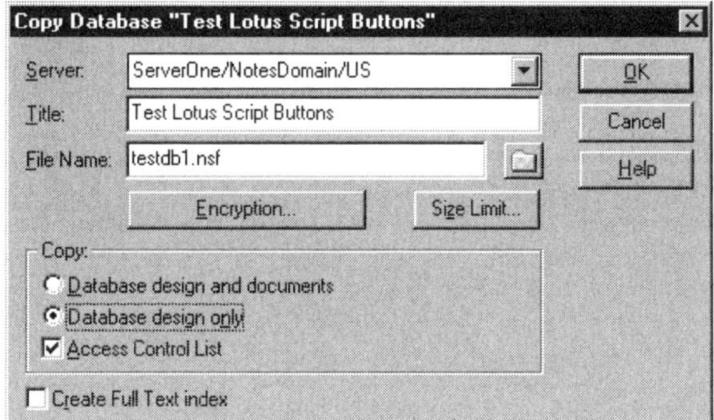

FIGURE 6.2

The Copy Database dialog box allows you to specify the destination server for the database copy.

After all of the appropriate fields are filled out and you've clicked the OK button, the database will get copied to the destination server you specified. When the copy process is complete, the database is ready for use, provided the ACL is set up to allow basic database usage.

Once you move a new database into production the database is ready to use. However, there are still a few more settings you should set before considering the database completely ready to use.

Setting the Maximum Database Size Limit

One of the first settings you and the developer need to consider with a new database is a setting for the maximum size limit for databases. Setting a maximum size limit allows you to control the growth of the database in a way that should keep it from taking over your server's entire hard drive.

Limiting a database's maximum size is done in 1 gigabyte increments and ends with a maximum limitation of 4 gigabytes. The size limitation is set when the database is created for the first time, or in this case, when a new copy or a new replica is created. Setting the database maximum size limit the first time you copy or replicate the database is done via the Size Limit button on the Copy Database or New Replica dialog box (see Figure 6.3). Select this button and then select the desired gigabyte limit from the Size Limit drop-down list.

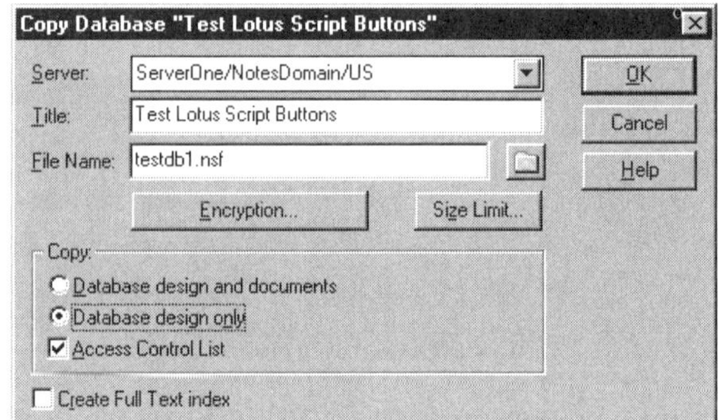

FIGURE 6.3
The Size Limit button is labeled and located in the same place on the New Replica dialog box as it is on the Copy Database dialog box shown here.

If an attempt is made to exceed a database's maximum size, Notes will prevent the attempt. An error message will be recorded in the Notes Log (LOG.NSF), and if the error occurred because of user interaction, such as a user creating a new document, a message will inform the user that an error has occurred.

A database maximum size can later be fine tuned using the Database Quota Tool found on the Server Administration screen, which is accessible by selecting File ➢ Tools ➢ Server Administration from the menu bar. With this tool, an administrator can adjust the total amount of disk space a selected database can consume and set a warning threshold which will record a message in the Notes Log when a specified size threshold has been crossed. The following steps outline how to access and use the Database Quota Tool:

1. From the menu bar, select File ➢ Tools ➢ Server Administration. The Server Administration screen appears.
2. Select the Database Tools icon on the right side of the screen. The Tools to Manage Notes Databases dialog box appears as shown in Figure 6.4).
3. Select the server on which the database you want to manage is located from the Server drop-down list.
4. In the Databases window below the Server drop-down list, select the database you want to manage.
5. From the Tool drop-down list, select the database tool you want to use. In this case we want to use the Quotas tool (see Figure 6.5).
6. The first option, Database Quota, is where you specify or adjust the maximum database size limit, or select the No Quota option if you don't want to set a quota. Keep in mind that you cannot increase a database size beyond what the original maximum size was first set to.
7. The Warning Threshold is where you specify a size that, once crossed, will record a warning message in the Notes Log. You can also select the No Warning option if you do not want threshold warnings recorded in the Notes Log.
8. If you have changed either of the quota settings, press the Update button to apply your changes.

If you just want to view the current quota settings for a selected database, follow steps 1 through 5 and then press the More Info button on the right side of the Tools to Manage Notes Domain dialog box. A screen with information similar to that shown in Figure 6.6 will appear.

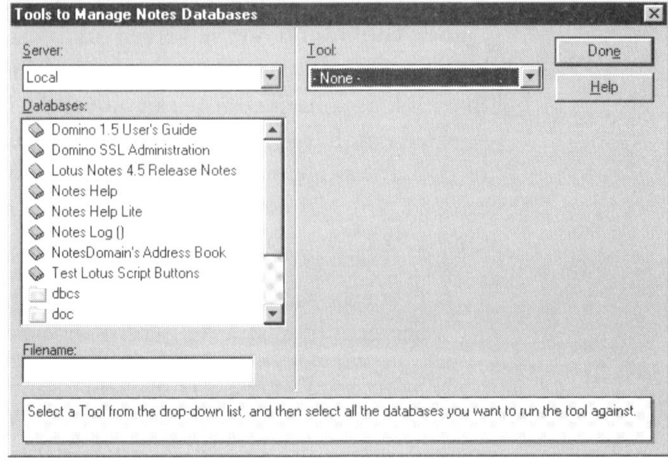

FIGURE 6.4

The Tools to Manage Notes Databases dialog box offers a convenient way to manage several databases from a single location.

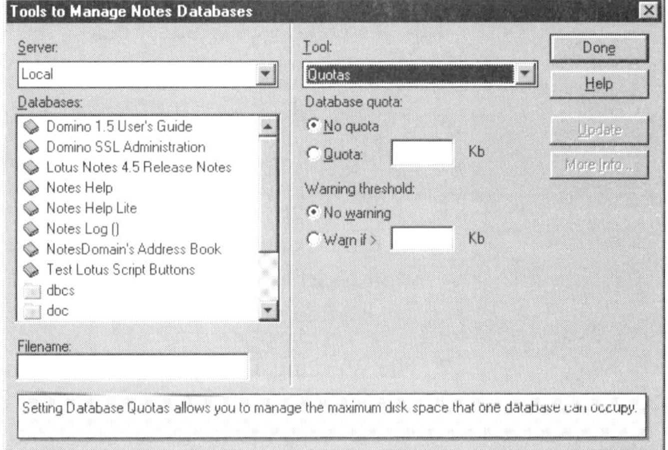

FIGURE 6.5

Once the Quotas tool is selected from the Tool drop-down list, the tool's options and settings are shown.

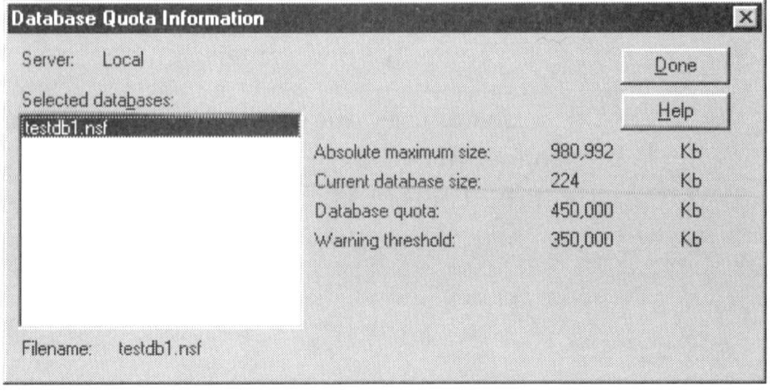

FIGURE 6.6

The More Info button opens the Database Quota Information dialog box, which displays quota details for the selected database.

Now that the new database is copied or replicated to its destination server and the maximum size limit has been set, you need to set, or just double-check, the database's ACL settings to make sure those users who should have access to this database do and those who shouldn't have access don't.

Setting the Access Control List

More than likely, the Notes developer has already set the ACL for the new database. If the developer hasn't set the ACL, chances are they have some type of document that outlines the ACL requirements for this database. The Notes administrator is expected to use this ACL requirements document and apply the settings accordingly.

Details about the access levels are covered in Chapter 7, *Notes Security*. For easy reference, however, here is a quick description of each access level:

- **No Access:** This is the lowest level of access because it doesn't allow any access. In security-conscience Notes environments, set the database access level of all databases to No Access. This way the risk of accidentally granting access is significantly reduced.
- **Depositor:** Users assigned Depositor access can actually create documents but have no means of seeing the documents they create (or any other documents, for that matter) in the database views. Why would anyone use this access level? This type of access is specifically for Notes applications that allow people to submit a document but not access it after submission. Such is the case for Notes databases that are designed to collect surveys, customer satisfaction reports, or training evaluations.
- **Reader:** Users assigned Reader access can read documents in the database but cannot create or edit documents. For example, a human resource policy manual would assign Reader access to all users in the organization so they could read the policies in the manual, but not edit or add to the manual.
- **Author:** Administrators and users assigned Author access can create documents and edit only the documents they create. Assign Author access to users that need the ability to create and edit their own documents, but not the documents of others.
- **Editor:** Administrators and users assigned Editor access can create documents and edit all documents in the database, including those created by others. Grant Editor access to anyone or any group that needs the ability to edit all documents in a particular database.

- **Designer:** Designer access can modify all database design elements—fields, forms, views, public agents, the database icon, and the Using This Database and About This Database documents. Designer access also grants the ability to modify replication formulas and create a full-text index. Designers can also perform all tasks allowed by lower access levels.

- **Manager:** This is the highest level of access. Manager access can modify ACL settings, encrypt the database, modify replication settings, and delete the database. Managers can also perform all tasks allowed by other access levels. Notes requires that each database have at least one person with Manager access.

To set a server, group, or user to any of the previously mentioned access levels follow the steps outlined below:

1. If the database is not added to your workspace, add an icon by selecting File ➢ Database ➢ Open from the menu bar.

2. In the Open Database dialog box, select the server where the database is located and then the database itself, and click the Add Icon button.

3. Once the database is on your workspace, click it once to select it.

4. From the menu bar, select File ➢ Database ➢ Access Control. The Access Control List dialog box appears as shown in Figure 6.7. (Another quick way to open the Access Control List dialog box for a database is to click the database once with your right mouse button. A short drop-down menu appears from which you can select Access Control to quickly open the Access Control List.)

5. Click the Add button to display the Add User dialog box. In this dialog box, you can manually type in the name of a server, group, or user that you want to add to the ACL.

6. If you don't want to manually enter the name of a server, group, or user, click the Person button to open the Names dialog box where you can browse the names or servers, groups, and users listed in the Public Address Book.

7. In the Names dialog box (see Figure 6.8), select servers, groups, or users and click the Add button to add them to the Added window. Once you have added everyone you want to add, click OK.

8. Individually select each new entry in the Access Control List dialog box and select the desired access level from the Access drop-down list.

9. Repeat step 8 for each new entry in the Access Control List dialog box. Once the appropriate access level is set for each new entry, click OK.

Further details about additional security settings beyond the access level can be found in Chapter 7, *Notes Security*.

FIGURE 6.7

The Access Control List is where you specify the level of access for servers, groups, and users.

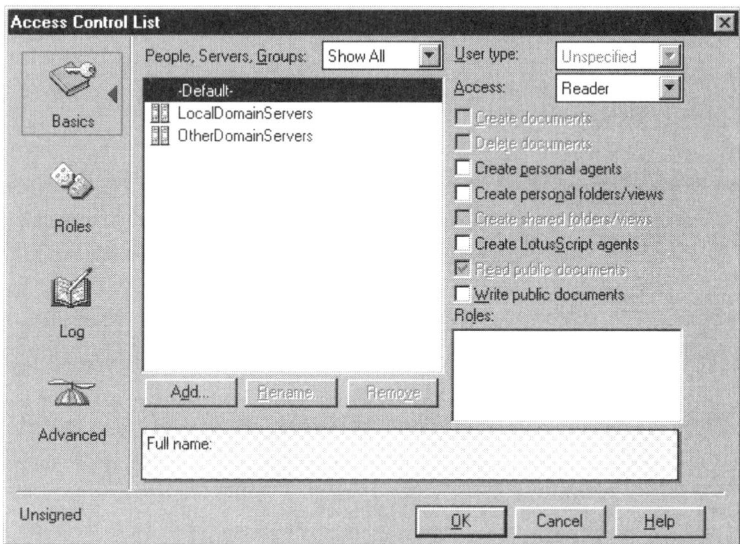

Whether the ACL has already been set or you have to apply the ACL settings according to the developer's specifications, you should still get together with the developer and double check the ACL settings before officially making the new database available to the users. Reviewing the ACL settings with the developer before the official roll-out should reduce the risk of excessive access caused by a misunderstanding about what the developer intended or what a particular access level allows.

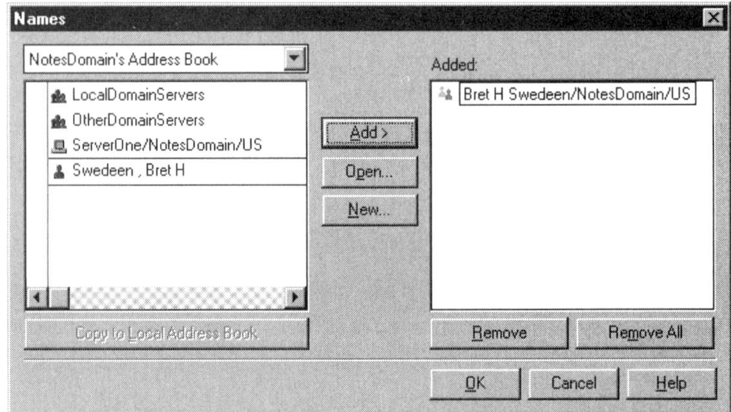

FIGURE 6.8

Using the Names dialog box to add servers, groups, and users is much faster than manually typing each entry in the Add User dialog box.

Once the database is located on its destination server, the database's maximum size limit is set, and the ACL is correctly set up you can start to replicate the database to all of the appropriate servers within your Notes network.

Replicating a Database to All Servers

If you have several Notes servers in your network, you may need to replicate a copy of this new database to each server. This decision depends on the overall purpose of each of these servers in your Notes network. For example, if these additional servers are dedicated to functions such as the various Message Transfer Agents (MTAs) or pager gateway (a Notes add-on product that allows you to send mail messages from Notes directly to an alphanumeric pager), then replicating a copy of this new database to these servers isn't necessary. If, however, these servers support users in a particular department or remote office location, then replicating a copy of this new database to these servers makes perfect sense.

Details on how to replicate are explained in Chapter 8, *Replication*.

Knowing how to replicate, initialize replication, and maintain the replication schedule is the responsibility of the Notes administrator. Even though the developer may have outlined some guidelines for replication in a database design document, don't expect the developer to take responsibility for setting up and monitoring replication for his or her database. As the Notes administrator you can work with the developer to implement replication according to the requirements of the database. Keep in mind, however, that ultimately the responsibility of replication rests on your shoulders.

Replicating the Design Template to All Servers

The Notes developer may have created this new database based on a previously created design template. A design template is a complete database minus the data. Using a template is a quick way to create a new database with minimal developmental effort.

If your developers used a template to create their new database and plan to use the template as a way to easily update the design of the database itself, then you'll need to make sure you copy the design template to the destination server the same way you did for the new database itself. You'll also have to make sure that you replicate the design template to all of the servers that the database is being replicated to.

You replicate a design template the same way you replicate any other database in your Notes network.

Distributing Encryption Keys

Any new database that you roll out may or may not use encryption as part of its design. Using encryption in a database allows developers to selectively grant access to certain fields within a form. A field can be encrypted using an encryption key, which makes the field accessible to only those who have received a copy of the encryption key. This security feature is very useful for fields that contain information such as someone's salary or social security number. The down side to this additional security capability is that the Notes administrator must distribute the security keys to only those users who have been identified as needing access to this secure information.

You can distribute encryption keys through Notes mail or by exporting the keys to a file and then distributing the file through any number of methods. For example, you could send the file as an attachment in any e-mail program that supports attachments. You could also distribute the file to users on a floppy disk or make the file accessible on a shared network drive.

Sending encryption keys via Notes mail is very simple and is described in the steps listed below. These steps assume you have already created an encryption key to send (see the sidebar *Creating an Encryption Key* for details):

1. Select File ➢ Tools ➢ User ID from the menu bar.
2. Select the Encryption icon shown in Figure 6.9 to display the encryption options in the User ID dialog box.

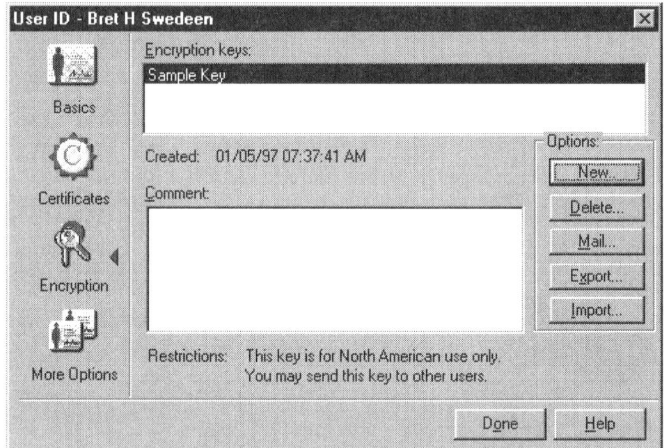

FIGURE 6.9

Available keys will be shown in the Encryption Keys window.

3. Select the encryption key you want to distribute and click the Mail button.
4. Enter the names of all recipients in the To field and then enter a subject or accept the default subject (see Figure 6.10).
5. Finally, click the Send button. You will be prompted with the message "Should recipients be allowed to send this key to other users?" You can select Yes or No. Selecting Yes allows the recipients to send this encryption key to other users, which will give those users access to the encrypted information. More than likely, you don't want users distributing encryption keys because it probably undermines the reason encryption was used in the first place.

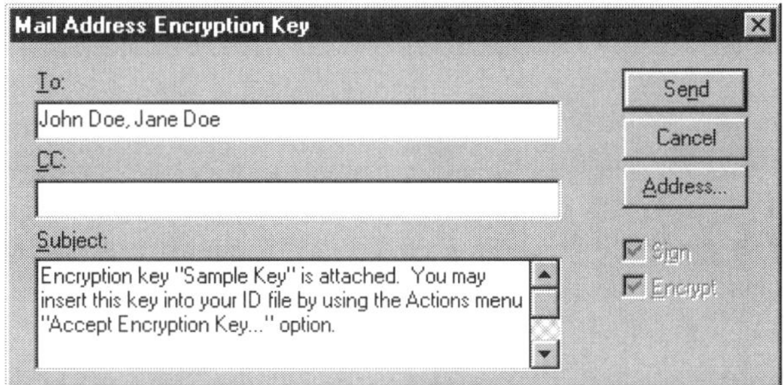

FIGURE 6.10

The Mail Address Encryption Key dialog box is where you can enter the names of all encryption key recipients.

Creating an Encryption Key

Encryption keys are easy to make and are based on the ID file you were using when you made them. The following steps detail how to make an encryption key:

1. From the menu bar, select File ➢ Tools ➢ User ID. The User ID dialog box appears.
2. From the dialog box, select the Encryption subsection.
3. Click the New button and the Add Encryption Key dialog box appears.
4. In this dialog box, enter a name for the new key and choose North American or International license type. Click OK.
5. The new encryption key is created and you are returned to the Encryption subsection of the User ID dialog box. From here you can create additional keys or click Done to close the dialog box.

The other way you can distribute encryption keys is to export them to a file. Once exported to a file you can then e-mail that file using a mail system other than Notes. You can also copy the file to a diskette and hand out the diskette to those users who need it. Or you could just place the file on a shared network drive and tell users where to get the file. Whatever way you choose to distribute the file, you still have to export the encryption key to a file first. The steps listed below describe the export process:

1. Select File ➢ Tools ➢ User ID from the menu bar.

2. Select the Encryption icon shown in Figure 6.9 to display the encryption options in the User ID dialog box.

3. Select the encryption key you want to distribute and click the Export button to display the User ID Encryption Key Export dialog box.

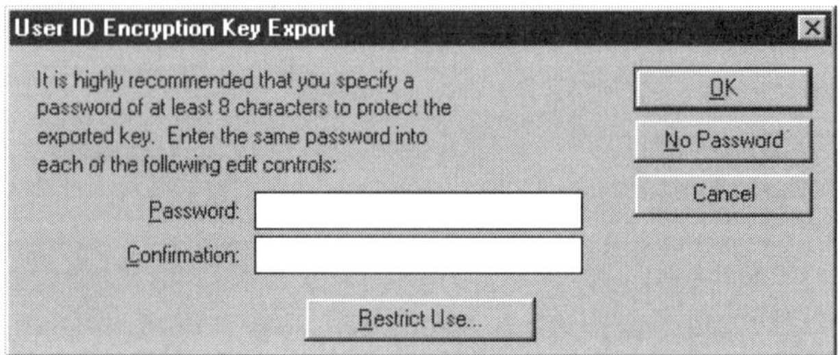

4. If you want to restrict the use of this exported key, click the Restrict Use button and enter the name of the user who should be allowed to use this exported key in the Encryption Key Restriction dialog box.

5. If you want to allow the user entered in step 4 to export or forward this key, place a check mark in the Allow That Person to Export the Key or Forward It to Others checkbox.

6. Once you are finished entering information in the Encryption Key Restrictions dialog box, click OK to return to the User ID Encryption Key Export dialog box.

7. If you want to apply a password to this exported key (I strongly recommend applying a password to keep the exported key safe from those who shouldn't have access to it), then type a password in the Password field and confirm that password in the Confirmation field by retyping it. If you don't want to apply a password to the exported key, click the No Password button.

8. Click OK and the Specify File for the Exported Key dialog box appears (see Figure 6.11), which allows you to select the directory and specify the name for the exported file.

9. Once you have selected the directory for the exported key and given it a name, click Save.

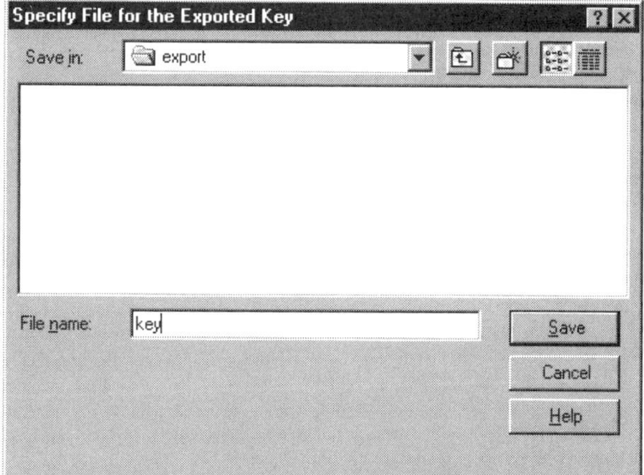

FIGURE 6.11

The Specify File for the Exported Key dialog box is similar to a standard Windows File Save dialog box where you can select a destination directory and enter a name for the file you are saving.

The exported file is saved in the specified directory with the given name and the file extension .KEY. Now you can distribute this file the same way you would distribute any other file.

Merging Encryption Keys with User IDs

Once users receive an encryption through Notes mail or through an exported file given to them on disk or sent as an e-mail attachment, they need to merge it into their user ID. The following steps explain how to merge an encryption key into a user ID:

1. If the key was sent through Notes mail, open the mail message and select Actions ➢ Accept Encryption from the menu bar.
2. Enter the user's password, if prompted.
3. Add any additional comments for the encryption key and then click Accept.
4. If the key was received in the form of an exported file, choose File ➢ Tools ➢ User ID from the menu bar.
5. Enter the user's password, if prompted.
6. Click the Encryption icon in the User ID dialog box.
7. Click the Import button to display the Specify File Containing the Key dialog box (see Figure 6.12).

8. Locate the exported key file, select it, and click the Open button. The Accept Encryption Key dialog box will appear.

9. Enter any additional comments in the Comment field of the Accept Encryption Key dialog box and click Accept.

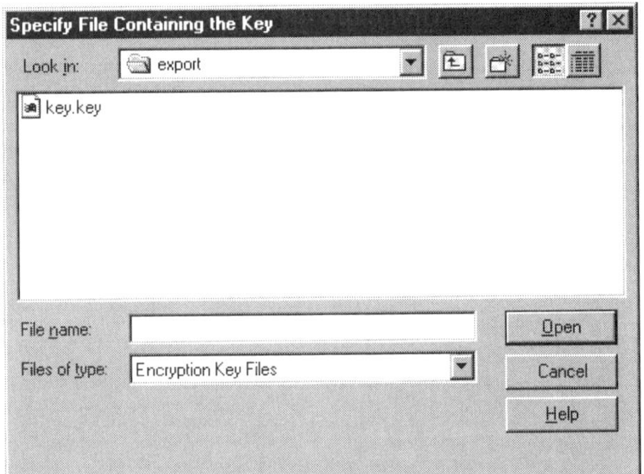

FIGURE 6.12

Traverse the directories shown in the Specify File Containing the Key dialog box and locate the exported key file to import.

If you distribute encryption keys on a regular basis, you should create your own "how-to accept encryption keys" document. Once this document is created, you can distribute it along with the encryption keys. Hopefully, users will read this document and manage the encryption key acceptance process without any further assistance.

Creating a Mail-In Database Document

Some new databases rolled out in your Notes network might be designed for mail-in use. These databases often are designed to collect surveys, instructor-led training evaluations, or electronic versions of the all-popular suggestion box. No matter what the database's design purpose is, if it is a mail-in database by design, the administrator is responsible for creating the Mail-In Database document in the Public Address Book to support the database.

To create a Mail-In Database document, start by opening the Public Address Book and selecting Create ➢ Server ➢ Mail-In Database from the menu bar. A blank Mail-In Database document appears. Fill out this document by entering the name of the database in the Mail-In Name field, the domain name for the database in the Domain field, the name of the server where the database is located in the Server field, and the actual filename of the database in the Filename field. The Description field is optional but I recommend adding something in this field so other administrators can quickly understand the purpose of this document.

When you have finished entering the required information into the various fields, click the Save button on the Action bar. The final document should appear similar to the document shown in Figure 6.13.

FIGURE 6.13

Sample Mail-In Database document

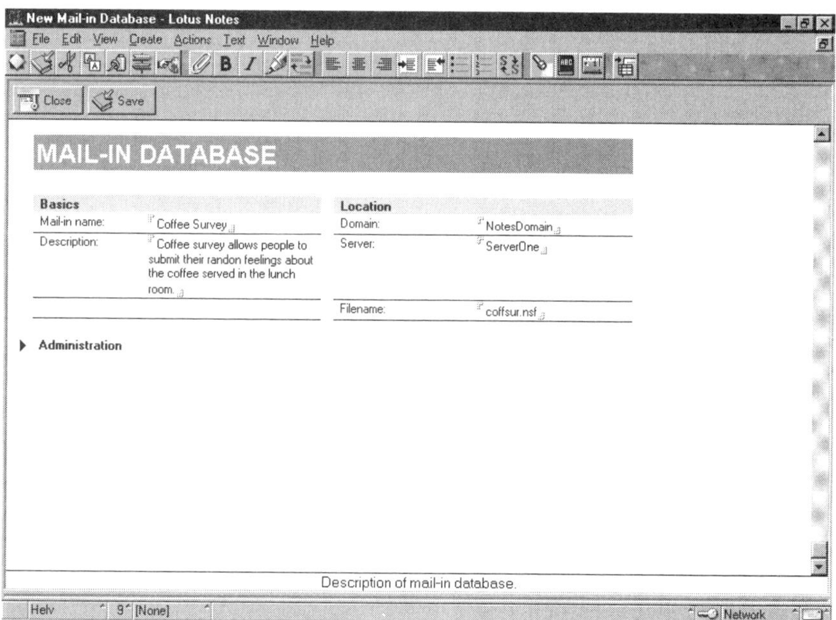

The final step is to inform everyone what the name for this mail-in database is and how to use it. Normally, using a mail-in database is just a matter of creating a new e-mail message and addressing the message to the mail-in database name the same way you would address a message to a regular user.

Including the New Database in the Database Catalog

Another important part of rolling out a new database is to include it in your domain's database catalog. If you haven't already created a Database Catalog, you should consider doing so because it is a very convenient way to list all of the databases in a Notes network from a single location. Creating a Database Catalog is described in the following steps:

1. From the menu bar, select File ➢ Database ➢ New.
2. In the New Database dialog box, shown in Figure 6.14, enter the server where you want the catalog located.
3. Give the catalog a title in the Title field.
4. Specify CATALOG.NSF as the filename in the File Name field.
5. In the template window near the bottom of the New Database dialog box, select the Database Catalog template.
6. Click OK.

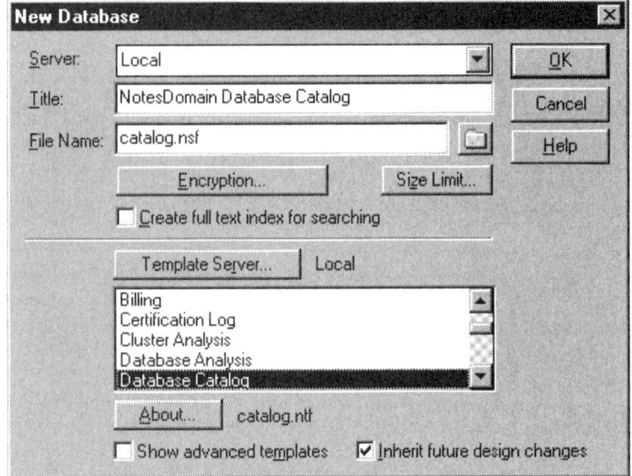

FIGURE 6.14
The New Database dialog box allows you not only to create a new database but also to indicate which server to locate it on.

After the Database Catalog is created it will open the About This Database form. There is useful information on this form which you should review to make sure you set the ACL for the Database Catalog correctly.

The next time the Catalog server task runs, it will update the Database Catalog with all of the databases that have been set for inclusion in the Database Catalog. If you want to set a current database or new database for inclusion in the Database Catalog, follow the steps listed below:

1. Select the database you want to include in the Database Catalog.

2. From the menu bar, select Edit ➢ Properties to display the Properties dialog box (see Figure 6.15).

3. Click the Design tab and place a check mark next to List in Database Catalog.

4. Enter one or more of the categories for the database and close the Properties dialog box. Entering a category determines how this database will appear in the Database Catalog.

5. At this point, you can either wait for the Catalog server task to run as scheduled or load it yourself and force the catalog update. If you want to force an update, go to the server console and type **Load catalog**. The Catalog server task will load and update the Database Catalog immediately.

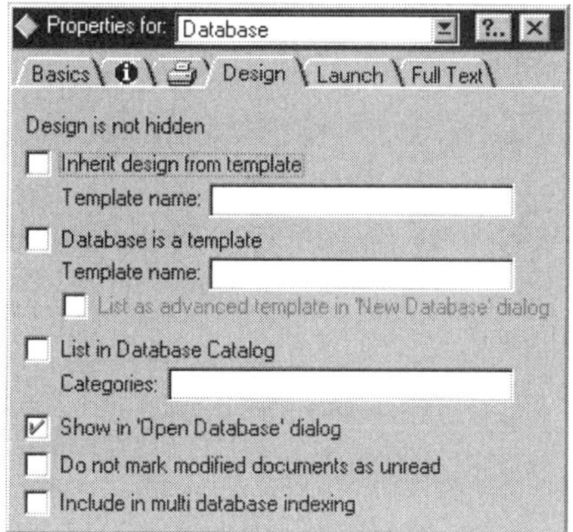

FIGURE 6.15
The Properties dialog box for a sample database

Notify Users That There Is a New Database to Use

The last, and probably most important, step in rolling out a new database is informing the users that a new database is available and letting them know how to get to it. Hopefully, most users will know how to follow the simple steps required to add a new database to their workspace. However, if you want to make things easier for your users, consider sending a Notes mail message with a button that automates the process of opening a new database. You can do this by following the steps listed below:

1. Create a new Notes mail message and address it to all of the users that should know about this new database.

2. Enter a subject that indicates what this message is about.
3. In the body portion of the message, include a brief explanation about this new database and what the button in this form will do.
4. Then, from the menu bar, select Create ➢ Hotspot ➢ Button.
5. Give the button a meaningful label, such as “Click here to open database.”
6. In the Formula box, enter any one of the following formulas:

```
@Command([FileOpenDatabase];"Server Name Here":"Database
Name Here";)
```

```
@Command([FileOpenDBRepID];"Replica ID Number Here")
```

If you’d rather just add the database to the user’s workspace and not open it, then use either of the following commands:

```
@Command([AddDatabase];"Server Name Here": "Database
Name Here")
```

```
@Command([AddDatabaseRepID];"Server Name Here"; "Replica
ID Number Here")
```

7. Close the Button Formula Edit screen. Your message should appear similar to what is shown in Figure 6.16.
8. When you are satisfied with the message, click the Send button on the Action bar.

E-mail messages are probably the quickest way to inform users that a new database is available. However, e-mail is not the only way to disseminate information. You may find it easier to send out an actual interoffice memo, post a message in a Notes discussion database, or post the news on your corporate Web site. Choose the method your users are accustom to.

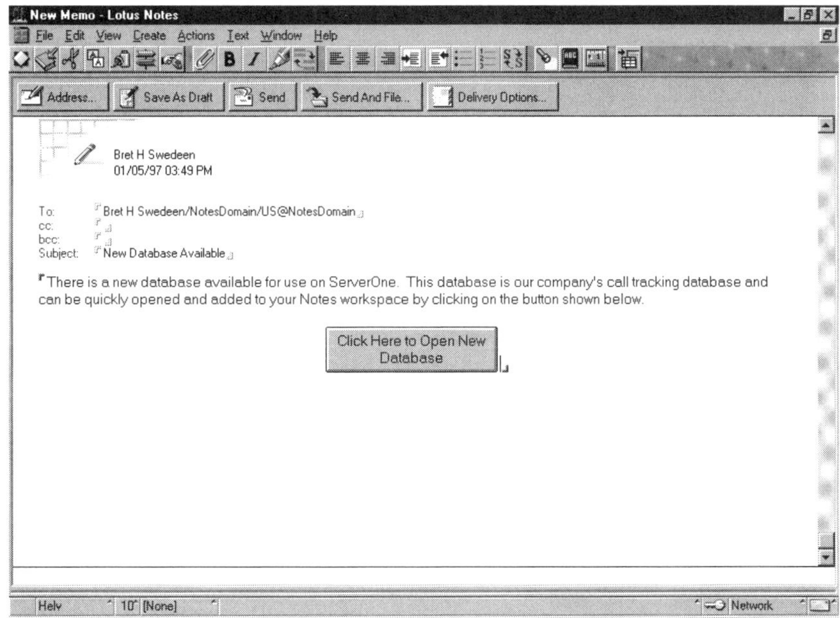

FIGURE 6.16 A sample new database notification message including a button to help users quickly open the new database

Maintaining Database Integrity

Whether a database is new or old, it must be maintained. Users don't like to use databases that frequently become corrupted, perform slowly, or contain extremely old and out of date information. For those simple reasons, Notes administrators are expected to keep a watchful eye on their network's databases and make sure they are accessible, perform well, and are populated with meaningful up to date information.

Basic database maintenance in Notes usually encompasses more than just running a couple database utilities to keep things running. Normally, any task that falls outside the scope of database development and daily usage is considered database maintenance. Such typical tasks include the following:

- Creating and maintaining full text indexes
- Updating databases after their design template has been changed

- Running database analysis to collect useful database information
- Locating missing response documents
- Monitoring database activity
- Managing database size
- Moving databases
- Repairing corrupted databases
- Troubleshooting general database performance problems

Some of these tasks are made significantly easier with the tools included in Lotus Notes. For example, analyzing a database to collect useful information is made easy with the help of the Database Analysis tool available from the Server Administration screen. In the case where no obvious tool is provided, the effort required to complete the task is insignificant. However, seeing (or reading, in this case) is believing. Therefore, the following sections address each of the previously mentioned database maintenance tasks in greater detail.

Creating and Maintaining Full Text Indexes

The ability to quickly locate information in a database is very important to most users. However, the steps involved in locating that information must also be easy. Most users don't want to enter long, complex search commands to locate their information. What they want to do is type a couple of words, press a search button, and in a few seconds see a list of matching documents.

Creating a Full Text Index

Lotus Notes makes ad hoc text searching possible by allowing you to build a full text index of the database. A full text index is a collection of files that indexes a particular database, which allows users the ability to type a few words and click a search button. The results displayed are a list of all documents that contain those words no matter which fields those words are in. To create a full text index for a database, follow the steps outlined below:

1. Select the database you want to index and select File ➢ Database ➢ Properties from the menu bar.

2. Click the Full Text tab.

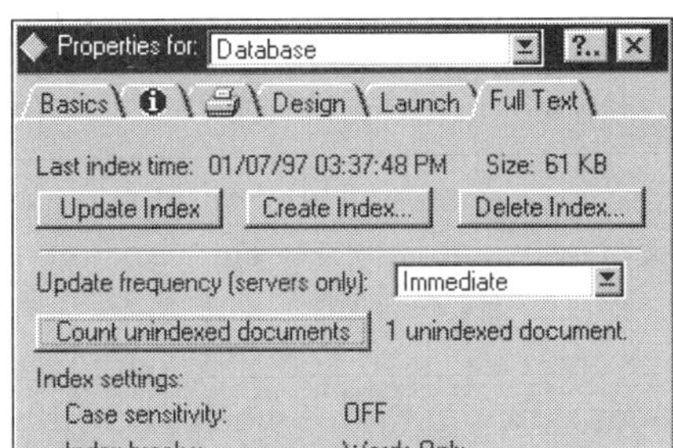

3. Click the Create Index button and the Full Text Create Index dialog box appears (see Figure 6.17).

4. There are several options to choose from on the Full Text Create Index dialog box. Each option is explained below:

   - **Case sensitive index**: This option causes Notes to index a word for each different character case occurrence of the word. For example, the word "Notes" and "notes" would both get indexed if this option is selected. This option allows users to create case-specific searches and also adds to the overall size of the index by approximately five to ten percent.

   - **Index attachments**: You can include text in attachments in your index with this option selected. In situations such as document library databases, this option is useful. Keep in mind, however, that this option also increases the size of your index by the amount of attachments in a database and the text those attachments contain.

   - **Index encrypted fields**: This option includes encrypted fields in the index. Normally encrypted fields are not indexed because doing so compromises the security of the encrypted field (see the *Indexing Encrypted Fields* sidebar for details).

   - **Exclude words in Stop Word file**: A Stop Word file is a file that contains words that you don't want included in an index. Notes provides a default Stop Word file called DEFAULT.STP which contains a set of predefined words to skip and the digits 0-9. You can add to or remove from this file using a simple text editor or you can create your own Stop Word file. Using a Stop Word file when creating an index can reduce the overall index size by fifteen to twenty percent.

- **Word breaks only**: This option allows searches to find a word regardless of where it is in a document. This option also causes the index size to be fifty percent of the space consisting of text. If, for example, your database is 10 MB and contains mostly text and few graphics, the index will be approximately 5 MB. Leave this option on for the most flexible general searching.
- **Word, sentence, and paragraph**: With this option you can create searches that use "proximity" operators. For example, you could create a search that returns all the documents that have the words "Domino" and "Intranet" in the same paragraph with the command **domino paragraph intranet**. This type of searching is a little more complex than most users need, but it does provide the ability to create very effective searches. This option also causes the index size to be seventy-five percent of the space consisting of text. Once again, if your database is 10 MB consisting mostly of text, then your index will be approximately 7.5 MB.

5. After you select the appropriate index options, click OK.

FIGURE 6.17

The Full Text Create Index dialog box provides several options for customizing an index creation.

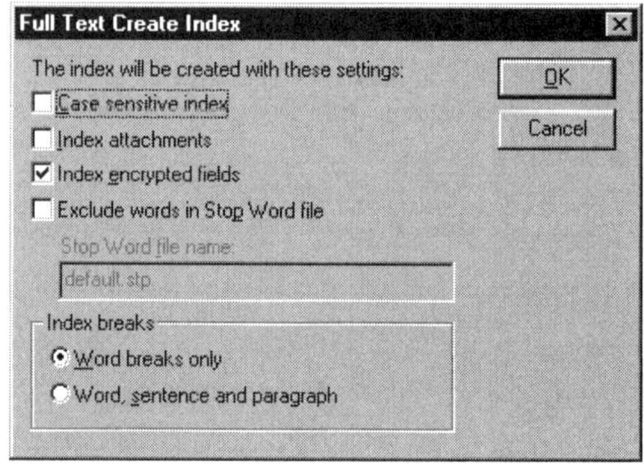

Indexing Encrypted Fields

When you create a new full text index, the Index Encrypted Fields option is selected by default. If you have encrypted fields in a database, including these fields in an index can compromise the security of the encrypted field in two simple ways.

- Any user who can access the database can also create a search based on information contained in the encrypted field even though they don't have the encryption key for that field. The encrypted information isn't viewable. However, if the search is specific enough, you won't have to see it to know what it is. For example, in a database that has an encrypted field for an employee's annual salary, you could create a search that returns all documents that have the number 50,000.
- Creating a full text index creates a plain text file that is not encrypted. If someone understands how indexes are created, then that person also knows where and how to get to the plain text index file itself and read the encrypted information.

Notes indexes the database which creates a subdirectory to store the index files. This subdirectory is located in the same directory where the database is located and has the same name as the database being indexed, except that it has an .FT extension instead of an .NSF extension.

When creating a full text index, especially on databases where the size exceeds double digit MBs, make sure you have a rough idea of how much disk space this index will consume before making it. Full text indexes can take up a significant amount of disk space, which you may not want to give away if your disk space is already limited.

How do you calculate the total size of an index? Unfortunately, you can't calculate the exact size of an index but you can do a fair estimation if you understand the two basic factors that determine the size of a full text index:

1. What percentage of the database is text? This percentage usually ranges from twenty-five to seventy-five percent.

2. Which of the previously described index options were selected?

Use these two basic factors as a foundation for a simple estimation matrix similar to the one shown in Table 6.1.

TABLE 6.1 Estimating Index Size

Database Size	Percentage Text	Index Option: Word Breaks Only	Index Option: Case Sensitive Index	Index Option: Exclude Words in Stop File
10 MB	25% = 2.5 MB	1.25 MB	2.75 MB	2 MB
10 MB	50% = 5.0 MB	2.50 MB	5.50 MB	4 MB
10 MB	75% = 7.5 MB	3.75 MB	8.25 MB	6 MB

Using a similar matrix to estimate index size, you'll have a good idea of your worst and best case scenario.

Updating a Full Text Index

After a full text index is created, you'll want to periodically update it to reflect any changes made in the source database. Indexes located on a server are updated automatically according to the frequency that you specify, which is done in the following manner:

1. Select the database on your workspace and then select File ➢ Database ➢ Properties from the menu bar.
2. Click the Full Text tab.
3. From the Update Frequency drop-down list, select one of the four available update options (Figure 6.18).
   - **Daily:** This setting updates the index every night when the server Updall runs.
   - **Scheduled:** This setting updates the index according to a schedule set in a Program document for the Updall server task. This document is located in the Pubic Address Book and if the document doesn't exist the scheduled update never happens.

- **Hourly:** This setting will update the index every hour.
- **Immediate:** This setting updates the index as soon as possible after the database is closed.

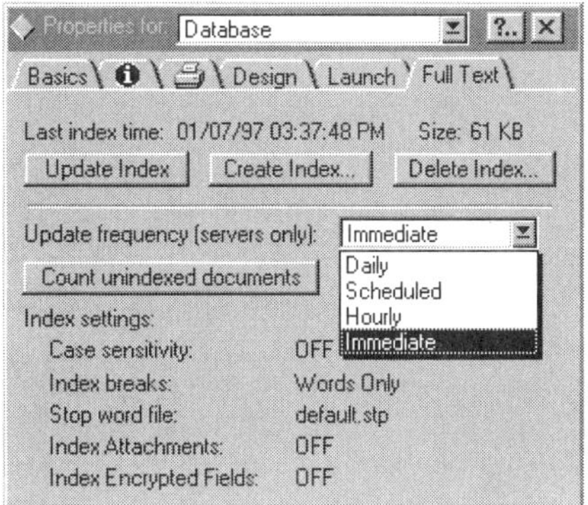

FIGURE 6.18

The Full Text tab of the Properties dialog box allows you to set the update frequency for an index. There are four update frequency settings available.

After selecting the update frequency, close the Properties dialog box. The updates will occur according to the new setting. If, however, you set the frequency to Scheduled, follow the steps listed below to create a Program document to support the schedule:

1. Select or open the Public Address Book and select Create ➢ Server ➢ Program from the menu bar.
2. In the Program Name field, give this document a name.
3. In the Command Line field, enter the command or program that you want to execute.
4. Select the server to run on from the Server to Run On field.
5. Choose to enable, disable, or run only at server startup from the Enabled/Disabled field.
6. Specify when to run this command or program in the Run at Times field.
7. Specify the repeat interval in minutes in the Repeat Interval Of field.
8. Select the days of the week to run from the Days of Week field.
9. Enter additional descriptive comments in the Comments field.

Your Program document should appear similar to the one shown in Figure 6.19. I have set up this document to run the Updall server task every night at midnight and to repeat every six hours. Your document may differ depending on what you specified in the Documents fields.

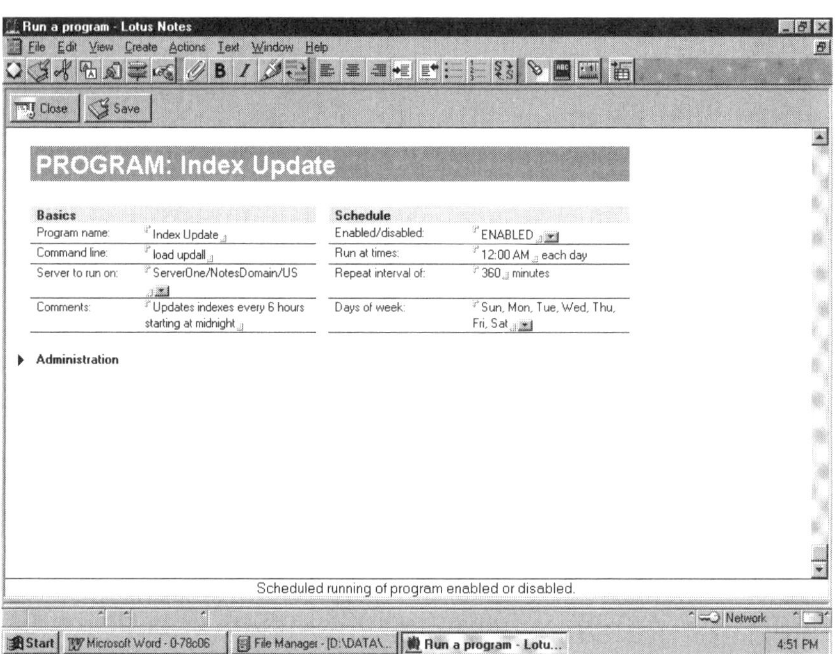

FIGURE 6.19

A sample Program document that runs the Updall server task every night at midnight and repeats every six hours after that

If, when viewing the Full Text tab in the Properties dialog box, you notice several unindexed documents, you can manually update the index to immediately index these documents. To do so, press the Update Index button.

Removing a Full Text Index

Aside from creating and updating full text indexes, you will also delete them in three particular situations. These situations include changing index options, fixing index problems, and removing unnecessary indexes.

From time to time the need will arise for an existing index to support other index options. Perhaps an index was created as case insensitive but daily usage has revealed that creating searches that are case sensitive would be much more effective. In a situation such as this one, the only way to add this functionality is to delete the index, create a new one, and select Case Sensitive in the Full Text Create Index dialog box.

There may be times when full text searches don't respond correctly and don't return documents that you know should be in your results set. This problem could be caused by a corrupted index. Full text indexes are just text files, which, like any other file, can become corrupted. If you suspect that the integrity of an index has been compromised, delete it and create a new one.

You don't ever need to update the options for an index or create a new one due to corruption. However, chances are you will need to delete an index at some time. Perhaps the database has been removed, the index is no longer needed, or you're running out of space on your Notes server and removing an index is a quick way to recover some disk space. Whatever the reason, the action taken is the same.

Listed below are the steps describing how to remove a full text index for any of the previous situations:

1. Select the database that has an index you want to remove and select File ➢ Database ➢ Properties from the menu bar.
2. Click the Full Text tab.
3. Click the Delete Index button and a dialog box appears asking if you are sure you want to delete this index.

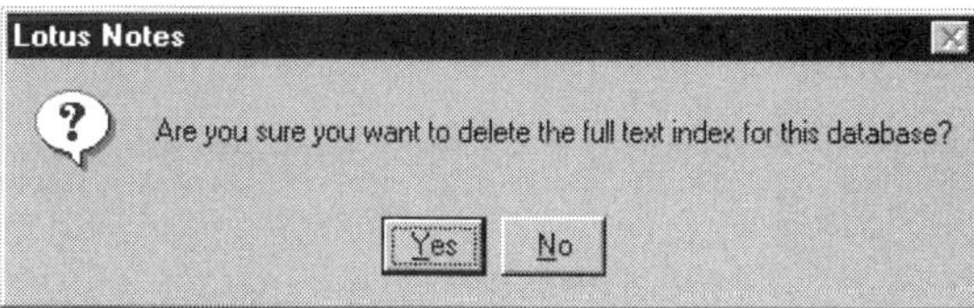

4. After the index is gone, most of the options on the Full Text tab will be dimmed out.

Updating a Database Design

Some Notes developers like to create databases based on a Notes template. A template is essentially a Notes database that contains no data but has all of the forms, views, folders, and agents ready for use (you supply the data). One benefit to using templates is that a developer can make changes to a template and test those changes in a controlled environment. If all the testing is successful, the developer can move the upgraded template into the production environment and refresh the design of the database based on that template.

Refreshing a database design requires that the Inherit Design From Template field in the database's Properties dialog box be checked. A name for the design template must also be supplied.

As a Notes administrator, you probably won't have much to do with upgrading database templates, but you will assist with other aspects of managing database templates. For example, if you have a master design template that is used for design updates, you'll be responsible for creating replicas of this template on all servers in your Notes network that need the template. Creating and replicating a design template throughout your organization is exactly the same as replicating a regular database. (Refer to Chapter 8 for details on how to replicate.)

Another possible aspect of template management that you might get involved with is helping to refresh database designs. By default, there is a setting in the NOTES.INI file, ServerTasksAt1, which runs the Design task every day at 1 AM. Unless you've edited this setting, databases based on a design template will get refreshed every morning at 1 AM. In most cases this setting is sufficient. However, if there is a better time for that task to run in your particular environment, you can change this setting by editing the ServerTasksAt1 to another time that is better, such as ServerTasksAt3. This new setting would cause the Design task to run at 3 AM instead of 1 AM.

For more information about the ServerTasksAt setting, refer to Appendix D.

If there is a situation in which a database design needs refreshing before the scheduled running of the Design server task, there are two ways to manually start the Design server task.

The first way to manually refresh a database design is very specific and probably the best way if you only have one database design to refresh.

1. If the database isn't already on your Notes workspace, add the database by selecting File ➢ Database ➢ Open.

2. From the Open Database dialog box, select the appropriate server and database and click the Add Icon button.

3. Once the database is added to your workspace, select the database by clicking it once with the left mouse button.

4. From the menu bar, select File ➢ Database ➢ Refresh Design. The Refresh Database Design dialog box appears.

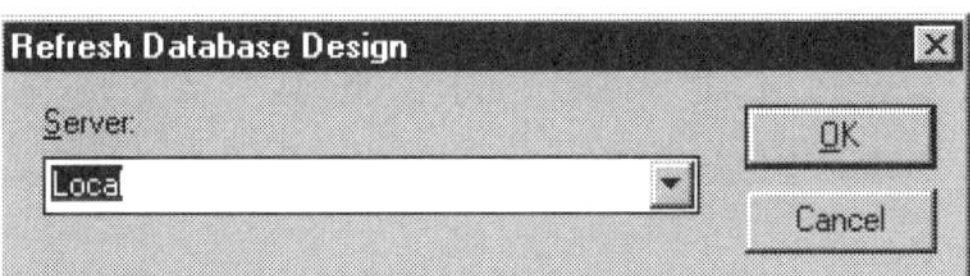

5. Select the server where the Design template is located; click OK and a warning dialog box appears.

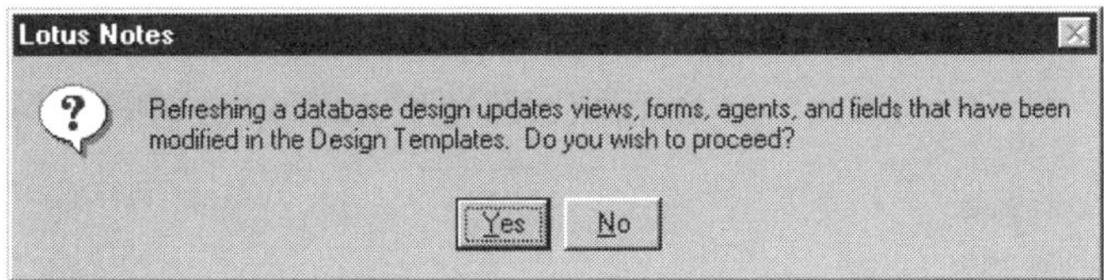

6. Click the Yes button and the design refreshing begins. When the process is complete, a message appears in the workspace status bar to indicate that the refresh is complete.

This way of manually refreshing a database design only updates the database you have selected, which can be quicker than the way that will be presented next.

Refreshing a database design from the Notes workspace requires that you have at least Designer access to the database.

The other way to refresh a database design is a little less specific than the previous way, and also requires that you have direct access to the server console or have access to send console commands to the server remotely.

1. From the server console of the server where the database you want to refresh is located, type the following command:

   Load Design

2. The Design server task loads and begins refreshing database designs.

If you don't have direct access to the server console, try to send the command remotely following the steps listed below:

1. From the menu bar, select File ➢ Tools ➢ Server Administration and select the Console button and the Remote Server Console appears (see Figure 6.20).
2. When the Remote Server Console dialog box appears, select the server from the drop-down list. Make sure the server you select is the one in which the database you want to refresh is located.
3. Enter the command **Load Design** in the Server Console Command box and click the Send button.
4. The server response and progress to your command is displayed in the Server Output box.

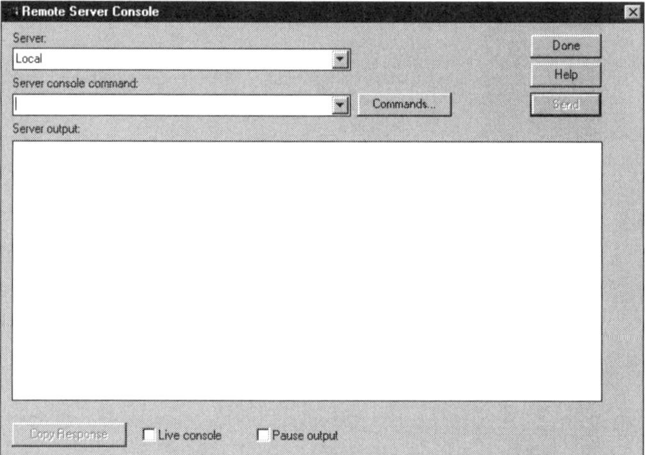

FIGURE 6.20 The Console button on the Server Administration screen opens the Remote Server Console dialog box.

Additional details about sending server commands remotely are located in Appendix C.

The only two drawbacks to refreshing a database design with the server console command is that all of the databases on that server, which are based on design templates, get refreshed. Refreshing all of the databases based on a template can have a serious impact on your server's CPU utilization. Also, after running the Design task, you should run the Updall task to rebuild the views that might have been replaced by the updated design. This task is also a CPU-intensive operation.

Unless you absolutely have to refresh a design immediately, try to let the scheduled Design task handle the task of refreshing a design. Doing a design refresh in the middle of the day can have a negative performance impact on your server.

Running a Database Analysis

As the Notes administrator, the developers in your organization may come to you from time to time and request a simple informational report about the databases they've created. Such information might include replication history, database usage, or design updates. All of this information is available, but it is scattered in different places. Fortunately, Notes provides a database analysis tool that enables you to collect this scattered information and put it in a single location.

The Database Analysis Tool collects information about one or more databases from that database's Replication History dialog box and User Activity dialog box, and the Notes Log (LOG.NSF). After the tool gathers this information together, it stores the information in a single results database created from the Database Analysis template (DBA4.NTF).

The database analysis tool can collect the following information about one or more databases:

- Replication history
- User document reads and writes
- Document creations, edits, or deletions
- Design changes
- Replication additions, updates, and deletions
- Mail messages delivered by the router

Aside from analyzing one or more databases, you can also analyze the selected information on other replicas of the database(s).

Analyzing a large database or multiple replicas can take a long time.

Follow the steps listed below to perform a database analysis:

1. From the menu bar, select File ➢ Tools ➢ Server Administration.
2. Click the Database Tools icon to display the Tools to Manage Notes Databases dialog box.

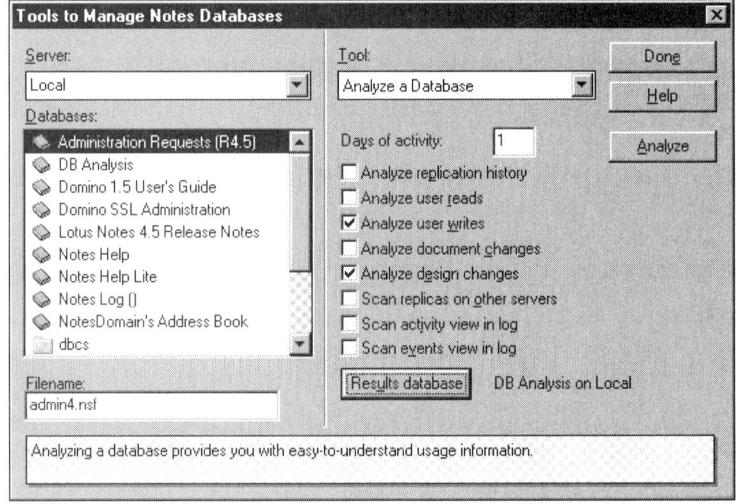

3. From the Server drop-down list, select the server that stores the database, or databases, you want to analyze.
4. In the Databases box, select one or more databases to analyze.
5. From the Tool drop-down list, select Analyze a Database.
6. In the Days of Activity field, enter the number of days to report on. The higher the number entered here, the longer it takes to generate the results.

7. Select one or more of the following options:

   - **Analyze replication history:** Reports successful replications of the database as recorded in the Replication History dialog box for the database.

   - **Analyze user reads:** Reports the number of times users opened documents in the database and the number of times servers read documents.

   - **Analyze user writes:** Reports the number of times users or servers created, modified, or deleted documents based on information in the database User Activity dialog box. Also reports the number of documents the Mail Router delivered to the database.

   - **Analyze document changes:** Reports details of document additions, edits, and deletions.

   - **Analyze design changes:** Reports changes to database Access Control List and database design.

   - **Scan replicas on other servers:** Reports information from other replicas for the specified database. Depending on the number of databases and replicas analyzed, the time required to create an analysis can increase significantly.

   - **Scan activity view in log:** Reports database activity from the Usage By User view of the Notes Log.

   - **Scan events view in log:** Reports events relating to the selected database from the Miscellaneous Events view of the Notes Log.

8. Click the Results Database button to display the Results Database dialog box. Specify a server, title, and filename for the database where you want to store the results (see Figure 6.21). If the specified Results database already exists, you can decide whether the new results will overwrite this database or append to it. Then click OK to return to the Tools to Manage Notes Databases dialog box.

9. When all of the appropriate options are selected, click the Analyze button in the Tools to Manage Notes Databases dialog box.

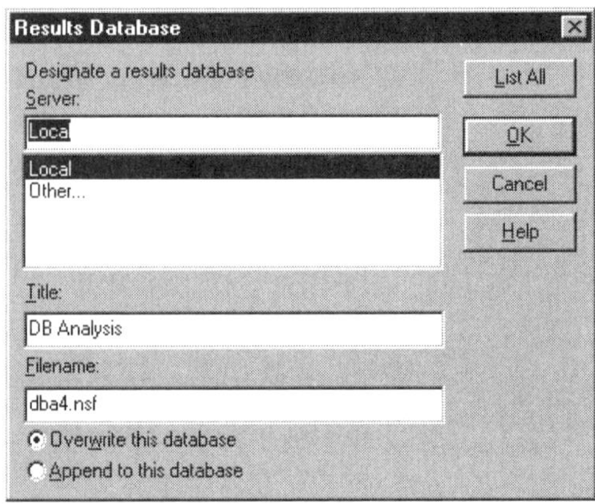

FIGURE 6.21
The Results Database dialog box

Once the database analysis is complete, you can view the results in the database you specified as the Results database, which contains four primary views defined as follows:

- **By Date:** This view categorizes documents by the date that the reported event occurred.
- **By Event:** This view categorizes documents by the type of event.
- **By Source:** This view categorizes documents according to the server on which the event occurred.
- **By Source Database:** This view categorizes documents by the source database for the event.

Each of these views contain several documents that capture specific analysis information. A typical document might appear similar to the one shown in Figure 6.22.

The informational fields in this document are defined as follows:

- **Date:** This field contains the date the event occurred.
- **Time:** This field contains the time the event occurred.
- **Source of Event Information:** This field is either the analyzed database, its replicas, or the Notes Log (LOG.NSF) on the server.

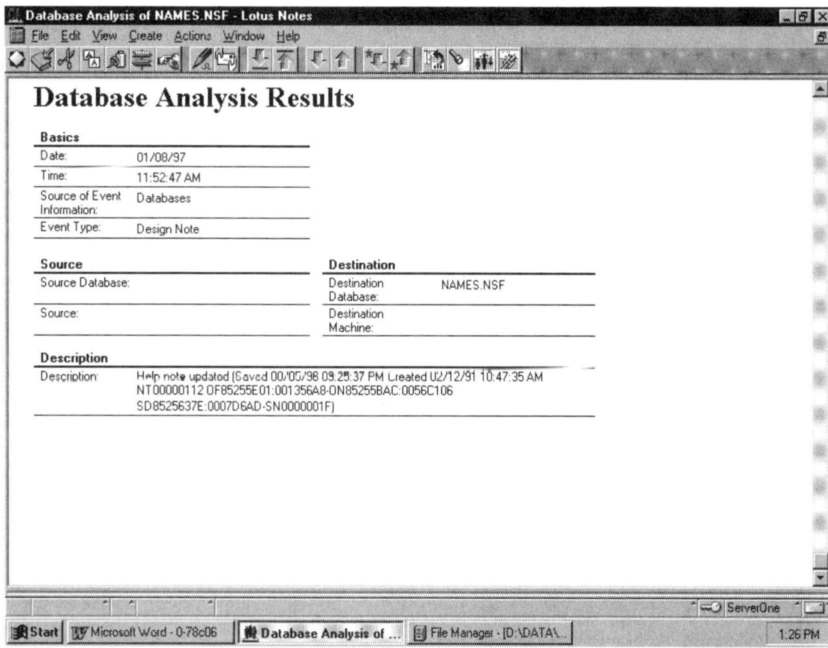

FIGURE 6.22 Here is what a typical document from the Results database looks like after running the database analysis tool.

- **Event Type:** This field is one of the following seven event types:
  - **Activity:** This event type is the number of times users or servers read and write to the database as recorded in the database's User Activity report. These events appear if you select User Reads and User Writes options.
  - **+Activity:** This event type is the number of times users read and write to the database as recorded in the database and in the Notes Log. These events appear if you select the Log File Activity and User Reads or User Writes options.
  - **Mail Router:** This event type is the number of documents delivered to the database. These events appear if you select the User Writes option.
  - **Data Note:** This event type displays details about document creations, edits, or deletions. These events appear if you select the Changes to Documents option.

- **Design Note**: This event type displays details about changes to the database Access Control List or design. These events appear if you select the Changes to Design option.
- **Replicator**: This event type displays the replication history as recorded in the database's Replication History dialog box indicating successful replications. These events appear if you select the Replication History option.
- **+Replicator**: This event type is the number of replication additions, updates, and deletions as recorded in the Notes Log. These events appear if you select the Log File Activity option.

- **Source Database:** This field displays the name of a database containing documents that were read. For database replication events, this field displays the name of the database from which information was pulled.
- **Source:** This field displays the name of the server where the database containing documents that were read or written is located. For database replication events, this field displays the name of the server where the database from which information is pulled is located.
- **Destination:** This field displays the name of a database where documents were updated. For database replication events, this field displays the name of the database to which information was replicated.
- **Destination machine:** This field displays the name of a server where the database that was updated is located. For database replication events, this field displays the name of a server where the database to which information is replicated is located.
- **Description:** This field contains a description of the event shown in the Event field.

Running a database analysis is a great way to pull a lot of information together into a single location. However, all of the information contained in the Results database is readily available from sources like the Notes Log (LOG.NSF) and a database's Replication History dialog box. So if you're only interested in a single piece of information, you're better off using a different resource because you'll get what you need much faster.

Locating Missing Response Documents

Most Notes databases have some type of hierarchical document structure. There are main documents, which are often referred to as parent documents, and response documents, which are also referred to as child documents. And there are response-to-response documents, which are also known as child documents. Each child, or response document, is tied to a parent document, and when the parent document is deleted the child document becomes an orphan. Orphan documents can take up disk space unnecessarily and can even hide information that someone might need.

Managing orphan documents isn't difficult; it really only involves three simple activities:

1. Finding the documents that are orphans.
2. Deleting the documents if they are no longer needed.
3. Finding a new parent for an orphan if the orphan document is still needed.

Finding orphan documents will usually require that you work with the database developer to create a non-hierarchical view. This type of view will show all of the documents in the database regardless of other document dependencies. Use this type of view in the following manner to locate orphaned documents:

1. Select all of the documents in a non-hierarchical view.
2. Switch to a hierarchical view and deselect all of the documents. Keep in mind that you must hold down the CTRL key when you switch from one view to another in order to maintain the check marks placed next to the selections you've made.
3. Switch back, while holding down the CTRL key, to the non-hierarchical view. The documents that remain selected are orphaned documents.

At this point, you can delete the remaining selected documents by pressing the DEL key. Then, either press the F9 key to refresh the view or close the database. In either situation a dialog box will appear and warn you that you are about to delete a certain number of documents. If you are sure you want to continue and delete these documents, press OK.

If you'd rather not delete the remaining selected documents, you can always reassign them to a new parent document. To give an orphan document a new parent, follow the steps listed below:

1. Select the orphan document.
2. From the menu bar, select Edit ➢ Cut.
3. Select a parent document, which is also known as a main document.
4. From the menu bar, select Edit ➢ Paste.

Now the orphan document has a new parent and will once again appear in hierarchical views.

Monitoring Database Activity

Monitoring database activity is an important part of database management. If a database is heavily used, you might want to create a replica on another server to balance the load. If, on the other hand, a database is under-used or sits idle for weeks at a time, you might consider removing that database from the server to make room for a more popular database. To make these judgments you need to monitor the usage of a database, and you can do so in the following manner:

1. Select the Database icon from the Notes workspace by clicking it once with the left mouse button.
2. From the menu bar, select File ➢ Database ➢ Properties.
3. Select the Info tab (see Figure 6.23).
4. Press the User Activity button and the User Activity dialog box shown in Figure 6.24 appears.
5. Place a check mark in the Record Activity check box and then press the OK button.

Once you've completed the previous steps, you'll need to give the database some time to start collecting information. Wait about a week and then return to the User Activity dialog box. The dialog box should contain some usage information, which you can easily copy and paste into any word processor document by pressing the Copy to Clipboard button. Also contained in the User Activity dialog box is a quick breakdown on the number of uses, reads, and writes for this database.

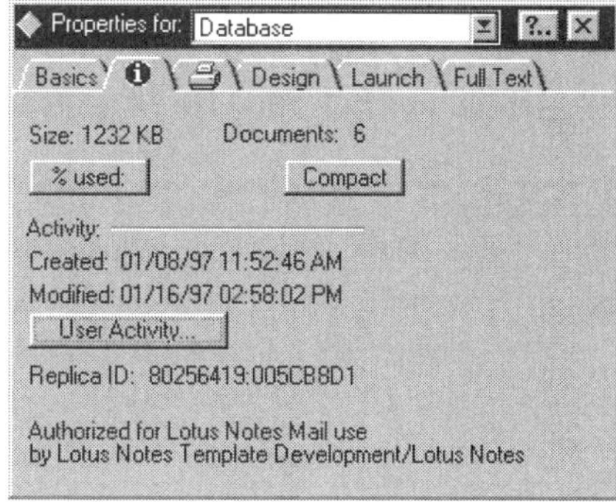

FIGURE 6.23

The User Activity button on the Info tab of the Properties dialog box opens dialog boxes with additional information.

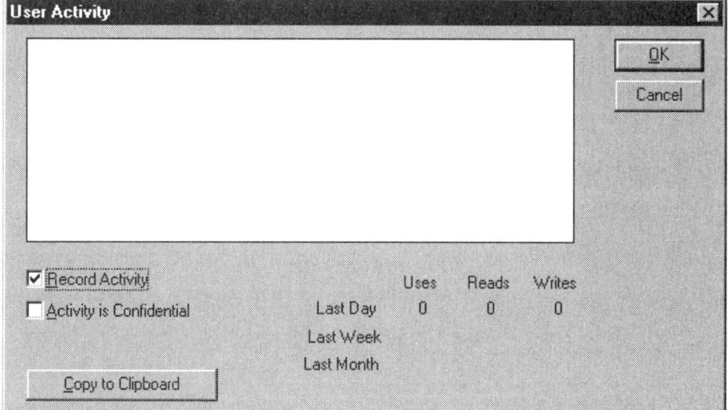

FIGURE 6.24

The User Activity dialog box displays activity information.

While the information contained in the User Activity dialog box is useful, this dialog box is not the only place this information is located. In the Notes Log (LOG.NSF) and in the server, the Database view sorts database usage information by usage and size:

- **By Usage:** This view shows each use of a database by users and servers. Session documents show the number of documents read and written for each session. Activity documents show the number of times a database was used (including uses at the view level where no documents were opened) and the number of documents read and written to over a period of days, weeks, or months.

- **By Size:** This view has a Weekly Usage column containing the number of times the database has been used during the last week.

Aside from the Database view in the Notes Log, you should also look at the Usage By User view. This view lists each session between a user and a server. Documents in the view also show all the documents used during those sessions.

Recording user activity using the settings in the Database Properties dialog box adds 64 k to the overall size of a database. If disk space is tight on your server, you might want to just rely on the Notes Log for usage information.

Managing Database Size

Managing the size of the databases in your Notes network is important no matter how much disk space you have. If disk space is limited, the need for database size management is obvious. However, if you have ample disk space, you still need to manage database size because the bigger a database gets the slower it responds for the users.

In the *Rolling Out a New Database* section of this chapter, we looked at setting a maximum database size and setting database quotas. However, these are not the only ways to control a database's size. You can also control the size of a database by compacting it when necessary or archiving old documents.

As documents get deleted from a database, the percentage of unused space starts to increase. Compacting a database is a process that reclaims this unused space by creating a temporary copy of the database and then copying that database back over the original. From the user's point of view, nothing has changed after a database has been compacted. However, if the user tries to access the database while it's being compacted, they will see a message indicating that the database is in use.

Compacting a database makes a copy of that database, so make sure you have enough disk space before compacting a database. If you don't have enough room, you may not be able to compact the database.

Determining whether a database needs compacting is done by finding out what percentage of the database is unused. The following steps describe how to make this determination:

1. Select the database in question from the Notes workspace by clicking it once with your left mouse button.
2. From the menu bar, select File ➢ Database ➢ Properties and click the Info tab in the Properties dialog box (see Figure 6.25).

3. Click the % Used button and the percentage of used space is displayed.
4. If the percentage used is less than ninety percent, which means ten percent is unused, click the Compact button. However, if the database is in use by someone, you won't be able to compact it.

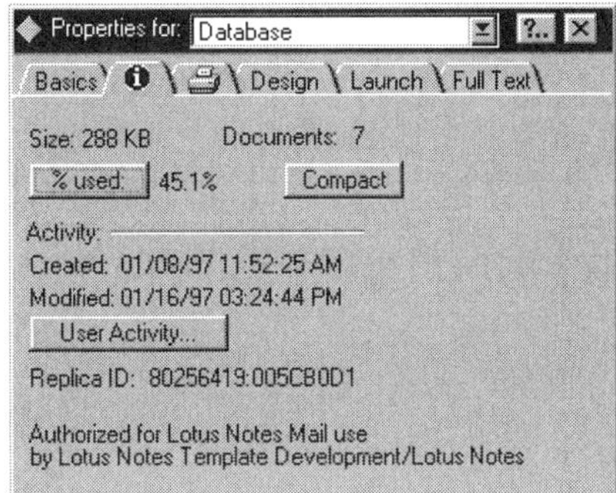

FIGURE 6.25
The percentage of the database that is used is shown in the % Used portion of the Info tab of the Properties dialog box. In this example, the database should be compacted because % Used is well below ninety percent.

Compacting a database can disrupt the Notes user in your environment. I suggest that you try to compact databases during off hours or add the Compact server task to one of the ServerTasksAt settings in your NOTES.INI file and have it run nightly at a predetermined time. For example, adding **ServerTasksAt3=Compact** to the NOTES.INI file runs the compact task at 3 AM when the likelihood that someone is using the databases is greatly reduced.

Aside from compacting a database, you should also consider archiving old documents to keep the size of the database within reason. Archiving documents from a database in an automated manner requires the design of a specialized Agent. Since Agent design is beyond the scope of this book, I recommend you get together with a Notes developer for assistance or review the *Lotus Notes Database Manager Guide* for further details.

Moving Databases

Moving databases from one server to another within your Notes network isn't something you'll do often. However, when you install new server hardware or relocate users is usually the time when moving databases also becomes necessary.

The steps involved in moving a database are simple, and they're similar to the steps you took when rolling out a new database.

1. If the database you are moving has replicas on other servers, delete those replicas first.
2. Go to the destination server and add the database to the Notes workspace by selecting File ➢ Database ➢ Open.
3. Select the appropriate server and database, and click the Add Icon button.
4. Select the new icon by clicking it once with your left mouse button.
5. From the menu bar, select File ➢ Database ➢ New Copy.
6. The default settings in the Copy Database dialog box should be correct. You may have to change the filename and destination directory. Otherwise, your dialog box should be similar to the one shown in Figure 6.26.
7. If everything is correct in the Copy Database dialog box, click OK.
8. Once the database has reached its new destination, double check the ACL settings.
9. Finally, create new replicas of this database if they existed previously.

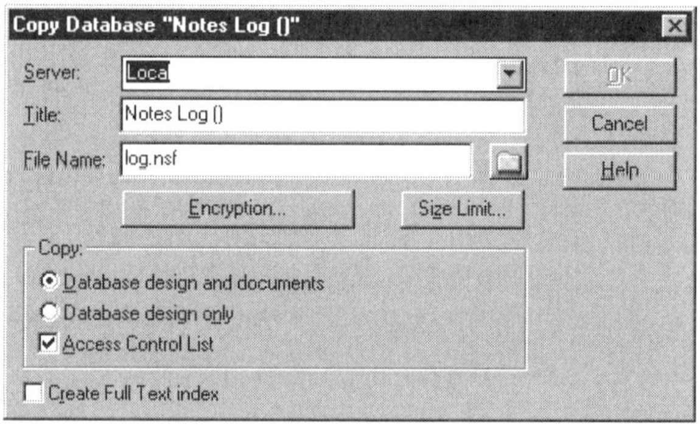

FIGURE 6.26
The default settings in the Copy Database dialog box should not need to be changed. Make sure, however, that Database Design and Documents is selected.

Another quick way to move a database involves using the Database tools available from the Server Administration screen.

1. From the menu bar, select File ➢ Tools ➢ Server Administration.

2. Click the Database Tools icon to display the Tools to Manage Notes Databases dialog box.
3. From the Server drop-down list, select the server that stores the database, or databases, you want to move.
4. In the Databases box, select one or more databases to analyze.
5. From the Tool drop-down list, select Move a Database.
6. From the Destination Servers box, select the appropriate server.
7. Click the Create button.

Either way you choose to move a database, you'll still need to inform the Notes user community that the database has been moved. You can send them a simple e-mail message or an e-mail message that contains a button that automatically adds the database icon to their desktop. Also, if this database is a mail-in database, you'll have to update the Mail-In Database document as well.

Sending an e-mail message with a button to automate the adding or opening of a database for a user was covered in the *Rolling Out a New Database* section at the beginning of this chapter.

Repairing Corrupted Databases

Notes databases are basically just files like any other data file on your computer. And like any other data file, Notes databases can become corrupted. Improperly shutting down the operating system, a system crash, a power failure, or improper access to a database through the Notes API are all causes of database corruption. Fortunately, if a database becomes corrupted you can usually repair it.

Part of being able to repair a corrupted database is simply taking precautionary measures before corruption occurs. Tape backups are usually your first precautionary measure, but the last place to turn when correcting database corruption. Adding a tape backup device to your Notes server is an easy to implement safety precaution. However, restoring a database from tape is typically a last resort for correcting database corruption because it usually means that a certain amount of data is going to be lost (the tape backup is normally older than the database just lost).

Aside from tape backups, a replica copy from another server is also a great precautionary measure to take. Sometimes it might make sense to add a dedicated backup server to your Notes network. This server would be inaccessible to average users. This server's primary purpose would be to have a fairly current replica copy of every database in your environment. If a database becomes corrupted, you can replicate a fresh copy from this dedicated server and you're problem is solved.

When tape backups and replica copies are not an option, use the Fixup utility. This utility is a server task that checks databases for corrupted documents and tries to fix them, if possible, to prevent server crashes. You can run Fixup in one of two ways.

1. Automatically, each time the server starts.
2. Manually from the server console, specifying one or more databases.

To run Fixup manually, type the following command at the server console:

Load fixup ***filename arguments***

The filename is optional and it specifies the name of the database that you want to check. If you don't specify a database, Fixup checks all databases on the server. If the Notes Log is closed when you run Fixup, then the Notes Log is checked first. If needed, the Notes Log is repaired so all subsequent repairs can be recorded in the Notes Log. After the Notes Log, Fixup checks and repairs any other Notes databases that were improperly closed.

As with filenames, arguments are optional. Available arguments include one or more of the following:

- -L: This argument reports every database that Fixup opens and checks for corruption to the Notes Log. Without this argument, Fixup logs only actual problems encountered.
- -V: This argument prevents Fixup from running on views, which reduces the time Fixup takes to run.
- -I: This argument causes Fixup to check only those documents modified since the last time Fixup ran.
- -N: This argument prevents Fixup from purging corrupted documents so that the next time Fixup runs or the next time a user opens the database, Fixup must check the database again. Use this argument when you run

Fixup on a specific database. You can also use this argument when you want to copy and paste the corrupted documents into another database in an attempt to salvage the data if no tape backup or replica copy exists.

Each argument requires a preceding hyphen as shown above.

Fixup runs automatically in the background each time the Notes server starts. Fixup starts with the Notes Log (LOG.NSF) so that the Log can record reports of subsequent database repairs.

When Fixup runs at server startup, it does not detect and rebuild corrupted views.

When the server starts, all databases are quickly scanned to determine which ones require Fixup. This quick scan allows the server to start up quickly. Any databases requiring Fixup are fixed a few minutes after the server starts. If users attempt to access a database that has not yet been fixed, they will receive the error message, "This database cannot be opened because a consistency check of it is in progress."

Multiple Fixup tasks run simultaneously at server startup to reduce the time required to fix databases. The default number of Fixup tasks that run at startup is equal to two times the number of processors available on the server. The default behavior should be adequate for most Notes servers. However, should you need to increase the number of Fixup tasks, you can add the line **Fixup_Tasks = *number*** to the NOTES.INI file (*number* is any valid number). The actual number of tasks that run are never more than what is set in the .INI file and never more than is actually needed to fix corrupted databases. For example, if you have **Fixup_Task = 3** set in the NOTES.INI file but only one database needs to be repaired, then only one Fixup task is started.

Running Fixup can consume a significant amount of CPU resources. Run Fixup manually only when necessary.

You can also schedule Fixup to run as an automatic server program. This approach is a happy medium between the manual and server startup ways to run Fixup. With a schedule, you can avoid consuming significant amounts of

CPU resources during peak server usage and get the benefit of Fixup detecting and fixing corrupted views and documents the same way it does when it's run manually.

To schedule Fixup to run automatically during off hours, you can create a Program document in the Public Address Book (see Figure 6.27) or add Fixup to one of the ServerTasksAt settings in the NOTES.INI file.

FIGURE 6.27

A sample Program document for running Fixup every night at midnight and reporting all activity to the Notes Log with the -L argument

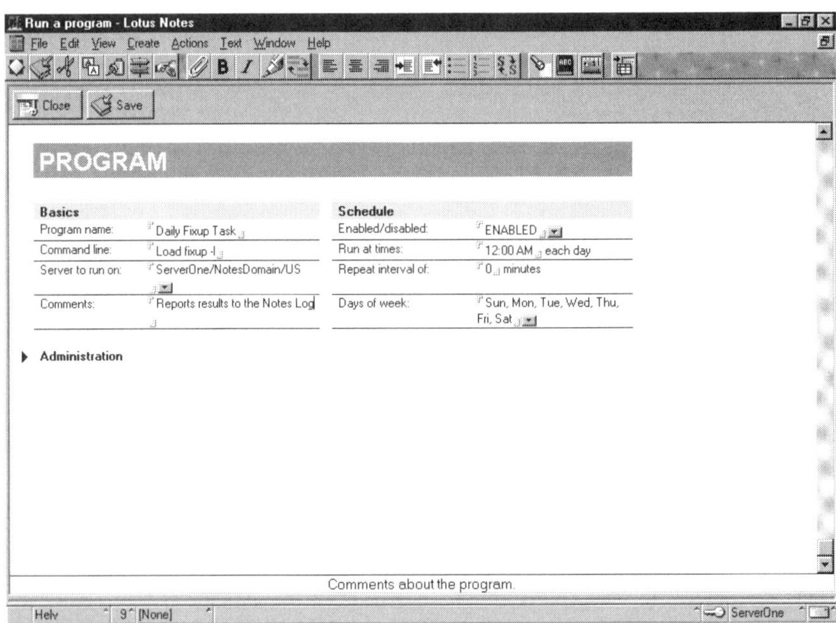

Occasionally, individual views will become corrupted. Restoring from a tape backup, replica copy, or running Fixup on the database can repair a corrupted view. However, there are still two other options that might be a little simpler.

- Run Updall from the server console.
- Rebuild the view from the workspace.

Updall is a server task that updates all views that have been accessed at least once, and runs by default every morning at 2 AM (determined by the NOTES.INI setting ServerTasksAt2). When Updall is run manually or through a program document, there are additional arguments that determine how the task works. Of these argument options, the ones most useful when attempting to repair corrupted views are shown below:

- -R: This argument rebuilds from scratch all database views that have been accessed at least once and updates all full text indexes. This is a very time consuming process and may affect server performance, so use this argument sparingly (for example, **Load Updall -R**).
- *-database* -T *viewtitle*: This argument updates a specified view in the specified database (for example, **Load Updall DISCUSS.NSF -T "Mail View"**).

Using Updall from the server console or listing the task in the Command Line field of a Program document requires that you precede the task with the **LOAD** command and all arguments must be preceded with a hyphen.

You can also attempt to rebuild the Notes workspace by selecting the view and then pressing SHIFT + F9. Or, if you need to, you can rebuild all corrupted views and update all views in a single database by pressing CTRL + SHIFT + F9.

Troubleshooting Database Performance

I've often found that end-users' performance expectations are much greater than systems administrators' or application developers'. People who work with technology every day understand and have accepted the limitations of the technology they work with. The typical end-user, however, does not know where the limitations are. Therefore, they completely expect the technology to perform robustly and reliably all the time.

The Notes user community is a tough audience to please. They seldom want to hear excuses and technical explanations for why a database can't be accessed or why it's so slow. They simply want the database to work.

There are two common complaints about Notes databases often heard from users:

1. Why can't I access this database?
2. Why is this database so slow?

Keep in mind one thing as you tackle these problems: troubleshooting database problems is not an exact science. A lot of what you'll do to solve a problem is just going to be trial and error. I recommend being methodical; start with the simplest solution and work your way up to the more complex solutions.

As for database access problems, the problem could be several things. Here is a list of possible places to start:

- **ACL not set correctly:** The ACL is the single most important control device for databases. First, confirm that the user can access the server. If they can, verify that they are listed in that database's ACL either explicitly or implicitly. (See Chapter 7 for more details about security.)
- **The server is down:** If the server is not available, no one can get to the databases stored there. Because you're the Notes administrator, you should know if the server is up or down.
- **The database is being compacted:** Remember, whenever a database is being compacted it is not available for use. If compacting starts to cause a regular problem, make sure the compact task is not starting automatically at inappropriate times. Check the Public Address Book for a Program document that runs this task and check the start time and repeat interval. Also, check the NOTES.INI file and look at the ServerTasksAt settings for times that coincide with the problem.
- **Server is updating an index:** Updating an index is a fairly CPU-intensive operation. Check the update frequency setting in all of the databases that have indexes and make sure that the update isn't happening too often.
- **Views are being rebuilt:** The Updall server task is another CPU-intensive operation. Check the Public Address Book for a Program document that runs this task and check the start time and repeat interval. Also, check the NOTES.INI file and look at the ServerTasksAt settings for times that coincide with the problem.

If database access isn't a problem but database performance is, here are a couple of suggestions for resolving this problem:

- **Very busy database:** Check the database activity in the Notes Log. If you notice that the database is very busy, consider creating a replica on another server and splitting the usage load. You could also consider upgrading the server hardware for better performance. Notes is a fairly CPU- and memory-intensive program. Upgrading to a faster processor and adding more memory will usually help.

- **Too many views in the database:** Views require indexes and each view gets one. The more views you have the more indexes there are for the server to create and update. Work with the Notes developer to consolidate the views.
- **View indexes are being refreshed too frequently:** Views, much the same as full text indexes, have an update frequency that can be set. Work with the Notes developer to adjust the frequency for view updating.
- **Complex database:** When complex calculations, computed fields, and DB lookup functions are all in one database they can impact how quickly the database performs. As the Notes administrator, you probably can't do much to resolve this type of problem other than inform the Notes developers and hope that they make some changes.

These are only a couple of places to start when trying to resolve common database problems in your Notes network. Each Notes network is a little different than the next. Therefore, common problems and the methods used to resolve those problems will be a little different for each environment. Most problems, however, seem to occur because of a lack of communication with the user community about the database administration schedule. The users don't need to know the details about database administration. However, they should know when database administration takes place and how they will be impacted by that administration.

Removing a Database

When it comes time to take a database out of production, you'll probably find that it takes you longer to get ready to remove the database than to actually remove it. Even though the database is being removed for one reason or another, the database was used at one time and probably still contains some important information. Therefore, you can't just delete the database without proper preparation.

- **Freeze the database:** Remove all of the ACL entries, except LocalDomain-Servers and the administration entry, and set the default access to Reader. People can still view the information in the database, but they can't add or remove anything from it.
- **Notify the users:** Send out an e-mail that informs everyone that the specified database is going to be removed from the system on a specific date. Include the explanation for the database and removal. And include proper points of contact for questions or objections.
- **Backup the database to a Notes server:** If you have a dedicated backup Notes server, replicate the database to this server one last time and set the default ACL to No Access. Chances are someone in your organization is going to object to the database deletion months after it's gone. Having a backup on a Notes server allows you to quickly resurrect the database.
- **Backup the database to tape:** Make a permanent copy of the database to a tape device. Catalog the contents of the tape and store it in a safe location.
- **Create a deletion notification database:** This is a database that contains the same information that you included in your e-mail notification message. I like to add this information to the "About this database" document. I set the database properties to always open the document. Then I set the default ACL to Reader.
- **Delete the database:** Select the database from the Notes workspace. Then, from the menu bar, select File ➢ Database ➢ Delete. Answer Yes to the warning box. The database is now gone. Then place the previously created deletion notification database into this database's place. The notification database should have the same path, filename, and database title as the one just deleted.

Permanently deleting a database from your Notes network can have unpredictable results. Users could become outraged or they could care less. You could successfully delete the database and months could go by before anyone notices. If you follow the preparatory steps listed above, you'll be ready for whatever happens after the database is gone.

Summary

As the Notes administrator, you will often find yourself responsible for the production databases in your Notes environment. You may also be very fortunate and actually have someone dedicated to the role of Notes database administrator. Either way, you need to be familiar with what is involved with Notes database management so you can assume the responsibility on a full time basis or whenever the dedicated resource is not available.

Aside from knowing what is involved with Notes database management, I also recommend that you create some simple procedure documents that record this information. These documents should address the three basic database management functions:

- **Rolling out a new database:** This document should briefly outline the steps to follow when rolling out a new database in your Notes environment.
- **Maintaining databases:** This document should describe the daily or weekly routine that you follow to ensure database integrity, performance, and availability.
- **Removing a database from production:** This document should list the steps involved in removing a database from the production Notes environment.

A day may come when you, or the dedicated Notes database manager, is not available. Inevitably, that day is the one day that everything goes wrong, or the day that a critical database has to be rolled out. So when the documentation is complete, make sure it is available to everyone who may need it in both electronic and hard copy format.

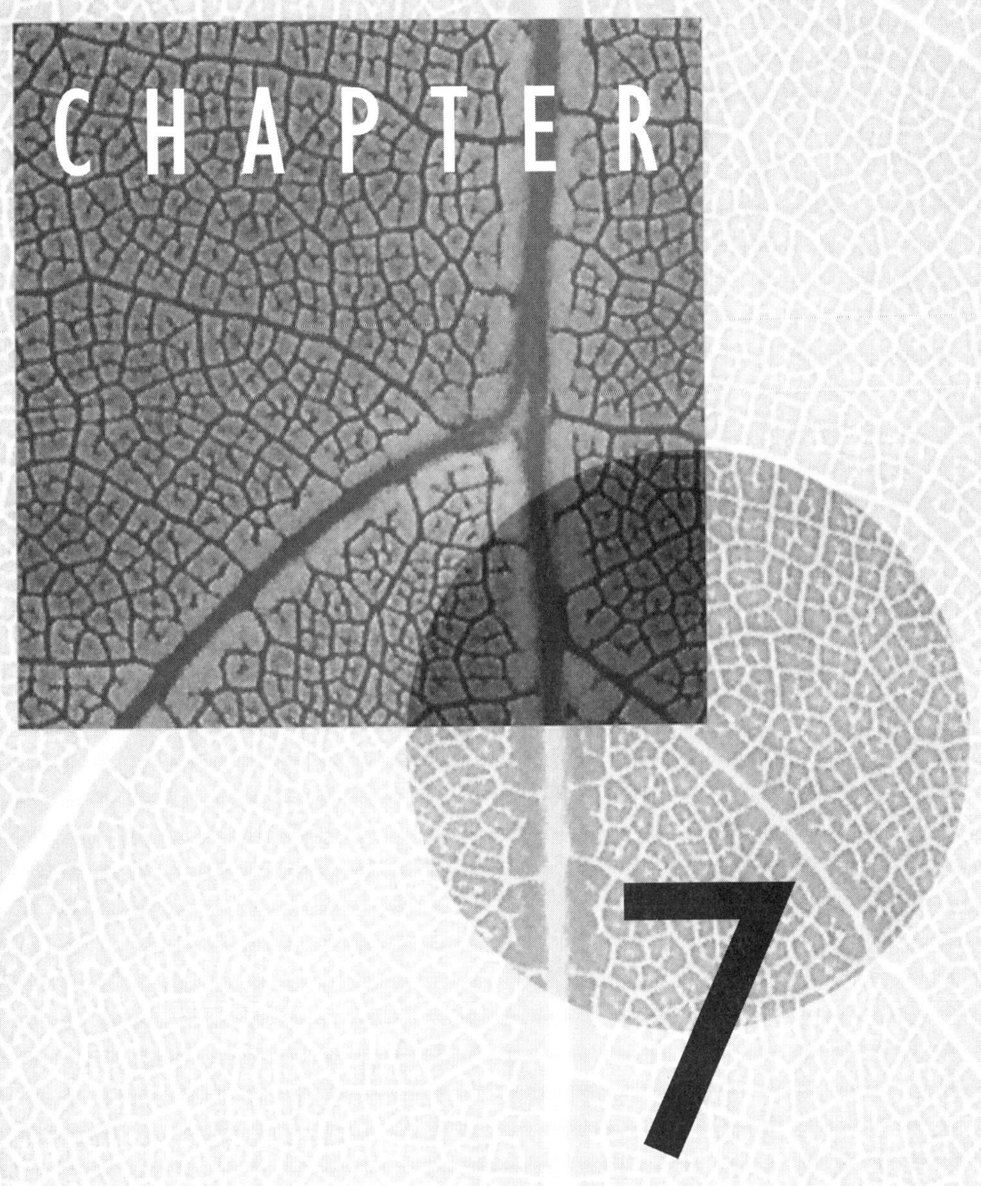

CHAPTER 7

Notes Security

One of the fundamental purposes of Lotus Notes is to enable groups of people to work together more effectively. This intended purpose might imply an open and unsecure environment. Fortunately, Lotus has built into Notes a wide variety of security options which allow the Notes administrator to implement as much or as little security as is required in his or her environment.

Security for nearly any type of computer system usually invokes one of two human emotions: love or hate. If you're a systems administrator, you either love the elevated level of power that security gives you, or you hate the tedious work that implementing and maintaining a secure system creates for you. And if you're a user of a secure system, you usually hate the seemingly endless hoops you have to jump through just to gain access to network resources. Of course, users of unsecure systems don't love the absence of seemingly endless hoops because they simply aren't aware that these hoops are missing. Users often think that easy access to a system is the way it is supposed to be.

Security for nearly any type of network system, whether it is a file server or a client server application, often consists of three basic elements: granting access, denying access, and controlling how much a user can do once access has been granted. These basic elements also apply to a Lotus Notes network.

Lotus Notes is fundamentally a network-based client server application. A Notes network is a grouping of Notes servers that contains Notes databases and services. Users in a Notes network are granted or denied access to these servers. Once access is granted to a server, further access to the databases or services on that server are controlled through the Access Control List (ACL). This list is associated with each database or configuration document, which in turn is associated with the service or database.

Notes security is a very straightforward security model to understand. Notes security is an inverted pyramid starting at the broadest level of access. Once server access is granted, access to individual databases is granted or denied. Inside of those databases, access to forms, views, and folders is either granted or denied. Finally, inside of the forms, access to individual sections and fields is at the bottom of the inverted pyramid (see Figure 7.1).

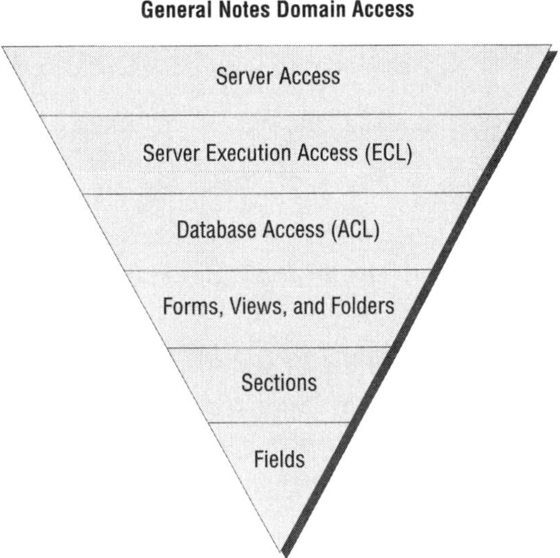

FIGURE 7.1
Notes security is an inverted pyramid.

As a Notes administrator, you'll need to completely understand this inverted pyramid—the dependencies between each level and how to manage the levels.

Server Access

At the top of the inverted security pyramid pictured in Figure 7.1 is server access. This access is at the top for good reason; if a user hasn't been granted access to a server, they're not going to get into that server and therefore all the remaining levels of the inverted security pyramid don't come into play. I like to split this level into two sections starting with the two step process of validation and authentication (the server validating who you are and authenticating that you are who you say you are) and then move on to actual server access.

Basic Server Security

Notes provides the technical features of server security, but you as the Notes administrator must provide the physical security to the Notes server. Here are a few tips to ensure the physical security of your Notes server:

- Keep the server in a locked, well ventilated room.
- Password protect your server ID unless you want your server to be able to restart automatically.
- Use the Set Secure command at the server console to password protect the Notes server console.
- Use the Local Security option to encrypt databases to protect them from unauthorized access—even when copied to a local machine (see the *Notes Encryption* section later in this chapter for details about Notes' encryption.)

Validation and Authentication

Validation and authentication is like going to a very popular bar. When you go there, the bouncers at the door typically card everyone coming in. No matter how old you might appear, these bouncers usually don't believe it until they see that little, official piece of plastic. Once your license confirms your age, the bouncers let you in. These bouncers aren't concerned with whether you can actually buy a drink. They are only concerned about validating and authenticating your age and identity, which is exactly what this two step process is all about.

Validation

Validation consists of establishing trust of a public key found in the Public Address Book, which, in a hierarchical naming scheme, is guided by three specific rules.

1. **Trust the public key of any of your ancestors in the hierarchical name tree.** For example, ServerOne/NotesDomain reads the NotesDomain public key from its own ID file and trusts the public key of NotesDomain because it is an ancestor in the hierarchical name tree. Therefore, ServerOne will trust any other server or user public key obtained from NotesDomain.

2. **Trust any public key obtained from a valid certificate issued by any ancestor in your hierarchical name tree.** This means that since ServerOne trusts NotesDomain, it will also trust any public key obtained from OrgOne/NotesDomain because OrgOne/NotesDomain is a certificate issued by a common, trusted ancestor, which is NotesDomain in this case.

3. **Trust any public key certified by any trusted certifier and belonging to one of the certifier's descendants.** This means that ServerOne will trust a public key such as John Doe/OrgOne/NotesDomain because it was certified by a trusted certifier, which is OrgOne/NotesDomain in this case.

Authentication

Authentication consists of an encryption and decryption random-number challenge between either user and server, or server and server. This challenge process involves the user or server encrypting a random number with their private key associated with their ID file. This encrypted number is then passed to the other side—server or user—and decrypted using the public key found in the Public Address Book for that very same ID. If decrypting is successful, the process is repeated for the other server or user. An example of this is explained further in the next section.

An Example of Validation and Authentication

Validation and authentication sounds great when described in a quick bulleted list or in the popular bar analogy, but how does it really work? The following example attempts to place validation and authentication into context by describing how John Doe, a user in the domain called NotesDomain, is trying to access ServerOne in the same domain:

1. John Doe/OrgOne/NotesDomain wants to access some databases on ServerOne/NotesDomain. The user starts by executing a traditional File ➢ Database ➢ Open. He selects ServerOne/NotesDomain from the list of servers.

2. By selecting ServerOne, John Doe establishes a connection with ServerOne and now both user and server exchange certificates and try to validate one another.

3. ServerOne knows that its ancestor is NotesDomain and that it should trust other users and servers that have this same ancestor. ServerOne looks at John Doe's ID for a certificate issued from NotesDomain.

4. ServerOne finds that NotesDomain issued a certificate to OrgOne and therefore takes the NotesDomain public key and verifies that the OrgOne certificate is valid.
5. The certificate is valid and now ServerOne trusts public keys obtained from OrgOne.
6. ServerOne looks at John Doe's ID again, but this time it looks for a certificate issued by OrgOne.
7. ServerOne finds that OrgOne issued a certificate to John Doe, and therefore takes the OrgOne public key and verifies that John Doe's certificate is valid.
8. The certificate is valid and now ServerOne trusts John Doe, and the authentication process begins.
9. ServerOne sends a random-number challenge to John Doe.
10. John Doe's workstation encrypts the random number with his private key and sends it back to ServerOne.
11. ServerOne uses John Doe's public key to decrypt the encrypted random number. If, after decryption, the same random number that was originally sent is found, ServerOne knows that John Doe is who he claims to be.

Once the entire process of validation and authentication is complete for the server, ServerOne, it is repeated so the user, John Doe, can validate and authenticate the server. Furthermore, this process of validating and authenticating for both server and user is exactly the same one that's used between two servers.

Controlling Server Access

The second section of gaining access to a server has to do with being listed in the appropriate Server Document field, either explicitly or implicitly, through group membership. How or for what reason a user or server is trying to access another server will determine which Server Document field they need to be included in. Figure 7.2 displays the Restrictions section of the Server Document where these important fields are located.

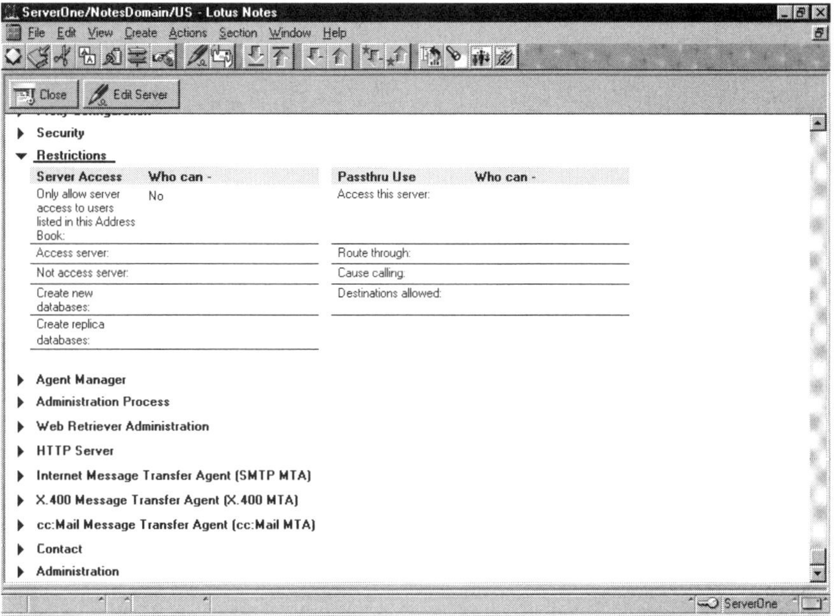

FIGURE 7.2 Important access fields in the Server Document determine whether a user or server can access a server and what basic actions they can perform on that server.

As you can tell from Figure 7.2, there is more to the Server Document than just allowing and denying access. Below is a field-by-field listing with definitions.

- **Only allow server access to users listed in this Address Book:** This field prevents users and servers not listed in the Public Address Book from accessing your server. Selecting Yes enables prevention and selecting No allows users and servers not listed in the Public Address Book access to the server. The default is No.

- **Access server:** This is one of the two most important access fields in the Restrictions section of the Server Document. By default, this field is blank, which allows any certified user or server access to this server. I don't advise leaving this field blank even if you want everyone to access the server because it's a sloppy administration habit. At the very least, create a group called Everyone, which includes every user and server in your Notes network. Then, add this group to the Access Server field. Using a group also helps speed up log performance because Notes just checks to see if a particular user or server is a member of the listed group. Another approach you can use is specifying a view from the Public Address Book in this field; but this approach is much slower than a group because essentially it has to open the view and search for the user or server trying to gain access. You could also use a branch of the hierarchy to specify a group of users and/or servers. For example, you can add */OrgOne/NotesDomain to the Access Server field and then all users and servers at that level of the hierarchy will have access. Finally, you could just place an asterisk (*) in the Access Server field. An asterisk (*) allows everyone in the Public Address Book to gain access to the server. However, I don't recommend this approach because it gives access too easily to a large group of users. Using groups to grant bulk access is better because you can selectively add and remove certain users from groups rather than make changes directly in the Server document. With the group method your changes are immediate, whereas using the Server document requires restarting the server for the individual additions or deletions to take effect.

- **Not access server:** This is the second of the two most important fields in the Restrictions section of the Server Document. As with the Access Server field this field is also blank by default, which means no one is denied access. As you might suspect, any user or server listed in this field cannot access the server. Be careful how you use this field because what is listed in this field overrides what is listed in the Access Server field. The traditional use of this field is to list a group called something like "DenyGroup." As users leave your organization, their Person documents are deleted from the Public Address Book and they are added to the DenyGroup. This way, if the users takes their Notes ID file with them, they won't be able to dial in and gain access after they've left. A "deny access" group of some sorts should be added to every server in your organization.

- **Create new databases:** This field is also blank by default, which means anyone that can access your server can create a new database on it (imagine the mess that could cause). I recommend adding a group of high level Notes developers in this field. This group should only include those developers who completely understand the ramifications of adding new databases to a server. In theory, you only want production-ready databases on your Notes servers. In practice, it might not be possible to keep "under-construction" databases off a production server. However, if you can dedicate a single server to development that is only accessible to Notes developers, then by all means do it. Databases under construction might require a server to be frequently restarted to test a new feature, or these under-construction databases might inadvertently cause your server to crash. Do what your resources allow in your Notes network, but at the very least add some type of development group to the Create New Databases field.

- **Create replica databases:** This is another blank by default field that should be changed immediately. You only want Notes administrators, some developers, and the LocalDomainServers group listed in this field. I prefer only adding administrators to this field, that way I maintain the highest level of control over what is getting replicated across the organization.

In the Passthru Use column of the Server Document's Restrictions section there are also several fields for controlling passthru server access. With a passthru server, workstations and servers can access other servers that they don't share a common network protocol with by using the passthru server as a sort of router. Passthru servers also allow administrators to set up a single dial-in server that allows remote users access to their home server even though that server is not dialed into directly.

If you're not planning to use a passthru server in your Notes network, you can accept the defaults for the fields in this section. However, if your current or future plans call for setting up a passthru server, review the following field definitions to familiarize yourself with the level of control you can impose on a passthru server:

- **Access this server:** List users, servers, and groups that should be allowed passthru access to this server. By default, this field is blank, which means no one can access this server via a passthru connection.

- **Route through:** This is another blank field by default, which means the server is not a passthru server. If you want to enable this server as one to be used for passthru access, just list the users, servers, or groups that will have that access in this field. Keep in mind that just because someone has been given access to the server doesn't mean they can use it for passthru functionality.

- **Cause calling:** This field allows you to control whether users or servers can force this server to call another server in order to complete a passthru connection. By default, this field is blank, which means no one can force this server to place a call to another server.

- **Destinations allowed:** If you want to restrict passthru destinations to specific servers, enter those server destinations here. If this field is blank, which is the default, all servers are reachable through this passthru server.

Additional Security Settings

In the Security section (see Figure 7.3) of the Server Document there are three fields that provide an additional level of security to a server (listed below). The default settings for these additional fields are perfectly acceptable. However, for those who administer security-conscience environments, such as certain branches of government or law enforcement, these additional fields are worth investigating.

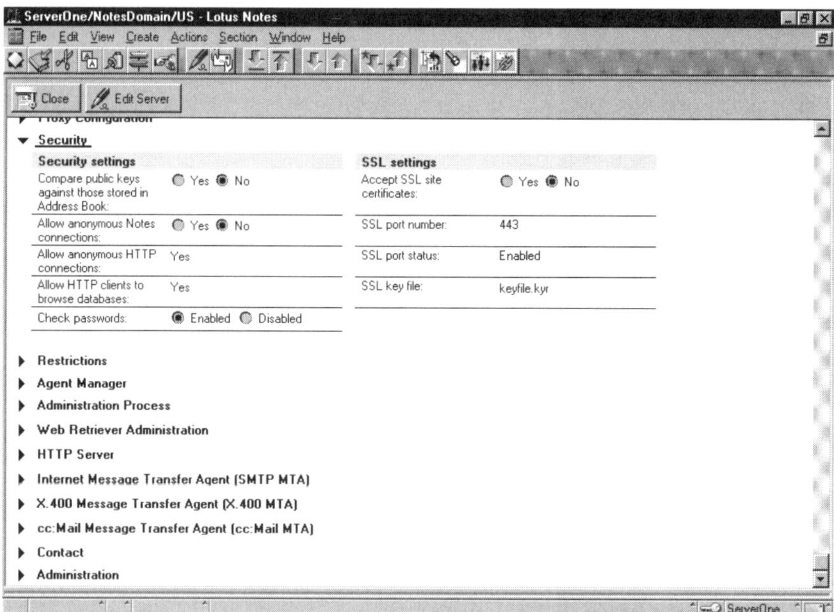

FIGURE 7.3
Three additional fields in the Security section allow an extra level of security for those environments that need it.

- **Compare public keys against those stored in Address Book:** This field allows administrators to add yet another level of safety. When this field is set to Yes the Notes Server will automatically verify that public keys in the server and user ID files are the same as their counterparts in the Public Address Book. This level of double-checking is useful if a user believes there are copies of his or her ID file floating around and that someone is possibly misusing their ID to gain access to servers and information. In this case, a user would create a new public key and send a safe copy of it to the Notes administrator to recertify. After recertification the user merges the returned ID into his or her present ID. Now, older copies of the ID are useless, because with this field set to Yes the Notes server would compare public keys and reject these older keys.

- **Allow anonymous Notes connections:** The default for this field is No and should remain that way unless you plan to use this server as a public access server. Setting this field to Yes allows users and other servers access to this server without having to pass through the validation and authentication process. In other words, users and server need not share a common certificate with this server to access it. If the default database's ACL setting is No Access, you'll also need to add the word "Anonymous" to the database's ACL and grant it the appropriate access to allow anonymous users into this database. Likewise, you can deny anonymous access to a database by adding the word "Anonymous" to the database's ACL and setting the access level to No Access.
- **Check passwords:** By default, this field is set to Disabled, which means that passwords won't be created during the validation authentication process. If enabled, the server will verify during authentication that passwords for the IDs have not expired. And if a Required Change Interval has been specified, users will be prompted to change their password when the change interval approaches.

Forcing Password Changes

The Check Passwords field in the Server Document works in conjunction with a similar field in the Person Document, and both of these settings must be set to Yes to enable password checking. The Person Document also allows administrators to set a Required Change Interval, which specifies how long a password will remain valid, and then the Grace Period, which indicates the length of time (measured in days) that a user has after the required change interval has passed before they will be locked if they haven't changed their password. Both the Required Change Interval and Grace Period fields are optional. Keep in mind that if a user has more than one copy of his or her USER.ID file, they'll need to keep all of their copies in sync whenever a password is changed.

You've probably noticed in Figure 7.3 that there are several other fields that I didn't define with the other three. These fields are specific to the Internet capabilities of Lotus Notes and will be covered in Chapter 12.

Controlling Port Access

The Security and Restrictions section of the Server Document is where you'll control most of the actual server access, but there are still a few oddball settings that can only be made through the NOTES.INI file. Two .INI settings in particular have to do with allowing and denying access to actual network ports:

- **Allow_Access_*portname***: This setting allows you to specify whether a user or server can gain access to this server through this port. Keep in mind that a user or server allowed to access a server through a specified port must still be listed in the Access Server field. Refer to Appendix C for syntax details regarding this .INI setting.
- **Deny_Access_*portname***: This setting allows you to specify which users or servers can't access the server through this port. Even if a user or server is listed in the Access Server field of the Server Document, they still won't be able to gain access through the port specified in this setting.

Why would anyone use these two .INI settings? The answer is simple. Imagine a server that has only one modem attached. If this attached modem is dedicated for server-to-server replication and mail routing, how do you prevent users from using it for dial-in access? Easy. Just add the following line to the NOTES.INI file:

```
Deny_Access_COM1=NotesUsers
```

This setting indicates that all users listed in the NotesUsers group won't be able to access the server through COM port number 1. Now you've preserved your modem connection for just server-to-server activity.

Execution Control List

The Execution Control List, referred to as the ECL, is a list of control settings that determine what can be executed on workstations in your Notes network. The ECL is new to Release 4.5 and can limit the actions of a user's formulas or scripts when run on a workstation other than their own. I've placed the ECL in the next level of the inverted security pyramid in Figure 7.1 because it determines what can be executed in the Notes environment once access to that environment has been granted.

Default settings for each workstation's ECL are determined by the settings that you, as the Notes administrator, impose on your Public Address Book. To view the current ECL settings for the Public Address Book, select the Public Address Book icon from your workspace. Then, from the menu bar, select Actions ➢ Edit Administrations ECL. After you make these selections, the Workstation Security dialog box shown in Figure 7.4 appears.

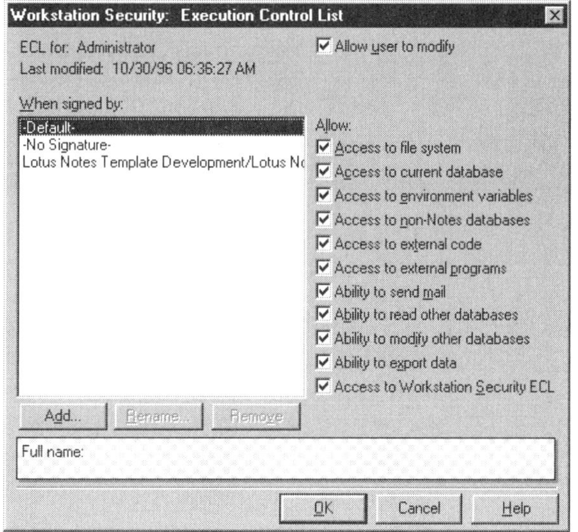

FIGURE 7.4

Set the defaults for the ECL of your Notes network in the Workstation Security dialog box. Note that the Lotus Notes Template signature must be manually added; by default, it is not automatically listed.

Starting in the upper left corner of the dialog box you'll notice some general information about who these settings are for and the last time these settings were modified. Moving down the left side of the dialog box you'll see the When Signed By section. This section lists the signatures for which some type of execution control is imposed. By default, two signatures are already listed (see the *What Are Signatures* sidebar for more information about signatures).

- **Default:** As the name indicates, this is the default for signatures that haven't been previously listed. When you first open the ECL dialog box you'll notice that Default has no restrictions applied. If you have a very secure environment, you may want to impose the following restrictions as suggested by Lotus:

- Access to current database
- Access to environment variables
- Ability to read other databases
- Access to non-Notes databases

- **No Signature:** Once again, as the name indicates, the execution access restrictions applied to No Signature are used for situations when something hasn't been signed. As with Default, No Signature is allowed to do everything. Lotus recommends granting minimal execution access to things with no signature, which are as follows:
  - Access to current database
  - Access to environment variables
  - Ability to read other databases
  - Access to non-Notes databases

There is also a third default signature, but it is one that you have to add to the When Signed By section yourself. This third signature is Lotus Notes Template Development/Lotus Notes. This signature is provided by Lotus as the signature applied to the development templates that come with Notes. Lotus recommends allowing all execution access to this signature. Even if you don't plan to develop any databases based on Lotus templates, make sure you follow this recommendation because the Public Address Book, mail databases, and your Notes Log database are all based on templates. Restricting access to the Lotus template signature could have adverse effects on other areas of your Notes environment.

In the ECL dialog box shown in Figure 7.4, in the upper right corner you'll notice a checkbox called Allow User To Modify. By default, this box is checked; this will allow any user to modify the ECL settings associated with their individual workstation. Depending on the security requirements for your Notes network, you may want to check this box so you, as the Notes administrator, can control the ECL settings throughout your Notes environment.

What Are Signatures?

Signatures in Notes are similar to hand written signatures in that they both uniquely identify a person as being who they say they are. In the real world, people place their signatures on items, such as personal checks, and then someone else visually checks this signature against a signed piece of identification like a driver's license. If the signature appears close enough, then it usually passes. In the Notes environment, placing a signature on something and passing it along for validation is much more involved:

1. Notes starts a signature by generating a 128-bit fingerprint of the data being signed and then encrypts the scrambled fingerprint with the private key of the author of the data.
2. Notes attaches the encrypted fingerprint to the data.
3. Notes takes the signer's public key and certificates and attaches them to the data.
4. When someone accesses the signed data, Notes verifies that the signer has a common certificate or common certificate ancestor with and from a certifier that the reader trusts. If a common certificate exists, Notes attempts to decrypt the signed data using the public key that corresponds to the private key with which the data was signed.
5. If decryption is successful, Notes indicates who signed the message. If decryption is not successful, Notes indicates that it could not verify the signature. If Notes fails to decrypt a signature, chances are the data has been tampered with. The typical reason for a failed decryption is simply that the sender does not have a certificate trusted by the reader, which would be the case if a user receives mail from a user in another company and that user doesn't have a cross-certificate.

As you can see from the signature process, Notes' signatures are closely associated with Notes' encryption scheme. These signatures are like electronic stamps that you can place on mail messages, fields, sections of documents, and now, in Release 4.5, entire databases or Notes applications.

Finally, below the Allow User To Modify checkbox are the eleven categories of execution that you can control:

- **Access to file system:** allows specified user(s) to attach, detach, read to, and write from workstation files.
- **Access to current database:** allows specified user(s) to read and modify the current database.
- **Access to environment variables:** allows specified user(s) to access the NOTES.INI file on a workstation through @Set Environment and @Get Environment variables, and through LotusScript methods.
- **Access to non-Notes databases:** allows specified user(s) Read access to databases through @DBLookup, @DBColumn, and @DBCommand. This setting is only applicable when the first parameter for these three @DB functions specifies a non-Notes database driver.
- **Access to external code:** allows specified user(s) to run LotusScript classes and DLLs unknown to Notes.
- **Access to external programs:** allows specified user(s) to access other applications, including activating any OLE object.
- **Ability to send mail:** allows specified user(s) to use, for example, @MailSend, to send mail.
- **Ability to read other databases:** allows specified user(s) to read information in databases other than the current database.
- **Ability to modify other databases:** allows specified user(s) to modify information in databases other than the current database.
- **Ability to export data:** allows specified user(s) to print, copy to the clipboard, and import and export data on the workstation.
- **Access to Workstation Security ECL:** allows specified user(s) to modify the ECL Certifier name.

Even though Notes has two default signatures listed and a third available to those who develop databases based on Notes templates, Lotus suggests coming up with your own signature scheme. The Lotus Notes Template Development/Lotus Notes signature is a great signature model to follow.

1. Start by creating a new User ID with a name that identifies it as an ID for Notes development (for example, Acme Developers/NotesDomain) and certify it at the top, or near the top, of your organizational hierarchy.

2. Save this User ID to disk during its creation and protect it with at least one password.

3. This new User ID is for your Notes development team to sign the internal Notes databases they create and the external databases that have been tested and deemed safe for your Notes network.

Add this new signature to the ECL of the Public Address Book and grant it all execution access. Figure 7.5 shows what the ECL for the Public Address Book might look like for what has just been described. Notice it provides minimal access to Default and No Signature and all access to the signature used by the Acme Developers. The Lotus Notes Template Development/Lotus Notes signature is also included to make sure that Notes-specific databases such as LOG.NSF and mail databases work properly.

FIGURE 7.5

The ECL for a secure Notes environment

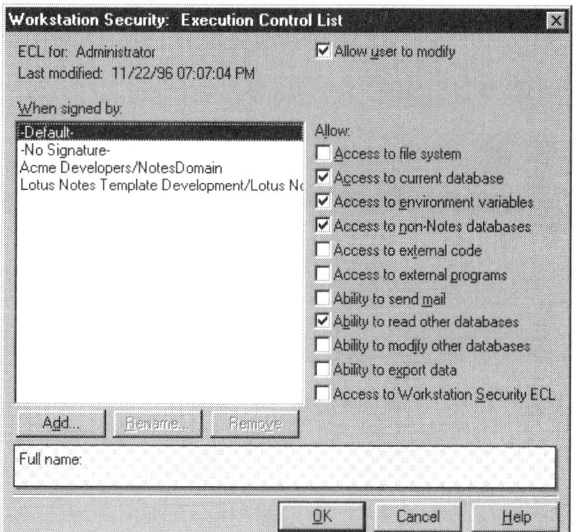

To use this new ID to sign Notes databases that have been created either internally or tested and approved externally, Lotus provides a utility file called SIGNNSF.EXE. Follow the steps listed below to use this utility:

1. If your newly created Notes ID is not your current ID, switch to it by selecting File ➢ Tools ➢ Switch ID from the menu bar and then selecting the correct ID from the dialog box.

2. Open a command prompt window and change to the directory containing the Notes program files (for example, C:\NOTES).

3. To sign a specific database or template, type the following command:

   ```
   SIGNNSF path\filename
   ```

   where *path\filename* refers to the path and filename of the database or template you want to sign. For example, if I wanted to sign a database called Customer Contacts located in my Notes data directory with an actual filename of CUSCONT.NSF, I'd type the following command:

   ```
   SIGNNSF C:\NOTES\DATA\SERVICE.NTF
   ```

   You can also use wild cards to sign all templates or databases in the same directory. For example, to sign all of the databases in my Notes data directory, I'd type the following command:

   ```
   SIGNNSF C:\NOTES\DATA\*.NSF
   ```

Signing a design template can take a considerable amount of time to perform. Therefore, you might want to wait until after hours before executing the SIGNNSF command.

One last important point about the ECL: If you make changes to the Public Address Book ECL but have already set up individual workstations, how do you update the ECL on each of those workstations? You could go around to each machine and manually update each user's ECL. A better way, however, is to send a mail message to all the users that you need to update with a button that executes the following formula:

```
@RefreshEcl (""; "")
```

Include in this memo a brief description of what this button is for.

To ensure that these users both got the message and pressed the button, do the following:

1. Check the return receipt option when you send the message. This option will cause a message to be sent to you once the user has read the message.

2. Add the following @MailSend function to the button formula. This added formula will cause a message to be sent to you automatically once the button is pressed, thus confirming the ECL update was executed.

```
@MailSend("Your Name Here";"";"";ECL Update;""; "ECL
update execution is complete")
```

Refer to the Notes online Help guide for syntax and detailed explanations of @RefreshECL and @MailSend.

Keep track of your return receipts. Once an ECL update message is received for that user, delete both messages. Any outstanding return receipts with no matching ECL update message are indications that you might have to actually visit these users and perform the update yourself.

Access Control List

The next level of the inverted pyramid is the Access Control List, which is more commonly referred to as the ACL. The ACL comes next because it determines which databases individual users can access and exactly what this access allows them to do with the databases. The ACL also controls what information servers can replicate.

Each database has its own ACL. There are seven levels of access control defined as follows:

- **No Access:** This is the lowest level of access because it doesn't allow any access. In security-conscience Notes environments I like to set the default database access level of all databases to No Access. This way, the risk of accidentally granting access is significantly reduced.
- **Depositor:** Users assigned Depositor access can actually create documents but have no means of seeing the documents they create (or any other documents for that matter) in the database views. Why would anyone use this access level? Personally, I have never used it, but I have seen Notes applications that required that people be able to submit a document but not access it after creation. Such is the case for Notes

databases that are designed to collect surveys, customer satisfaction reports, or training evaluations. The idea is that once you have filled out a form and submitted it to this type of database, you shouldn't be able to change it.

- **Reader:** Users assigned Reader access can read documents in the database but cannot create or edit documents. For example, a human resource policy manual would assign Reader access to all users in the organization so they could read the policies in the manual but not edit or add to the manual.

Even though Reader access only allows users to read the contents of a database, they can create personal agents in the database if the database manager selects the Create Personal Agents option in the server's ACL. However, users can only run agents that perform tasks allowed by their access levels.

- **Author:** Servers and users assigned Author access can create documents and edit only the documents they create. Assign Author access to users who need the ability to create and edit their own documents but not the documents of others.
- **Editor:** Servers and users assigned Editor access can create documents and edit all documents in the database, including those created by others. Grant Editor access to anyone or any group that needs the ability to edit all documents in a particular database.
- **Designer:** Designer access can modify all database design elements—fields, forms, views, public agents, the database icon, and the Using This Database and About This Database. Designer access also grants the ability to modify replication formulas, and can create a full-text index. Designers can also perform all tasks allowed by lower access levels. I like to create a group called NotesDev, which is a group I list as designer in all of the Notes databases created internally. Creating a developer group like this one places the responsibility of database design and functionality on someone other than the Notes administrator.
- **Manager:** This is the highest level of access. Manager access can modify ACL settings, encrypt the database, modify replication settings, and delete the database. Managers can also perform all tasks allowed by other access

levels. Notes requires that each database have at least one Manager. I like to create a group called NotesAdmins and set this group to Manager access in all of the Notes databases. By adding and deleting users to and from the NotesAdmins group, I can quickly update Manager access to all of the databases in my Notes environment. I also recommend having at least two people in this group so that if one person is out sick or on vacation someone else has Manager access in case it is required.

These seven levels of control are accessible by selecting a database icon and then, from the menu bar, selecting File ➢ Database ➢ Access Control. The level of Access is in the top right corner of the Access Control List dialog box (see Figure 7.6). Any user that has at least Depositor access to a database can view its ACL settings, but to actually make any changes to the ACL a user must have Manager access.

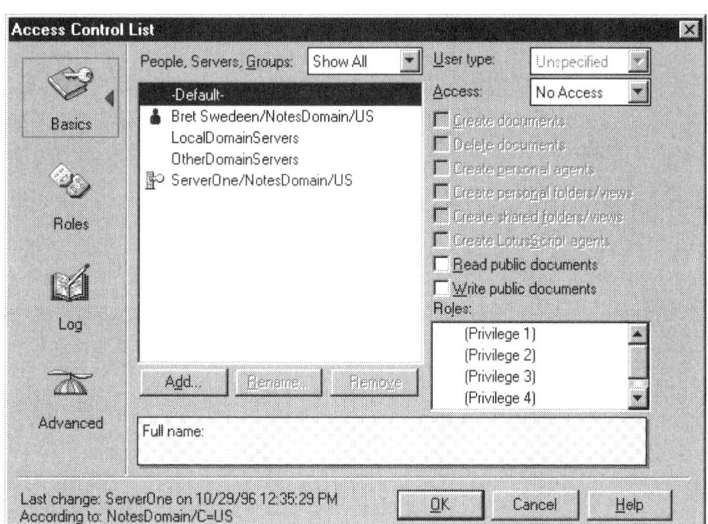

FIGURE 7.6

The Access Control List dialog box for my personal mail database

There is a considerable amount of information in this dialog box, which is divided into four sections identified by the four stacked icons on the left side of the dialog box. Each of these sections is explained in the following sections.

The Access Control List Basics Section

The Access Control List dialog box opens up to the Basics section (see Figure 7.7).

FIGURE 7.7

The Access Control List Basics section

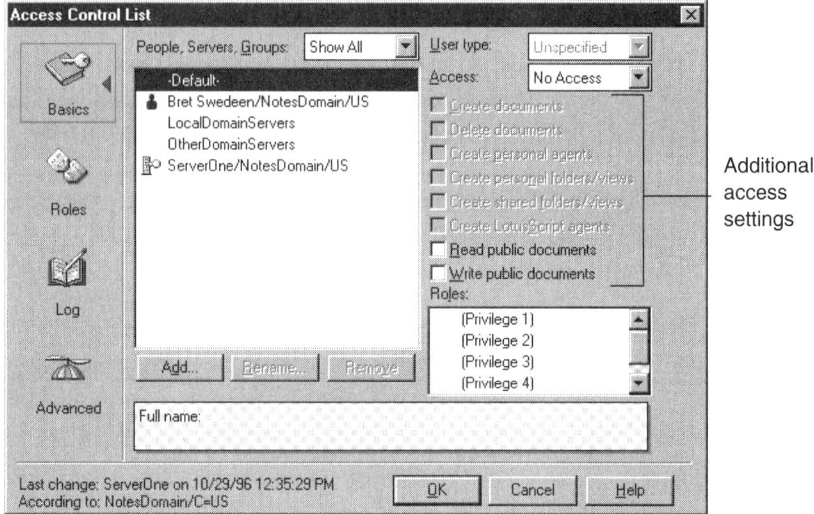

Additional Access Settings

Each of the key elements in the ACL Basics section is described below:

- **People, Servers, Groups:** Allows you to select which access level to view in the display box below. By default, Show All is selected, but you can choose to just display people, servers, or groups with Manager access or any other access level. This feature is very helpful when you want to troubleshoot access problems, because you can quickly identify excessive access as well as no access.
- **Display Box:** Displays who has what level of access.
- **Add, Rename, and Remove Buttons:** Use these buttons to quickly add, rename, or remove a user, server, or group from the display box. A new user, server, or group added will inherit the default access level, but can quickly be changed by highlighting the name just added and then selecting the appropriate level from the Access drop-down list.

- **Full Name:** Displays the full name of the user, server, or group as it is highlighted in the display box.
- **User type:** Each listing in the display box has a corresponding user type. If no type has been assigned, Unspecified is displayed (see the *User Type Explained* sidebar). You can manually change a user type by highlighting a listing in the display box and selecting the appropriate type from the drop-down list.
- **Access:** Here is where you select the desired level of access for whatever user, server, or group is highlighted in the display box.
- **Roles:** Some databases will have defined roles while others will not. Roles are infrequently used because most people find it easier to use groups as a means to define roles. However, if roles are defined for a particular database, they can be assigned to any of the users, servers, or groups found in the display box.
- **Additional Access Settings:** The benefit of the additional settings is that you can give someone an access level such as Author, but prevent them from deleting their documents. The need for these additional settings is usually dictated by the database developer and the overall purpose of the database. The additional settings are self-explanatory, but their availability depends on which access level you selected. Table 7.1 lists all additional settings and when they are selected, deselected, or available for you to decide.

TABLE 7.1 Additional Access Settings

Additional Setting	Automatically selected when the access level is set to...	Automatically deselected when the access level is set to...	Available for selecting or deselecting when the access level is set to...
Create documents	Manager, Designer, Editor, and Depositor	Reader and No Access	Author
Delete documents	Manager, Designer, Editor, and Author	Reader, Depositor, and No Access	Manager, Designer, Editor, and Author
Create personal agents	Manager and Designer	Depositor and No Access	Editor, Author, and Reader

TABLE 7.1 *(cont.)* Additional Access Settings

Additional Setting	Automatically selected when the access level is set to...	Automatically deselected when the access level is set to...	Available for selecting or deselecting when the access level is set to...
Create personal folders/views	Manager and Designer	Depositor and No Access	Editor, Author, and Reader
Create shared folders/views	Manager and Designer	Author, Reader, Depositor, and No Access	Editor
Create LotusScript agents	Manager	Depositor and No Access	Designer, Editor, Author, and Reader
Read public documents	Manager, Designer, Editor, Author, and Reader		No Access, Depositor
Write public documents	Manager, Designer, and Editor		No Access, Author, Reader, and Depositor

When an additional setting is available for selecting or deselecting, what determines whether it is selected or deselected by default will differ from one database to the next.

The Access Control List Roles Section

Database roles traditionally haven't been used that much in Notes development. Most people find it much easier to just define groups and assign different levels of access accordingly. If the security scheme for a Notes database is simple, then using groups works just fine. However, if you have a database that controls access to certain views, forms, sections, and fields then using roles is actually a much easier way to maintain security for the database.

User Type Explained

Assigning a user type to names shown in the Access Control List (ACL) adds additional security. Possible type selections are as follows:

- **Person**: A single user
- **Server**: A single server
- **Mixed group**: Users, servers, and even other groups
- **Person group**: Several users
- **Server group**: Several servers
- **Unspecified**: Unknown

This feature is new to Notes Release 4.*x*. The feature allows you to clearly indicate whether a name is that of a person, server, or group. If a type is set to Person in the ACL it prevents someone from creating a group in the Public Address Book with the same name, adding his or her name to the group, and accessing the database through the group name. Also, if a type is set to Server or Server Group it prevents someone from accessing the database from a Notes workstation using the Server ID.

Keep in mind, however, that setting the name to Server or Server Group is not a foolproof security method. Someone could still create a Notes add-in program that gains access to the database from a workstation through the Server ID, because add-in programs behave like servers.

You can assign a user type on a case-by-case basis or assign a user type to all Unspecified names, except for the Default entry, which is always listed as Unspecified.

The Roles section shown in Figure 7.8 is where you can easily add, rename, and remove roles to and from the database. Normally, the Notes administrator will work closely with the database developer to define roles for the database if that developer chose to use them. See the sidebar *Making Security Maintenance Easier with Roles* for more information about roles.

FIGURE 7.8
The Access Control List Roles section is where roles are added, renamed, and deleted from the database.

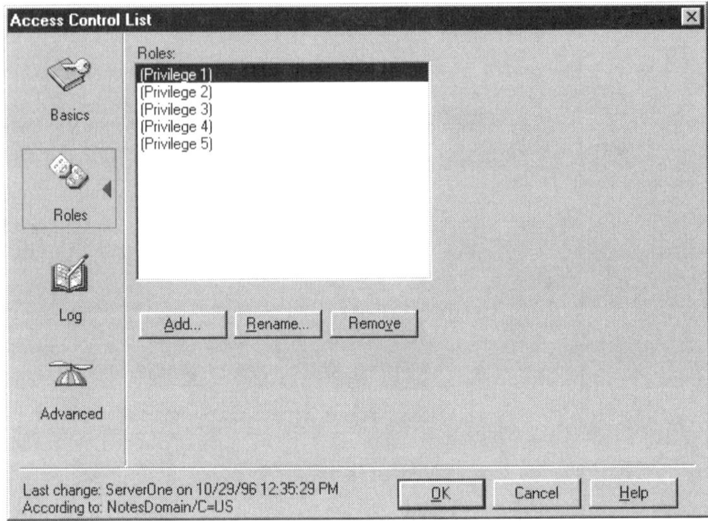

The key elements of the Access Control List Roles section is described below:

- **Roles:** This is the display box where all of the current roles are listed.
- **Add, Rename, and Remove buttons:** Press the Add button to add an additional role to the database or highlight one of the roles listed and press Rename or Remove to perform the indicated action.

The Access Control List Log Section

Click the Log icon in the Access Control List dialog box and a history of ACL changes is displayed (see Figure 7.9). This section is for monitoring changes to the ACL.

If someone can access the database one day and the next day they can't, check the ACL log for changes that may be denying that person access. However, before chasing after ACL changes, verify that the user's connection to the Notes server is actually functional.

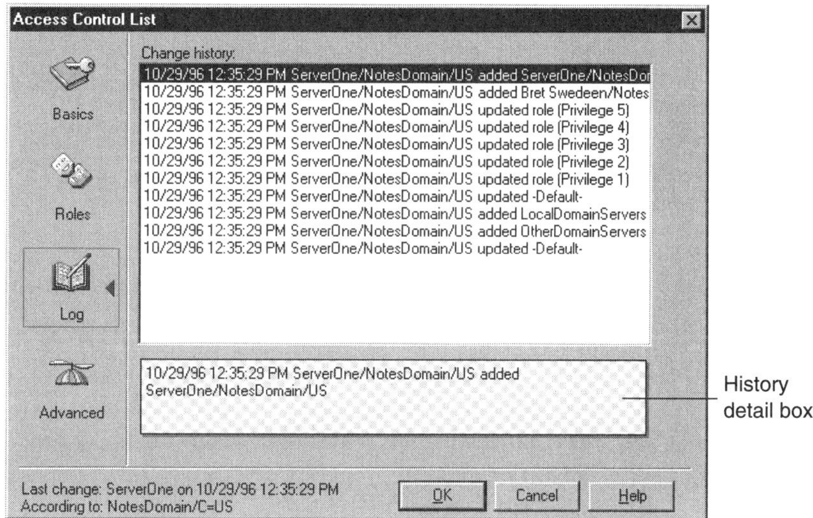

FIGURE 7.9 The Access Control List Log section

The key elements of the Log section of the Access Control List dialog box are described below:

- **Change History:** The chronological listing of changes to the ACL. To actually see how this history is updated try adding a role in the Roles section, click OK, and then open the Access Control List dialog box again and go to the Log section. You should see a new listing in the Change History box that corresponds to the date and time that you added the role.
- **History Detail Box:** Displays whatever history entry is currently highlighted. This box is helpful if a history entry is not completely visible in the Change History box.

The Access Control List Advanced Section

The final section of the Access Control List dialog box is the Advanced section. The title for this section is a bit misleading. The options contained in this section are advanced, but not so advanced that you would want to accept the default settings and forget about them. A more appropriate title might be Enterprise Security Options because most of the options in this section have an impact on the enterprise-wide distribution of the database. Take a closer look at the options displayed in Figure 7.10 and you'll see what I mean.

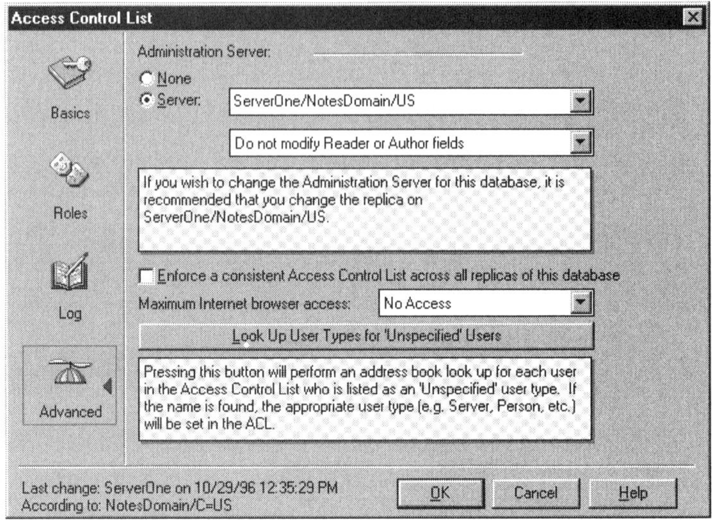

FIGURE 7.10 The Access Control List Advanced section. These settings have an enterprise-wide effect on the database.

The key elements in the Access Control List dialog box's Advanced section are described below:

- **Administration Server:** Located at the top of the dialog box, this option has two possible settings: None and Server (which is an actual administration server). Specifying an administration server helps with the Administration Process, which is a process that runs on a specific server at startup time. With the Administration Process, you can initiate certain administration tasks and the Administration Process will complete them for you. (Details on the Administration Process are available in Chapter 4.) The Administration Server can have a specific impact on a database's ACL when a user, server, or group is deleted. When a deletion request is made, the Administration Process posts a "Delete in Access Control List" request. If you specified an Administration Server in the Advanced section of the Access Control List, that server then has the ability to update the database's ACL and remove the user, server, or group that has been deleted. If no Administration Server is specified, updates to the ACL, such as deletions, have to be done manually.

Making Security Maintenance Easier with Roles

To better illustrate how using Roles can make security maintenance easier, consider the following scenario:

You have a Notes database called Sales Tracking, which helps track and qualify sales leads. The database has three basic forms.

1. **Company Profile:** This document records basic company information such as name, address, and contact person.
2. **New Opportunity:** A company profile must exist before a New Opportunity is created. In this response document, a sales person will record details of a new sales opportunity and track it through its different status phases.
3. **Opportunity Review:** This form is for sales managers to review the success and failures of their sales reps.

There are several views that are part of this database, but they are not important for this security illustration.

The previous form definitions make it clear that there are various levels of access required within this database. Sales reps need Author access to create Company Profiles and New Opportunities. Sales managers need Author access to certain sections within the New Opportunity form to approve or reject demonstration requests. Sales managers also need Author access to create Opportunity Review documents, and Sales reps need to be able to read those reviews without being able to create or edit them. To accomplish this variety of access I'd create a SalesRep group and a SalesManager group as a simple way to manage the required access levels within this database.

The security requirements for this database are easy to understand, but not so easy to maintain if you port this database to a different Notes environment. If this new Notes environment doesn't have a SalesReps or SalesManagers group, you'll have to create them. Creating new groups is simple, but what happens if these groups already exist under a different name? You could still create the required groups and place these existing groups into them. That solution works, but it gets a little messy and can be confusing. A better solution is to use Roles in the database and assign the existing groups to these Roles in the Access Control List dialog box. If your database has a detailed design document that explains its security model, then any Notes administrator or other Notes developer can quickly understand the overall purpose of these different Roles in your database.

Roles are most helpful to Notes developers, but as a Notes administrator you'll need to understand how they work and why someone might use them.

- **Do not modify Reader or Author fields:** This option is a drop-down list box located right below the drop-down list box that you use to specify an Administration Server. This list box offers two options: Do Not Modify Reader or Author Fields, and Modify All Reader and Author Fields. These two options add further functionality to the previously described option. If you specified an Administration Server then that server can update the ACL for the database but nothing else. If you select the option Modify All Reader and Author Fields, then the Administration Server can also update Reader and Author fields when it updates the ACL. For example, if user John Doe was listed explicitly in the ACL for a database and in several Reader and Author fields in documents contained in that database, then these fields would also be updated by the Administration Process.
- **Enforce a consistent Access Control List across all replicas of this database:** This option is a very important security option because it allows a certain amount of centralized control in what can be a very decentralized environment. To use this setting, you must have Manager access to the database. If you have that access and have selected this option, then the ACL will remain the same for all replicas of a database, including those replicas made on workstations or laptops.
- **Maximum Internet browser access:** This option applies to those databases that you plan to make available for Web browsing via Domino. The drop-down list displays all of the access levels previously defined. By default, No Access is selected. Keep in mind, however, that if Domino is not running on this server, and if this database is not replicated to a server that is running Domino, this option doesn't come into play.

- **Look Up User Types for "Unspecified" Users:** This button comes with its own explanation in the box right below it. Pressing this button will check all of the users, servers, and groups listed in the ACL whose User Type is unspecified and attempt to assign the appropriate User Type.

It's important to understand completely the different levels of access you can grant in the ACL (Author, Editor, and so forth) because some of these access levels come into play with Document Compose access and View access. Without a doubt, the ACL is a critical part of Notes' security scheme.

I was once told by someone at Lotus to live and die by the ACL. I'm not sure exactly what he was driving at, but I think it was his way of stressing the importance of the ACL in Notes security. I recommend you live and die by the ACL as well.

Form, View, Folder, Section, and Field-Level Access Control

The next level in the inverted pyramid is access to forms, views, and sections. As a Notes administrator you probably won't have much control over access to forms, views, and sections because the database designer will probably control that capability. Nevertheless, it is important that you understand that access control at this level is possible and how it is done.

Form Access Control

Each form in a database has a certain amount of customizable security that is accessible when the form is in Design mode. To help demonstrate the security options for a form, I opened the Design section of my mail database and double-clicked on the Memo form. Because my mail database inherits its design from a template, Notes warns me that any changes I make to this form may be lost. Click OK to ignore this message if you don't intend to make any changes.

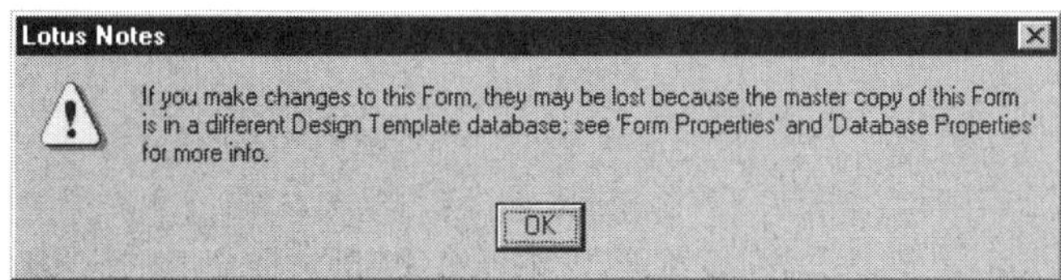

Once the form is open in Design mode you can view its security options by selecting Design ➢ Form Properties from the menu bar. Figure 7.11 shows the Form portion of the Properties dialog box for the Memo form from my mail database.

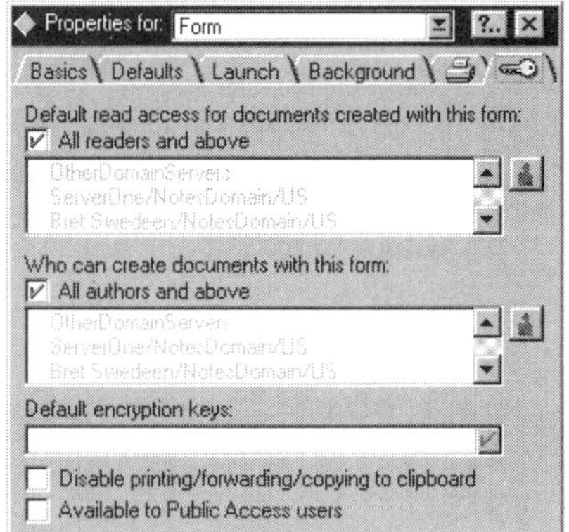

FIGURE 7.11
In the Form portion of the Properties dialog box, you can access form-specific security options on the tab with the key icon.

The Key tab of the Form portion of the Properties dialog box offers the following security options:

- **Default read access for documents created with this form**: By default, there is a check mark next to All Readers and Above. However, you can deselect the default by clicking the check mark once and then specifically listing users, servers, or groups. This option is useful if you have a form that you only want a certain user or group to have Reader access to. For example, if I only wanted the SalesManagers group to have Reader access to the Employee Review form, then I would deselect the default and specifically list that group in the list box below.
- **Who can create documents with this form**: The default setting for this option is All Authors and Above, which means that anyone with Author access to the database can create documents based on this form. As with the previous setting, you can deselect the default and specifically list users, servers, and groups. This option is used frequently by developers. Keep that in mind when you run across a Document Compose problem. It is a good possibility that the developer may have assigned limited access to this form.

- **Default encryption keys:** This option allows designers to assign one or more encryption keys to this form. When a document is created with this form, it will automatically be encrypted using this default encryption key. Only those users who have merged the key into their ID will have the ability to decrypt these documents.
- **Disable printing/forwarding/copying to clipboard:** When this option is selected it prevents documents based on this form from being printed, forwarded using Notes Mail, and copied.
- **Available to Public Access users:** If this database is made available to Public Access, you can determine which forms inside that database will also be available by selecting or deselecting this option.

There are still two more form options that you should be aware of. On the Basics tab of the Form Properties dialog box there are two options that affect the availability of a form. In Figure 7.12, notice the two options listed under the Include In section.

FIGURE 7.12

Under the Include In section there are two options that affect a form's availability.

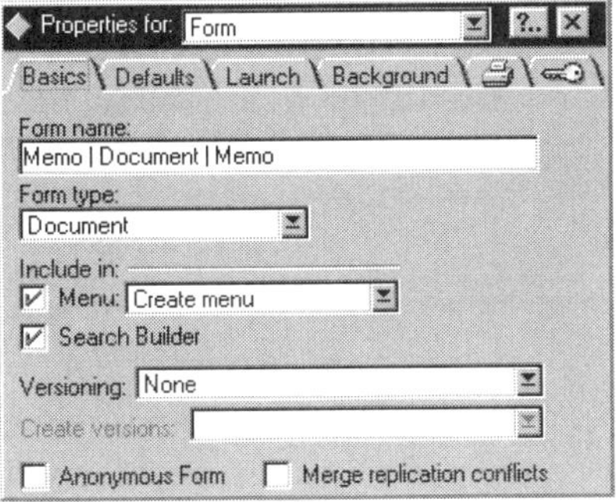

The two options available under the Include In section are:

- **Menu:** If you deselect the check mark placed next to this option, the form is not available in the Create menu. I've used this option in the past when I was trying to force a particular usage flow for a database. I wanted people to have to compose a Final Report before composing a new Resource Request so I removed the check mark from this option in the Form portion of the Properties dialog box for my Resource Request. I then added a button to the Final Report that allowed the creation of a

Resource Request. Users couldn't create a Resource Request without first starting a Final Report. For the most part this solution worked, but there were still some users who created a Final Report only to access the button and then never completed the rest of the Final Report.

- **Search Builder**: You can create complex searches based on a form. If you don't want users doing this then remove the check mark from the box. This is not so much a security feature as a design feature. Nevertheless, it helps to know why a form may not be available to the Search Builder.

Once again, designers will be making most of the form-level security decisions, so you shouldn't have to worry much about why or when to use these security options. You should, however, have a clear understanding of form-level security so that you can troubleshoot access problems and assist developers in implementing complex security requirements for a database.

View Access Control

Controlling access to a specific view isn't done so much for security reasons as for application appearance. Developers may need to create views that are used only for @DBLookUp functions. If users had access to these views, it wouldn't necessarily harm anything; it would just clutter up the View menu or the navigation pane with information that is unnecessary for the user.

If you plan to use view security as an actual security measure, don't. View security is very easy to defeat by anyone who wants to defeat it. If I was denied access to a view but really want to see it, I would copy the database design and create a private view based on what I learn from the design. The only things that could really stop me are if the database design is hidden, if I've been denied Reader access to a form in the ACL, or if the fields I want to see have been encrypted.

Even though view security isn't really a security measure, you still need to be aware of what security can be imposed on a view. As I did with the Form Access Control, I opened my mail database and double-clicked one of the views in the Design section. And as before, I am reminded that this database inherits its design from a template and any changes I make may not stick.

Once the view is open in Design mode you can view its security options by selecting Design ➢ View Properties from the menu bar. Figure 7.13 shows the View portion of the Properties dialog box for the All Documents view from my mail database.

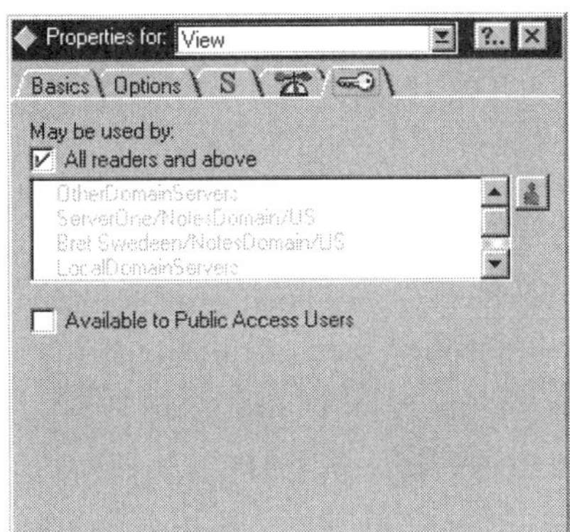

FIGURE 7.13

The View portion of the Properties dialog box is where you can access view-specific security options, which are viewable if you select the tab with the key icon.

You only have two security options to use in the View portion of the Properties dialog box:

- **May be used by**: The default setting here is All Readers and Above. As with the similar Form Security options, you can deselect this default and specifically list users, servers, or groups that should have access to this view. If someone doesn't have access to a view, they will still see it listed but will be unable to use it.
- **Available to Public Access Users**: If the database is going to be made available to Public Access, then you can select this option to make this view useable by the Public. Otherwise, you can just leave it deselected to prevent Public Access users from viewing the information contained in the view.

As you can see, there is not much to choose from when it comes to view-level security because, like I said previously, view-level security isn't very secure.

There is still one last View option that isn't really a security option, but it is a way to prevent users from using a specific view. On the Options tab of the View portion of the Properties dialog box there is an option to Show in View Menu (see Figure 7.14). If this option is selected, the view appears on the View menu. If this option is not selected, the view does not appear on the View menu and is therefore unavailable to the user.

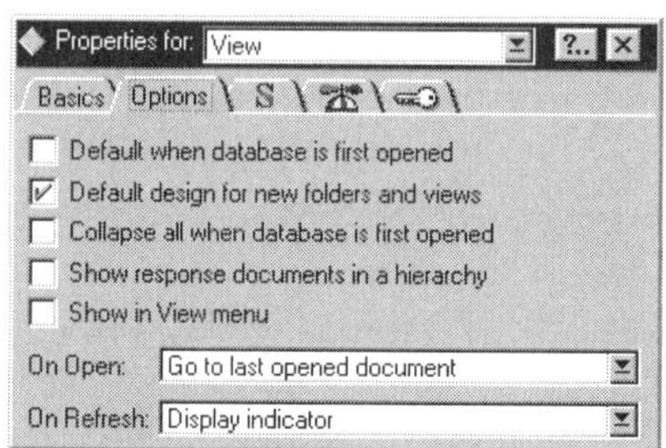

FIGURE 7.14
On the Options tab of the View portion of the Properties dialog box you can determine whether or not a particular view is included in the View menu.

View security, in general, really isn't secure. And as with Form security, most of these decisions will probably be made by the database designer and not the Notes administrator.

Folder Access Control

Folders are very similar in their functionality to views, but resemble forms in their level of access control. As with forms and views, determining folder security is usually done by the developer, but as an administrator you should know what the access options are and where they are.

As I did before with both Form Access Control and View Access Control, I opened my mail database and double-clicked on one of the folders in the Design section to help demonstrate the folder-level access options.

Once I double-click on the ($Alarms) folder I am reminded that this database inherits its design from a template and any changes I make may not stick.

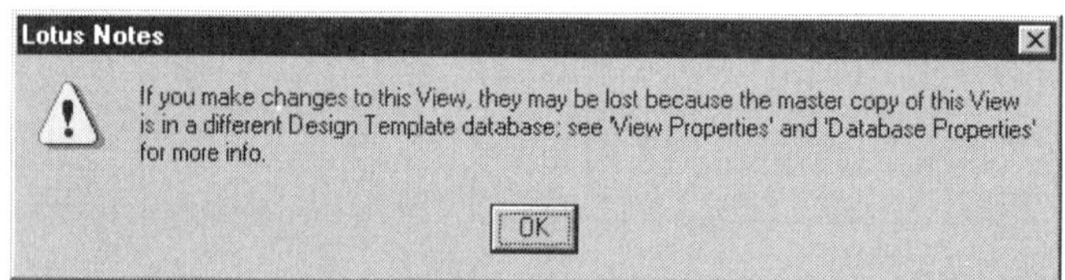

Once the folder is open in Design mode, you can view its security options by selecting Design ➢ Folder Properties from the menu bar. Figure 7.15 shows the Folder portion of the Properties dialog box for the ($Alarms) folder from my mail database.

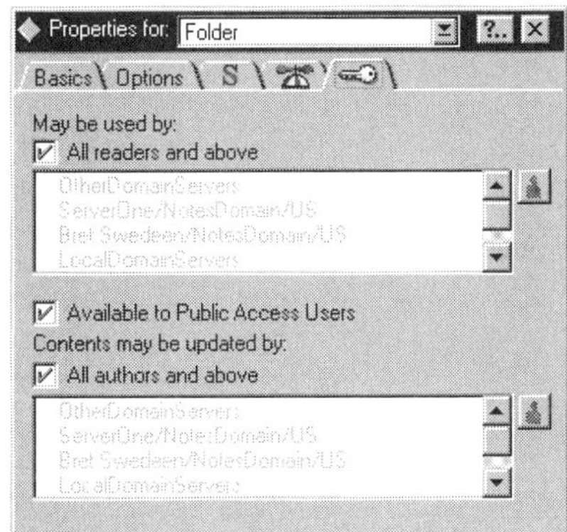

FIGURE 7.15

The Folder portion of the Properties dialog box is where you can access folder-specific security options, which are viewable if you select the tab with the key icon.

In the Folder portion of the Properties dialog box you only have three security options:

- **May be used by**: The default setting here is All Readers and Above. As with the similar view security options, you can deselect the default and specifically list users, servers, or groups that should have Reader access to this folder.
- **Available to Public Access Users**: If the database is going to be made available to Public Access, then you can select this option to make this folder useable by the public. Otherwise, you can deselect it, which prevents Public Access users from viewing the information contained in the folder.
- **Contents may be updated by**: You can either use the default All Authors and Above option when selected, or deselect this option and specifically list those users, servers, or groups that you want to have access to update the contents of this folder.

Along with these three security options you can also decide whether to include the folder in the View menu as you did with view-level access control. Figure 7.16 shows where this option is located.

Also, you can hide a folder by enclosing its title in parenthesis, just as you hide a form by enclosing its title in parenthesis. And don't forget that there were two additional security settings in the Basics section of the Access Control List dialog box: Create Personal Folders/Views and Create Shared Folders/Views. These two additional settings apply to views as well.

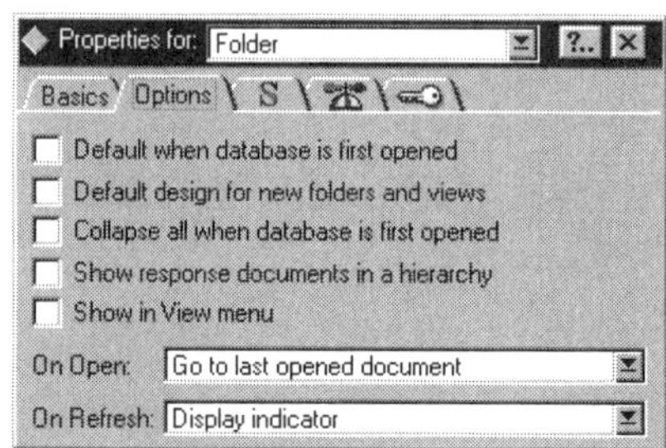

FIGURE 7.16
On the Options tab of the Folder portion of the Properties dialog box, you can determine whether or not a particular folder is included in the View menu.

Section Access Control

If you have Author access to a form, you'd think that you'd have access to the entire form, right? Wrong. Access to actual sections within a form can also be controlled. As with form, view, and folder access control, section access control is something that a database designer will implement. However, as with form, view, and folder access control it is worthwhile to at least understand how section access control works.

Sections break up a form and restrict access to all fields below a section break to those with Editor access. Section access control doesn't affect who can create a document based on a particular form, and it doesn't affect whether someone can or cannot read a section of a document that they may already have Reader access to. Section access control determines who can edit a particular section of a document. This security option is usually implemented in work flow applications that use forms with "approval" sections. For example, if I had a vacation request form, I might include a manager approval section and give the Managers group Editor access to the database. Any user could create a vacation document, but only members of the Managers group could enter the approval section and actually approve the request.

Designers will normally insert sections into forms as needed; however, you might want to play around with a simple database of your own and add some sections to see how it affects the overall use of a form.

Field Access Control

The final and most finite area of access control is at the field level. A designer places each field into a form with three important security options of its own:

- **Signed if mail or saved in a section**: Selecting this option signs this particular field with the author's digital signature explained in the *What Are Signatures?* sidebar earlier in this chapter.

- **Enable encryption for this field:** Select this option and you can encrypt this field with an encryption key that is part of the form properties, or select an encryption key from a field used to store a list of frequently used encryption keys.
- **Must have at least Editor access to use:** Like the option says, users must have at least Editor access to use this field. This option is sort of like making a single-field section.

These access options are available on the Options tab of the Field portion of the Properties dialog box (see Figure 7.17).

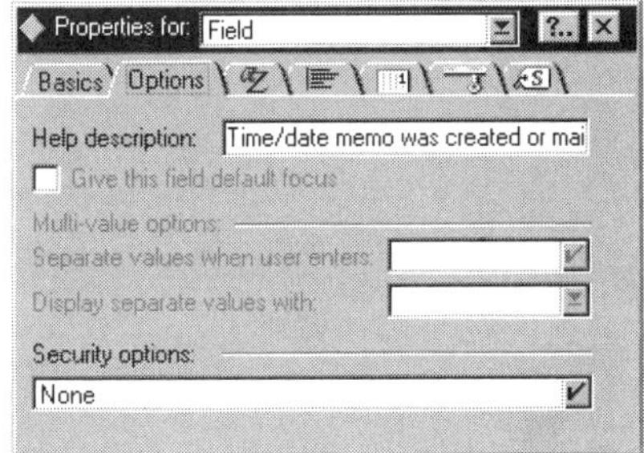

FIGURE 7.17

The Options tab of the Field portion of the Properties dialog box is where you can find additional field-level security options.

I know I sound like a broken record (or should I say a faulty CD?), but field-level access control is the same as forms, views, and folders in that the designer will determine how to implement access control. You shouldn't have to worry too much about this level of access, but since it does have to do with security and Notes administrators often end up doing a little Notes development on the side, you should spend some time with it and understand what you can do with field-level access control. And the best way to spend some time with this level of access control is to make a simple database and experiment with it.

Access Is Like a Filter

The previous sections in this chapter have taken you through the different levels of the inverted security pyramid shown way back in Figure 7.1. For the sake of convenience, here is that diagram again (see Figure 7.18).

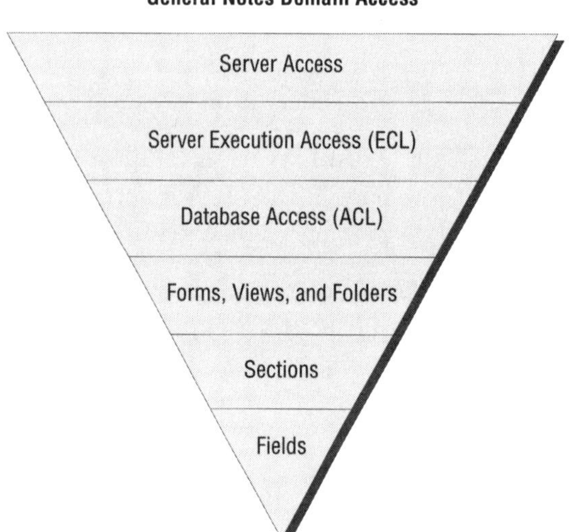

FIGURE 7.18
Server access is the broadest range of access. Once server access is granted, access to individual databases is granted. Inside of those databases, access to forms, views, and folders is then granted or denied. Finally, inside of the forms, access to individual sections and fields is determined.

The reason I used an inverted pyramid to illustrate access control is that the access at each level keeps getting more and more detailed until finally you arrive at the smallest element, which is the field. While the access keeps getting more and more specific, it is also acting as a sort of filter. For example, if you can't pass through the first level and authenticate with the server, you certainly won't be able to access a database on the server even if you've been explicitly listed in the ACL as a Manager. Simply put, you can't gain access at a lower level if you haven't been granted the appropriate access at a higher level.

Quick Security Quiz

Consider the user access matrix shown on the next page and answer the following questions:

1. If the Employee Profile form contains a field for annual salary, and that field is in a section, who can view that field?
2. Who can't view the Company Profile view? Who can?
3. If John wants to view a list of all of the employees and their home phone numbers, which is all contained in the Employee Profile form, can he?
4. Can Jane compose a new Company Profile? Explain.

5. There is a new group called SeniorSalesReps that needs Editor access to the database. Which user can make that change? Why?

	John Doe	Jane Smith	Bret Swedeen
Level 1: Authentication/ Validation	Yes	No	Yes
Level 2: Server Access	Yes	Yes	Yes
Level 3: ECL Settings	NA	NA	NA
Level 4: ACL Setting (default is reader)	Author	Not Listed	Manager
Level 5: Form Access	Access to all	Access to all	Access to all
Level 6: View Access	Company Profile view only displays documents created with the Company Profile form	Access to all	Access to all
Level 7: Folder Access	NA	NA	NA
Level 8: Section Access	Depends on ACL setting	Depends on ACL setting	Depends on ACL setting
Level 9: Field Access	NA	NA	NA

So how did you do? Here are the answers:

1. **If the Employee Profile form contains a field for annual salary, and that field is in a section, who can view that field?** Only Bret can view the contents of that field because Jane can't authenticate with the server and John doesn't have access to a view that contains documents based on the Employee Profile form.

2. **Who can't view the Company Profile view? Who can?** Jane can't view the Company Profile because she can't even authenticate with the server. John and Bret can both use this view.

3. **If John wants to view a list of all of the employees and their home phone numbers, which is all contained in the Employee Profile form, can he?** No, the reason is similar to the answer for question number 1. However, John could copy the design of the database to his local machine and look at the different forms and build his own private view that uses the Employee Profile form. John could also replicate the database to his local machine and promote himself to Manager and have access to everything so long as nothing is encrypted and the option to Enforce a Consistent Access Control List Across All Replicas of This Database was not selected in the Advanced section of the Access Control List dialog box.

4. **Can Jane compose a new Company Profile? Explain.** No. Jane can't even authenticate with the server so she can't pass through to the lower levels of access control even if she has been given explicit Compose access to a particular form.

5. **There is a new group called SeniorSalesReps that needs Editor access to the database. Which user can make that change? Why?** Bret is the only one who can add a new group to the ACL because he has Manager access, which is required to make changes to the ACL.

The ACL and the various levels and ways to control access can get a bit confusing at times, but a complete understanding of it is critical for Notes administrators. If you don't have a firm grasp on the ACL and general access control, you could be in charge of a security nightmare waiting to happen.

Access Roles for the Public Address Book

Aside from the actual machine that your Notes server runs on, the Public Address Book is the most important part of your Notes network. The best way to maintain the integrity of this database is by limiting access to it. Unfortunately, limiting access to the Public Address Book via the ACL can sometimes mean more work for the Notes administrator. For example, if you wanted to designate one person to be responsible for certifying users in a domain, that person would need to be able to create and edit Person documents, which requires at least Editor access. This level of access would also allow that person to create and edit not only Person documents, but also every other document in the Public Address Book as well. Not a very secure way to do things.

In Notes Release 4.*x*, the usage of roles in the ACL of the Public Address Book has added some tremendous flexibility for situations like the one just described. Now, using roles, you can more precisely delegate authority for manipulating documents in the Public Address Book. Roles work in conjunction with access levels and allow you the ability to assign an individual a low access level for most document types, but higher levels of access for other documents.

The solution to the previous example described in the Notes 4 environment would be to assign the user the UserCreator and UserModifier roles to create and edit Person documents. Now, the user can create and edit Person documents as much as they want without having the same access to other documents in the Public Address Book.

To see the available roles in the Public Address Book, click the Public Address Book icon and select File ➢ Database ➢ Access Control from the menu bar. In the Basics section of the Access Control List dialog box you'll see all of the roles listed in the Roles display box. The available options are listed and briefly defined below. You should also know that the Creator role must be assigned at all levels in order for users to create documents, but the Modifier role only applies at the Author level. The reason for this is that users at the Editor, Manager, and Designer level are automatically granted Modifier rights.

- **GroupCreator**: Can create new Group documents
- **GroupModifier**: Can edit or delete existing Group documents
- **NetCreator**: Can create all documents except Person, Group, and Server documents
- **NetModifier**: Can edit or delete all existing documents except Person, Group, and Server documents
- **ServerCreator**: Can create new Server documents
- **ServerModifier**: Can edit existing Server documents
- **UserCreator**: Can create new Person documents
- **UserModifier**: Can edit existing Person documents

Whether you use roles in the Public Address Book to reduce the administrative burden is entirely up to you and depends largely on the organizational structure of your Notes support team or M.I.S. department.

Keep in mind that if you choose to use roles in the Public Address Book, you should also make a document explaining how and why you are using roles and support that document with an organizational chart of your department. This document should help avoid any potential confusion over who is doing what.

Notes Encryption

One of the most powerful security aspects for any system is encryption. In a nutshell, encryption protects data from unauthorized access by scrambling it with a special programming algorithm. This algorithm utilizes a very long number (or numbers) referred to as a key (or keys) to help encrypt the data. In order for someone to decrypt the data and view it, that person needs to have the key that was used to encrypt. (In a two key encryption scheme, one key is used to encrypt and the other key is used to decrypt.)

Notes implements the dual-key RSA (Rivest, Shamir, and Adleman) Cryptosystem to encrypt data. The RSA technology assigns a unique pair of keys to each user:

- **Private key**: This key is part of the USER.ID file.
- **Public key**: This key is stored in the Public Address Book and is publicly available.

These two keys are mathematically related, so data encrypted with one key can be decrypted by the other key. In this implementation of encryption the same key cannot be used to encrypt and decrypt data. Notes, however, does also use a single key encryption scheme based on the RC2 and RC4 algorithms where the same key is used to encrypt and decrypt data. This key is referred to as a "secret" key.

A quick reminder about using encryption. If a user forgets his or her password or loses his or her ID file, then any mail encrypted using their private key is lost forever. If you have a backup copy of the ID file, you can avoid a situation such as this one. Personally, I don't like to keep backup copies of ID files because, in my opinion, it compromises ID-based security. I recommend doing your best to educate the users, and if they don't listen, they'll have to suffer the loss. However, suffering the loss may not be acceptable in your Notes environment. In this case, consider backing up the ID files to a secured network drive, diskette, tape, zip disk, or some other type of securable computer media.

The authentication process described earlier in the *Validation and Authentication* section of this chapter uses encryption technology. Aside from the authentication process, encryption can also be used on mail files, fields, documents, databases, and network ports.

One of the most significant uses of encryption in Notes 4.5 is the option to enable local encryption, which protects a database from unauthorized access even when copied or replicated to a local workstation. On the Basics tab of the Database Properties dialog box is the Encryption button. Press this button and it displays the option to enable local encryption. You can select Simple, Medium, or Strong encryption. The higher the level the more secure the encryption, but it also means that the database access speed also slows down. I recommend at least enabling local encryption on the Public Address Book and setting the level to Medium. This setting protects your most important database while also allowing quick access to it.

Keep in mind that the Medium and Strong encryption settings don't allow the database to be compressed.

Summary

Notes provides a tremendous amount of security for those who need it. The available security is flexible and can be implemented in a way that best suits your Notes network. When deciding how much security to implement, let the nature of what your business does and the role that Notes plays in your business processes drive your decision. I do, however, recommend erring on the side of too much security. The worst thing that can happen is that someone complains that they can't access something and you correct the problem. The alternative is that you leave the system wide open and someone gets into something that they shouldn't have, which you can't readily undo.

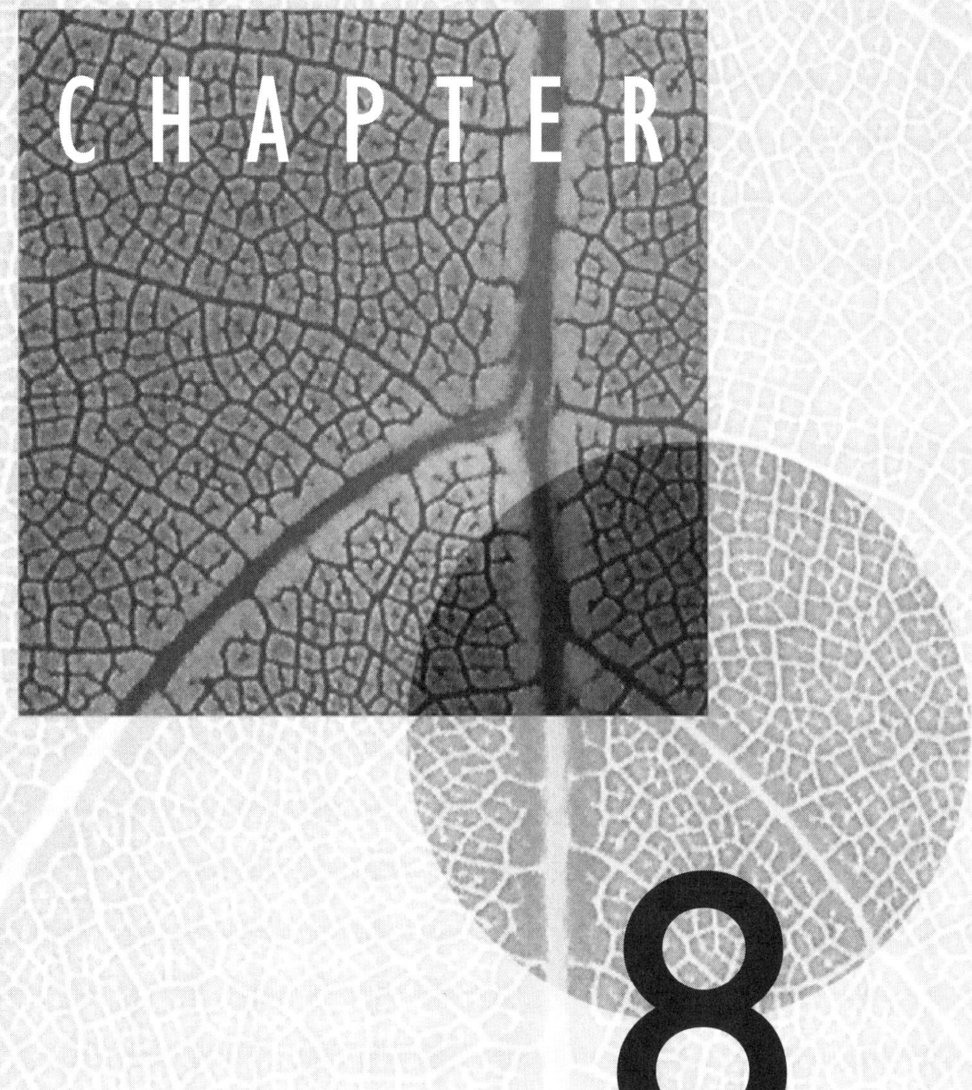

CHAPTER 8

Replication

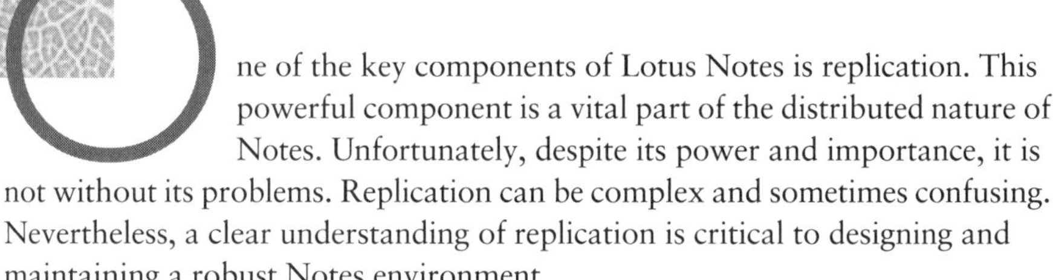

One of the key components of Lotus Notes is replication. This powerful component is a vital part of the distributed nature of Notes. Unfortunately, despite its power and importance, it is not without its problems. Replication can be complex and sometimes confusing. Nevertheless, a clear understanding of replication is critical to designing and maintaining a robust Notes environment.

Replication is the functional component of Lotus Notes that periodically synchronizes databases spread across multiple servers and/or workstations. A replica of a database is an exact or selective copy of another database. Unlike a standard file copy where the source always overwrites the target, replication synchronizes the source and the target so that changes made to either database are reflected in both.

How Replication Works

Replication between servers is handled by the *replica task* that runs on the server. Each time the server starts the replica task also starts (see Figure 8.1) but remains idle either until a scheduled replication event or until it is manually initiated at the server console or the Notes workspace. Once started, the replica task begins the process of replication based on the settings specified in the Server Configuration document and individual replication settings for each database. When the replication process is complete, replica returns to its idle state and waits for the next scheduled event or manual initiation.

```
Lotus Notes Server: ServerOne/NotesDomain/US

Lotus Notes r Server, Build 144.5  (Test Build 2), October 3, 1996
Copyright c 1985-1996, Lotus Development Corporation, All Rights Reserved

11/19/96 06:18:19 AM  Begin scan of databases to be consistency checked
11/19/96 06:18:19 AM  End scan of databases: 17 found
11/19/96 06:18:28 AM  Billing started
11/19/96 06:18:28 AM  Cluster Administration Process started
11/19/96 06:18:31 AM  This system is a NetBIOS name server for port LAN0
11/19/96 06:18:33 AM  Database Replicator started
11/19/96 06:18:39 AM  Mail Router started for domain NOTESDOMAIN
11/19/96 06:18:39 AM  Router: Internet SMTP host pentium in domain
11/19/96 06:18:43 AM  Index update process started
11/19/96 06:18:49 AM  Stats agent shutdown
```

FIGURE 8.1
The replica task is one of several tasks initiated when the server starts.

Replication between Servers

When two servers replicate they have four different ways to do so:

- Pull-Pull
- Pull-Push
- Push Only
- Pull Only

Pull-Pull Replication

In Pull-Pull replication, Server A pulls changes from Server B and Server B pulls changes from Server A. This action can take place simultaneously (see Figure 8.2).

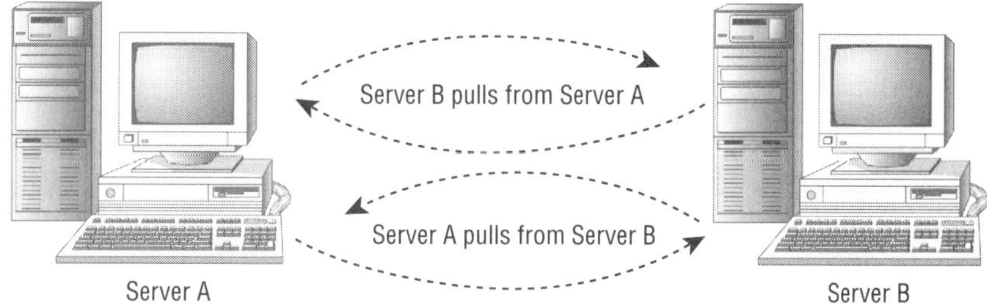

FIGURE 8.2
With Pull-Pull replication, Server A pulls from Server B and Server B pulls from Server A.

- **Benefits:** Under the right hardware and bandwidth conditions, it has the potential to be an extremely fast method of replication.
- **Weaknesses:** It's very CPU intensive on more than one machine at a time.
- **When to use:** It's best used when all servers replicating are configured with high-end hardware (my personal preference is an SMP Pentium machine with 128 MB of RAM) and when fast replication is a requirement.

Pull-Push Replication

In Pull-Push replication, Server A pulls changes from Server B and then Server A pushes its changes onto Server B. Server B is a passive participant (see Figure 8.3).

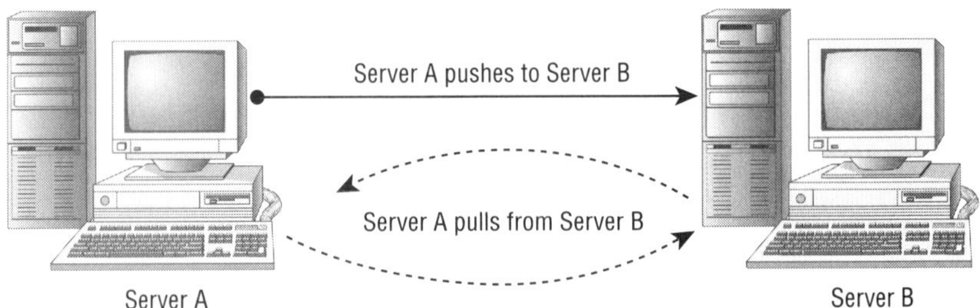

FIGURE 8.3
With Pull-Push replication, Server A pulls from Server B and pushes to Server B.

- **Benefits:** One machine carries the primary load of replication. Only Server A in this situation needs to be configured with high-end hardware, making this replication method more cost effective than the Pull-Pull method.
- **Weaknesses:** In a large Notes environment, Server A would end up dedicated to the task of replicating and provide no direct client services. This lack of direct client service might be compared to a file server that does not serve any files to end-users.
- **When to use:** This type of replication is best in a large Hub and Spoke Notes environment that can afford dedicating one machine to the task of replication.

Push Only Replication

In Push Only replication, Server A pushes changes to Server B. Nothing new or altered is allowed to transfer from Server B back to Server A (see Figure 8.4).

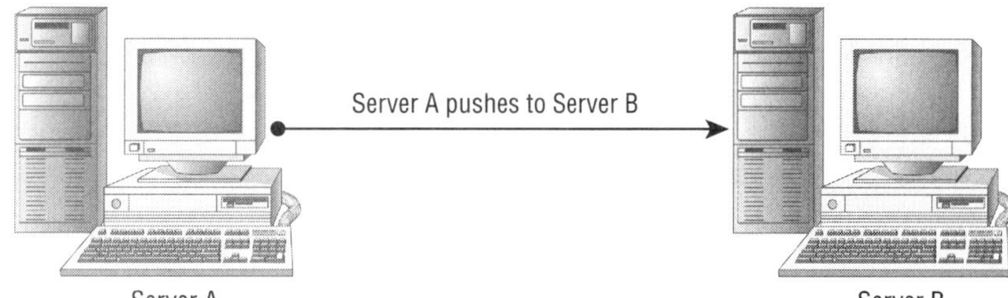

FIGURE 8.4
With Push Only replication, Server A pushes to Server B.

- **Benefits:** It's an ideal way to isolate where changes to particular databases can be made.
- **Weaknesses:** Careful planning of database use and location is required before implementing this type of replication; otherwise, the results can be frustrating to the Notes users because additions or changes made to the database on one server won't get replicated to other servers in the organization.
- **When to use:** I prefer this replication method as a way to control changes to the Public Address Book. One location is responsible for creating users, groups, new servers, and other important documents. These changes and additions are then replicated throughout the organization. This design works well for small to medium-sized Notes environments, but becomes an administrative burden in larger organizations.

Pull Only Replication

In Pull Only replication, Server A pulls changes from Server B. Changes made on Server A are never sent to Server B (see Figure 8.5).

- **Benefits:** This replication is useful for distributing the administration of replication. Each server is responsible for pulling down the latest changes or updates to a particular database.
- **Weaknesses:** Distributing the administration of replication reduces an administrator's ability to evenly distribute the replication load throughout the day.

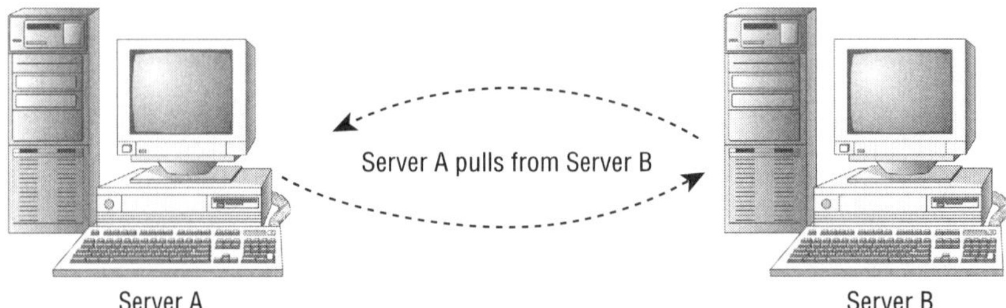

FIGURE 8.5 With Pull Only replication, Server A pulls from Server B.

- **When to use:** If you have an infrequently updated informational database that you want to make available to customers this model will work best. You can give the customer the connection information and let them replicate as they wish.

These four replication methods only work between servers. Workstation-to-server replication does not allow the same range of options.

Replication between a Workstation and a Server

When a workstation replicates with a server the replica task on the server remains idle because all of the work is being performed by the workstation. The end result is the same, but in this situation the server is passive while the workstation does all of the work of pulling and pushing changes. Of course, actual database security still determines what a workstation is allowed to push and pull from the database to the server.

What Gets Replicated?

Initially when you think of replicating databases, you'll probably think of data synchronization. Replication does keep data in sync between databases, but it also keeps all other database items in sync as well. These other items include forms, subforms, views, navigators, agents, the Access Control List, and any fields or properties associated with them.

Let's think of a simple file copy. To reflect changes made in a source file in the target file, you have to completely recopy the file. Simple file copies are an *all or nothing* operation. Imagine that restriction applied to replication. Any time a change is made to even one field in a document, the whole database would have to be recopied to keep the replica copy in sync. Not bad if your database is very small. If your database is large however, a simple file copy becomes an impractical approach to synchronization. Fortunately, replication only needs to exchange items that have been changed since the last replication. Change a field in one document and only the information in that one field is exchanged during replication.

Release 3 of Lotus Notes did not allow field-level replication. If a change was made to a document, the entire document was exchanged during replication. Field-level replication, introduced in Release 4, allows just the data of individual fields to be exchanged instead of the entire document. This level of granularity allows for much quicker replication and also helps reduce replication/save conflicts.

During a typical replication session the following events take place:

1. The replication session begins by one server contacting another server and going through the process of validation and authentication the same way it was described in Chapter 7. Once the connection has been established, the servers compare replica IDs on all the databases and database templates to determine which ones they have in common.

2. Once a commonality has been established for a replication session, the two servers replicate the Public Address Book. This database is the first database replicated because it contains the Server Configuration document and Connection documents that contain settings that may affect the remainder of the replication session.

3. After the Public Address Book has been replicated, the servers move first numerically then alphabetically through either the rest of the databases and database templates they have in common or just the ones specified in the Connection document related to this session.

4. Design changes, database properties, and the Access Control List (ACL)—which is actually a design document—are pulled for each database. The same way changes to the Public Address Book can affect the remainder of the replication session, so too can changes made to an ACL at this point.

5. If changes to the ACL don't stop replication at this point, it then moves ahead and looks at the date and time of the last successful replication.

This date is compared to each document creation date in the source database (the one being pulled from). If the document creation date is after the last successful replication date then the document is pulled to the target database.

6. Next, the document modification date is checked. If the modification date is after the last successful replication date then individual fields in the document are checked. Each field has a sequence number, and each time a field is modified its sequence number is incremented by one. If a sequence number for a field in the source database (the one being pulled from) is greater than the target database, the field contents are pulled into the same field in the target document. If the field has been modified in both databases, the entire document is pulled into the target database and saved as a main document and the other document in the target database is saved as a replication conflict.

Replication and Save Conflicts

Notes does not provide any means of record or file locking the documents contained in its databases. Locking a record or file prevents more than one person from editing the same information at the same time. For example, if I open a database record or file in edit mode, I put a lock on that information while I have it open. When I have finished making changes I save the changes, which releases the lock and allows others to edit the information. Because Notes does not provide a locking feature, it is possible for more than one person at a time to edit the same document. When this happens, a replication or save conflict can occur.

Replication Conflict This type of conflict occurs when two users open and edit the same field in the same document on different servers between replication sessions. During the next replication process, Notes detects an update conflict and selects the document with the most changes as the main document and saves the other as a response document. In the case where both documents have had the same amount of changes applied, Notes selects the document with the most recent modification date as the main document and the other becomes a response document.

Save Conflict This type of conflict occurs for the same reason as a replication conflict except that both users accessed the same server instead of different servers. When Notes detects the conflict, the document saved first is the main document. When the second document is saved, a dialog box appears prompting the user to save the changes and the document becomes a response document with a diamond-shaped symbol. The document author or editor can then go back and review both of these documents and determine which document, or combination of the two, should be saved.

Preventing Replication and Save Conflicts

Field-level replication helps reduce replication save conflicts that users, developers, and administrators experienced with Release 3. Developers can leverage field-level replication features to further reduce replication save conflicts by selecting the Merge Replication Conflicts option in the Form portion of the Properties dialog box (see Figure 8.6). This option forces conflicting documents to be merged into one. The developer can then add code to each field that will programmatically determine which of the two conflicting fields should be saved.

FIGURE 8.6 The Form portion of the Properties dialog box provides a means for forcing replication conflicts to be merged into one document.

Replication and Deleted Documents

The replication process just described talks about replicating new and modified documents. What about deleted documents? If replication is the process of synchronizing databases, then if a document is removed from one database but still exists in another, what stops this document from coming back into the database again?

Deleted documents are really just modified documents. When a document is deleted, a stub known as the *Deletion stub* is left in its place. The stub still has the original document ID. When the databases are replicated the deleted document is recognized as being modified and the modifications are pulled over to the database. In this case, the modification is the Deletion stub. The target database now contains the Deletion stub, and the document associated with that stub disappears from that server's database.

Deletion stubs don't remain in the database forever. These stubs are aged out of the database as determined by the purge interval. This interval defaults to ninety days but can be extended or shortened depending on your environment.

Be careful when changing the purge interval. An interval set to a time that is very short can result in deleted documents reappearing in the database. This interval is the first place to check when you encounter reappearing deleted documents.

Planning for Replication

Now that you understand the fundamentals of replication you're ready to start spreading replica copies of databases throughout your organization...right? Wrong!

Replication can make your Notes environment a rich and robust distributed world of information and communication. Unfortunately, replication also has the ability to drag the performance and usefulness of your Notes environment back into the stone ages. Careful replication topology planning is critical for your Notes environment. Up-front planning can make the difference between success and failure.

Do not neglect careful planning of every aspect of your Notes environment. I've seen too many Notes projects fail because of poor planning.

Determining Which Databases to Replicate

Part of designing a replication topology is determining which databases to replicate. This decision is very simple, and the driving factors that should be considered include which databases are essential for the user community, how heavy the usage of each database is, where databases should be located, and where a replica copy of each database should be kept.

Location

If your Notes environment is dispersed geographically, then you have to replicate databases between servers just to make them accessible to everyone, everywhere. Not all databases, however, are needed by everyone. Determine which ones are needed by everyone and which ones are location- or department-specific and replicate accordingly.

Usage

If a database on a single server is getting heavy usage (determined through database usage statistics), you should replicate it to another server to distribute the load. Setting up statistics reporting is covered in Chapter 4.

Hot Copy

Having a replica copy of a database is like having a hot copy of it. If the database becomes corrupted or is deleted from one server, then you can quickly replicate a new copy and you're back in business. Please note that replica copies are no substitution for tape backups. If all replica copies fail, you'll need some type of offline copy that you can quickly restore.

Essential

Which databases are essential largely depends on your particular Notes network. The simplest way to determine whether a database is essential is if it must be available to everyone in your Notes network. As you determine whether each database is essential, don't forget to consider the Public Address Book, the Database Catalog, and template files. These databases are considered essential because they contain important information that either keeps your Notes network running or helps users use it more effectively.

Replication Topology Options

Once you've determined which databases to replicate, you can start designing a replication topology to support your needs. There are four basic schemes to choose from:

- Hub and Spoke
- End-to-End
- Ring
- Mesh

You can mix and match these schemes as necessary or even create your own. However, I've never seen anyone create a replication topology that wasn't a derivative of at least one of the previously mentioned designs.

All of the different Notes network topologies were covered in Chapter 2. Refer back to that chapter to see figures that visually describe these four options.

Hub and Spoke

Hub and Spoke is the most popular and effective scheme of the four previously mentioned (it also happens to be my personal favorite). The Hub and Spoke scheme uses a central Notes server that schedules and initiates all replication with all other servers (known as spokes) in the organization. The hub server is like the captain of your Notes environment—managing system resources and making sure that each server in the organization is replicated in an orderly way. This model is very sizable and can be as simple as a single hub servicing a couple of spokes or as complex as several hubs in a tiered designed servicing a high number of servers (see Figure 8.7).

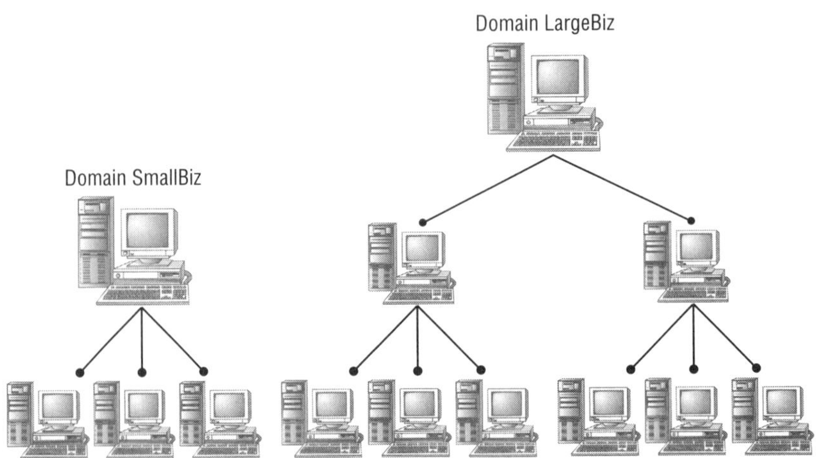

FIGURE 8.7 Domain SmallBiz demonstrates a single hub to many spokes while Domain LargeBiz demonstrates a tiered Hub and Spoke design.

The Hub and Spoke model is also very useful in a heterogeneous network environment. For example, you might have a group of Macintosh computers communicating with AppleTalk, a group of PCs in a NetWare environment using IPX/SPX to communicate, and finally a group of UNIX machines using

TCP/IP. A hub server could handle replication across these dissimilar environments with two network cards installed and three protocols enabled. One card would handle SPX and the other card would handle TCP/IP and AppleTalk.

End-to-End

End-to-End, sometimes known as peer-to-peer, is a topology in which each server in a Notes environment communicates directly with the servers that have databases that it wants. This design works best in small Notes environments or where ad hoc replication doesn't adversely affect performance or administration.

End-to-End replication requires several Server Connection documents which can be calculated with the formula $n * (n - 1) / 2$ where n is the number of servers. If this scheme is used in a large Notes environment, administration can be difficult for two main reasons. First, connections must be carefully planned to avoid overlapping replication schedules. Second, security mistakes are easy to make because there is no "real" standardized ACL requirement.

Avoid using an End-to-End topology unless your Notes environment is small and simple. Be prepared, however, with a plan for migration to a Hub and Spoke model in the event your Notes environment starts to grow larger than originally anticipated.

Ring

With the Ring topology, Server A replicates with Server B, and Server B replicates with Server C, and so on until the final server in the ring, Server x, replicates with Server A. This scheme is useful when simplicity is required and timely updates are not necessary. The down side to a Ring topology is that if one server in the ring fails, subsequent servers are adversely affected. Close replication monitoring is needed to avoid such failures.

Mesh

In the Mesh replication topology, every server replicates with all servers in the organization. This is obviously not the best replication scheme. Often this scheme isn't planned; it just happens because every Notes server has its own administrator, none of whom communicate with each other.

In small Notes networks where future growth is a very unlikely prospect, the Mesh topology is probably useful. Let me emphasize, however, the word *probably*. I'm not a big fan of this replication scheme because from my point of view it implies chaos and poor planning. Even if your Notes environment is small, take the time to implement a replication design with some type of order. You might never know if and when your Notes network might grow. Doing things right from the start makes unplanned future growth much easier to handle.

Planning, Planning, Planning

I hate to kick a dead horse, but let me reiterate the importance of planning one last time.

Selecting a replication topology is not something to take lightly. This decision impacts nearly every aspect of your Notes network. Overall Notes network performance, administration efforts, and hardware requirements are a few areas impacted by your topology selection.

If you're unsure what you should think about when planning your replication topology, start with the following questions:

- What is the current strategy for Notes in my organization, and might that strategy change in the future? If so, how?
- What is the current Notes user base, and is that number expected to grow?
- What is the intended use of the Notes network? E-mail, static information databases, message enabled workflow applications, and so on.
- Are any of the Notes databases expected to be accessible from the Internet?

There may be more questions to ask than the ones above, but these are a good place to start. Each time you answer a question follow it up by asking yourself which replication topology best supports this answer. For example, if the answer to the future strategy of Notes in your organization is to have every one of your company's ten offices across the country sharing information through Notes, then the Hub and Spoke topology is probably the best.

Once again, take the time to plan your replication topology before you start replicating databases all over your network. You could get lucky and find that your ad hoc strategy satisfies the needs of your organization. You may also find, however, that your ad hoc solution is a full time administration nightmare. In that case, is the replication strategy actually working? Remember the old saying, "If it isn't broken, don't fix it?" That may be true, but who determines what constitutes being broken?

Creating New Replica Copies

This book assumes that you have some experience with Lotus Notes and hopefully with Notes administration. Even with that assumption, parts of this book focus on what some readers might consider beginner topics. This section might be considered one such section. Therefore, if you have a clear understanding on how to create replica copies in Notes Release 4, skip ahead to the next section.

The following steps describe the simple process of creating a replica copy of a database.

1. Start by adding a database icon from a Notes server to your workspace (any database will do, but preferably something small). I used the Release Notes database for this example.

2. Select the database icon by clicking it once with the left mouse button.

3. From the menu bar, select File ➢ Replication ➢ New Replica.

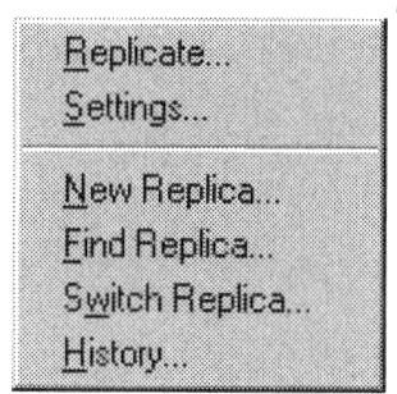

4. Change the name listed in the Filename field (this will help illustrate an important point later).

5. Select OK and an iconless database appears in the current workspace with a message in the status bar indicating that initialization will occur during the next replication (see Figure 8.8).

6. Select the new iconless database if it isn't already selected.

7. Select File ➢ Replication ➢ Replicate to initialize the replica copy.

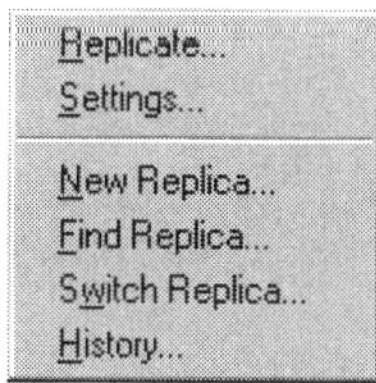

8. A replicate dialog box appears offering two additional options: Replicate Via Background Replicator and Replicate with Options.

9. Accept the default setting and click OK.

10. Switch to the Replicator tab and watch the replication progress (see Figure 8.9).

FIGURE 8.8

The database without an icon (ServerOne names.nsf on Local) is selected and the status bar message indicates when initialization will occur.

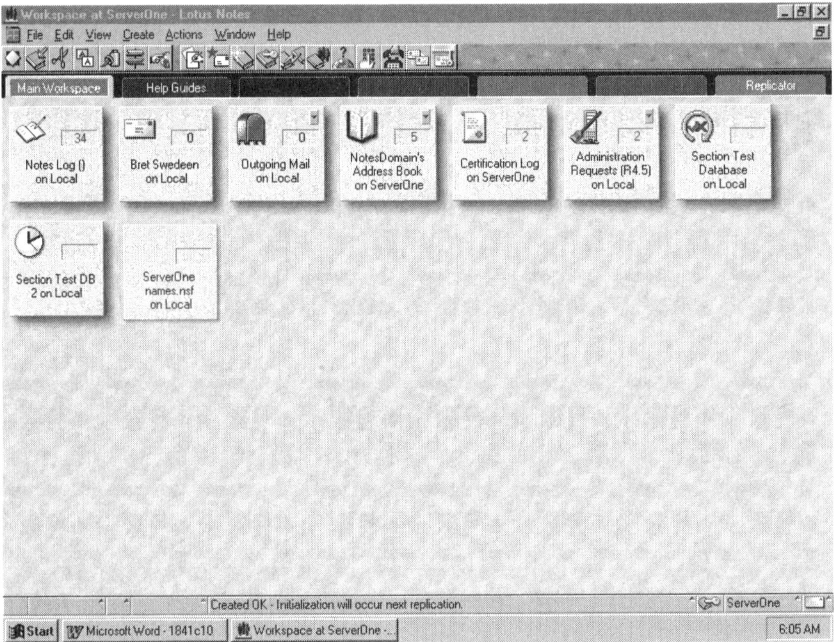

Which database you selected to replicate and your ACL setting for that database will determine your success or failure. If replication was successful, you should see a new database icon on the workspace from which you initiated the replication. If you don't see a new icon, select View from the menu bar and see if there is a check mark next to Stack Replica Icons. If there is a check mark, select this option to remove the check mark. When the workspace is displayed now, it will show the original source icon and the new replica icon.

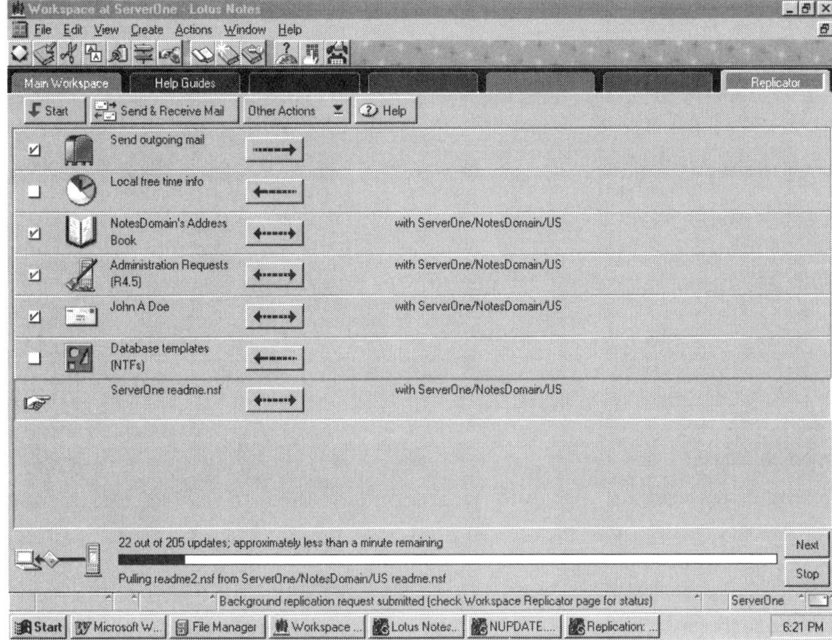

FIGURE 8.9

The Replicator tab. The items displayed may differ from one Notes environment to the next.

Replica Copies versus Regular Copies

Now that you have a new database replica on your workspace, this is a great time to learn how Notes distinguishes between a replica copy and a regular copy.

A key identifier for Notes when performing replication is the replica ID. Select the source database of the database you just replicated and choose Edit ➢ Properties from the menu bar. In the Properties dialog box select the Information tab (the one with the letter "i" inside a circle) and take note of the replica ID (see Figure 8.10).

Close the Properties dialog box and select the replica database; open the Properties dialog box the same way you did for the source database (see Figure 8.11).

Notice that the replica ID is identical to the source database. Even though you changed the filename before replicating, the replica IDs are the same. You can even change the database title for either the source or the replica and the replica IDs will remain the same. Even if you create a selective replica copy of another database, the IDs will always be the same because this is what Notes uses to locate commonality among databases when replicating.

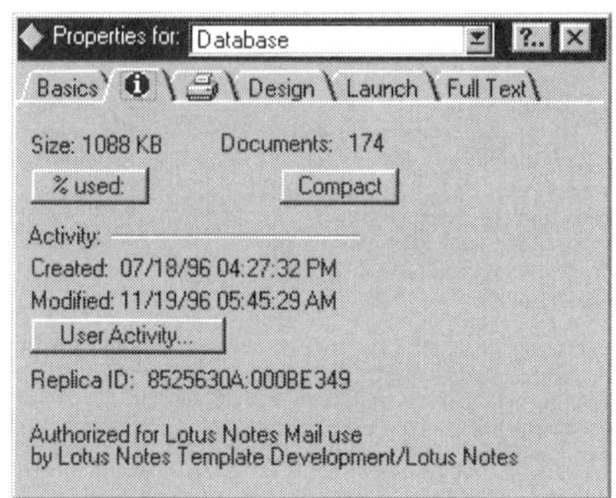

FIGURE 8.10 The Information tab of the Database portion of the Properties dialog box for the source database

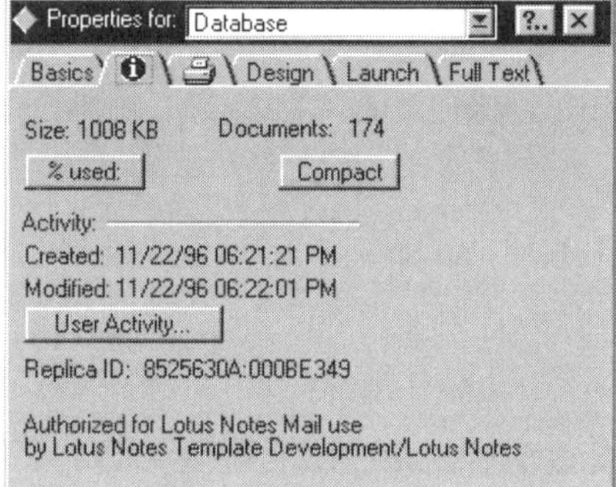

FIGURE 8.11 The database properties for the target database. Notice that the Replica ID is the same as the ID for the source database.

If you have several databases on your workspace and need to quickly locate ones with local replica copies, from the menu bar, select View ➢ Stack Replica Icons. Stacked icons are databases with local replica copies. This is also a typical way to troubleshoot some replication problems. If more than two icons appear on a stack, you have more than one replica copy, which could be causing some problems–or at least some confusion.

Now let's create a normal database copy and compare replica IDs. Start by selecting the source database previously used to create a new replica. From the menu bar, select File ➢ Database ➢ New Copy and then press OK in the Copy Database dialog box. After the copy process is complete, check the replica ID in the Database portion of the Properties dialog box the same way you did in the previous example and notice how the replica ID is different from its source (see Figure 8.12).

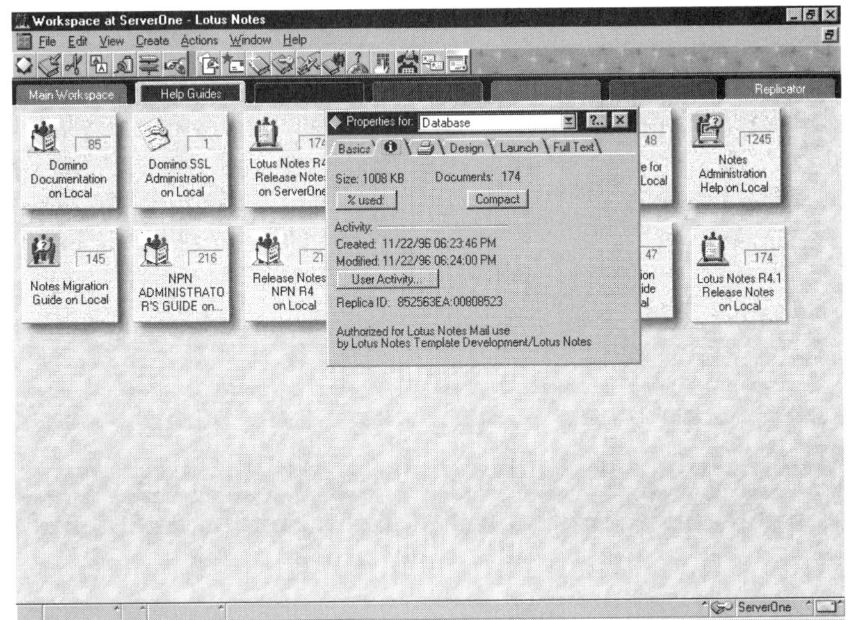

FIGURE 8.12 The database properties for a normal database copy. Notice that the replica ID differs from the replica ID for the source.

Initiating Replication

Creating a database replica is a very easy process, as you have just seen. Once the replica is created, however, keeping it in sync with its source does not occur automatically. In the previous example we had to manually initiate replication. This type of manual intervention can be very time consuming in a large Notes environment, not to mention a bothersome administrative duty. Thankfully, Notes provides a way to automate the process of replication through the creation of a Server Connection document.

Scheduled Replication with the Server Connection Document

For the Notes administrator, the Server Connection document is the key component for controlling when replication occurs (see Figure 8.13).

The Basics portion of the document includes the following fields:

- **Connection type:** Choose a connection method. Available options are Local Area Network, Dial-up Modem, Passthru Server, Remote LAN Service, X.25, SMTP, X.400, cc:Mail, and SNA.
- **Source server:** Name of the server that the connection is initiated from.
- **Source domain:** Name of the domain for the source server.

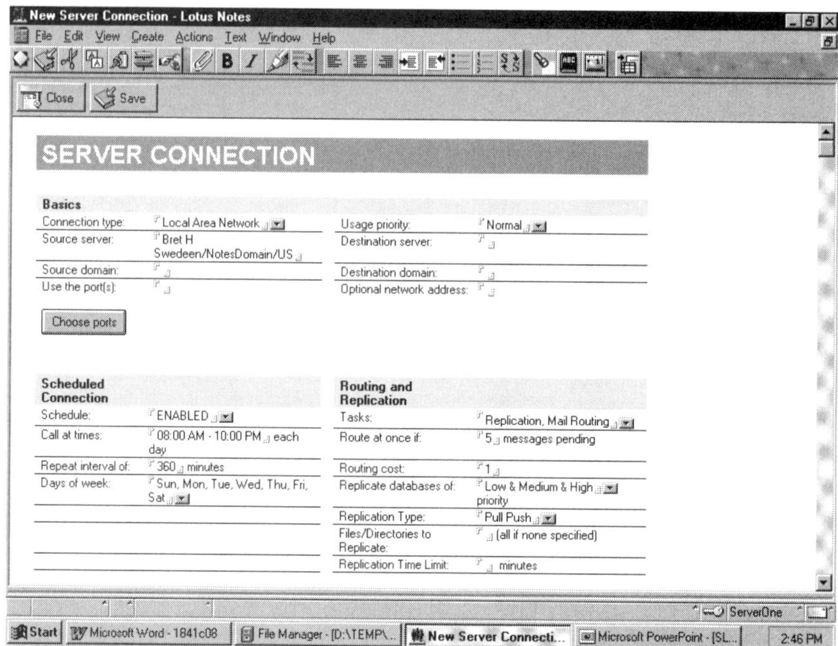

FIGURE 8.13 A blank Server Connection document with the default values filled in

- **Use the port(s):** Name of port to use for this connection. Useful if you connect to other servers using more than one port, such as COM1 for a Dial-up Modem connection or LAN0 for a Local Area Network connection.
- **Usage priority:** Supports settings Normal and Low. When set to Normal it forces Notes to use the port specified in the Connection document. If this field is set to Low, Notes looks at the Connection document as a means to identify which port to use. Using this option is only helpful if your Notes server has more than one port enabled in the same Notes named network.
- **Destination server:** Name of the server that the source server is going to contact.
- **Destination domain:** Name of the domain for the destination server.
- **Optional network address:** Typically where you enter complete numeric addresses such as an IP address.

The Scheduled Connection section of the document includes the following fields:

- **Schedule:** Choose whether to Enable or Disable replication. Selecting Enable without editing any of the other fields in the Scheduled Connection or Routing and Replication section of the document will simply cause the document defaults to become active. Selecting Disabled has the opposite effect. Disabling a Server Connection document is useful when a network connection is down or you're having some replication problems and you need to narrow the possible causes in order to resolve the problem.
- **Call at times:** Specify how often you want this connection to occur:
    - You can enter a specific time. For example, you could select 2:00 AM as a connection time. If the connection is unsuccessful, the server will keep trying over the course of the next hour. Each connection attempt will be at random, with each attempt waiting progressively longer than the last. Regardless of whether the connection was successful, once the one hour retry period is up the connection attempts stop. A connection will not be attempted again until the next scheduled connection time.
    - You can enter multiple times. For example, if you need to keep servers across an organization current with minimal disruption to Notes users, you might enter 7:30 AM, 12:00 PM, and 7:00 PM. This schedule causes replication to occur once in the morning (before most users are using the system), once in the afternoon (when most users are at lunch), and once in the evening (when most users have gone home). Failed connections are handled the same way as they were for a specific time connection.
    - You can enter a range of time. For example, if you need frequent replication and don't want to enter each time individually, you can enter a range and specify a repeat interval. The repeat interval field specifies how long a server will wait after its first successful replication before replicating again. Imagine a range of time from 8:00 AM to 5:00 PM with a repeat interval of 120 minutes. The first connection for the day is attempted at 8:00 AM. If successful, replication occurs. Once replication is complete, the server will wait 120 minutes before attempting to replicate again. This process will continue throughout the day until 5:00 PM when the range of time is complete. If at any point during

the range of time a connection is unsuccessful, the server will keep trying to connect in much the same way as a single time connection. The difference is that the server will not stop attempting after one hour but will keep trying until connection/replication is successful or the range of time has ended. If you enter a range of time and do not enter a repeat interval, then once connection/replication is successful the server will not connect again until the next day during the same range of time. This is much the same as a single time connection except that if a server is unsuccessful at connecting it will keep trying to connect while the range of time is valid. Once it is successful, it is done until the next scheduled connection, which in this case is between 8:00 AM and 5:00 PM of the next day.

- **Repeat interval of:** The amount of time in minutes the server should wait before replicating again after the last successful replication. If the interval is set to sixty minutes and the replication started at 7:30 AM and ended at 7:43 AM, the next replication event will start at 8:43 AM.
- **Days of week:** Specify which days of the week this schedule applies to. Enter the first three letters of each day and separate them with a comma.

The Routing and Replication section of the document includes the following fields that deal with mail:

- **Tasks:** Select one or more than one of the listed tasks (Mail Routing, Replication, X.400 Mail Routing, SMTP Routing, or cc:Mail Routing) that are handled by this Server Connection document.
- **Replicate databases of:** Priority levels of High, Medium, and Low can be assigned to each database. You can leverage this setting by specifying a certain priority level associated with this Server Connection document. Select High and only databases with a priority level of high will be replicated with this Server Connection document. You can create a separate Server Connection document for each priority level.
- **Replication Type:** Here is where you can specify a replication method of Pull-Pull, Pull-Push, Pull Only, or Push Only.
- **Files/Directories to Replicate:** A new feature to Release 4, this field allows you to specify by filename exactly which files to replicate. The replication will occur in the order that the databases are entered in this field. If this field is left blank, then all databases are replicated unless, of course, you specified a priority level for this Server Connection document.

- **Replication Time Limit:** Another new feature to Release 4. This field allows you to specify a maximum time limit for replication. Once the time limit is reached, replication stops. If you choose to set a replication time limit, make sure you know what you're doing and why you're doing it. Don't use a feature just because it is there.

Once the Server Connection document is complete, replication will start to take place as specified in the document and will continue to do so until the document is changed or removed.

Manually Initiating Replication

If updates to a particular database are needed before the next scheduled replication event, you can always manually start replication.

If you have physical access to the Notes server and no other security restrictions stand in your way, you can manually start replication by entering one of three replication commands, the name of the server you want to replicate with, and an optional filename. Table 8.1 shows an example of each possibility.

TABLE 8.1 Replication Commands for the Server Console

Server Console Command	Description
Replicate ServerOne/NotesDomain	Causes a Pull-Pull replication session with ServerOne of every database replica
Pull ServerOne/NotesDomain names.nsf	Causes a Pull-Only replication of names.nsf, the Public Address Book from ServerOne
Push ServerOne/NotesDomain names.nsf	Causes a Push-Only replication of names.nsf, the Public Address Book from the current server, to ServerOne

Notice that a Pull-Push replication method is not supported as a console command line option.

Keep in mind when replicating from the server console that wild card characters on the command line are supported when used in filenames and all ACL restrictions still apply.

If you don't have direct access to the server console, you can still execute the previous commands through the use of the Remote Server Console. The following instructions explain how this is done:

1. From the Notes workspace, select from the menu bar File ➤ Tools ➤ Server Administration. The Administration Control Panel appears (see Figure 8.14).
2. Click the Console icon and the Remote Server Console appears (see Figure 8.15).
3. Select the name of the server from which you want to issue the command.
4. Enter one of the previously described server console replication commands shown in Table 8.1 above.
5. Click the Send button and the command will be executed (provided you have the right level of access).

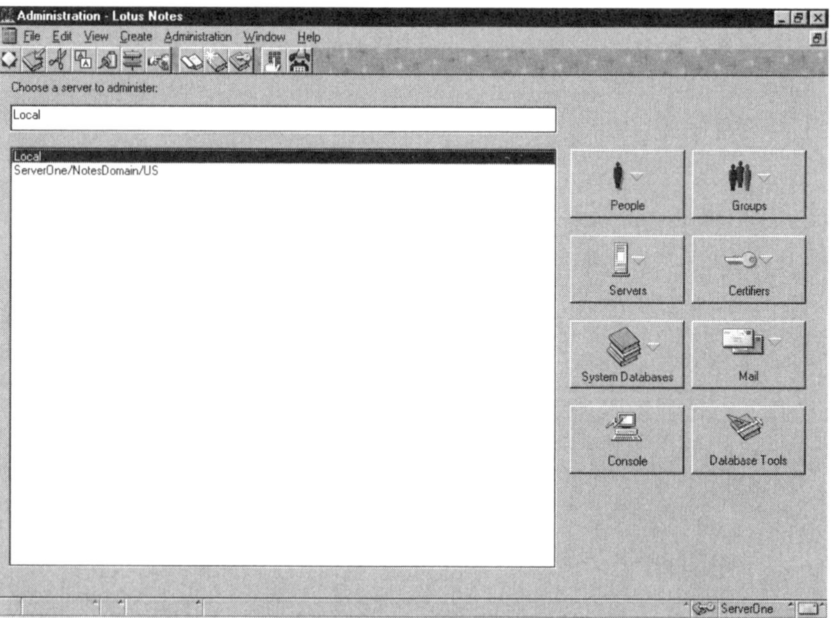

FIGURE 8.14

The Administration control panel offers eight areas of control over any of the servers listed.

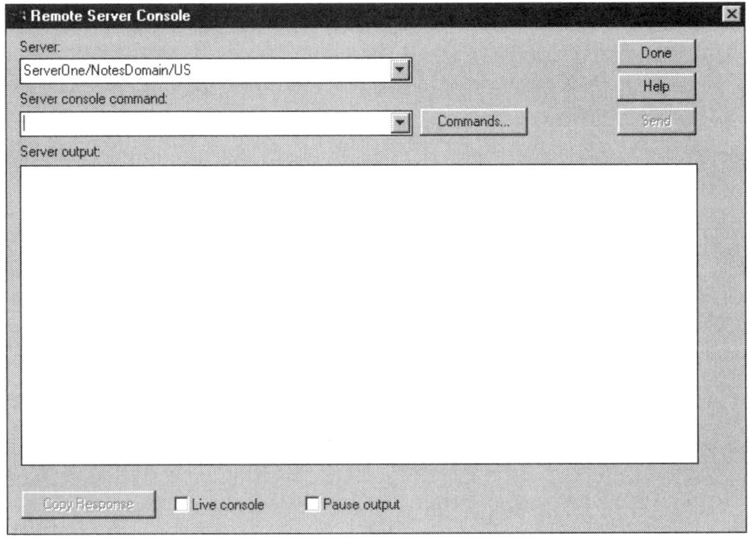

FIGURE 8.15
Server console commands can be executed through the Remote Server Console.

Initiating Workstation-to-Server Replication

Replication between a workstation and server may not be part of a Notes administrator's daily responsibilities, but it is part of user support. Whether you like it or not, Notes users will come to you (if they haven't already) seeking your wisdom and guidance on the elusive subject of workstation-to-server replication.

Initiating replication from a workstation is quite similar to the way replication is done between servers. You can manually force it to occur by selecting the Replica icon on the Notes workspace and then in the menu bar choosing File ➢ Replication ➢ Replicate.

Users can also create replication schedules similar to the way they are created between servers. Scheduled workstation initiated replication relies on two components: a Location document (found in the user's Personal Address Book) and the Replicator tab, which is the last tabbed workspace page on the user's Notes desktop.

The Location Document The Location document is similar to the Server Connection document except that there are no options for selecting which databases get replicated. The Replication section of the Location document allows you to do the following:

- Enable or disable the Schedule.

- Specify the time to call the server for replication or to replicate daily between a range of time.
- Determine if you want to repeat every so many minutes, accept the default of 60, or set it to 0 to only call once.
- Specify which days of the week you want this schedule executed on.

The first time a user creates a Location document they don't have to do much more than enable the replication schedule. This document is easily accessible from the Replicator workspace when further customization is required.

Once the schedule is enabled on the Location document, move to the Replicator workspace to specify which databases to include in this schedule.

The Replicator Workspace The Replicator workspace (see Figure 8.16) is where the user decides which databases to include in the replication schedule and customizes either individual or all replication sessions. Take some time to walk users through this workspace or provide a "how to" document.

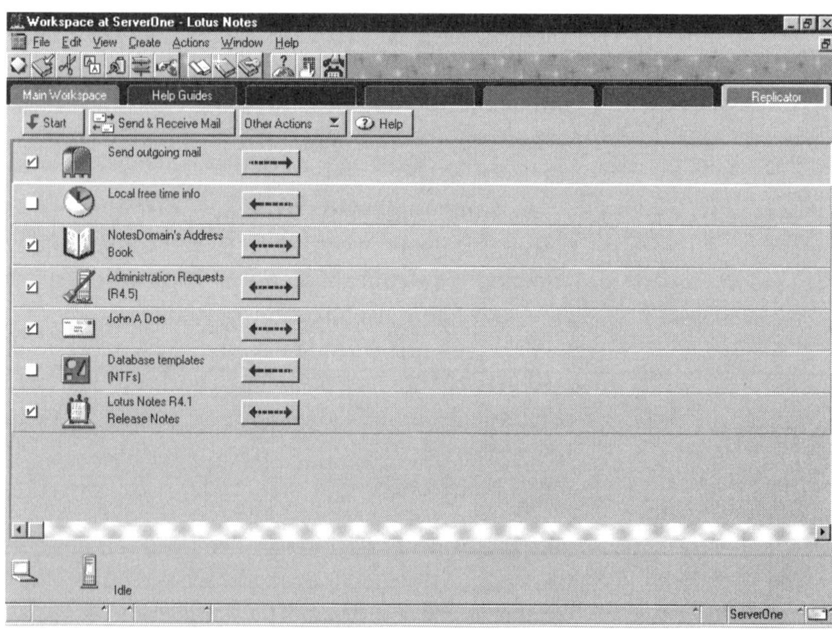

FIGURE 8.16

The Replicator workspace is where users specify which databases to include in their workstation-based replication.

Moving from top to bottom, the Replicator workspace (shown in Figure 8.16) has an Action bar that contains the following buttons:

- **Start:** Initiates replication for the databases and options set on this workspace.
- **Send & Receive Mail:** A welcomed improvement over Release 3. Now, with the click of a button, users can quickly route mail held in their outgoing mailbox to the server and retrieve any new mail from the in box in their server-based mail database. This entire process is done without having to initiate replication.
- **Other Actions:** Lets you perform the following specific replication tasks:
    - **Replicate High Priority Databases:** Similar to the parameter on the Server Connection document where you can specify which priority databases to associate with the schedule. In this case, however, you only get to specify high priority databases.
    - **Replicate with Server:** Allows you to specify which server to use for replication.
    - **Replicate Selected Databases:** Allows you to replicate only those databases you've selected on this workspace.
    - **Send Outgoing Mail:** Allows you to just send and not receive mail. Useful when you know there is no mail waiting or when you don't have time to retrieve your mail but have important messages to send.
    - **Help:** Activates Notes help.

Next on the workspace you'll notice several rows. Each of these rows contains a checkbox, an icon, descriptive text, a button, and (on some rows) more text reporting on the status of the last replication.

- The checkbox allows you to select or deselect a particular database to include in this replication.
- The icon is just a visual description and has no functional purpose.
- The descriptive text complements the icon.
- The button allows further replication customization. Click the button next to the clock icon and the Location document appears. Click the button for other databases and a dialog box appears offering more replication options (see Figure 8.17).

FIGURE 8.17

Detailed replication settings

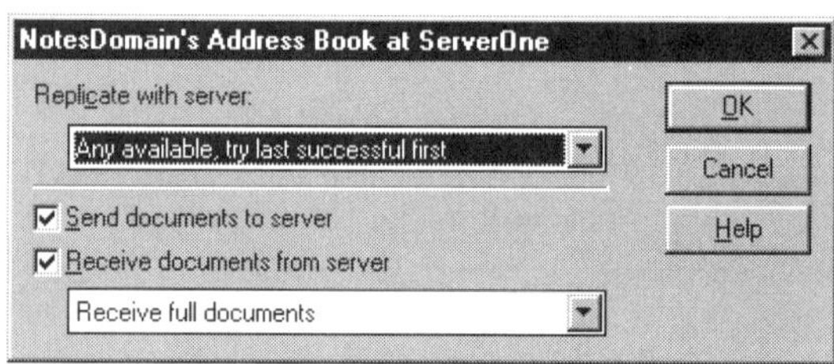

This dialog box allows the user to specify which server to replicate with. Options provided are as follows: Any Available, Try Last Successful First; Any Available, Try <*Server Name*> First, <*Server Name*>.

The user can select whether they want to Send Documents To The Server or Receive Documents From The Server. Users can also determine at the bottom of the dialog box if they want to Receive Full Documents, Receive Summary and 40 KB of Rich Text, or Receive Summary Only. These options are extremely useful for remote connections when time spent online must be kept to a minimum.

Further replication customization can be done on any database on this workspace by simply clicking your right mouse button anywhere in the row to display more options.

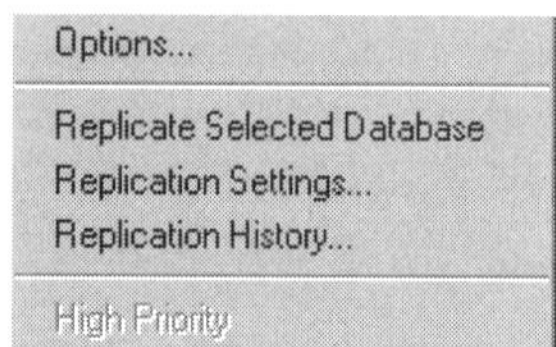

The displayed options have been covered in one way or another in this chapter, so I won't cover them again here. Make sure, however, that when teaching users how to use this workspace you point out that this pop-up list is a quick way to set a database to high priority, which is helpful if they choose to utilize the Other Actions and Replicate High Priority Databases options.

Finally, at the very bottom of this workspace a status bar appears when replication is started. Notes estimates how long each database will take to replicate while it's replicating. This number is dynamic and Notes is always recalculating it as more documents are pulled in. Two additional buttons appear on this status line: Next and Stop.

Selecting Next stops the current database replication and moves on to the next one shown on the workspace. Selecting Stop has the obvious effect: it stops the entire replication session.

After you've taken users on a tour of the workspace, take a few moments to explain the two ways databases are placed here. The first way happens whenever users manually initiate replication from any workspace by selecting a database and then clicking File ➢ Replication ➢ Replicate, the database automatically appears on the Replicator workspace. The other way is to select any database and drag it to this workspace the same way they drag databases to any other workspace. The difference is that the original icon remains where it was found.

Once users understand the individual components of this workspace, they should have no problem scheduling replication, selecting which databases to replicate, and rearranging the order by simply dragging the individual rows up or down the workspace.

Using Multiple Replicators

As a Notes administrator you'll typically be working with scheduled replication. As you create a schedule to support your selected replication topology you may find that there is no elegant way to avoid overlapping replication schedules. Fortunately, Release 4 offers a solution to this problem: multiple replicators. This new feature handles overlapping replication sessions by enabling more than one replica server task to run at a time, which not only solves a big problem, but also makes efficient use of server resources, and can even shorten replication cycles.

When multiple replicators are enabled each one handles a single server-to-server replication session. For example, if Server A is scheduled to replicate with Server B and Server C at the same time, there would be a replicator to handle the session with Server B and one to handle the session with Server C. Keep in mind that this feature enables single databases between multiple simultaneous server sessions (see Figure 8.18) and not simultaneous databases between a single server-to-server session (see Figure 8.19).

Enabling Multiple Replicators

Now that you know about the power of multiple replicators, how do you make them work? There are two ways to enable multiple replicators: manually edit the NOTES.INI file to include more than one replicator and restart the server, or load additional replicators at the server console.

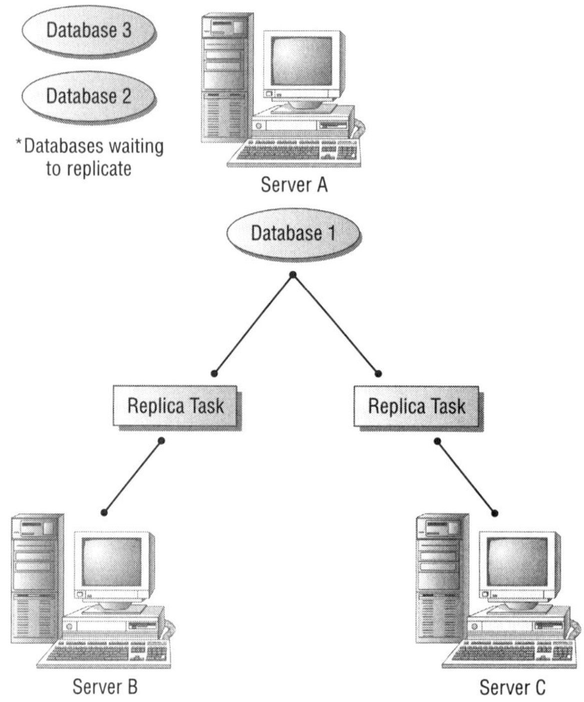

FIGURE 8.18

The multiple replicator enables Server A to replicate with Servers B and C simultaneously. Notice that Databases 2 and 3 are waiting to be replicated after Database 1 is finished.

The NOTES.INI File To enable multiple replicators every time you start the Notes server, edit the Replicators value in the NOTES.INI file. The default value is 1 but can be set higher depending on how many replicators you need.

Don't be careless and set the Replicators setting in the NOTES.INI file to an arbitrary number. Each replicator consumes a certain amount of system resources. Even though this server task sits idle until replication is initiated, it still requires some resources just to sit idle.

In order for the changes to the Replicators value to take effect, the server needs to be restarted. If you prefer, you can change this value through the Server Configuration document using the Set/Modify Parameter button.

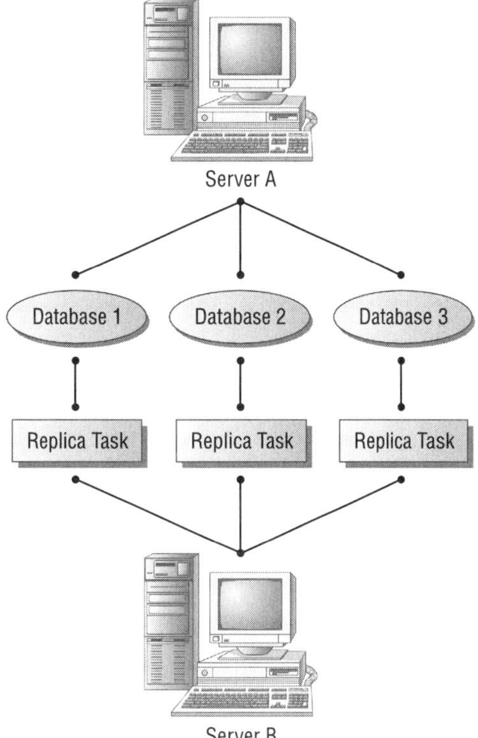

FIGURE 8.19
Multiple replicators do not allow Databases 1, 2, and 3 to be replicated simultaneously between Server A and Server B.

From the Server Console If you'd prefer not to shut the server down to enable multiple replicators, then simply load another replica task. From the server console type the command **Load Replica**.

This command loads another instance of the replica task. To verify that this task is loaded type **Show Tasks** from the server console and you'll see more than one instance of the replicator task listed (see Figure 8.20).

If you need another replica task to run only once, you can specify the name of the server after the Load Replica command **Load Replica *ServerName*** where *ServerName* is the name of the server that you want this server to replicate with.

Once the replication with the specified server is complete, the replica task will exit. This command is similar to initiating replication from the server console except that it starts another instance of the replica task to service the one time session.

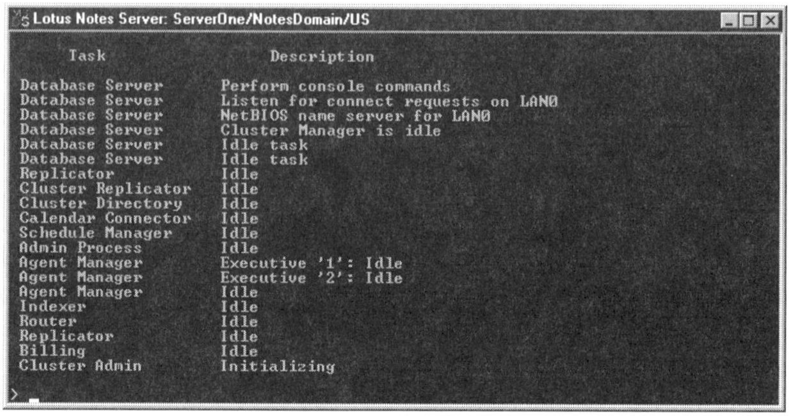

```
Lotus Notes Server: ServerOne/NotesDomain/US

     Task                      Description

Database Server          Perform console commands
Database Server          Listen for connect requests on LAN0
Database Server          NetBIOS name server for LAN0
Database Server          Cluster Manager is idle
Database Server          Idle task
Database Server          Idle task
Replicator               Idle
Cluster Replicator       Idle
Cluster Directory        Idle
Calendar Connector       Idle
Schedule Manager         Idle
Admin Process            Idle
Agent Manager            Executive '1': Idle
Agent Manager            Executive '2': Idle
Agent Manager            Idle
Indexer                  Idle
Router                   Idle
Replicator               Idle
Billing                  Idle
Cluster Admin            Initializing
>
```

FIGURE 8.20
Server console tasks show more than one replicator task loaded.

Controlling What Gets Replicated

Scheduled server-to-server replication through a Connection document provides a fair amount of control over what gets replicated. Most of the control, however, is over when replication occurs and which databases to replicate. This approach is basically binary. Either a database gets replicated or it doesn't. Fortunately, Notes allows an even finer level of control over replication by allowing you to specify exactly which items within a database get replicated and which items do not.

The Access Control List and Replication

Before you start customizing the replication settings for each database, you need to have a clear understanding of how the Access Control List affects replication or all of your customization efforts could be for nothing. The ACL is covered in detail in Chapter 7. However, here is a quick refresher.

Notes defines seven access levels:

- **No Access:** No access whatsoever. Users and servers can't even add this database to their workspace.
- **Depositor:** Users can compose and save documents in the database but can't read any documents, not even the ones they composed.

- **Reader:** Users can read documents but can't compose any. Servers with this access can receive documents but can't replicate anything back to a replica source.
- **Author:** Users can compose documents, read all documents, and edit documents that they composed. Servers with this access can replicate new documents to the source and can even delete documents if specific access is granted.
- **Editor:** Users can compose documents, read all documents, and edit any document in the database regardless of who composed the document. Servers with this access get the same control as if they were authors with the additional ability to change any document and replicate those changes back to the source.
- **Designer:** Users get the same access control as editors with the additional ability to make changes to the database design elements. Servers with this access can replicate changes to a database design element back to the replica source.
- **Manager:** Users get the same access as designers plus they can make changes to a database's ACL and delete the database altogether. Servers with this access level can replicate all changes to a database back to the replica source, even deletion of the database.

When you think of the ACL, keep in mind that it applies to servers much the same way as it does to users. Servers are created, registered, and have IDs the same as users do, so the same access rules that apply to users apply to servers.

How the Access Control List Affects Replication

To better understand how the ACL affects a server's ability to replicate, here are a few example scenarios with explanations for each. In all of the examples, Server A is the source server and Servers B and C are the target servers.

Scenario #1: Blocking Replication with No Access

Server A has a discussion database (DISCUSS.NSF) that grants access to the sales group and John P. Doe. The default access level is set to No Access. Server B tries to create a replica copy. What happens?

Nothing. Access is denied to Server B because Server B is not explicitly or implicitly granted through group membership listed in the ACL. Since the default access level is No Access, Server B is completely blocked from making a replica copy. The same results occur when a user not listed in the ACL or part of the sales group tries to perform the same operation because they can't even open or add the database to their workspace.

Scenario #2: Controlling Replicated Changes

Server B is listed in the discussion database's (DISCUSS.NSF) ACL as a Reader. Server B successfully replicates the database from Server A. Changes are made to the database on Server B and a Pull–Pull replication is initiated. What happens?

Any new changes made on the copy at Server A are brought over to Server B's copy. However, the changes made on Server B are not allowed to replicate back to Server A because Server B is only a Reader, which means it is not allowed to create new documents or edit current ones.

Scenario #3: Ring Replication Topology and Unusual Access Control List Settings

Server C is listed in the discussion database's (DISCUSS.NSF) ACL as an Editor. Server B is still listed as a Reader. Server B replicates the database from Server A, and Server C replicates the database from Server B. Changes are made to a document in the replica copy on Server C. Server C replicates with Server B and Server B replicates with Server A. What happens?

Changes made at Server C are replicated to the copy on Server B, but when Server B tries to replicate with Server A the changes are refused because Server B only has Reader access and therefore cannot send changes to Server A. However, since Server C is an Editor it can send its changes to Server B but, of course, that's as far as the changes go in this scenario.

This scenario might be somewhat unusual. It is doubtful that you would ever see, in a well designed Notes environment, servers in the same domain with such unusual restrictions applied. However, this scenario does help illustrate how the ACL directly affects replication.

Determining What Gets Replicated

The Server Connection document, as you previously learned, primarily controls when replication occurs and which databases get replicated. What can you do, however, if you need a greater level of control over the replication process? Notes does provide an answer to this question and it can be found in the replication settings for each database.

To view or edit the replication settings for a particular database, start by selecting the replica copy of the particular database. In this example I've selected the replica copy of the database we created to illustrate the importance of the Replica ID. Now select from the menu bar File ➢ Replication ➢ Settings. The Replication Settings dialog box appears and displays the Space Savers setting first (see Figure 8.21).

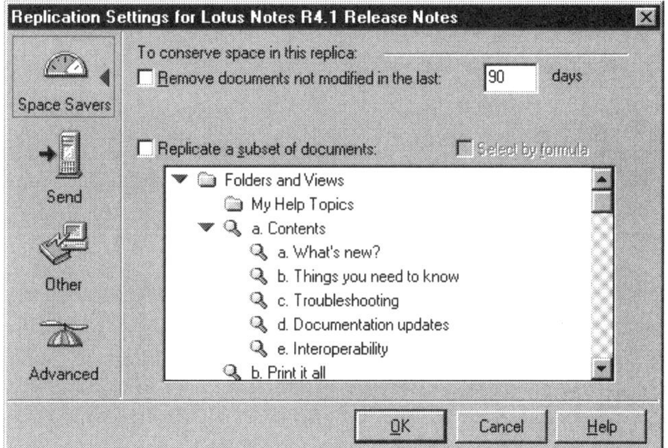

FIGURE 8.21
The Space Savers subsection of the Replication Settings dialog box

Many of the menu bar options described in all of the examples are easily accessible by pointing to an item and then clicking once with the right mouse button.

Space Savers

The Space Savers settings are very useful for mobile users that need to carry certain databases with them wherever they go. Available options for space savers are as follows:

- **Remove documents not modified in the last 90 days:** Documents that have a modification date that is ninety or more days old are removed during replication. This number can be increased or decreased depending on your situation and can be completely different than the source database. A great use for this setting is for mobile users who replicate their mail database. They can enable this setting on their local replica copy and leave it disabled on the server source copy. This approach allows them to conserve disk space without permanently losing access to old documents.

- **Replicate a subset of documents:** This option allows you to select a certain folder or view and only the documents in that folder or view will be replicated.
- **Select by formula:** Used in conjunction with Replicate a Subset of Documents, this option allows you to enter a selection formula similar to those used for views as a means to select a subset of documents. Only those documents that meet the selection formula will be replicated.

If you plan to replicate based on a selection formula, test it by creating a simple view based on the formula. This approach is a quick way to determine whether the formula will deliver what you want during replication. The restrictions that apply to selection formulas for views also apply to formulas for replication.

Send

The Replication Settings' Send options are self explanatory and their overall usefulness depends largely on the unique needs of your Notes environment (see Figure 8.22).

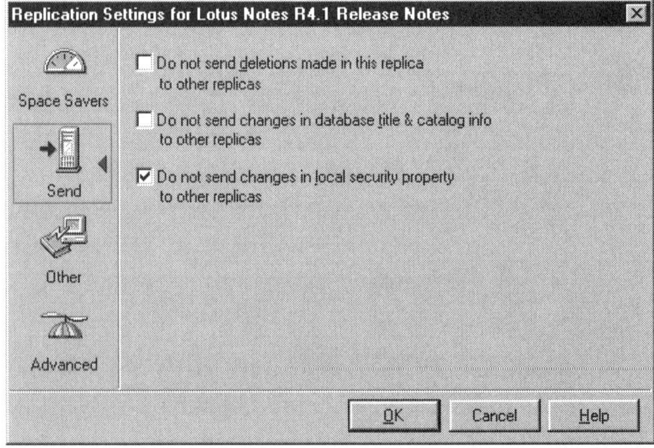

FIGURE 8.22
The Send subsection of the Replication Settings dialog box

- **Do not send deletions made in this replica to other replicas:** Allows documents to be deleted without sending the Deletion stub back to the source during replication.
- **Do not send changes in database title & catalog info to other replicas:** Allows you to change the database title or catalog information without sending that information to other replica copies.
- **Do not send changes in local security property to other replicas:** Allows you to make changes to the ACL on a replica copy without sending those changes back to the source server. This option is useful if the ACL needs to be fine tuned—depending on which server it is located on and which groups of users that server services.

Other

The Replication Settings' Other options contain a few useful administrative options (see Figure 8.23).

- **Temporarily disable replication:** As the option indicates, you can turn replication on and off for the selected database.
- **Scheduled replication priority (Low, Medium, High):** Here is where you set the database priority that can be used in the Server Connection document.
- **Only replicate incoming documents saved or modified after:** Since replication relies heavily on the creation and modification date, you can use that to your advantage by setting a cutoff date. Any documents created or modified after the date set will not be replicated. This is a useful option when you only want to have a replica copy of the most recent documents.
- **CD-ROM publishing date:** If you publish this database to a CD-ROM, you can set the date for that to occur.

Advanced

The options in this subsection let you create selective replication settings for other servers from one location (see Figure 8.24).

- **When computer:** This is the destination server or the location for the target database.

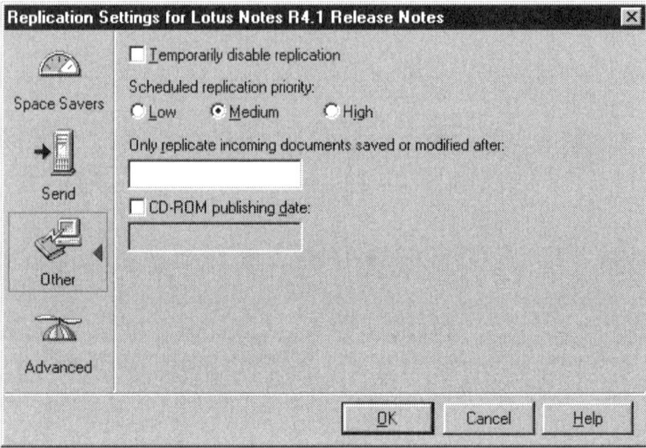

FIGURE 8.23
The Other subsection of the Replication Settings dialog box

- **Receives from:** This is the source server or the server that is initiating the replication session.
- **Replicate a subset of documents:** This setting does the same thing it does in the Space Savers subsection.
- **Select by formula:** This setting works in conjunction with Replicate a Subset of Documents the same way it does in the Space Savers subsection.
- **Replicate incoming:** You can select various database items to replicate by placing a check mark next to them. The available database items include the following (an asterisk after the item indicates that it is selected by default):
  - Forms, Views, Etc. *
  - Agents *
  - Replication Formula
  - Access Control List *
  - Deletions *
  - Fields

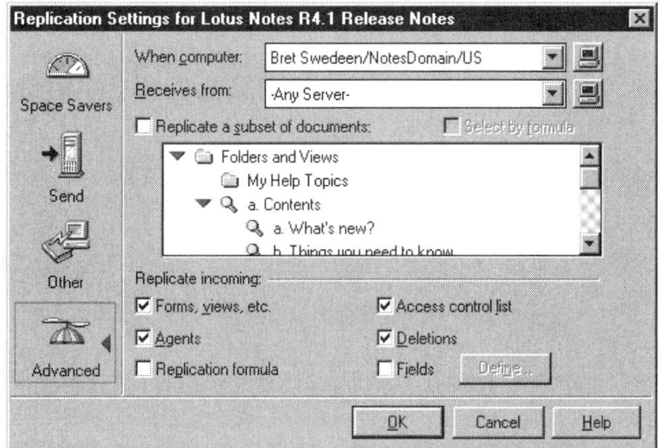

FIGURE 8.24
The Advanced subsection of the Replication Settings dialog box

If you select the Fields options in the Advanced subsection of the Replication Settings dialog box, the Define button becomes available. Select this button and you can specify All Fields or Custom from the drop-down list in the Replicate Selected Fields dialog box that appears. If you select Custom, a list of fields from the database appears in which you can specify exactly which fields the replica copy should receive.

Address book databases have additional settings available in the drop-down list found on the Replicate Selected Fields dialog box: Minimal Address Book, Minimal Address Book - Encryption, Minimal Address Book - Person Info, and Minimal Address Book - Person Info - Encryption. These additional settings make it easy for mobile users to take a local replica copy of the Public Address Book that won't consume all of their free disk space.

These different replication settings can easily be combined in a variety of ways to execute replication in a way best suited for your unique situation.

Replication Settings Scenarios

What follows are a few scenarios that help illustrate the ways to effectively use replication settings. In each of the scenarios, assume that the ACL settings are correct and that a Server Connection document has been created.

Scenario #1: Replication Settings in a Multi-Protocol Environment

Server A is located in a Novell NetWare environment using IPX/SPX as the only network protocol. Server B is in a Windows NT network using IP as its only network protocol for all of its clients, and SPX and IP for all of its servers regardless of their function. On Server A there is a database used for order entry by the sales force. When an order is finished by the sales force the status on the order is set to Ready. This status informs the warehouse crew that an order is waiting to be filled. Server B, in the NT environment, has IP and SPX loaded while the clients in this environment only have IP loaded. Server B replicates the order entry database from Server A periodically throughout the day. Unfortunately, this database is somewhat large and replication can sometimes be slow. Is there a way to speed up replication in this situation?

Yes. Using the replication settings for the order entry database, Server B would select Replicate a Subset of Documents from the Space Savers subsection. If there were a view available that only displayed orders with a status of Ready, then this view would be the selected subset. Otherwise, a selection formula would be created that only selects documents where status equaled Ready. The reason users in the warehouse crew don't directly access Server A is because their workstations don't load SPX as a protocol. Server B loads SPX, which is used to communicate with Server A, and IP, which allows users to communicate with Server B. There could be other reasons for not directly accessing Server A, but in this scenario the reason is a lack of network protocols on the user's workstation.

Scenario #2: Disabling Replication to Prevent Disaster

The order entry database on Server A is the source database, and Server B and Server C both have replica copies. The Server Connection document has a schedule that replicates this database at 8:30 AM, 12:00 PM, and 5:00 PM. Two Notes developers, Mutt and Jeff, started making alterations to the database early one morning around 7:00 AM. By 8:15 AM they realized that they did not understand what the other one was doing and had inadvertently written over each other's changes. This caused save conflicts to several key database forms which rendered the database forms temporarily useless. Replication was about to start in a matter of minutes and the warehouse crew was about to start filling orders left over from yesterday. What can developers Mutt and Jeff do to isolate their mistake and prevent it from spreading through the Notes environment before they can fix it?

Mutt and Jeff have two options. They can open the Server Connection document and disable the schedule or, if they have the proper access to Server B and Server C, they can open the replication settings and in the Other subsection place a check next to the Temporarily Disable Replication option. This way, if replication starts the copies on Server B and Server C won't replicate during that session. When the corrections are made they can change the replication settings and enable replication of that database. Then they can manually initiate a replication session or wait until the next scheduled event to bring the databases up to date.

Scenario #3: Controlling the Content of Replica Copies

Server A has a discussion database that gets replicated to all servers in the Notes environment. In the Windows NT environment of Server B there is a manager who is a bit of a control freak. He wants the ability to censor documents. The rest of the company doesn't want to be subject to his censorship but no one wants to tell him how to manage his employees. Is there a way to solve this problem? (This scenario is more of a diplomatic lesson than a technical lesson, but worthwhile nonetheless.)

Fortunately, Notes does provide a way for this control freak to get what he wants without affecting anyone outside of his area. In the Send subsection of the discussion database's Replication Settings, he can place a check mark next to the Do Not Send Deletions Made in This Replica (to Other Replicas) option. This option allows the censorship czar to delete documents to his heart's content without affecting other replica copies throughout the Notes environment.

If the manager only has Author access to this database, however, then he won't have the level of control he needs to randomly delete documents. To solve this potential problem, increase his access to Editor locally. Then on the Send subsection place a check next to the Do Not Send Changes in Local Security Property to Other Replicas option. This option will prevent ACL changes made to the local replica copy from affecting any other replicas.

Monitoring Replication

Notes replication is a fairly reliable operation. Once it is configured and scheduled, it tends to work the way one would expect. Unfortunately, there are times when careless mistakes are made and unpredictable events occur. As a Notes administrator it is your job to make sure that replication takes place as scheduled, and when it doesn't take place you should be the first one to know.

Tools for Monitoring Replication

If you're serious about administering your Notes environment, then take the time in the beginning to establish good administration habits. One of those habits should be a daily routine of monitoring replication activity within the Notes environment.

Lotus provides the following tools built into Notes to help make daily replication monitoring easy and quick:

- Notes Log
- Reporter Task
- Event Task
- Replication History

The Notes Log

Every server in your Notes environment has a Notes Log which is created the first time you start the server. This log contains useful information about databases, users, and daily activity on the server. The log is the first place to look each day to make sure replication is occurring as scheduled.

There are three views that provide detailed information about replication:

- **Replication Events:** This view provides such details as the starting time, ending time, and total session time in minutes for each replication event that takes place. Open any one of these replication events in the view and information about each database replicated is displayed.
- **Miscellaneous Events:** This view displays a range of time that events were recorded. Open any of these range documents and you'll see such things as when user sessions were opened and what server console commands were executed, just to name a few.
- **Phone Calls:** This view can be sorted by date or by user. Information about phone calls made are displayed here and are useful if you connect to other servers and replicate over phone lines. If you're having replication problems when Server A calls Server B it may be a problem with the phone call that was placed and not a problem with the replica task.

Take some time to familiarize yourself with these three views so you understand what information they present and how to use that information to quickly spot strange replication behavior.

Along with these three views, Notes allows you to further customize what is recorded about replication in the log by making some adjustments to the Log_Replication value in the NOTES.INI file. You can set this value to six different numeric values, each of which determines a different level of replication detail logging (see Table 8.2).

TABLE 8.2 Level of Replication Based on the Numeric Value

Number	Level of Replication Detail Logging
0	Do not log replication events
1	Log server replication events
2	Log replication activity at the database level
3	Log replication activity at the level of database elements (views, documents, and so on)
4	Log replication at the field level
5	Log summary information

These NOTES.INI values apply to servers only and can not be set on individual workstations.

The online Notes Administration Help Guide indicates that there is no default value for the Log_Replication value. This statement, however, is a bit misleading.

When you installed your Notes server and entered the information about the administrator and the network protocol you may recall there was an Advanced button in this dialog box. Selecting the Advanced button provides a list of items you can choose to have logged, one of which is replication events. By default, the replication option is not selected. Therefore, if you accept the defaults, replication events are not logged. Hence the misleading statement in the Notes Administration Help Guide. On the other hand, however, if you place a check mark next to this option, the Log_Replication NOTES.INI value is set to 1, which logs server replication events. With values 2 through 5, you must make changes through a manual edit of the NOTES.INI file or modify the appropriate parameter in the Server Configuration document.

The Reporter Task

The Reporter task runs on the server and collects server statistics which it feeds to the Statistics Reporting database (STATREP.NSF). Once these statistics are placed in the database, they can be used the same way any other database would be used.

The Reporter task does not run on a server automatically, so if you want to utilize this tool you'll have to add it to your server's StartUp tasks (details about how to do this are covered in Chapter 4).

There are ten different statistical items recorded in the Statistics Reporting database but the ones of most interest at this time are those related to replication. Take some time to examine the System view (by selecting Statistics Reports ➢ System) in this database because it displays information useful for replication monitoring. Many of these statistics can have alarms set for them so that when a particular action occurs or a threshold is reached a failure report is generated, which can be e-mailed to you, sent to a mail-in problem reporting database, or sent to an alphanumeric pager if you have the additional software required.

The Event Task

As Chapter 4 explained, the Event task is a server task that is used to monitor certain events that occur on the server. The administrator creates a monitor document for a particular event and sets thresholds appropriate for his or her Notes environment. When the threshold set in the monitor document is crossed, a notification is sent and the administrator can take action.

You can create a monitor document to track replication failures. If replication fails for whatever reason, you can have a notification message sent to a mail-in database, an individual, or a group. My favorite use for Events Monitoring is to have messages sent to the Lotus Notes Pager Gateway (one of my all-time favorite Notes add-on products). This way I can have a message sent to my alphanumeric pager, which informs me of the error no matter where I am. Provided I have some type of Notes access available to me, I can take action quickly and correct the problem (or at least start correcting the problem).

Details explaining how to set up events monitoring are covered in Chapter 4.

Replication History

The replication history maintained for each database is another useful tool for monitoring replication activity. The history is automatically created for any database that has successfully replicated at least once. If a database hasn't yet been replicated, the Replication History dialog box is empty.

At the beginning of this chapter the steps that occur during replication were outlined. If you recall, the date and time of the last successful replication is critical to determining what gets replicated during a replication session. That important information is recorded in the Replication History dialog box (shown in Figure 8.25).

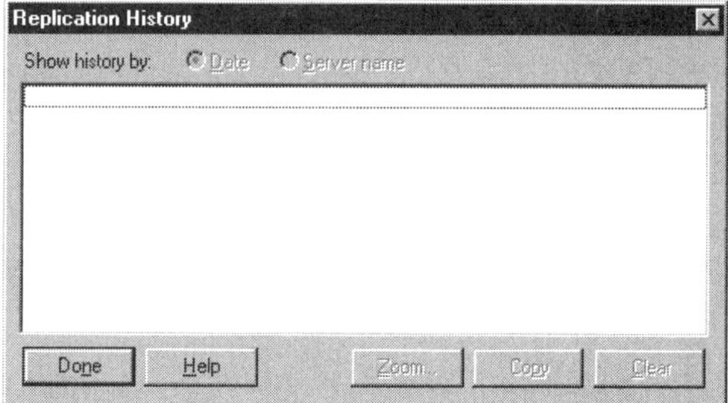

FIGURE 8.25

The Replication History dialog displays information about the last successful replication.

The best use of the Replication History dialog box is to verify when replication was last performed. If problems have occurred, or if you believe that the database is somehow out of sync with its source, you can clear the replication history. When the history is cleared, Notes no longer has a record of when the last replication occurred. Without knowing the last successful replication, Notes is forced to replicate everything since the last cutoff date (see Figure 8.26) instead of just replicating changes since the last replication.

The cutoff date is defined on the Other tab of the Replication Settings dialog box. The option Only Replicate Incoming Documents Saved or Modified After specifies the cutoff date.

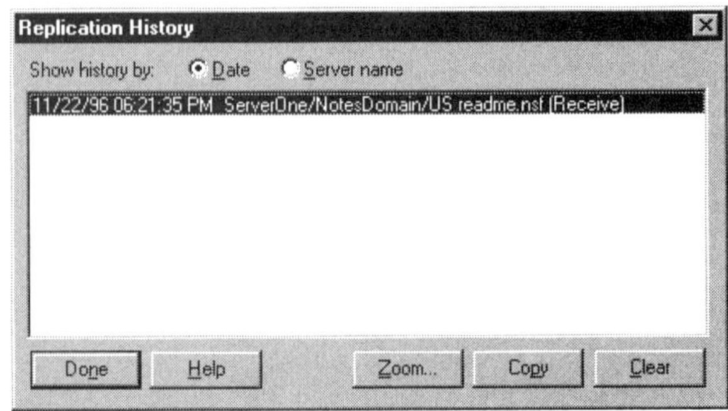

FIGURE 8.26
The Other tab of the Replication Settings dialog box is where the cutoff date is specified.

Establishing a Replication Monitoring Routine

You now know how replication works, how to set it up, and the tools to use to ensure that replication is occurring as scheduled. Unfortunately, even with all of this knowledge you probably haven't taken the necessary time to establish a good daily replication monitoring routine. The absence of such a routine shouldn't surprise you or make you feel stupid. It is the nature of the job. Few administrators have the time to sit down and sketch out such a routine for themselves. Let's face it, Notes administrators and systems administrators, in general, spend most of their time fighting fires and catering to the end-user community (a full time job, second only to eating and sleeping). When administrators do have time, creating a replication monitoring routine doesn't top their list of fun things to do. Quite honestly, creating one of these daily routines is about as much fun as watching cars rust (my sincere apologizes to anyone who actually enjoys watching cars rust).

A Framework for Routine Replication Monitoring

If you're not sure how to get started with a replication monitoring routine, try to use the framework outlined below. More organizational than technical, the framework provides a good starting place for what each administrator should do on a daily basis to make sure replication is working properly:

1. Create a spreadsheet that displays the replication schedule for your Notes servers. Include times and which databases are replicated.

2. Post this schedule near the Notes servers.

3. Every morning, scan the Replication Events view in the Notes Log and make sure that events listed correspond to the times listed in your schedule spreadsheet.

4. Automatically have the server load the Reporter and Event tasks and utilize these tools to prevent problems before they occur or to quickly notify you in the event of a problem.
5. When problems do occur that can't quickly be diagnosed, try clearing the replication history or completely removing the replica copy and starting fresh.
6. Create a simple document of your daily routine for other administrators and include a list of people to contact "when all hell breaks loose."

Basic Replication Troubleshooting

When it comes to troubleshooting, there are no absolutes. I'd love to say, "Here is exactly what you do each and every time there is a problem with replication." Unfortunately, I can't. What I can tell you, however, is a few basic places to start looking when replication problems occur.

When Replication Just Isn't Happening

When replication just isn't happening between two servers, start with the obvious; it just might surprise you:

- **Is the server down?** The reason the server might be offline could be as simple as someone turned it off, or as bothersome as a total hardware failure. The first action to take in this situation is to verify that both servers are on and totally functional.
- **Is the network in general having a problem?** The larger the network, the more hardware devices it requires to keep connected, which means more points of failure. Check other aspects of the network (access to file servers and availability of printers) and verify that your Notes servers are the only devices experiencing problems.
- **If the server-to-server connection is made across a modem, are the modems working and are the phone lines functional?** Make sure that neither server shares its modem line with some other device, such as a fax machine.
- **Is there enough disk space on both servers?** Check both servers and make sure they have ample disk space. At the server console or through the Remote Server Console type **SHOW DISKSPACE** ***(drive letter)***.

If the obvious solutions don't do the trick, it's time to dig a little deeper, but not too deep:

- **Does the calling server actually have a Server Connection document for the receiving server?** If the document does exist, are all of the fields filled out correctly? Does the Task field have replication listed and does the Port field specify the correct port? Carefully comb through each field and verify that each is correct.
- **If the Notes network is large and layered, do these two servers share a common certificate?** It's easy to overlook this detail in a deeply layered Notes network. Select File ➢ Tools ➢ Users ID from the menu bar and then click Certificates. The certificates are displayed. Repeat these steps for the other server.

You've tried the previous suggestions, but still no luck. The fact is that you can replicate a single database between two servers initiated from the server console, but scheduled replication just doesn't make it:

- **Back to the Server Connection document!** Chances are that if you can manually initiate replication but scheduled replication doesn't work, you probably have a typo in the Server Connection document.
- **Are there any overlapping schedules?** Overlapping schedules are perfectly legal; however, they require multiple replicators. If overlapping schedules are the root of the problem either add additional replicators or rearrange the schedules and remove the conflict(s).
- **Is the server overburdened?** If your Notes network has more users than your servers can service, and each server is doing double duty (file server and Notes server), then you need to add more servers. A heavy server load shouldn't completely stop replication, but it can slow down the step in replication where Notes builds a list of databases that two servers have in common. If this step takes too long, it can severely throw off a scheduled replication. This problem can also occur if you have an unusually large number of databases on one server. In this case, move some of the databases to other servers and reduce the load.

Common Replication Error Messages

So, you can replicate manually and your replication schedule even works. However, there is this one database that just won't cooperate and error messages keep appearing in the Notes Log. The following are some common error messages you might encounter and how to deal with them.

- **Access control is set to not allow replication:** This error message is fairly common, especially when more than one Notes domain is involved. An incorrect ACL setting is typically the root of the problem in this situation. Review the previous section on the ACL and replication and make sure each server in the loop has the correct ACL setting. Keep in mind, however, that an incorrect ACL setting won't completely stop replication. For example, if Server A has Reader access to the source database on Server B, Server A can receive documents from Server B—it just can't send any changes back to Server B. Part of replication (but not all of it) occurs, and therefore the error message appears in the Notes Log.
- **Unable to copy document:** Isolated problems such as this one, in any context, can often be the result of a corrupt file. Run the server program Fixup. If that doesn't help, delete the problematic database and restore a clean copy from a tape backup or create a new replica copy from another server.
- **Replication disabled:** An error message such as this one states the obvious. Check the databases replication settings and deselect Temporarily Disable Replication in the Other subsection of the Replication Settings dialog box.

The suggestions above are only a place to start. Always go after the obvious possibilities first, especially when replication worked at one time but doesn't anymore. If the problem persists, utilize the tools Notes provides (Notes Log, Statistics Reporter, Events Monitoring, and Replication History) and methodically work your way through the problem. Good troubleshooting skills are grounded in common sense and methodical behavior.

Don't randomly investigate the bizarre before ruling out the obvious.

Personal Replication Experiences

Most of the problems with replication you'll encounter are typically caused by careless mistakes: typos in the Server Connection document, not setting the ACL correctly, or trying to replicate between servers that don't have a port in common. That is not to say that all of the problems with replication are careless in nature. There are times when you'll come across an unusual problem. What follows are a few examples of some of the unusual replication problems that I've personally encountered.

Personal Experience #1: Incorrect Access Control List Setting Affecting Replication

As discussed in the section *How the Access Control List Affects Replication* of this chapter, the ACL can seriously affect whether databases get replicated. The following personal experience describes an ACL setting problem that is all too common.

Problem I added several databases on remote server Frodo from the Administration client on local server Bilbo (the domain, oddly enough, was called Middle Earth). Replication was deferred until the next replication session, which was scheduled for 1:00 AM the next day. The next day I checked server Frodo only to find that the replica copies had not initialized. I reviewed the Notes Log and found the following error message:

> Access Control is Set in Change Management to Not Allow Replication from Bilbo. Not Replicating Bilbo Change Management. (Not Authorized to Read Change Management.)

One message for each failed database replication was listed.

The problem was where I had created the replica copy, and not an obvious ACL setting problem. Since I had created the replica copies on remote server Frodo from the Administration client on server Bilbo, my user ID was added to the new replica ACL as user type Person instead of adding the server ID to the ACL as user type Server. This ID problem wouldn't have occurred if the LocalDomainServer group was in the ACL for the database Change Management. Unfortunately, it wasn't. To further add to the problem, the default setting on the database was for No Access.

Solution I added the LocalDomainServer group to the ACL and gave it Manager access.

Personal Experience #2: Notes Server Log Incorrectly Reporting Failed Replication

Every so often you'll come across a replication problem that, by all indications, points to a severe problem but turns out to be nothing.

Problem A customer was having problems getting their scheduled replication to work. They were using Notes 4 and kept seeing the following message show up in the Notes Server Log:

> Missing Scheduled Replication with Server BOST_MRKT 6/28/96 1:00:00 am. Last replication Completion Time: Unknown.

I checked the Server Connection document and made note of the schedule times. I then compared these times to the replication history for the replicated databases. They all appeared to be replicating as scheduled.

One of the scheduled replication sessions was approaching so I made a few changes to one of the databases. The session kicked off as scheduled and everything appeared to work. I checked the replica copy of the database I had just changed and my alterations were there. I looked at the Notes Log and found a similar error message to the one shown above. Upon closer examination, I discovered that the replication time recorded was incorrect.

Solution Something as odd as this problem requires additional resources. Fortunately, I had access to the Lotus Notes KnowledgeBase.

The tech note (Document Number 138936) describes a problem similar to the one my client was experiencing. The tech notes explains that the Notes Log is the problem. Replication is occurring, but is not being recorded correctly in the Notes Log. Details explaining what caused this were not available. No work-arounds were offered. The problem has been reported to Lotus Quality Engineering and by the time you're reading this it will probably be resolved.

Personal Experience #3: Using Fully Distinguished Names to Resolve Replication Problems

At one time or another everyone has chased after a problem that occurred because of a typo. Traditionally, the problem was finally solved by painfully typing each letter very slowly and saying it out loud. The following experience isn't exactly the same, but it comes pretty close.

Problem At a recent client visit I met a new and nervous Notes administrator who claimed he couldn't initialize replication from the server console. No matter which server he tried to replicate with, it failed to work. I was somewhat puzzled and began to prepare myself for a really weird one.

We went over to one of the Notes servers in his lab and he proceeded to demonstrate exactly what was happening (see Figure 8.27).

It appeared to be an ACL problem, so I asked the administrator to show me the ACL setting for the specific database. The server was listed except that its hierarchical name was used.

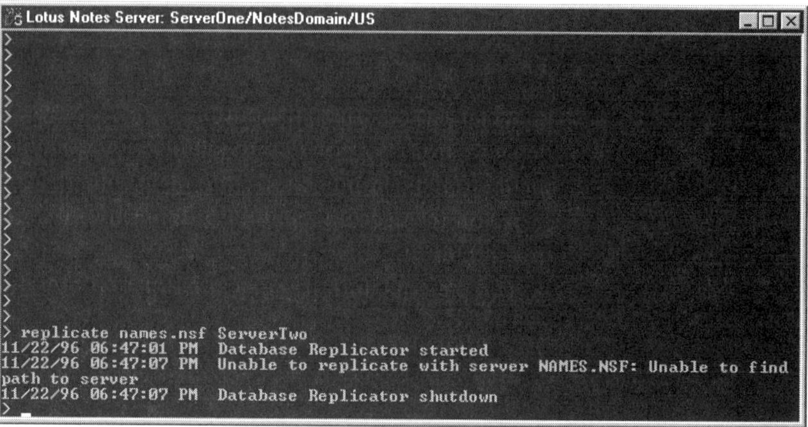

Lotus Notes Server: ServerOne/NotesDomain/US
> replicate names.nsf ServerTwo
11/22/96 06:47:01 PM Database Replicator started
11/22/96 06:47:07 PM Unable to replicate with server NAMES.NSF: Unable to find path to server
11/22/96 06:47:07 PM Database Replicator shutdown

FIGURE 8.27 Re–creation of what the Notes administrator typed in the server console and the error message received

We returned to the server console and tried again. The same problem occurred. I asked the administrator to try it one more time, but this time to use the entire hierarchical name. It worked!

Solution Each server listed in each database's ACL was listed using its hierarchical name. The administrator was using the server's common name, which was not listed in the ACL; therefore, the server was denied access when it tried to replicate.

Important NOTES.INI Replication Settings

Controlling replication settings will typically be handled through the Server Connection document, Server Configuration document, and individual database replication settings. There are, however, situations where you'll want (or even need) to edit certain NOTES.INI replication values directly. What follows is a laundry list of the NOTES.INI values you'll want to be familiar with.

Changing most .INI values requires restarting the server before the changes take affect.

The following are replication setting .INI values:

- **Repl_Error_Tolerance**: This value indicates the number of replication errors of the same type between two databases that a server tolerates before it terminates replication. The default value is 2. Setting this value higher increases the server's replication error tolerance level.

- **ReplicationTimeLimit:** Indicates a maximum time allowed, in minutes, that replication can take between servers. There is no default value so there is no initial time limit. Typically, this value is set in the Server Connection document.
- **Replicators:** Specifies the number of replica tasks that can run simultaneously. The default is 1.
- **Repl_Push_Retries:** Specifies the number of times that the server will attempt to try a push replication method with a Release 3 server.
- **ServerNoReplRequests:** Forces the server to refuse all replication requests from other servers except for pull-push requests. A value of 0 disables this feature and a setting of 1 enables it. By default, this feature is disabled. If the setting was previously enabled and setting it back to 0 does not disable it, try removing the setting altogether.
- **ServerPullReplication:** Specifies that all scheduled replications from this server use the pull-push method. There are two values for this setting, 0 and 1. A value of 0 enables normal replication. A value of 1 forces this server to pull changes from other servers but does not allow other servers to pull from it. There is no default setting and this setting only affects scheduled replication.
- **ServerPushReplication:** Specifies that all scheduled replications from this server use the push-pull method. There are two values for this setting, 0 and 1. A value of 0 enables normal replication. A value of 1 forces other server to pull changes from this server but does not allow this server to pull changes from those servers. There is no default value.

The following are security-specific INI values:

- **Allow_Access:** Specifies the servers, users, and groups allowed to access this server. An asterisk means everyone listed in the Public Address Book can access the server. Specific names must be listed in hierarchical format. Hierarchical names can also use the wild card asterisk. For example, */SALES_BOST means everyone certified with the SALES_BOST certifier is allowed access. Keep in mind that these settings are also made in the Server document, which takes precedence over the settings in the NOTES.INI file. This INI setting is only used when the Access Server field in the Server document is empty.

- **Create_Replica_Access**: Specifies the groups that can create replica copies on the server. This .INI setting is only used when its Server document Counterpartl, the Create Replica Databases field, is empty. The Server document setting, however, takes precedence over the .INI setting. Naming restrictions for Allow_Access also apply to this setting.
- **Deny_Access**: Specifies the servers, users, and groups that are denied access to this server. This .INI setting is used only when the Not Access Server field in the Server document is empty. Otherwise, the Server document setting takes precedence. Naming restrictions for Allow_Access also apply to this setting. This setting overrides the Allow_Access setting. For example, servers listed in both Allow_Access and Deny_Access are denied access.

These three .INI settings are the most useful with regard to replication and security. However, you should familiarize yourself with the other Allow and Deny settings listed in Appendix D because they may also affect replication.

Here are the server information .INI values:

- **Domain**: Specifies the name of the domain for the server. This setting must have at least one value listed and by default is the name of the domain you specified when you set up the server.
- **KeyFilename**: Specifies the server ID or the user ID. This setting allows the administrator to use one ID to run the server. The default is the ID for the administrator you specified when you created this server.
- **ServerKeyFilename**: Specifies the server ID file used on a machine that is both a workstation and a server.
- **ServerName**: Specifics the server's complete hierarchical name. May not appear particularly useful at first, but refer back to *Personal Experience #3* earlier in this chapter and you'll quickly see how a complete hierarchical name can affect replication.

There's only one server task .INI value:

- **ServerTasks**: Lists the tasks that begin automatically when the server first starts. All of these tasks can be manually started at the server console. However, if a certain task must always run, it should be listed here.

By default Replica, Router, Updall, and Stats are listed. If replication isn't listed at the server console as a running task, make sure it is part of this .INI value's list of startup tasks.

And one troubleshooting .INI value:

- **Log_Replication**: Turns replication logging on and off. A value of 0 turns logging off and a value of 1 turns logging on. The default depends on what you select when you first install your server. If you never go into the Advanced section, then the default is 0 (or off).

Summary

Since the beginning of Notes, replication has been one of the product's most powerful and flexible features. Even in Release 4.5, with all of its new Internet-specific enhancements, replication remains one of the most important capabilities of Notes.

The ability to synchronize databases across several servers regardless of location, operating system platform, and network protocols is a feature that no other software product to date has done as well as Notes. With this power and flexibility comes some complexity. Understanding the intricacies of replication, however, is possible with a little time, patience, and experimentation. As a Notes administrator, you'll be expected to know replication backwards and forwards. Make sure you do what it takes to attain that level of mastery.

9

Notes Mail

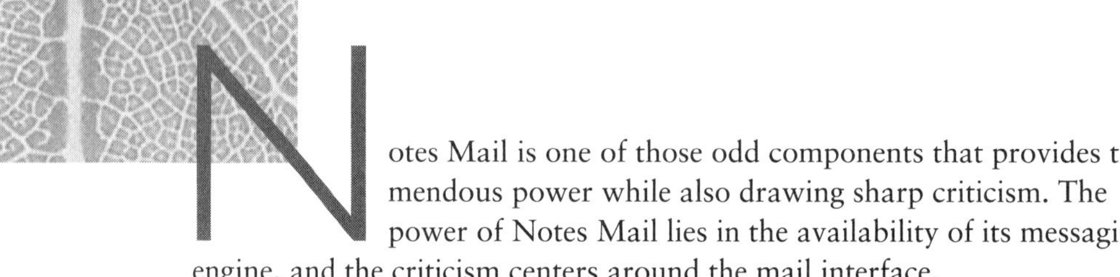

Notes Mail is one of those odd components that provides tremendous power while also drawing sharp criticism. The power of Notes Mail lies in the availability of its messaging engine, and the criticism centers around the mail interface.

The Notes messaging engine is available to all applications and databases built in Notes. Simple databases can now be "mail enabled," which allows any documents, not just e-mail messages, to flow throughout an organization. Developers can easily add mail functionality to their form design through a simple button or a calculated formula. Developers don't need to understand the complexities of an organization's e-mail system to add this functionality, nor do organizations have to have a formal e-mail system to support such a feature.

Even though the availability of the Notes messaging engine enables feature-rich databases and applications, "messaging purists" (people who firmly believe that particular features must exist in a product before it can be called a messaging product) tend to disregard this feature. The actual complaints against Notes Mail are vague. Typically, criticisms center around the mail interface and the lack of certain end-user features.

Try not to think of Notes Mail in terms of a "pure" electronic mail package. Release 4.5 has improved the often criticized mail interface, but Notes Mail is still only one piece of a much larger product. Doing a feature by feature comparison with other mail products may not distinguish Notes Mail as an exceptional program, because such a comparison only reveals part of what Notes really is.

The Fundamentals of Notes Mail

Making the most of Notes Mail for yourself and your Notes environment relies heavily on your understanding of the Notes Mail basics. I suggest acquiring a basic understanding of the four major components that make up Notes Mail and how those components work together before you begin to design your Notes network. This fundamental understanding will help you design a robust Notes network.

Notes Mail Components

Notes Mail is made up of four major components that work together to deliver and route mail to its destination. Regardless of whether mail is sent within the same Notes network or to a foreign mail system, the basic mail process and the four major components that enable that process remain the same. To effectively administer the Notes Mail component of Lotus Notes, it is of paramount importance to thoroughly understand the four major mail components and the roles they play. The four components are: Public Address Book, MAIL.BOX, Mail Router, and user mail database.

Public Address Book

The Public Address Book is a critical component of nearly every aspect of Lotus Notes, and Notes Mail is no exception. The Public Address Book is where users, servers, and Server Connection documents are stored. Users often reference the Public Address Book to look up the addresses of users or groups, and the Mail Router also uses the Public Address Book to help determine the routing path to a user's or group's mail database.

MAIL.BOX (The Mailbox Database)

Each server in your Notes environment will have a MAIL.BOX. This file is a Notes database that temporarily stores mail messages before the Mail Router picks them up and delivers them to their destination. Like any other Notes database, the MAIL.BOX can be corrupted, which adversely affects the delivery of mail within a Notes network. How to correct a MAIL.BOX corruption is covered later in this chapter.

The Mail Router

The Mail Router is a *server task* that automatically starts each time the Notes server is started. Like other automatic server tasks, the Mail Router can be stopped from the server console with the following command:

TELL ROUTER EXIT

This command stops the Mail Router until the server is rebooted. If you want to prevent the Mail Router from restarting, you can remove it from the list in the ServerTasks parameter in the NOTES.INI file.

The Mail Router's sole purpose is to look for pending messages in the MAIL.BOX database and deliver them according to connection information detailed in the Server Connection document(s).

User Mail Database

Each user in a Notes network has a personal mail database that resides on a Notes server. They may also have a replica copy of this database on their local machine. Mail messages received are stored in this database and copies of mail messages sent can also be saved here.

How Notes Mail Gets Delivered

The four previously mentioned components work together to deliver mail from point A to point B and much more. Completely understanding how mail gets delivered is important knowledge to have when designing your Notes network and when troubleshooting mail problems. If you don't understand how mail gets delivered, you'll never know how to fix it if it doesn't get delivered.

What follows is a step-by-step description of what happens when a mail message is sent:

1. A user clicks once on his or her mail icon to select it.
2. From the menu bar the user selects Create ➢ Memo and a blank memo form appears (see Figure 9.1). (A shortcut that combines the first two steps is to press the New Memo button on the Action bar.)
3. The user selects the Address button from the Action bar (see Figure 9.2) to locate the addressee in the Public Address Book (see Figure 9.3).

FIGURE 9.1

A blank Notes Mail memo

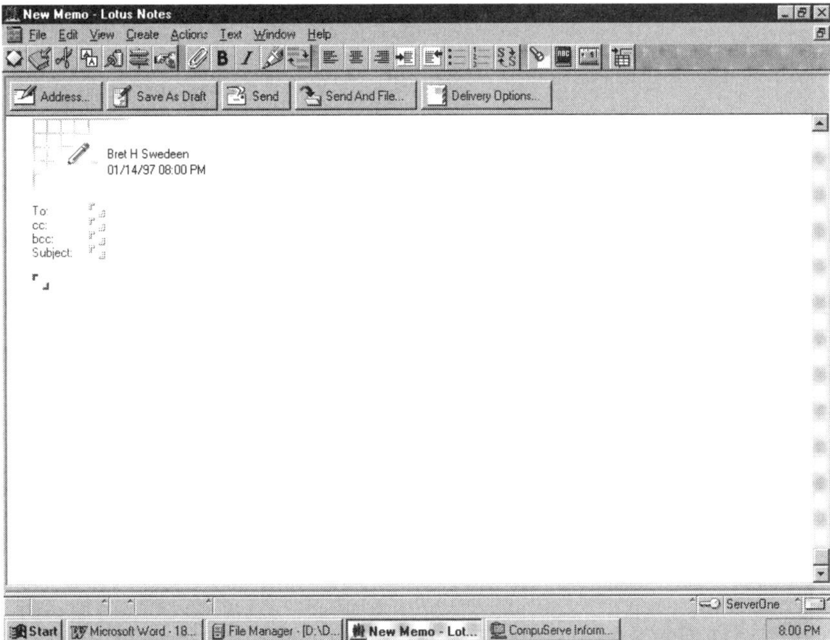

FIGURE 9.2

The Action bar provides shortcuts to common mail commands such as Address.

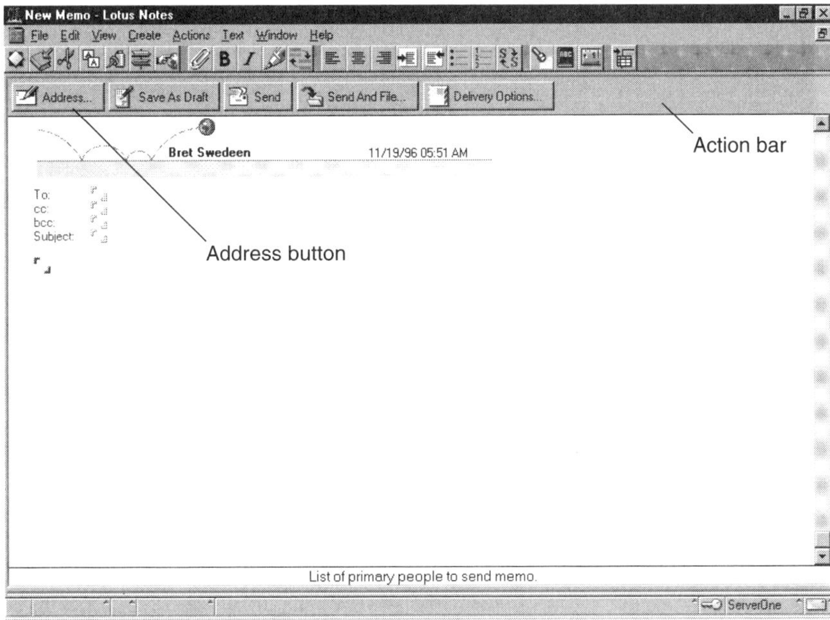

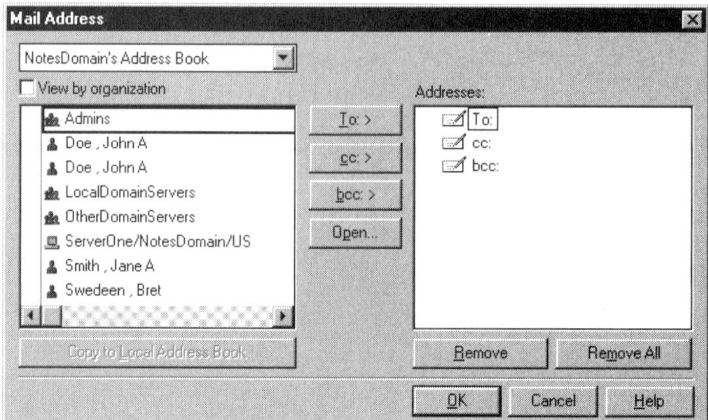

FIGURE 9.3

The Mail Address dialog box is where a user can select individual users or groups to mail a message to.

4. Once an addressee is selected, a user can select addressees for the CC (copy) and BCC (blind copy) fields, if desired. Then the user clicks OK to proceed.
5. The user types the message and then selects the Send button on the Action bar.
6. If the proper options are set in the User Preferences dialog box, a copy of the message is saved in the user's mail database.

The User Preferences dialog box can be accessed from the menu bar by selecting File ➢ Tools ➢ User Preferences. By selecting the Mail subsection of this dialog box, users can further control how their individual workstation interacts with the Notes Mail system.

7. The message is placed in the server's MAIL.BOX database and waits to be delivered.
8. The Mail Router takes over at this point and examines the message to find the location of the addressee's mail database.
9. Depending on where the addressee is located, one of the following actions takes place:
   - **A.** If the addressee's mail database is located on the same server as the sender, the Mail Router delivers the message immediately to the addressee's mail database.

B. If the addressee's mail database is located on a different server in the same Notes named network, the Mail Router delivers the message to the MAIL.BOX database on the addressee's server and then the Mail Router running on that server delivers the message to the addressee's mail database.

C. If the addressee is located on a different server in a different Notes named network and the sender's server has a Server Connection document making a connection to that server possible, then that connection information is used to make a connection to the addressee's server and the message is delivered in the same manner as described in the previous example.

D. If the sender's server does not have a Server Connection document that enables a direct connection to the addressee's server but servers do exist that enable an indirect connection, then the Mail Router sends the message to the MAIL.BOX on the next server. That server's Mail Router in turn picks up the message and sends it to the MAIL.BOX on the next server. This process continues until the message arrives on the addressee's server where that Mail Router finally delivers the message to the addressee's mail database.

E. If there is more than one possible route to get to the addressee's server, the Mail Router on the sender's server calculates the least expensive route based on the connection cost defined in the Server Connection document. Each server involved in the message transfer performs the same calculation to determine the least expensive route to the addressee's server. Then the least expensive route is taken to deliver the message.

When a message moves from one server to another to get to its destination server, the action is called a "hop."

Now that you've read through the steps that occur when mail gets delivered, it probably seems very obvious. That is the right attitude to have. Mail delivery isn't rocket science, so don't let yourself get flustered when delivery problems occur. Remember the steps you once thought so obvious and you can methodically break down any problems that occur.

Setting Up Notes Mail

When it comes to setting up Notes Mail, the actual work involved depends on how large and complex your Notes network is. If you administer a single Notes named network with a single Notes server, then no mail setup is required. Notes Mail delivery happens automatically. If, however, your Notes network has several servers, more than one Notes named network, and connections to foreign Notes domains or other external mail systems, then setting up Notes Mail becomes a little more involved. For example, in a simple Notes network with one server, mail delivery happens automatically. If mail isn't getting delivered in this situation, it is probably one of two things:

- The Mail Router server task is not running.
- Mail databases, including the MAIL.BOX on the server, are corrupted.

The solution to the first problem is to start the Mail Router server task, and the solution to the second problem is to run FIXUP on the mail databases. If, however, your Notes network is more complex, then the possibilities get larger. Delivery problems in a complex environment could be a number of things:

- The Mail Router server task is not running.
- Mail databases are corrupted.
- The connection documents to the other Notes named networks don't exist.
- Connection documents exist but are incorrect.
- No cross-certificate with an external Notes domain exists.
- Network links are down.
- The modem is not functioning correctly.
- The modem is not compatible with the other server's modem.
- There is a problem with the phone line.
- Important documents such as Person, Server, Foreign Domain, or Non-adjacent Domain don't exist.
- Important documents such as Person, Server, Foreign Domain, or Non-adjacent Domain exist but are incorrect.

- Changes to the Public Address Book are not replicating throughout the domain.
- The Public Address Book design is not uniform across all replicas.
- Mail settings in the User Preferences dialog box are incorrect.
- The user's Personal Address Book setup is incorrect.
- The sender's workstation is set up incorrectly.
- There is insufficient memory or disk space on the recipient's home server or destination server.

With every connection you add to support mail delivery in your Notes network, you also add another possible point of failure that has to be considered if mail problems occur.

Notes Network Topology and Mail

Designing a system that ensures quick and reliable mail delivery depends heavily on how you design your Notes network. The *Replication Topology Options* section in Chapter 8 covers the various replication topologies, but I've listed them again here for quick reference.

- **Hub and Spoke:** A central Notes server schedules and initiates all mail routing with all other servers (known as spokes) in the organization.
- **End-to-End:** Sometimes known as peer-to-peer. In this topology, each server in a Notes environment communicates directly with the next server in a chain until the final server is reached.
- **Ring:** This topology is the same as the End-to-End model except that the final server in the chain closes the loop by communicating directly with the first server in the chain.
- **Mesh:** Every server exchanges mail with every other server in the domain. This model has very limited appeal.

The benefits and drawbacks of these topologies are addressed thoroughly in Chapter 8.

If you recall from Chapter 8, replication relies on Server Connection documents to make connections and determine the schedule for replication. Mail delivery also relies on Server Connection documents to make connections between servers for mail routing.

As with replication, Hub and Spoke is still the most flexible Notes network topology. Hub and Spoke allows for the greatest amount of Notes network flexibility for current and future server-to-server connection, which enables quick mail delivery. However, if you're working with a single Notes named network, then any topology works as well as the Hub and Spoke model for mail delivery because in a single Notes named network mail delivery is automatic and therefore doesn't require any thoughtful arrangement of servers. On the other hand, if there is more than one Notes named network, some type of coherent topology is required to ensure quick mail delivery. Consider Figures 9.4 and 9.5 to better understand how the Notes network topology affects mail delivery.

A "hop" is counted each time a messages passes through a server.

FIGURE 9.4

Mail delivery in the Hub and Spoke topology. There are three Notes named networks in this topology.

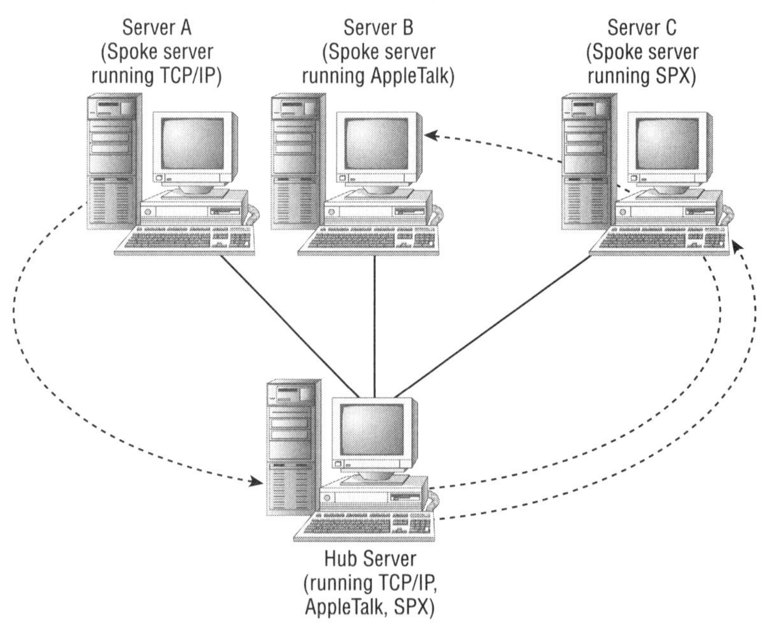

Hub and Spoke

Mail sent from Server A passes through the hub and gets delivered to its destination server.

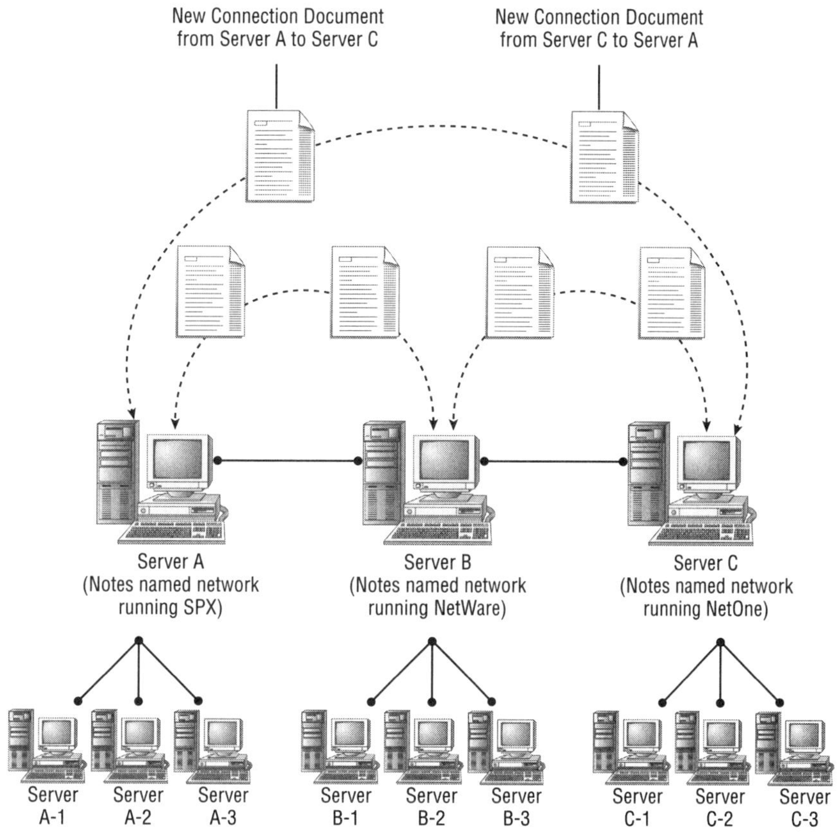

FIGURE 9.5
Mail delivery in the End-to-End topology. There are several Notes named networks in this topology.

The Hub and Spoke topology has three Notes named networks in place. Mail sent from a user on Server A moves from that server to the hub and then to a destination server, which could be Server B or Server C. The same message sent from Server A to Server B or C is delivered in two hops. Even though neither Server B or C resides on the same Notes named network as Server A, or as each other for that matter, the hub server allows for quick mail delivery because it maintains connections between each Notes named network.

The End-to-End topology has several Notes named networks. The same message sent from Server A to Servers B and C does not arrive in the same amount of hops. Server B is two hops while Server C is three hops. And when more servers are involved, a message sent from Server A to Server B-2 has a hop count of three. When that same message is sent from Server A to Server C the count is three. What happens when the message is sent to Server C-2? Four hops! Of course the excessive hops could be solved in this End-to-End topology by rearranging the Server Connection documents as shown in Figure 9.6.

FIGURE 9.6

A Server Connection document scheme in an End-to-End topology that improves mail delivery

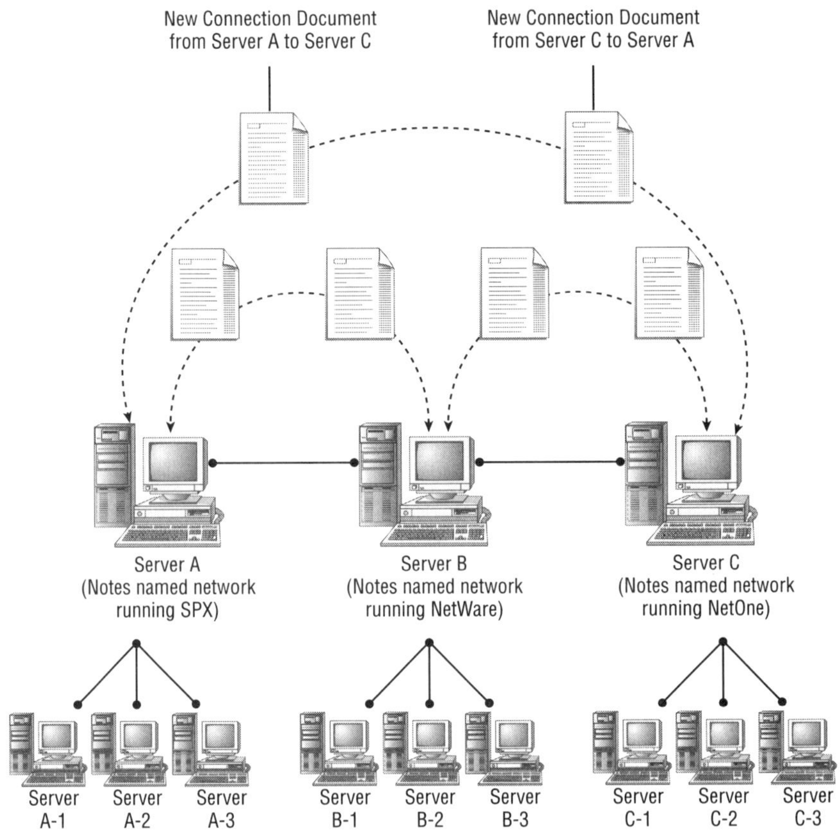

Now, when a message is sent from Server A to Server C-2, the hop count is only three. Reducing a hop count by one isn't an amazing improvement, but when considering that the Mail Router can only make twenty-five server hops before it returns a message back to a sender, it is an improvement nonetheless.

You're probably saying right now that an End-to-End topology isn't too bad for mail delivery. This observation is true, and it brings us back to what I said at the beginning of this section: designing a system that ensures quick and reliable mail delivery heavily depends on how you design your Notes network. Furthermore, your Notes network design is determined by your unique network environment. Whatever that design may be, try not to let it grow organically. If you do, you may end up with a topology similar to the one shown in Figure 9.7. Can you figure out how many hops a message from Server A to Server D might have to make?

FIGURE 9.7

An organically grown Notes network design. This network is clearly a nightmare to administer.

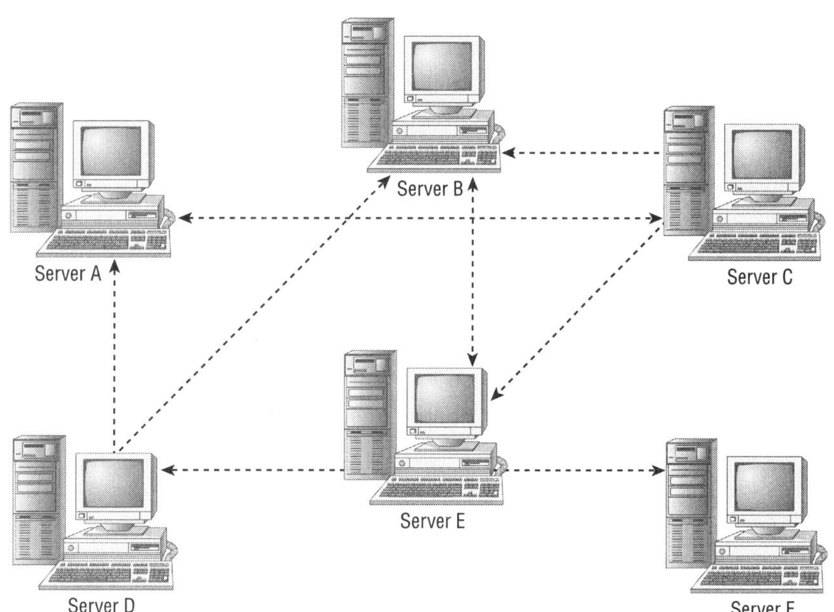

Planning is Critical

Planning is so critical to the success of your Notes environment I can't stress it enough. Even though you may not have a clear idea of where Notes fits into your organization, or if it will at all, draw up some type of design document that clearly identifies the current Notes design and a proposed future design for when and if Notes really takes off in your organization. Such a document should help you avoid a topology similar to the one in Figure 9.7.

Dedicated Mail Server

Regardless of which Notes network topology you've selected, you may want to consider setting up a dedicated Notes Mail server. This type of server doesn't do anything other than store the user's mail databases and route mail to other mail servers or other mail systems. The benefits of setting up a dedicated servers are easy to sum up:

- Easier mail administration because mail and application databases reside on separate servers.
- Easier to troubleshoot mail routing problems because fewer servers are involved.
- Reduces network traffic because fewer, if any, Server Connection documents are involved, which means mail delivery is handled within one or only a few servers.
- Better mail routing performance because mail servers can be set up on the same Notes named network, which routes mail immediately.

But when should you set up a dedicated mail server and how many should you have? The answer to both of these questions, like most answers, depends on your unique Notes network. The following two questions, however, should help you decide whether or not to create dedicated Notes Mail servers (answer "yes" to both questions and a dedicated mail server is for you):

1. Do you have the available hardware and software resources for a dedicated machine?
2. Is Notes Mail the primary messaging system in your organization?

In regard to the first question, I've read countless articles in various industry trade publications that assume every network is large, with a massive MIS department. The focus of the article could have been Lotus Notes network planning, NetWare-to-NT migration plans, or a complete network topology design and implementation. No matter what the focus was, the emphasis and the target audience were always the same: large-scale situations with thousands of users and endless amounts of money to spend. Although the articles were very informative and well written, they made the assumption that every network is large, with a massive MIS department to support it, and a budget that has no end. This assumption couldn't be further from reality.

If your company is one of the majority of small to medium-sized companies with strict budgets and limited available resources, then answering the first question is critical. To put it plainly, if you don't have the available hardware and software resources to dedicate to a single Notes server task, then dedicated mail servers are out of the question for you. Just because the resources aren't available today, however, doesn't mean they won't be available in the future. Make sure your Notes network plan has a place in it for future inclusion of dedicated Notes Mail servers.

Now let's look at the second question you need to answer before deciding on setting up a dedicated Notes server: is Notes Mail your primary messaging system in your organization? We'll assume for the moment that you've heard the criticisms of the Notes Mail interface. You've looked at Notes Mail in Release 4. You've considered the criticisms and what you've seen, and decided that Notes Mail is going to be the primary messaging system for your company. Great! The people at Lotus Development love you. And I, a Notes consultant/network integrator, would love to talk to you about your project (please pardon the shameless plug). However, this decision also drives another decision: the need for dedicated Notes Mail servers.

When Notes serves the role as primary messaging system, treat it the same way you would treat any other primary messaging system: give it dedicated machines to run on and dedicated professionals to keep it running smoothly.

The Server Connection Document

Once you've selected the supporting Notes network topology, you're ready to create or edit the Server Connection documents to enable mail routing between servers, which can be done using one of two approaches:

- Select the Public Address Book and then select Create ➢ Server ➢ Connection from the menu bar.
- Open the Public Address Book, expand the Server view in the navigation pane, click once on Connections, and click the Add Connection button on the Action bar.

Whether you'll create a new Server Connection document or edit an existing one depends on a few things:

- If you've previously set up a schedule for replication between servers, you can use the same Server Connection document and add mail routing to the Tasks field that already has replication listed.

- If you've set up dedicated mail servers within the same Notes named network, you won't need any Server Connection documents because mail routing happens automatically between servers in the same Notes named network.
- If you have servers on different Notes named networks and don't already have an existing Server Connection document, you'll need to create a new document with mail routing selected in the Tasks field.
- If you've previously set up a schedule for replication between servers but want to schedule mail routing to occur at different times than replication, you can create another Server Connection document, select mail routing in the Tasks field, and fill out the remainder of the schedule according to your particular needs.

Regardless of whether you're creating new Server Connection documents or editing an existing one, there are three important fields under the Routing and Replication section of the Server Connection document that directly affect mail routing. These fields are defined below and shown in Figure 9.8.

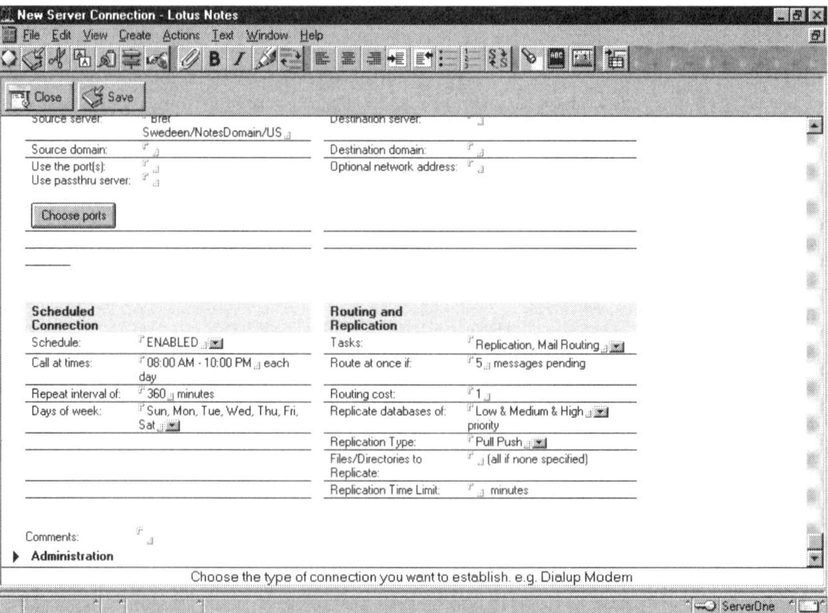

FIGURE 9.8

The Routing and Replication section of the Server Connection document displays three fields that directly affect mail routing.

- **Tasks:** As with replication, this is where you can select Mail Routing from a list of tasks to be included as a task for this Server Connection document.
- **Route at once if:** You can set the number of pending mail messages that forces routing to occur on this server. The default is five but can be increased or decreased depending on your situation. Trial and error is the best way to find what number works best. Remember, you want mail routing to occur frequently enough that mail gets delivered quickly, but not so frequently that your server is always busy connecting to another server to route mail.
- **Routing cost:** This is where the cost of this connection is set. This number is used by the mail router to determine the least expensive route for mail delivery when more than one route is available. Routing costs are computed by the mail router and then stored in the router's internal routing tables. The larger the number the higher the cost, and you can increase or decrease this number to force particular connections from being chosen over others.

Mail Routing

If you've read the previous section, then you're no stranger to the Server Connection document and should already be well aware of which fields are important with regard to mail routing. However, the question still remains: how should you configure the Server Connection document to ensure quick and efficient mail routing? As usual, the answer is not simple and not the same for every Notes network. The only way to really answer the question is to have a clear understanding of the different ways mail routing works in different situations. Once you're armed with that knowledge, you should be able to handle the rest.

Routing Mail within the Same Notes Named Network

The situation for mail routing is simplest when messages are being sent between users in the same Notes named network. In this situation, Server Connection documents are unnecessary because mail routing happens automatically. Figure 9.9 illustrates this arrangement. When a message from

User A on Server A is sent to User B on Server A, the Notes workstation locates User B's address in the Public Address Book. Then the Mail Router examines the address of the location of User B's mail database and delivers the message directly to the addressee's mail database.

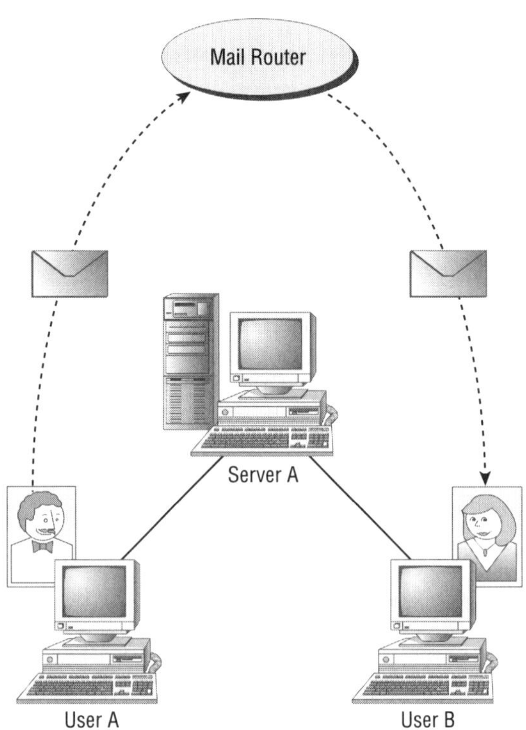

FIGURE 9.9
Mail routing within the same Notes named network to an addressee on the same server

If User B were located on Server B in the same Notes named network as User A, the Mail Router would place the message in the MAIL.BOX on Server B. Then the Mail Router on Server B would pick up the message from its MAIL.BOX file and place it in User B's mail database (see Figure 9.10).

Routing Mail between Different Notes Named Networks

Routing mail between different Notes named networks is the first situation where you'll need to utilize Server Connection documents. If you previously set up scheduled replication between two servers in different Notes named networks, you can use these previously existing Server Connection documents

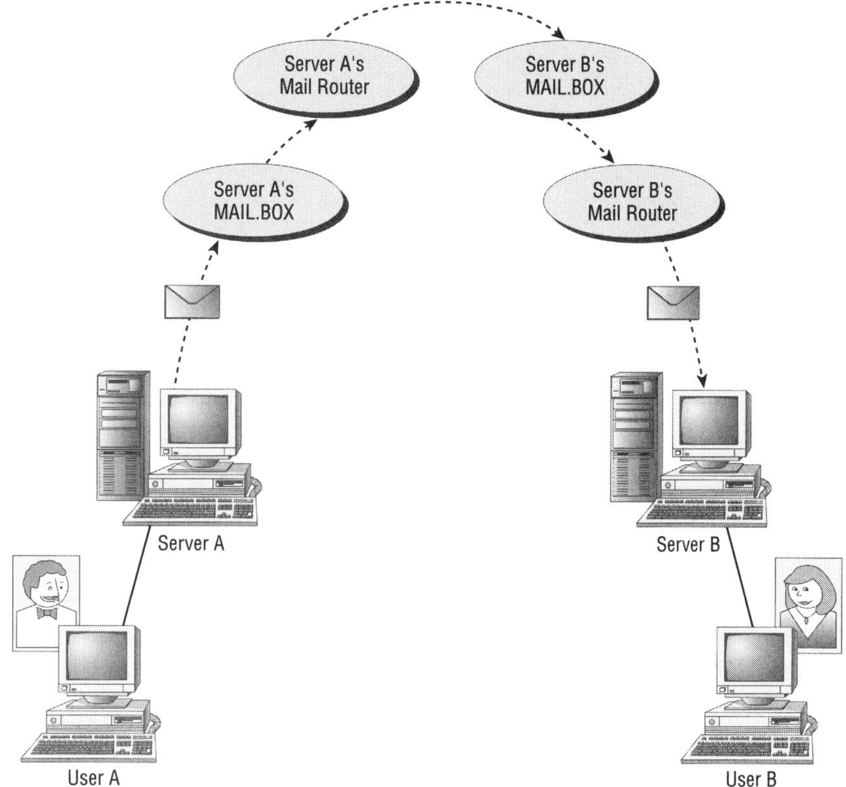

FIGURE 9.10
Mail routing within the same Notes named network to an addressee on a different server

for mail routing by simply selecting Mail Routing in the Tasks field of the Server Connection document (see Figure 9.11). Keep in mind, however, that mail routing is different than replication.

With replication you only needed one Server Connection document to enable two-way replication between servers. In this situation, one server was responsible for establishing the connection, but after the connection was established both servers could exchange information both ways as long as security and the replication method were set correctly.

Mail routing works differently. With mail routing, you need to make sure that there is a Server Connection document on both servers, otherwise mail routing becomes a one-way operation. If a Server Connection document enables Server A to connect with Server B, but there is no such document

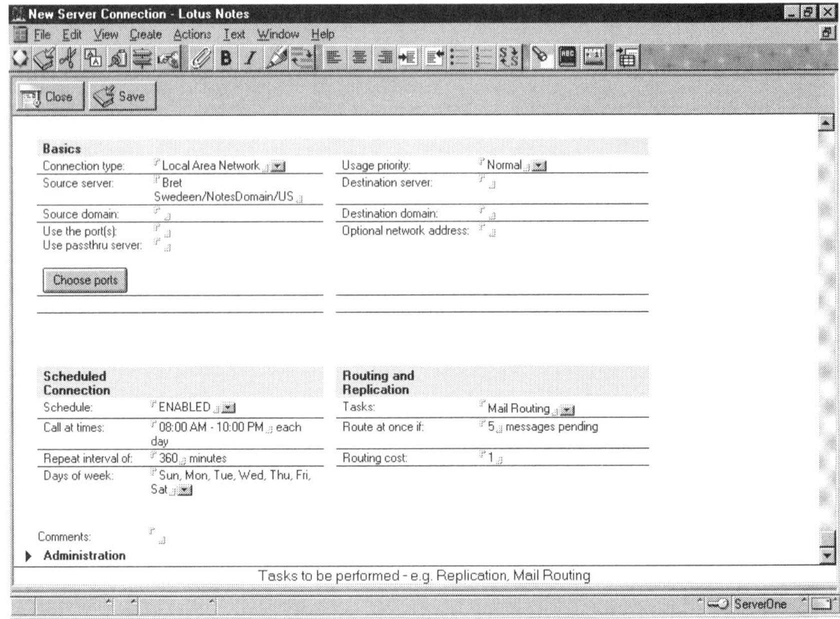

FIGURE 9.11 Select Mail Routing from the Tasks field in the Routing and Replication section of the Server Connection document to enable mail routing with the same document used to enable replication.

enabling any type of connection from Server B to Server A, then Server A can send mail to Server B, but Server B can't send any mail to Server A because its Mail Router doesn't know where Server A is.

When you administer a complex Notes network that requires a considerable amount of mail routing to deliver messages to their final destination, it is critical that you completely understand how mail routing works in order to avoid and/or troubleshoot problems. Remember, the Mail Router examines the address to determine the location of the addressee's mail database location. When that location is a different server on a different Notes named network, the Mail Router needs to know not only that the server exists but also how to get to that server. It is the same as if you had heard about a store called Acme Five & Dime but didn't know where it was; you could think about going there, but until you knew where it was you'd never get there.

Establishing Server Connection documents between servers in the same domain ensures a direct route for mail between each server. If, however, there is a server that is part of both Notes named networks, and if Server Connection documents exist between that server and servers in each of the Notes named networks, then that server can be used as an intermediary mail routing server without adding additional Server Connection documents. In this situation, a message delivered from Server A to Server C in the same domain but on a different Notes named network will use Server B as an intermediary routing hop to reach its destination, because the Mail Router on Server A knows that the way to Server C is through Server B (see Figure 9.12).

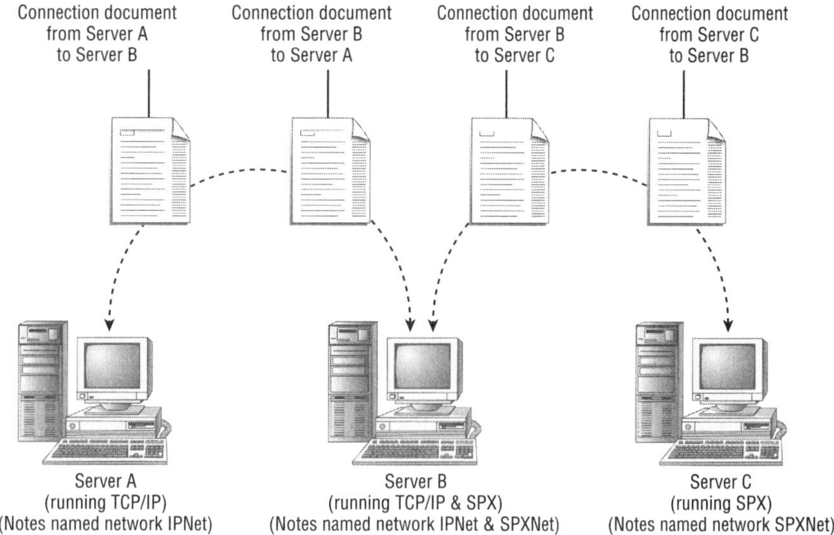

FIGURE 9.12
Routing mail using an intermediary server as a routing mechanism

A mail message travels through the connection illustrated in Figure 9.12 in the following manner:

1. User A on Server A creates a message to User C on Server C and sends it.
2. The message is sent to the MAIL.BOX on Server A.
3. The Mail Router on Server A picks up the message from the MAIL.BOX and checks the address and locates the Person document for the addressee in the Public Address Book. By examining the Person document, the Mail Router discovers that the addressee's mail database is located on Server C.
4. Server C is located in a different Notes named network so the Mail Router looks through the Server Connection documents in the Public Address Book for a connection between Server A's Notes named network and Server C's Notes named network.

5. The Mail Router locates a Server Connection document from Server A to the Notes named network of Server C through Server B which has a connection to both Notes named networks.

6. Server A's Mail Router delivers the message to the MAIL.BOX on Server B.

7. Server B's Mail Router picks up the message from its MAIL.BOX and, because it has a Server Connection document to Server C, sends it to the MAIL.BOX on Server C.

8. Server C's Mail Router picks up the message from its MAIL.BOX and places it in the addressee's mail database to complete the process.

Each mail message delivered between servers in different Notes named networks follows the previously described steps. Even if you have several Notes named networks, the basic process is the same. The critical part of this process occurs at the beginning when the first server is looking for a route to deliver its message. If, in the previous example, there were no intermediary server to provide a route for the message, the message would never have made it to its destination. Even if the two servers were physically next to each other on the same network segment, the message would still never have found its destination, because the Public Address Book had no Server Connection document to link the two servers.

Creating a Server Connection Document Explicitly for Mail Routing

Now that you understand the details of how mail routing works within the same and different Notes named networks, you can proceed creating or editing the appropriate Server Connection documents to enable mail routing within your Notes domain. Creating a new Server Connection document isn't much different for mail routing as it is for replication, but, as a quick refresher and future reference, here are the steps to follow:

1. Select the Public Address Book.

2. From the menu bar select Create ➢ Server ➢ Connection (as shown in Figure 9.8).

3. In the Connection Type field select Local Area Network from the drop-down list for servers that are physically connected to the same LAN, or select Dial-up Modem for servers that connect across a modem. If you

select Dial-up Modem, options relating to the modem's serial port and phone numbers will appear and need to be completed. (Dial-up connection is typically used for connecting to servers in other domains, which will be covered later in this chapter.)

4. Confirm that the correct server is listed in the Source Server field and change it if necessary.
5. In the Source Domain field enter the correct domain (this field becomes more important as you start to connect with other Notes domains or foreign domains).
6. Enter the name of the server you want to connect with in the Destination Server field.
7. Enter the name of the domain for the destination server in the Destination Domain field.
8. In the Use the Port(s) field enter the port to use for this document. This is an important field when connecting servers on different Notes named networks. You'll want to enter the port that is common between the two servers. For example, if Server A is using Netbios over LAN0 and Server B is using Netbios over LAN0 and NetWare SPX over the SPX port, then you'd enter LAN0 as the port to use. You can also enable several ports using the same document by separating them with a comma or entering an asterisk to use the first port in the list of enabled ports.
9. In the Tasks field, make sure that Mail Routing is entered.

Although you have a great deal of flexibility with selecting ports, I suggest you use one port per document because it makes administration and mail troubleshooting much easier.

That is all you need to fill out if you're connecting servers on the same physical network. If, however, you're connecting servers across modems, then you'll want to fill out a couple more fields. The following steps pick up where the last set left off:

1. Enable the Schedule field if it is disabled.

2. In the Call at Times field you can enter a range of time or specific times for this connection to occur (this is much the same as what you would do to enable a replication schedule).

3. In the Repeat Interval Of field enter a time range, in minutes, if you entered a range of time in step 2.

4. In the Days of the Week field enter the days that this connection is valid for. Since this connection is for mail routing, I suggest leaving every day listed.

5. Back in the Routing and Replication section you may also want to adjust the value for the Route at Once If field. The default is 5, which means that a connection will occur and mail will be transferred if five or more mail messages are pending. You can increase or decrease this number depending on your unique situation.

As a final point, I suggest filling out the Comments field. Even though comments are not required, I suggest entering some explanatory information here about the creation of this particular Server Connection document. This comment may help others that need to administer your Notes network while you're on vacation, out sick, or after you've been fired—oops, I mean after you've moved on to a higher paying, more important position elsewhere.

Mail Routing between Adjacent Domains

Mail routing between adjacent domains isn't much different from mail routing between different Notes named networks, except that in the Server Connection document you'll enter a different domain name in the Destination Domain field.

Adjacent domains are basically two different Notes domains connected directly to each other and cross-certified accordingly. The direct connection can be either a common LAN, a shared WAN backbone, or a dial-up connection. (Typically, adjacent domains are connected to one another over a dial-up connection.) Figure 9.13 illustrates what adjacent domains look like between fictional companies Acme Widgets and Bret's SuperStores.

The actions that take place when mail gets routed between adjacent domains is exactly the same as when mail is routed between different Notes named networks. Server Connection documents are still the key for the Mail Router to find the path to route mail through. The only real difference is that

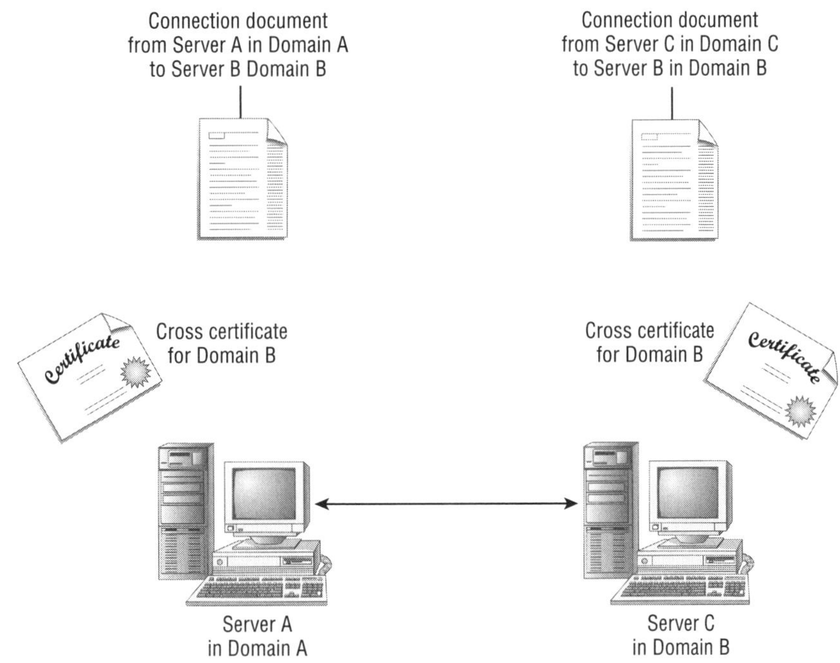

FIGURE 9.13

Acme Widgets is Domain A, which is adjacent to Domain B, Bret's SuperStores. These two domains know about each other through a Server Connection document and have cross-certified each other so that they can exchange mail and replicate selected databases.

all mail typically passes through the same server to reach the other domain because you usually only enable one server to connect to the adjacent domain. The steps listed below detail the actions to create the situation illustrated in Figure 9.13.

1. User A on Server A in the Acme Widgets domain sends a message to User B on Server B in the Bret's SuperStores domain.

2. The Mail Router on Server A looks in the Public Address Book to find out how to get to Server B in Domain B. Server A finds out that it has a Server Connection document to Server B in Domain B.

3. Server A holds the message in its MAIL.BOX and waits for the next connection to Server B before further routing takes place.

When messages are queued up in the MAIL.BOX you can take a look at this database to see the pending mail by opening this database and looking at the default view.

1. Select File ➢ Database ➢ Open from the menu bar.
2. Select the server whose MAIL.BOX you want to view.
3. In the Filename field, type **MAIL.BOX** and press Open.
4. The database is added to your workspace and opened for you to view (see Figure 9.14).

FIGURE 9.14

Pending mail in the MAIL.BOX on Server A

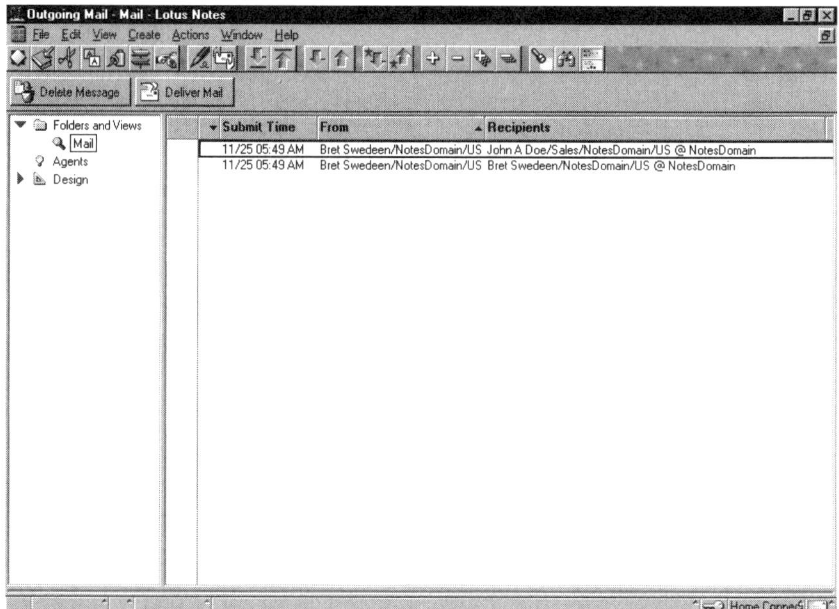

Pending mail gets routed to its next hop according to connection details in the Server Connection document as follows:

- If it's time for a scheduled connection that has mail routing listed in its Tasks field, the message is routed to its next hop (in this case, Server B in Domain B).

- If the Route at Once If threshold has been reached, then a connection is forced and mail is routed.
- If the message priority has been set to High, and the MailDisablePriority in the NOTES.INI hasn't been set to 1, then a connection is forced and the mail is routed.

Once a connection is established between Server A and Server B, the message is placed in the MAIL.BOX on Server B and then that server's Router task picks it up and routing continues the same way it does between different Notes named networks.

Mail Routing between Non-Adjacent Domains

Before you can set up mail routing between non-adjacent domains, you first have to know what a non-adjacent domain is. Fortunately, this means exactly what it says: a non-adjacent domain is a domain that is not adjacent to yours. In other words, you have no direct connection to it and probably have not cross-certified with it. However, the two non-adjacent domains can communicate with each other through a third domain to which each is adjacent (see Figure 9.15).

Mail routing to a non-adjacent domain travels from your domain to an adjacent domain and from that adjacent domain to the non-adjacent domain. The adjacent domain is what your domain and the non-adjacent domain have in common. At one time, you cross-certified with this adjacent domain and the non-adjacent domain also cross-certified with this adjacent domain. Since you know about Domain C shown in Figure 9.15, you can create a non-adjacent domain document to simplify mail addressing. Now, if you create a non-adjacent domain document for Domain C, then instead of sending mail to John Doe @ Domain C @ Domain B you can just type John Doe @ Domain C. The non-adjacent domain document specifies that all mail sent to Domain C is routed through Domain B.

Most Internet mail addresses consist of one long string of text with names and Internet abbreviations separated by periods, underscores, and @ signs. Spaces, especially around the @ sign, usually aren't found in Internet mail addresses. Notes mail addressing between different Notes domains is similar to Internet mail addressing except that spaces around an @ sign are normal. Usually, if you enter a Notes mail address such as, JohnDoe@DomainA, Notes will actually add the missing spaces so the address looks like this: John Doe @ Domain A.

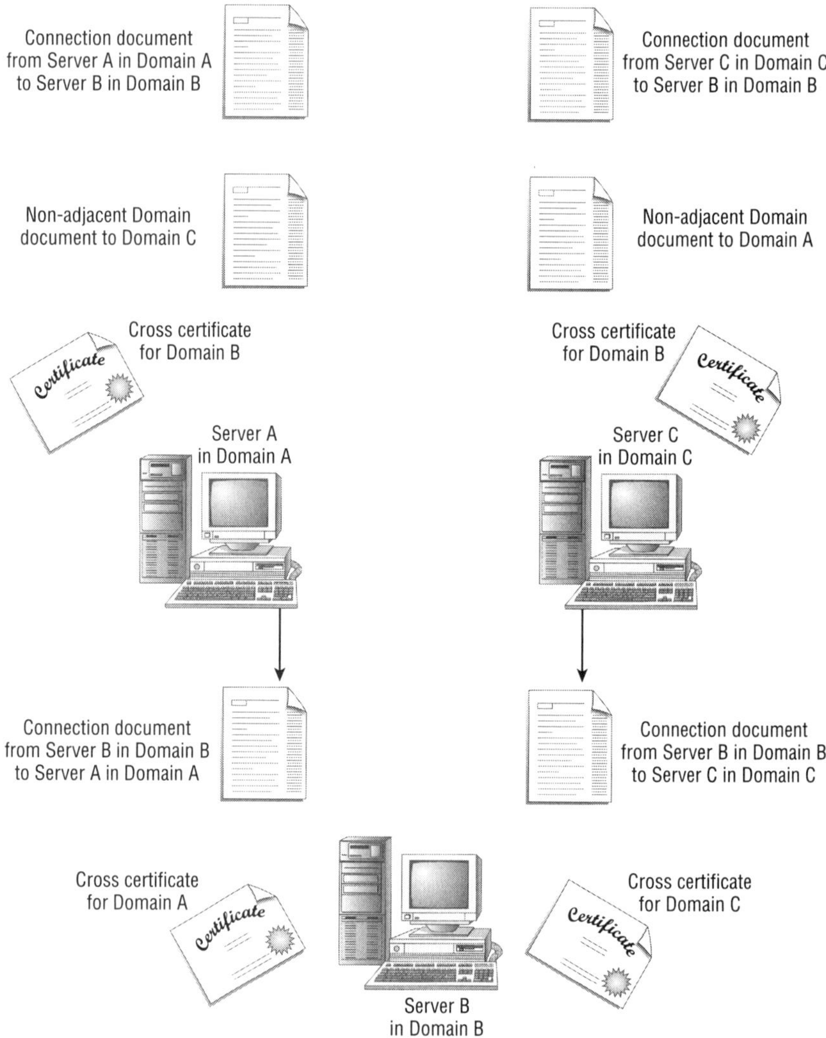

FIGURE 9.15 Domain C is a non-adjacent domain to Domain A. In this example, Domain B is adjacent to Domain A and Domain C, which allows it to serve as the common domain between A and C.

Non-Adjacent Domain Document

To enable mail routing to this non-adjacent domain, you need to create a Non-adjacent Domain document (see Figure 9.16).

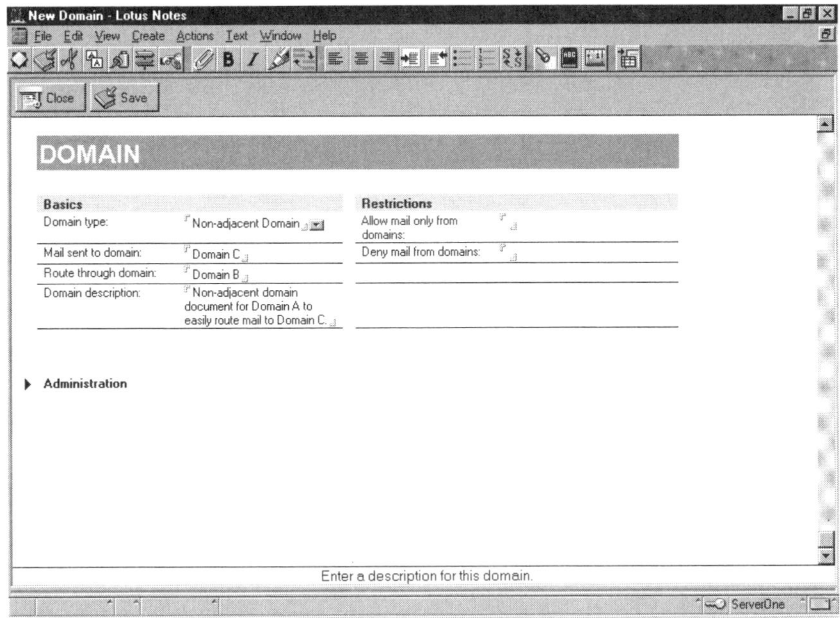

FIGURE 9.16
A New Domain document for a non-adjacent domain

1. Select the Public Address Book and then select Create ➢ Server ➢ Domain.
2. From the Domain Type drop-down list, choose Non-adjacent Domain.
3. In the Mail Sent to Domain field enter the name of the non-adjacent domain. In the case of the examples I've been using, I would enter **Domain C**.
4. In the Route through Domain field enter the name of the adjacent domain you have in common with the non-adjacent domain. In the case of the examples I've been using, I would enter **Domain B**.
5. Enter an optional description in the Domain Description field and save the document.

The new Domain document instructs the Mail Router to send any mail addressed to the non-adjacent domain to the intermediary adjacent domain. The adjacent domain will complete the mail routing process because it has a direct connection to the destination domain.

The Non-Adjacent Domain Document reads and acts much like a routing instruction. The following list defines the fields found in the Basics section of the Domain document mentioned in the previous step-by step instructions:

- **Domain type:** A pop-up keyword list of domain types. Select Non-adjacent Domain and some of the fields shown on the document will change.
- **Mail sent to domain:** Name of the non-adjacent domain you want to route mail to.
- **Route through domain:** Name of the adjacent domain you have in common with the non-adjacent domain. The adjacent domain acts as an intermediary between your domain and the non-adjacent domain.
- **Domain description:** Optional field that helps quickly explain the reason for this document to other Notes administrators.

A quick way to understand a Non-adjacent Domain document is to string together the second and third field names and read it just like a complete sentence. For example, if Domain A were the value for the second field and Domain B were the value for the third field, it would read as follows: Mail sent to Domain A route through Domain B.

How Messages Are Routed between Non-Adjacent Domains

Once a Non-adjacent Domain document has been created, messages sent to this domain are handled in the following manner:

1. User A on Server A in Domain A sends a message to User C on Server C in Domain C.
2. The Mail Router on Server A looks in the Public Address Book to find the location for User C. The router does not find a User C, so it looks for a connection to Server C. The router does not find a connection to Server C, so it looks for a Domain document for Domain C. The router finds the Non-adjacent Domain document for Domain C and learns that mail sent to this domain should be routed through Domain B. The router looks for a Server Connection document to a server in Domain B and finds one.

3. Server A holds the message in its MAIL.BOX and waits for the next connection to Server B before further routing takes place.

4. When a connection between Server A and Server B is established, the message is passed from Server A to Server B. The message is queued in Server B's MAIL.BOX.

5. From this point, the message is handled as if it were a message sent to an adjacent domain. Server B eventually connects to Server C, passes the message to that server, and the message is delivered to its final destination (see Figure 9.17).

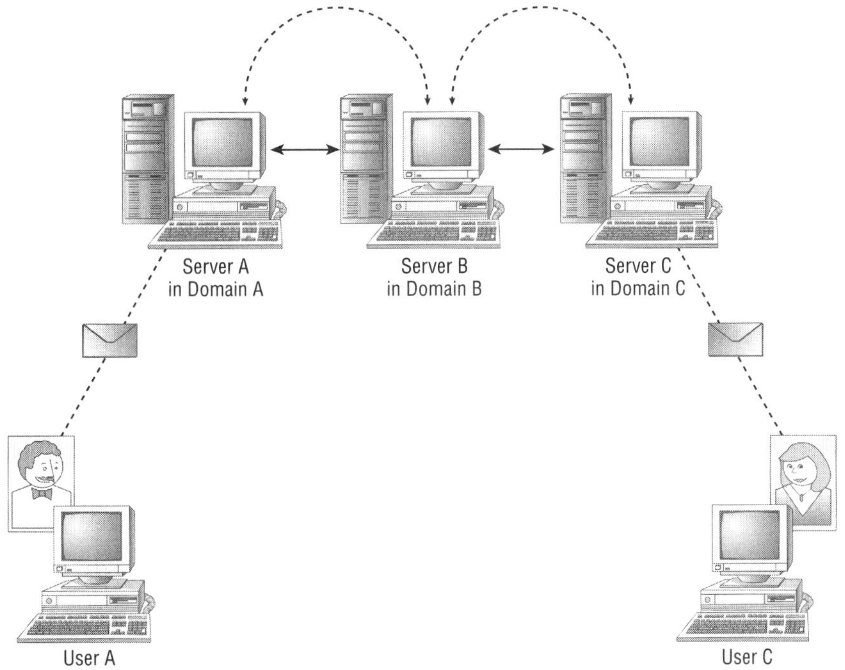

FIGURE 9.17

Messages flow from User A on Server A in Domain A to User C on Server C in Domain C. Server B in Domain B is an adjacent domain to Domain A and Domain C and acts as a routing intermediary between these two non-adjacent domains.

Don't forget that for mail routing between non-adjacent domains (as well as adjacent domains) to deliver mail in both directions, the appropriate Domain and Server Connection documents must exist on the connecting servers in both domains. Each server's Router task relies on these documents to locate a route to the destination server.

Connecting with Foreign Domains

Adjacent domains, non-adjacent domains, and now foreign domains? Yes, there is yet another domain type to consider when setting up mail routing. Fortunately, you'll only have to deal with foreign domains if you plan to route mail to a foreign mail system.

A foreign mail system has nothing to do with a mail system in a foreign country; it refers to any mail system that is not Notes Mail. The issue with exchanging mail with foreign systems is the actual format of a message. Notes will format a message one way, cc:Mail will format a message another way, and so on. Gateways, or Message Transfer Agents (MTA), assist with the translation of a message from one format to another.

Prior to Notes Release 4, gateways were used to exchange messages with foreign systems. Gateways translated, as best they could, messages from one format to another. With the introduction of Release 4 came the MTA, which can provide the same functionality as a gateway, but can also exchange a message in native Notes format.

If you've decided to connect to a foreign mail system and exchange mail, you'll have to set up a couple of documents in the Public Address Book first. Fortunately, most of what you've learned about routing mail to other adjacent domains, non-adjacent domains, and other Notes named networks is also applicable here.

The first document needed to enable foreign mail exchange is a new Domain document with Foreign Domain selected as the Domain Type. Then simply fill in the remaining fields in the Basics section of the new Domain document. Figure 9.18 shows a new Foreign Domain document.

The following list describes each of the required fields to make this document work:

- **Domain type:** Since this is a Domain document for a foreign domain the Foreign Domain value should be selected for this field. By default, Foreign Domain is selected when you create a new Domain document.

- **Foreign domain name:** Enter the domain name for the foreign mail system. Usually this name was determined when the gateway, or MTA, was installed. If you haven't installed the gateway at this point, cancel the creation of this document and install the gateway, then come back and create this domain document.

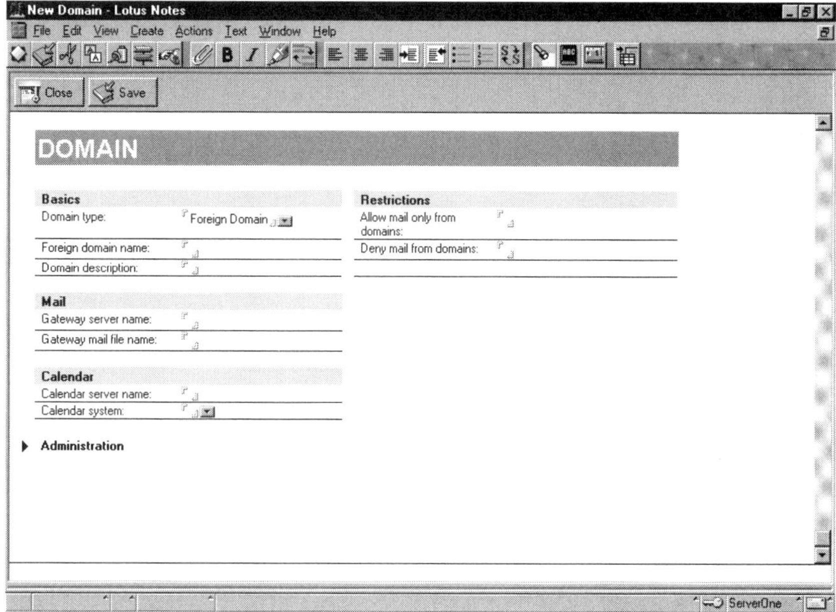

FIGURE 9.18

Create a new Domain document and select Foreign Domain from the Domain Type field.

- **Gateway server name**: When you set up a gateway it will typically be located on one server. Enter the name of that server in this field.
- **Gateway mail file name:** Like the field name suggests, enter the gateway's mail file here. The name of this file should be provided in the documentation that came with the gateway.
- **Domain description:** This field is not required, but I strongly suggest that you enter in some type of description here so that Notes administrators can quickly understand the purpose for this document.

After you create the Domain Document for the foreign mail system you should be all set. Keep in mind that a Server Connection document is not needed because the Foreign Domain document has already specified the server's name and that server's mail file that supports the gateway. You'll also notice that with a Foreign Domain connection no cross-certification is required. The reason is that certification is a Notes-specific operation and foreign domains have no means of certifying with a Notes server the way that Notes does.

The cc:Mail, SMTP, and X.400 Message Transfer Agents

Notes Release 4.5 includes three Message Transfer Agents that were previously sold separately. Each MTA exchanges Notes Mail with a specific mail system.

- **cc:Mail MTA**: Allows Notes servers and workstations to synchronize directories and exchange messages between Notes and cc:Mail. While you can use this MTA to exchange mail between cc:Mail and Notes Mail, you can also use it as an intermediate solution during a cc:Mail to Notes Mail migration.
- **SMTP MTA**: Allows Notes servers and workstations to exchange mail over the Internet. With the increasing popularity of the Internet, this MTA is becoming more and more important and is also required to enable the Notes POP3 mail support (see the *Notes POP3 Mail Support* sidebar for details).
- **X.400 MTA**: You can use this MTA to connect to an X.400 and allow Notes servers and workstations to exchange mail with users on foreign mail systems.

Since POP3 Mail support relies on the existence of the SMTP MTA, which is not covered here, actual POP3 configuration details are beyond the scope of this book.

Because these three MTAs are not mail gateways, they operate a little differently. A mail gateway translates messages from Notes Mail format to the mail format of the foreign system and vice versa. An MTA, on the other hand, can either translate a mail message the same way a gateway does or it can send a message in native Notes format.

Getting into the details of configuration and operation of these MTAs is beyond the scope of this book. Therefore, for further details refer to the appropriate documentation for each MTA.

Notes POP3 Mail Support

POP3 mail (Post Office Protocol Version 3) is an Internet protocol that allows a workstation running POP3 software, such as Netscape Navigator, Eudora, or Pegasus Mail to retrieve messages from a host server (typically a UNIX machine) also running POP3. In Release 4.5, Notes servers can now act as host servers for workstations running POP3 software. These workstations don't need the Notes client software, but must have a Notes mail file on a Notes server that has been configured as a POP3 server.

In a nutshell, using a Notes server as a POP3 server requires the Notes server to be configured with TCP/IP, run the POP3 server task, and create server-based mail files and Person documents for each POP3 client that will use the Notes server as its POP3 host. Also, at least one server in the Notes network must have the SMTP MTA installed to handle the transport of POP3 mail.

Once everything is configured, POP3 support works in the following manner:

- The Notes POP3 server listens for connection requests from POP3 clients over TCP/IP port 110.
- POP3 clients establish a connection with the Notes POP3 server over TCP/IP.
- The Notes POP3 server authenticates the client using standard POP3 authentication (the user name and password contained in the Person document).
- If authentication is successful, the Notes server gives the client access to his or her Notes mail file.

Standard POP3 authentication is used between client and server because POP3 clients do not use Notes IDs and their Person documents don't contain public keys. Therefore, they can't authenticate using Notes authentication (discussed in Chapter 7) and can't receive encrypted mail.

Multi-Threaded Mail Routing

Now that you know how to route your mail within your domain, with another domain, with external mail systems, and so forth, you may find that with all this routing your server needs a little help to make sure that it can route things quickly. Remember, one of the main objectives of a mail system, whether it be Notes Mail or some other, is for the mail to be delivered quickly to its destination. One way to ensure that your server routes mail quickly is to take advantage of Notes' multi-threaded mail routing ability.

Multi-threaded mail routing is a feature that allows a Notes server to initiate mail routing connections to multiple servers simultaneously. In much the same way that you can enabled multiple replica tasks to run on the server, you can also enable multiple mail routing connections through a setting in your NOTES.INI file.

In the NOTES.INI file a setting called MailMaxThreads determines the maximum number of transfer threads that the Mail Router task can create per server port. The obvious default for this parameter is 1 thread per port, but that can easily be increased by editing this value.

How many threads should you specify? Well, I've got some good news and some bad news for you. The bad news is that the maximum number of threads really depends on your operating system. Can the OS you've selected support multiple threads (or on some systems multiple processes)? Does your server have adequate resources to efficiently support more than one thread? You'll have to experiment with this value to find a happy medium. The good news, however, is that you can experiment with high values because the mail transfer threads are only created when there are actual messages waiting to be transferred.

My suggested value for MailMaxThreads is based on how many servers you exchange mail with. If your Notes network has twenty-five servers, then enter **25** as the value. With this value you're anticipating twenty-five messages going out all at once to twenty-five different servers all across the same server port. The chances of this situation happening are very unlikely so you'll probably never create that many threads at once, which means your server will never get bogged down with multiple mail transfer threads.

Controlling Mail Routing

As you've set up mail routing to other adjacent, non-adjacent, and foreign domains you've probably noticed that while you can route mail through these domains to other domains, there's nothing to stop these domains from treating your domain in the same manner. The fact is, you might only be interested in receiving incoming mail that is explicitly for your domain and prefer that your domain not act as an intermediary between domains. If this level of control is something you'd like to have, Notes does provide a means to do so through the use of restriction settings available in the Domain document.

Options to Prevent Mail Routing

If you think back to when we created the different types of Domain documents, there was a section called Restrictions (as shown in Figure 9.18). This section has two specific fields that directly affect who can route mail to the domain for which this document was created. These two fields are described below:

- **Allow mail only from domains:** List the domains that can send mail to the domain specified in the Domain Name field (the actual field name may vary depending on which Domain type you selected for this Domain document). Keep in mind that this restriction applies to mail for which the previous hop is one of the listed domains. For example, if you list Domain A in this field, then only mail coming from Domain A is allowed. The mail does not have to originate in Domain A, it only has to pass through Domain A to be allowed in.

- **Deny mail from domains:** List the names of the domains that will be denied mail routing access to the domain listed in the Domain Name field. This particular field is most useful when you are creating Adjacent Domain documents as a security means to deny explicit mail routing. Explicit mail routing is when someone uses a complete domain addressing scheme so that the Mail Router doesn't have to rely on Non-adjacent Domain documents to resolve the destination for a message. For example, a user in Domain A addresses a message to User D in Domain D in the following manner:

  User D @ Domain D @ Domain C @ Domain B

A message addressed in this manner could bypass the restriction applied in the Allow Mail Only from Domain field because the Non-adjacent Domain document would not be referenced to resolve routing. The reason for this is because the address itself told the router exactly what to do. The routing actions that take place are listed below:

1. The router in Domain A sees that this message is for Domain B and passes it along according to its Server Connection document.

2. The router in Domain B picks up the message and sees that it is for Domain C and passes it along according to its Server Connection document.

3. Then the router in Domain C picks up the message and sees that the message is addressed to someone in Domain D so the router passes it along according to its Server Connection document.

4. Finally, the router in Domain D receives the message and delivers it to the addressee.

To prevent explicit mail routing between domains you can create an Adjacent Domain document and in the Deny Mail from Domains field list the names of the domains that you want to deny mail from.

Mail Routing and Priority Levels

The last part of controlling mail routing has to do with users and message priority levels.

Priority levels only affect mail that relies on a Server Connection document or Domain document to make it to its destination. Priority levels have no affect on messages sent to destinations within the same Notes named network.

Each mail message can be set to one of three priority levels before it's sent: High, Normal, or Low.

- A message set to High priority will disregard any connection schedules you've created and force a connection to route itself immediately.
- Normal is the default setting and causes mail to behave according to the routing guidelines you've established.
- A setting of Low, by default, causes mail to be routed only between midnight and 6 AM. Even if low priority mail is pending and a connection is established to route normal and high priority mail, the low priority mail will just sit and wait until its designated time. You can, however, alter the default time for low priority mail by changing the MailLowPriorityTime setting in the NOTES.INI file.

Different priority levels are helpful when used wisely, but they can also cause excessive server-to-server connections, which might overburden your server or cause low priority messages to not get sent. To override the priority setting of a mail message, use the MailDisablePriority setting in the NOTES.INI file and set it to 1. This setting will cause all mail to be treated as if it were normal priority.

Shared Mail

Lotus Notes Release 4 introduced a new mail feature called Shared Mail, also referred to as "single copy object store." This new feature is a space-saving enhancement that allows administrators to set up a single database for mail storage. This database can be configured to store all mail messages or just mail messages sent to two or more people on the same server. The feature is transparent to users and basically acts the same as non-Shared Mail.

Enabling Shared Mail

The real kicker for Shared Mail is getting started. Fortunately, setting up Shared Mail is a very simple process. All you need to do is to create a Shared Mail database and tell the Mail Router to use it. The following server console command does just that:

TELL ROUTER USE *SHARMAIL.NSF*

SHARMAIL.NSF is simply a suggestion for the name of the Shared Mail database that you want to create. Any valid filename for your operating system will work.

The previous command does the following:

- Creates a database with the specified name.
- Sets the Shared_Mail parameter in the NOTES.INI file to 2, which enables Shared Mail delivery for new mail delivered to this server and for new mail transferred through this server. This parameter can also be set to 0, which disables Shared Mail, or set to 1, which uses the Shared Mail database for new mail delivered to this server but not for mail transferred through this server.

- Creates a file called MAILOBJ.NSF in the Notes data directory. MAILOBJ.NSF is a database link that points to the Shared Mail database currently in use. This database is important because, as you'll learn later, you can create new or additional Shared Mail databases and MAILOBJ.NSF helps the Mail Router send mail to the current Shared Mail database.

Once Shared Mail is enabled, mail sent to the server using Shared Mail is handled in the following manner:

1. The Mail Router separates the message header from the message body, which also can include attachments, and stores a copy of the header in each recipient's mail database and then stores the message body in the Shared Mail database.
2. When a user opens the message, a link to the message is activated and the user can read the message unaware that the message is stored in a Shared Mail database.
3. When the user deletes the message, it is actually the header in his or her personal mail database that is deleted. The body of the message remains in the Shared Mail database.
4. When all of the users have deleted the header from the mail databases, the body of the message is removed from the Shared Mail database by the Object Collect task, which runs by default on the server every day at 2 AM.

Security Considerations for Shared Mail

OK, so enabling Shared Mail is fairly easy, but something about shared doesn't sound very secure. It is true that the word "share" doesn't really imply safe or secure; however, in the case of Shared Mail, "shared" refers to a single object store as a method for conserving disk space.

Don't be alarmed. "Shared," in terms of Notes mail, doesn't mean everyone can read everyone's mail. "Shared" in this situation is just a quicker way to say "single copy object store."

The Shared Mail database is encrypted so only the server ID that created it can access it. Unlike the MAIL.BOX, the Shared Mail databases isn't something you're going to add to your workspace even as an administrator. Even if you took the server ID file and tried to add the database to your workspace, it won't work. This approach fails because the database's Access Control List (ACL) specifies that the server ID can only be used as a server and not a workstation. Furthermore, even if you could add the database to your workspace, it doesn't have any views and none can be added to it.

OK, so now Shared Mail sounds pretty secure, but you'd still rather not take a chance with all of your users. The fact is, your boss, despite your explanations, just doesn't believe Shared Mail is secure. Therefore, excluding his mail from the Shared Mail database would be much easier than trying to change his mind. Fortunately, Notes allows you to selectively exclude certain mail databases from being shared using the following server console command:

LOAD OBJECT SET -NEVER *BOSSMAIL.NSF*

BOSSMAIL.NSF can be the name of any valid mail database on the server where Shared Mail has been enabled.

If Shared Mail causes the paranoid population of your user community to throw a conniption because they believe their Encrypt Incoming Mail setting is being compromised, tell them to get a grip. Any user that has enabled Encrypt Incoming Mail in the user preferences will be excluded from Shared Mail. Any messages sent directly to them or through group membership will be stored in their personal mail database and encrypted, just as they would without Shared Mail enabled on their mail server.

Creating a New Shared Mail Database

There may be a point where you'll need to create another Shared Mail database. Perhaps your Shared Mail database has grown quickly and you find it easier to administer, or to avoid problems altogether, when the database is small. For this reason or others, you can easily create another Shared Mail database with the following server console command:

LOAD OBJECT CREATE *SHRMAIL2.NSF*

SHRMAIL2.NSF is the name of another Shared Mail database that you may want to create. SHRMAIL2.NSF is only an example and any valid filename for your operating system will work.

After you create a new Shared Mail database, you'll need to tell the router that this is where to deliver Shared Mail. Issue the following server console command and the MAILOBJ.NSF will direct mail from the Mail Router to the new Shared Mail database:

TELL ROUTER USE *SHRMAIL2.NSF*

Now the Mail Router will deliver Shared Mail to this database instead of the previous database. The first Shared Mail database is still around, it's just not receiving new mail deliveries. If users still have message headers pointing to messages in the first Shared Mail database, they'll still work. Remember, all we've done with the new Shared Mail database is redirect MAILOBJ.NSF to this new database. The old database is still around and any valid message headers still point to this older database and can still open the entire message.

Shared Mail Maintenance

Aside from creating new Shared Mail databases you'll also find yourself manually purging messages from the Shared Mail database, unlinking mail files when you remove users from the system, and sometimes deleting the Shared Mail database completely.

Purging Old Mail

Manually purging old messages is easy. While the Object Collect task purges old messages every day at 2 AM by default, you may find some occasions when you'll want to do it yourself. The following server console command will forcibly remove obsolete messages from the Shared Mail database:

LOAD OBJECT COLLECT *SHARMAIL.NSF*

Removing Mail from Old Users

When a user is removed from the Notes environment where Shared Mail was being used, his or her mail messages will still be in the Shared Mail database. Since these messages don't belong to anyone anymore you'll want to remove them to conserve disk space. Start by unlinking the user's mail from the Shared Mail database with the following command:

LOAD OBJECT UNLINK *USERMAIL.NSF*

Now delete the user's mail database as you would any other file on your system. Finally, force the Object Collect task to run just in case there is any space to be reclaimed in the Shared Mail database.

If, for whatever reason, you delete the user's mail database before unlinking it from the Shared Mail database you'll have dangling messages with no headers pointing to them. This situation causes a space problem because with no headers pointing to the message contents there is no way for the Object Collect task to know that these messages should be purged. When this situation occurs, manually run the Object Collect task with the "force" parameter:

LOAD OBJECT COLLECT -FORCE *SHARMAIL.NSF*

Running the Object Collect task with the additional option forces it to purge all messages associated with a mail file that cannot be located or successfully opened.

Use the "force" option with extreme caution. You run the risk of deleting messages that belong to mail files that are only temporally unavailable. Make sure you back up all mail files and the shared mail database before manually executing the Object Collect task with the "force" option.

Removing the Shared Mail Database

Removing the Shared Mail database is much like removing a single user from the Shared Mail database.

1. Start by disabling Shared Mail by setting Shared_Mail in the NOTES.INI to 0.

2. Unlink all of the user's mail from the Shared Mail database with the following command:

   LOAD OBJECT UNLINK *SHARMAIL.NSF*

3. Finish by deleting the Shared Mail database as you would any other file.

When to Use Shared Mail

I'm sure it's obvious that Shared Mail can be a very powerful feature; however, I don't recommend using it just because it's there. Shared Mail has the potential of adding extra administration, so you want to implement it only when there is a clear need for it.

Consider setting up Shared Mail when one or more of the following situations is true for your Notes environment:

- A high volume of mail is sent to mailing lists of users on the same mail server. Shared Mail will save disk space by only having one copy of a message for several users to share.
- A high volume of mail messages is being forwarded between users on the same mail server. Shared Mail allows people to easily share a personal message by moving that message to a common folder instead of forwarding a copy of it to everyone who wants to see it.
- A high volume of messages with attachments regularly being sent to two or more people at a time. Once again, Shared Mail allows you to save disk space in this situation by only storing one copy of the message and attachment.

One final note about Shared Mail: keep this mail feature in the back of your mind when planning your Notes network. Don't let the knowledge of Shared Mail drive your Notes network design just because you think Shared Mail is a great new feature that you have to implement. Use Shared Mail in your Notes network when it makes sense. In some cases you may want to get the Notes environment going and then let the server-by-server mail usage drive the decision to implement Shared Mail. And if you do decide to use Shared Mail, make sure you only set it up on the servers that will truly benefit from it.

Troubleshooting Mail Problems

When messages fail to reach their destination, you usually hear about it pretty quickly. Second only to printing, mail delivery failures can cause the greatest amount of frustration and panic. E-mail is quickly becoming the preferred way to exchange documents and when the mail doesn't get delivered, people get upset.

As the Notes administrator, you'll be the one expected to resolve any mail problem no matter how simple. Here are a few tips to help you troubleshoot a delivery problem. In many cases these steps have to be done from the user's workstation:

- **Try it again:** More often than not sending a message a second time usually does the trick.
- **Check the address:** Make sure the destination address is entered correctly. The slightest syntactical mistake can cause a message to stop dead in its tracks.
- **Send a message yourself:** Make sure mail in general is working and that nothing weird is going on.
- **Try sending a message to someone else from the problematic location:** Make sure the user with the problem can send messages to other locations. If they can't but others can, then you know you have a very localized problem.
- **Run a trace:** Reserve this for when all else fails.

Running a Trace to Troubleshoot Mail Delivery Problems

Sending a mail trace is an administrative tool (new in Release 4) that you can use to test whether a mail message can be successfully delivered without actually sending the message. Sending a mail trace is useful in situations where mail delivery is failing, or if you set up a new Server Connection document for mail routing and want to test the new routes. To run a trace, follow the steps listed below:

1. From the menu bar select File ➢ Tools ➢ Server Administration (see Figure 9.19).
2. Click the Mail icon and choose Send Mail Trace from the drop-down menu.
3. Enter the mail address of a particular user (see Figure 9.20).
4. Select one of two options in the Send Delivery Report From field:
   - **Each router on path:** Select this option to receive a delivery report from each router on the path. This option is helpful when you have a very complex Notes Mail environment with lots of possible routes.

- **Last router only**: This option sends a delivery report only from the last router on the path, which is useful in a simple Notes Mail environment or in situations where you just want to see how far the message is getting.

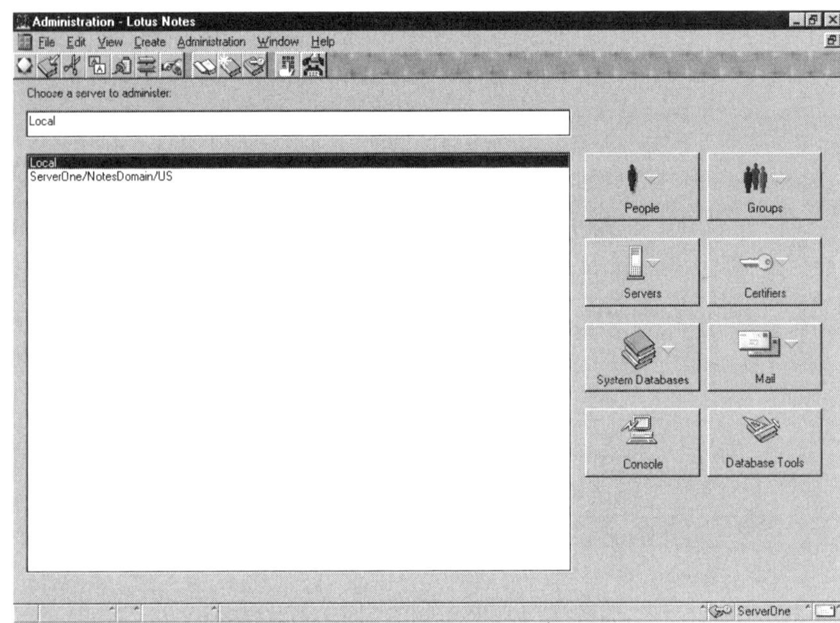

FIGURE 9.19
The Server Administration screen provides several administration options.

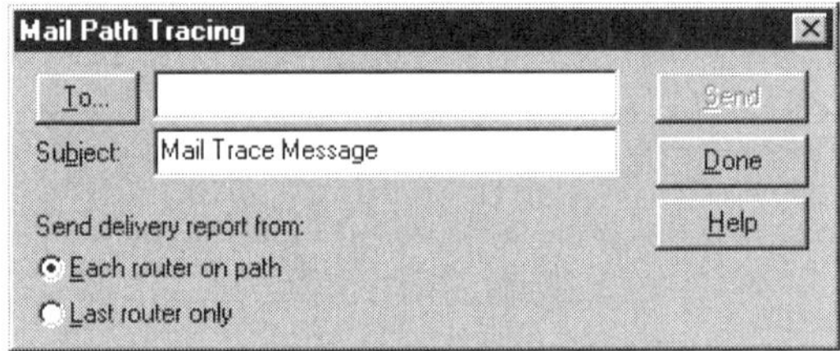

FIGURE 9.20
The Mail Path Tracing dialog box appears when you choose the Send Mail Trace option from the Mail button on the Server Administration screen.

5. Finally, click the Send button and wait for a trace report (see Figure 9.21).

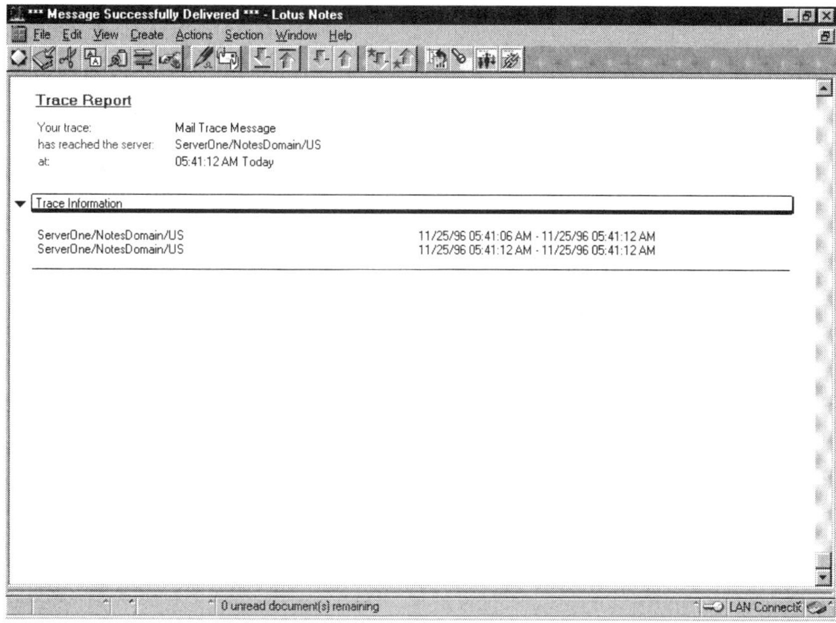

FIGURE 9.21
A sample Trace Report, which is unique to each Notes network

The Trace Report is a very useful tool for tracking delivery problems because you can quickly learn where in the route the message is failing and you can focus in on that one area instead of looking everywhere. You should also notice that knowing how mail gets delivered is very useful in deciphering a Trace Report.

As I said before, electronic mail isn't rocket science, although some people would like you to think that it is. In the Notes environment, electronic mail is made up of three to five elements:

- A user's personal mail database.
- The MAIL.BOX on the server.
- The router task running on the server.
- Server Connection documents to facilitate mail routing.
- Domain documents also to facilitate mail routing.

Mail routing is the action whereby all or just some of these elements interact together and pass messages from one location to another. If you break down Notes Mail into its basic elements and don't lose sight of how these elements work together, you should have no problem keeping your Notes Mail system up and running.

Summary

Notes Mail functionally hasn't changed a tremendous amount since Release 3. Personal mail databases, the MAIL.BOX, and the Mail Router still exist. And Server Connection documents and Domain documents still help messages reach their destination. What Release 4.5 has provided in the way of mail is a superior user interface, built-in Message Transfer Agents, Shared Mail capabilities, POP3 mail support, and better troubleshooting tools, like Send Mail Trace. Hopefully, the new mail features and enhancements will quiet the critics of Notes Mail and help them see that Notes Mail is a powerful solution for today's, and tomorrow's, enterprise-wide messaging needs.

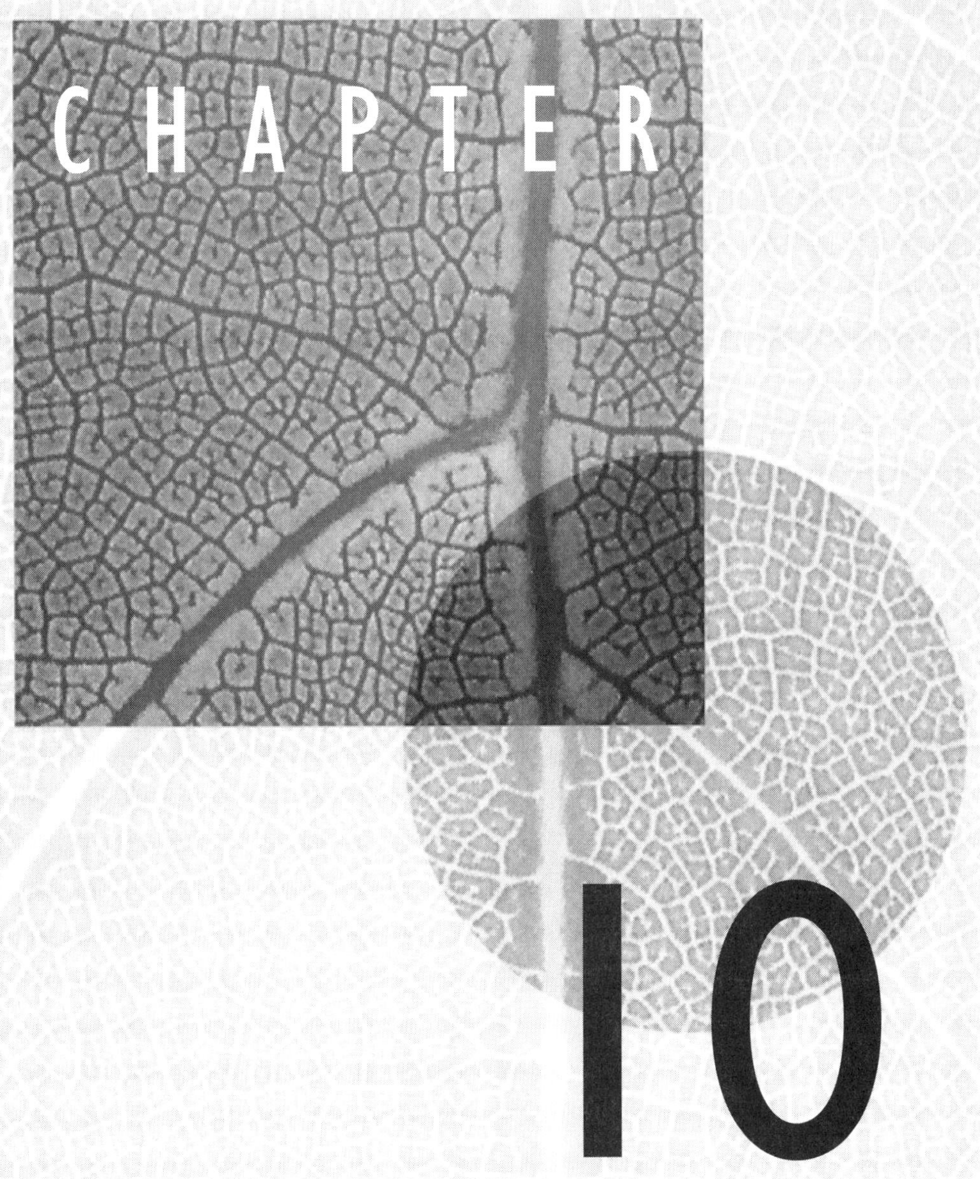

Notes Calendaring and Scheduling

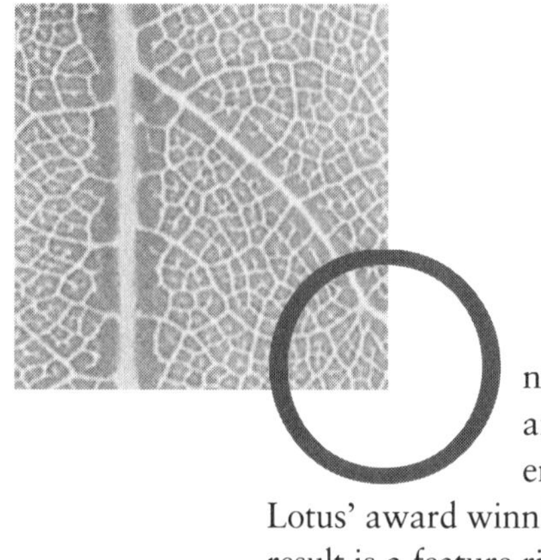

One of the most anticipated features in Notes 4.5 is calendaring and scheduling. This new feature combines IBM's expertise in enterprise-wide, host-based calendaring and scheduling with Lotus' award winning personal information manager (PIM), Organizer. The result is a feature rich calendaring and scheduling solution delivered to the Notes user community through the familiar Notes mail interface.

This new feature brings additional functionality to the To Do view and adds the Calendar view and the Meetings view to the user's mail database. These views allow users to leverage the groupware and client server architecture of Notes to make calendaring and scheduling a collaborative activity not possible with a standard, single-user PIM.

Users can now schedule appointments, events, and anniversaries and share that information with all, or just some, Notes users. This shared information makes it possible for users to more effectively coordinate meetings by performing a "free time" search. This new search feature allows users to view when other users and common resources, such as conference rooms, are available.

The end result might appear to be time management nirvana. Unfortunately, despite the power that calendaring and scheduling provides, time management utopia is possible, but not guaranteed. In order for these features to work effectively, people must participate by keeping their calendars current with appointments, meetings, and any other time commitments. Without full user participation, free time searches aren't reliable. Hence, conference rooms are reserved when they're already in use. And users, thought to be available, are busy with other commitments.

As a Notes administrator, your responsibility for calendaring and scheduling is different from your responsibility for other aspects of Notes. There is, of course, some technical responsibility, such as ensuring that the server-based scheduling task is running. However, now there is also a non-technical responsibility which requires that you step outside or your traditional technical role and become what I like to call a calendaring and scheduling evangelist.

The calendaring and scheduling evangelist is a "feature champion" who spreads the word about calendaring and scheduling by helping users learn how to unleash all of the power captured in this feature. Through proactive feature demonstration and daily personal usage of their own, evangelists help calendaring and scheduling take hold in the Notes environment.

Even if you have someone else in your M.I.S. organization who is going to take on the role of calendaring and scheduling evangelist, as the Notes administrator you'll still have to fill this role from time to time. If you don't, users looking for an excuse not to use calendaring and scheduling will point to your lack of enthusiasm as justification for their non-participation. Don't be an excuse for someone. Take charge and be a feature champion. Otherwise, calendaring and scheduling will fail and some people may try to blame you and the product.

How Calendaring and Scheduling Works

Before you can take on the non-technical responsibilities of calendaring and scheduling, you'll first need to fulfill your technical responsibilities. You'll need to understand how calendaring and scheduling does its behind the scenes work and make sure that the required server tasks are up and running.

The Free Time Manager

Notes keeps track of all of the schedules for users and resources with the Free Time Manager, which relies on two server tasks that run on the Notes server: the Schedule Manager (SCHED.EXE) and the Calendar Connector (CALCONN.EXE). The Schedule Manager is a server task that maintains the Schedule database on the server where busy time information is collected. The Calendar Connector connects Notes servers with one another to perform free and busy time searches. During a standard Notes server installation these tasks are added to the ServerTasks setting in the NOTES.INI file and start up automatically whenever the Notes server starts.

When Schedule Manager first starts it creates a database on the server called BUSYTIME.NSF (if one doesn't already exist). Then it adds an entry to this database for each user that has a mail database on that server. This database acts as a central repository for busy times and is what gets referenced when users search for free and busy time of other users and resources. This start up process is repeated for each Notes server in your environment that contains users' mail databases.

When users search for free time to arrange a meeting, the Busy Time database is referenced for the available time data. If a user invited to the meeting has a mail database on a server other than the one currently being referenced, the Free Time Manager calls the Calendar Connector task which in turn refers to the Public Address Book to find the path between the user doing the inviting and the invitee's mail server. When this path is established, the Busy Time database (BUSYTIME.NSF) for the invitee is searched for free time and the results are returned to the user performing the free time search.

With the appropriate systems in place, the Free Time system can also search free time availability for users who are using Lotus Organizer or IBM's Office Vision.

Making Sure Calendaring and Scheduling Is Running

On the Notes server, calendaring and scheduling is driven by two server tasks: SCHED.EXE and CALCONN.EXE. Therefore, you can easily make sure that calendaring and scheduling is working in your environment by periodically checking the status of these tasks with the **Show Tasks** command at the server prompt or through the remote server console (see Figure 10.1).

FIGURE 10.1 Entering **Show Tasks** at the server console reveals that the Schedule Manager and Calendar Connector tasks are idle, which also means they are fully functional.

```
Lotus Notes Server: ServerOne/NotesDomain/US

    Task                  Description

Database Server       Perform console commands
Database Server       Listen for connect requests on LAN0
Database Server       NetBIOS name server for LAN0
Database Server       Cluster Manager is idle
Database Server       Idle task
Database Server       Idle task
Replicator            Idle
Cluster Replicator    Idle
Cluster Directory     Idle
Calendar Connector    Idle
Schedule Manager      Idle
Admin Process         Idle
Agent Manager         Executive '1': Idle
Agent Manager         Executive '2': Idle
Agent Manager         Idle
Indexer               Idle
Router                Idle
Replicator            Idle
Billing               Idle
Cluster Admin         Initializing

> _
```

Setting Up Calendaring and Scheduling

There isn't much to actually setting up calendaring and scheduling in your Notes environment. As explained in the section *How Calendaring and Scheduling Works*, the required server tasks are automatically started. What else could there be? Well, at this point users can start using the new feature but you'll probably want to set up the Resource Reservation database first. This database is not mandatory but it does help users benefit from all that calendaring and scheduling has to offer.

The Resource Reservations Database

The Resource Reservations database is an important piece of calendaring and scheduling. This database is available to all users and acts as a catalog of company resources. Items such as conference rooms, overhead projectors, and teleconferencing equipment are listed in this database and made available to all Notes users.

As the Notes administrator, you'll need to create this database based on the Resource Reservations template (RESRC45.NTF) in the following manner:

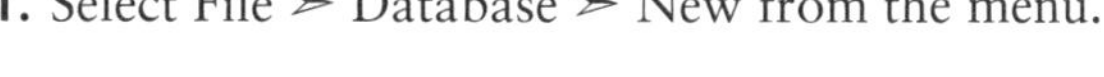

1. Select File ➢ Database ➢ New from the menu.

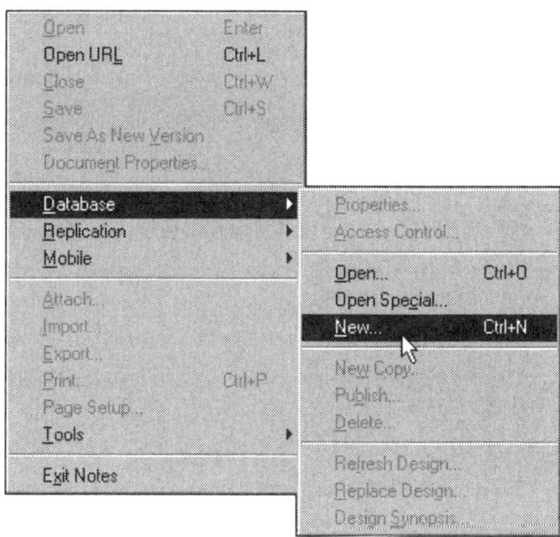

2. Make sure the server name listed in the Server field is for the correct server.

3. In the Title field, type the name of the database (for example, Room Reservation). Notice that the name entered in the File Name field automatically gets an extension of .NSF (in this example, the filename is ROOMRESE.NSF).
4. At the bottom of the dialog box, click Show Advanced Templates.
5. In the scrollable selection box, select Resource Reservations (4.5) with the template name and the filename of RESCR45.NTF.
6. Click OK to create the database (see Figure 10.2).

FIGURE 10.2

The New Database dialog box with information to create the Room Reservation database

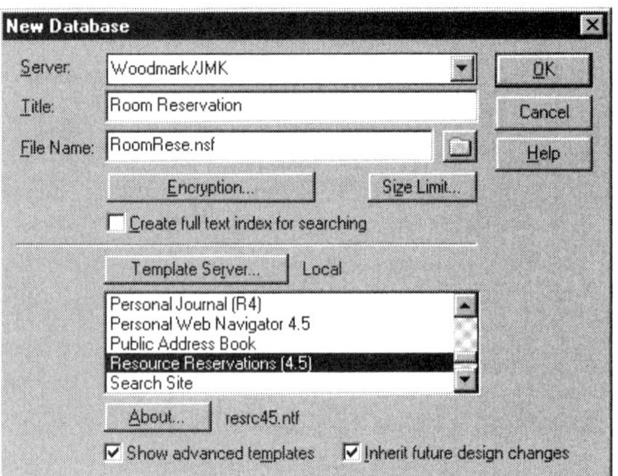

Once the Resource Reservation database is created on the server, your job is far from over. Next you'll need to utilize the Site Profile, Resource, and Reservation forms to list and manage company resources.

Creating a Site Profile

Start with the Site Profile form. In order to fill out the Site Profile document you must be named in the CreateResource role in the ACL of the database. To name yourself in the CreateResource role, select File ➢ Database ➢ Access Control and when the Access Control List dialog box is displayed, select your name on the left and click the CreateResource role on the right. Click OK when you're done. Once you have proper access, select Create ➢ Site Profile from the menu bar in the Resource Reservation database.

The Site Profile form is required before any of the other forms can be created because resources must be associated with a site.

The Site Profile form requires the information pertaining to the site name (for example, Building 10), the domain name of your Notes server, the server name, and the resource reservation filename.

Creating a Resource

After creating the Site Profile, you can create a new resource by filling out a Resource form. From the menu bar in the Resource database, select Create ➢ Resource. Fill out the Resource form by giving the resource a name and selecting what type of resource it is. If the resource is a room, you will need to fill out the times when the room will be available and provide a detailed description of the room.

When these resource documents are created, a corresponding record is created in the Public Address Book for each resource. This gives the Free Time Manager the ability to track the available time for the resources.

Keep in mind, if you have multiple replicas of the Resource Reservations database, the resource will only be available after the Administration Process adds the resource to the Public Address Book and it is replicated to all of the replicas.

By default, if a resource is invited to a meeting, it automatically gets booked and cannot be double booked. For example, if you schedule a meeting and invite ten people, and you schedule a conference room and an overhead projector for that meeting, the conference room and overhead will automatically be invited and that meeting time will be blocked out for those resources. If you would prefer to have someone manage the calendars for the conference room or the overhead, that can be accomplished by giving someone access to that calendar. Details regarding how to do this are discussed in the *Advanced Calendar Options* section later in this chapter.

Creating a Reservation

Finally, after you create a Site Profile and create resources associated with that profile, you can create a reservation in order to reserve a resource for a specific time. Here is the first instance of the role of the calendaring and scheduling evangelist. You, and anyone else fulfilling this role, will have to completely understand how to create a reservation so you can disseminate this knowledge to the masses.

To get started, highlight a resource in the Resource Reservation database and select Create ➢ Reservation from the menu bar. Then fill out the Resource form by entering the name and phone number of the person who this reservation is for. Next, select either Room or Resource. Click the Continue button, and depending on which resource you selected, Room or Resource, the form will bring up the available times for the room or resource. Continue by entering the date, time, and site for the reservation. Depending on what you selected, insert the resource or the number of attendees for a room reservation in the corresponding field. Finally, click the Search button to continue and Notes will search for available times. Close and save the document.

Ideally, you will reserve a resource or schedule a meeting using the Calendar entry in your mail file.

Changing or Deleting a Resource

If you want to change anything other than the resources or the times and days the resources can be scheduled, then you must delete the Resource document and create a new Resource document. If you want to change a resource's availability, just highlight the document and in the Action bar, click the Edit Document button.

If you want to delete a resource, highlight the resource and click the Delete Resource button in the Action bar. Do not use the Delete key to delete the resource from the database because if you do a request gets sent to the Administration Request database and then you must go into the Public Name and Address Book and approve the request for deletion.

If you have a company that acquires new resources on a regular basis, you might consider delegating the responsibility of maintaining site profiles and resources to someone other than yourself.

Setting Up Users for Calendaring and Scheduling

Setting up calendaring and scheduling for users is a cross between Notes administration and typical end-user desktop support. The administration aspect is the understanding you have of how calendaring and scheduling works in your environment. Thus, you can easily comprehend and explain what the various user setup options mean. The end-user desktop support portion is the direct user contact that this setup requires. You can't really sit in your secure data center and configure everyone's calendaring and scheduling options. You have to actually work with the end-user face to face (or over the phone) to set up their options. Try not to think of direct end-user contact as something negative, but rather as the perfect opportunity to spread the word about calendaring and scheduling.

Keep in mind that the person who helps users during this configuration process will be identified by the user community as the first person to look to for additional help. While I strongly advocate getting involved in this process, be careful whom you assist. Helping the wrong person could make the wrong friend for life, while helping the right person (for example, the CEO), could help further the cause of calendaring and scheduling.

The Calendar Profile

The heart of calendaring and scheduling for the end-user is the Calendar Profile. This form determines such things as who can view the user's calendar, when the user is available, and whether or not certain invitations are automatically accepted. To create a Calendar Profile, select the user's mail database and then select Actions ➢ Calendar Tools ➢ Calendar Profile from the menu bar (see Figure 10.3).

Notice that the Mail File Owner field is automatically filled in for the user. If you are setting up someone's mail file you should make sure the person who owns the mail file has their name in this field. Notes makes it quite easy to select someone else's name. To do so, click the down arrow next to the Mail File Owner field. Choose the name from the Public Address Book and click OK.

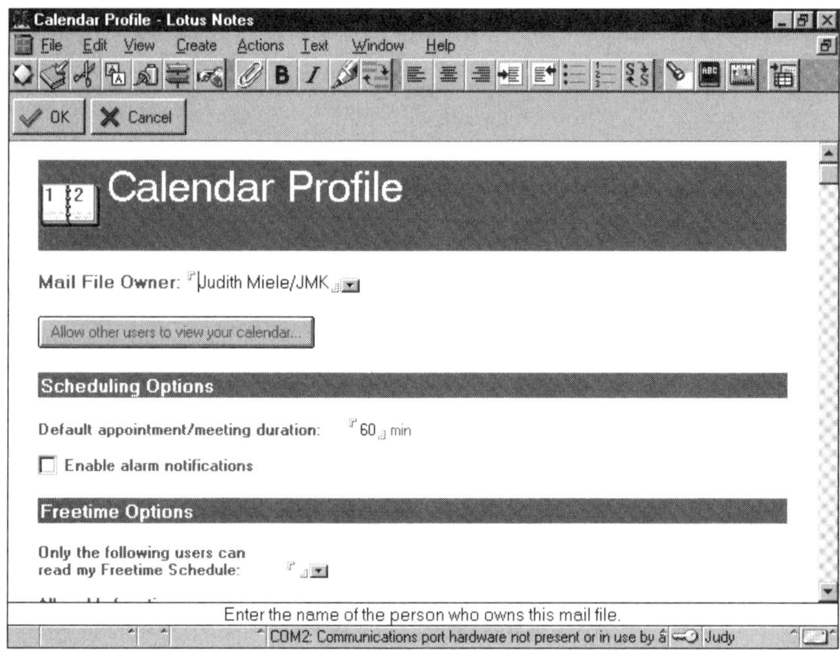

FIGURE 10.3 The Calendar Profile document automatically fills in the Mail File Owner field with the information from the user ID.

Scheduling Options

The first section displayed in the Calendar Profile document in Figure 10.3 is the Scheduling Options section. This section is used to specify the length of time for meetings, which, by default, is set to sixty minutes. For example, when you create a meeting for 1 PM your time will be blocked out until 2 PM. If your meetings typically run longer than sixty minutes, change the default number accordingly.

Below the Default Appointment/Meeting Duration box is the Enable Alarm Notifications checkbox. Placing a check in this box enables alarms for invitations, events, anniversaries, or reminders. By default, this option is not checked.

If you decide to enable alarms, you'll notice that another checkbox appears: Automatically Set Alarm(s) For. This additional checkbox, when checked, causes yet another set of checkboxes to appear. With these additional boxes you can specify the amount of time prior to appointments, meetings, reminders, events, or anniversaries that an alarm should sound.

Freetime Options

The second half of the Calendar Profile document (see Figure 10.4) is the Freetime Options section. This section starts with the Only The Following Users Can Read My Freetime Schedule field, which is left blank by default, allowing everyone access to your free and busy time. Keep in mind, however, that other users can only see the times which you are available, which has nothing to do with actually reading your meetings from your calendar. If you prefer for only certain people to have access to your free and busy times, then designate those people by clicking the down arrow next to this first field and selecting their names from the Public Address Book.

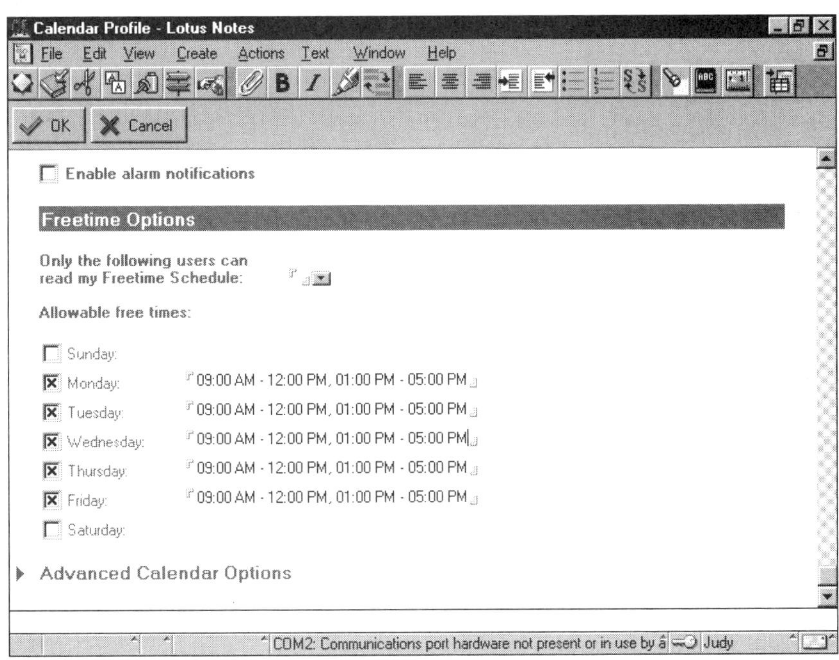

FIGURE 10.4 The Calendar Profile includes the default settings for the Freetime Options section.

In the Allowable Free Times section, select and deselect the days of the week for which this person (or room or resource) is available. For example, if your company has flex time and you work Monday through Thursday for ten hours a day, then you would deselect Friday and type in **8:00 AM - 6:00 PM** next to Monday, Tuesday, Wednesday and Thursday. Then, when free time searches are done, only these days and times are checked.

Advanced Calendar Options

Advanced Calendar Options appear next in the Calendar Profile document (see Figure 10.5). This section is collapsed, which prevents you from viewing the additional options that this section contains. However, simply click the section heading and the additional options appear.

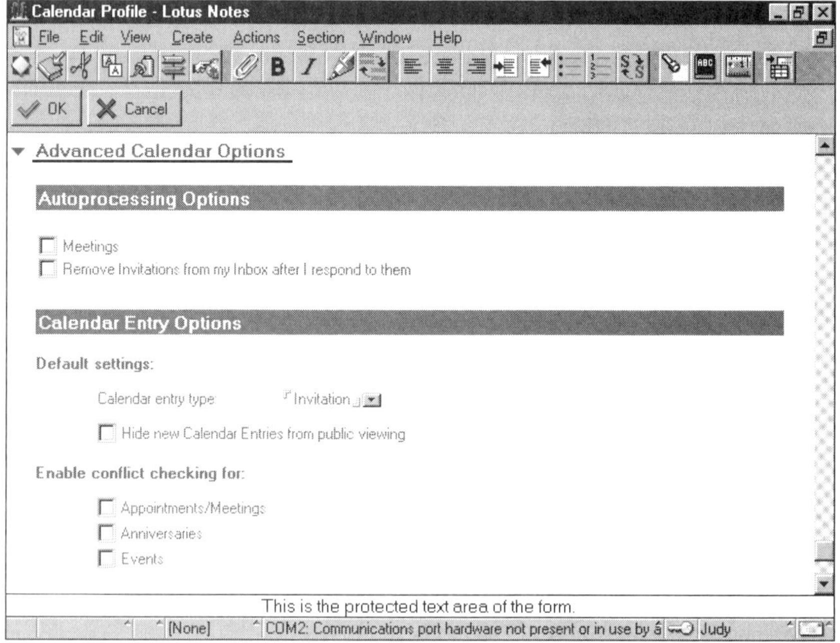

FIGURE 10.5 By clicking the section heading Advanced Calendar Option, all of the information for the section is displayed.

The additional options available in the Advanced Calendar Options section are contained in two smaller sections: Autoprocessing Options and Calendar Entry Options.

By default, all the meeting invitations must be processed manually by the user. When a user receives an invitation, they can either accept it, decline it, or delegate it. The Autoprocessing Options section provides an option for users to automatically accept all invitations. Checking the Meetings box enables this time saving feature. Normally, however, this feature is used for auto-processing resources and room availability. Generally, a room or resource can be scheduled for a meeting and if someone invites (or schedules) a certain VCR or room for the meeting, Notes will automatically accept the invitation if there are no conflicts. However, in some cases, someone might be in charge of designating training rooms or equipment. In this situation the designated person can be given the authority to manage a resource's calendar. Therefore, you would uncheck the Meetings option in the resource's Calendar Profile to allow the person to manage the calendar.

Another time saving feature available in the Autoprocessing Options section is the Remove Invitations from My Inbox After I Respond to Them option, which automatically deletes invitations from the user's in box. Normally, when invitations are sent to users, they appear in that user's in box and stay there until the user puts them in the trash or moves them to a folder. If, however, users would like invitations to automatically be deleted once they respond to them, they can check the Remove Invitations from My Inbox After I Respond to Them option. Even with this option checked, a user can still view these invitations in their Meetings view or Calendar view.

If you get an invitation which does not require you to respond (a Broadcast invitation) then Notes will delete this message from your in box after you add it to your calendar.

The second of the two smaller sections in the Advanced Calendar Options section is the Calendar Entry Options. This section allows users to specify the type of entry they create most often. The default is Invitation but can easily be changed to Appointment, Event, Reminder, or Anniversary depending on which entry type they prefer.

This section also allows users to easily hide their calendar from public viewing by placing a check in the box preceding Hide New Calendar Entries from Public Viewing. Selecting this option makes every new calendar entry confidential and does not allow the entries to be viewed by others, even when someone else is given access to the calendar.

The final option in the Calendar Entry Options section is for conflict checking. Users can enable conflict checking for Appointments/Meetings, Anniversaries, and Events. When a user accepts an invitation or places an entry into their calendar with this feature enabled, Notes will inform the user when they have a conflicting engagement.

The Delegation Profile

Complementing the Calendar Profile document and completing the calendaring and scheduling set up process for the end-user is the Delegation Profile. This profile allows the user to designate other users to have Read and Write access to public documents (calendar meetings, responses, events, and anniversaries) in their mail file. This profile can be created by either clicking the Allow Other Users to View Your Calendar button in the first section of the Calendar Profile (as shown in Figure 10.3), or from the menu bar by selecting Actions ➢ Mail Tools ➢ Delegation Profile (see Figure 10.6).

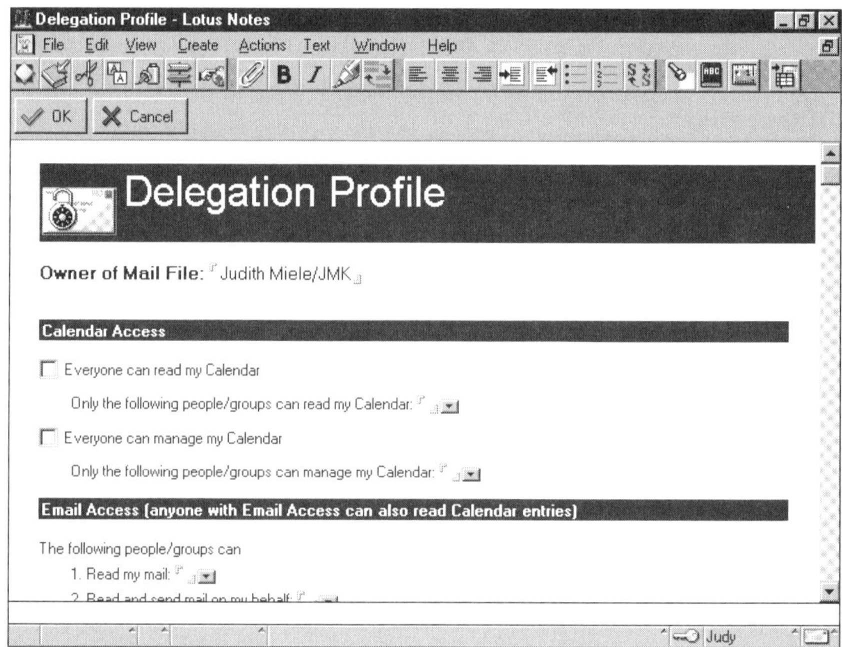

FIGURE 10.6 The Delegation Profile allows the user to designate other users to have access to their calendar.

The Delegation Profile allows users to designate other users to have Read and Write access to public documents (calendar meetings, responses, events, and anniversaries) in your mail file. Notes calendaring and scheduling allows users to keep track of their appointments and meetings in the Calendar view of their mail database. In addition, users can also delegate someone to maintain their calendar without giving them the capabilities to read all of their e-mail.

Under the Delegation Profile heading is the Owner of Mail File field, which contains the ID name of the person whose mail file you are currently using and two additional sections: Calendar Access and Email Access.

The Calendar Access Section

This section is where users control access to their calendars. There are two checkboxes in this section, which are both unchecked by default.

- **Everyone can read my calendar:** When this button is not checked, no one can read calendar entries in the Calendar view, Meeting view, or To Do view. Just to clarify, calendar entries consist of only appointments, invitations, responses, events, reminders, and anniversaries. However, the Everyone Can Read My Calendar option will give access to free and busy time unless otherwise specified in the Freetime Options section of the Calendar Profile. If this box is checked, it will allow everyone to read your calendar entries unless a calendar entry is specified as not for public viewing. In addition, under this checkbox option, you can specify a specific group or person who will have access to read your calendar entries. If you allow everyone to read your calendar, the option to specify a specific group or person becomes unavailable.
- **Everyone can manage my calendar:** If this option is not checked, no one is allowed to read, write, create, or delete entries in your Calendar, Meetings, and To Do views. As mentioned above, calendar entries consist of only appointments, invitations, responses, events, reminders, and anniversaries. However, access will be given to free and busy time unless otherwise specified in the Freetime Options section of the Calendar Profile. If you check this box, it will allow everyone to read, write, edit, or delete your calendar entries. Under this checkbox option, you can specify a specific group or person who will have access to your calendar entries. If you allow everyone to manage your calendar, the option to specify a specific group or person becomes unavailable.

The Email Access Section

The Email Access section (shown in Figure 10.7) allows for you to specify specific groups or people from the Public Name and Address Book who are allowed access to your Calendar entries, as well as access to your e-mail. This might be used by an administrative assistant who has been given "ownership" of a manager's calendar, as well as the manager's mail file.

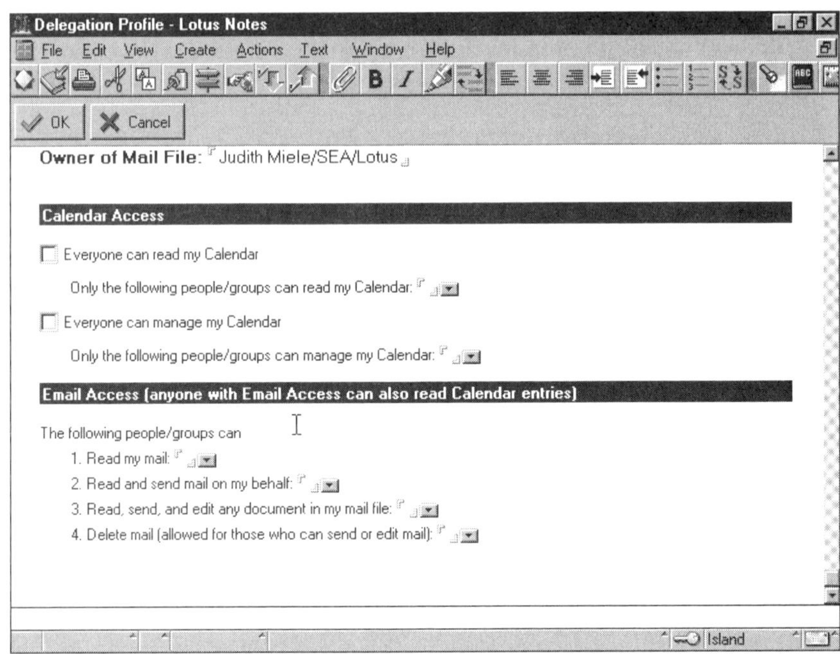

FIGURE 10.7 The Email Access section of the Delegation Profile screen

Under this section, there are four levels of access to your e-mail that you can give. Keep in mind, if you specify anyone in any of these options, they also have access to your calendar entries.

- **Read my mail**: The names listed in this field have access to read your mail as well as access to read your calendar entries.
- **Read and send mail on my behalf**: The names listed in this field have access to read your mail as well as send e-mail on your behalf. Sending e-mail on your behalf shows both the name of the sender and the person for whom they are sending the e-mail. Also, this person has access to read your calendar entries.
- **Read, send, and edit any document in my mail file**: The names listed in this field have access to read and edit your mail as well as send e-mail on your behalf. Sending e-mail on your behalf shows both the name of the sender and the person for whom they are sending the e-mail. Also, this person has access to read your calendar entries.

- **Delete mail (allowed for those who can send or edit mail):** The names listed in this field have access to read, edit, and delete your mail as well as send e-mail on your behalf. Sending e-mail on your behalf shows both the name of the sender and the person for whom they are sending the e-mail. Also, this person has access to read your calendar entries.

Once you have completed the Delegation Profile, click the OK button in the Action bar.

Should You Train Users to Configure Their Own Profiles?

Now that you understand how to configure the Calendar and Delegation profile documents, you can conduct group training sessions for your Notes user community. Group training sessions for a feature such as calendaring and scheduling are effective. However, try to complement group training with some individual training. One on one interaction is one of the best ways to demonstrate the power of this new feature. Users, reluctant to ask questions in group settings, will inquire about features and functions they're interested in during a personal training session. During these one on one meetings, you'll make the most headway in spreading the word about calendaring and scheduling. You'll also build a strong following, which will ensure this feature's success in your Notes environment.

Basic Features of Calendaring and Scheduling

Once you've finished assisting a user to configure their Calendar and Delegation profiles, you might also want to give them a brief tour of the different features of calendaring and scheduling. This brief overview shouldn't take long and only needs to walk a user through the three primary views and what each one means.

The Calendar View

Start with the Calendar view (see Figure 10.8) where the user can pick from four specific ways to present dates in the view: Two Days, One Week, Two Weeks, One Month. Each of these date arrangements is accessible through their respective buttons on the Action bar. Regardless of which arrangement of time the user has selected to view, the Calendar view is where they will create any one of five different calendar entries: Appointments, Invitations, Events, Reminders, Anniversaries.

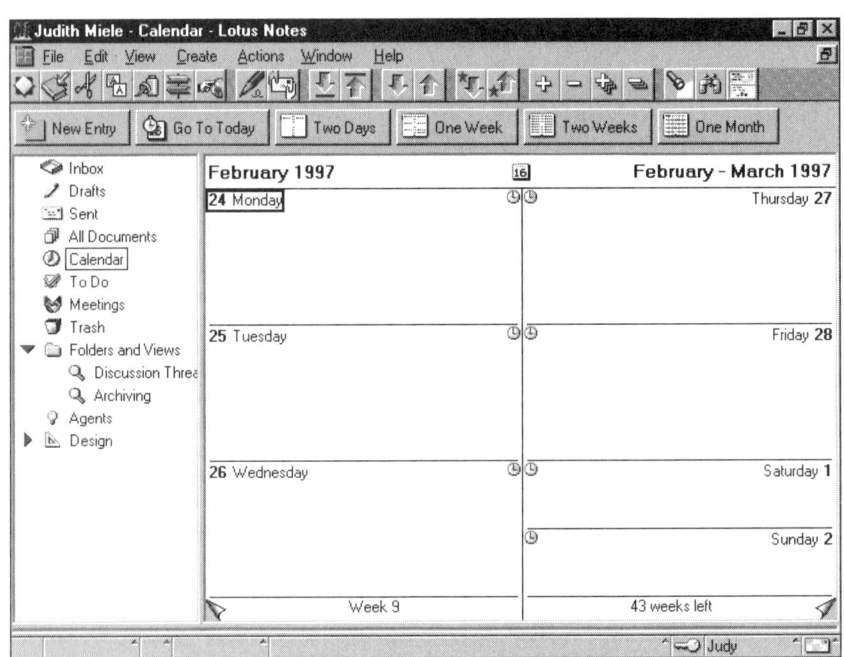

FIGURE 10.8
The Notes Calendar view is a new view style. It comes in the Mail template, but can be copied and used in other databases.

To create any of these calendar entries, select Create ➢ Calendar Entry to display the Calendar Entry form, or click the New Entry button in the Action bar of the Calendar view.

Appointments

Appointments (see Figure 10.9) have start and end times, and a description. They also have repeat functionality. For example, users can create appointments for meetings that occur every Monday or for a conference call that occurs every third Tuesday of each month. Appointments are mainly for the user's use. If an appointment needs to be scheduled with someone else, then it becomes an invitation. (The *Invitations* section provides more information.)

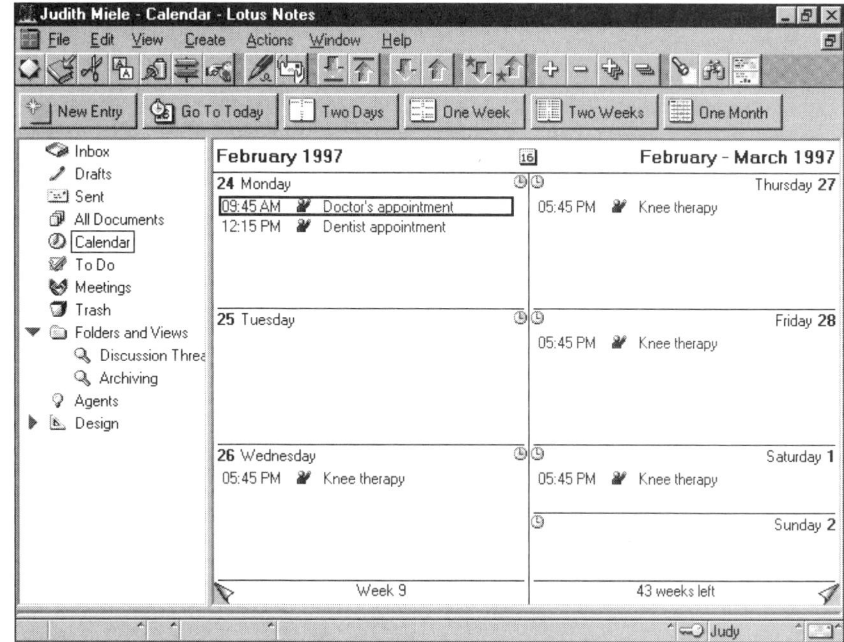

FIGURE 10.9 This Notes Calendar shows calendar entries that are only Appointments. Notice that the icon next to each appointment is a person with an arm raised.

In the Calendar view, people typically keep track of their own appointments and meetings. However, users can also keep track and allow for scheduling among all of the users. In addition, users can delegate someone to maintain their calendar without giving them the capabilities to read all of their e-mail (previously described in the section *The Delegation Profile*).

Invitations

Invitations are created to schedule meetings and to invite other users to those meetings. Like Appointments, Invitations have a start and end time as well as repeating and alarm functionality. The creator of the meeting is called the Chairperson. The people the Chairperson invites are called the Invitees. Refer to Figure 10.10 for several examples of invitations created in the Calendar view.

Events

Events are similar to appointments with start and end times, and a description (see Figure 10.11). But Events might encompass the whole day or even several days. Training, trade shows, and vacations are all perfect examples of an event.

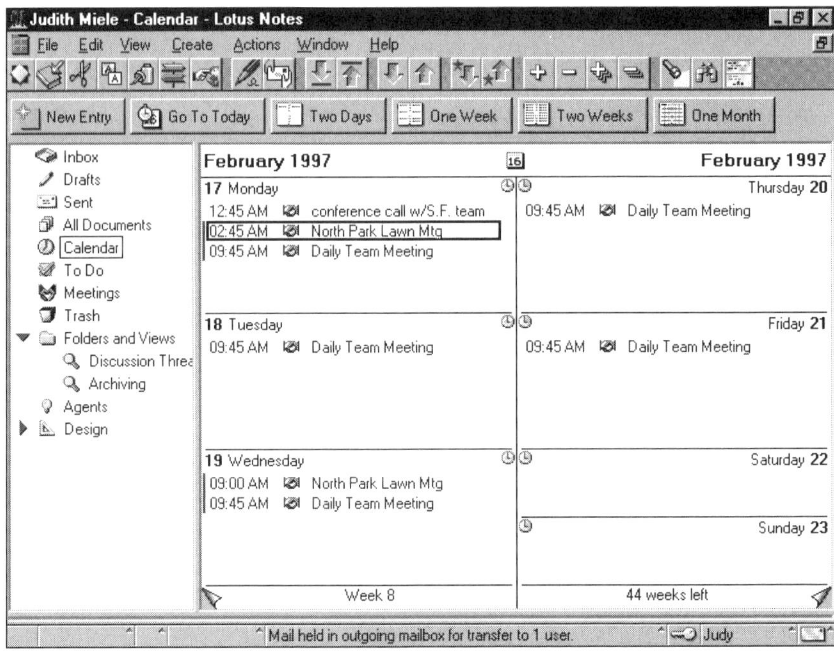

FIGURE 10.10
This Notes Calendar shows calendar entries that are Invitations which have been accepted and entered on this user's calendar. The icon to the left of the brief description of the scheduled meeting is two hands shaking; this indicates that it is an invitation to a meeting.

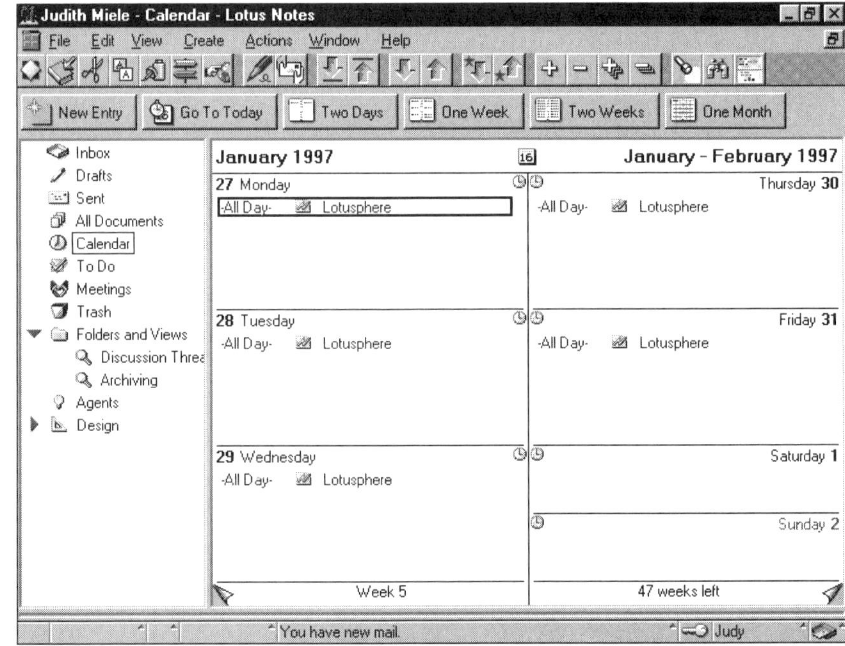

FIGURE 10.11
This Notes Calendar shows a calendar entry that is an Event. This Event spans over five days. The icon to the left of the brief description, which indicates that the entry is a scheduled event, is a chart with a lightning bolt.

Different than Appointments, Events don't get displayed during the free and busy time searches when scheduling a meeting. Free and busy time searching is a feature in Notes that allows the user to review the available and busy times of someone else's calendar without the ability to actually read the appointment information. Free and busy time searching will display a time bar that indicates when the person is available (no bar indicator) and unavailable (bar indicator).

Reminders

Reminders are only for the user creating the reminder (see Figure 10.12). They are placed on the user's calendar as a visual reminder of a meeting or event that might be coming up. For example, if you need to know that next week is the company meeting but you don't want to set an alarm a week ahead of time on that entry, create a reminder for the Friday before. Reminders can be used in conjunction with alarms, but in the case of the company meeting example, a reminder was used instead of an alarm.

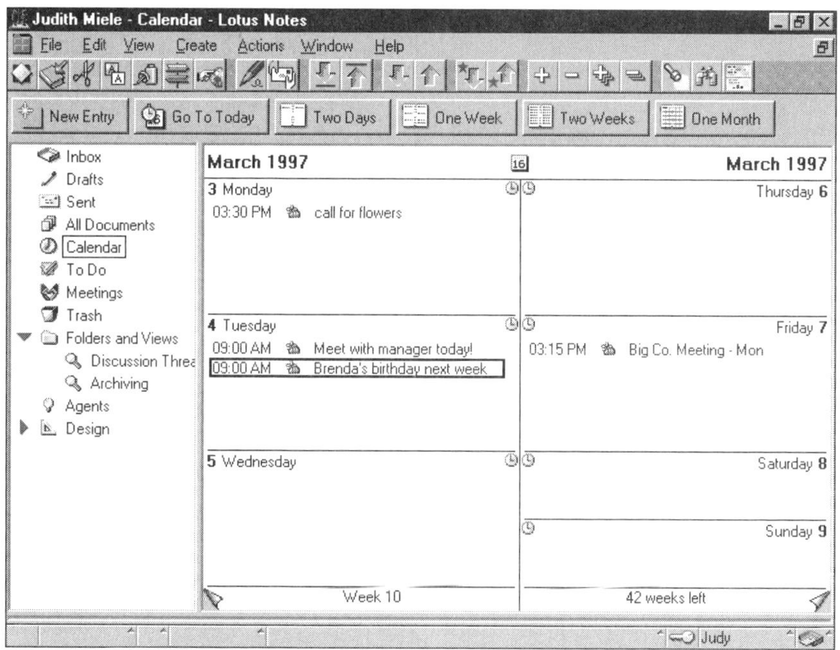

FIGURE 10.12

This Notes Calendar view shows calendar entries that are Reminders. The icon to the left of the brief description, a finger with a bow tied around it, indicates that this is a scheduled reminder.

Anniversaries

Anniversaries are just that. Generally, anniversaries repeat yearly (see Figure 10.13). For example, an anniversary entry might be a birthday, a wedding date, Boxing day in Canada, or some other special day to remember.

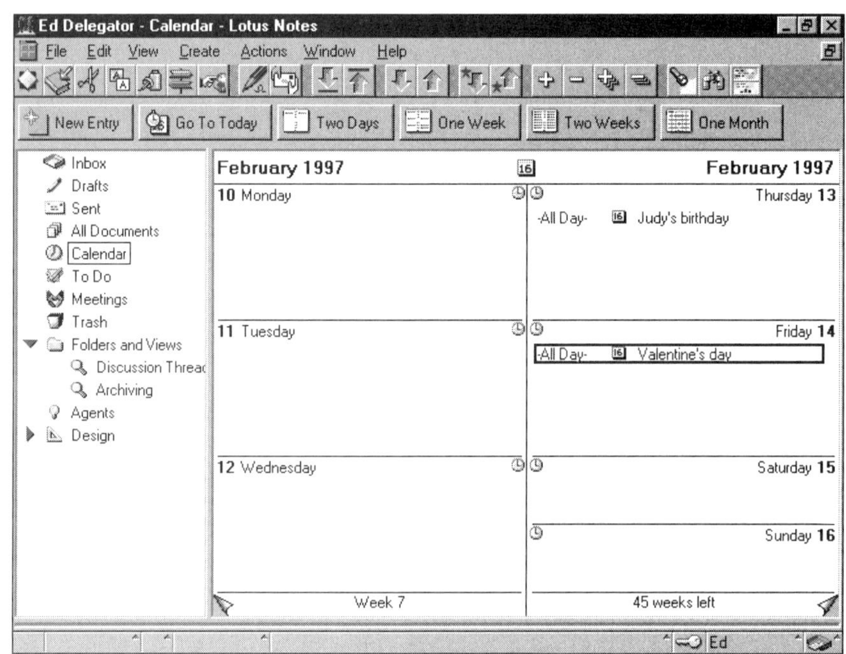

FIGURE 10.13 This Notes Calendar shows calendar entries that are Anniversaries. Generally, anniversaries are special dates which repeat yearly. The icon indicating a scheduled anniversary is a small torn off calendar to the left of the brief description.

To Do View

After walking a user through the Calendar view and explaining the various entries that can appear in it, move on to the To Do view. This view is not new to Release 4.5; it has been around since Release 4.0. The To Do view (see Figure 10.14) keeps track of the tasks that a user enters, which might be things that need to get done or things that require assistance from someone else. In the latter case, the user would want to enter a task and then assign it to someone.

FIGURE 10.14

This Task form is for creating a task for the user that hasn't been assigned to someone else. You can assign the task to someone else and/or display the task on your calendar by selecting the appropriate button(s) in the Action bar.

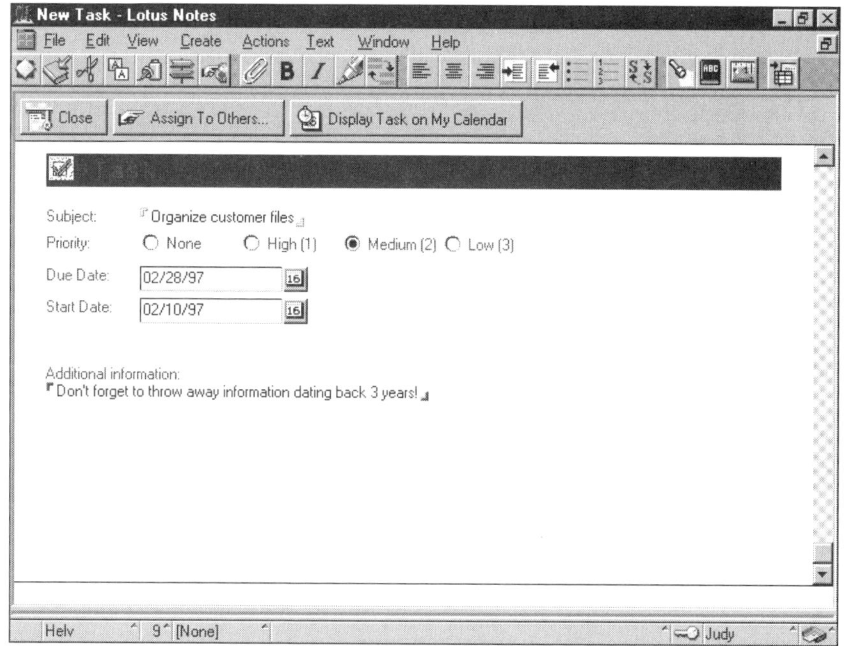

Tasks have a description, a priority of either High, Medium, or Low, options for a start date and due date, and a field for additional information. By clicking two different buttons in the Action bar, users can display the task on their calendar and/or assign the task to other users.

In Figure 10.15, each task is categorized in the Overdue, Current, Future, or Complete section. This view also displays the due date and who the task is assigned to.

The To Do view is not the only place to view tasks. If a user has created a task and clicked the Display Task on My Calendar button during creation, then those tasks are also shown in the Calendar view (see Figure 10.16).

Remember, to view tasks in the Calendar view you must click the Display Task on My Calendar button in the New Task dialog box when you create the task.

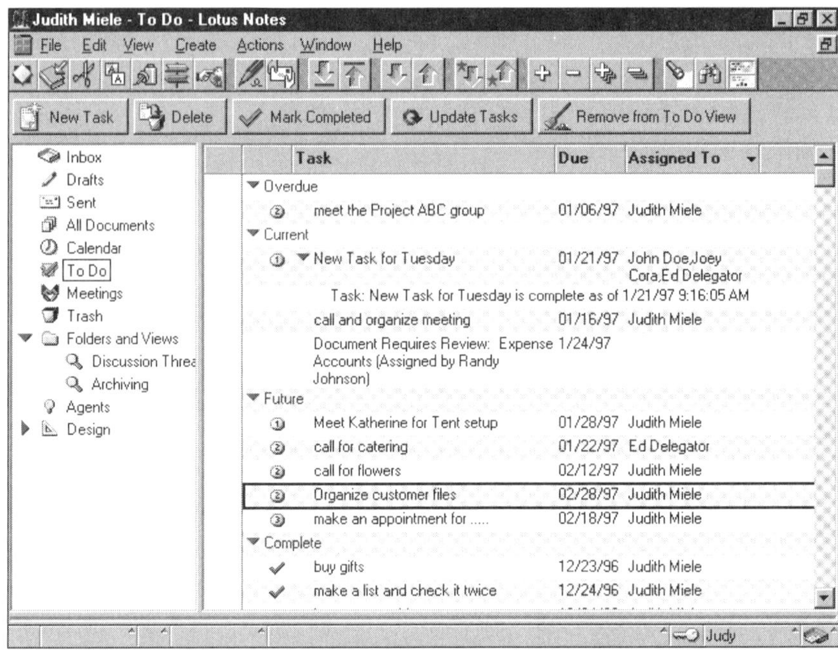

FIGURE 10.15 The To Do view displays each task. Notice the task created in Figure 10.14 is now displayed in the To Do view.

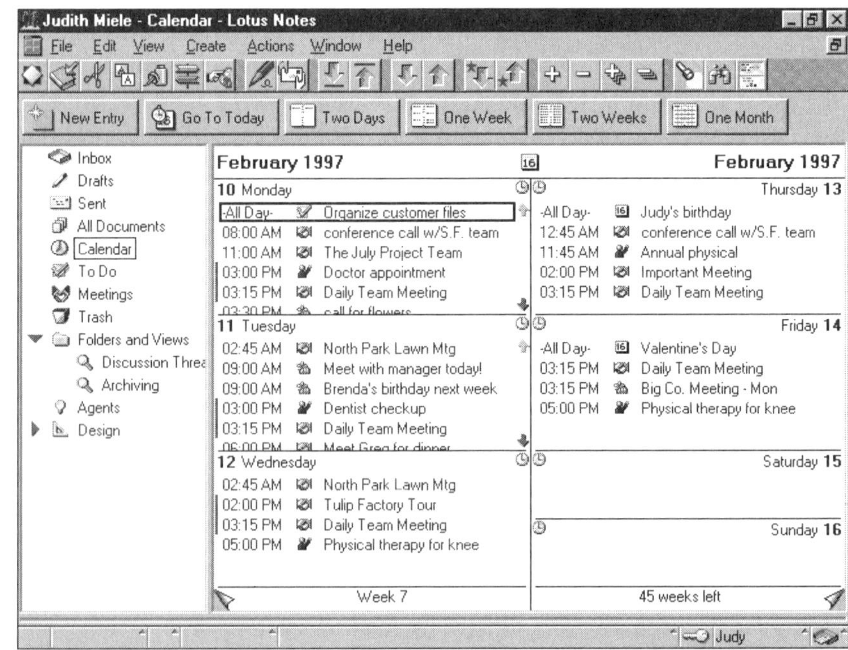

FIGURE 10.16 The Calendar view displays tasks that were created in the New Task dialog box. The task that was created in Figure 10.14 is highlighted here along with other Calendar entry types, such as Anniversaries, Invitations, Reminders, and Appointments.

Meetings View

The final view to walk a user through is the Meetings view. This view is a central place to create and view meetings. Generally, this is where users will review all of their meetings, and any notifications from these meetings will be "threaded" in this view for information tracking purposes. Threading allows the user to read all meeting notifications as they pertain to one another, regardless of when the meeting invitation is sent and when the invitee responds. With e-mail, there could be several pieces of mail between the first invitation and the response. Notes threads each piece of e-mail together to make the progression of information more accessible for the user. Figure 10.17 shows the Meeting view once you have created several meetings.

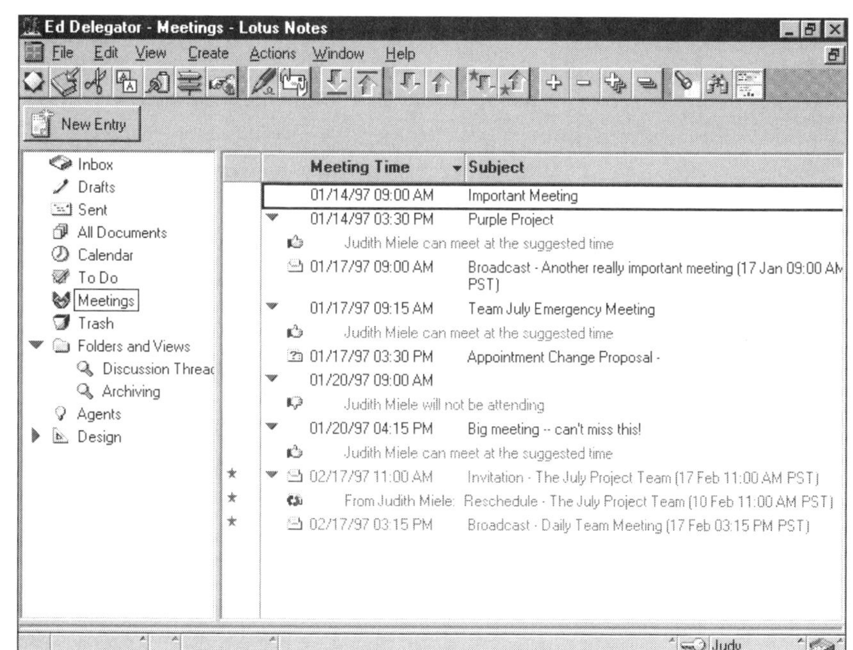

FIGURE 10.17

The Meeting view displays the invitations and any responses regarding the scheduled meeting. The threads are indicated by the indented responses to the meetings. A thumbs up or thumbs down indicates to the Chairperson whether or not the invitee will be attending.

Using Calendaring and Scheduling

The real key to making calendaring and scheduling take off like a rocket in your Notes environment is user participation. Like every other software application on a user's computer, the ones that get used are the ones the user knows how to use or absolutely has to use whether they like it or not (except for games of course).

A word processing application gets used when a user needs to type any number of things, such as a business letter, a report, or a resume. The value of the word processing application is based on usage. Only one user needs to use the application for it to demonstrate its value. Calendaring and scheduling in Notes, however, requires that everyone participate before its value is fully realized.

I've advocated the concept of acting as product champion (also referred to as calendaring and scheduling evangelist) throughout this chapter. Administrators get their first shot at this concept when they assist users with configuring their Calendar and Delegation profiles. The next opportunity is when you are walking a user through the basic features of calendaring and scheduling. Now, the final and most important time to spread the word about this exciting feature has come. You must train users and demonstrate how to use all of the functionality of calendaring and scheduling

Formal group training is the best way to get started, but make sure you follow that training with proactive one on one assistance. How receptive people are to this feature will determine how much one on one contact you'll have to have. But make no mistake, you will have to get out into the trenches and make sure people are using this feature and using it right. And the only way to accomplish this is to completely understand how to use and navigate this feature for yourself.

Navigating through the Calendar View

Get started learning all there is to this new feature by navigating around the Calendar view (shown in Figure 10.18). Click the Calendar folder from the Folder pane on the left side of your mail file to go to the Calendar view. By default, the view is set up to display one week's worth of information. However, you can change the view setup to display two days, one week, two weeks, or one month by clicking the appropriate button in the Action bar. In addition to the activities for each day, Notes displays the number of days, weeks, or months into the year and the number of days, weeks, or months left in the year at the bottom of the page.

Regardless of how many days, weeks, or months you are displaying, at the bottom of the calendar the pages are turned up. If you click these turned up pages, the calendar will turn to the next days, weeks, or months. If you want to return to the current date, click the button in the Action bar called Go To Today.

FIGURE 10.18

By clicking the Calendar folder on the left side of your Notes mail file database, you will open the Calendar view.

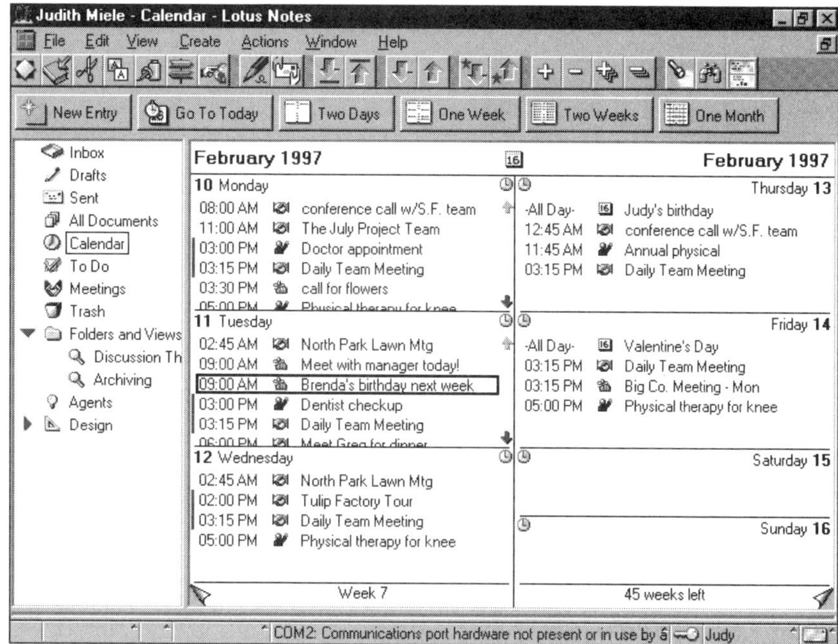

If you are in any of the views except the One Month view, centered on the top of the page between the month and year is a smaller calendar page with the number 16. This indicator allows you to bring up a monthly calendar to navigate through the months. In the One Month view, this small calendar is located on the top left side of the screen.

To move to a day, just click the day you want to move to. To quickly move to the next month, click the right-pointing triangle to the right of the month's name. To go back, click the left-pointing triangle on the left side of the month's name. If you want to move through the months by using your keyboard, you can use your page down key to go forward, and your page up key to go backward. Hold down the Ctrl key and press the Page Up or Page Down key to move through the years.

In order to show the time slots during each day, go back to the Calendar view and click the small clock in the upper right corner of each day. Figure 10.19 demonstrates how the day's time slots will look when you click the small clock for that day. Also, if you double-click a specific time in the time slot, that time will automatically get entered in the calendar entry when you create the entry, whether it is an Invitation, Appointment, Event, or Anniversary.

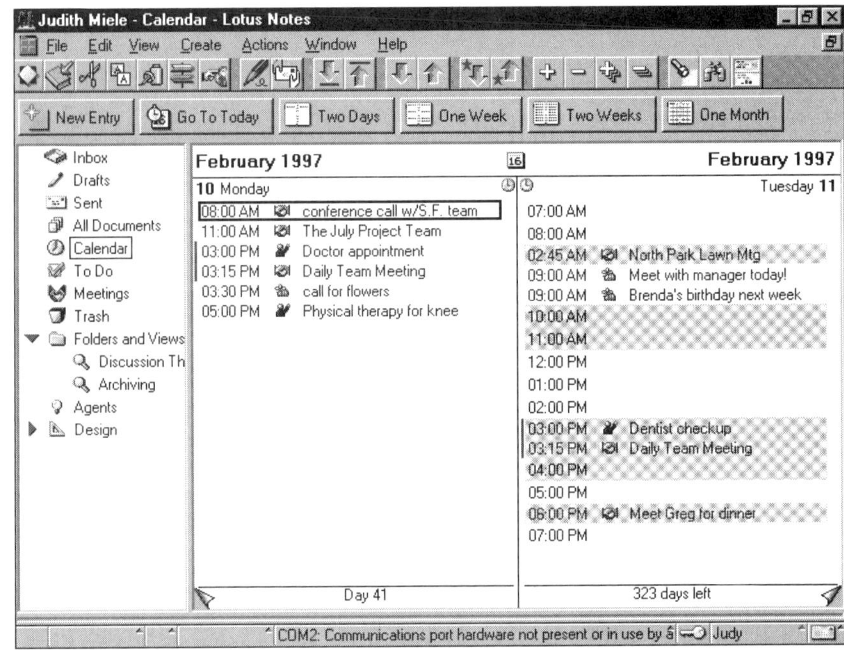

FIGURE 10.19

Click the small clock in one of the days to display the times during that day. This will also display your scheduled appointments and their duration. In this figure, the clock for February 11th has been clicked.

Another way to change the way the display looks for the time slots of a particular day is to right-click the day to bring up a menu and choose Show Time Slots. Also, notice that in this menu you can choose which view you would like to display: Two Day, One Week, Two Weeks, or One Month.

The One Month view is a little different from the other views. Because there is so much displayed in the view, the entries are truncated. However, if you place the mouse over an entry and leave it for a few seconds (called hovering), then the full entry will be displayed in a larger pop-up box (see Figure 10.20).

Creating a Meeting Invitation

Now that you know how to navigate around the Calendar view, it's time to learn about the many ways to create a calendar entry. You can be in any of the views in your Notes mail database, and, by selecting from the menu bar Create ➢ Calendar Entry you will bring up the Calendar Entry form to be filled out. You can also click the New Entry button on the Action bar or double-click the day and/or time in which you want to create the entry.

The Calendar Entry form will be displayed, and depending on how you set up your Calendar Profile and what day and time you clicked, the corresponding information will be displayed automatically in the Time and Date fields of the form (see Figure 10.21).

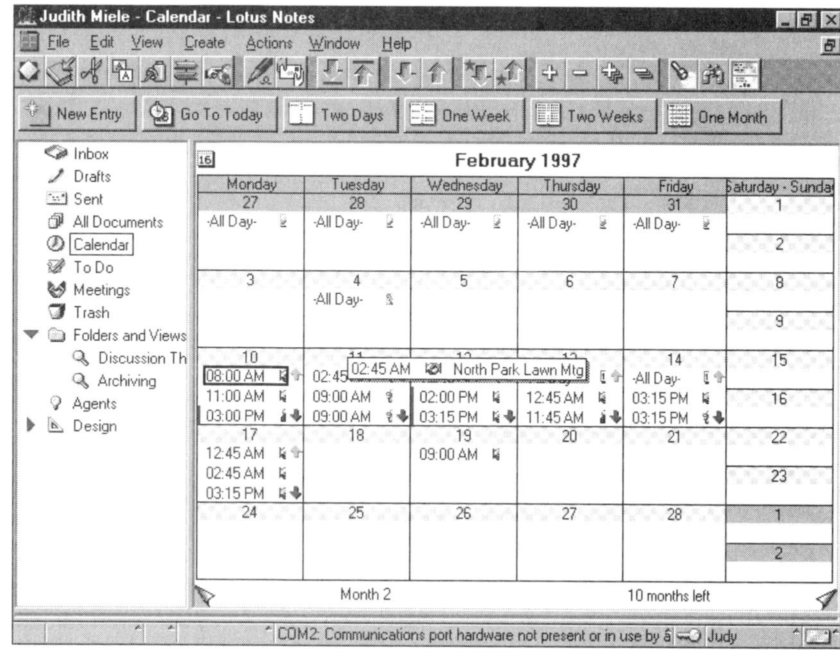

FIGURE 10.20

In the One Month view, because of the amount of information being displayed, a technique called hovering is used to display the information regarding the scheduled meetings. To hover, place your mouse over an entry and leave it there for a couple of seconds. The entry will pop-up the description of the scheduled meeting.

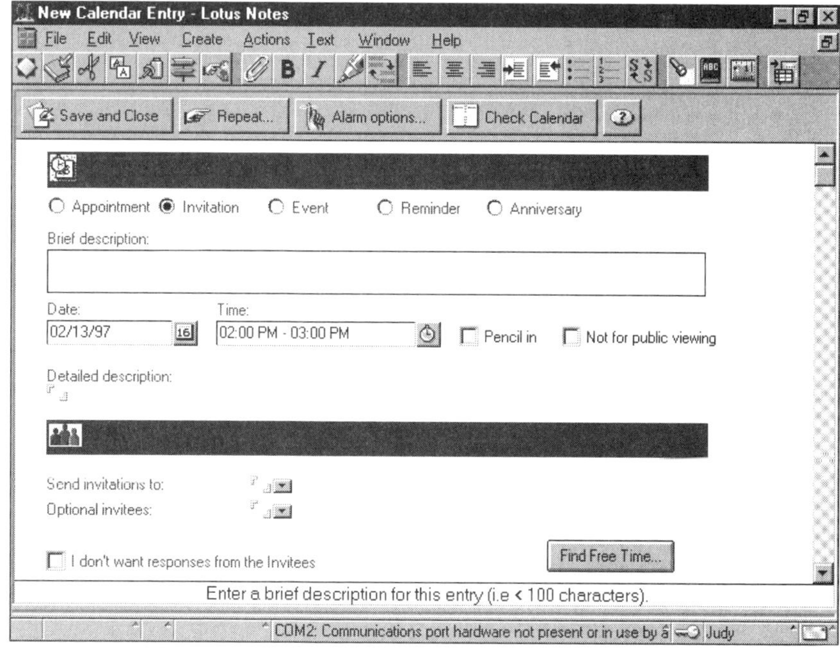

FIGURE 10.21

This Calendar Entry form was created by double-clicking on 2:00 PM for the date February 13th. The Calendar Entry form can also be created by clicking the New Entry button in the Action menu of the Calendar view.

The steps for creating an Appointment, Event, Reminder, or Anniversary are very similar but generally less complex than the steps for creating an Invitation. For that reason, the key elements of the New Calendar Entry dialog box are covered in detail in this section and only the different elements are covered in the sections that discuss the creation of other engagements.

The first thing you'll want to do when creating a new calendar entry is select the entry type. By default, Invitation is the type selected unless you specified otherwise in the Calendar Profile. However, you can easily select any of the other entry types (Appointment, Event, Reminder, or Anniversary).

After you've selected an entry type, you can include a brief description in the Brief Description text box. While this field is optional, it is important to include a description because that is what appears in the Subject field of the e-mail invitation that is sent to invitees. The Date and Time fields are the next fields to complete for a new calendar entry. A pop-up calendar makes it easy to select a date and the scrollable "time bar" allows you to easily drag the start and stop times up and down depending on your requirements (see Figure 10.22).

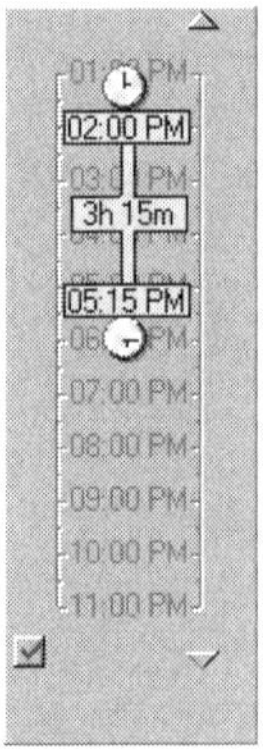

FIGURE 10.22 The Time bar allows you to scroll through times by dragging the top clock, the bottom clock, or the middle bar.

The Pencil In checkbox allows you to schedule a tentative meeting. The key concept here is that when you "pencil in" an invitation, that time is still available to others when they search your calendar for free and busy time. Once you edit the calendar entry and remove the check from the Pencil In option, the time becomes blocked off.

The Not for Public Viewing checkbox is unchecked by default. However, if you do not want anyone to see the calendar entry you are making, then check this box by clicking it. Even though you might have delegated someone to be able to read your calendar entries, the Not for Public Viewing option will keep the delegated person or group from actually seeing this entry.

If you have given a person or group Reader access to your mail file in the ACL, that person or group will have access to any entry marked with the Not for Public Viewing option.

In the Detailed Description area, you can enter additional details about the meeting or attach a file, such as a meeting agenda. To attach a file, click the Paperclip button in the SmartIcons bar or select File ➢ Attach from the menu bar to display the Create Attachment dialog box.

Make sure you are in the Detailed Description box when creating an attachment. Otherwise, you won't get the option to create an attachment from the menu.

Search through the Create Attachment dialog box for the file you want to attach and highlight it by clicking it once; then click the Create button. Notes will place an attachment icon with the name of the file underneath the attachment. Figure 10.23 shows the Create Attachment dialog box with the file Agenda selected. By clicking the Create button, the Agenda file will become attached to the invitation.

FIGURE 10.23

To attach a file, find the file in the Create Attachment dialog box, highlight it, and click the Create button to attach it.

After clicking the Create button, the file in Figure 10.23 is attached to the Detailed Description box of the New Calendar Entry dialog box. You can see the attached file in Figure 10.24. It is stored in the Detailed Description box and is designated by a notepad icon and the filename under the Here's the Agenda section. Below that section, you can specify who to invite to the meeting.

FIGURE 10.24
The attached file is in the Here's the Agenda box in the Detailed Description area. It is designated by a notepad icon with the filename underneath. And below the attached file is where you can list who to invite to a meeting and reserve rooms and resources.

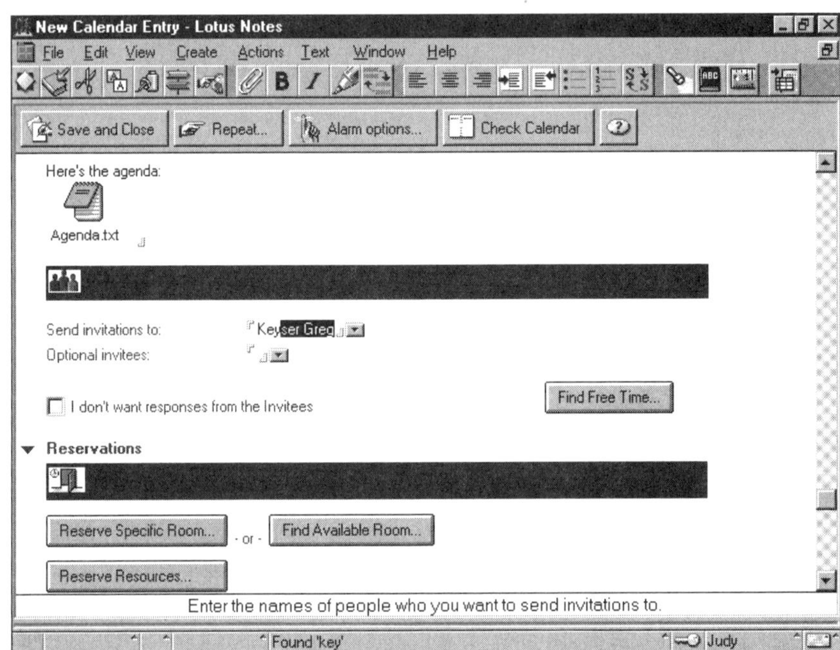

To invite someone to a meeting, click the down arrow next to the Send Invitations To option. This will bring up the Names dialog box, which accesses the Public Address Book or the Personal Address Book. In this dialog box, you can select people or groups by placing a check mark to the left of the name of the person or group. Do this by clicking once in the empty column to the left of the Send Invitations option. You can also deselect people or groups by clicking on them again. Once all of the invitees are selected, add them to the invitation by clicking the Add button. Click OK.

You can also invite people by typing their names or the group's name into the Send Invitation To field. Notes has automatic addressing, which allows you to begin typing a person's name and autoaddressing will search through the Public Address Book to find the name of the person. Refer to the *Autoaddressing* sidebar for more information.

Autoaddressing

You can invite people or a group to a meeting just by typing their first or last name or the group's name. Notes has automatic addressing, which allows you to begin typing the person's name and it will search through the Public Address Book to find the name faster than you type it. It will pop up the person's name as you keep typing; once it has found the name you are looking for, just press the Enter key and Notes will insert the rest of the name for you. For example, if you need to invite John Doe to your meeting, but you can't remember if his name is John or James, but you definitely know his last name is Doe, begin typing his last name in the Send Invitations To field and each time you type a letter, Notes pops up names beginning with those letters until Notes finally reaches Doe, John. Once Notes reaches that point, press Enter. Autoaddressing also works any time you are e-mailing someone.

The Optional Invitees field allows you to invite people who are not obligated to attend the meeting. In addition, this meeting notice allows you to receive the invitation without having to respond as to whether or not you will be attending the meeting.

The I Don't Want Responses from the Invitees option is not checked by default. If you check this option, when the Invitee receives the invitation to the meeting they do not have to respond as to whether or not they will be attending the meeting.

Once you decide who will be invited to your meeting, who is required to attend, and who is not required to attend, click the Find Free Time button. This button will bring up the Free Time dialog box (shown in Figure 10.25). In this dialog box, Notes calculates all of the schedules for each invitee, including the Chairperson (the person calling the meeting), and their available and blocked out schedule times. The Free Time dialog box will display the date and time of the meeting in the corresponding fields, and below that information it will either state, "Scheduled time is OK for everyone" or "Scheduled time is NOT OK for everyone."

This dialog box will also display up to two weeks of available dates and times in the Recommended Meeting Times section. Therefore, if there is a conflict, just click one of the next available times and Notes will change the information to that time. Once the scheduled time for the meeting is okay for everyone, click the OK button.

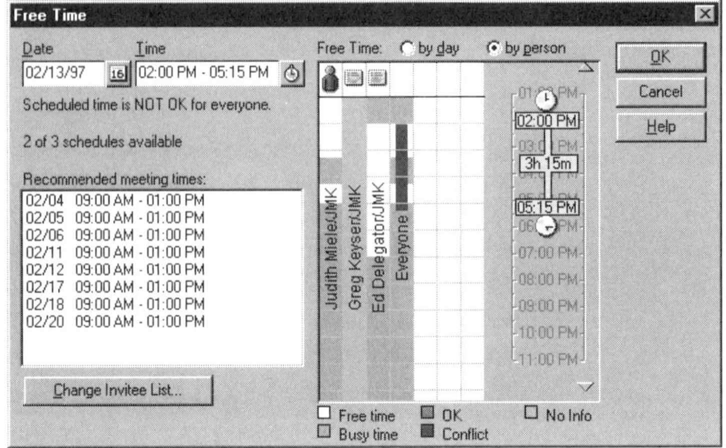

FIGURE 10.25 The Free Time dialog box is displayed by clicking the Find Free Time button.

Other information in the Free Time dialog box includes a graphical representation of the schedules for all of the attendees. By default, the graphic is displayed by person, which means that each person's calendar entries are noted here with a bar indicating the busy time as marked in his or her calendar; available time is indicated with a white bar. The Chairperson is indicated by a generic person icon with no neck (there's a joke there somewhere), while all of the invited people are indicated by an invitation icon over their schedules. Notes will automatically consolidate all of the schedules into an Everyone block and display either a green bar, meaning the time is available for everyone, or a red bar, indicating the time is not available for everyone. And finally, if a user has a gray bar it could mean one of two things: the user's file is on a different Notes server or the user is using Organizer or IBM Profs, or there isn't a Calendar profile set up for this user.

Another option you have for viewing free time is to view it by day; to do this, simply click the By Day button in the Free Time area. What the By Day button does is consolidate all of the schedules for each day and display a week's worth of information to you in the graphical area. This way, you can look at Sunday through Saturday to quickly determine which day might be best for your meeting.

In the Free Time dialog box, Notes gives you the option to click the Change the List of Invitees button to change the list of invitees. This brings up the Names dialog box, which by this time you should be familiar with. Then, click OK to return to the Calendar Entry form.

In the Calendar Entry form, the I Don't Want Responses from the Invitees checkbox isn't checked by default. However, if you select this option, the invitation becomes a Broadcast, which means that the meeting is announced but user's don't need to respond.

The I Don't Want Responses from the Invitees checkbox is a great option if you schedule a meeting with 500 people in a department or company and you don't want to know if everyone will be attending.

If you need to reserve a room or a resource for this meeting, click the arrow indicator next to the word Reservations at the bottom of the Calendar Entry form. This section includes three buttons which, once clicked, allow you to reserve or find a specific room or resource for your meeting. Once the Calendar Entry form is completed, click the Save button and then the Close button on the Action bar.

If this is a meeting that will occur regularly, you can create a repeating meeting by clicking the Repeat button on the Action bar. Invitees will only be notified of the meeting the first time, but a broadcast message can be sent for subsequent meetings as a reminder.

Notes will ask you if you want to send invitations to your invitees by displaying the Close dialog box.

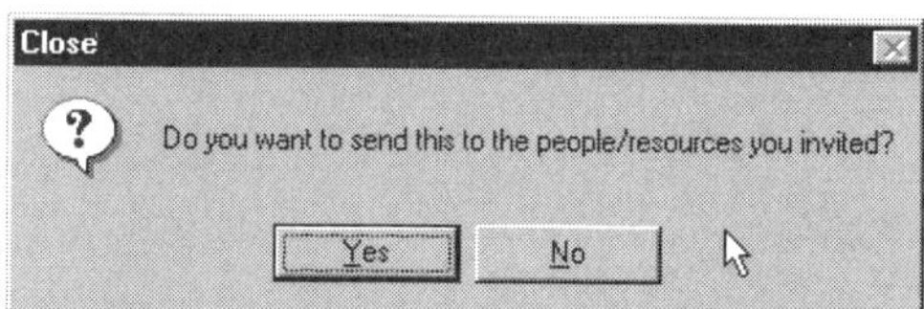

If you click Yes, an invitation will be sent to everyone you invited and the resources you specified, if any, will be booked for your meeting. In the section *Responding to Meeting Invitations*, you can read about how to respond to these invitations when you receive them.

Creating an Appointment

Creating an Appointment is similar to, but less complex than, creating an Invitation. As you did to create an Invitation, select Create ➢ Calendar

Entry from the menu bar to open a new Calendar Entry form. With the new calendar entry started, click the Appointment button (see Figure 10.26). Notice that once the Appointment button is selected most of the options in the Calendar Entry form are eliminated. This change occurs because those options only pertain to Invitations.

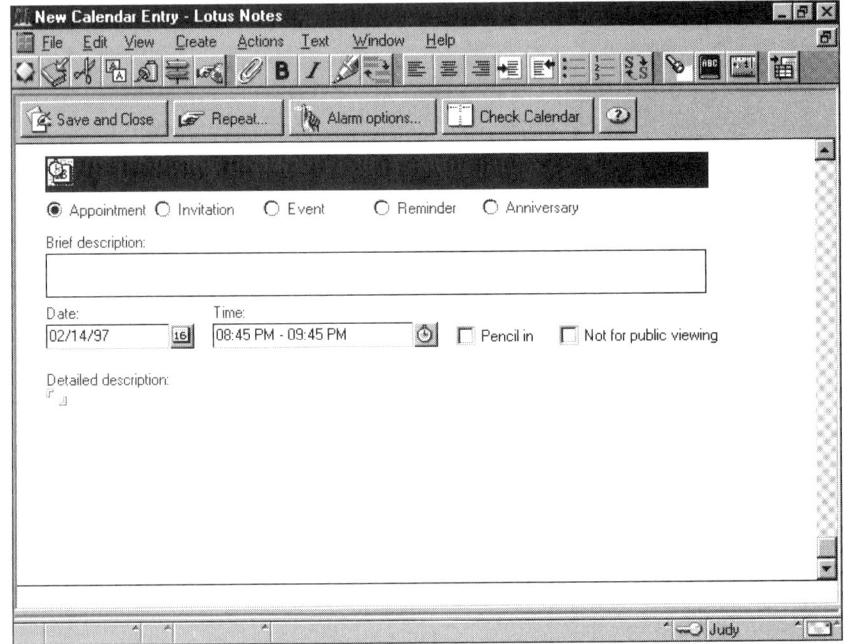

FIGURE 10.26

The Calendar Entry form for an Appointment. Notice most of the options are eliminated because they only pertain to the Invitation type of Calendar Entry.

Click in the Brief Description box and enter a description for this entry. This brief description is what will be displayed in the Subject field of the e-mail and on your calendar. Also, the Date and Time fields, which use the pop-up calendar and the Time bar respectively, allow you to choose the date and scroll through times for the appointment.

The Pencil In checkbox allows you to schedule a tentative appointment. Once again, the key element here is that when you pencil in the appointment, the time designated for the appointment is still available to others when they search your calendar for free and busy time. Once you edit the calendar entry and remove the check from the Pencil In option, the time becomes blocked off.

As with the meeting invitation, the Not for Public Viewing checkbox is unchecked by default in an Appointment entry. However, if you do not want anyone to see the calendar entry you are making, check this box. Even though you might have delegated someone to be able to read your calendar entries, the Not for Public Viewing option will keep the delegated person or group from actually seeing this entry. If you want to make this option enabled for every new calendar entry, refer back to the section *Advanced Calendar Options*.

If you have given a person or group Reader access to your mail file in the ACL, that person or group will have access to any entry marked with the Not for Public Viewing option.

The Detailed Description box is where you enter additional information regarding this appointment. You can also attach a file that pertains to the appointment, such as a resume. For instructions on how to attach a file, refer back to the section *Creating a Meeting Invitation*.

Creating an Event

Creating an Event, like an Appointment, is similar to creating an Invitation. As with Appointments and Invitations, simply click the New Entry button on the Action bar to start a new Calendar Entry document.

When the new Calendar Entry document appears, select Event and notice that most of the options on this document are eliminated (see Figure 10.27). The options left are only those that pertain to the Event entry type. In addition, there is a Duration field rather than a Time field. The automatic default for this field is 1 day, but can be adjusted as needed.

Creating a Reminder

Creating a Reminder is similar to all of the previously described entry types (see Figure 10.28). The only thing to note with regard to creating a Reminder is that a finger with a bow tied around it is displayed with the Reminder in the Calendar view.

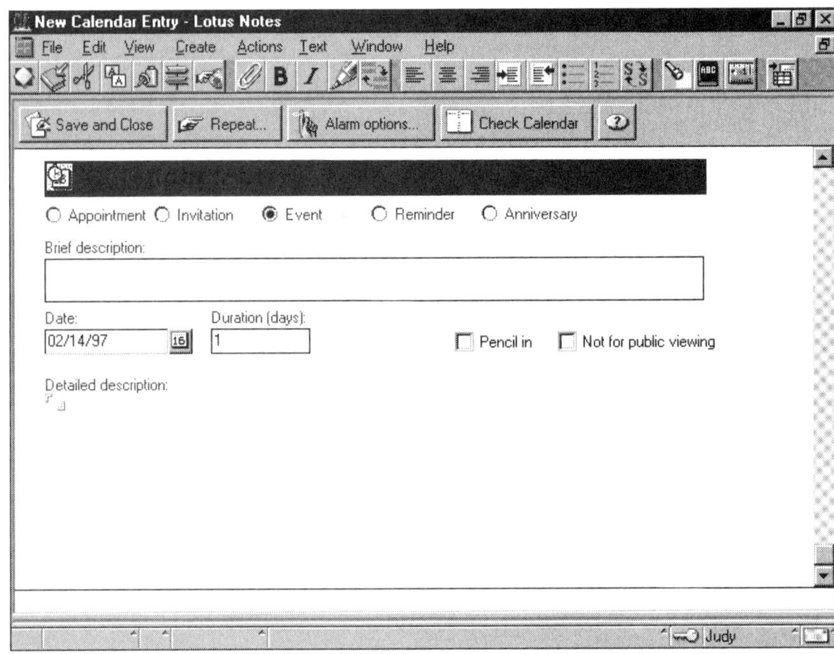

FIGURE 10.27

The Calendar Entry form for an Event

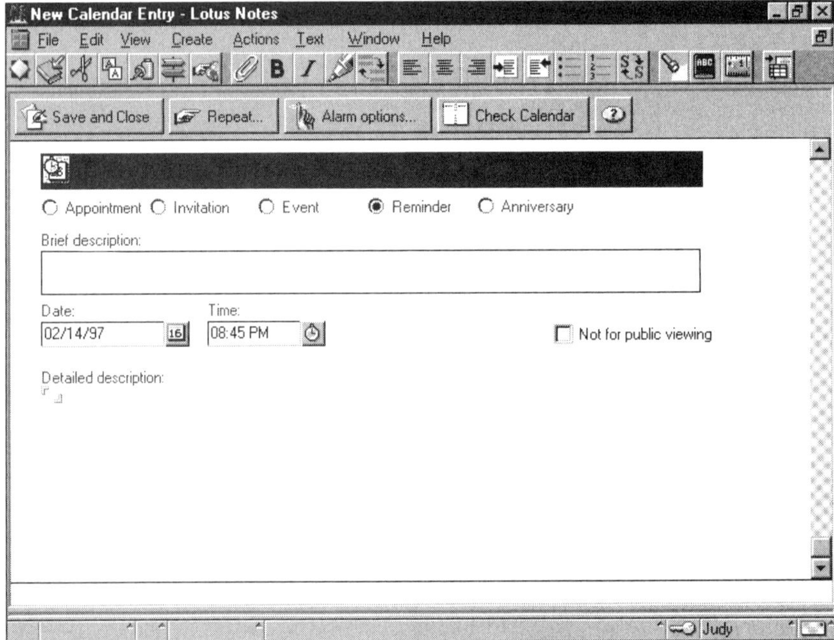

FIGURE 10.28

The Calendar Entry form for a Reminder

Creating an Anniversary

Finally, as with all other calendar entries, an Anniversary can be created by selecting the New Entry button on the Action bar or from the menu bar by selecting Create ➢ Calendar Entry. Once a new Calendar Entry document appears, select Anniversary (see Figure 10.29). Several of the fields on the document disappear and what remains are only those fields relevant to an Anniversary entry type.

The Brief Description field is used to describe the anniversary (birthday, wedding, super bowl). Select the date from the pop-up calendar for the Date field. The Pencil In checkbox allows you to schedule a tentative calendar entry, which means this time still appears in free and busy time searches. In the case of an Anniversary, this time may or may not be available depending on the type of Anniversary. For example, some users may want to be available on their birthday, while other users may consider Canadian Boxing day sacred and wish to be unavailable during that time. If you want an Anniversary to be blocked out of free time searches, just remove the check mark from the Pencil In option.

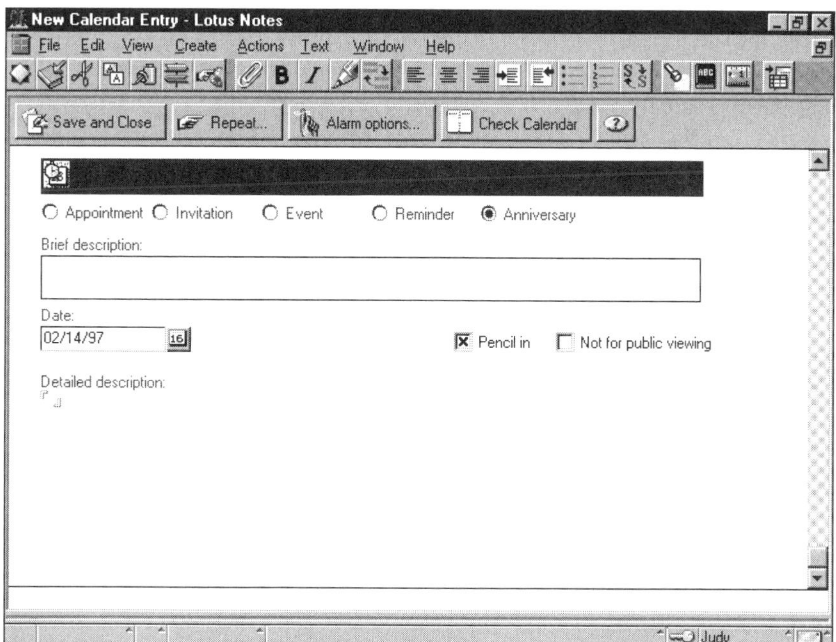

FIGURE 10.29

The Calendar Entry form for an Anniversary

Responding to Meeting Notices

The ability to schedule meetings through Notes is probably the feature users will like the most. However, scheduling meetings is really a two part activity. First, you invite people to your meeting (covered in the *Creating a Meeting Invitation* section). Then, people have to respond to the invitation.

Since invitations are sent out to users through Notes mail, that is where users will read and respond to the invitations they receive. A typical meeting invitation might begin with "Invitation – Important Meeting 13 Feb 02:00 PM PST" (see Figure 10.30).

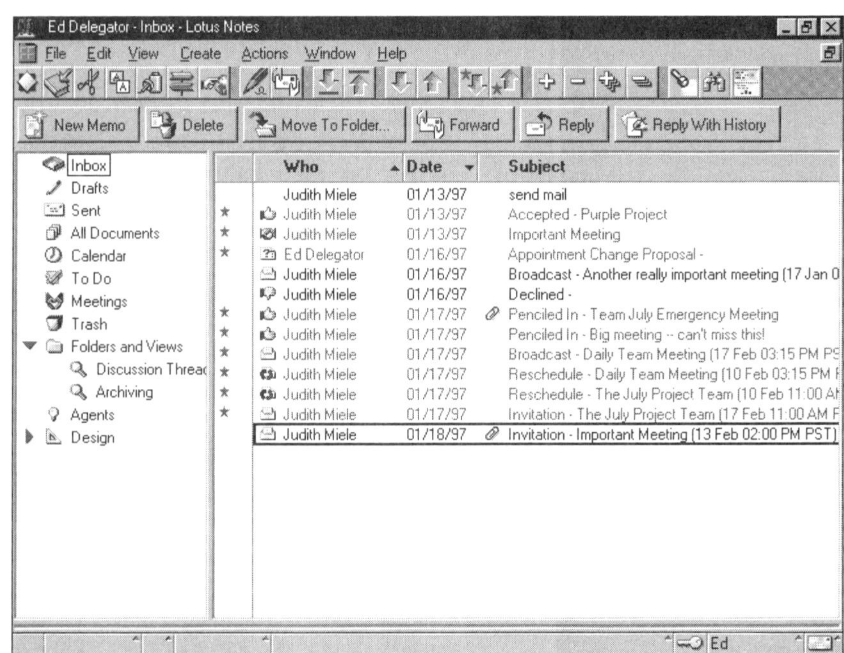

FIGURE 10.30 E-mail of a typical Notes user, in which the user receives an Invitation to a meeting

Once you double-click the e-mail to read it, you will see that you have been invited to a meeting. In this example, you are asked to respond to this meeting invitation. This is indicated by the buttons on the Action bar: Accept, Decline, and Other (see Figure 10.31).

- **Accept**: If you click the Accept button, Notes will send a notification back to the Chairperson indicating on the Chairperson's Invitee Responses list that you accepted the invitation. See the sidebar *The Invitee Responses List* for more information.

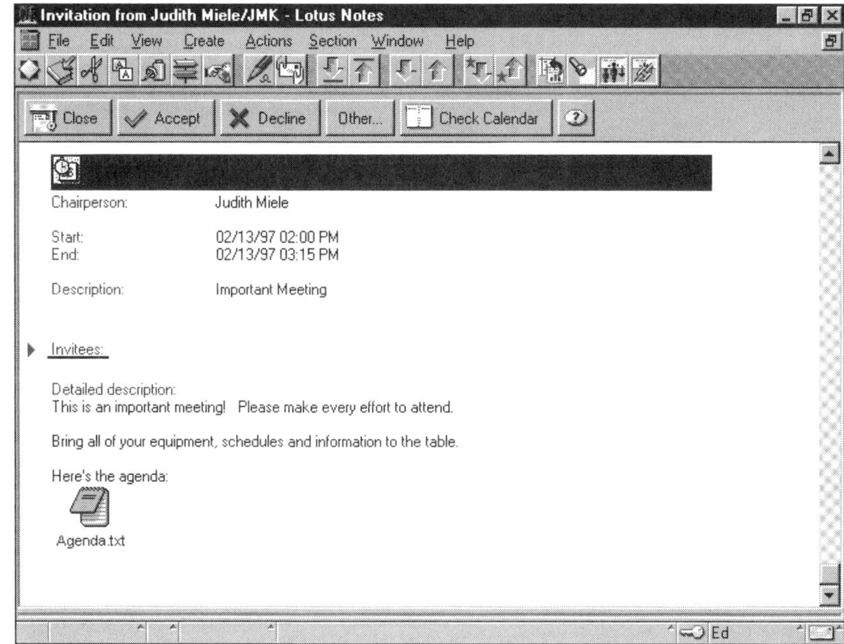

FIGURE 10.31
This user has been asked to respond to the meeting invitation, as indicated by the options displayed in the Action bar: Accept, Decline, and Other.

- **Decline:** If you click the Decline button, Notes will send a notification back to the Chairperson indicating on the Chairperson's Invited Responses list that you declined the invitation to the meeting.
- **Other:** If you click the Other button, you have three more options to choose from: Delegate, Propose Alternative Time/Location, or Pencil In. Click OK to send an invitation to the delegated person and an e-mail to the Chairperson informing them of the change.
  - **Delegate:** If you choose Delegate under the Other button and click OK, Notes will prompt you to enter the name of the person whom you would like to attend this meeting in your place in the Delegate To dialog box. The Delegate To dialog box with a person icon button for the Names dialog box is displayed. Type the person's name or choose the person icon button to display the Names dialog box. Click OK. Type in comments in the comment section, if applicable.

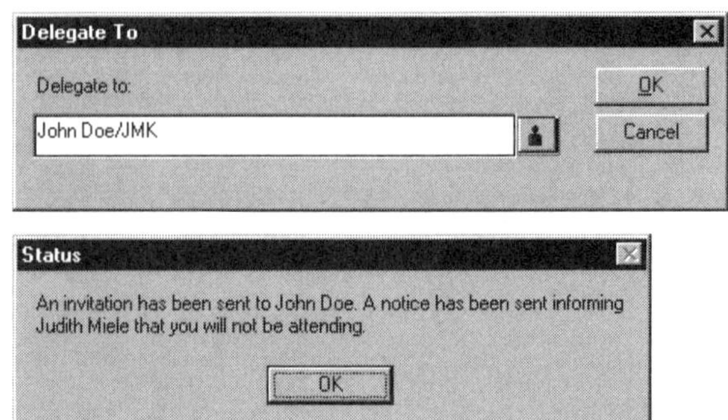

- **Pencil In:** If you choose this option under the Other button, type in your comments about why you are tentatively scheduling this meeting. When you click OK, a dialog box appears informing you that a notice has been sent informing the Chairperson that you will be attending and that a meeting document has been added to your calendar. A Calendar Entry is added to your mail file, and Pencil In is checked off. An e-mail will be sent back to the Chairperson indicating that you plan to attend and have penciled in the meeting.
- **Propose Alternative Time/Location:** If you choose this option under the Other button and click OK, Notes will bring you back to the original invitation with the Proposed Change section displayed. In this section you can enter the information describing your reason for suggesting the change along with a suggested time, date, and location for the new meeting. Figure 10.32 shows what the Chairperson will receive from the person who is proposing the change in the meeting time.

The Invitee Responses List

As the Chairperson, when you invite many different people to several different meetings, you can keep track of who is coming and who is not coming to the meetings by double-clicking on the particular entry in your calendar for the meeting. This will bring up the Calendar Entry form which you previously completed and sent out to your invitees. As the invitees respond, Notes will calculate that information into an Invitee Responses list. At the bottom of the Calendar Entry form, click the Display Invitee Response button to display this list. Within this dialog box, you can print this list as well as send a confirmation to the accepted invitees all with a click of a button or two. Refer to Figure 10.33 for an example of the Invitee Responses list.

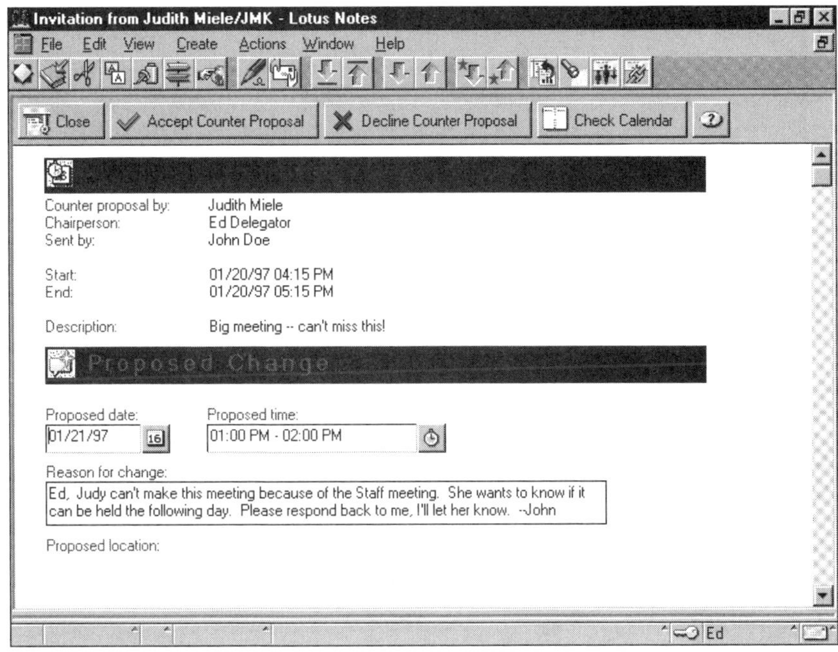

FIGURE 10.32

This is the response the Chairperson receives back from the invitee who proposed an alternate time and/or location for the meeting.

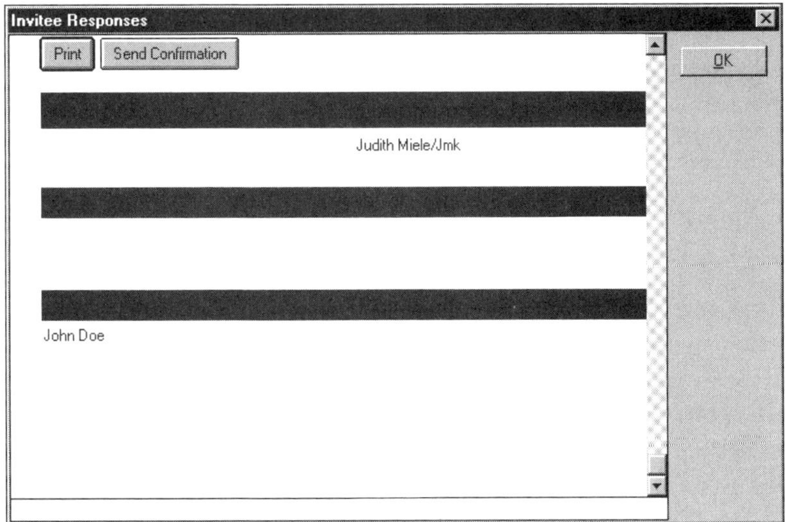

FIGURE 10.33

An example of the Invitee Responses list. To display this dialog box, double-click your calendar entry for the scheduled meeting and click the Display Invitee Responses button.

Not Responding to Meeting Notices

Even if the invitees don't respond to meeting notices, the Chairperson can still send out a confirmation to all invitees. After a meeting invitation has been sent out the Chairperson might want to send a reminder about the meeting to those who have and haven't responded. If you are the Chairperson, you can do this by double-clicking the calendar entry for the meeting and then in the Action bar clicking the Send Confirmation button. Clicking this button sends an e-mail to all of the invitees, which includes a list of the status of each invitee response.

The Optional Invitees field, which is in the Invitation type of Calendar entry, allows the Chairperson to invite people who are not obligated to attend the meeting. In addition, this meeting notice allows the invitees to receive the invitation and add it to their calendar, but the optional invitees do not have to respond to the invitation. Figure 10.34 indicates that this invitee is an optional invitee because the buttons to Accept, Decline, or Other are not displayed in the Action bar.

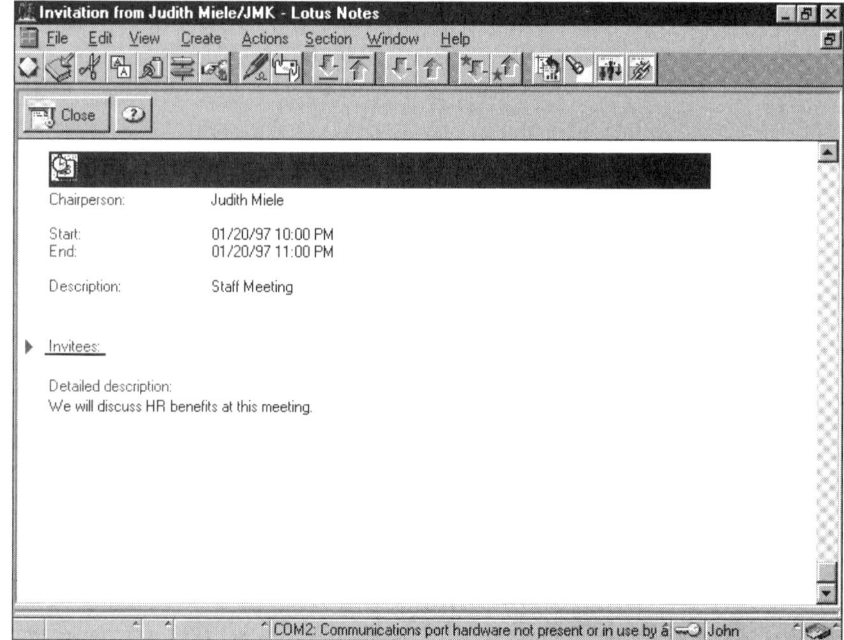

FIGURE 10.34 This is an Invitation sent to an optional invitee. This type of invitee is notified about the meeting but does not have to respond to the invitation. This is indicated by the fact that the Action bar menu does not include options to respond (Accept, Decline, and Other).

Troubleshooting

One of the most frequently asked questions concerning creating an invitation has to be when the invitee's free and busy time comes up in the graphical information as grayed or "No Info." If you have scheduled meetings with this person many times before, here are some things you might want to check:

1. Go to the Server Console or use the Remote Server Console to see if the server is running.
2. Next, at the Server Console, type **SH TA** for Show Tasks and make sure that the Schedule Manager is running on the server. You can also do this through the Remote Server Console. If the Schedule Manager isn't running, type **LOAD SCHED** to load the Schedule Manager.
3. Determine where the invitee's home server is located and perform steps 1 and 2 on that server. If the invitee's server is down, Notes will not be able to access the BUSYTIME.NSF database on the invitee's server.
4. Check the Calendar Profile under the Freetime Options for the invitee. Did the invitee change his or her Calendar Profile to mistakenly not include User access to free and busy time?
5. Check for a calendar created for this invitee and make sure Notes 4.5 is running on this invitee's home server.

When scheduling a room or resource a user might receive the message, "No room was found during the specified time." This error message means that the time specified for the meeting invitation is not available for that particular resource. Either check the Room or Resource document in the Resource Reservations database to make sure that the times are properly set up.

Summary

Understanding how Notes' calendaring and scheduling works in your Notes environment is not complex. There are two server tasks that drive this process, which start automatically every time the server starts: Schedule Manager and Calendar Connector. The Schedule Manager assists with free time searches and keeps the busy time database (BUSYTIME.NSF) up to date. In a multi-server Notes environment, the Calendar Connector enables free time searches across each Notes server that has a Busy Time database. These tasks work continuously with little intervention from you, the Notes administrator.

Most of your administrative duties when it comes to calendaring and scheduling can be broken down into two parts. First, there is the basic configuration of calendaring and scheduling. This part includes setting up the Resource Reservation database on the Notes server and helping individual users configure their Calendar and Delegation Profile documents. The second part of your administrative duties is far less technical but extremely important. This part is where you work at making sure calendaring and scheduling takes hold in your environment by working with users one on one to spread the word about this great new feature.

Calendaring and scheduling, as I've said throughout this chapter, relies heavily on user participation. If all users don't use this new feature, free time searches and group schedule coordination won't work. For this reason, you, as the administrator, have to get out into the trenches and teach people about this powerful new feature. Because if you don't proactively push this feature, you might as well have everyone just use a computer-based PIM or the old paper appointment method. The choice is yours.

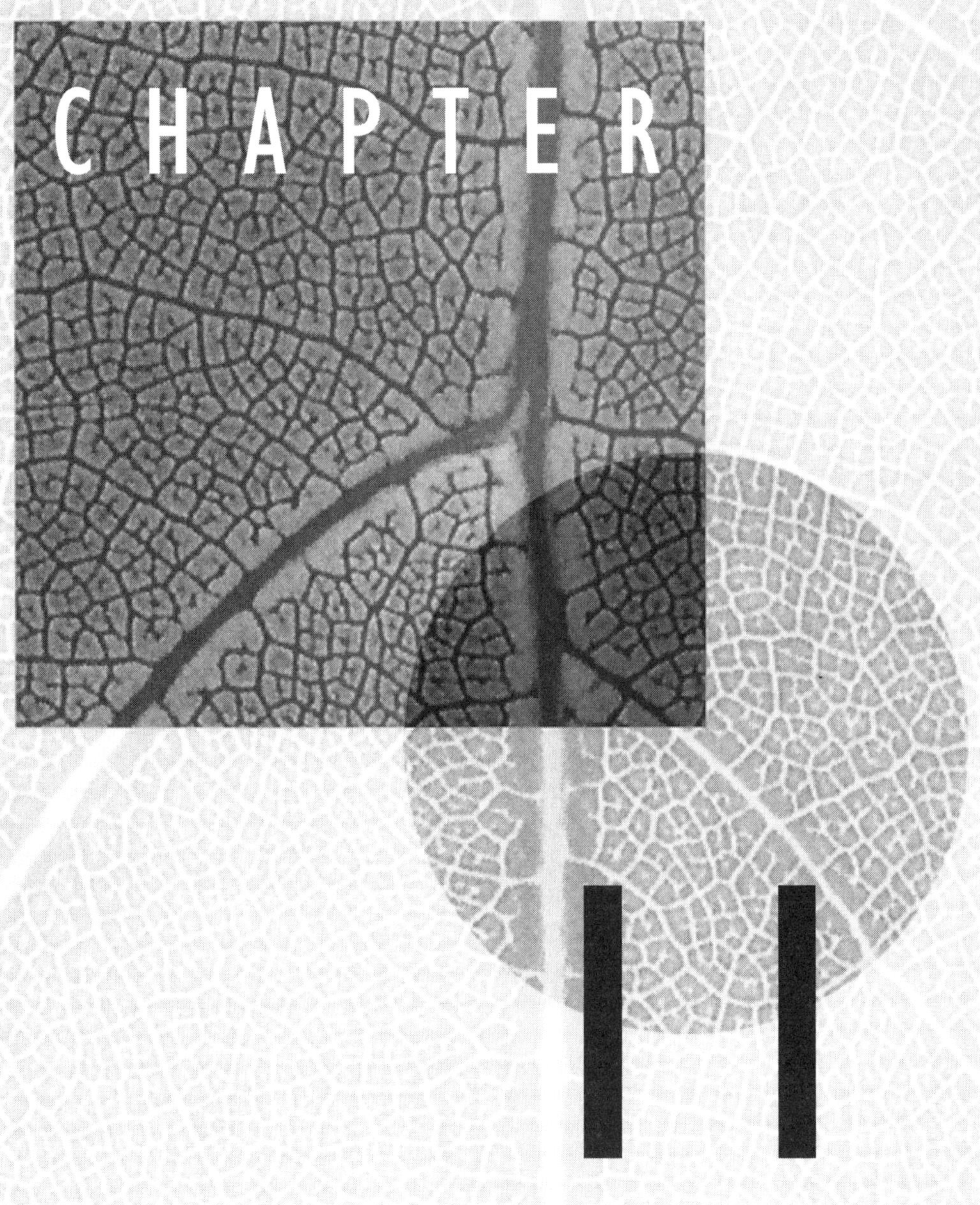

Notes Web Navigator

One of the first Internet-specific features included with Notes Release 4.0 was the Notes Web Navigator. This feature enabled Notes users to browse the Internet through the familiar interface of a Notes database. Powered by a Notes server configured as an InterNotes server, the Notes Web Publisher retrieved requested Web pages from the Internet and stored them in a Notes database. This database was then made available to users for viewing.

The benefit of this particular feature over a standard Web browser such as Netscape's Navigator or Microsoft's Internet Explorer was that each user on the network didn't have to be configured with TCP/IP to communicate with the Internet. Since the Web retrieval process was being handled by the Notes server, only that machine had to have TPC/IP running. If Notes clients currently communicated with their Notes server via SPX, for example, they could continue to do so and still access the Web through the Notes server configured as an InterNotes server.

Besides a lack of protocol dependency, this feature also had a sort of Web proxy functionality. Since each Web page retrieved was stored in a Notes database, these pages were quickly available to other users who wanted to view them.

The down side to this technology was that at least one Notes server had to be configured as an InterNotes server. Fortunately, with Release 4.5 this requirement is no longer a limitation. Now the Web Navigator feature has the added functionality of being able to work independently. This capability does call for the TCP/IP protocol dependency, but this requirement is hardly seen as a limitation these days because so many networks are enabling TCP/IP in one way or another.

Since the Web Navigator can now be run independently of a Notes server, you might ask, "What administrative responsibilities are there?" Well, there are two basic roles that a Notes administrator plays with this enhanced feature. First, the Web Navigator can still be run dependent on an InterNotes server. If your network doesn't have TCP/IP enabled on each workstation, you will want to exploit this way of enabling the Web Navigator. Second, your administrative responsibilities depend largely on the support you've decided to provide for running the Web Navigator independently of the Notes server.

Your network environment may already use Netscape's Navigator or Microsoft's Internet Explorer as its standard desktop Web browser. In this situation, your Notes support infrastructure probably won't provide any assistance for users who want to use the Web Navigator because of the current browser standard. However, if there is no Web browser standard for your company, then you'll need to support this enhanced Notes feature. For the purpose of support, you will have to understand the stand-alone usage of the Web Navigator as well as the server-based implementation of this feature.

The Server-Based Web Navigator

Setting up the Web Navigator on your Notes server is a very simple process. It requires only a Notes server configured with TCP/IP to run the InterNotes process on, and that you have a leased line connection to an Internet Service Provider (ISP) or a connection to a Web proxy server that then connects to an ISP. If these requirements are in place, it should take you about fifteen minutes to get the server-based Web Navigator up and running.

Web Navigator Setup in the Server Document

Once the basic requirements, TCP/IP and Internet access, are met you'll need to edit the Server document in the Public Address Book for the Notes server that will run the InterNotes process. In this document there is a section called Proxy Configuration that must be filled out if your connections to the Internet are made through proxy machines (see Figure 11.1).

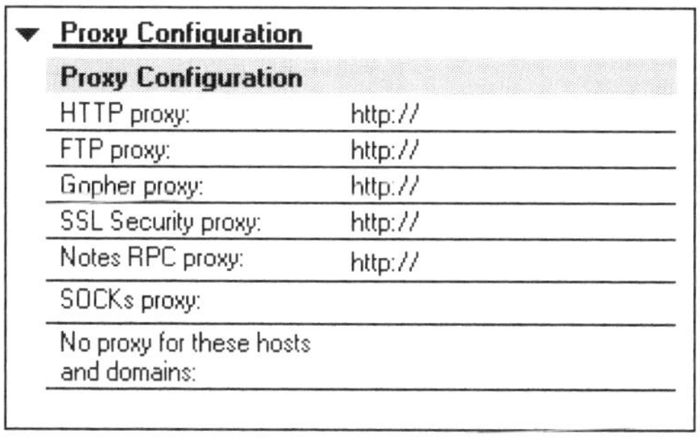

FIGURE 11.1

Each of the popular Internet services can be configured as a proxy server.

The various Internet services defined in this section of the document are defined below:

- **HTTP proxy**: This field is where you list the name or IP address of the proxy and the port to access Web pages using the HTTP protocol. Such an address for a fictional company called Acme Widgets might appear as `Webproxy.acmewidgets.com`. If that proxy server were on a specific IP port, such as 8001, then the address would be `Webproxy.acmewidgets.com:8001`.
- **FTP proxy**: This field is where you enter the name or IP address of the proxy and the port to access FTP (File Transfer Protocol) services. Here again, a fictional company called Acme Widgets might have an address such as `ftpproxy.acmewidgets.com`. If the port were different than the default FTP port, you would add a colon to the end of the address and then the number.
- **Gopher proxy**: As with HTTP and FTP proxy fields, this field is where you enter the name or IP address of the proxy and the port to go through when accessing Gopher pages through a proxy. The Acme Widgets address might be `gopherproxy.acmewidgets.com`.
- **SSL Security proxy**: In this field, enter the name or IP address of the proxy and the port you want to go through for pages on Internet servers using SSL (Secure Sockets Layer). SSL is a method of transaction security that offers authentication of servers and clients, and message confidentiality and integrity.
- **Notes RPC proxy**: This field is specific to Notes-to-Notes communication over the Internet.
- **SOCKS proxy**: In this field, enter the name or IP address of the proxy and the port.
- **No proxy for these hosts and domains:** If your company has implemented a corporate intranet, then you can list the domain(s) for those intranet machines so that the Web Navigator knows to skip the HTTP proxy to reach these specific internal machines. In the case of the fictional company Acme Widgets, this field might appear as `acmewidgets.com`.

In all of the previous fields, numeric IP addresses are perfectly acceptable if no internal DNS (Domain Name Server) is available to resolve the host names to IP numbers. Also note that your company may use only some of the proxies listed above. If you're not sure what types of proxies are implemented in your network environment, check with your network or LAN administrator.

Aside from filling in the required information in the Proxy Configuration section of the Server document, you also need to enter some basic information in the Web Retriever Administration section of this document. This additional section controls how the Web retriever process runs on your Notes server.

▼ Web Retriever Administration

Web Retriever Management	
Web Navigator database:	web.nsf
Services:	HTTP, FTP, GOPHER
Concurrent retrievers:	25
Retriever log level:	None
Update cache:	Never
SMTP Domain:	

Internet Site Access Control	
Allow access to these Internet sites:	*
Deny access to these Internet sites:	

In this section, there are several fields you need to understand. They are described below:

- **Web Navigator database:** By default, this field is already populated with WEB.NSF. I suggest you leave this default unless you have a really compelling reason to change it.
- **Services:** This field is important because it specifies the Internet services that the Notes server will allow. By default, this field includes HTTP, FTP, and Gopher. However, you might want to enable one of the other services such as HTTPS or Finger. You may also want to disable one of the default services, such as FTP, as a means of preventing users from downloading shareware or freeware programs from the Internet, thus reducing the risk of violating copyright laws or bringing infected programs into your corporate LAN.

- **Concurrent retrievers:** This field specifies how many users can use the Web retriever services on the server. By default, this value is set to 25, which should be sufficient. However, if the Web retriever performance lags, you might want to reduce this number.
- **Retriever log level:** This field specifies whether messages sent by the Web retriever process should go to the InterNotes server console and to the server or local log file (LOG.NSF). The default setting is None, which sends no messages. However, you also have the option of Terse, which sends only minimal messages, and Verbose, which sends all messages to your log.
- **Update cache:** As Web pages are retrieved from the Internet they are stored in the server's Web database (WEB.NSF). The Update Cache field determines how often Notes checks the Internet to see if a page stored in the Web database has changed. Your options for this field are limited to three possible settings:
  - **Never:** Notes will never check the Internet to determine if the requested Web page stored in the Web database (WEB.NSF) has changed. This setting is the default.
  - **Once per session:** Notes will check the Internet to determine if the requested Web page stored in the Web database (WEB.NSF) has changed the first time a Web page is requested. The next time that page is requested during the same Web Navigator session, Notes will not check the Internet for changes and will simply show the user the page as it now appears in the Web Navigator database.
  - **Every time:** This setting causes Notes to check the Internet for changes to a requested Web page stored in the Web database (WEB.NSF) each time the page is requested.
- **SMTP Domain:** Some Web pages have Mail-to buttons attached to them. When a user clicks one of these buttons, Notes starts a new Notes mail message and enters the Internet address specified by the Mail-to button in the To field of the mail message. If you're using the Notes SMTP MTA, the automatic address added to the new message will be handled correctly. However, if you're using the older Lotus SMTP Mail Gateway, you'll have to append the foreign domain name for that gateway to the address in the To field of the new message. So users don't have to append this foreign domain each time, add the name of that gateway in the SMTP Domain field.

- **Allow access to these Internet sites**: As the field label indicates, you can control which Web sites users can access by explicitly listing them in this field. By default, an asterisk (*) is added to this field indicating that all Web sites are accessible. Specific Web site names or IP addresses are acceptable entries in this field. Normally, you will accept this field's default and use the Deny Access to These Internet Sites to control what users can get to.

- **Deny access to these Internet sites**: This field, as the label indicates, controls which Web sites users cannot access. By default, this field is blank, which denies access to nothing. This field has precedence over the previously described Allow Access to These Internet Sites field. Therefore, you can accept the default in the first field and then deny specific sites in the Deny Access to These Internet Sites field, which overrides the access to all.

Once you've completed the Proxy Configuration and Web Retriever Administration sections of the Server document for the server that will become the InterNotes server in your Notes environment, you're just about ready to go. The only steps left are to specify the location of the InterNotes server so users can find it and to start the InterNotes task on the Notes server.

Specifying the Location of the InterNotes Server

When users open Web pages in Notes, Notes opens those pages based on settings found in the user's Location document (see Figure 11.2) stored in the Personal Address Book. The settings that determine how Notes opens Web pages are found in the Internet Browser and Servers sections of the document. The relevant fields are listed below:

- **Internet browser**: This field specifies whether to use Notes or some other Web browser that is installed in the system. If you select another Web browser, such as Netscape Navigator, then the Retrieve/Open Pages and InterNotes Server fields (described next) disappear because they are not needed if users select an external browser.

- **Retrieve/open pages**: This field allows users to specify whether to retrieve and open pages from the InterNotes server or the Notes workstation, or whether to not retrieve pages at all. Select the From InterNotes Server option.

- **InterNotes server:** When the user selects From InterNotes Server in the previous field, the InterNotes Server field appears. In this field, users specify the name of the Notes server that you set up as the InterNotes server. The name entered here must be in hierarchical format (for example, ServerOne/NotesDomain/US).

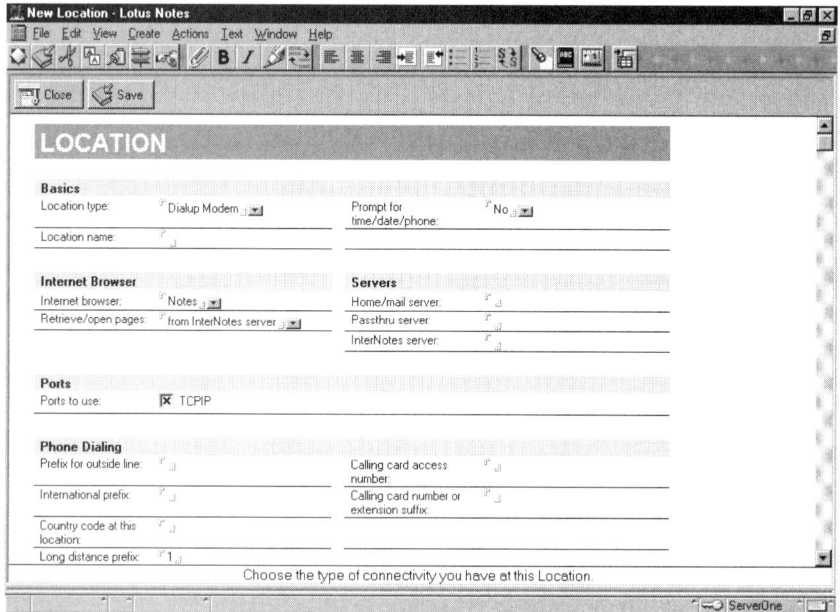

FIGURE 11.2

The Location document in a user's Personal Address Book contains fields where users can specify how to retrieve and open Web pages.

If these fields in the user's Location document are blank, Notes will check the Server Location Information section of the Server document for the user's home/mail server (see Figure 11.3). In this section, there is a field where you, the Notes administrator, can specify the name in hierarchical format of the Notes server that is also the InterNotes server. If, however, this field is blank, Notes returns an error message to the user and the user is unable to open Web pages through Notes.

The Web Server

If all of the appropriate information is entered into the Server document of the soon-to-be InterNotes server and the location for this server is specified in the user's Location document or in all of the home/mail servers in your Notes

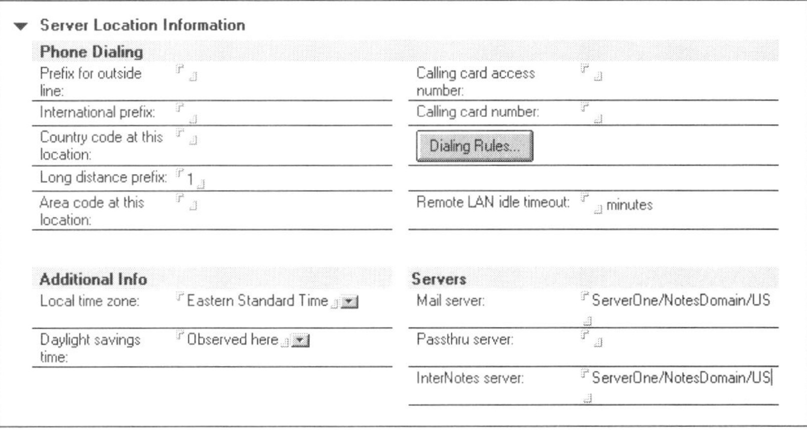

FIGURE 11.3

The Server document for a Notes server that is also a home/mail server for users should also specify the name of the InterNotes server in your Notes environment.

environment, then you're ready for the last step to enabling Web navigation through your InterNotes server: loading the Web server task.

The Web server task is what makes Web navigation through the familiar interface of a Notes database (WEB.NSF) possible. From the Notes server console or remote server console of your soon-to-be InterNotes server, type **load web** (see Figure 11.4). This command starts the Web server task so users can start to browse the Web using the InterNotes server.

FIGURE 11.4

The server console shows the Web task starting.

```
Lotus Domino Server: ServerOne/NotesDomain/US
>
>
>
> sh server

Lotus Domino r Server (Release 4.5a for Windows/32) 03/19/97 05:11:17 PM

Server name:            ServerOne/NotesDomain/US
Server directory:       d:\apps\notes
Partition number:       1
Elapsed time:           00:02:04
Transactions/minute:    Last minute: 0; Last hour: 0; Peak: 0
Peak # of sessions:     0 at
Transactions:           0
Shared mail:            Not enabled
Pending mail:  0        Dead mail:  0
>
> load web
03/19/97 05:11:23 PM  WEB(1): InterNotes(R) WEB Retriever starting for
'ServerOne/NotesDomain/US'...
03/19/97 05:11:23 PM  WEB(1): Creating InterNotes database 'web.nsf', using
template 'pubweb45.ntf'
03/19/97 05:11:34 PM  WEB(1): Creating InterNotes Navigator administration
options for server 'CN=ServerOne/O=NotesDomain/C=US'
> _
```

If you want the Web server task to load every time the Notes server starts, add Web to the ServerTasks setting in the server's NOTES.INI file.

Managing the Web Retriever Database

Getting the InterNotes server running in your Notes environment is only part of Notes Web navigator administration. The other part of administration for this feature includes customization of the Web Retriever database (WEB.NSF). Customizing this database will help you effectively retrieve and store Web pages.

Setting the Access Control List for the Web Navigator Database

When you started the Web server task, it created the Web Navigator database on your server and named it according to the filename you specified in the Server document of your InterNotes server. This database is where all of the retrieved Web pages are stored. Like any other Notes database, the Web Navigator database has an Access Control List (ACL) that needs to be customized for your Notes environment (details about the ACL can be found in Chapter 7).

View the current ACL settings for the Web Navigator database by selecting the database and then, from the menu bar, selecting File ➢ Database ➢ Access Control. The ACL dialog box appears and displays the current settings.

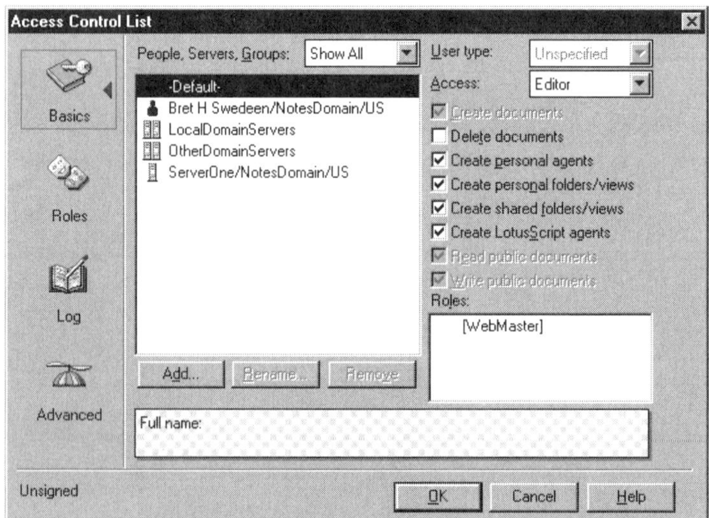

The default ACL settings should be sufficient for this database unless you only want to give Web access to select people. If this is the situation, adjust the ACL accordingly, but be sure you give these selected users enough access and deny access to other users. You can choose the level of access in the Access drop-down list in the top right corner of the screen. The following list outlines the ACL settings that you need to set for this database:

- **Default:** By default, all users have Editor access. This level might seem a bit excessive. However, a setting this high is required so users can fill out HTML forms, create Recommendation documents, and create Web Tours (both Recommendation documents and Web Tours are discussed later in this chapter).
- **LocalDomainServers:** This group should be set to Manager access so all servers can easily replicate this database throughout your Notes domain.
- **OtherDomainServers:** This group is set to No Access for the simple reason that outside domains probably shouldn't be surfing the Web through your InterNotes server. This type of activity would place unnecessary burden on your server.
- **Administration:** Someone or some group needs to be assigned the Web Master role. Usually, you'll give your Notes administrator(s) Manager access to this database and assign them this special role as well. The Web Master role allows that person to access and edit the Web Navigator Administration document (discussed in detail shortly).

Once you have checked the ACL settings and they meet your environment's requirements, you should create an Administration document.

The Web Navigator Administration Document

The Administration document for the Web Navigator database is a special document that allows you to access certain aspects of this database. Database size, document purge settings for the database, and control aspects of Web page appearance are all things that you can control through this document. Before you can access this document, you have to create it.

1. Select the Web Navigator database and, from the menu bar, select Create ➢ Other.

2. The Other dialog box appears and presents three choices: Admin, Launch URL, and Web Tour. Select Admin and click OK.

3. The Administration Document appears (see Figure 11.5).

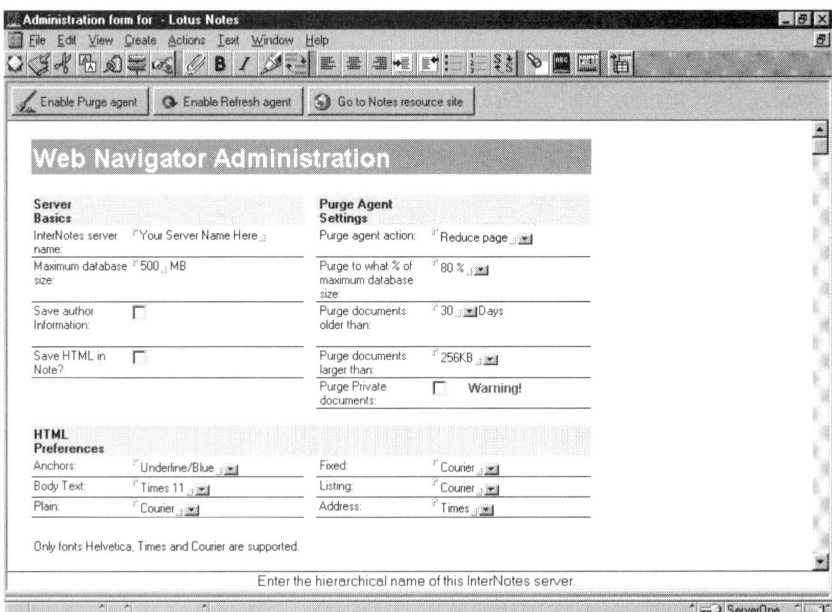

FIGURE 11.5

The Web Navigation Administration document has three sections: Server Basics, HTML Preferences, and Purge Agent Settings.

Server Basics

As the section title suggests, the Server Basics section is for basic settings such as size and the InterNotes server name.

- **InterNotes server name:** Enter the hierarchical name of the InterNotes server (for example, ServerOne/NotesDomain/US).
- **Maximum database size:** Web page retrieval can cause significant growth in a database. Control that growth by limiting the database's size in this field. The increments of measure are megabytes and the default is 500.

- **Save author information:** Each person who requests a Web page is considered the author of that page when it becomes a document in the database. By default, the author information is not saved when documents are created. Place a check next to this option to override the default and cause each new document to save author information about who requested the document.
- **Save HTML in Note:** This option allows you to save the HTML source for each Web page retrieved. By default, this option is turned off. Placing a check next to this option will enable it and save all HTML source code in a field called HTMLSource.

HTML Preferences

This section of the Administration document allows you to control how certain HTML tags are interpreted by the Web Navigator. Keep in mind that the HTML standard tags for Web page creation keep evolving and expanding. Therefore, while most HTML tags are supported by the Web Navigator, some tags such as frames and tables are still unsupported at this time.

- **Anchors:** Links to other Web sites embedded in a Web page are normally identified by a different color or some other textual characteristic. This field allows you to specify the appearance of those links once they are retrieved into the Web Navigator database. The default is Underline/Blue.
- **Body Text:** This field allows you to specify the font and size of any element not defined in any of the other fields of this section. The default is Times 11.
- **Plain:** This field allows you to specify the font type for text within the <PLAINTEXT>, <PRE>, and <EXAMPLE> tags. The default is Courier.
- **Fixed:** This field allows you to specify the font type for text within the <CODE>, <SAMPLE>, <KBD>, and <TT> tags. The default is Courier.
- **Listing:** This field allows you to specify the font type for text within the <LISTING> tag. The default is Courier.
- **Address:** This field allows you to specify the font type for text within the <ADDRESS> tag. The default is Times.

Purge Agent Settings

As previously mentioned, the size of the Web Navigator database can grow significantly. Although you can limit the size of the database, you shouldn't rely on the size limitation as a way to keep this database under control. A better way to control the database size is to use the built-in Purge agent. This agent removes documents from the Web Navigator database according to the settings in this section of the Administration document.

- **Purge agent action:** This field determines what action is taken on documents in the Web Navigator database when the Purge agent runs. You can select from two options:
  - **Reduce:** This option, which is the default setting, deletes the contents of the Web page but saves the URL so the page still appears in database views. If someone selects a "reduced" document to view, InterNotes will retrieve the content from the Internet based on the URL that was saved.
  - **Delete:** Select this option and the Web page will be deleted by the Purge agent if the page meets the rest of the criteria defined in this section of the Administration document.
- **Purge to what % of maximum database size:** This field specifies the percent of the maximum database size (specified in the Maximum Database Size field in the Server Basics section) that you want the Purge agent to reach. For example, if the maximum database size was set to 100 MB and you accepted the default of 80 percent for the Purge to What % of Maximum Database Size field, then when the Purge agent runs it will remove documents until the database total size is less than 80 MB (details about the Purge agent are in *The Purge Agent* section).
- **Purge documents older than:** This field specifies when to delete or reduce documents based on the number of days they have been in the database. The default is 30, but you can also select 60, 90, 120, or enter a number of your own.
- **Purge documents larger than:** This field specifies when to delete or reduce a document based on its size. The default is 256 KB, but you can also select 512 KB or 1024 KB.

- **Purge Private documents:** There is a warning sign in bright red letters next to this field. This warning is to remind you that selecting this option will include documents previously moved to a private folder in the Purge agent's scope of execution. Purging documents in private folders can cause quite a surprise for some users. If you decide to enable this feature, make sure you inform each user who uses this database that documents which meet a certain criteria will be purged from the system. By default, this option is disabled.

Aside from these three configuration sections in the Administration document, there are two specialized agents that go hand-in-hand with this document: the Purge Agent and the Refresh agent. These two agents help control the size of the Web Navigator database and the currency of the documents contained in that database.

The Purge Agent

As users browse the Web using the InterNotes server, the Web Navigator database will become populated with Web pages. These pages can cause this database to quickly grow in size. To manage the size of this database you'll need to activate the Purge agent. This agent removes documents from the Web Navigator database according to the settings specified in the Purge Agent Settings section of the Administration document.

To activate the Purge agent you'll need to set agent security on the InterNotes server, set the Purge agent criteria, and then enable the Purge agent. The following steps detail how to accomplish each of these tasks:

1. Open the Public Address Book and then open the Server document for the InterNotes server in Edit mode.

2. In the Agent Manager section of the Server document, enter your name in both the Run Restricted LotusScript Agents and Run Unrestricted LotusScript Agents fields.

3. In the Nighttime Parameters section of the Server document, enter 360 in the Max LotusScript Execution Time field and 80 in the Max % Busy Before Delay field.

4. Save the changes to the Server document and close the document.

5. Set up the Purge agent criteria (described in the previous section).

6. Open the Web Navigator Administration document if it isn't already open, and click the Start Purge Agent button on the Action bar. This button enables the Purge agent.

When the Purge agent has been activated, it will run every day at 1 AM and make several passes over the Web Navigator database to purge documents. During the first pass over the database, the Purge agent checks the header from each Web page in the database. If the Web page has expired, the Purge agent deletes the page. During the second pass, document creation dates for each Web page are checked and deleted if the page is older than the date specified in the Purge Documents Older Than field. During the final pass, the Purge agent checks for Web pages that are larger than the size specified in the Purge Documents Larger Than field and deletes them.

The Refresh Agent

The Purge agent, as you just learned, helps manage the size of the Web Navigator database. This agent is a very useful administration tool but doesn't do much to manage the currency of the documents in the database. For that task, the Web Navigator has another agent called the Refresh agent.

The Refresh agent compares the date of each Web page contained in the Web Navigator database with the date of the same Web page on its Internet server. If the Web page on the Internet server is newer, the Refresh agent replaces the Web page inside the database.

The Refresh agent only works on HTTP pages. FTP pages, Gopher pages, or pages stored in a user's private folder in the database are not refreshed by this agent.

Setting up the Refresh agent is very simple. Start by reviewing steps 1 through 4 in the previous section, *The Purge Agent.* If you haven't executed those steps, do so now. Once those steps are complete, open the Administration document in the Web Navigator database and click the Start Refresh Agent button on the Action bar. This button enables this agent to run every day at 3 AM.

The Workstation-Based Web Navigator

As a Notes administrator, you'll work with the Web Navigator when it is set up on an InterNotes server. You won't need to know much about this feature if an InterNotes server isn't planned for your Notes environment or if your company has standardized on a non-Notes Web browser. However, when neither of the previously described situations is true, users may want to use the Personal Web Navigator in stand-alone mode\. For this type of situation, you'll need to understand how to set up and use the stand-alone implementation of the Personal Web Navigator.

Creating the Personal Web Navigator

To get started, create the Personal Web Navigator database on your local hard drive by selecting File ➢ Database ➢ New. In the New Database dialog box, select the template for the Personal Web Navigator 4.5 (PERWEB45.NTF). Complete the New Database dialog box with the server name, the name of the database, and the filename for the database. Click OK to create the database.

The server equivalent of the Personal Web Navigator is the Server Web Navigator database, which can be created on the server. The template for the Server Web Navigator is PUBWEB45.NTF. Essentially, it has all the aspects of the Personal Web Navigator, but it resides on the Notes server to allow groups of people to access and share Web pages.

When you enter the database for the first time, you are prompted by a Welcome dialog box (as shown in Figure 11.6). The Welcome dialog box will ask you if you want to fill out the Internet Options profile at this time. Click Yes to fill out the profile.

Internet Options

When entering the Web Navigator for the first time, if you chose Yes from the Welcome dialog box, Notes will display the Internet Options profile (see Figure 11.7). However, if you chose No in the Welcome dialog box, you can access the Internet Options profile by selecting Actions ➢ Internet Options from the menu bar.

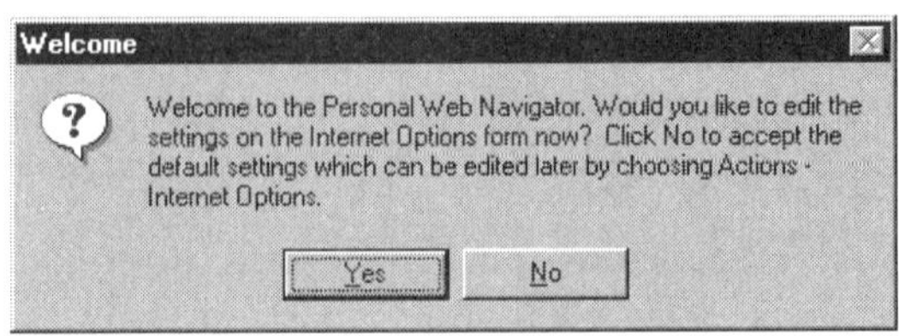

FIGURE 11.6

The Welcome dialog box greets you the first time you enter the Personal Web Navigator 4.5 database. Click Yes to edit the Internet Options profile.

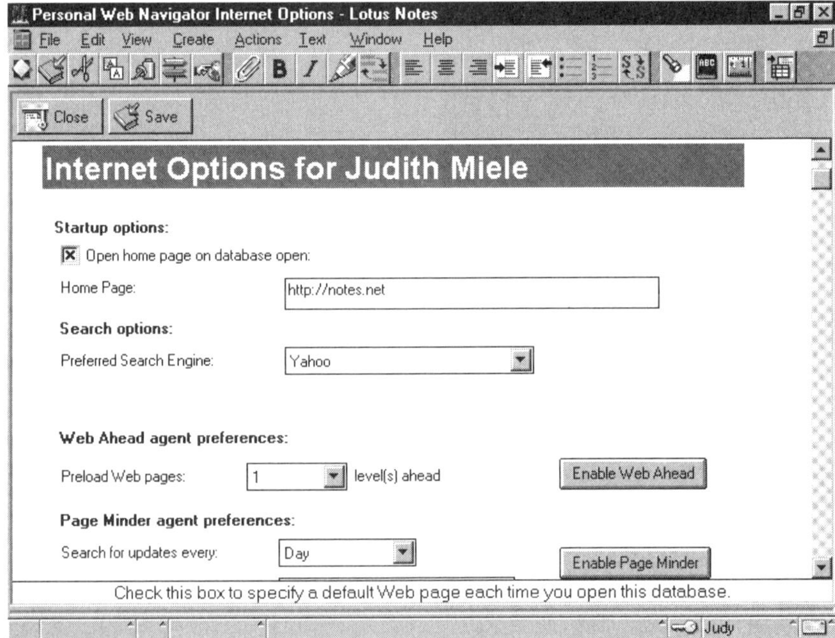

FIGURE 11.7

The first portion of the Internet Options profile in the Web Navigator database

Startup Options

Under the Startup Options section, the checkbox for Open Home Page on Database is checked by default. When you enter the database, it displays the Web site you specified in the Home Page field information line.

Search Options

Under this section, specify your favorite Internet search engine in the Preferred Search Engine field. When you are using the Web Navigator, click the Search button and it will take you to whichever search engine you specify: Yahoo, Excite, Alta Vista, Lycos, or another search engine of your choice.

If you choose Other as your preferred search engine, Notes will provide you with a field to fill in the search engine's URL.

Web Ahead Agent Preferences

The Web Ahead feature is an agent that runs on your computer and stores Web pages up to four links away from whichever Web page you specify. Click the Enable Web Ahead button to enable the agent process. It then stores all of these Web pages in the Personal Web Navigator database. To use the Web Ahead feature, load a Web site in the Personal Web Navigator database and then drag the Web page to the Web Ahead folder. Notes reviews the Web pages that have been placed in the Web Ahead folder. Then the agent replicates pages of HTML documents either 1, 2, 3, or 4 levels deep (depending on what you specified in the Preload Web Pages drop-down list in the Web Ahead Agent Preferences section of the Internet Options profile).

To enable the Web Ahead feature, in addition to clicking the Enable Web Ahead button, you must select File ➢ Tools ➢ User Preferences, and in the Startup section, select the Enable Scheduled Local Agents checkbox.

Page Minder Agent Preferences

Like the Web Ahead feature, the Page Minder is an agent that reviews documents placed in the Page Minder folder. Once the Web pages are in the folder, if there is any change to that Web page, the Page Minder agent will send you (or whomever you specify) an e-mail message informing you of the change.

In addition to clicking the Enable Page Minder button, select File ➢ Tools ➢ User Preferences and in the Startup section, click the checkbox to enable Scheduled Local Agents.

There are also options you can set to determine how often searches are done for updates (see Figure 11.8). In the If an Update Is Found area, choose to send either an e-mail with the actual Web page or a summary with doc links. Either specify who this e-mail should be sent to in the Send To field or click the Address button to obtain the Names dialog box to select a name from the Public Name and Address Book. (Make sure you click the Enable Page Minder button to enable the agent.)

FIGURE 11.8

The second part of the Internet Options profile

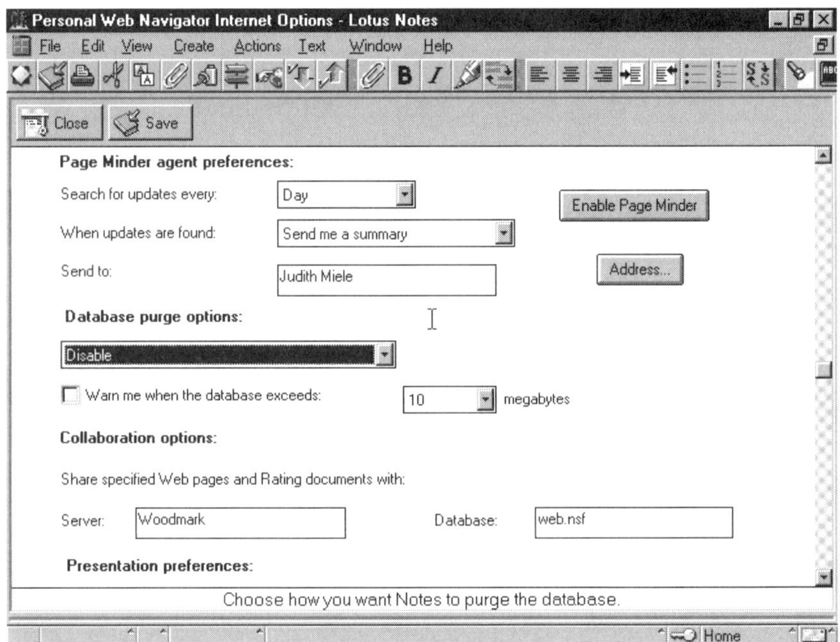

Database Purge Options

The Database Purge options are the default specification for the Housekeeping Agent, which allows the database manager to maintain a document's deletion schedule. This agent will keep the Web Navigator database to a reasonable size, by deleting or reducing the size of documents that have not been read for the number of days you specify. By default, the Database Purge options are disabled. But if you enable them, you can purge Web pages that haven't been read within fifteen, thirty, sixty, or ninety days. You also have the option to reduce the pages to links if they haven't been read within fifteen, thirty, sixty, or ninety days.

In addition, click the Warn Me When the Database Exceeds checkbox, and then choose 5, 10, 25, or 50 megabytes. Make sure you click the Enable Housekeeping button and select the server to run it on. This agent runs each night at 1 AM.

Collaborations Options

The Collaboration Options section allows you to click the Share button in the Personal Web Navigator and either share a Web page to the specified Notes server and the Server Web Navigator database, or create a recommendation for a Web site (see Figure 11.9). Enter the name of the server in the Server field and the name of the database in the Database field.

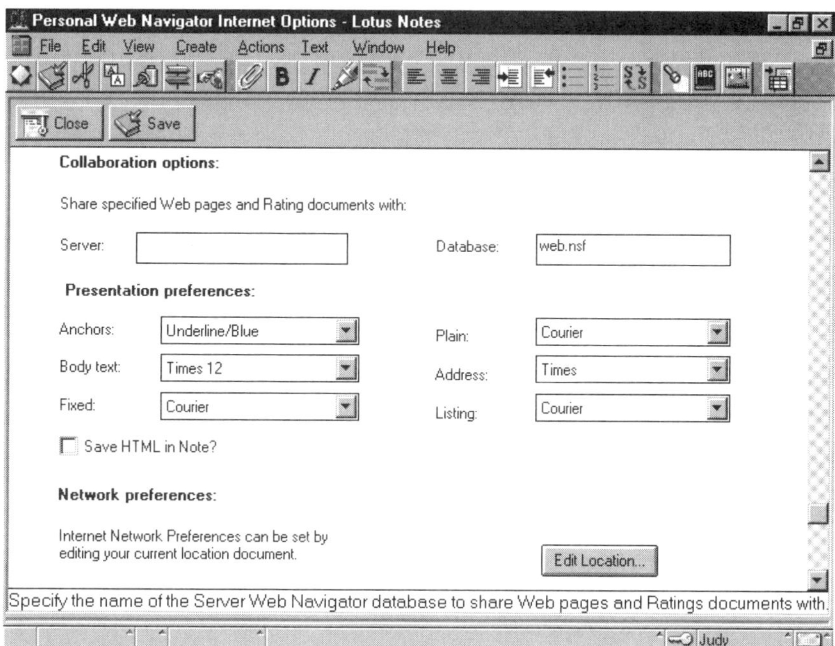

FIGURE 11.9

Refer to this last section of the Internet Options profile for the Collaborations Options and Presentation Preferences sections.

Presentation Preferences

The Presentation Preferences section shown in Figure 11.9 has the same functionality as the HTML Preferences of the server-based Web Navigator database (refer to *The Web Navigator Administration Document* section for details about these preferences).

Most Web browsers allow you to view the HTML source code for any page currently displayed in the browser. The Web Navigator, however, does not allow this feature unless you check the Save HTML in Note option in the Presentation Preferences section.

Network Preferences

The Network Preferences section includes a button that takes you to the current Location document in the Personal Address Book. This document needs to be edited before you can successfully connect to the Web.

Editing the Location Document

Location documents are stored in the Personal Address Book in the View by Locations folder. These documents specify important information regarding the network, ports, default servers, replication settings, and location of USER.ID files. An example of the Office Location document appears in Figure 11.10.

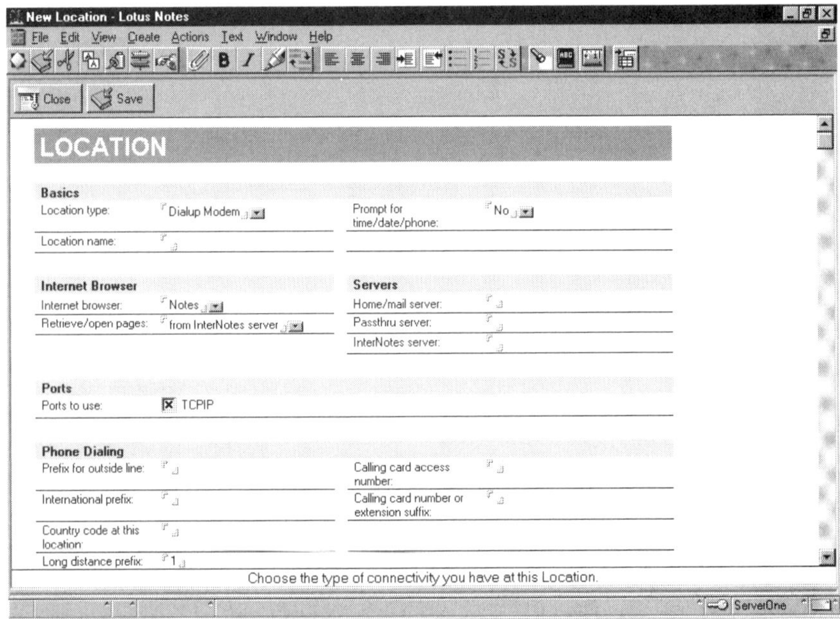

FIGURE 11.10

The Location document is where the user can specify information regarding the network, ports, default servers, replication settings, and location of USER.ID files.

Basics Section

When you select Local Area Network, or Both Dialup and Local Area Network for the Location Type field, Notes displays an additional option called the Web Proxy field. This field allows users to enter the IP and port of the proxy server, if one is used in your network environment.

After you enter the default HTTP proxy in the Web Proxy field, click the button with the icon that looks like a hat with a propeller to display the Proxy Server Configuration dialog box (see Figure 11.11). Notes makes it easy for the administrator by using the same proxy name that will be used for FTP, Gopher, and SSL Security. If you do not want to use that same proxy name, uncheck the Use Same Proxy for Internet Protocols checkbox and enter the proxy names you prefer to use.

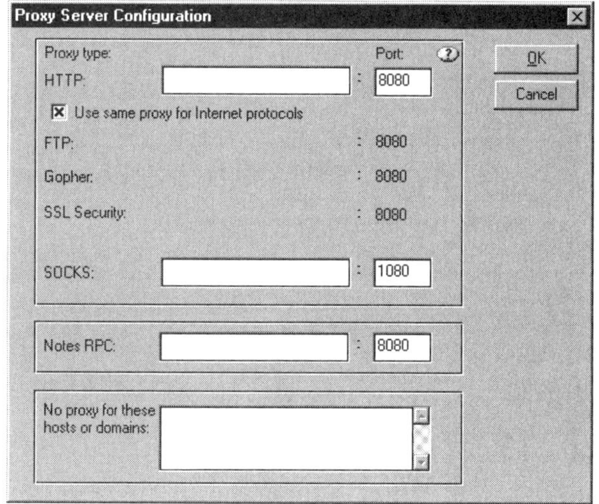

FIGURE 11.11 The Proxy Server Configuration dialog box is displayed when you click the icon next to the Web Proxy field in the Location document. Whatever proxy information the administrator has entered will be repeated within the FTP, Gopher, and SSL Security Internet Protocols Settings fields. You can also fill in your own settings.

- **Hypertext Transfer Protocol (HTTP)**: a protocol used on the World Wide Web to transfer information between servers and browsers. An example of a Hypertext Transfer Protocol would be when you are in a browser and you enter, **http://www.simplyshareware.com**. This is the URL for the HTTP protocol.

- **File Transfer Protocol (FTP)**: a protocol that allows you to transfer or download files from the Internet.
- **Gopher**: a type of server that resides on the Internet. It is only text-based and has no graphics or links.
- **Secure Socket Layer (SSL)**: servers running SSL (details about this type of proxy can be found in the *Server-Based Web Navigator* section).

Other fields in this dialog box include SOCKS, Notes RPC Proxy, and No Proxy for these hosts or domains.

- If you enter information in the SOCKS proxy option, it will take precedence over the HTTP proxy.
- Notes RPC proxy allows Notes servers to talk with other Notes servers over the Internet.
- If you want to bypass the proxy servers, enter the exact name of the host or domain in the No Proxies For These Hosts or Domains field, or use wild cards to specify different elements of the address, for example **ftp.*.org**.

Internet Browser Section

In this section, choose which Internet browser you prefer to use. Here you have the option to use the Notes Web Navigator, Netscape Navigator, Microsoft's Internet Explorer, or another browser of your choosing. This option brings up the browser of your choice when you are in Notes and want to browse the Web.

For example, if someone e-mails you a URL which reads, "Found this information on http:/www.lotus.com/seminars," the underlined URL is green, or whichever color you designated in the Internet Options profile. If you double-click the URL, it launches the browser you specified and loads the Web page.

The Retrieve/Open Pages field refers to where the Web pages will be retrieved from. There are three options: From the InterNotes Server, From the Notes workstation, or No Retrievals. Since we're discussing the workstation version of the Web Navigator, the correct selection here would be From Notes workstation.

Java Applet Security

Notes has Java applet support and the applets will run when browsing with the Notes Web Navigator as long as the Java support files are installed on the workstation and you have enabled the Java applets option under File ➢ Tools ➢ User Preferences.

The Java Applet Security section lets you designate the level of access for your workstation to run the applets (see Figure 11.12). By default, all Java applets will run on your system. If the default is acceptable, don't change anything in this section. However, if you prefer for only certain hosts to load Java applets on your machine, then specify that information in the Trusted Hosts field.

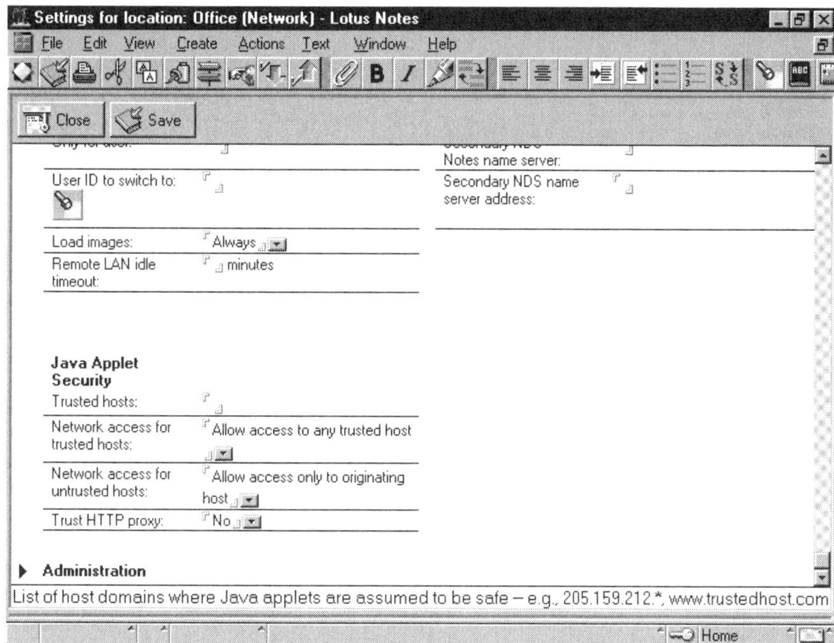

FIGURE 11.12 A Location document showing the Java Applet Security section

Once you enter host names in the Trusted Host section, give network access to these hosts by choosing one of the following options in the Network Access for Trusted Hosts field:

- **Disable Java**: Java applets will not run on your workstation.

- **No access allowed:** the trusted host (listed in the Trusted Host field) will not have access to make HTTP connections, but will run Java applets on your workstation.
- **Allow access to any originating host:** any Java applet will run from the host.
- **Allow access to any trusted host:** the Java applets will only run when the name of the host is designated in the Trusted Host field.
- **Allow access to any host:** allows all Java applets to run from any host.

Other options under the Java Applet Security section include: Network Access for Untrusted Hosts, and Trust HTTP proxy. The Network Access for untrusted hosts pertains to all of the hosts that were not specified in the Trusted Host section. This field has three choices: Disable Java, No Access Allowed, and Allow Access to Any Originating Host.

Trust HTTP Proxy is the last option in the Java Applet Security section. Only choose Yes in this field if you have specified an HTTP proxy in the Web Proxy field under the Basics section in the Location document.

Using the Personal Web Navigator

Once the Personal Web Navigation database is set up on the workstation and the appropriate settings have been made in the Location document, you're ready to get started with the Notes Web Navigator. Keep in mind as you use this feature, however, that the Personal Web Navigator database is just another Notes database. The database is a container that stores Web pages as Notes documents. These documents are accessible regardless of whether or not you're connected to a LAN or phone line. The beauty of the Personal Web Navigator is that the documents that it stores are Web pages! You can access the pages stored in the database no matter where you are (in a plane, on the beach, or even sitting on your roof).

Using the Personal Web Navigator Database

When you open the Personal Web Navigator database, you may recognize the contact-sensitive menu bar. Below the menu are the smart icons and the Action bar buttons that make browsing easy. There are also three window panes of information: the Folder, View, and Preview panes. The Folder pane contains the folders within this database. The View pane is located below the Folder pane and contains a listing of the Web pages in whichever folder you have selected. The View pane categorizes the Web pages by their host names. The Preview pane to the right of the Folder and View panes contains the Web page that is selected in the View pane.

Opening Web Pages

When you open the Personal Web Navigator, it will default to the Web page you specified in the Internet Options profile under the Startup Options section. Refer to the *Internet Options* section previously in this chapter.

Once you are in the Web Navigator, you can open a Web page by entering the page's URL. Select File ➣ Open URL from the menu bar and you will receive the dialog box shown in Figure 11.13.

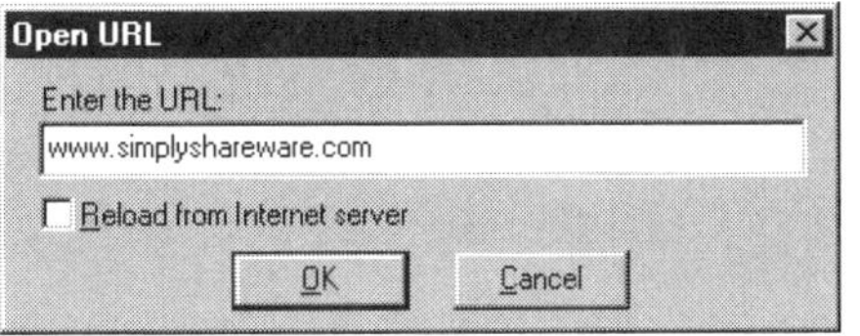

FIGURE 11.13
The Open URL dialog box appears when you select File ➣ Open URL from the File menu. Enter the URL in the Enter the URL box.

If you begin to retrieve a Web page and decide that you actually don't want to retrieve that page or decide that you just want to cancel the process, press the ESC key to cancel opening the page. Or, you can press the icon with the flying paper image to the right of the URL window to cancel the retrieval of a Web page.

Saving Web Pages

Once you open the Web page of your choice, you may decide that you are really interested in this particular page and that you want to save it. To do this, click the Bookmarks button in the Action bar. The dialog box will display a list of folders; select the Bookmark folder and click the Add button.

Notes also supports the drag and drop feature. By clicking and dragging the Web page from the View pane to the Folder pane, you can drop the page into the Bookmark folder.

If you prefer to save a Web page in a different folder than the Bookmark folder, you will need to create the folder you want to save the Web page in by selecting Create ➢ Folder. The Create Folder dialog box will prompt you to name the folder. Type the name for the folder and click OK. The new folder appears under the Folders and Views in the Folder pane. Now click and drag your Web page from the View pane into the newly created folder.

Forwarding Web Pages

If you come across a Web page you'd like others to see, you can forward the entire Web page to someone or a group of people. To forward a page, click the Forward button in the Action bar. A new mail message will appear, which you complete as you would any other e-mail message. Address the e-mail message, place a subject in the Subject line, and provide additional explanatory text if required.

Searching within the Personal Web Navigator

Once the Web pages are stored in the Web Navigator database, you can perform a full text search on them. First, make sure the database is indexed by selecting File ➢ Database ➢ Properties from the menu bar to display the Properties dialog box. Inside the Properties dialog box, click the Full Text tab and click the Create button to create a full text index on the Notes database. After the database is indexed, the Search bar will appear below the menu bar. The Search bar is indicated by an icon of a finger pointing to a book (or a finger pointing to a planet when used for URL entries). Next to the icon, type in the text you are looking for. For example, if you want to see all the Web pages contained in this database that have the word "Organizer" in them, type **Organizer** in the text box and click the Search button (see Figure 11.14). Notes' search engine will search through the database and will filter only the Web pages that have the word "Organizer" in them.

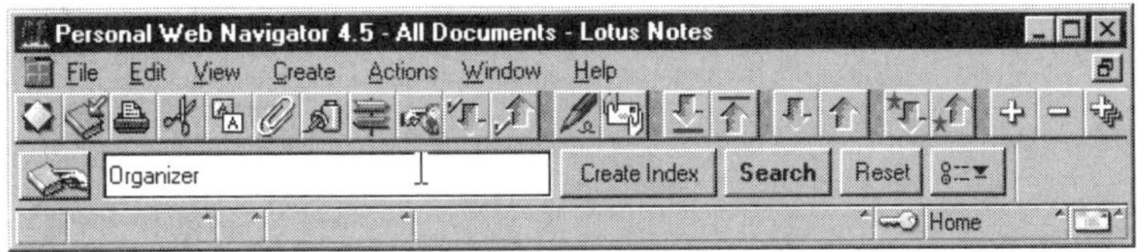

FIGURE 11.14

The Search bar has a button with a finger pointing to a book icon on the left. In the text box next to this button you can enter key words for a search.

The Search bar is indicated by an icon with a finger pointing to a book. If you only see an icon with a finger pointing to a globe, that means the Navigational bar is active. Click the icon—whichever one appears—to toggle between the Search bar and the Navigational bar.

Searching the View Pane of the Personal Web Navigator

You can perform a quick search of a document that has been categorized in the View pane. To do this, select a Web page in the View pane by beginning to type the word you are looking for. For example, if you are looking for `www.sybex.com`, just begin typing each letter of the address. The Quick Search dialog box (see Figure 11.15) will appear and will display whatever you are typing in the Search Text box.

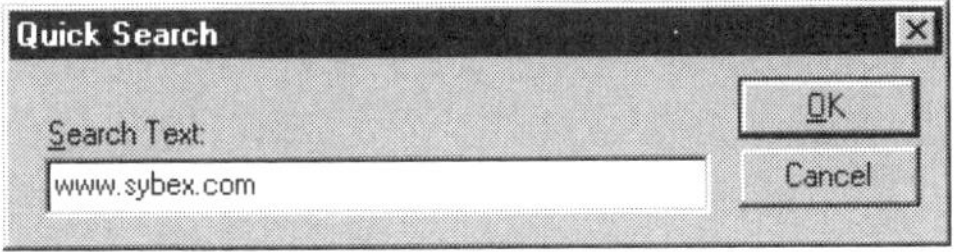

FIGURE 11.15

The Quick Search dialog box will appear when you begin typing the word you are looking for. This will only find the category the document is listed under in the View pane.

Viewing the Source Code

In order to view the source code of the HTML document, first check the Internet Options profile. Select Actions ➢ Internet Options and make sure that the checkbox for Save HTML in Note is checked. Highlight the document of the source code you want to review and then bring up the Document

Properties dialog box by selecting File ➢ Document Properties. Click the Fields tab and on the left side and a listing of field names will be displayed. Click HTML Source. On the right side, the HTML source code will display. To view the HTML source code information more easily, highlight the source code and press Ctrl+C to copy the highlighted information and paste it into an e-mail or the Notepad.

Agents for the Workstation-Based Personal Web Navigator

Simple Web browsing with the Notes Web Navigator is not much different than browsing with any other browser. So why not just use a regular browser? If the Notes Web Navigator were just another browser, the answer would be difficult. However, this feature is not just another Web browser. There are two very significant agents provided with the Personal Web Navigator database that make Web browsing more intelligent and productive.

Page Minder

One of the two important agents included in the Personal Web Navigator database is the Page Minder agent. This agent keeps track of changes made to Web pages you place in the Page Minder folder. If a page in the folder changes in any way, the Page Minder agent will send you (or whomever you specify) an e-mail message informing you of the change.

Your workstation must be running in order for Page Minder to collect Web page information.

Page Minder will search for updates either every hour, every four hours, every day, or every week depending on what you specify in the Page Minder preferences in the Internet Options profile. If an update is found, either an e-mail with the actual Web page is sent or a summary with doc links is sent.

To get started with Page Minder, you'll need to enable it. First go into the Internet Options profile by selecting Actions ➢ Internet Options and fill out the Page Minder preferences section. Refer back to the *Internet Options Profile* section earlier in this chapter for details about the fields in the Page Minder section.

Click the Enable Page Minder button to enable the Page Minder agent. Then select Local for the server to run it on and click OK (notice how the button has changed to Disable Page Minder). Next, select File ➢ Tools ➢ User Preferences and make sure that the checkbox for Enable Scheduled Local Agents is checked.

From the Web Navigator View pane, select the Web pages that you want to be notified about when they change. Select them by highlighting the document and pressing your space bar, which places a check next to the document. You can also select the document by clicking your mouse in the column to the left of the document. Either way, a check mark will appear to indicate that it has been selected.

Next, click and drag the selected pages from the View pane to the Folder pane and drop them into the Page Minder folder. Page Minder will begin informing you when new information arrives on the Web pages you designated.

If at any point you want to disable Page Minder, select from the menu bar, Actions ➢ Internet Options and in the Internet Options profile click the Disable Page Minder button.

Web Ahead

The other built-in agent that makes Web browsing smarter is the Web Ahead agent. When you select a Web page and place it into the Web Ahead folder, this agent will follow the URLs on that Web page to subsequent Web pages. Those subsequent Web pages get placed into the Web Ahead folder.

In the Internet Options profile, the Web Ahead agent preferences allow you to select the number of levels of Web pages you would like the agent to place in the Web Ahead folder. Then when you place one Web page into the Web Ahead folder and this preference is set to two levels, every URL on that Web page is followed by the Web Navigator. Each page that is returned while the Web Navigator is following links is placed in the Web Ahead folder.

For example, if you drag into the Web Ahead folder a home page that has ten URL links to other home pages, the Web Navigator will place all ten of those Web pages into the folder. Now, with two levels ahead selected, if each of those secondary Web pages have ten URLs on them, then the Web Navigator would end up with ten more pages for each of the ten first pages—hence, about 111 pages will be placed in the Web Ahead folder. The number of Web pages could be astronomical if you place many Web pages in the Web Ahead folder and select a very high number of levels ahead that you want to gather.

Make sure you understand the ramifications of selecting a high number of levels for the Web Ahead feature to gather. Also, limit the number of Web pages you place in your Web Ahead folder to keep the number of Web pages gathered at a reasonable number.

Click the Enable Web Ahead button to enable the process and select Local for the server to run it on. Notice that the button has now changed to Disable Web Ahead. Next, check to make sure that the Enable Scheduled Local Agents option is selected under File ➢ Tools ➢ User Preferences.

If at any time you decide that you don't want to continue using the Web Ahead agent, you can easily turn it off. Select from the menu bar, Actions ➢ Internet Options, and in the Internet Options profile, click the Disable Web Ahead button.

Importing Bookmarks

If you use Netscape Navigator or Microsoft Internet Explorer and would like to permanently switch to Notes Web Navigator, you can easily take your bookmarks with you. To get started, select from the menu bar, Actions ➢ Import Microsoft Favorites or Actions ➢ Import Netscape Bookmarks. Both of these menus display a dialog box. If you are importing from Microsoft's Explorer, you will get the Import Favorites dialog box. If you are importing from Netscape's Navigator, then the Import Bookmarks dialog box will appear. Both of these dialog boxes prompt you to enter the path leading to where these files are stored. This importing technology allows you to migrate all of your bookmarks or favorites in one step.

Creating Web Tours

As you are surfing the Net, the Notes Personal Web Navigator creates a history of each Web page you have visited. You can create a Web Tour with this history list by selecting Actions ➢ History from the menu bar.

The History dialog box will appear with the listings of all of the pages you have visited. Click the Save button to create a Web Tour. Fill out the information presented in the Web Tour document. Type the title of the tour and fill in any comments regarding the Web pages on the tour. Click the Save button and this tour will be stored in the Web Tours folder.

Troubleshooting

Once it is properly set up, the Web Navigator and all of its features are great to use. However, users might come across some error messages. Make sure they are not confused between Internet error messages such as "404 URL Not Found," and problems they might encounter using the Personal Web Navigator.

Here are some issues and suggestions to help you get beyond the error messages and problems:

- Why don't I get the hypertext link green line?
    - Make sure the right option in the User Preferences dialog box is selected. Select File ➢ Tools ➢ User Preferences and then go to the Advanced Options section. The Make Internet URLs (http://…) into Hotspots option should be checked. If it is, Notes will automatically create the links.
    - Check the Internet Options profile. Select Actions ➢ Internet Options and review what colors are selected in the Presentation Preferences section.
- I launched a page that had Java applets, why weren't they moving?
    - Check under the User Preferences section to make sure the Enable Java Applets option is checked by selecting File ➢ Tools ➢ User Preferences.
- I was using Web Ahead, but it didn't bring in any pages when I dragged a page to the Web Ahead folder. Why not?
    - Check the Internet Options profile. Select Actions ➢ Internet Options and click the Enable Web Ahead agent button.
    - Select File ➢ Tools ➢ User Preferences to check under the User Preferences section to make sure Enable Scheduled Local Agents is checked.
- Why isn't Page Minder giving me any updates?
    - Check the Internet Options profile. Select Actions ➢ Internet Options and click the Enable Page Minder agent button.

    - Check under the User Preferences by selecting File ➢ Tools ➢ User Preferences and make sure Enable Scheduled Local Agents is checked.

- Why aren't Java applets running?

    - The Java support files must first be installed on the machine. You can access and download the Java support files from the Internet.

    - Select File ➢ Tools ➢ User Preferences and make sure Enable Java Applets is checked.

    - Check the Location document. Select Actions ➢ Internet Options and at the bottom, select the Edit Location button. Make sure a proxy is specified in the Basics section and that in the Java section you set up security to allow applets to run on the workstation.

Summary

The Notes Web Navigator has come a long way in a very short time. You can run the server-based version by setting up an InterNotes server, or you can enable users to exploit this feature without the need for an InterNotes server. Either way, the functionality contained in the Web Navigator database is essentially the same.

Even if your company has a Web browser standard other than Notes, you may still want to experiment with this feature. There are some aspects of the Notes Web Navigator that still don't exist in any other product. The most significant feature that Notes has is the mobility of the Web Navigator database. Now users can take a replica copy of their favorite Web site with them wherever they go. This is undoubtedly a powerful feature worth knowing about as a Notes administrator, because you never know when someone will need this type of flexibility.

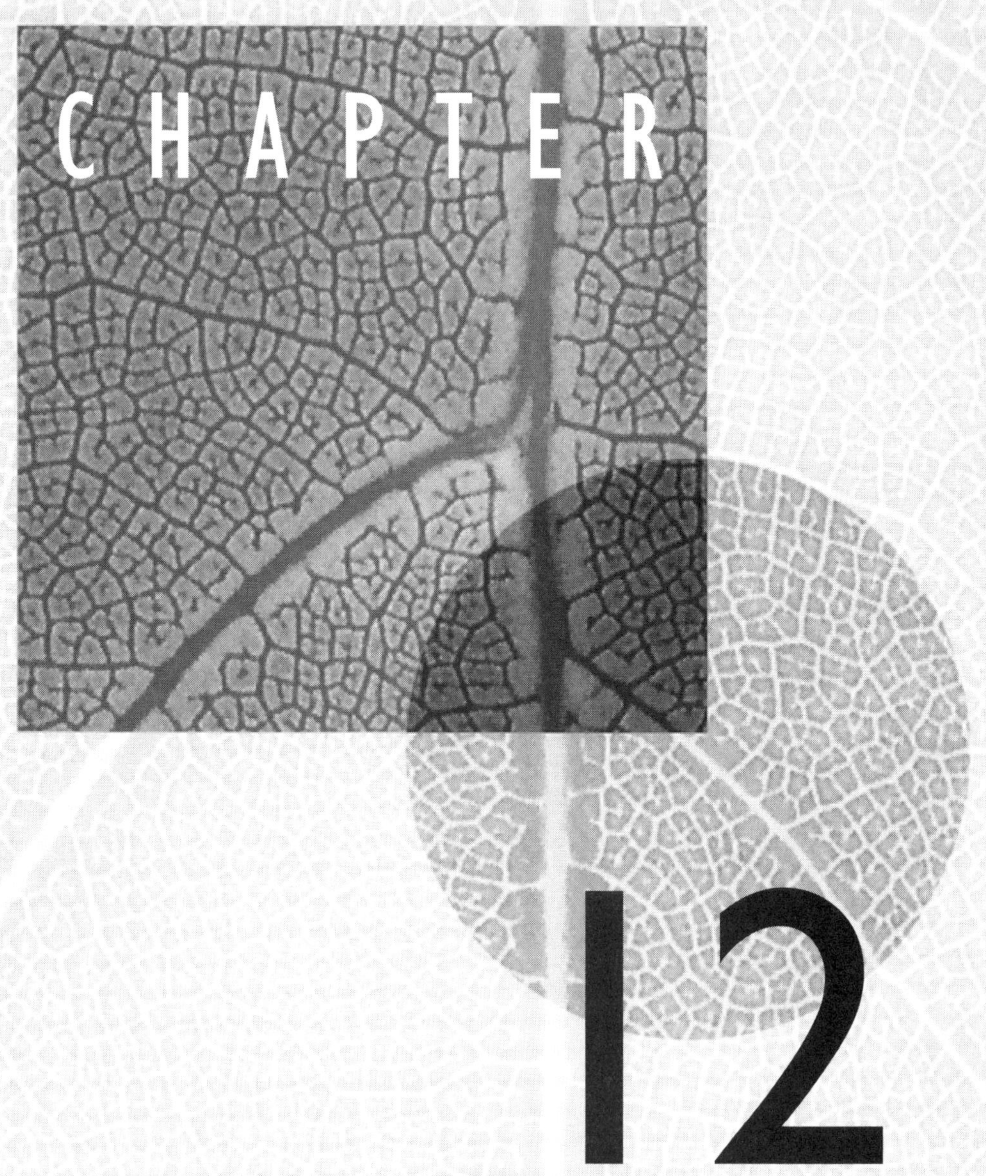

The Notes Domino Server

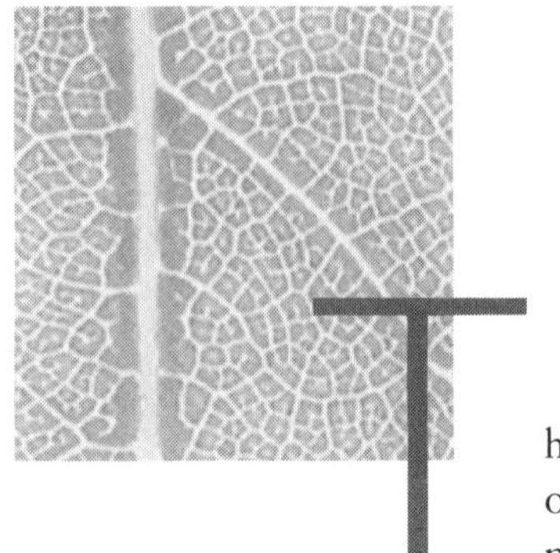

The one new feature in Notes Release 4.5 that has caught the eye of nearly everyone in the computer industry is Domino. This new feature has become so significant that Lotus has redesigned their entire naming scheme for Notes around it. Now, the Notes server is known as the Domino server and the Notes client as simply Notes. The name change helps Lotus let everyone know that Notes is a serious product for the Internet and not just a proprietary groupware product.

The power of Domino is its ability to make a Notes database accessible to a standard Web browser. By loading the HTTP Notes server task, the Notes server is transformed into a fully functional Web server. The combination of Web server functionality with a Notes server is the marriage of a superior and secure publishing environment, Notes, with an intuitive navigational interface, the Web.

Despite the power and importance of Domino, the complete name change for Notes is confusing. Domino was and still is a feature, and now Domino is also Notes.

But with or without the name change, the Domino feature within the Notes server requires administration. As the Notes administrator, I doubt that your Notes network won't use Domino to some extent. Therefore, you'll need to know how to set up Domino, configure it, start it, and keep it running.

Since this book has referred to the Notes server and the Notes client by their older names, this practice will continue in this chapter. When Domino is mentioned it refers to the new feature that runs as a server task.

Introduction to Domino

Domino takes a Notes server beyond the level of a proprietary groupware product. Now your standard Notes server can also be an Internet or Intranet application server. Using Domino, Notes developers can create databases and applications that leverage the Notes Access Control List (ACL), views, forms, and fields and then deliver those databases and applications across the Internet to anyone with a standard Web browser.

Notes developers creating Notes databases and applications specifically for the Internet will have to develop a little differently than they do today. An introduction to Notes development for Domino is available in the *Domino User's Guide*. As for administration, the Domino server task is just another task that you can run on the Notes server and configure using the Notes Server document.

How Domino Works

On the Internet, the Hypertext Transfer Protocol (HTTP), a standard Internet protocol, enables Web clients to talk to Web servers. On a Notes server, the HTTP server task provides the same functionality and enables communication between Web clients and the Notes server.

The Uniform Resource Locator (URL) interface is the standard Internet protocol that enables Web clients to tell Web servers what item they are requesting. The Domino HTTP server examines the URL in the incoming request and determines if the request is for an item in a Notes database or if it's for an HTML file in the file system.

If the request is for an HTML file, Domino acts just like any other HTTP server and serves the file to the Web client. When the request is for something in a Notes database, Domino interacts with the Notes database and translates items such as navigators, views, and documents into HTML and serves the translated information to the Web client. If the request comes from the Web client to put information into the Notes database the process is reversed.

All of this impressive power is activated when you load a single Notes server task, **HTTP**, at the server console. This task is driven by the configuration options set in the Server document, which control how the tasks operate and determine basic browser access to the server.

Setting Up Domino

Even though Domino has impressive powers and features, Domino is really no different than any other server task you already run on your Notes server. Start by selecting a Notes server that you want to be accessible across the Internet. Then you'll have to make some configuration changes to each database's ACL that you want accessible via the Web. Next, as you might expect, there are configuration settings to make in the Server document. Finally, load the HTTP server task and you're on the Internet with Domino.

Selecting Your Domino Server

To run Domino on your Notes server you first need a connection to the Internet. Typically, this connection is enabled with the help of an Internet Service Provider (ISP). Once this connection exists you'll also need to make sure your Notes server's primary network protocol is TCP/IP. This protocol is the de facto network protocol for the Internet and is what makes services such as Web browsing possible. Aside from the Internet connection and TCP/IP there are no other special requirements for Domino. Any machine that meets the minimum hardware and software requirements to run the Notes server can also run Domino.

More is always better. Don't just use the Notes minimum hardware requirements as your guide. Try to adhere to the recommended hardware configuration. And, if possible, try to exceed the recommendations. Domino can place a significant load on any computer. Therefore, the more RAM you have and the faster your CPU the better Domino will run.

Basic Database ACL Settings

Once you've selected the Notes server to run Domino, you'll need to select which databases you want to be accessible across the Web. Each database has an Access Control List (ACL). This list determines what type of access to the database each user in your Notes environment has. However, controlling access to a database over the Web is separate from regular Notes client access.

Security options for Domino, which will be covered in the *Domino Security* section of this chapter, are very flexible. However, basic Web access to each database on your Domino server is handled in the Advanced section of the Access Control List dialog box (see Figure 12.1). This section provides a Maximum Internet Browser Access drop-down list with access levels identical to the Notes client access levels to choose from. This setting allows you to have a database on your Notes server that is available to Notes clients but not to Web browsers.

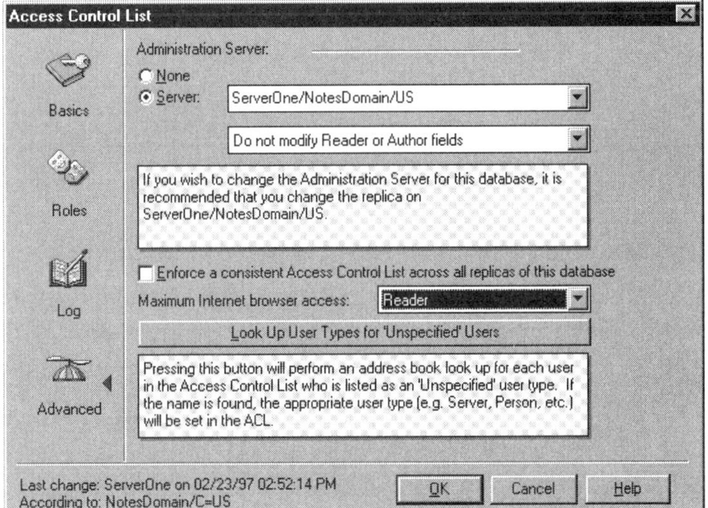

FIGURE 12.1

The Advanced section in the Access Control List dialog box allows you to set a default Web access level.

Configuring Domino

After setting the maximum Internet browser access for each database on your Notes server, you can start to set the Domino configuration options found in the HTTP Server section of the Server document. The several configuration options in the Server document start with the Basics and Operational Information subsections (see Figure 12.2).

FIGURE 12.2

Start configuring Domino by setting the options in the Basics and Operational Information subsections.

▾ HTTP Server

Basics		Operational Information	
TCP/IP port number:	80	Cache directory (for GIFs and file attachments):	domino\cache
TCP/IP port status:	Enabled	Garbage collection:	Enabled
SSL port number:	443	Garbage collection interval:	60 minutes
SSL port status:	Enabled	Maximum cache size:	50 (MB)
Host name:		Delete cache on shutdown:	Disabled
DNS lookup:	Disabled	Image conversion format:	GIF
Default home page:	default.htm	Interlaced rendering:	Enabled
Maximum active threads:	40		
Minimum active threads:	20	Default lines per view:	30
		Default character set group:	Western

Basics

The Basics configuration provides nine options to set. In most cases the default settings are probably acceptable. However, each option is defined below to help you better understand what is available to you:

- **TCP/IP port number:** The default for this field is 80. However, you can specify any port that you've selected for Domino to listen for HTTP requests. The only restriction for this field is to avoid using port numbers less than 1024, except for the default of 80. Port numbers less than 1024 are reserved for other TCP/IP applications. The default setting is probably the best port to use because any other port requires that clients trying to contact your server will have to include the specific port number after the URL. For example, www.acme.com on port 8008 translates into the URL `http://www.acme.com:8008/`.
- **TCP/IP port status:** This field is either enabled or disabled, which means that it acts as an on/off switch for the port. By default, this option is enabled. If you disable this option, the SSL port must be enabled, otherwise connections to Domino are not possible.
- **SSL port number:** In this field you can specify the SSL port number. This port is used for SSL security and is where HTTPS requests are listened for. As with the TCP/IP port number, you change the SSL port number

from the default of 443. This port is different from the TCP/IP port, so changing this number won't affect the normal unsecure HTTP requests from being serviced by the TCP/IP port specified in this option.

- **SSL port status:** This option allows you to enable the SSL port, which is the default, or disable the SSL port. Disabling this port won't affect TCP/IP. However, at least one or both of these ports has to be active, otherwise no one can communicate with Domino.
- **Host name:** This field is used for your Domino machine's fully qualified host name. This name is what clients use when they are entering a URL in their Web browser to establish a connection. You can use a name alias, but that name needs to be defined in your Domain Name Server (DNS). If your machine does not have a host name registered in a DNS, you can enter the machine's IP address in this field. By default, this field is blank and if left that way, Domino will use the host name specified in the operating system's TCP/IP stack.
- **DNS lookup:** This field is where you specify whether you want Domino to look up the DNS host name of the requesting client. Your choice is to enable or disable this field (default is disabled). Accepting the default improves the performance of Domino because the server does not use any resources to perform host name look ups. However, disabling this feature will cause Web client activity to be logged by IP address and not host name. Enabling the feature slows Domino's performance because Domino frequently refers to the DNS to resolve IP numbers to names, which can consume additional server resources. The benefit to enabling this option, however, is that Web client activity is logged by name and not by IP number.
- **Default home page:** By default, this field is set to Default.htm. However, if you would rather use a page such as Home.htm or Index.htm you can specify that page in this field. Keep in mind that an alternative home page needs to be located in the Domino HTML directory and the Home URL field in the Mapping portion of the HTTP Server section must be blank.
- **Maximum active threads:** This field is used to specify the maximum number of threads you want to have active at one time (the default is 40). When the maximum is reached, Domino holds new requests until another request finishes and threads become available.

- **Minimum active threads:** If threads aren't being used, Domino will close them one by one and re-create them as needed. This field allows you to specify the point where Domino will stop closing threads, whether they're being used or not. The default is 20.

Most of the default settings for the Basics portion of the HTTP Server section in the Server document are perfectly acceptable. To get started, I suggest accepting these defaults and making adjustments as needed.

Operational Information

The next portion of the HTTP Server section to look at is the Operational Information subsection (refer back to Figure 12.2). This area allows you to set caching options for managing disk space and improving performance as well as image options for the format and display style of Web images, views, and character sets:

- **Cache directory:** This option is used to specify the directory for Domino to use for storing image files and file attachments. The cache directory improves Domino performance by making frequently requested images and attachments readily available. The default is Domino\Cache.

- **Garbage collection:** Garbage collection is the process that deletes files that should no longer be cached and thereby keeps the cache small and efficient. Files are removed based on their request frequency. The more infrequently a file is requested by a client, the more likely that file is to be removed from the cache. By default, this option is enabled.

- **Garbage collection interval:** This option controls the interval at which the garbage collection process runs. The default is 60 minutes but can be increased or decreased. However, if the cache reaches its maximum size, the garbage collection process kicks in automatically.

- **Maximum cache size:** This field allows you to set the maximum size of the cache. The cache will not grow beyond this maximum size, which is maintained by the garbage collection process. By default, this size is 50 MB, which should be sufficient. However, if disk space is limited on your Domino machine you can reduce this size.

- **Delete cache on shutdown:** This option determines whether Domino will delete the cache when it's shut down or leave it as is. The default is disabled.

- **Image Conversion Format:** Images contained in a Notes document are converted by Domino before served to a Web client. This field is used to specify the conversion format. By default this field is set to GIF but JPEG is also available.

- **Interlaced rendering:** This option allows you to enable or disable the interlaced rendering for .GIF or .JPEG images. Normally, browsers display a .GIF image while it is being loaded. An interlaced .GIF file displays an image through a sequence of lines. For example, an interlaced .GIF might display every eighth row, then every fourth row, then every second row, and so on. The image seems to appear quickly to users because their eyes tend to fill in the missing pieces. As for .JPEG images, they are displayed in a Web page all at once. This method of image delivery usually leaves large blank frames in a Web page while the image is being sent across the Net. Progressive rendering causes the image to appear immediately on the page. However, the sudden image is out of focus to start, and progressively becomes clearer as the rest of the image is sent. By default, this field is enabled.

- **JPEG image quality:** This option appears if you select JPEG as your image conversion format. This field allows you to specify a percentage for the JPEG image quality. The higher the value the better the image quality, the larger the file size, and the longer it takes to send across the Internet. The smaller the value the lower the image quality, the smaller the file size, and the faster the image travels across the Internet. The range is 5 to 100 percent and the default is 75.

- **Default lines per view:** This option is used to set the number of lines Domino uses to show a Notes view to Web clients. This setting defaults to 30.

- **Default character set:** This field is used to specify the default character set that Web clients need to access Domino. The default is Western but selecting Multilingual allows you to service clients from around the world without much trouble.

Mapping

The next portion in the HTTP Server section of the Server document to configure is the Mapping area (see Figure 12.3). The fields associated with the Mapping area are used to determine the location of HTML files for Domino.

FIGURE 12.3

Additional areas for configuration in the HTTP Server section of the Server document include Mapping, Logging, Timeouts, and Character Set Mapping.

Mapping	
HTML directory:	domino\html
Home URL:	/?Open
CGI URL path:	/cgi-bin
CGI directory:	domino\cgi-bin
Icon URL path:	/icons
Path to icons:	domino\icons

Logging	
Access log:	
Error log:	
Time stamp:	LocalTime
No log:	

Timeouts	
Idle thread timeout:	0 minutes
Input timeout:	2 minutes
Output timeout:	20 minutes
CGI timeout:	5 minutes

Character Set Mapping	
Western:	Latin 1(ISO-8859-1)

- **HTML directory:** This is where you set the location for HTML files. By default, this option is set to Domino\html, which is below the directory specified as the Notes data directory. You can change this setting to any other directory on the Domino machine. However, if the directory you specify is not below the Notes data directory, you need to include the complete path.

- **Home URL:** This option specifies the URL for the About document, navigator, or database you want Domino to send to Web clients when they enter the basic URL of your site. For example, a Web client that enters the URL `www.acme.com` gets the page that is specified in this field. The default is Default=/?Open, which returns a list of databases on the server (equivalent to the File ➢ Database ➢ Open command in Notes). If you already have a default home page specified, leave this field blank.

- **CGI URL path:** Use this field to specify the URL path to the CGI directory. This option relates to URLs such as `www.acme.com/cgi` and not directory paths such as c:\notes\data\domino\cgi. The default for this option is /cgi-bin.

- **CGI directory:** This field is where you indicate the directory location for CGI program files. This path is relative to the Notes data directory and defaults to Domino\cgi-bin. If your CGI program files are located in a directory that is not below the Notes data directory, you need to supply the complete path in this field (for example, c:\web\cgi).

- **Icon URL path:** This field is where you specify the URL path to the Domino icons directory. Keep in mind that this path relates to URLs and not the file system. Normally, you won't need to modify the icons fields. However, if you have an existing icons directory, specify the path to the directory here. The default for this field is /icons.

- **Path to icons:** This final field is where you specify the directory location for the icons directory. By default, this field is set to Domino\icons, which is relative to the Notes data directory. If your icons files are located in a directory that is not below the Notes data directory, you need to supply the complete path in this field (for example, c:\web\icons).

Logging

The Logging portion of the HTTP Server section of the Server document is where you customize activity logging for Domino. Figure 12.3 shows the Logging area and the following list describes each field in that area:

- **Access log:** This field specifies the path and/or the filename where you want Domino to log access statistics. By default, this field is blank and if left this way will cause Domino to not log access requests. However, if you add a path and/or filename here, that path and/or filename is below the directory specified as the Notes data directory unless you explicitly add an entire path (for example, c:\web\logs).

- **Error log:** This field specifies the path and the filename where you want Domino to log internal errors. Domino also places the CGI error log, Cgi_error, in this area. However, if you add a path and filename here, that path and filename are below the directory specified as the Notes data directory unless you explicitly add an entire path (for example, c:\web\logs).

- **Time stamp:** This field is where you specify what time should be used when logging errors. Your choices are Local Time (the default) or Greenwich Mean Time (GMT).

- **No log:** Normally, all client activity is logged in the log files. However, if you don't want to log activity from one or several users, you can specify which hosts to exclude from logging in this field. You can enter entire IP numbers, or part of an IP number using wild cards for the rest of the number (for example, 204.141.*.*). You can also exclude logging based on a complete host name or partial host name (notes.acme.com or *.acme.com are perfectly acceptable). However, excluding by host name requires that you enable DNS Lookup in the Basics area of the HTTP Server section.

Timeouts

A Web client connection can be disrupted or unresponsive for any number of reasons. If a Web client drops its connection for some reason, it may leave an idle thread on the server or leave a CGI program in static state. As the Notes administration, you'll use this area of the HTTP Server section to control when Domino should timeout on certain activities. Figure 12.3 displays this area and what follows defines the fields associated with the Timeouts area.

- **Idle thread timeout**: This field specifies the length of time in minutes that Domino will keep an idle thread available. By default, this field is set to zero, which prevents Domino from ever closing an idle thread. Once the thread is open it stays open. However, entering a time in this field will cause Domino to close an idle thread after the specified time has elapsed. A thread is considered idle after the last request to it is completed.

- **Input timeout**: This setting indicates the amount of time in minutes that a Web client has to send a request after connecting to Domino. By default, this field is set to 2 minutes. If a connected Web client does not send a request within that time, Domino drops the connection.

- **Output timeout**: This field specifies the maximum time in minutes that Domino has to send output to a client. This limit applies to requests for local files. Requests that start a local CGI program are not affected by this setting. The default for this field is 20 minutes and if Domino does not send the complete request within the amount of time specified, the server drops the connection.

- **CGI timeout**: This option sets the maximum time, in minutes, that a CGI program started by Domino has to finish. By default, this field is set to 5 minutes and when the time runs out, Domino kills the program.

Character Set Mapping

The Default Character Set Group set in the Operational Information area determines what additional options appear in the Character Set Mapping area. Character sets that have several options, such as Multilingual, require that you specify which set to use for each language. These character sets determine how to generate HTML text to and from the Web client.

Running Domino

Once you have selected the machine to run Domino, set the basic Web access for each database on that machine, set the configuration options in the HTTP Server section of the Server document, and you're ready to go. To get Domino up and running, simply go to the server console, type **Load HTTP**, and press Enter. Domino will start and you are ready to go.

There isn't too much involved in getting Domino running. However, the various configurations in the Server document can be intimidating. Therefore, I suggest setting up a small Domino test machine and accepting all of the defaults in the Server document. Then start Domino and experiment with the various Server document settings. Keep in mind, however, that nearly all of the options in the HTTP Server section require you to restart your server in order for them to take effect. For that simple reason, a test machine is a good way to get started with Domino.

Once you are running with Domino there are still a few things you'll need to know:

- **How do I know that Domino is working?** Use a standard Web browser and attempt a connection the same way you would for any other Web site.
- **How do I stop Domino?** From the server console, type **Tell HTTP Quit** and press Enter.
- **How do I enable Domino to start each time my Notes server starts?** Add **HTTP** to the ServerTasks statement in the NOTES.INI file.

Multiple Web Sites with Domino

One of the really exciting things about Domino is a feature that allows you to host several Domino based Web sites on the same machine. You might need this type of power if you're in the business of providing Internet access to consumers or if you're an Intranet administrator for your company. In either case, Notes has the ability to make multiple Web site hosting possible.

Unfortunately, you can't give multiple names to the same IP number. The good news is that IP numbers normally shouldn't cost you any more money than having individual servers for each site would. To get started, you need to make sure that every Web site you want to host has its own IP address.

The next step in hosting multiple Web sites is to create a Virtual Server document in the Domino Web Server Configuration database. You probably don't already have a Domino Web Server Configuration database so you'll need to create one, which is very simple. From the menu bar, select File ➢ Database ➢ New and complete the New Database dialog box options as shown in Figure 12.4.

The options you set in the Virtual Server document override the corresponding settings made in the Server document.

FIGURE 12.4

To create the Domino Web Server Configuration database, select the Domino Configuration template and then add a title and the filename DOMCFG.NSF.

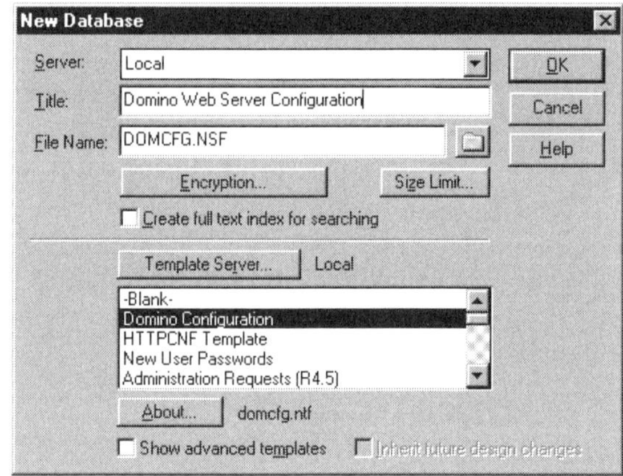

Once this database is created you're ready to start creating Virtual Server documents:

1. Open the Domino Web Server Configuration database and from the menu bar, select Create ➢ Virtual Server.

2. In the new document, add a valid IP address in the IP Address field.

3. In the Comment field, enter a meaningful description of this virtual site. This step is optional but highly recommended to help differentiate virtual servers from one another.

4. In the Default Home Page field, assign a home URL for this virtual server.

5. The Mapping section of the document is similar in purpose to the Mapping area described in the *Configuring Domino* section. Refer to that section for detailed descriptions of each field. However, if you plan to host different sites on this one machine, you should make these mapping fields unique for each virtual server you create, otherwise one site might inadvertently delete or overwrite the data of another site. Unique mappings also make content management much easier.

6. Save the Virtual Server document (shown in Figure 12.5) and repeat steps 1 through 6 for subsequent virtual servers.

FIGURE 12.5

A Virtual Server document configured for Acme Widgets

VIRTUAL SERVER

Site Information

IP Address:	123.123.123.123
Comment:	Acme Widgets Sales Department Server
Default home page:	default.htm

Mapping

HTML directory:	c:\acmesales\html
Home URL:	/?Open
CGI URL path:	/cgi-bin
CGI directory:	c:\acmesales\cgi-bin
Icon URL path:	/icons
Path to icons:	c:\acmesales\icons

The Virtual Server document is what makes hosting multiple servers on a single Domino machine possible. Normally this document is enough to utilize this feature. However, there are some additional documents in the Domino Web Server Configuration database that provide additional flexibility when hosting multiple sites.

The Mapping and Redirection documents in the Domino Web Server Configuration database allow you to keep HTML files, CGI scripts, and other related Web files in multiple locations without breaking URL links or changing Server or Virtual Server documents. Use these documents when you need to do the following:

- Hide the actual location of a directory and specify Read or Execute access to its files. Use the Directory Mapping document.
- Map collections of URLs from their old location to a new location. Use the URL Mapping document.
- Redirect one URL to another URL. Use the URL Redirection document.

Each of these documents are easy to use and create. For example, to map all requests for URLs ending with /scripts to a directory that contains my custom CGI scripts, I would create a Directory Mapping document (see Figure 12.6). To create this document, select the Domino Web Server Configuration database and then, from the menu bar, select Create ➢ Mapping URL -> Directory.

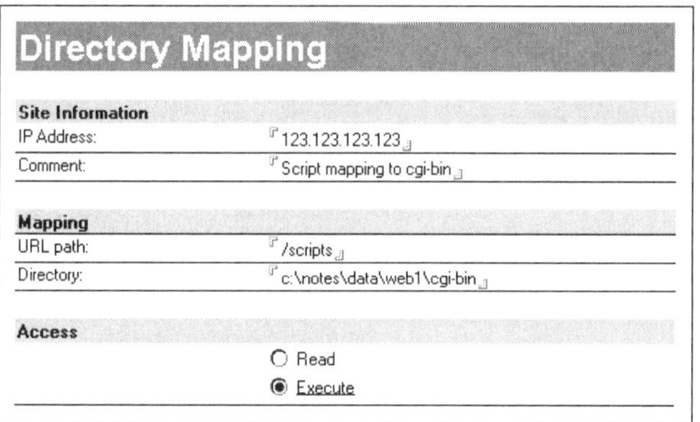

FIGURE 12.6 This document sends all requests for URLs ending with /scripts to the c:\notes\data\web1\cgibin where users only have Execute access.

If, instead of mapping to a directory, I needed to map URLs ending with /scripts to URLs ending with /cgi, then I'd create a URL Mapping document (see Figure 12.7). To create this document, select the Domino Web Server Configuration database and then, from the menu bar, select Create ➢ Mapping URL -> URL.

Finally, if my Web site's URL changes from `www.acme.com` to `www.acmewidgets.com`, then I would create a URL Redirection document (see Figure 12.8). To create this document, select the Domino Web Server Configuration database and then, from the menu bar, select Create ➢ Redirection URL -> URL.

FIGURE 12.7

Users with bookmarks pointing to URLs ending with /script get automatically redirected to URLs ending with /cgi.

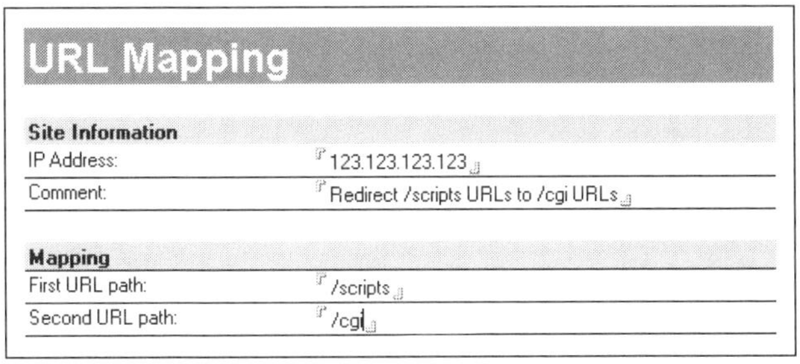

URL Mapping

Site Information

IP Address:	123.123.123.123
Comment:	Redirect /scripts URLs to /cgi URLs

Mapping

First URL path:	/scripts
Second URL path:	/cgi

FIGURE 12.8

Redirecting an old URL to a new one is easy with the URL Redirection document.

URL Redirection

Site Information

IP Address:	123.123.123.123
Comment:	Redirect old URL to the new one

Mapping

URL path:	www.acme.com
Redirection URL:	http://www.acmewidgets.com

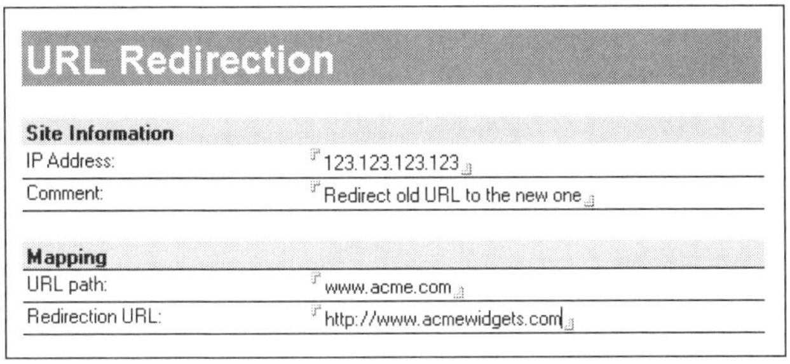

The Virtual Server document and the additional redirection documents make hosting multiple Web sites on a single machine very easy. Keep in mind that each virtual site you add will probably increase the amount of user traffic on your Domino machine. Therefore, make sure that the machine you've selected for Domino is a machine with plenty of disk space, RAM, and CPU horse power.

Domino Security

In the *Setting Up Domino* section, the essentials for getting Domino running in your Notes environment were covered. You may have noticed that outside of the database ACL settings there weren't many other security options. Domino looked like a fairly unsecure Web server. Fortunately, that impression couldn't be further from the truth. Domino provides a variety of ways to control access to its services and is perhaps one of the most secure ways to host a Web site.

When you begin to configure the security for Domino, there are four basic areas to consider: managing anonymous access, managing access for registered users, database security, and managing advanced security, if required.

Anonymous Access

Most Web sites today allow anyone to connect. There is no need to supply a user name or a password. A Web page is requested by a browser and that Web page is returned. With Domino you can easily enable the same type of anonymous access by enabling the Allow Anonymous HTTP Connection option in the Security section of the Server document (see Figure 12.9).

FIGURE 12.9

Enabling and disabling anonymous access to Domino is handled in the Security section of the Server document.

▼ Security

Security settings		SSL settings	
Compare public keys against those stored in Address Book:	○ Yes ◉ No	Accept SSL site certificates:	○ Yes ◉ No
Allow anonymous Notes connections:	○ Yes ◉ No	SSL key file:	keyfile.kyr
Allow anonymous HTTP connections:	◉ Yes ○ No		
Allow HTTP clients to browse databases:	◉ Yes ○ No		
Check passwords:	○ Enabled ◉ Disabled		

Another field in the Server document Security section worth considering is the Allow HTTP Clients to Browse Databases. If set to yes, Web clients can use the OpenServer URL command to see a list of databases they can browse. If this option is disabled, users can only access the databases to which they have specific access.

Registered Users

If you want to allow access to everyone but want to know who those people are, you can implement a user registration process. This process requires that you create a Person document that contains an HTTP password for each user that you will allow to access Domino. However, creating Person documents for everyone on the Web doesn't sound like an easy task. Fortunately, Lotus has removed the burden of manually creating each of these documents with a sample registration application.

The Domino Web site, `domino.lotus.com`, has an application that anyone can download free of change and use for Web based user registration. This application allows any Web user to register with your site and supply their user name and password. The process then adds a Person document for this user to the Public Address Book. Now, when this user attempts to access your site they are prompted for a user name and password. If the user enters the correct information, they are allowed access.

Database Security

Controlling which databases users can access is another feature of Domino. In the *Setting Up Domino* section, the Maximum Internet Browser Access field was discussed. This setting in the Advanced area of the Access Control List dialog box allowed you to set the maximum access for Internet browsing. You can also fine tune this access if your users must register before browsing.

In the Basics area of the Access Control List dialog box, access for Notes users is specified. If, however, Web clients must register before accessing Domino, then they'll be listed in the Public Address Book. Once users are listed in the Public Address Book, their access to a database can be specified as it is for any other Notes user. This access method allows you to specify different levels of access for different users or groups of users instead of just using the Maximum Internet Browser Access field in the Advanced section of the Access Control List dialog box to provide general access for everyone (for more details about the ACL and Notes security refer to Chapter 7).

Advanced Security with Secure Sockets Layer

Transaction security across the Internet is a very hot topic. Everyone wants to do commerce across the Internet but also wants to keep the information required for commerce, such as credit card numbers, confidential. To meet the needs of confidentiality, most Web sites use a piece of technology known as Secure Sockets Layer (SSL).

SSL is a security protocol that provides communications privacy and authentication over the Internet. When Domino is configured for SSL transactions, Domino can encrypt data that passes between Web clients and the server. Using SSL, data sent during a transaction can be encrypted and thus kept private. SSL also allows the inclusion of an encoded message digest with messages, which provides a way to detect if a message has been tampered with. Finally, SSL enables authentication by sending the server's digital signature with each message to assure the client that the server's identity is authentic.

SSL uses a similar encryption scheme to the one used by Notes: the public/private RSA-based cryptosystem. In this system the server holds a private key and a public key, which are a unique pair of mathematically related keys. These keys are used to initiate SSL-encrypted transactions.

Instead of using USER.ID files to store private keys and the Public Address Book to store public keys, key ring files are used. These files, held by clients and servers, store the information needed for encrypted transactions: the owner's private and public key and one or more certificates. The encryption process that occurs between the Domino Web server and a Web client is based on the relationship between the key pairs and the certificates.

In a Notes network, trust is established between a client and a server when they both share a common certificate. SSL uses a similar process based on a certificate issued by a Certificate Authority (CA). This authority is typically an external, commercial certifier, such as VeriSign. The certificate that is issued to a server or client also includes a trusted root key that contains the server's or client's name and public key. An SSL transaction is authenticated only if the client can verify the server's identity (because the server has a trusted root key from the same CA).

Web clients that need to access an SSL-controlled Domino Web server need to have a Web browser that supports the use of SSL and a certificate in common with the server issued by a Certificate Authority, and need to use HTTPS to precede the URL of the server. On the server side, an SSL port must be specified and enabled in the Server document before SSL transactions can occur.

Clearly you can see that at the core of SSL and Notes security is a certificate. With SSL you normally use a Certificate Authority to acquire this certificate and with Notes you create the certificate yourself. Fortunately, however, Domino allows the best of both worlds. You can use a Certificate Authority to obtain a certificate or you can do it the old Notes way and create your own.

The Domino SSL Administration database is where you create and administer certificates to use with SSL. Add this database to your workspace by selecting from the menu bar, File ➢ Database ➢ Open. Select Local or a Notes server and then the listing for Domino SSL Administration, and click Open. When the database opens, the About database document appears. Click where indicated on this page (see Figure 12.10).

The SSL Administration document (see Figure 12.11) provides a variety of easy to follow instructions and buttons to help walk you through the process of creating certified key rings. In this document you can create key rings for testing, minimal security requirements, key rings to send to a Certificate Authority, and certificates based on your key rings for use in SSL transactions. The options on this document are flexible and easy to follow.

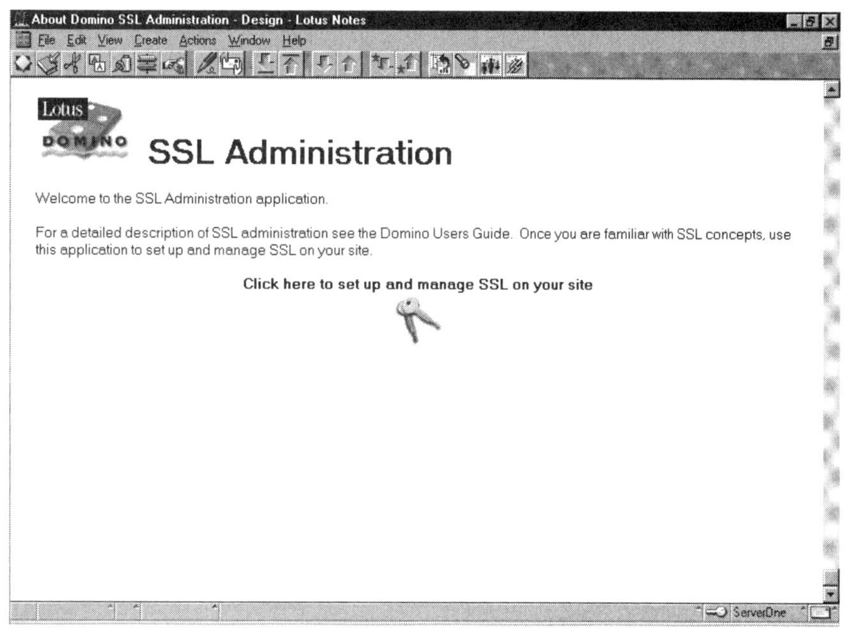

FIGURE 12.10

Click where indicated on this page to view the SSL Administration document.

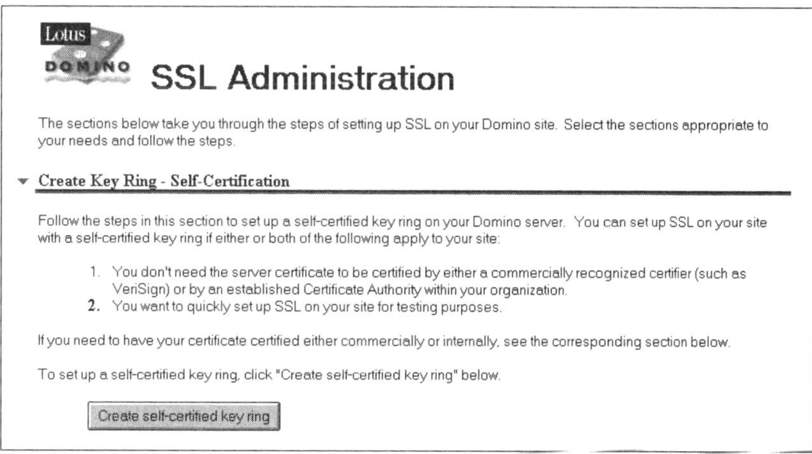

FIGURE 12.11

The SSL Administration document helps you through the process of creating a self-certified key ring.

For example, to create a self-certified key ring select the Create Self-Certified Key Ring button in the SSL Administration document. This button displays the dialog box shown in Figure 12.12. Fill in the appropriate information and click OK. A self-certified key ring is created and ready to use for creating certificates.

Much the same as you can do with Notes, you can create Certification ID files used to register users and servers. This process is where you create a key that is used to create certificates that are distributed to users and sometimes servers for SSL transactions.

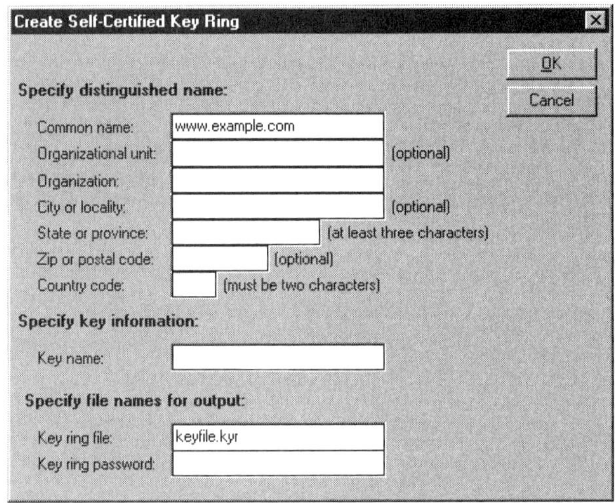

FIGURE 12.12 The Create Self-Certified Key Ring dialog box requires some information which is used during key generation.

Domino Activity Logging

Nothing is perfect, and that goes for Domino also. Fortunately, most of the troubleshooting skills you use for common Notes problems can also be applied when dealing with a Domino problem. However, to effectively solve a problem you need to know as much as you can about the problem. That begins with knowing where Domino logs come in.

Setting Up Logging for Domino

The Domino log is one of the first places to check when things don't seem to be running correctly. Activity between Domino and Web clients is captured in the log. The format of the information is the same as any other Web server on the market today. A general Web server reference can help you decipher the information contained in these logs. However, even though the information captured in the logs is similar to other Web servers, Domino does allow you to choose between a standard text file and a Notes database for where the information is to be captured.

Standard Text Log

Domino can write activity and error information to a standard ASCII text file in the same format as most other Web servers in use today. The benefit to using this format is that there are several products on the market today that can analyze and provide reports for the information contained in these standard Web logs.

To use just the text file log method, refer back to the *Configuring Domino* section in this chapter and review the area that describes the available fields in the Logging area of the Server document. The Access Log and Error Log fields in this area are where you specify the names of the standard text log files.

Leave the Access Log and Error Log fields blank if you don't want to capture log information in a standard text file.

Notes Database Log

If you prefer to view log information in a regular Notes database, you can do that as well. Simply create a new database based on the Domino Log template and you're on your way.

1. From the menu bar, select File ➢ Database ➢ New.
2. Select the Domino Log template, give the database a title, give it the filename DOMLOG.NSF, and click OK (see Figure 12.13).

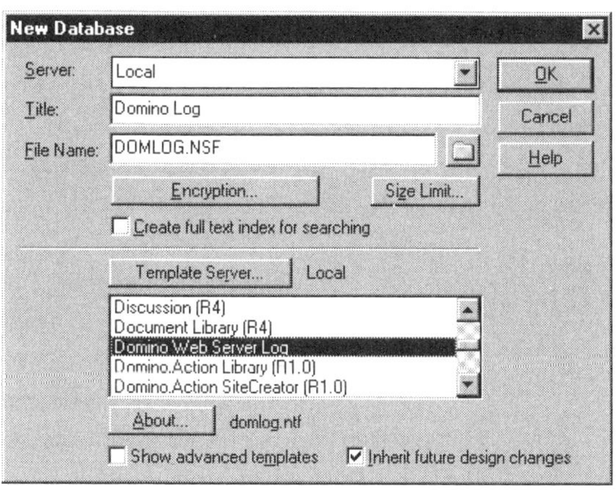

FIGURE 12.13
Creating a Domino Log database requires that you use the filename DOMLOG.NSF.

Once this database is created, Domino events are automatically sent to it. Since this database is a Notes database, you can use it the same way you would use any other database. For example, you can create agents that monitor for certain events and alert you when these events occur. You can also create custom views that present event information in a way that is useful to you.

The main drawback to using the Notes Domino log is that capturing event information in the log usually takes longer than sending the same information to a plain text file. If your Domino machine is very active, you might want to disable the Notes Domino log database. To do so, simply delete the database and Domino will stop sending activity information to it.

You can capture activity information in both a plain text file and a Notes Domino log database by enabling both methods as previously described.

Regardless of which logging method you choose, make a point to review these logs daily to catch any odd or harmful activity before it can cause a real problem.

Summary

As far as most computer industry experts can guess, the Web is the future of computing. To remain competitive, companies of all types will have to get involved with the Web in one way or another. Lotus is well aware of the future of computing and the importance of the Web, and has been one step ahead of the game for some time now.

For Lotus, the future is Domino. This powerful feature is a serious Web server with an emphasis on running a business on the Web. Domino is so important to Lotus that it has also become the new name for their long-standing product, Notes. Some of us may find the name change unnecessary and confusing. However, the name change simply helps state a direction for Notes, and has no affect on the underlying power and flexibility of the "groupware standard."

Will your Notes network be running Domino? If your Notes environment is based on Release 4.5 technology, I can't imagine that you won't be using Domino. The feature has received so much attention in the press that once users know you have it, they'll want to see it in action. Therefore, if you haven't gotten started with Domino, you should start experimenting with it soon. The time isn't far away when if you don't know Domino, you won't know Notes.

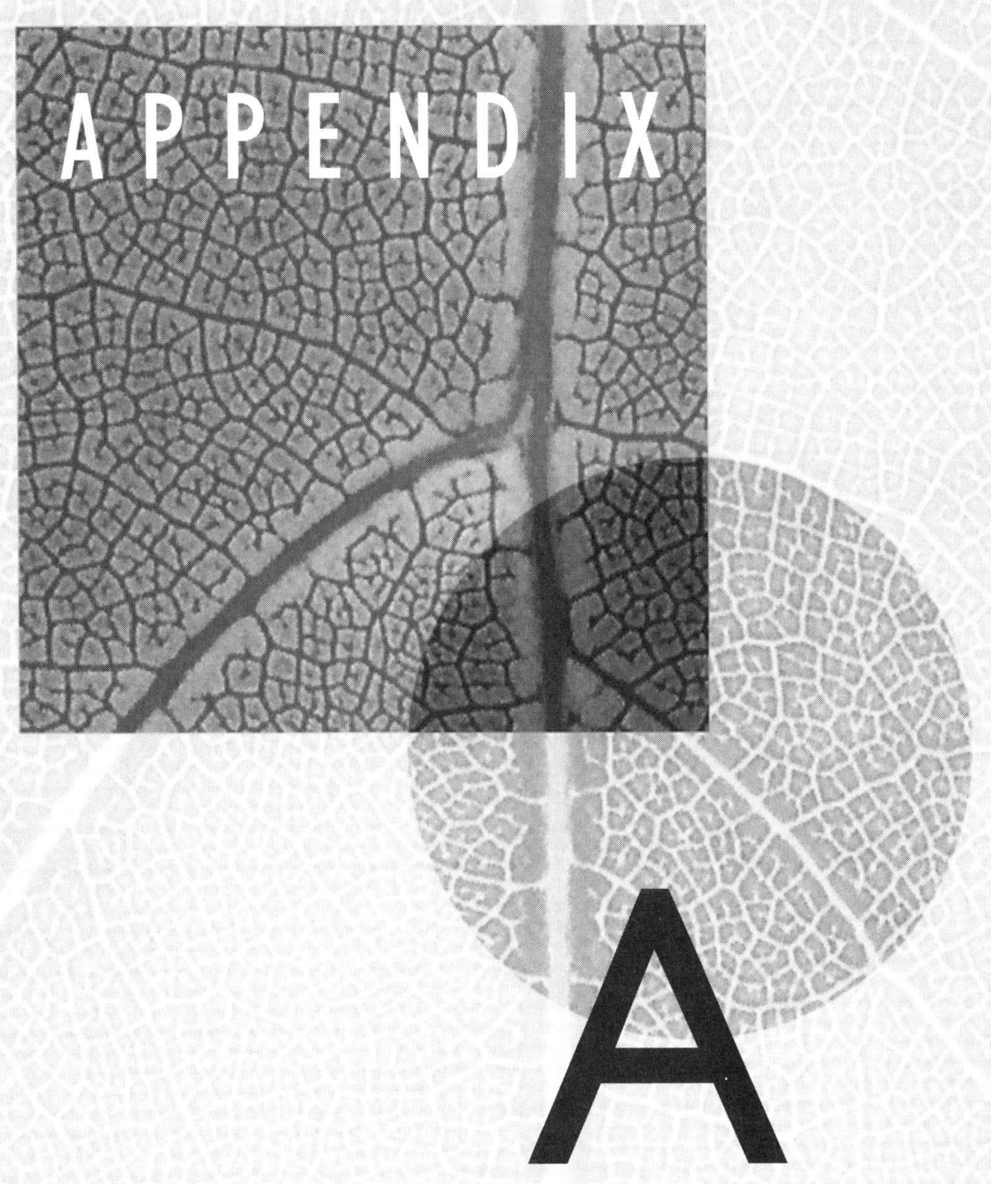

APPENDIX A

Lotus Notes Certification

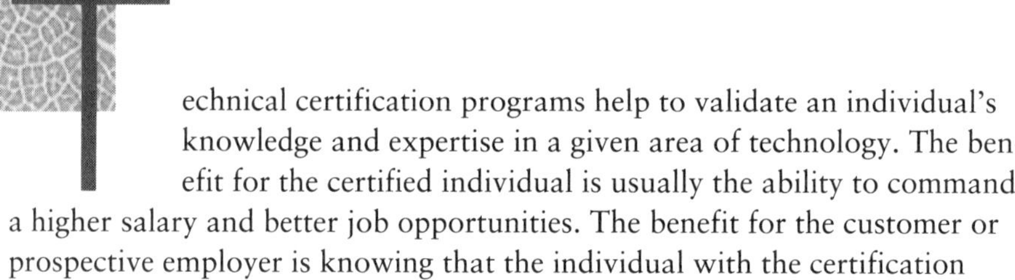

Technical certification programs help to validate an individual's knowledge and expertise in a given area of technology. The benefit for the certified individual is usually the ability to command a higher salary and better job opportunities. The benefit for the customer or prospective employer is knowing that the individual with the certification probably knows what he or she is talking about and can actually do the job.

Technical certification programs in the computer industry have been on a steady climb upward ever since Novell introduced its Certified NetWare Engineer (CNE) program. Undoubtedly, Novell's CNE program is still the most widely recognized technical certification in the industry today, and at one time was the most coveted certification.

The down side to technical certifications is that there is no way to completely test an individual's actual technical ability. Since certification is achieved through a series of tests, anyone with enough time and perseverance can obtain a certification without ever having worked with the product in a "real life" situation. Novell's CNE program was, at one time, sharply criticized for making it too easy for people with no real life experience to achieve certification. These people were referred to as "paper CNEs." Novell responded to the complaints by revamping their certification program.

To illustrate the growing popularity in certification programs, just look around the computer industry today and pick a popular product. Take Microsoft Word, for example. You can become a certified Microsoft Product Specialist by taking a Microsoft Word exam and one Microsoft operating system exam. You say you like to develop in PowerBuilder? Fear not. You won't be left out of the exciting world of certification because PowerBuilder also offers a PowerBuilder developer certification. You don't like software? You'd rather be certified on network hardware such as routers, bridges, and switches? Bay Networks, Cisco, and 3Com all offer network engineering certification.

Nearly every major hardware or software product today offers some form of certification. One reason that so many companies offer certification programs is that providing certification helps companies sell their products; manufacturers that have computer professionals certified on their products means that there are resources available to install and maintain these products besides the manufacturer. What good is the greatest computer hardware or software if only a couple of people know how to install and maintain it? Availability of knowledgeable resources for products in the computer industry does have an affect on purchasing decisions. Another reason for offering certification is that products today—especially network-centric products—are extremely complex and benefit from someone who has received more training than what can be gathered from the product documentation. I'm not trying to knock certifications. I'm just pointing out how widespread certification programs are, and their increasing importance in the industry today.

Certified Lotus Professional Program

Lotus, like every other major software manufacturer, has a professional certification program: The Certified Lotus Professional. This program helps participants demonstrate their broad depth of knowledge in Lotus Notes or cc:Mail and, through a series of examinations, earn certification directly from Lotus recognizing them as technical professionals.

Lotus has designed their program to be sensitive to the variety of different certification requirements within the industry without being difficult to understand. If you ever pursued a NetWare certification, you probably remember mulling over the CNE matrix chart trying to decipher which classes you had to take. Once you figured out which classes you needed, you had to figure out how you were going to pay for them. Finally, it was a grand day when you figured out that you didn't need to take any classes; you just needed to take the tests. (Novell wasn't very forthcoming with information about the classes not being required.)

Certification Options and Examinations

Whether you're currently working as a Notes Administrator or exploring the career opportunities for systems administration in general, it's important for you to be aware of the types of Notes certification available from Lotus. In some cases, such as working for a Lotus Business Partner or Lotus Authorized Education Center, Notes certification may actually be required. In other cases, such as working for a company with a large MIS (Management Information Systems) organization or looking for a new Notes administration job, Notes certification is highly recommended because it will help distinguish you from others in your field of specialty.

Fortunately, figuring out which classes to take and which exams to sign up for is much easier with the CLP (Certified Lotus Professional) program. Lotus is very clear that the classes are not required. Passing the tests is all it takes. Lotus offers five different certification titles. The titles and corresponding examinations are presented in Table A.1.

TABLE A.1 Lotus Notes Release 4 Certification and Examinations

Certification	Examinations
CLP Application Developer	• System Administration 1 • Application Development 1 • Application Development 2
CLP Principal Application Developer	• System Administration 1 • Application Development 1 • Application Development 2 • Elective (for example, Application Development 3)
CLP System Administrator	• Application Development 1 • System Administration 1 • System Administrator 2
CLP Principal System Administrator	• Application Development 1 • System Administration 1 • System Administrator 2 • Elective (for example, cc:Mail System Administration)
cc:Mail Certification	• cc:Mail Examinations
CLP cc:Mail Specialist	• System Administration 1 • System Administration 2

Each of the examinations listed in the above chart has a corresponding class with the exact same name.

CLP Application Developer

This certification is directed towards individuals responsible for building multiple database Notes applications that facilitate the business processes between several departments within the same organization. If you plan to pursue this certification path, you should be well versed in application architecture, application development, application security, and application documentation.

CLP Principal Application Developer

This certification is directed towards individuals who have probably already achieved the CLP Application Developer certification but want to take their certification to the next level. The status of "Principal" is usually for those individuals responsible for building enterprise-wide Notes applications that encompass multiple databases, departments, and tasks inside and outside of Notes while using programming language functionality. Advanced competencies expected at this level of certification include application planning, complex application security issues, object-oriented programming expertise, and troubleshooting.

CLP System Administrator

This certification is directed towards individuals who are currently Notes administrators or are working towards becoming Notes administrators. These individuals typically have experience in Notes server installation configuration, monitoring, maintenance, operations, certification, Notes communications, and managing multiple domains. The expected areas of competencies include infrastructure, planning, design, server installation/setup, systems security, application security, and troubleshooting.

CLP Principal System Administrator

This certification is directed towards individuals who have probably already achieved the CLP System Administrator certification but want to take their certification to the next level. The status of "Principal" is usually reserved for those individuals with proven expertise in the integration of additional communications product technology. As of the writing of this book, the only option elective is the cc:Mail administration test. Since Lotus has several communication products, I imagine that additional tests will become available as time goes on.

Since this book is about Lotus Notes administration and not cc:Mail, I'm not going to cover the cc:Mail certification program. I only included it in the certification matrix to show that Lotus has other certification programs besides Notes.

Certification Preparation

If I could tell people with absolute certainty the best way to prepare for certification examinations, I'd be rich. Unfortunately, I don't have the perfect answer because preparing for a certification examination is such a personal thing. Some people may respond best to classroom-led instruction. Others may prefer a self-guided approach such as a CBT (Computer Based Training). And others may choose to read manuals and experiment on their own.

Formalized classes are available directly from Lotus or through a Lotus Authorized Education Center (LAEC). The courses taught at these facilities follow courseware designed by Lotus which prepares people for certification examinations and teaches them role-related and job-related tasks. Having gone through some of the courseware myself, I can personally testify that the material covered is extremely relevant for the work you'll be doing as a Notes administrator. These courses don't merely teach about the "world of Notes according to Lotus." The material is practical and beneficial.

Computer Based Training (CBT) courses seek to mirror the classroom experience, minus the instructor. The real benefit of taking a CBT instead of a class is time. You can do the class on your time and repeat a module as often as you want. The down side to a CBT is twofold: no instruction, which often translates into no additional insight beyond the course material, and no access to classroom equipment and software.

The final approach is the total self-study method. This approach usually relies on a complete set of third party books, Notes manuals, and experimentation. I often find myself using this approach not because I prefer to work alone, but because of available time and resources. I usually don't have the time to attend a class; and purchasing a CBT or self-study kit is usually too expensive, and it's too much hassle to convince my employer to buy it for me. If you choose this approach to certification preparation, do yourself a favor and purchase the self-assessment exams. One major part of taking a certification test from any program is being comfortable with the examination format. Self-assessment examinations are the best way to get familiar with the format and to identify which areas you might need more work on. These tests aren't cheap, but they help reduce the risk of having to repeat a test.

The best advice I can offer to help you be more successful at taking certification tests is to try to identify the areas in which you are weakest and work at getting better in those areas.

Regardless of whether you're taking courses or using a CBT, additional sources of information are always helpful. The Lotus Notes KnowledgeBase, the Web, Lotus forums on CompuServe, and magazines and books are great sources of additional information. Refer to Appendix E for a complete listing of Notes resources.

Aside from courses, CBTs, and additional sources of information nothing quite beats hands on experience in a real world situation. If you haven't been using Lotus Notes as a developer or administrator for at least six months, don't bother taking the certification tests. You might pass, but it is doubtful that you'll really have a firm understanding of what you were tested on. Take your time. The CLP program isn't going away.

When You're Ready to Take the Exam

When you're ready to take your first examination, call Sylvan Prometric Testing Centers at (800) 745-6887 and register. Sylvan Prometric provides you with instructions concerning cancellation policy and testing requirements. A confirmation notice is sent to you in the mail which includes the test time, test location, directions to the testing center, and exam procedures.

All of the Lotus Notes exams are closed book which means no printed material, no electronic material, no computers other than the ones supplied, and no calculators. All of the exams are computer-based and most take between one hour and one and one half hours. However, the update combination exams are longer.

Examination scoring is done instantly on the screen. And you are given a hard copy of your test results showing whether you passed or failed (keep a copy of this report for your records). Your test scores are then automatically sent to Lotus within five business days. When you complete all of the examination requirements for a certification, Lotus Education automatically sends you a certificate of completion along with a welcome kit.

If you fail your examination, you have to re-register for the exam through Sylvan Prometric and pay the exam fee all over again.

The Benefits of Certification

What are the benefits of certification? From a professional perspective you are recognized by an industry software leader as having achieved a certain level of expertise with one of their products. Employment opportunities should be better and so should your salary. Unfortunately, there is no guarantee of either.

Aside from the professional benefits, the self satisfaction, and a cool-looking lapel pin with a logo, there isn't much else. NetWare gives all of their CNEs a couple of free incident calls. Microsoft gives their Microsoft Certified Systems Engineers (MCSE) a one year subscription to TechNet (a CD-ROM–based technical knowledge base) which is about a $300 value. Lotus, unfortunately, doesn't provide free incident calls or a free subscription to the Lotus Notes KnowledgeBase. The lack of any extra perk for certification is the only real complaint about the program. I wish Lotus would give their certified professionals something extra for getting certified. Hopefully Lotus Education is aware of this shortcoming and will correct it.

Recertification for Notes 3 Professionals

If you're already a Certified Lotus Professional for the Notes Release 3 environment, you need to consider updating your certification to Release 4. As it stands right now, Lotus is not making it mandatory to update your certification, but they are strongly encouraging you to do so (this requirement is subject to change). If, however, your business is a Lotus Business Partner, you should check with your partner representative to find out if the LBP program has different certification requirements. You may have to update your certification to remain in the LBP program.

The requirements for updating a certification for any certification program are not always easy to understand. Recertification requirements always have to be flexible for people who have certification and people right in the middle of certification. What often results from this flexibility is a confusing matrix of conditions. Fortunately, Lotus has done a pretty good job at keeping this matrix of conditions as clear as possible.

In review, the Certified Lotus Professional program previously had four levels of certification (see Table A.2).

TABLE A.2 Notes Release 3 Certification Titles and Examinations

Certification	Examination
Lotus Certified Notes Consultant (LCNC)	• Notes Technical User • Application Developer 1 • System Administration 1
Lotus Certified Notes System Administrator (LCNSA)	• Notes Technical User • System Administration 1 • System Administration 2
Lotus Certified Notes Application Developer (LCNAD)	• Notes Technical User • Application Developer 1 • Application Developer 2
Lotus Certified Notes Specialist (LCNS)	• Notes Technical User • Application Developer 1 • Application Developer 2 • System Administration 1 • System Administration 2

There are seven possible update examinations available along with the five new Release 4 exams. They are defined in Table A.3.

TABLE A.3 Examination Names and Codes

Update Exam Title	Exam Code
Application Development Update 1 (ADU1) Exam	190-161
Application Development Update 2 (ADU2) Exam	190-162
Application Development (AD) Recertification Exam	190-163
System Administration Update 1 (SAU1) Exam	190-164
System Administration Update 2 (SAU2) Exam	190-165
System Administration (SA) Recertification Exam	190-166
Lotus Certified Notes Consultant (LCNC) Recertification Exam	190-167
System Administration 1 for Release 4 Exam	190-174
System Administration 2 for Release 4 Exam	190-175

TABLE A.3 *(cont.)* Examination Names and Codes

Update Exam Title	Exam Code
Application Developer 1 for Release 4 Exam	190-171
Application Developer 2 for Release 4 Exam	190-172
Application Developer 3 for Release 4 Exam	190-173
cc:Mail System Administrator 1 Exam	190-051
cc:Mail System Administrator 2 Exam	190-052

Which level of certification you achieved determines which update examinations you need to take to recertify for Release 4. Table A.4 should help clarify which you'll need to take.

TABLE A.4 Update Requirements for Notes Release 3 Certifications

R3 Status	To Become a Notes Release 4...	Required Test for Release 4
LCNC	CLP System Administrator	• Lotus Certified Notes Consultant (LCNC) Recertification Exam • System Administration 2 for Release 4 Exam
LCNC	CLP Application Developer	• Lotus Certified Notes Consultant (LCNC) Recertification Exam • Application Developer 2 for Release 4 Exam
LCNSA	CLP Application Developer	• System Administration (SA) Recertification Exam • Application Developer 1 for Release 4 Exam
LCNAD	CLP System Administrator	• Application Development (AD) Recertification Exam • System Administration 1 for Release 4 Exam
LCNS	CLP System Administrator	• Lotus Certified Notes Consultant (LCNC) Recertification Exam • System Administration Update 2 (SAU2) Exam
LCNS	CLP Application Developer	• Lotus Certified Notes Consultant (LCNC) Recertification Exam • Application Development Update 2 (ADU2) Exam

Once you recertify and achieve either CLP System Administrator or CLP Application Developer, you can upgrade your certification to the status of "Principal" in the corresponding category with the following exams:

CLP System Administrator	190-051 to achieve CLP Principal System Administrator
CLP Application Developer	190-173 to achieve CLP Principal Application Developer

Further Certification Information

You can get more information about the Certified Lotus Professional program (such as sample questions and test objectives) through the mediums listed below.

On the World Wide Web

Check out `http://www.lotus.com/` and follow the links to Lotus Education or Support, where you can access the Lotus Notes KnowledgeBase.

The certification program continues to expand with new course offerings and innovative testing methods. I recommend checking the education pages on Lotus' Web site, or periodically checking the Lotus Notes KnowledgeBase and searching for education and/or certification.

By Phone

Call the Lotus Education Help line. In the United States call (800) 346-6409 or (617) 693-4436 (Monday through Friday, 8:30AM – 5:30PM Eastern Standard Time).

APPENDIX B

Notes Documents

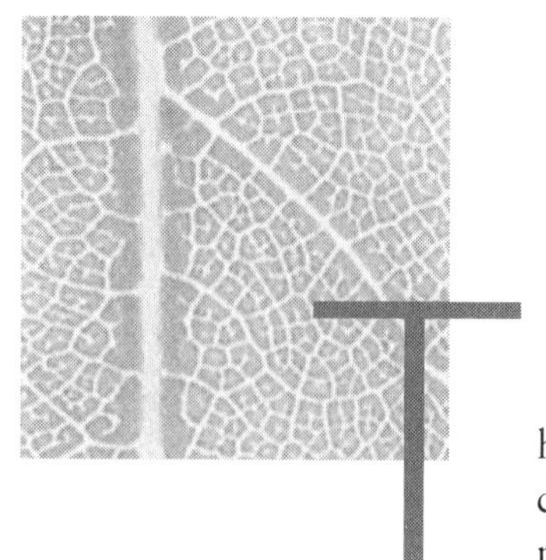

The importance of the Public Address Book in a Notes network can't be stressed enough. All Notes databases contain documents, but the Public Address Book contains the documents that define most of your Notes network.

In most Notes databases, someone has to create an actual document before it exists. Some of the documents in the Public Address Book, however, appear automatically as a result of the server setup or because of an administrative task that you perform. For example, when you register a new user, Notes automatically creates a new Person document; when you register a new server, Notes automatically creates a new Server document.

Because the documents contained in the Public Address Book are so important to your Notes network, you should have a basic familiarity with the essential documents contained in this database. What follows is a brief description of each document contained in the Public Address Book.

The Certifier Document

This document describes a certifier ID with information such as its public key. Each certificate issued to any Notes server in your network will have a corresponding document.

CERTIFIER

Basics

Certifier type:	Notes Certifier
Certifier name:	
Issued by:	
Certified public key:	

Contact

Company:	
Department:	
Location:	
Office phone:	
Comment:	

E-Mail

Notes mail server:	
Notes mail filename:	
Other mail address:	

The Connection Document

After the Server document, the Connection document is probably the most important document in the Public Address Book. This document is the driving force behind how and when servers connect with one another, replicate databases, and route mail. The Connection document also makes communication with other Notes domains possible and helps with certain Message Transfer Agents and foreign mail gateway products.

As a Notes administrator you'll want to become very familiar with the Connection document. You'll need to have a deep understanding of the various fields in this document and when more than one Connection document is needed. For instance, when two servers are routing mail back and forth both servers need to have a Connection document to the other server to enable mail delivery in both ways.

The available fields on a Connection document can change depending on which connection type is selected. I suggest creating Connection documents specifying different connection types to see how the document changes.

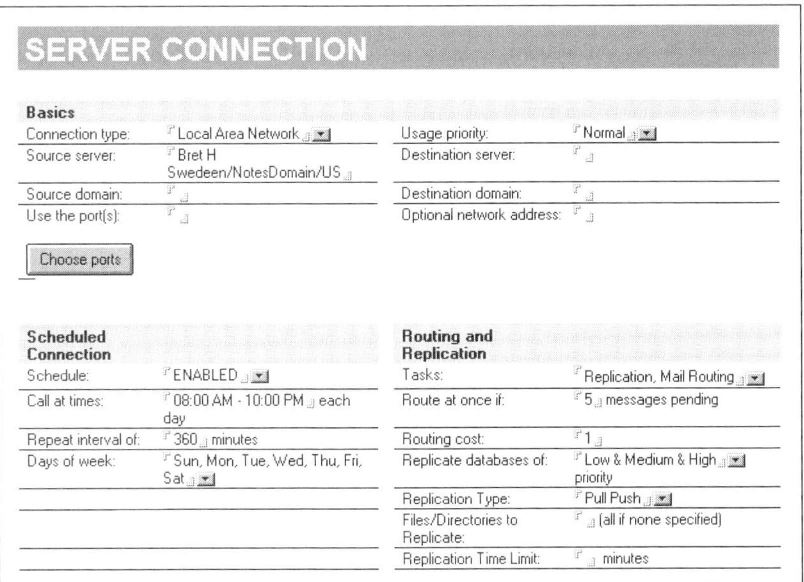

The Domain Document

The Domain document defines the name, location, and access to adjacent and non-adjacent Notes domains and non-Notes domains. Sending e-mail to other Notes domains, non-Notes domains, or Message Transfer Agents (MTAs) requires a Domain document.

The critical field in any Domain document is the Domain Type. This field provides seven possible options: Foreign Domain, Non-adjacent Domain, Adjacent Domain, Foreign X.400 Domain, Foreign SMTP Domain, Foreign cc:Mail Domain, Global Domain. The remaining fields in the Domain document will appear and disappear depending on the Domain Type selected.

DOMAIN

Basics
Domain type: Foreign Domain
Foreign domain name:
Domain description:

Mail
Gateway server name:
Gateway mail file name:

Calendar
Calendar server name:
Calendar system:

Restrictions
Allow mail only from domains:
Deny mail from domains:

The Group Document

Group documents are used to group together users, servers, and sometimes other groups. Using groups is an easy way to send e-mail to several users at once, as well as quickly grant and revoke access to servers and databases.

The Group document is a very easy document to use because there are only a few fields to fill in and those fields are fairly self-explanatory. The most important field on the form is the Group Type field. The field determines how you can use the group defined within the context of your Notes environment. There are four group types to choose from:

- **Multi-Purpose**: This type of group can be used as a mailing list and as an entry in an Access Control List.
- **Access Control List Only**: This type of group is only used as an ACL entry. You can't send e-mail to this group.
- **Mail Only**: This type of group is only a mailing list and can't be used as an ACL entry.
- **Deny List Only**: This type of group is a collection of Notes users that are denied access to the Notes server. You normally use these groups in the Restrictions section of a Server document. Groups of this type also only show up in the Server - Deny Access Groups view.

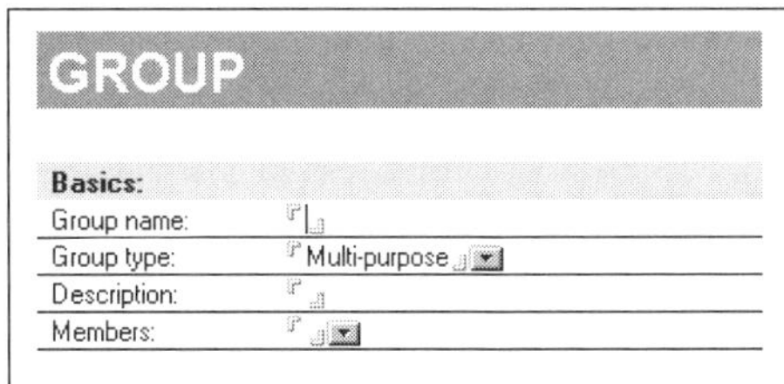
GROUP

Basics:

Group name:	
Group type:	Multi-purpose
Description:	
Members:	

The Location Document

Although you will find Location documents in the Public Address Book, the most common use of these documents is to provide an easy way to define different location scenarios for mobile Notes users. For example, a mobile Notes user might need a Location document that defines their home dial-up configuration as well as a dial-up configuration they can use in a hotel. There are several sections to a Location document starting with the general settings.

After the general locations setting section, the following section, Phone Dialing, allows you to define the dial-up settings for this particular location. In addition, further customization for a particular Location document can be made in the way a particular location handles mail and replication. This can be determined in the Mail and Replication sections of the Location document. Advanced features such as time zone configuration and Java applet security can be chosen from the Advanced and Java Applet Security sections of the screen.

The Mail-In Database Document

Notes can send mail to more than just a user's mail database. Developers can create databases that can receive mail. However, developers that create such databases will need your help in completely enabling their database to receive mail. You'll have to create a Mail-In Database document so that their database has an addressable name.

The Mail-In Database document defines the location and properties of a database that needs to receive mail. As an administrator, you won't create this type of document too often and once you do you might want to delegate the responsibility for this document type to the developer who created the database.

MAIL-IN DATABASE

Basics		Location	
Mail-in name:		Domain:	
Description:		Server:	
		Filename:	

The Person Document

The Person document contains important information about the registered users in your Notes environment. General information about the user, such as home server and mail file name, are found in the first section of the document. Personal and professional information can easily be recorded about each user in the Work, Home, and Misc (miscellaneous) sections of the Person document. And the final sections of the Person document, Public Keys and Administration, contain information about encryption keys and administrative settings for password expiration and Notes license type.

PERSON

Name		Mail	
First name:		Mail system:	Notes
Middle initial:		Domain:	
Last name:		Mail server:	
User name:		Mail file:	
Short name and/or Internet address:		Forwarding address:	
HTTP password:			

The Program Document

Program documents allow you to automate the task of running server tasks or other executable programs. Such tasks or programs can be scheduled with this document allowing you to run programs whenever it is convenient for you.

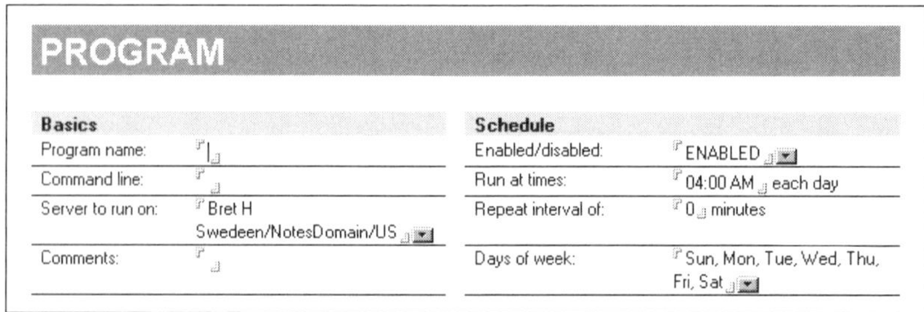
PROGRAM

Basics		Schedule	
Program name:		Enabled/disabled:	ENABLED
Command line:		Run at times:	04:00 AM each day
Server to run on:	Bret H Swedeen/NotesDomain/US	Repeat interval of:	0 minutes
Comments:		Days of week:	Sun, Mon, Tue, Wed, Thu, Fri, Sat

The Resource Document

This document helps with calendaring and scheduling. You can define resources in your organization that people can reserve for meetings or other activities.

RESOURCE

Basics		Reservations Database	
Resource type:	Room	Domain:	
Resource name:		Server:	
Capacity:		Filename:	

Resource Description:
Comments:

The Server Document

This is the most important document as far as Notes administration goes, and probably the most complex. As an administrator, you'll frequently use this document to perform such tasks as granting and revoking access to the server, and configuring general settings for the Message Transfer Agents.

There are several sections to a Server document starting with the Basics section, which contains general server information. This section is the only section where all of its fields are viewable when you open the Server document for the first time. The remaining sections of the document, defined below, are collapsed and can be expanded by clicking the arrow to the left of the section title to show which fields are available.

- **Server Location Information**: This section defines server location information which is used for server-to-server dial up connections.
- **Network Configuration**: This section contains information that provides details about enabling network ports and their associated Notes named network.
- **Proxy Configuration**: This section provides information about various Internet-related resources.
- **Security**: This section contains general security information for the server.
- **Restrictions**: This section contains specific information about who can access the server and use the server for passthru.
- **Agent Manager**: This section is where you set options that control the execution of server-based agents.

- **Administration Process:** The Administration process running on the server is configured and controlled in this section.
- **Web Retriever Administration:** Web-related configuration information is available in this section.
- **HTTP Server:** This section contains HTTP configuration information.

The final sections, Internet Message Transfer Agent (SMTP MTA), X.400 Message Transfer Agent (X.400 MTA), and cc:Mail Message Transfer Agent, are sections that allow you to configure the corresponding Message Transfer Agent once it is installed.

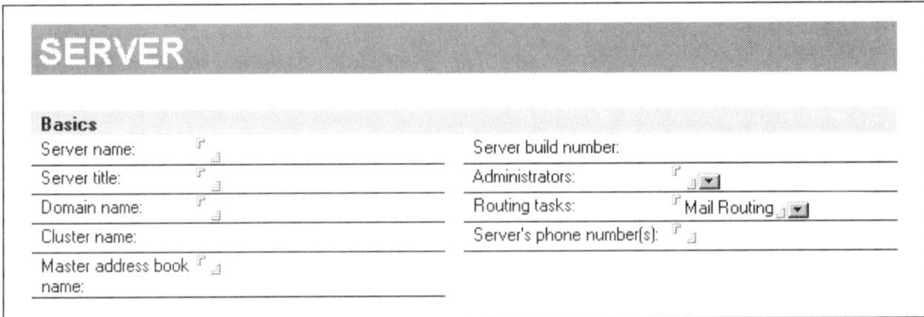

The Server Configuration Document

This document is used to change and add certain settings to the NOTES.INI file. Using this document you can quickly make any INI change across several servers without having to visit each server. Changes or additions made using this document are saved and can be used for future configuration reference.

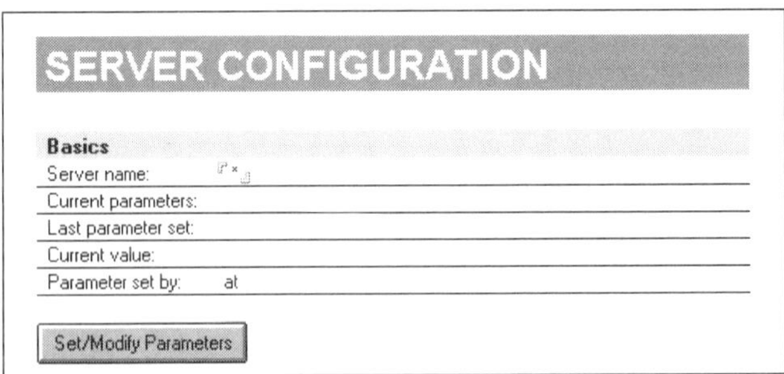

The User Setup Profile Document

This document identifies a standard set of connections that you provide for users when you register them. Whether you enter information in all or some of these fields depends on the user profile you are trying to create. You are not restricted to only one user profile and can create as many different profiles as your unique Notes network requires.

USER SETUP PROFILE

Basics

Profile name:	
Internet browser:	Notes
Retrieve/open pages:	from Notes workstation

Default Databases

Database links:	

Default Passthru Server

Server name:	
Country code:	
Area code:	
Phone number:	

Default Connections to Other Remote Servers

Server Names	Country Codes	Area Codes	Phone Number

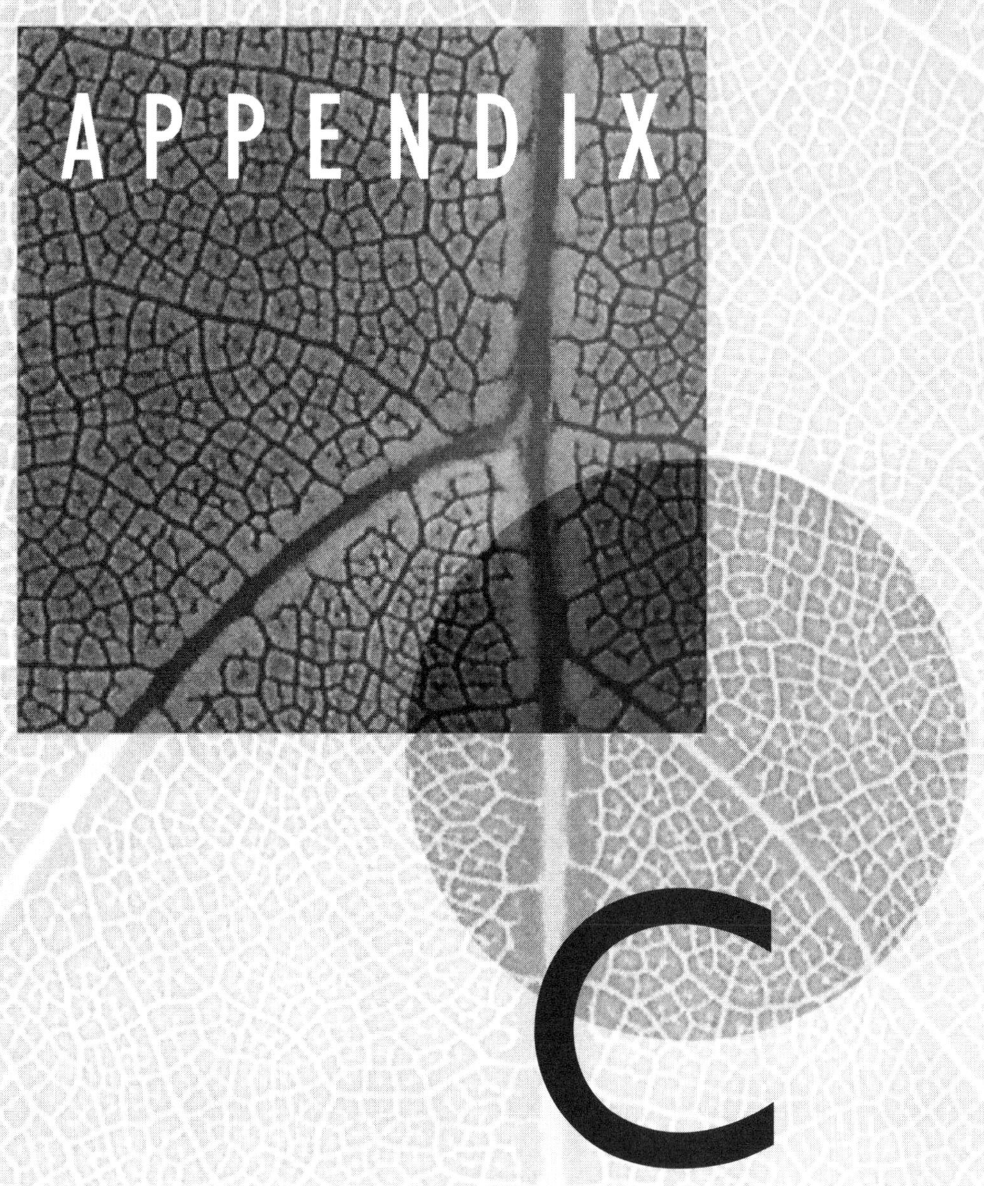

APPENDIX C

Server Console Commands

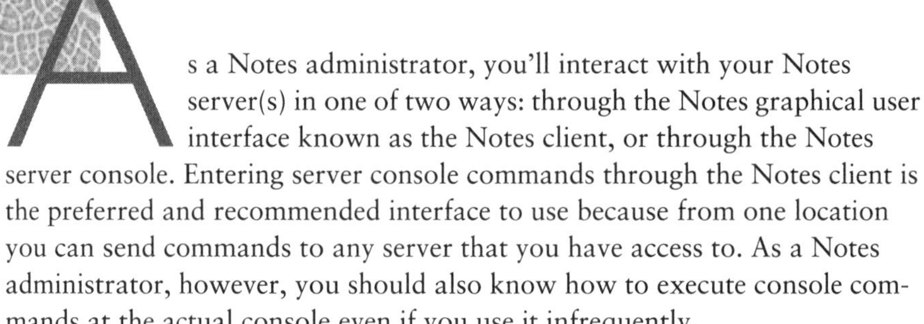

As a Notes administrator, you'll interact with your Notes server(s) in one of two ways: through the Notes graphical user interface known as the Notes client, or through the Notes server console. Entering server console commands through the Notes client is the preferred and recommended interface to use because from one location you can send commands to any server that you have access to. As a Notes administrator, however, you should also know how to execute console commands at the actual console even if you use it infrequently.

Entering Server Console Commands from the Notes Client

Entering server console commands from the Notes client is very easy. From the menu bar, select File ➢ Tools ➢ Server Administration. The Server Administration screen provides eight topical buttons that provide additional tools and/or options (see Figure C.1).

From these two columns of buttons, select Console. This button opens the Remote Server Console screen (see Figure C.2).

Each of the key elements on the Remote Server Console screen is described below:

- **Server:** This is a drop-down list box with all of the available Notes servers in the same Notes-named network. Select the server that you want to interact with from this drop-down list.
- **Server console command:** This is where you enter actual server console commands. You are limited to a command string that is equal to or less than 255 characters. All of the console commands listed later in this appendix can be abbreviated, so the 255 character limit shouldn't ever be a problem.

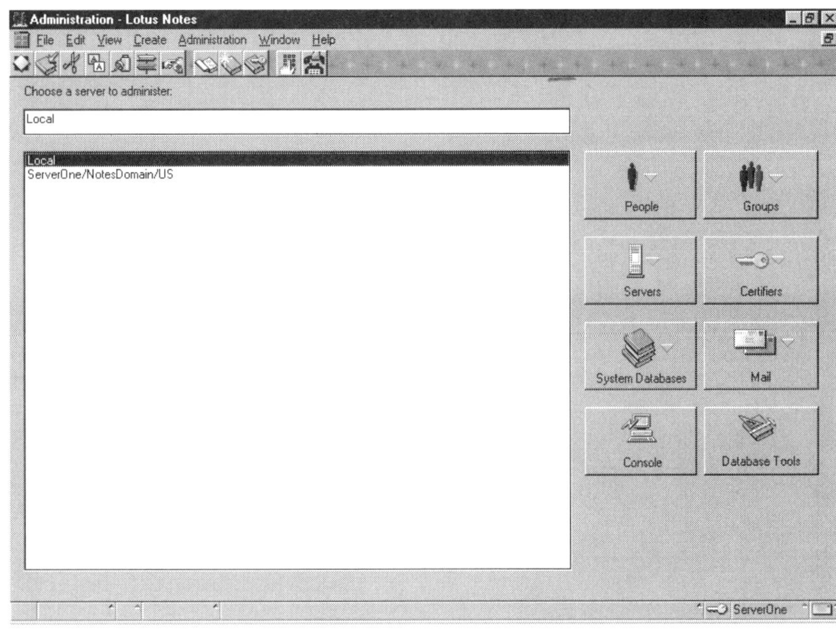

FIGURE C.1

The Server Administration screen is the access point to the Remote Server Console.

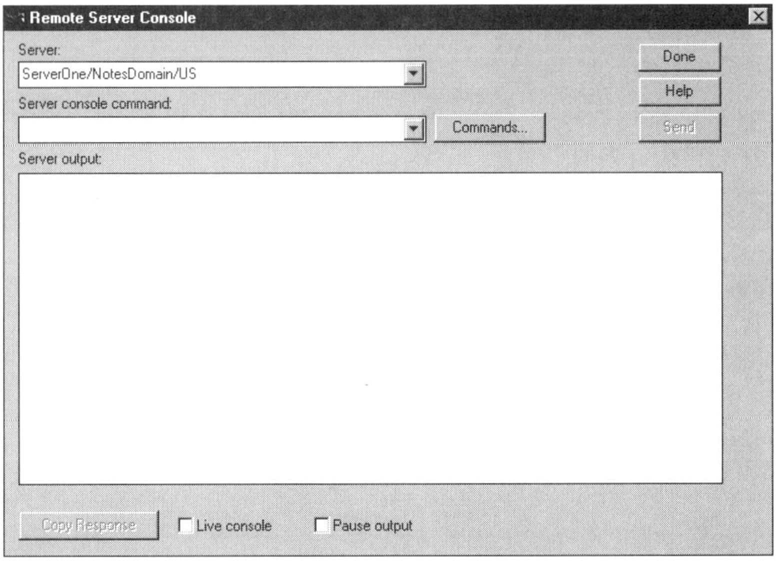

FIGURE C.2

In the Remote Server Console you can enter server console commands without actually being at the server.

- **Commands:** If you select this button, a dialog box appears displaying all of the available commands with brief dynamic descriptions (see Figure C.3). As you highlight a command, a brief description is displayed in a box below the command. Click OK and the command you highlighted is placed in the Server Console Command text box. Any required parameters are described in square brackets ([ ]) and optional parameters are described in angled brackets (< >).

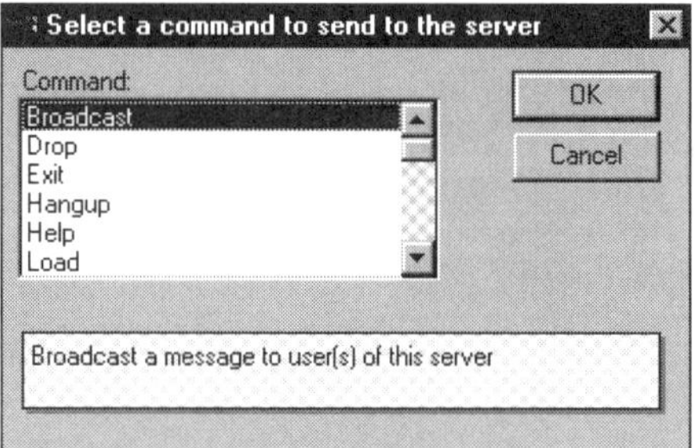

FIGURE C.3 Click the Commands button and all available console commands are displayed.

- **Server output:** This is the area where the server response to your command is displayed. If the server response doesn't fit in this area, horizontal and vertical scroll bars appear to help view the response (see Figure C.4).

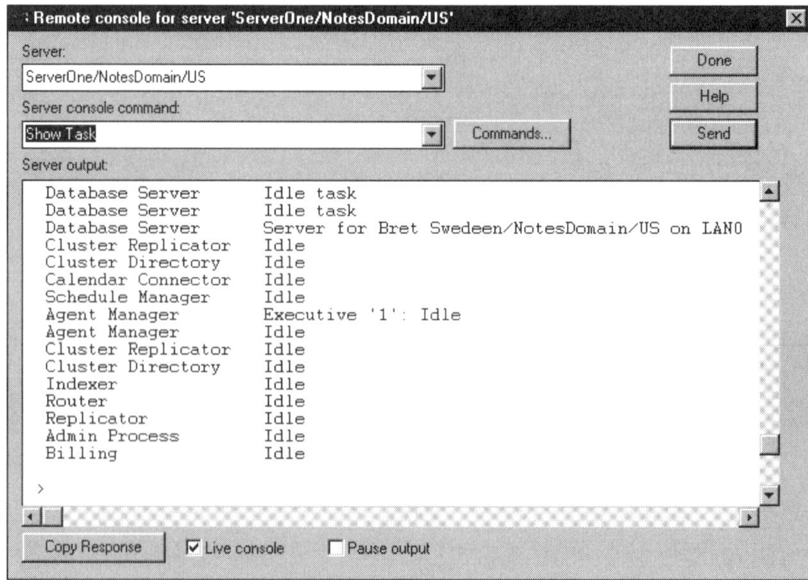

FIGURE C.4 The results of the Show Tasks console command. Notice the horizontal and vertical scroll bars, which enable you to view results that are not in the viewable portion of the Server Output window.

- **Copy Response:** This button is a handy way to quickly copy the output in the Server Output window. It's helpful if you need to place this information into a report or e-mail message.
- **Live console:** This check box turns the Server Output window into a remote duplicate of the actual server console. Server activity that is displayed at the actual server console is also displayed here.
- **Pause output:** This check box pauses the scrolling information in the Server Output window.
- **Send:** This button sends the command type in the Server Console Command text box to the selected server for execution.
- **Help:** This button activates context-sensitive help for the Remote Console screen.
- **Done:** This button closes the Remote Console screen and ends the session.

Entering Server Console Commands at the Server Console

Entering console commands at the actual server console is not much different than doing it from the Remote Server Console screen in the Notes client. The real difference is that the added features, such as the Command... button and context-sensitive help, are not available from the actual server console.

To enter a simple console command such as **Show Tasks**, do the following:

1. Go to the Notes server machine and make the Notes server program the active window on the screen.
   - On the Windows server, double-click the Notes server icon or switch to the console
   - On a NetWare server, enter **load notessrv**
   - On a UNIX server, log into the server account, change to the server's Notes directory, and enter **server**

2. Press Enter to get to a command prompt, which can be seen in Figure C.5 at the bottom left side of the screen as a right angled bracket (>).This bracket is sometimes referred to as a right arrow or a greater than sign.

3. Type your command and press Enter. In Figure C.5, the command results for Show Tasks are displayed in the server console program window.

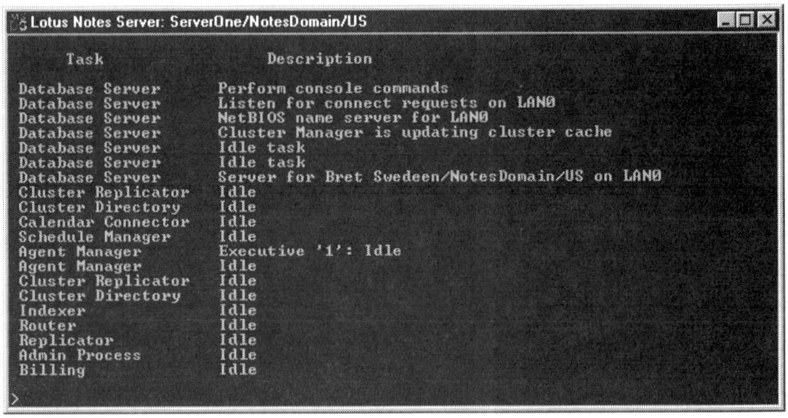

```
Lotus Notes Server: ServerOne/NotesDomain/US

     Task                     Description

Database Server      Perform console commands
Database Server      Listen for connect requests on LAN0
Database Server      NetBIOS name server for LAN0
Database Server      Cluster Manager is updating cluster cache
Database Server      Idle task
Database Server      Idle task
Database Server      Server for Bret Swedeen/NotesDomain/US on LAN0
Cluster Replicator   Idle
Cluster Directory    Idle
Calendar Connector   Idle
Schedule Manager     Idle
Agent Manager        Executive '1': Idle
Agent Manager        Idle
Cluster Replicator   Idle
Cluster Directory    Idle
Indexer              Idle
Router               Idle
Replicator           Idle
Admin Process        Idle
Billing              Idle
>
```

FIGURE C.5
The Notes Server program displayed in a command prompt on a Windows NT server machine

When entering console commands from the Remote Server Console screen, you can copy the server response with the click of a button. Unfortunately, there is no button at the actual server console, but you can redirect the server response to a text file by following the command with a right angled bracket and the name of a text file to write to. The Show Tasks command redirected to a text file called OUTPUT.TXT would appear as:

```
show tasks > output.txt
```

When typing commands at the server console, here are a few things to keep in mind to make entering commands a little easier and quicker:

- You are limited to 255 characters for a single command.
- If the server console prompt doesn't appear, press Enter.
- To quickly retype the last command you entered, press the up arrow (↑).
- If a command you are typing gets disrupted by a server activity message, type CTRL+R to restore the command line you started.

- If server names or other command parameters include spaces, make sure to enclose them in quotation marks.
- To stop the server console messages and suspend both access to the server and events in progress, press CTRL+Q or PAUSE. Pressing CTRL+R will resume activity display, access, and events-processing on the server.

Graphical administrative interfaces such as the Notes client are normally a great way to use administrative tasks. However, sometimes graphical interfaces are too cumbersome and you'd just rather type a command the old-fashioned way. For those times when typing is faster, Table C.1 provides a list of "case-insensitive" server console commands followed by their syntax, abbreviation, and definition.

TABLE C.1 Server Console Commands

Server Command	Command Abbreviation	Command Definition
Broadcast "msg" ["user"]	B "msg" ["user"]	Sends a message to users of this server. The message appears on the Status Message section of the Notes client
Drop ["username"] [All]	D	Closes one or more user sessions
Exit	E	Shuts the server down
Hangup [Portname]	Ha [portname]	Hangs up the specified communications port
Help	H	Displays all available server console commands
Load [Program name]	L	Loads and runs the specified program on the server
Pull [ServerName] <database>	P	Forces replication in one direction from the server specified to the source server. A particular database can also be specified

TABLE C.1 *(cont.)* Server Console Commands

Server Command	Command Abbreviation	Command Definition
Push [ServerName] <database>	PUS	Forces replication in one direction from the source server to the specified server. A particular database can also be specified
Quit	Q	Shuts the server down
Replicate [ServerName] <database>	REP	Forces two-way replication with the specified server. A particular database can also be specified
Route [ServerName]	RO	Forces mail routing with the specified server
Set Configuration <parameter = value>	SE C	Creates or resets a NOTES.INI setting
Set Secure <new password>	SE SE	Sets password protection for the server console
Set Statistics	SE ST	Resets the numeric-additive statistics
Show Cluster	SH CL	Displays a list of cluster members and their current status
Show Configuration <parameter>	SH C	Displays the current NOTES.INI setting for the specified parameter
Show Database <database> [D or V]	SH DA <database> [D] or [V]	Displays the named database information regarding both the document type and view sizes. Using option [D] will only display the document type with live and deleted information; using option [V] will only display the view sizes and bytes

TABLE C.1 *(cont.)* Server Console Commands

Server Command	Command Abbreviation	Command Definition
Show Directory	SH DIR	Lists all Notes databases in the data directory. Only works on the Notes data directory. You can't specify any other directory
Show Diskspace [drive]	SH DIS	Shows the current disk space available on the specified drive
Show Memory	SH ME	Shows available RAM plus boot drives swapping memory
Show Performance	SH PE	Changes the SERVER_SHOW_ PERFORMANCE parameter from 1 (active) to 0 (not active)
Show Port <portname>	SH PO	Shows traffic and error statistics for the specified port. Great way to quickly see whether a port is working or not
Show Schedule	SH SC	Shows the next time that a server, program, or location will run
Show Server	SH SER	Shows server status information
Show Tasks	SH TA	Shows the status of all the active server tasks
Show Users	SH U	Shows a list of all users currently accessing the server, and the databases those users are using
Tell [task] [command string]	T	Issues a command to a server task such as the Replicator, Router, or Indexer

All of the commands are useful and worth knowing because they can be helpful, especially when you are trying to troubleshoot a problem. However, the replication commands and the Show Tasks, Show Users, and Show Port commands are ones that I use on a regular basis. The three "show" commands provide quick feedback on the overall activity on the server. And the replication commands are frequently used because they help distribute important changes quickly to a database during unscheduled replication times.

I recommend you become familiar with these server console commands and practice using them from both the Notes client and the actual server console.

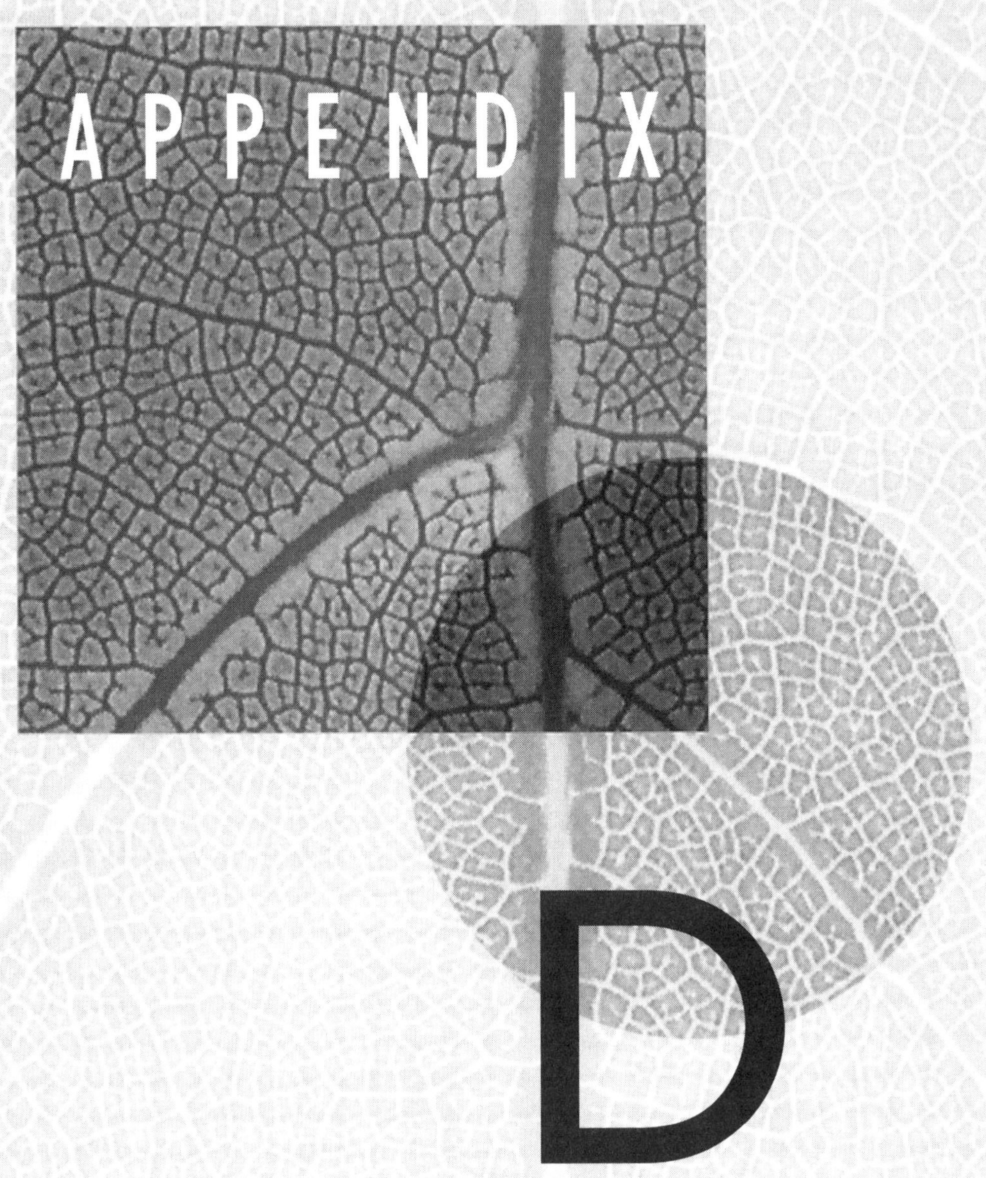

APPENDIX D

The NOTES.INI File

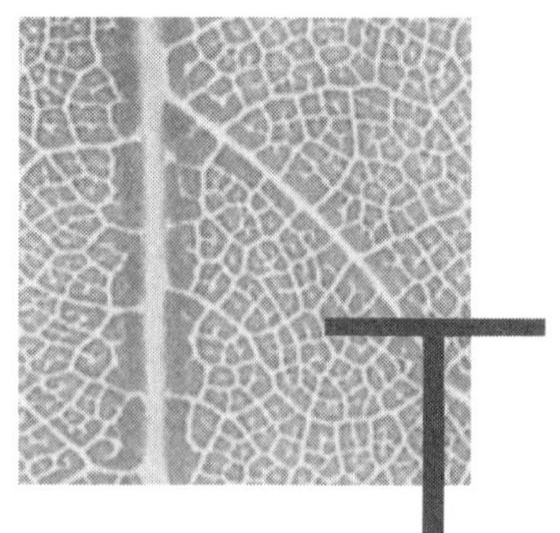

The NOTES.INI file is a basic initialization file that provides all of the functional settings for a Notes server or client. The .INI file is accessed during server or workstation startup and checked for information about which tasks to run and how to set up the Notes environment. Some of the settings contained in the NOTES.INI file are made during server or workstation installation. Still other settings are made when certain documents in the Public Address Book are created.

How to Edit the NOTES.INI File

The NOTES.INI file is a standard text file and can be edited directly with a simple test editor such as Notepad, which is supplied with all flavors of Windows (see Figure D.1). When the .INI file is open in a text editor, you can make changes to any of the settings by simply typing them in. Once you've finished your changes, save the file.

Since most .INI settings are read only, during server or workstation startup, you might have to restart your Notes server or workstation for your changes to take affect.

Another way to make changes to the settings in the NOTES.INI is directly at the server console or indirectly through the remote server console. Use the Set Configuration command followed by the .INI setting that you want to change or add. The same syntax is applicable when using either the direct or indirect method and is illustrated in Figure D.2.

FIGURE D.1

Using Notepad, or any other text editor, is a quick and easy way to make changes or add settings to the NOTES.INI file.

```
notes - Notepad
File Edit Search Help
[Notes]
Directory=d:\apps\notes45\data4
$$HasLANPort=1
CertifierIDFile=d:\apps\notes45\data4\cert.id
FileDlgDirectory=D:\apps\notes45\data4
MailServer=CN=ServerOne/O=NotesDomain/C=US
KitType=2
NPN=1
WinNTIconPath=d:\apps\notes45\data4\W32
EnablePlugins=1
Preferences=-2146957199
Passthru_LogLevel=0
Console_LogLevel=2
VIEWIMP1=Lotus 1-2-3 Worksheet,0,_IWKSV,,.WKS,.WK1,.WR1,.WRK,.WK3,.WK4,
VIEWIMP3=Structured Text,0,_ISTR,,.LTR,.CGN,.STR,
VIEWIMP4=Tabular Text,0,_ITAB,,.PRN,.RPT,.TXT,.TAB,
VIEWEXP1=Lotus 1-2-3 Worksheet,0,_XWKS,,.WKS,.WK1,.WR1,.WRK,
VIEWEXP3=Structured Text,0,_XSTR,,.LTR,.CGN,.STR,
VIEWEXP4=Tabular Text,1,_XTAB,,.LTR,.RPT,.CGN,.TAB,
EDITIMP1=ASCII Text,0,_ITEXT,,.TXT,.PRN,.C,.H,.RIP,
EDITIMP2=MicrosoftWord RTF,0,_IRTF,,.DOC,.RTF,
EDITIMP3=Lotus 1-2-3 Worksheet,0,_IWKSE,,.WKS,.WK1,.WR1,.WRK,.WK3,.WK4,
```

FIGURE D.2

From the server console, use the Set Configuration command to change or add .INI settings to the NOTES.INI file.

```
Lotus Domino Server: ServerOne/NotesDomain/US
Peak # of sessions:      0 at
Transactions:            0
Shared mail:             Not enabled
Pending mail:  0         Dead mail:  0

     Task                     Description

 Database Server      Consistency check will start in 8 seconds
 Database Server      Perform console commands
 Database Server      Listen for connect requests on LAN0
 Database Server      NetBIOS name server for LAN0
 Database Server      Idle task
 Database Server      Idle task
 Event                Idle
 Calendar Connector   Idle
 Schedule Manager     Idle
 Admin Process        Idle
 Agent Manager        Executive '1': Idle
 Agent Manager        Idle
 Indexer              Idle
 Router               Idle
 Replicator           Idle
 Billing              Idle

> set configuration "AdminPInterval=30"
```

The final method available to set the values of certain .INI setting is through the use of the Server Configuration document in the Public Address Book. This method allows you to easily set or change an .INI setting on any of your Notes servers from a single location. To use this method, follow these directions:

1. Open or select the Public Address Book.

2. From the menu bar, select Create ➢ Server ➢ Configuration.

3. A Server Configuration document appears.

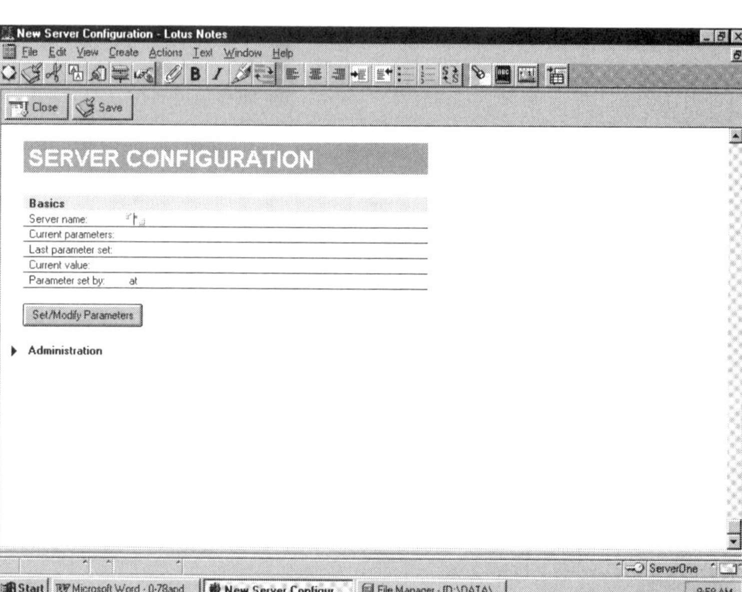

4. Enter the name, or names, of the server(s) you want to apply this change or addition to in the Server Name field.

5. Press the Set/Modify Parameters button.

6. The Server Configuration Parameters dialog box appears.

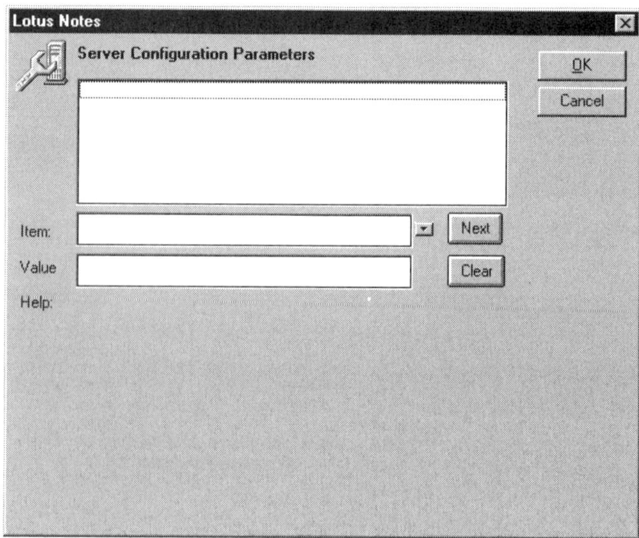

7. From the drop-down list next to the Item field, select an .INI setting, such as Shared_Mail.
8. Enter the value for this setting in the Value field. If I had selected Shared_Mail, I would enter **2** to enable shared mail for delivery and transfer of mail messages.
9. Press the Next button and repeat steps 7 and 8 to change or add additional .INI settings.
10. When complete, press the OK button and save the document.

Location of the NOTES.INI File

Where the NOTES.INI file is located depends on the operating system. Therefore, each Notes platform is listed below indicating where the NOTES.INI file is located:

- **NetWare**: The NOTES.INI is located in the Notes directory.
- **OS/2**: The NOTES.INI is located in the Notes data directory.
- **Windows**: The NOTES.INI is located in the Windows directory or Notes data directory.
- **Macintosh**: The NOTES.INI is represented by the Notes Preferences file located in the Preferences folder in the System folder.
- **UNIX**: The NOTES.INI file is placed, by default, in the user's or server's Notes directory, but can be moved anywhere in the path.

NOTES.INI Settings

What follows is an alphabetical listing of NOTES.INI settings for quick reference. Additional information about the .INI settings listed here can be found in the *Notes Administration Help* guide. This guide comes with the product and is also available in a Notes database format as online documentation.

Each listing shown below includes a brief description of the setting, available parameters, and its proper syntax. Not every .INI setting that exists is listed here simply because Lotus doesn't always document every .INI setting available. It might be a good idea to pencil into this appendix any additional .INI settings that you learn about on your own for future reference.

ActionPaneEnabled

This setting determines whether the Action Pane appears when opening an item in Design mode. This setting applies to workstations and has a default setting of 0, which causes the Action Pane not to appear.

Syntax: ActionPaneEnabled = <*value*>

0 = Action Pane not does not appear in Design mode.

1 = Action Pane appears in Design mode.

Admin

This setting applies to servers and indicates the name of the server administrator in canonical format with each part being separated by a slash.

Syntax: Admin= CN=<*common name*>/OU=<*organization unit*>/O=<*organization*>

AdminPInterval

This setting specifies the interval cycle for the Administration Process to carry out requests. The interval is measured in minutes and applies to servers only.

Syntax: AdminPinterval= <*time in minutes*>

AdminPModifyPersonDocumentsAt

This setting determines the hour at which the Administration Process modifies Person documents in the Public Address Book. The value for the setting must be in twenty-four hour format. If this setting doesn't exist and no value is specified in the Server document, the Administration Process modifies Person documents at midnight.

Syntax: AdminPModifyPersonDocumentsAt = <*24 hour value*>

Admin_Access

This setting must contain at least one name by default that specifies which users or groups can administer the server. The entries for this setting must be in canonical format.

Syntax: Admin_Access = CN=<*common name*>/OU=<*organization unit*>/O=<organization>

Allow_Access

This setting applies to servers and indicates which servers, users, and groups can access the server. Names must be entered in hierarchical format, with a comma separating entries. An asterisk represents everyone listed in the Public Address Book. An asterisk followed by a view name represents everyone listed in that view of the Public Address Book. An asterisk followed by a slash (/) and a hierarchical certifier's name represents everyone certified by that certifier.

Syntax: Allow_Access = <*names*>

Allow_Access_[Portname]

This setting applies to servers and specifies which servers, users, and groups can access a particular port on the server. Names must be entered in hierarchical format, with a comma separating entries. An asterisk represents everyone listed in the Public Address Book. An asterisk followed by a view name represents everyone listed in that view of the Public Address Book. An asterisk followed by a slash (/) and a hierarchical certifier's name represents everyone certified by that certifier.

Syntax: Allow_Access_[*Portname*] = <*names*>

Allow_Passthru_Access

This setting applies to servers and specifies the servers, users, and groups that can access the server using passthru. If you don't specify a name, no one can access the server using passthru. Use an asterisk to represent everyone listed in the Public Address Book. Use an asterisk followed by a view name to represent everyone listed in that view of the Public Address Book. An asterisk followed by a slash (/) and a hierarchical certifier's name represents everyone certified by that certifier.

Syntax: Allow_Passthru_Access = <*names*>

Allow_Passthru_Callers

This setting applies to servers and specifies the servers, users, and groups that can instruct the server to establish a connection to call a destination server. If you don't enter a name, no calling is allowed. An asterisk represents everyone listed in the Public Address Book. An asterisk followed by a view name represents everyone listed in that view of the Public Address Book. An asterisk followed by a slash (/) and a hierarchical certifier's name represents everyone certified by that certifier.

Syntax: Allow_Passthru_Callers = <*names*>

Allow_Passthru_Clients

This setting applies to servers and specifies the servers, users, and groups that can use a passthru server to connect to this server. If you don't specify a name, passthru is not allowed. An asterisk represents everyone listed in the Public Address Book. An asterisk followed by a view name represents everyone listed in that view of the Public Address Book. An asterisk followed by a slash and a hierarchical certifier's name represents everyone certified by that certifier.

Syntax: Allow_Passthru_Clients = <*names*>

Allow_Passthru_Targets

This setting applies to servers and specifies the destination servers that this server can connect to using passthru. If you don't specify a name, this server can route to all servers.

Syntax: Allow_Passthru_Targets = <*names*>

AMgr_DisableMailLookup

This setting applies to servers and is used to disable mail lookup agents from running on the server. By default, a mail-triggered agent performs a mail lookup of the user who last modified it and only runs if the server running the agent is also the user's mail server. If a user creates or modifies a mail-triggered agent on a server other than his or her mail server, use this setting on the server to disable mail lookup so that the agent can run. There are two possible settings defined as follows:

0 = Perform mail lookups when running mail-triggered agents.

1 = Do not perform mail lookups when running mail-triggered agents.

Syntax: AMgr_DisableMailLookup = <*value*>

AMgr_DocUpdateAgentMinInterval

This setting applies to both workstations and servers and specifies the minimum elapsed time, in minutes, between the execution of the same document update-triggered agent. By default, this setting is set to thirty minutes.

Syntax: AMgr_DocUpdateAgentMinInterval = <*time in minutes*>

AMgr_DocUpdateEventDelay

This setting applies to both workstations and servers and specifies the delay time, in minutes, that the agent manager schedules a document update-triggered agent after a document update event. By default, this setting is set to five minutes.

Syntax: AMgr_DocUpdateEventDelay = <*time in minutes*>

AMgr_NewMailAgentMinInterval

This setting applies to both workstations and servers and specifies the minimum elapsed time, in minutes, between execution of the same new mail-triggered agent. By default, the minimum time is set to zero.

Syntax: AMgr_NewMailAgentMinInterval = <*time in minutes*>

AMgr_NewMailEventDelay

This setting applies to both workstations and servers and specifies the time, in minutes, that the Agent Manager delays before scheduling a new mail-triggered agent after new mail is delivered. The default value is one minute.

Syntax: AMgr_NewMailEventDelay = <*time in minutes*>

AMgr_WeekendDays

This setting applies to both workstations and servers and is referenced when agents use the On Schedule trigger and the Don't Run on Weekends checkbox option is checked. When you select this option, the agent will not run on weekend days. The default value for weekend days is Saturday (7) and Sunday (1). You can specify any number of days, up to 7.

Syntax: AMgr_WeekendDays = <*1,2, and so on*>

AppleTalkNameServer

This setting applies to workstations and servers that are AppleTalk users only. This setting identifies the name of the user's secondary AppleTalk server. Consult your AppleTalk network documentation for more information.

Syntax: AppleTalkNameServer = <*server name*>

AutoLogoffMinutes

This setting applies to workstations and is used to set the number of inactive minutes before a user is automatically logged off.

Syntax: AutoLogoffMinutes = <*time in minutes*>

BillingAddinOutput

This setting applies to servers and specifies where Notes records billing events. There three possible values defined as follows:

1 = Billing database (BILLING.NSF)

8 = Binary file (BILLING.NBF)

9 = Both the billing database and the binary file

Notes creates the BILLING.NSF database and/or the BILLING.NBF file the first time the billing add-in task is started with BillingAddinOutput set.

Syntax: BillingAddinOutput = <*value*>

BillingAddinRuntime

This setting applies to servers and specifies how long the billing add-in task runs, which, by default, is ten seconds. After the specified time has elapsed, the billing add-in stops processing records, even if there are additional records to be processed. The BillingAddinRuntime value must be less than the value you specify for the BillingAddinWakeup variable.

Syntax: BillingAddinRuntime = <*time in seconds*>

BillingAddinWakeup

This setting applies to servers and specifies how often the billing add-in task runs; the default is sixty seconds. The BillingAddinWakeup value must be greater than the value you specify for BillingAddinRuntime. If BillingAddin-Wakeup is less than BillingAddinRuntime, the billing task will already be running when the BillingAddingWakup kicks in to start the billing task again.

Syntax: BillingAddinWakeup = <*time in seconds*>

BillingClass

This setting applies to servers and specifies one or more of five classes of billing activity defined as follows:

- Database
- Document
- Mail
- Replication
- Session

The Notes billing process tracks only the Notes activities that you specify in the BillingClass variable. BillingSuppressTime only applies to session and database billing.

Syntax: BillingClass = <*class or classes*>

BillingSuppressTime

This setting applies to servers and specifies the frequency of record stamping during session and database activities if session and database activities are specified for the BillingClass variable. If you want billing data collected more frequently, decrease the default value of fifteen minutes. To minimize the billing workload on your system, increase the value.

Syntax: BillingSuppressTime = <*time in minutes*>

CertificateExpChecked

This setting applies to servers and workstations. This setting specifies the path for the Notes ID and its certification expiration date. The ID file requires its complete path and filename. The expiration date that appears after the ID file is the expiration date of the ID. If you have more than one ID file, the last ID file used is the one that gets checked.

Syntax: CertificateExpChecked = <*ID filename* and *expiration date*>

CertifierIDFile

This setting applies to servers and specifies the path and ID file for the certifier ID. The path must contain the drive letter, network drive, and directories. The ID file is the actual name of the certifier ID file.

Syntax: CertifierIDFile = <*drive letter*, *directory path*, and *ID filename*>

COM[number]

This setting applies to workstations and servers. This setting specifies information for modems connected to the ports you set in the Ports dialog box. Up to five ports can be defined (COM1 through COM5). Each port accepts the series of additional parameters defined as follows:

Syntax: COM[*port number 1-5*] = <*driver*, *unit_ID*, *max_sessions*, *buffer_size*, *others…*>

driver: Driver name (required)

unit_ID: Unit ID (required)

max_sessions: Maximum number of concurrent sessions (required)

buffer_size: Size of buffer in kilobytes (required)

flags: Optional flags, such as secured channel, log modem I/O, enable RTS/CTS, and so on

modem_speed: Modem speed

modem_volume: Modem volume and dialing mode

modem_filename: Name of the modem command file

dial_timer: Connection timeout in seconds

hangup_timeout: Idle hang-up time in minutes

Config_DB

This setting identifies the location of the Statistics and Events database on the server and defaults to the Notes data directory.

Syntax: Config_DB = <*drive letter* and *directory path*>

Console_Loglevel

This setting applies to workstations and is used to control the level of information displayed on the status bar when you trace a connection. There are five possible values defined as follows:

0 = No information is displayed

1 = Only errors are displayed

2 = Summary progress information is displayed

3 = Detailed progress information is displayed

4 = Full trace information is displayed

The default value for this setting is 2

Syntax: Console_Loglevel = <*value*>

Create_File_Access

This setting applies to servers and is used to specify the users, servers, and groups that can create new databases on the server. Names must be listed in hierarchical format. If you don't specify a name, all certified users can create files. An asterisk (*) represents everyone listed in the Public Address Book. An asterisk followed by a view name represents everyone listed in that view of the Public Address Book. An asterisk followed by a slash (/) and a hierarchical certifier's name represents everyone certified by that certifier.

Syntax: Create_file_Access = <*name/organization/domain*>

Create_Replica_Access

This setting applies to servers and specifies the groups that can create replicas on the server. Names must be listed in hierarchical format. If you don't specify a group, all certified users can create replicas. An asterisk (*) represents everyone listed in the Public Address Book. An asterisk followed by a view name represents everyone listed in that view of the Public Address Book. An asterisk followed by a slash (/) and a hierarchical certifier's name represents everyone certified by that certifier.

Syntax: Create_Replica_Access = <*name/organization/domain*>

CTF

This setting applies to workstations and is used to specify the international import/export character set that Notes will use. By default, this setting is set to L_CPWIN.CLS.

Syntax: CTF = <*filename*>

DDE_Timeout

This setting applies to workstations. This setting is the amount of time (in seconds) Notes waits for another DDE application to respond to a DDE message. By default, this setting is ten seconds.

Syntax: DDE_Timeout = <*time in seconds*>

Default_Index_Lifetime_Days

This setting applies to servers and specifies a default lifetime for view indexes if none was selected by the database designer in the View Properties box. If the index is inactive for the specified number of days, the Indexer server task purges the index. The default value for this setting is forty-five days.

Syntax: Default_Index_Lifetime_Days = <*time in days*>

Deny_Access

This setting applies to servers and specifies the servers, users, and groups that are denied access to the server. Names listed after this setting must be in hierarchical format. An asterisk (*) represents everyone listed in the Public Address Book. An asterisk followed by a view name represents everyone listed in that view of the Public Address Book. An asterisk followed by a slash (/) and a hierarchical certifier's name represents everyone certified by that certifier. The Deny_Access setting overrides the Allow_Access setting.

Syntax: Deny_Access = <*name/organization/domain*>

Deny_Access_[Portname]

This setting applies to servers and specifies the servers, users, and groups that are denied access to a specific server port. The [*Portname*] parameter indicates the name of the port you enabled in the Port Setup dialog box and in the Server document. An asterisk (*) represents everyone listed in the Public Address Book. An asterisk followed by a view name represents everyone listed in that view of the Public Address Book. An asterisk followed by a slash and a hierarchical certifier's name represents everyone certified by that certifier.

Syntax: Deny_Access_[*Portname*] = <*name/organization/domain*>

Desktop

This setting applies to workstations and specifies the location of the DESKTOP.DSK file used to customize the Notes workspace. If this setting does not exist, Notes looks in the Notes data directory.

Syntax: Desktop = <*drive letter* and *path*>

Directory

This setting applies to workstations and specifies the Notes data directory's location. The default for this setting is set during the Notes installation and is usually C:\NOTES\DATA, unless you specify another directory during the Install program.

Syntax: Directory = <*path*>

Domain

This setting applies to workstations and servers. This setting defines the domain for a server. On a workstation, it specifies the domain of the user's mail server. The default for this setting is whatever was set during the Notes setup program.

Syntax: Domain = <*name*>

DST

This setting applies to workstations and servers. This setting specifies whether daylight savings time is observed; by default, it is. There are two available values defined as follows:

0 = Do not observe daylight savings time

1 = Observe daylight savings time

Syntax: DST = <*value*>

DSTlaw

This setting applies to workstations and servers. This setting specifies when daylight savings time (DST) is observed. By default, Notes defines the DST period as beginning the first Sunday in April and ending the last Sunday in October (DSTlaw = 4,1,1,10, -1,1).

If you need to change the range of time when daylight saving is observed, you can set the starting month, week, and day. Then set the ending month, week, and day where the months are 1 (January) through 12 (December); weeks are 1 through 4; days are 1 (Sunday) through 7 (Saturday).

Syntax: DSTlaw = <*begin month*, *week*, *day*, *ending month*, *week*, *day*>

DST_Begin_Date

This setting applies to servers and identifies the date when daylight savings time will begin, specified in dd/mm/year format.

Syntax: DST_Begin_Date = <*date*>

DST_End_Date

This setting applies to servers and identifies the date when daylight savings time will end, specified in dd/mm/year format.

Syntax: DST_End_Date = <*date*>

EditExpnumber

This setting applies to workstations and is used for file exports done at the document level. There are five possible values to include with this setting and they are defined as follows:

value1: Program name and file type

value2: The following append options:

0 = No append option offered

1 = Append option offered through a dialog box

2 = Automatically write to a temporary file to avoid the 64K limit

value3: Name of the export routine called

value4: Not currently used

value5: One or more file extensions used to automatically select a file type in the File Export dialog box

Syntax: EditExp = <*value1*, *value2*, *value3*, *value4*, *value5*, …>

EditImp

This setting applies to workstations and is used for file imports done at the document level. There are five possible values to include with this setting and they are defined as following:

value1: Program name and version

value2: Not used, always 0

value3: Name of the import routine called

value4: Not currently used

value5: One or more file extensions used to automatically select a file type in the File Import dialog box

Syntax: EditImp = <*value1*, *value2*, *value3*, *value4*, *value5*, ..>

EmptyTrash

This setting applies to workstations and specifies when and how the Trash folder will be purged of documents marked for deletion. The default value is 0. This value and the other two possible values are defined as follows:

0 = Prompt the user before closing the database

1 = Always empty the Trash folder before closing the database

2 = Empty the Trash folder manually

Syntax: EmptyTrash = <*value*>

ExtMgr_AddIns

This setting applies to servers and defines the list of add-in files for the Extension Manager. Notes reads this variable on initialization and then appends a platform-identifying suffix character to each name. Notes will then attempt to load the add-in library.

Syntax: ExtMgr_Addins = <*suffix1*, *suffix2*, *suffix3*, …>

FileDlgDirectory

This setting applies to servers and specifies the default directory for all file searches.

Syntax: FileDlgDirectory = <*drive letter* and *directory path*>

Fixup_Tasks

This setting applies to servers and, by default, is twice the number of CPUs on the system. The setting specifies the maximum number of fixup tasks, described in Chapter 6, that are created at server startup.

Syntax: Fixup_Tasks = <*value*>

FTV_Fields_[database]

This setting applies to both workstations and servers and specifies the numeric and date fields in a specific database that are full-text indexed. The database is defined where [*database*] appears. The path statement that follows this .INI setting is the complete path to a text file that defines the indexed numeric and date fields. The text filename must match the database name and have the extension DTS. The text file can be in the Notes directory or subdirectories or outside of the Notes directory; if it's in the Notes directory tree, you still must specify the complete path.

Syntax: FTV_Fields[*database name*] = <*complete path to index file*>

FTV_Max_Fields

This setting applies to workstations and servers. The setting specifies the number of numeric and date fields that are full-text indexed in each database on a server.

Syntax: FTV_Max_Fields = <*value*>

FT_Intl_Settings

This setting applies to workstations and imposes several limitations on full-text functionality to allow Notes to work properly with the Japanese language. When enabled (set to 1), this setting turns off stemming, makes all full-text indexes case-sensitive, and ignores the setting for the stop word file.

Syntax: FT_Intl_Settings = <*value*>

FT_Max_Instances

This setting applies to servers with a default of 100,000 words for a document that is full-text indexed. This settings specifies a maximum size (in words) of a database document that can be full-text indexed. Increase this setting to allow the Indexer server task to use more memory while indexing, especially when the server contains large databases. The amount of memory required for the Indexer is approximately ten times the number of words specified.

Syntax: FT_Max_Instances = <*value*>

KeyFilename

This setting applies to workstations and servers and specifies the location of the Server ID or the User ID file.

Syntax: KeyFileName = <*drive letter*, *path*, and *filename*>

KillProcess

This setting applies to partitioned servers only. The setting enables or disables the shutdown procedure that cleans up all processes related to a partitioned server in the event of an unplanned server shutdown. In order to perform the cleanup, the setting KillProcess = 1 must be set in the server's NOTES.INI file before the first process begins. The available values are defined below:

0 = Disables shutdown procedure

1 = Enables shutdown procedure

Syntax: KillProcess = <*value*>

KitType

This setting applies to workstations and servers and specifies whether Notes initializes a workstation or server setup. The available values are defined below:

1 = Workstation

2 = Server

Syntax: KitType = <*value*>

LAN[number]

This setting applies to workstations and servers and specifies information about the network ports. The LAN number starts at zero and increases by one for each port you have enabled.

Syntax: LAN[*number*] = <*port driver*, *unit ID*, *not used*, *buffer size*>

Location

This setting applies to workstations and identifies the user's current location as selected from the available locations defined in a user's Personal Address book (Office, Internet, Island, and so on).

Syntax: Location = <*location name*>

Log

This setting applies to servers and specifies the contents of the Notes Log and controls other logging actions. This setting has five different values, which are defined below:

logfilename: The Notes Log database filename, usually LOG.NSF

log_option:

1 = Log to the console

2 = Force database fixup when opening the Notes Log

4 = Full document scan

not_used: Always set to zero; this parameter is not currently used

days: The number of days to retain log documents

size: The size of log text in event documents

Syntax: Log = <*logfilename*, *log_option*, *not_used*, *days*, *size*>

The default setting for this .INI entry is show below:

Log=LOG.NSF,1,0,7,40000

Log_AgentManager

This setting applies to servers and specifies whether the start of an agent execution is recorded in the Notes Log and shown on the server console. There are two possible values defined as follows:

0 = Do not log agent execution events

1 = Log agent execution events

Syntax: Log_AgentManager = <*value*>

Log_MailRouting

This setting applies to servers; it specifies the level of information that you want to record in the Notes Log and controls other logging actions. The values for this setting are entered in increments of ten, and the default is 20. The possible values are defined as follows:

0 = Defaults to 20

10 = Displays only the errors, warning, and major routing events. For example, startup and shutdown, number of messages transferred to *x*, and occurrences of database compacting are displayed. Successful deliveries and transfers are not recorded in the Notes Log

20 = Same as for 10, except that successful deliveries and transfers are also logged

30 = Displays thread information

40 = Displays transfer messages, message queues, and full document information for MAIL.BOX

Syntax: Log_MailRouting = <*value*>

Log_Replication

This setting applies to servers. It specifies whether the start and end of replication sessions are recorded in the Notes Log and displayed on the console. There are six possible values defined as follows:

0 = Do not log replication events

1 = Log server replication events

2 = Log replication activity at the database level

3 = Log replication activity at the level of database elements (views, document, and so on)

4 = Log replication activity at the field level

5 = Log summary information

Syntax: Log_Replication = <*value*>

Log_Sessions

This setting applies to servers and is used to specify whether individual sessions are recorded in the Notes Log and displayed on the console. There are two possible values defined as follows:

0 = Do not log individual sessions

1 = Log individual sessions

Syntax: Log_Sessions = <*value*>

Log_Tasks

This setting applies to servers and specifies whether the current status of server tasks is recorded in the Notes Log and displayed on the console. There are two possible values defined as follows:

0 = Do not send status information

1 = Send the status of server tasks to the Notes Log and to the console

Syntax: Log_Tasks = <*value*>

Log_Update

This setting applies to servers and specifies the level of detail of Indexer events displayed at the server console and in the Notes Log. There are three possible values defined as follows:

0 = Records when the Indexer starts and shuts down

1 = Records when the Indexer starts and shuts down, and when the Indexer updates views and full-text indexes for specific databases

2 = Records when the Indexer starts and shuts down, and when the Indexer updates views and full-text indexes for specific databases. This value also records the names of views the Indexer is updating

Syntax: Log_Update = <*value*>

Log_View_Events

This setting applies to servers and is used to specify whether messages generated when views are rebuilt are recorded in the Notes Log. There are two possible values defined as follows:

0 = Do not log messages when views are rebuilt

1 = Log messages when views are rebuilt

If you remove this setting from the NOTES.INI file, logging of these messages is disabled

Syntax: Log_View_Events = <*value*>

MailClusterFailover

This setting applies to cluster servers and is used to enable or disable Mail Router request failover. If users have replicas of mail files located on multiple servers, you can set this variable in the NOTES.INI file of all Notes Release 4.*x* servers in the domain to enable users to receive mail from servers within and outside the cluster when their home servers are down. There are two possible values defined as follows:

0 = Disables Mail Router request failover

1 = Enables Mail Router request failover

Syntax: MailClusterFailover = <*value*>

MailCompactDisabled

This setting applies to servers and either enables or disables the routine compacting of the server's MAIL.BOX. Without this setting in the NOTES.INI file, MAIL.BOX is compacted routinely when the Compact server task runs. There are two available values defined as follows:

0 = Enables compacting of MAIL.BOX

1 = Disables compacting of MAIL.BOX

Syntax: MailCompactDisabled = <*value*>

MailDisablePriority

This setting applies to servers and when set to 1, it causes the Mail Router to ignore the delivery priority of mail messages set by the messages' senders. All messages are then delivered with normal priority. If this parameter is set to 0, which is the default setting, mail routes are determined according to the sender's parameter.

0 = The sender determines the delivery priority

1 = Delivers all mail messages with normal priority

Syntax: MailDisablePriority = <*value*>

MailDynamicCostReset

This setting applies to servers and has a default of 60. This setting determines the Mail Router's dynamic cost reset interval (in minutes). The dynamic cost reset interval allows the Mail Router to use the original least-cost route again after a server comes online.

Syntax: MailDynamicCostReset = <*time in minutes*>

MailEncryptIncoming

This setting applies to servers and is used to force encryption of all incoming mail received by all users of a mail server. This setting uses one of the following two values defined below:

0 = Does not force encryption

1 = Forces encryption

Syntax: MailEncryptIncoming = <*value*>

MailLowPriorityTime

This setting applies to servers and determines the time period when low-priority mail gets routed. A range must be entered using the twenty-four–hour format, not a single time. If you specify a single time, Notes won't deliver low-priority mail.

Syntax: MailLowPriorityTime = <*start time-end time*>

MailMaxThreads

This setting applies to servers, except servers running on a UNIX platform. This setting determines the maximum number of concurrent processes that the Mail Router can create to perform its mail transfers efficiently.

Use this setting in conjunction with the NOTES.INI Log_MailRouting setting, which shows detailed thread information.

Syntax: MailMaxThreads = *<value>*

MailServer

This setting applies to workstations and servers and specifies the server where the user's mail file resides.

Syntax: MailServer = *<server name>*

MailSystem

This setting applies to workstations and servers. It identifies the mail system that the user selected during the workstation setup procedure. The two available values are the following:

0 = Notes mail

1 = cc:Mail or a non-Lotus mail system

Syntax: MailSystem = *<value>*

MailTimeout

This setting applies to servers and specifies the number of days after which the Notes server returns undelivered mail to the sender. To specify a timeout period of less than one day, use the NOTES.INI MailTimeoutMinutes setting.

Syntax: MailTimeout = *<time in days>*

MailTimeoutMinutes

This setting applies to servers and specifies the number of minutes after which the Notes server returns undelivered mail to the sender. The maximum number of minutes is 1440 (twenty-four hours). To specify a timeout greater than a day, use the NOTES.INI MailTimeout setting.

Syntax: MailTimeoutMinutes = *<time in minutes>*

Mail_Log_To_MiscEvents

This setting applies to workstations and servers. It determines whether all mail event messages are displayed in the Miscellaneous Events view of the Notes Log. The two possible values for this setting are defined as follows:

0 = Does not display mail events in the Miscellaneous Events view

1 = Displays mail events in the Miscellaneous Events view

Syntax: Mail_Log_To_MiscEvents = <*value*>

Map_Retry_Delay

This setting applies to servers and is used to specify the number of minutes that a server waits after an unsuccessful attempt to call another server before it tries again.

Syntax: Map_Retry_Delay = <*time in minutes*>

Memory_Quota

This setting applies to workstations and servers and is for OS/2 machines only. This setting specifies the maximum number of megabytes of virtual memory that Notes is permitted to allocate. This setting allows more control over the growth of the swap file. The minimum value is 4MB. Without this setting in the NOTES.INI file, Notes uses all available memory.

Syntax: Memory_Quota = <*size in MB*>

ModemFileDirectory

This setting applies to workstations and specifies the path for the modem files. By default, the modem subdirectory in the Notes directory, as defined during the Notes Setup procedure, is used for this setting. Unless you changed the modem file directory, you don't need to change this file.

Syntax: ModemFileDirectory = <*drive letter and path*>

Names

This setting applies to servers and is used to specify the names of the secondary Public Address Books that Notes searches to verify recipient names in mail messages. By default, Notes searches only the primary Public Address Book, which is always named NAMES.NSF.

Use this NOTES.INI setting to list additional address books for the server to search when verifying a recipient's name in a mail message. The server stops searching as soon as it finds a match in one of the databases. The filenames can be up to 256 characters. Separate the list of address books with commas and do not specify the NSF file extension.

Syntax: Names = <list of address books>

Name_Change_Expiration_Days

This setting applies to servers and defaults to twenty-one days. This setting is used to specify the number of days that the Administration Process waits before deleting obsolete Change Requests. The acceptable range of values is fourteen to sixty days. A Change Request is issued when a user is renamed by the Administration Process. If a user does not accept the name change within the period specified by this setting, the Administration Process deletes the contents of the Change Request field from the user's Person document. However, the Administration Process does not purge the associated Rename request from the Administration Requests database (ADMIN4.NSF).

Syntax: Name_Change_Expiration_Days = <*number of days*>

NewMailInterval

This setting applies to workstations and determines how often (in minutes) Notes checks the user's inbox for new mail. The default is set to 1.

Syntax: NewMailInterval = <*time in minutes*>

NewMailTune

This setting applies to workstations and specifies the tune that plays when mail arrives. The file specified must be a sound file, usually a .WAV file.

Syntax: NewMailTune = <*drive letter*, *path*, and *filename*>

NoDesignMenu

This setting applies to workstations and is used to hide the Design menu.

0 = Shows the Design menu

1 = Hides the Design menu

Syntax: NoDesignMenu = <*value*>

NoExternalApps

This setting applies to workstations and protects against "mail bomb" viruses by disabling the following workstation features:

- OLE, DDE, DIP, @Command
- @DBLookup, @DB Column (when using non-Notes drivers)
- @MailSend, @DDExxx
- Launching file attachments
- Subscribe on a Macintosh workstation

Use the following values to set this variable:

0 = Enables the workstation features listed above

1 = Disables the workstation features listed above

Syntax: NoExternalApps = <*value*>

NoMailMenu

This setting applies to workstations and is used to hide the Mail menu. Hiding the menu with this setting also sets the user's mail system to None.

0 = Shows the Mail menu

1 = Hides the Mail menu

Syntax: NoMailMenu = <*value*>

No_Force_Activity_Logging

This setting applies to servers and is used to control whether the Statlog task automatically enables activity logging on all databases. You turn this feature on or off with one of the following values:

0 = Allows automatic activity logging on all databases

1 = Prevents automatic activity logging on all databases

Syntax: No_Force_Activity_Logging = <*value*>

Even when activity is not being recorded for the database, the information is still recorded in the Activity entry of the Database Usage view in the server's Notes Log.

NSF_Buffer_Pool_Size

This setting applies to workstations and servers and specifies the maximum size (in bytes) of the NSF buffer pool, which is a section of memory dedicated to buffering I/O transfers between the .NIF indexing functions and disk storage.

The maximum value you can set depends on your operating system. For Macintosh and Windows 3.1*x*, the maximum size is 16MB. All other operating systems can be set to a maximum of 256MB.

Syntax: NSF_Buffer_Pool_Size = <*size in MB*>

NSF_DbCache_Disable

This setting applies to servers and either enables or disables the database cache on a server. Acceptable values for this setting are defined as follows (by default, this setting is enabled):

0 = Enables the database cache

1 = Disables the database cache

Syntax: NSF_DbCache_Disable = <*value*>

NSF_DbCache_Maxentries

This setting applies to servers and determines the number of databases that a server can hold in its database cache at one time. Increasing the database cache size can improve system performance but requires additional memory. The minimum number of databases allowed in the cache at one time is twenty-five; the maximum is approximately 2000, depending on the server platform.

Syntax: NSF_DbCache_Maxentries = <*number of databases*>

OS2DDE_[Command]

This setting applies to workstations and should not be changed unless instructed by Lotus. This setting is a family of NOTES.INI settings that contain instructions to control the opening and closing of application files during dynamic data exchange (DDE) under OS/2. This allows for DDE between different environments and products.

Syntax: OS2_DDE_[*Command*] = <*value*>

Passthru_Hangup_Delay

This setting applies to servers and determines how long a passthru server maintains a dial-up connection after its last dial-up session ends. The value for this setting is set in seconds and defaults to 120 if no other value is set.

Syntax: Passthru_Hangup_Delay = <*time in seconds*>

Passthru_Loglevel

This setting applies to workstations and servers and defaults to 0, which means no information is recorded. This settings specifies the level of trace information recorded for all network connections (including passthru) in the Miscellaneous Events view of the Notes Log. The five possible values you can set are defined as follows:

0 = No information is recorded

1 = Only errors are recorded

2 = Summary progress information is recorded

3 = Detailed progress information is recorded

4 = Full trace information is recorded

Syntax: Passthru_Loglevel = <*value*>

PhoneLog

This setting applies to workstations and servers and defaults to 2. This setting specifies whether phone calls are recorded in the Notes Log and can be set to three possible values defined as follows:

0 = Does not record phone calls to the Notes Log

1 = Records all calls, except those that fail because of a busy signal

2 = Records all phone calls

Syntax: PhoneLog = <*value*>

POP3Domain

This setting applies to servers and specifies a TCP/IP Internet domain for a Notes POP3 server that is different than the Internet domain of the Notes server on which the POP3 server runs.

Syntax: POP3Domain = <*Internet domain*>

POP3Port

This setting applies to servers and is used to change the TCP/IP port that a Notes POP3 server uses to connect to POP3 clients. Specify a value for this setting if you want to use a non-standard port when Secure Sockets Layer (SSL) is enabled on a Notes POP3 server. Without this setting, a Notes POP3 server will use TCP/IP port 110.

Syntax: POP3Port = <*TCP/IP port number*>

POP3_Enable_SSL

This setting applies to servers and lets you use Secure Sockets Layer (SSL) on a Notes POP3 server to encrypt data transferred between the server and POP3 clients. There are two possible settings defined as follows:

0 = Do not use SSL

1 = Use SSL

Syntax: POP3_Enable_SSL = <*value*>

Ports

This setting applies to workstations and servers. The setting indicates which ports are enabled for the server or workstation.

Syntax: Ports = <*port name*>

ProgramMode

This setting applies to workstations and defaults to 0 for Full Notes. This setting determines which Notes desktop license type the user has. The three possible settings are defined as follows:

0 = Full Notes

1 = Notes Mail

8 = Desktop

Syntax: ProgramMode = <*value*>

ReplicationTimeLimit

This setting applies to servers and specifies a time limit (in minutes) for replication between one server and another. If this setting is not included in the NOTES.INI file, there is no time limit.

Syntax: ReplicationTimeLimit = <*time in minutes*>

Replicators

This setting applies to servers and specifies the number of Replicator tasks that can run concurrently on the server. The default value is 1.

Syntax: Replicators = <*value*>

Repl_Error_Tolerance

This setting applies to servers and defaults to 2. This setting is used to specify the number of replication errors of the same type that can occur between two databases before the server terminates replication.

Syntax: Repl_Error_Tolerance = <*value*>

Repl_Push_Retries

This setting has no default and applies to servers and specifies the number of times that you attempt to replicate (push) to a Notes Release 3 destination server. When you get the message "Database is currently being replicated or copied elsewhere," use this setting to make sure the replication occurs. The default retry wait period of thirty seconds cannot be changed.

Syntax: Repl_Push_Retries = <*value*>

ReportUseMail

This setting applies to servers and, by default, is set to 0, which means statistic reports are sent to another server via the network. You can also modify this setting to enable the Reporter server task to use the Mail Router to send statistics to another server in the same domain. The two values that direct the statistics route are the following:

0 = Use the network

1 = Use the Mail Router

Syntax: ReportUseMail = <*value*>

RTR_Cached_Handle_Disable

This setting applies to cluster servers and, by default, is enabled. It enables or disables the caching of open databases in a cluster. Enable or disable this setting with one of the following two options:

0 = Enables caching of open databases

1 = Disables caching of open databases

Syntax: RTR_Cached_Handle_Disable = <*value*>

RTR_Logging

This setting applies to cluster servers and enables or disables monitoring of Cluster Replicator activity. There are two possible values defined as follows:

0 = Disables monitoring of the Cluster Replicator

1 = Enables monitoring of the Cluster Replicator

Syntax: RTR_Logging = <*value*>

SecureMail

This setting applies to workstations and you can modify its value to force the Notes Mail program to sign and encrypt all mail sent from the workstation. The two possible values are defined as follows:

0 = Enables the Sign and Encrypt options

1 = Removes the Sign and Encrypt options from all dialog boxes

Syntax: SecureMail = <*value*>

ServerKeyFileName

This setting applies to servers, except NetWare-based Notes servers, and specifies the Server ID file to use on a machine that runs both the Notes workstation program and the Notes server program. Edit the NOTES.INI KeyFileName setting to specify your User ID as the ID to use when you run the Notes workstation or API programs on the server machine.

Syntax: ServerKeyFileName = *<ID filename>*

ServerName

This setting applies to servers and specifies its full hierarchical name.

Syntax: ServerName = *<name>*

ServerNoReplRequests

This setting applies to servers and forces them to refuse all replication requests from other servers. When it is enabled, to replicate with a server, the requesting server must perform Pull-Push replication. There are two possible values defined as follows:

0 = Accepts replication requests from other servers

1 = Refuses replication requests from other servers

Syntax: ServerNoReplRequests = *<value>*

ServerPullReplication

This setting applies to servers and specifies that all scheduled replication initiated from a server must be Pull-Push replication. The two possible values are defined as follows:

0 = Scheduled replication occurs normally (Push-Pull replication is not forced)

1 = This server pulls changes from other servers, but other servers cannot pull changes from this server

Syntax: ServerPullReplication = *<value>*

This setting affects only scheduled replication.

ServerPushReplication

This setting applies to servers and specifies that all scheduled replication initiated from a server must be Push-Pull replication. There are two possible values defined as follows:

0 = Scheduled replication occurs normally (Push-Pull replication is not forced)

1 = Other servers pull changes from this server, but this server cannot pull changes from other servers

Syntax: ServerPushReplication = <*value*>

ServerSetup

This setting applies to servers and identifies the server's operating system. The following numeric values represent the specified operating system and are incremented by one each time you install a point release:

1 = NetWare

2 = Windows

3 = OS/2

Syntax: ServerSetup = <*value*>

ServerTasks

This setting applies to servers and specifies the tasks that begin automatically at server startup and continue until the server is shut down. By default, the Replica, Router, Update, Stats, AMgr, Adminp, Sched, and CalConn tasks are listed after this setting. If you've installed the advanced server license, Billing, Cldbdir, and Clrepl are also listed.

Syntax: ServerTasks = <*tasks*>

ServerTasksAt[Time]

This setting applies to servers and can be used to schedule automatic server and database maintenance functions. Replace [*Time*] with a twenty-four–hour format value, where 0 is 12 AM (midnight), 23 is 11 PM, and so on. Three default entries for this setting are listed below. The time for these defaults can be changed or removed completely. If the time value is removed, the default time, which is 1 AM, is used:

- ServerTasksAt1 = Catalog, Design
- ServerTasksAt2 = Updall, Object Collect mailobj.nsf
- ServerTasksAt5 = Statlog

Syntax: ServerTasksAt[*Time*] = <*task*>

Server_Availability_Threshold

This setting applies to cluster servers and specifies the acceptable level of system resources available to a server. When you set this value for each server in a cluster, you determine how the workload is distributed among the cluster's members. Valid values are from 0 to 100, where the server availability ranges from fully available to BUSY. Notes compares this value against a server's availability index; when the availability index falls below the Server_Availability_Threshold value, the server becomes BUSY. When the server is BUSY, the Cluster Manager tries to redirect user requests to more available cluster members.

0 = Indicates a fully available state and workload balancing is disabled

100 = Indicates the server is BUSY

Syntax: Server_Availability_Threshold = <*value*>

Server_Cluster_Default_Port

This setting applies to a cluster server and specifies the port used for intra-cluster network traffic.

Syntax: Server_Cluster_Default_Port = <*value*>

Server_Console_Password

This setting applies to servers and before the encrypted password can be written to this setting in the NOTES.INI file, you must use the Set Configuration Server command to specify the password.

The password can be a combination of letters and numbers. When this setting is added to the NOTES.INI file, Notes activates the Set Secure command to secure the server console. The password provided should be different from the administrator's user password. If you forget the console password, delete this setting from the NOTES.INI file, and then specify another password.

Syntax: Server_Console_Password = <*encrypted password*>

Server_MaxSessions

This setting applies to servers and specifies the maximum number of sessions that can run concurrently on the server. To prevent server overload, decrease this number if you set up multiple Replicators or Mail Routers.

Syntax: Server_MaxSessions = <*value*>

Server_MaxUsers

This setting applies to servers and sets the maximum number of users that are allowed to access the server. When this number is reached, the server state becomes MAXUSERS, and the server stops accepting new Database Open requests. There are two options for this setting defined as follows:

0 = Unlimited access to server by users

n = Restricts number of active users to the number (*n*) you specify

Syntax: Server_MaxUsers = <*value*>

Server_Restricted

This setting applies to servers and enables or disables access to the server as determined by one of the following three values:

0 = Server access is unrestricted

1 = Server access is restricted for the current server session. Restarting the server clears the setting

2 = Server access is restricted persistently, even after the server restarts

Syntax: Server_Restricted = <*value*>

If access is disabled, the server does not accept new Open Database requests.

Server_Session_Timeout

This setting applies to servers and defaults to four hours on all network operating systems except for NetWare, where the default is thirty minutes. This setting specifies the number of minutes of inactivity after which the Notes server automatically terminates network and mobile connections. The recommended minimum setting is fifteen minutes. If, however, you specify a short time, the server must reopen database server sessions too frequently, which slows server performance. For mobile connections, XPC has its own internal timeout. If the XPC timeout value is shorter than the Server_Session_Timeout value, the XPC timeout takes precedence.

Syntax: Server_Session_Timeout = <*value in minutes*>

Server_Show_Performance

This setting applies to servers and specifies whether server performance events are displayed on the server console. There are two possible values defined as follows:

0 = Records server performance events in the Notes Log

1 = Displays server performance events on console

Syntax: Server_Show_Performance = <*value*>

Setup

This setting applies to workstations and servers. The setting identifies the version number of the Notes software. The setting is used by the Notes Install program to determine whether or not to run the Setup program. This variable also provides an upgrade audit.

Syntax: Setup = <*revision number*>

Shared_Mail

This setting applies to servers and specifies whether the shared mail feature is used for new mail delivered to this server. The three available values are defined as follows:

0 = The shared mail feature is not used for new mail

1 = The shared mail feature is used for new mail delivered to this server

2 = The shared mail feature is used for new mail delivered to this server and for new mail transferred through this server

Syntax: Shared_Mail = *<value>*

SwapPath

This setting applies to servers and specifies the location of the server's swap file. If this setting exists in the NOTES.INI file, the Reporter or Collector server task uses this location for the Server.Path.Swap statistic.

Syntax: SwapPath = <drive letter and directory path>

TCPIP_PortMapping*NN*

This setting applies only to partitioned servers using TCP/IP port mapping. This setting specifies the TCP/IP port number for each partitioned server sharing the IP address of the port mapper server. This entry is only valid in the NOTES.INI file of the port mapper server. *NN* is any number from 00 to 99. However, 00 to 04 are currently the only port numbers supported. These port numbers must be assigned in ascending order. If there is a break in the number sequence, subsequent port numbers entered in the NOTES.INI file are ignored. TCPIP is the name of the TCP port that is specified in the NOTES.INI file by the settings Ports=*TCPIP*.

Syntax: TCPIP_PortMappingNN=CN= *<servername>* /O= *<organization>*,*<IPaddress>*:*<TCP/IP portnumber>*

For example:

- TCPIP_PortMapping00=CN=ServerOne/O=Domain,204.55.10.169:13520

- TCPIP_PortMapping01=CN=ServerTwo/ O=Domain,204.55.10.169:13521

The last number is the port number assigned to each partitioned server. This number must be an available number as specified in Assigned Numbers RFC 1340. In this example, TCPIP is the name of the TCP port.

TCPIP_TCPIPAddress

This setting applies only to partitioned servers using TCP/IP. This setting defines the IP address and port number for a Notes server.

Syntax: TCPIP_TCPIPAddress = 0, <*IP address*>:<*TPC/IP port number*>

TimeZone

This setting applies to workstations and server and specifies the time zone for that machine. Time zones begin at Greenwich, England (0 = Greenwich Mean Time) and move westward around the world. They can be 15, 30, 45, or 60 minutes apart (not all zones are an hour apart).

Syntax: TimeZone = <*value*>

Updaters

This setting applies to servers and specifies the number of Update server tasks that can run concurrently on the server. If this setting is omitted from the NOTES.INI file, only a single Update task can run at a time.

1 = One update can run

2 = Two update tasks can run concurrently

n = *n* update tasks can run concurrently

Syntax: Updates = <*value*>

Update_No_BRP_Files

This setting applies to servers and determines whether the Fixup server task creates BRP files. Setting the value to 1 will cause the Fixup server task not to create a BRP file when it encounters an error in a view index.

1 = Disables the creation of BRP files

No value = BRP files are created when an error is encountered in a view index

Syntax: Update_No_BRP_Files = <*value*>

Update_Suppression_Limit

This setting applies to servers and overrides the NOTES.INI Update_Suppression_Time setting if the specified number of duplicate requests to update indexes and views are received.

Syntax: Update_Suppression_Limit = <*value*>

Update_Suppression_Time

This setting applies to servers and the default setting is 5. This setting specifies the delay of time, in minutes, between full-text index and view updates, even if immediate indexing is scheduled as a server task.

Syntax: Update_Suppression_Time = <*value in minutes*>

UseFontMapper

By default, this setting is enabled and applies to servers and workstations. This setting determines whether the font mapper is used to guess the closest mappings between the font face name in a CGM metafile and the currently installed fonts on a Notes workstation.

0 = Disables the font mapper

1 = Enables the font mapper

Syntax: UseFontMapper = <*value*>

ViewExpnumber

This setting applies to workstations and servers and specifies the parameters to be used by file exports done at the view level.

value1: Program name and file type

value2: The following append options:

0 = No append option offered

1 = Append option offered through a dialog box

2 = Automatically write to a temporary file to avoid the 64K limit

value3: Name of the export routine called

value4: Not currently used

value5: One or more file extensions used to automatically select a file type in the File Export dialog box

Syntax: ViewExpnumber = <*value1*>, <*value2*>, <*value3*>, <*value4*>, <*value5*>

ViewImpnumber

This setting applies to workstations and servers and specifies the parameters to be used by file imports done at the view level.

value1: Program name and version

value2: Not used, always 0

value3: Name of the import routine called

value4: Not currently used

value5: One or more file extensions used to automatically select a file type in the File Import dialog box

Syntax: ViewImpnumber = <*value1*>, <*value2*>, <*value3*>, <*value4*>, <*value5*>

Window_Title

This setting applies to servers and workstations and is used to replace "Lotus Notes" on the title bar.

Syntax: WindowTitle = <*text string*>

WinInfoboxPos

This setting applies to workstations and determines the position of an InfoBox. The default values are 85 and 193.

Syntax: WinInfoboxPos = <*value1*>, <*value2*>

XPC_Console

This setting applies to servers and workstations running Windows 95 and Windows NT. A setting of 1 will display the XPC console, which shows modem input and output (if logged).

0 = Hides the console

1 = Displays the console

Syntax: XPC_Console = <*value*>

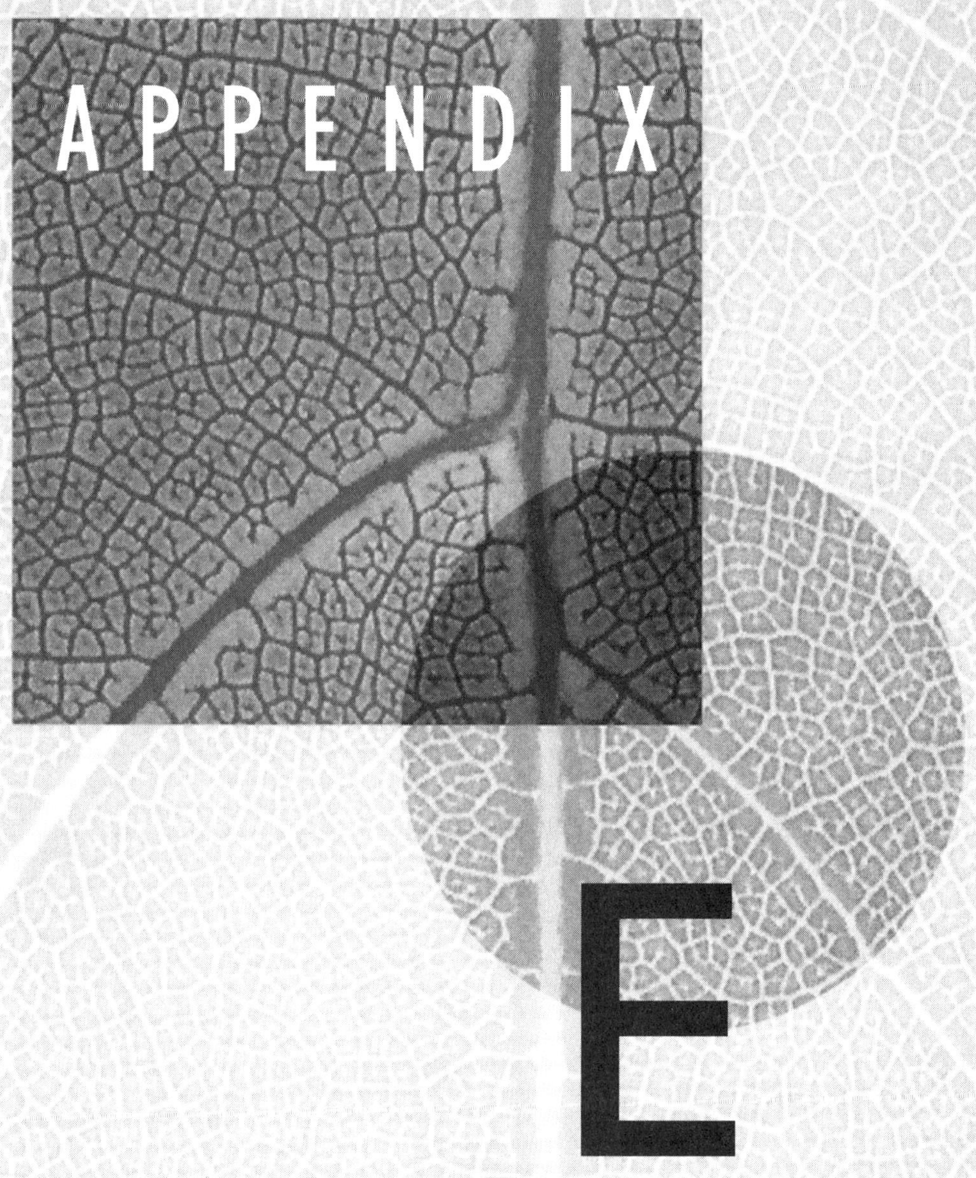

APPENDIX E

Notes Add-On Products

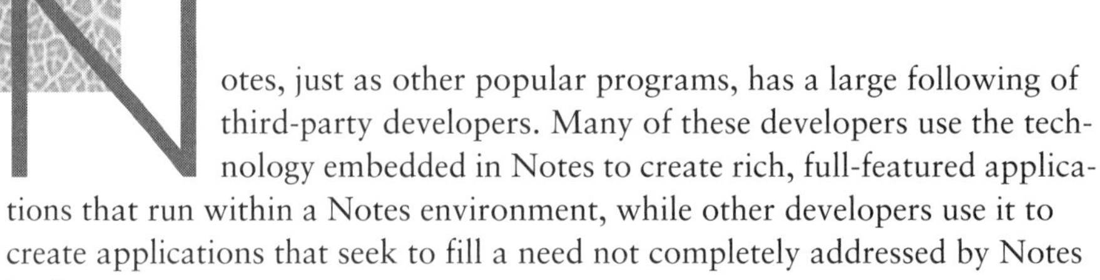

Notes, just as other popular programs, has a large following of third-party developers. Many of these developers use the technology embedded in Notes to create rich, full-featured applications that run within a Notes environment, while other developers use it to create applications that seek to fill a need not completely addressed by Notes itself.

Lotus relies on, and encourages, the third-party development community to further extend the capabilities of Notes. Support from third-party developers not only benefits the developer, but also extends the reach of Notes beyond what Lotus marketing can do on its own.

While most third-party development seems to target the Notes developer, there are still several exciting and powerful products that can help the Notes administrator. Some of these products are administrative tools while others help enhance your Notes environment by adding additional value. This appendix provides a list of some of my favorite third-party products as well as some of the more well known products.

ReCor Network-Based Training Solutions

The people at ReCor have developed a series of network-based computer training courses. The ReCor program offers several different training courses that you can make available to your user community over your Local Area Network. Users don't need to have Notes installed to benefit from ReCor's program, which allows you to train people before you start rolling out Notes.

ReCor doesn't try to position their product as a replacement to formalized classroom training, but rather as a complement to it. People can use the

ReCor courses to review material they previously learned or assess their level of knowledge with the online exercises.

I like this product because it is an excellent tool when performing a Notes Release 3 to Release 4 migration. In such situations, people already know how to use Notes, they just need additional training to introduce them to the new version. ReCor does an excellent job in these situations.

If you would like to contact ReCor for more information, they can be reached at:

ReCor

1-800-424-8700

E-mail: recor@nwu.edu

Web: `www.recor-corp.com`

Registration/Exchange

Registration/Exchange from Qxcom, Inc. helps automate ID registration tasks such as ID requests, verification, certification, password creation/ encryption, and archival. This product is intended to improve accuracy, increase productivity, and provide better security controls for the Notes administrator.

You can find out more about Registration/Exchange by contacting Qxcom, Inc. at:

Qxcom, Inc.

Phone: 818-991-8700

E-mail: sales@qx.com

Web: `www.qx.xom`

Remark! MessageCenter

Extend the accessibility of Notes Mail using the telephone. Remark! MessageCenter from Big Sky Technology reads a Notes text message to a caller and enables that person to respond instantly with a voice message. Aside from responding to messages with voice, messages can be faxed from your Notes mailbox to a fax machine anywhere. You can also have the MessageCenter send pager messages even if you know only the extension or last name of a MessageCenter user.

To contact Big Sky Technologies to learn more about Remark! MessageCenter, use the following contact information:

Big Sky Technologies

Phone: 800-REM-ARK1

Fax: 619-712-2310

E-mail: info@bigskytech.com

Web: `www.bigskytech.com`

Lotus Notes Fax Server

The Notes Fax Server enables Fax-based communication by allowing Notes users to send faxes the same way they send a Notes Mail message. Users are not restricted to Notes when sending faxes and can send them from any Windows-based application. Aside from sending faxes, the Fax Server can handle incoming faxes and route a fax automatically to a recipient's Notes mail database.

For more information about the Notes FaxServer, contact the Lotus Development Corporation at:

Lotus Development Corporation

Phone: 617-577-8500

Fax: 617-225-8097

Web: `www.lotus.com/imaging`

DocWatch

DocWatch from Sentor Communications provides a high level of security, auditing, and statistics for your Notes databases. DocWatch delivers real-time alerts for database changes and illegal copies. Full auditing trails that go down to the field level are also possible with DocWatch, as are detailed statistic reports describing document usage.

Sentor Communications can be reached at:

Sentor Communications

Phone: +61-2-9391-0544

Fax: +61-2-9391-0540

E-mail: productsales@sentor.com.au

Web: www.sentor.com.au

IntelliWatch

Formerly known as CleverWatch from CleverSoft, IntelliWatch from Candle is a family of products that help you deliver a high level of availability insurance for your Notes user community. IntelliWatch includes IntelliWatch Monitor which helps detect impending problems and automatically corrects them. Also included is IntelliWatch Analyzer which helps collect and analyze important server management data.

IntelliWatch is one of my all time favorite Notes administrative add-ons. Best of all, you can try IntelliWatch before you buy it by visiting their Web site and downloading a free thirty day trail copy of IntelliWatch.

You can find out more about IntelliWatch by contacting Candle at:

Candle (formerly CleverSoft)

Phone: 888-NOT-ES99

Fax: 603-433-2229

E-mail: prodinfo@cleversoft.com

Web: www.cleversoft.com

RemoteWare Essentials

This product helps reduce Notes replication time by up to eighty percent. Regardless of how many remote and mobile users you have using Lotus Notes, RemoteWare Essentials from XcelleNet can easily and quickly make your remote and mobile user's connection time less than it is today.

XcelleNet can be reached at:

XcelleNet

Phone: 800-322-3366

E-mail: info@xcellenet.com

Web: `www.xcellenet.com`

V-Bridge NT for Notes

V-Bridge NT for Notes by Computer Mail Services, Inc. is an e-mail gateway connecting Lotus Notes to Banyan VINES, which enables the exchange of messages and attachments between these two platforms.

To find out more about V-Bridge NT for Notes, contact Computer Mail Services, Inc. at:

Computer Mail Services, Inc.

Phone: 810-352-6700

E-mail: info@cmsconnect.com

Web: `www.cmsconnect.com`

Open File Manager

Open File Manager is not a Notes product but rather a backup software enhancement product. This product allows your backup system to capture open files in a transactionally complete state. Even if changes are made during the backup, your backup will contain a complete copy of your file. Open File Manager removes the need to shut down your Notes server to back up critical files such as the Public Address book (NAMES.NSF), and the shared mail database (MAILOBJ.NSF), if you implemented shared mail. Files such as these always remain open while the Notes server is running and consequently are skipped by most backup programs on the market today.

To find out more about Open File Manager, contact Saint Bernard Software at:

Saint Bernard Software

Phone: 1-800-782-3762 or 619-676-2277

E-mail: info@stbern.mhs.compuserve.com (for general sales information)

Web: `www.stbernard.com`

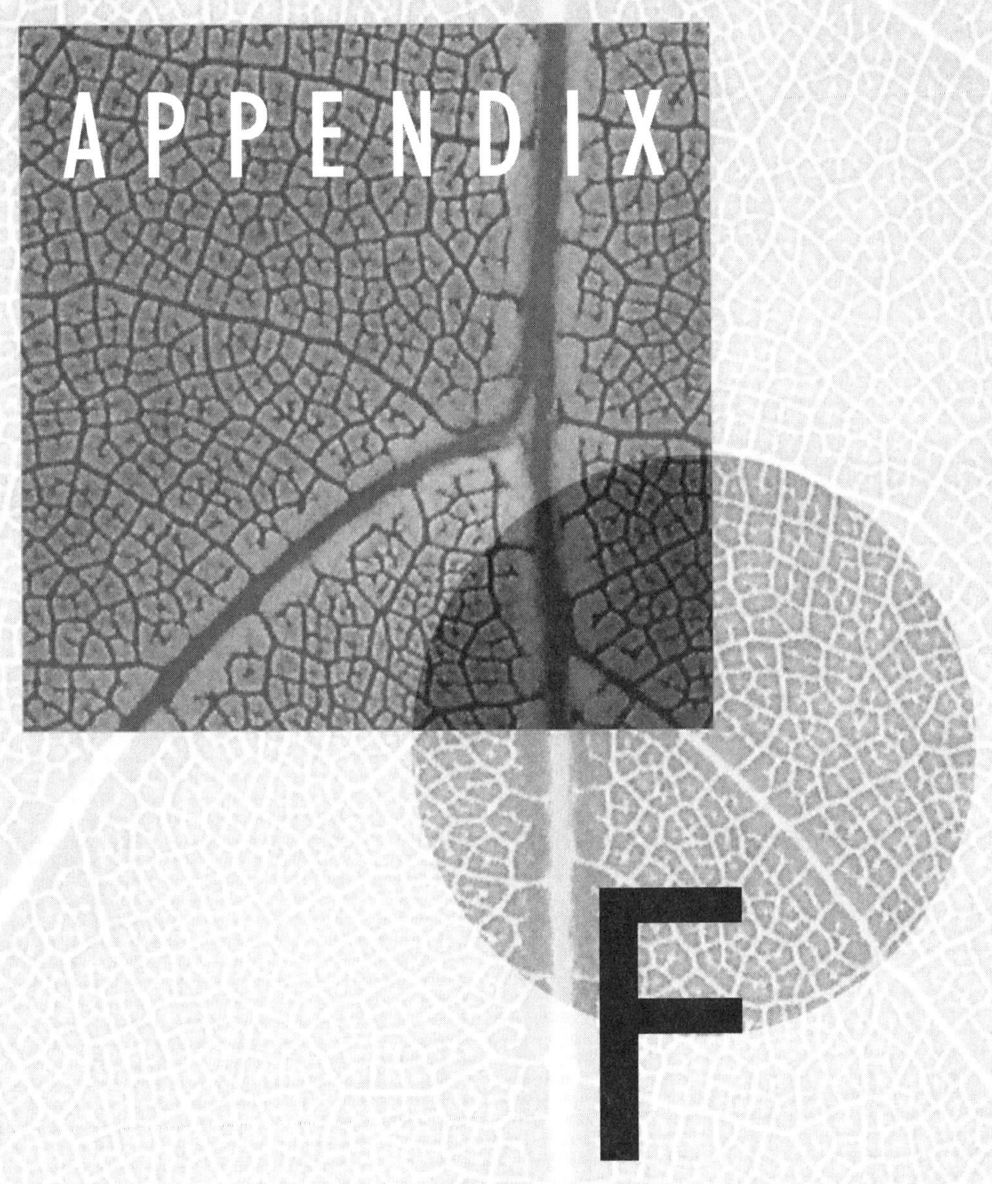

Administrator's Resource Guide

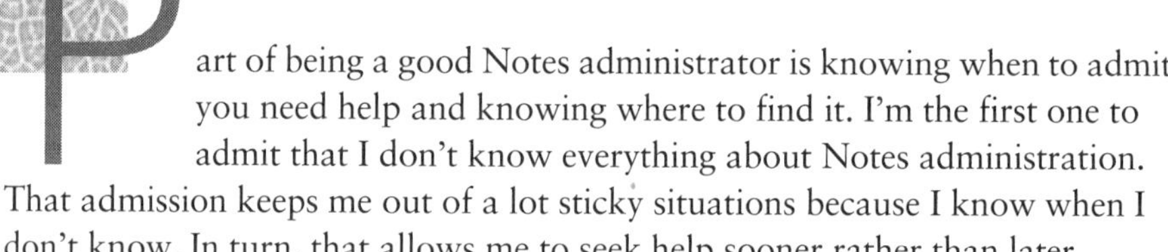

Part of being a good Notes administrator is knowing when to admit you need help and knowing where to find it. I'm the first one to admit that I don't know everything about Notes administration. That admission keeps me out of a lot sticky situations because I know when I don't know. In turn, that allows me to seek help sooner rather than later.

Fortunately, when you need help there are a number of places you can turn to get it; and that's what this appendix is all about.

Getting Help from Lotus

Before the debut of the World Wide Web and CompuServe technical forums, phone support was often the only way to get help. Most people have tried phone support at one time or another and personally know what it can be like. Calling for support can end in a wide range of results. Anything from fantastic, timely information to useless, confusing suggestions is possible. As for Lotus' phone support, unfortunately (or maybe fortunately for me) I haven't had to call it in nearly three years, so I can't tell you what to expect.

When you first purchase Notes, you should receive a time-limited support contract. However, remember, everyone purchasing Notes gets this support so it may not be a good indication of the actual support you receive when you purchase unlimited support. I suggest you use this support a couple of times. If your results are positive and you want an unlimited support contract, call Lotus at 1-800-553-4270 for more information about their support offerings. You can also visit the support Web site for more details at `http://www.support.lotus.com`.

Whether you like Lotus' phone support or not, you should try to at least get a subscription to the Lotus Notes KnowledgeBase. This KnowledgeBase is an invaluable informational resource for a Notes administrator or Notes developer. The latest technical notes, white papers, and product information is in this KnowledgeBase. It comes in the form of a Notes database and is received on CD-ROM or replicated via Notes Net. For more information about this resource, contact Lotus.

Information on the Web

There are several World Wide Web sites for Notes-related information. Here are few of my favorites:

- **`http://www.lotus.com`**: This corporate home page provides easy to follow links to a variety of Notes-related information. I make a habit of visiting this site whenever I can to read the latest information on Notes and other Lotus products.
- **`http://www.support.lotus.com`**: Another great Lotus Web page to visit is their support page. From this page, you can directly access the Lotus Notes KnowledgeBase, which has a wealth of technical information about Notes. The KnowledgeBase contains technical notes, white papers, and general product information—a must have for all Notes administrators. Aside from the KnowledgeBase, the support page has links to up-to-date product support information, downloadable files, and user-to-user discussions. These discussions are a great way to quickly learn from what others have already done and to find answers to problems of your own.
- **`http://domino.lotus.com`**: This page has all of the latest Domino information available. You can download the latest version of Domino, read the Domino FAQs (frequently asked questions), download Domino templates such as the mail and registration templates, and follow ongoing discussions from people actively using Domino.
- **`http://204.166.182.22`**: If you're interested primarily in the Lotus InterNotes Web Publisher, then visit this site. You'll find links to downloadable user guides, tips and techniques, Web Publisher samples, and other items of interest.

- **http://www.notes.net**: Here is a great link if you want to download the latest Notes maintenance release. This Web site makes the latest maintenance release available to all Notes users. The maintenance release is referred to as an "incremental installer." This installer expects the previous version of Notes to be installed already before it will run, so don't think you're going to download a free copy of Notes from this page.
- **http://www.support.lotus.com/css/wwsup.htm**: Lotus' world wide support offerings are accessible through this URL. Direct phone numbers to Lotus' sales and support, as well as other information about Lotus' product support programs can be located on this page.
- **http://www.st.rim.or.jp/~snash/Hotlist.html**: For non-Lotus hosted Web pages take a look at Scott Nash's bookmarks. I'm not sure how frequently these links are updated or even if they'll be around for long. However, I've been stopping by this page off and on for about a year. Scott has assembled a nice variety of links to other Notes related Web pages. Some of these pages are hosted by Lotus, but others are not. You can find links to Notes FAQs and other Internet informational sources from Scott's bookmarks.

All of the previously listed URLs are subject to change without notice. I suggest stopping by these URLs soon and often. Hopefully, this way, you'll be aware of an upcoming page move before it happens.

The Notes List Server

A List Server, for those of you who have never participated in one, is much like an automated group mailing list. Mail sent to the *list address* is redistributed to all *subscribers* of that list. People read the list mailings and sometimes respond directly to the individual or to the list address, depending on which seems appropriate.

The Notes List Server can be very useful. However, you need to read it nearly every day otherwise your e-mail might start overflowing with messages. You'll also need to be patient when waiting to receive an answer if you post a question. To participate in the Notes List Server you first have to subscribe to the list.

Subscribing to the Notes List Server

To subscribe to the Notes List Server send an e-mail message to the following address:

```
listproc@ozzie.lnotes.com
```

In the body of the message enter the following line:

SUBSCRIBE LNOTES-L <*your name*>

If I were subscribing for the first time, I would enter the following line:

SUBSCRIBE LNOTES-L Bret Swedeen

Acceptance to the list usually occurs within one day.

Unsubscribing to the Notes List Server

At some time or another you may want to unsubscribe to the Notes List Server. To do so, send an e-mail message to the following address:

```
listproc@ozzie.lnotes.com
```

In the body of the message enter the following line:

SIGNOFF LNOTES-L

Acknowledgment of your removal usually occurs within one day.

Sending a Message to the Notes List Server

If you've subscribed to the Notes List Server and want to submit a message, send e-mail to the following address:

```
lnotes-l@ozzie.lnotes.com
```

The message is automatically distributed to everyone subscribed to the list. A response could come to you directly or through the mailing list, so make sure you read the list daily.

When sending e-mail to the list, please don't request return receipts or carbon copy back to the list. Doing so can cause a flood of return receipts and duplicate messages.

Other List Server Commands

While subscribing, unsubscribing, and sending a message to a list server are the most important things to know about a list server, there are still a few other useful things you can do.

Temporarily Shutting Off E-Mail Delivery

Since the Notes List Server sends several message every day, your e-mail in-box can easily overflow with messages. Therefore, if you go on vacation or have an extended holiday, you might want to temporarily shut off the Notes List Server while still reserving your place in the queue. To do so, send an e-mail message to the following address:

```
lnotes-l-request@ozzie.lnotes.com
```

In the body of the message enter the following line:

SET NOMAIL

The Notes List Server will temporarily stop sending you e-mail until otherwise instructed. When you're ready to start receiving messages again, send an e-mail message to the same e-mail address. In the body of the message enter the following line:

MAIL

The Notes List Server will then resume sending you e-mail.

Retrieving Messages from a Specific Day

Anytime you want to retrieve all of the messages from a specific day, you can always do so by sending an e-mail message to the following address:

```
listproc@ozzie.lnotes.com
```

In the body of the message enter the following line:

GET LNOTES-L *<yymmdd>*

(With *<yymmdd>* representing the year, month, and date of the day you want to retrieve.)

For example, if I wanted to retrieve all of the messages sent on Christmas day for the year of 1996, I'd enter the following line in the body of the message sent to `listproc@ozzie.lnotes.com`:

GET LNOTES-L 961225

Searching for a Specific Topic

If you want to search the messages on the Notes List Server for a specific topic, send an e-mail to the following address:

`listproc@ozzie.lnotes.com`

Enter the following line in the body of the message where ***<topic>*** is the item you are looking for:

SEARCH LNOTES-L *<topic>*

Notes-Related Usenet Newsgroups

Internet Usenet newsgroups are like CompuServe discussion forums, except they are not nearly as well moderated as the ones found on CompuServe. The good thing about a newsgroup is that it won't send endless amounts of e-mail to your in-box, which is something the Notes List Server has a tendency to do. The real down side to a newsgroup, other than its lack of organization, is the signal-to-noise ratio. There is no way to stop unrelated postings from creeping into the newsgroup discussion thread. It is very common to find postings about "get rich quick" schemes and other annoying information. If you don't mind sifting through the junk, you will find useful information.

A couple of Notes related Newsgroups are:

- `comp.groupware.lotus-notes.misc`
- `comp.groupware.lotus-notes.admin`
- `comp.groupware.lotus-notes.programmer`
- `comp.groupware.lotus-notes.apps`

Notes Information on CompuServe

Even though most people are turning to the Internet these days to search for information and help on any number of topics, CompuServe is still a popular place to visit for technical information. The real benefit to CompuServe these days is its moderated discussion forum.

Unlike an Internet Usenet newsgroup where anything goes, a CompuServe discussion forum is closely monitored. This close monitoring doesn't mean things are censored. It simple means that the inappropriate nonsense and unrelated material is kept out while the technical stuff is keep in. Each visit to a CompuServe forum is well worth the time.

To find the latest Notes-related forums and information on CompuServe type **GO LOTUS** at the Go prompt from your CompuServe software.

Notes-Specific Books

If you learn well from just reading a book then you're in luck, because there are quite a few Notes-specific books on the market today. I've not personally reviewed many of these books, but I can recommend at least two that I have found very useful.

- *Mastering Lotus Notes 4* (Sybex, 1996). This book is aimed primarily at Notes development. Even if you're a Notes administrator you still need to know some development and this book has really come in handy for me.
- *Lotus Notes 4 Administrator's Survival Guide* by Andrew Dahl (Sams, 1996). A competitor to this book, however, an excellent book worth owning. A lot of higher level topics are addressed in this book which makes it a good choice for IS (Information Systems) managers.

There are several other books on the market. Check out your local book store for other Notes-related titles.

Notes-Specific Magazines

I used to be a magazine nut. At one time I had nearly ten computer-related magazines coming to my house, not to mention the half dozen I had arriving at work. I have since reduced my magazine consumption to one subscription and the rest I buy in an ad hoc manner, which makes my wife much happier.

Magazines are a great way to get additional technical information about Lotus Notes. You can find everything from quick, helpful tips to very focused and deep technical articles. There are three primary Notes magazines on the market today and they range from affordable to expensive.

- *The Notes Report*: I've only seen one issue of this magazine so I can only comment that it looked nice. It's approximately $295 a year. For subscription information call (617) 482-8634.
- *The View*: I've read this magazine from time to time. The articles are well written and very informative. People directly from Lotus can often be found writing in this magazine. It's approximately $295 a year. For subscription information call (800) 810-1800.
- *The Lotus Notes Advisor*: This is my favorite magazine for three reasons. First, they gave me my start in the world of freelance technical writing. Second, I'm a contributing writer for this magazine. And finally, I honestly believe they have the widest assortment of Notes articles from very experienced Notes professionals. It's approximately $45 a year. For subscription information call (800) 336-6060 or (619) 483-9851.

Aside from these magazines you'll occasionally find a Notes-related article in some of the network-specific magazines such as *LAN Magazine* and *Network World,* so keep your eyes open.

Index

Note to the Reader: First level entries are in **bold**. Page numbers in **bold** indicate the principal discussion of a topic or the definition of a term. Page numbers in *italic* indicate illustrations.

Symbols

@ (at sign) in Notes Mail addresses, 349

A

Access Control Lists (ACLs), 173–176, 216, 239–259, 262–264. *See also* security
- access control levels, 173–174, 239–241, 298–299
- Access Control List dialog box
  - Advanced section, 247–251, *248*
  - Basics section, 241–244, *241*
  - Log section, 246–247, *247*
  - overview of, 77, 115, 175–176, *175*, 241, *241*
  - Roles section, 244–246, *246*, 249–250
- access roles
  - overview of, **249–250**
  - for Public Address Book, 262–264
- database replication and
  - controlling replication, **298–300**
  - troubleshooting replication problems, 316, 317–318, *318*
- database settings, 173–176, *175*, *176*, 216
- Domino server settings, **454–455**, *455*
- user types and, 245
- Web Retriever database settings, 426–427, *426*

ActionPaneEnabled NOTES.INI setting, 512

adapter failures, 95–96

adding icons for Notes clients to the desktop, 151–152

Additional Server Setup dialog box, 90–92

add-on products, 552–557. *See also* applications; utilities
- DocWatch program, 555
- IntelliWatch program, 555
- Notes Fax Server software, 554
- Open File Manager program, 557
- ReCor network-based computer training courses, 40, 552–553
- Registration/Exchange program, 553
- Remark! MessageCenter program, 554
- RemoteWare Essentials software, 556
- V-Bridge NT for Notes software, 556

addresses, Mail addresses, 349

Admin NOTES.INI setting, 512

Admin_Access NOTES.INI setting, 513

administration, 5–7. *See also* Certified Lotus Professional (CLP) program; Lotus Notes servers

Administration document of Web Retriever database, creating, 427–428, *428*

Administration Process, 112–118. *See also* Lotus Notes servers
- assigning administrative servers to Public Address Book, 113–114
- configuring Notes servers for, 114–115
- console commands for, 117–118
- creating Certification Logs, 78–79
- defined, **112–113**
- monitoring, 115–116
- settings, 116–117, *117*

Administration Requests database (ADMIN4.NSF), 112

administration resources, 560–567
- books, 566
- on CompuServe, 566
- Lotus technical support, 560–561
- magazines, 567
- Notes List Server, **562–565**
  - overview of, 562

retrieving messages from a specific day, *564–565*
searching for a specific topic, *565*
sending messages to, *563*
subscribing to, *563*
temporarily shutting off, *564*
unsubscribing to, *563*
Usenet newsgroups, *565*
on the World Wide Web, 561–562
AdminPInterval NOTES.INI setting, 512
AdminPModifyPersonDocumentsAt NOTES.INI setting, 512
Advanced Calendar Options section, Calendar Profile documents, 382–383, *382*
Advanced options, Replication Settings dialog box, 303–305, *304*
Advanced section, Access Control List dialog box, 247–251, *248*
Advanced Server Setup Options dialog box, 74–77, *74*, 92, *92*
Agent Manager, 118–121. *See also* Lotus Notes servers
defined, **118–119**
limiting agent access on Notes servers, 119–121
Allow Other Users to View Your Calendar option, Calendar Profile documents, 384
Allow_Access NOTES.INI setting, 513
Allow_Access_[Portname] NOTES.INI setting, 513
Allow_Passthru_Access NOTES.INI setting, 513
Allow_Passthru_Callers NOTES.INI setting, 514
Allow_Passthru_Clients NOTES.INI setting, 514
Allow_Passthru_Targets NOTES.INI setting, 514
AMgr_DisableMailLookup NOTES.INI setting, 514
AMgr_DocUpdateAgentMinInterval NOTES.INI setting, 515
AMgr_DocUpdateEventDelay NOTES.INI setting, 515
AMgr_NewMailEventDelay NOTES.INI setting, 515
AMgr_WeekendDays NOTES.INI setting, 515
Anniversaries. *See also* calendaring and scheduling
creating, 400, 409, *409*
defined, **392**, *392*
anonymous access option for Domino server, 468, *468*
AppleTalkNameServer NOTES.INI setting, 516
Application Developer certification, 479
applications
add-on products, **552–557**
DocWatch program, 555
IntelliWatch program, 555
Notes Fax Server software, 554
Open File Manager program, 557
ReCor network-based computer training courses, 40, 552–553
Registration/Exchange program, 553
Remark! MessageCenter program, 554
RemoteWare Essentials software, 556
V-Bridge NT for Notes software, 556
Notes applications
application development, 2–3
defined, **4**
migrating from Notes Release 3 to 4, 65–66
Appointments. *See also* calendaring and scheduling
creating, 400, 405–407, *406*
defined, **388–389**, *389*
ASCII text logs for Domino server, 473
assigning administrative servers to Public Address Book, 113–114
at sign (@) in Notes Mail addresses, 349
Attach command, File menu, 401
authentication, 224–226
Author database access level, 173, 240
autoaddressing feature in Public Address Book, 402–403
AutoLogoffMinutes NOTES.INI setting, 516
Autoprocessing Options section, Calendar Profile documents, 382–383, *382*

B

backing up Notes servers, 79, 94–95
Basics section
Access Control List dialog box, 241–244, *241*
Location document, 439–440, *440*
Server document HTTP Server section, 456–458, *456*
Big Sky Technologies Remark! MessageCenter program, *554*
BillingAddinOutput NOTES.INI setting, 516
BillingAddinRuntime NOTES.INI setting, 516

BillingAddinWakeup NOTES.INI setting, 517
BillingClass NOTES.INI setting, 517
BillingSuppressTime NOTES.INI setting, 517
board failures, 95–96
bookmarks, importing from Netscape Navigator or Internet Explorer, 448
books about Lotus Notes, 566
broadcasting meeting Invitations, 405
browsers. *See* Lotus Notes Web Navigator
business purpose definition for Notes networks, 15–17
BUSYTIME.NSF database, 373–374

C

calendaring and scheduling, 2, 372–416
- Anniversaries
  - creating, 400, 409, *409*
  - defined, **392**, *392*
- Appointments
  - creating, 400, 405–407, *406*
  - defined, **388–389**, *389*
- basic features, **388–395**
- BUSYTIME.NSF database, 373–374
- Calendar Connector (CALCONN.EXE), 373–374, *374*
- Calendar Entry form
  - for Anniversaries, 409, *409*
  - for Appointments, 405–407, *406*
  - for Events, 407, *408*
  - for Invitations, 398–405, *399*
  - Not for Public Viewing option, 401, 407
  - Pencil In option, 400, 406, 409, 412
  - for Reminders, 407, *408*
- Calendar Profile documents, **379–383**
  - Advanced Calendar Options section, 382–383, *382*
  - Allow Other Users to View Your Calendar option, 384
  - Autoprocessing Options section, 382–383, *382*
  - Calendar Entry Options section, *382*, 383
  - defined, **379**, *380*
  - Freetime Options section, 381, *381*
  - Scheduling Options section, 380
- Calendar view
  - navigating, 396–398, *397*, *398*
  - overview of, 387–388, *388*
  - viewing tasks in, 393
- Delegation Profile documents, **384–387**
  - Calendar Access section, 385
  - defined, **384–385**, *384*
  - Email Access section, 385–387, *386*
- determining if calendaring and scheduling is running, 374, *374*
- Events
  - creating, 400, 407, *408*
  - defined, **389–391**, *390*
- Free Time Manager, 373–374, 377, 403–404, *404*
- how calendaring and scheduling works, **373–374**
- Invitations
  - autoaddressing feature, 402–403
  - broadcasting, 405
  - creating, **398–405**, *399*
  - defined, **389**, *390*
  - Free Time Manager and, 403–404, *404*
  - not responding to, 414, *414*
  - reserving rooms for meetings, 405, 415
  - responding to, 410–413, *410*, *411*, *413*
  - sending meeting confirmations to invitees, 414, *414*
  - troubleshooting, **415**
- Invitee Responses dialog box, 412, *413*
- Meetings view, **395**, *395*
- overview of, 2, 372–373, 395–396, 416
- Reminders
  - creating, 400, 407, *408*
  - defined, **391**, *391*
- Schedule Manager (SCHED.EXE), 373–374, *374*
- setting up, **375–378**
  - changing or deleting resources, 378
  - creating reservations, 377–378
  - creating Resource Reservations database, 375–376, *376*
  - creating resources, 377
  - creating Site Profiles, 376–377

setting up for users, **379–387**
creating Calendar Profile documents, 379–383, *380*
creating Delegation Profile documents, 384–387, *384*
training users to configure their own profiles, 387
To Do view and tasks
defined, **392–393**, *393*, *394*
viewing tasks in Calendar view, 393
troubleshooting, **415**
Candle IntelliWatch program, 555
card failures, 95–96
CBT (Computer Based Training) for Certified Lotus Professional program, 480–481
cc:Mail Mail Transfer Agents (MTAs), 356
Certificate Authorities (CAs), 470
CertificateExpChecked NOTES.INI setting, 518
Certification Logs, creating, 78–79
Certified Lotus Professional (CLP) program, 476–485. *See also* training
benefits of certification, 482
certification options and examinations, **477–485**
certification preparation, **480–481**
CLP Application Developer, 479
CLP Principal Application Developer, 479
CLP Principal System Administrator, 479
CLP System Administrator, 479
Computer Based Training (CBT), 480–481
Lotus Authorized Education Centers, 480–481
overview of, 477–478
recertification for Notes 3 professionals, **482–485**
self-study programs, 480–481
Sylvan Prometric Testing Centers and, 481–482
taking examinations, **481–482**, 483–484
Lotus Business Partners and, 482
overview of, 476–477
telephone numbers, 485
World Wide Web site, 485
Certifier documents, 488, *488*
certifier IDs
CertifierIDFile NOTES.INI setting, 518
and creating organizational unit certifiers, 84–86
Secure Sockets Layer (SSL) protocol and, 472
in user registration, 128–129, *128*
changing resources for calendaring and scheduling, 378
Character Set Mapping subsection, Server document HTTP Server section, *460*, 463
child documents in databases, 205–206
Choose Registration Server dialog box, 128
CleverSoft CleverWatch program, 555
clients. *See* Lotus Notes clients
CLP. *See* Certified Lotus Professional
clusters of Notes servers, 97
Collaborations Options section, Internet Options profile, 437, *437*
commands. *See* console commands
communications. *See* Lotus Notes communications
COM[number] NOTES.INI setting, 518–519
compacting databases, 208–209, 216
CompuServe Lotus Notes resources, 566
Computer Based Training (CBT) for Certified Lotus Professional program, 480–481
Computer Mail Services V-Bridge NT for Notes software, 556
Config_DB NOTES.INI setting, 519
configuring. *See also* installing; NOTES.INI file; setting up
Domino server, 455–463
Notes clients for Notes networks, 150–151, *151*
Notes servers for Administration Process, 114–115
Statistics Reporting, 111–112
conflicts, replication conflicts and save conflicts, 274–275, *275*
console commands, 498–506
for Administration Process, 117–118
entering, **498–503**
from Notes clients, 498–501, *499*, *500*
from the server console, 501–503, *502*
listed, **503–506**
Load HTTP, 463
Load Object Collect, 364, 365
Load Object Create, 363
Load Object Set -Never, 363
Load Object Unlink, 365
Load Replica, 297, *298*

Load Web, 425, *425*
Remote Server Console screen, 198, *198*, **498–501**, *499*, *500*
Show Time, 374, *374*
Tell Router Exit, 326
Tell Router Use, 361, 364
troubleshooting replication problems, 317–318, *318*
Updall, 214–215

Console_Loglevel NOTES.INI setting, 519

controlling
port access, 232
replication, **298–307**
Access Control Lists and, 298–300
controlling content of replica copies, 307
disabling replication to prevent disasters, 306–307
in multiprotocol environments, 306
with Replication Settings dialog box, 300–305, *301*, *302*, *304*, *305*
replication settings scenarios, 305–307
server access, **223–232**
controlling port access, 232
controlling with Server Document fields, 226–232, *227*, *230*
forcing password changes, 231
physical security, 224
validation and authentication, 224–226

Copy Database dialog box, 169, *169*, 170, *170*, 210, *210*

copying databases to Notes servers, 167–170, *168*, *169*

corrupted databases, repairing, 211–215, *214*

crashes, 94–95

Create Attachment dialog box, 401–402, *401*

Create Self-Certified Key Ring dialog box, 471–472, *472*

Create_File_Access NOTES.INI setting, 519

Create_Replica_Access NOTES.INI setting, 520

creating
Anniversaries, 400, 409, *409*
Appointments, 400, 405–407, *406*
Certification Logs, 78–79
current environment inventory for Notes 3 to 4 migration, 47
Database Catalogs, 183–184, *184*
Events, 400, 407, *408*
Events Monitoring documents, 104–108, *108*
full text indexes, 188–192, *190*
hierarchical naming schemes, 25–26
Mail-In Database documents, 182–183, *183*
meeting Invitations, 398–405, *399*
multiple users from a file, **135–147**. *See also* creating, users one at a time
creating user information files, 136–138
information you will need, 135–136
registering users from a file, 140–145, *140*
selecting mail type, 143–144
selecting passwords, license type, and user profiles, 143
selecting registration server, 141
storing user ID files, 144
user information file examples, 138–140
verifying user setup, 145–146, *146*, *147*
Notes 3 to 4 migration plan, 50
Notes 3 to 4 migration team, 47–48
Notes infrastructure, 39–40
Notes roll-out plans, **37–42**
allocating time for the roll-out, 37–38
creating Notes infrastructure, 39–40
determining who gets Notes first, 40
selecting a Notes feature to focus on, 41
supporting the infrastructure and users, 41–42
training users, 40–41
Notes standards documents, 24–26
NT accounts with Notes users, 129
organizational unit certifiers, 84–86
Personal Web Navigator database, 433
Reminders, 400, 407, *408*
replica copies of databases, **281–298**, **307**
controlling content of replica copies, 307
enabling multiple replicators, 295–297, *296*, *297*, *298*
initiating workstation-to-server replication, 291–295, *292*, *294*
manually initiating replication, 289–290, *290*, *291*
overview of, 281–282, *282*, *283*

replica copies versus regular copies, 283–284, *284*, *285*
replica IDs, 283–284
scheduling replication with Server Connection document, 285–289, *286*
a replication monitoring routine, 312–313
reservations in calendaring and scheduling, 377–378
Resource Reservations database, 375–376, *376*
resources in calendaring and scheduling, 377
Server Connection documents
for Lotus Notes Mail setup, 337–339, *338*
for routing mail, 344–346
shared mail databases, 363–364
Site Profiles in calendaring and scheduling, 376–377
test environment for Notes 3 to 4 migration, 48–49
users one at a time, **125–135**. *See also* creating, multiple users from a file
canceling user registration, 135
entering passwords, 130–131
information you will need, 125–126
selecting certifier IDs, 128–129
selecting mail type, 132–133, *132*
selecting North American versus international security types, 129
selecting Notes license types, 131
selecting registration server, 128, *128*
selecting user profiles, 132
storing user ID files, 130, 133–134
Web Navigator Administration document, 427–428, *428*
Web Tours, 448
CTF NOTES.INI setting, 520

D

Dahl, Andrew, 566
database logs for Domino server, 473–474, *473*
Database Purge Options section, Internet Options profile, 436–437
Database Quota Information dialog box, 171, *172*
database replication, 268–321. *See also* databases
controlling what gets replicated, **298–307**
Access Control Lists and, 298–300
controlling content of replica copies, 307
disabling replication to prevent disasters, 306–307
in multiprotocol environments, 306
with Replication Settings dialog box, 300–305, *301*, *302*, *304*, *305*
replication settings scenarios, 305–307
creating replica copies of databases, **281–298**, **307**
controlling content of replica copies, 307
enabling multiple replicators, 295–297, *296*, *297*, *298*
initiating workstation-to-server replication, 291–295, *292*, *294*
manually initiating replication, 289–290, *290*, *291*
overview of, 281–282, *282*, *283*
replica copies versus regular copies, 283–284, *284*, *285*
replica IDs, 283–284
scheduling replication with Server Connection document, 285–289, *286*
defined, **268**
deleted documents and, 275–276
field-level replication, 273
monitoring, **307–313**
creating a monitoring routine, 312–313
with Event tasks, 310
with Notes Logs, 308–309
with Replication History dialog box, 311, *311*, *312*
with Reporter tasks, 310
NOTES.INI settings
Create_Replica_Access, 520
Log_Replication, 528
Repl_Error_Tolerance, 539
ReplicationTimeLimit, 539
Replicators, 539
Repl_Push_Retries, 539
ServerNoReplRequests, 541
ServerPullReplication, 541–542
ServerPushReplication, 542
planning, **276–280**
determining which databases to replicate, 276–277

End-to-End replication topology, 279
Hub and Spoke replication topology, 278–279, *278*
Mesh replication topology, 279
Ring replication topology, 279
selecting replication topologies, 280
replica tasks
defined, **268**, *269*
loading, 297, *298*
replicating
database design templates to all servers, 177
databases to all servers, 176–177
replication conflicts and save conflicts, 274–275, *275*
Replication Settings dialog box, **300–307**
Advanced options, 303–305, *304*
Other options, 303, *304*
overview of, 300–301
Public Address Book settings, 55, 56
scenarios, 305–307
Send options, 302–303, *302*
Space Savers options, 301–302, *301*
Replication submenu, File menu
Replicate command, 281
Settings command, 301
Replicator workspace, 292–295, *292*
between servers, **269–272**
Pull Only replication, 271–272, *272*
Pull-Pull replication, 269–270, *269*
Pull-Push replication, 270, *270*
Push Only replication, 271, *271*
troubleshooting, **313–321**
Access Control List problems, 316, 317–318, *318*
console command problems, 317–318, *318*
error messages, 314–315
examples, 315–318, *318*
NOTES.INI replication settings, 318–321
Notes Log problems, 316–317
when replication isn't happening, 313–314
upgrading replica mail database, 65
what gets replicated, **272–274**
between workstations and servers, **272**
Database submenu, File menu
Access Control command, 77, 115, 241, 376
New command, 375
New Copy command, 169, 210
Open command, 168, 196, 210
Properties command, 185, 192–193, 196, 206, 208–209
Refresh Design command, 197
Replace Design command, 62
databases, 65–66, 93–94, 98, 166–219
access control options for Domino server, 469
BUSYTIME.NSF database, 373–374
compacting, **208–209**, 216
deleting, **217–219**
Deletion stubs, **275–276**
disaster planning for database failures, **93–94, 98**
freezing, 218
MAIL.BOX database, **325**
maintaining database integrity, **187–217**
creating full text indexes, 188–192, *190*
deleting full text indexes, 194–195
estimating index size, 191–192
finding missing response documents, 205–206
indexing encrypted fields, 191
managing database size, 208–209, *209*
monitoring database activity, 206–208, *207*
moving databases, 209–211, *210*
overview of, 187–188
repairing corrupted databases, 211–215, *214*
running database analyses, 199–204, *202*, *203*
troubleshooting performance problems, 215–217
updating database designs, 195–199, *198*
updating full text indexes, 192–194, *193*, *194*
migrating from Notes Release 3 to 4, **65–66**
NOTES.INI settings
Config_DB, 519
NSF_Buffer_Pool_Size, 536
NSF_DbCache_Disable, 536
NSF_DbCache_Maxentries, 536
parent and child documents, **205–206**
Properties dialog box
Database section, 185, *185*, 192–193, *193*, 196, 206, *206*, 208–209, *209*
Field section, 258–259, *259*
Folder section, 256–257, *257*, *258*

Form section, 251–254, *252*, *253*, *275*, *275*
Section section, 258
View section, 254–256, *255*
replica copies of
versus regular copies, **283–284**, *284*, *285*
upgrading replica mail database, 65
Resource Reservations database, 375–376, *376*
rolling out, **166–187**
copying new databases to Notes servers, 167–170, *168*, *169*
creating Database Catalogs, 183–184, *184*
creating Mail-In Database documents, 182–183, *183*
distributing encryption keys, 177–182, *178*, *179*, *181*
including databases in Database Catalogs, 183–185, *185*
merging encryption keys with user IDs, 181–182, *182*
notifying users about the new database, 185–186, *187*
overview of, 166–167
replicating database design templates to all servers, 177
replicating databases to all servers, 176–177
setting Access Control Lists (ACLs), 173–176, *175*, *176*, 216
setting maximum database size, 170–173, *170*, *172*
shared mail databases
creating, 363–364
deleting, 365
user mail database, **326**
WEB.NSF database, 425
DDE (Dynamic Data Exchange)
DDE_Timeout NOTES.INI setting, 520
OS2DDE_[Command] NOTES.INI setting, 536–537
dedicated Mail servers, setting up, 336–337
Default_Index_Lifetime_Days NOTES.INI setting, 520
defining business purpose for Notes networks, 15–17
Delegation Profile documents, 384–387. *See also* calendaring and scheduling; profiles
Calendar Access section, 385
defined, **384–385**, *384*
Email Access section, 385–387, *386*
deleted documents, replication and, 275–276
deleting
databases, 217–219
full text indexes, 194–195
resources for calendaring and scheduling, 378
shared mail, 364–365
shared mail databases, 365
users, 161–163
Deletion stubs, 275–276
delivery problems in Notes Mail
overview of, 366–367
sending a trace for delivery problems, 367–370, *368*, *369*
Deny_Access NOTES.INI setting, 520–521
Deny_Access_[Portname] NOTES.INI setting, 521
Depositor database access level, 173, 239–240
Designer database access level, 174, 240
desktop
adding Notes client icons to, 151–152
Desktop NOTES.INI setting, 521
determining
if calendaring and scheduling is running, 374, *374*
which databases to replicate, 276–277
Directory Mapping documents, 466–467, *466*
Directory NOTES.INI setting, 521
disabling
Notes List Server temporarily, 564
replication to prevent disasters, 306–307
disaster planning for Notes servers, 93–98, 306–307
database failures, 93–94
disabling replication to prevent disasters, 306–307
documenting disaster plans, 97–98
double-site synchronization disaster plans, 98
external power failures, 96
hard drive crashes, 94–95
motherboard and other computer card failures, 95–96
Notes clusters, 97
disaster prevention for Notes servers, 98–112
Events Monitoring, **102–108**, **310**
creating Events Monitoring documents, 104–108, *108*

loading Events server task, 103–104
monitoring replication with, 310
versus Notes Logs, 102–103
Notes Logs
database size and, 170
defined, **99–101**, *99*, *101*
versus Events Monitoring, 102–103
monitoring database activity, 207–208
monitoring replication, 308–309
troubleshooting replication problems, 316–317
overview of, 98–99
Statistics Reporting, **109–112**, **310**
configuring statistics reporting, 111–112
loading Report server task, 110
monitoring replication, 310
setting up, 109
disk crashes, 94–95
distributing encryption keys
by e-mail, 177–179, *178*, *179*
by exporting to files, 179–182, *181*
documenting disaster plans, 97–98
documents, 488–495. *See also* Server Connection documents; Server documents
Certifier documents, 488, *488*
creating Events Monitoring documents, 104–108, *108*
database replication and deleted documents, 275–276
Delegation Profile documents, **384–387**
Calendar Access section, 385
defined, **384–385**, *384*
Email Access section, 385–387, *386*
Deletion stubs, **275–276**
Directory Mapping documents, 466–467, *466*
Domain documents, 489–490, *490*
Domino SSL Administration documents, 470–472, *471*
Foreign Domain documents, 354–355, *355*
Group documents, 490, *491*
Location document, for workstation-to-server replication, 291–292
Location documents, **423–424**, **438–442**. *See also* documents; Lotus Notes Web Navigator
Basics section, 439–440, *440*
defined, **491**
Internet Browser and Servers section, 423–424, *424*, 440
Java Applet Security section, 441–442, *442*
overview of, 438, *438*
for workstation-to-server replication, 291–292
Mail-In Database documents, 182–183, *183*, 491, *491*
main documents in databases, **205**
Non-adjacent Domain documents, 349–352, *351*
Person documents, 492, *492*
Program documents, 492, *492*
Resource documents, 492, *492*
response documents in databases, **205–206**
Server Configuration documents, 494, *494*
Server Connection documents, 489, *489*
standards documents
creating, 24–26
and naming servers, 73–74
updating, 67
URL Mapping documents, 466–467, *466*
URL Redirection documents, 466–467, *466*
User Setup Profile documents, 495, *495*
Virtual Server documents, 464–467, *465*
Web Navigator Administration document, **427–432**
creating, 427–428, *428*
HTML Preferences section, 429
Purge Agent Settings section, 430–431
Server Basics section, 428–429
DocWatch program, 555
domains
Domain documents, 489–490, *490*
Domain NOTES.INI setting, 521
routing mail
between adjacent domains, 346–349, *347*, *348*
to foreign domains, 354–357, *355*
between non-adjacent domains, 349–353, *350*, *351*, *353*

Domino server. *See* Lotus Notes Domino server
double-site synchronization disaster plans, 98
drive crashes, 94–95
DST NOTES.INI setting, 522
DST_Begin_Date NOTES.INI setting, 522
DST_End_Date NOTES.INI setting, 522
DSTlaw NOTES.INI setting, 522
Dynamic Data Exchange (DDE)
DDE_Timeout NOTES.INI setting, 520
OS2DDE_[Command] NOTES.INI setting, 536–537

E

ECLs (Execution Control Lists) for workstation security, 232–239, *237*
EditExpnumber NOTES.INI setting, 523
EditImp NOTES.INI setting, 523
editing
NOTES.INI file, 508–511, *509*
Server Connection documents for Lotus Notes Mail setup, 337–339, *338*
Editor database access level, 173, 240
education programs. *See* Certified Lotus Professional (CLP) program
e-mail. *See* Lotus Notes Mail
Email Access section, Delegation Profile documents, 385–387, *386*
EmptyTrash NOTES.INI setting, 524
enabling
multiple replicators, 295–297, *296*, *297*, *298*
shared mail, 361–362
encryption. *See also* security
defined, **264**
encryption keys
distributing by e-mail, 177–179, *179*
distributing by exporting to files, 177, 179–181, *181*
ID files and, 265
merging with user IDs, 181–182, *182*
passwords and, 265
private and public keys, 264–265
indexing encrypted fields in databases, 191
North American versus international encryption, **129**
overview of, **264–265**
RSA Cryptosystem, 264
Simple, Medium, and Strong encryption, **265**
End-to-End network topology. *See also* topologies
defined, **19**, *20*
and setting up Notes Mail, 333–335, *333*, *334*
End-to-End replication topology, 279
end-users. *See* users
entering server console commands, 498–503
from Notes clients, 498–501, *499*, *500*
from the server console, 501–503, *502*
error messages
for database replication, 314–315
for meeting room reservations, 415
estimating index size, 191–192
Events. *See also* calendaring and scheduling
creating, 400, 407, *408*
defined, **389–391**, *390*
Events Monitoring, 102–108. *See also* disaster prevention; Lotus Notes servers
creating Events Monitoring documents, 104–108, *108*
loading Events server task, 103–104
monitoring replication with, 310
versus Notes Logs, 102–103
examinations for Lotus certification. *See* Certified Lotus Professional (CLP) program
Execution Control Lists (ECLs) for workstation security, 232–239, *237*
exporting encryption keys to files, 179–181, *181*
external power failures, 96
ExtMgr_AddIn NOTES.INI setting, 524

F

Fax Server software for Notes, 554
field access control, 258–259, *259*
field-level replication, 273

File menu
Attach command, 401
Database submenu
Access Control command, 77, 115, 241, 376
New command, 375
New Copy command, 169, 210
Open command, 168, 196, 210
Properties command, 185, 192–193, 196, 206, 208–209
Refresh Design command, 197
Replace Design command, 62
Open URL command, 443
Replication submenu
Replicate command, 281
Settings command, 301
Tools submenu
User ID command, 178
User Preferences command, 328
filename extensions
.FT, 191
.NSF, 191
File Replication menu, New Replica command, 167
FileDlgDirectory NOTES.INI setting, 524
finding
information in Personal Web Navigator database, 444–445, *445*
missing database response documents, 205–206
a specific Notes List Server topic, 565
Fixup utility, 212–214, *214*
Fixup_Tasks NOTES.INI setting, 524
folder access control, 256–257, *257, 258*
foreign domains, routing mail to, 354–357, *355*
foreign mail systems, defined, **354**
form access control, 251–254, *252, 253*
forwarding Web pages, 444
Free Time Manager, 373–374, 377, 403–404, *404*
Freetime Options section, Calendar Profile documents, 381, *381*
freezing databases, 218
.FT file extension, 191
FT_Intl_Settings NOTES.INI setting, 525
FT_Max_Instances NOTES.INI setting, 525
FTV_Fields_[database] NOTES.INI setting, 524–525
FTV_Max_Fields NOTES.INI setting, 525
full text indexes, 188–195, 524–525
creating, 188–192, *190*
deleting, 194–195
estimating index size, 191–192
.FT file extension and, 191
indexing encrypted fields in databases, 191
NOTES.INI settings
FT_Intl_Settings, 525
FT_Max_Instances, 525
FTV_Fields_[database], 524–525
FTV_Max_Fields, 525
updating, 192–194, *193, 194*

G

gateways, V-Bridge NT for Notes software, 556
Group documents, 490, *491*
group scheduling. *See* calendaring and scheduling

H

hard disk drive crashes, 94–95
hardware
hardware requirements for Domino server, 454
upgrading for Notes 3 to 4 migration, 47
hierarchical naming schemes
creating, 25–26
moving users in, 156–159
hop counts, 332
hosting multiple Web sites with Domino server, 463–467
HTML documents. *See also* Lotus Notes Web Navigator
HTML Preferences section in Web Navigator Administration document, 429
viewing source code, 445–446
HTTP (Hypertext Transfer Protocol)
HTTP server task, 452, 453
Load HTTP console command, 463
Hub and Spoke network topology
defined, **18–19,** *18, 19, 20*
and setting up Notes Mail, 332–333, *332*
Hub and Spoke replication topology, 278–279, *278*

I

icons, adding Notes client icons to desktop, 151–152
ID files
encryption keys and, 265
merging encryption keys with user IDs, 181–182, *182*
storing in individual user registration, 133–134
storing in multiple user registration, 144
importing bookmarks from Netscape Navigator or Internet Explorer, 448
including databases in Database Catalogs, 183–185, *185*
indexes. *See* full text indexes
infrastructure
creating, 39–40
supporting, 41–42
version migrations and, 46
initiating replication, 285–295. *See also* replication
manually initiating replication, 289–290, *290*, *291*
scheduling replication with Server Connection document, 285–289, *286*
workstation-to-server replication, 291–295, *292*, *294*
installing. *See also* configuring; setting up
additional Notes servers, **87–92**
installing server software, 90
registering new servers, 87–89
server setup, 90–92, *92*
the first Notes server, **70–79**
Advanced Server Setup Options dialog box, 74–77, *74*
creating Certification Logs, 78–79
optional server setup steps, 77–79
Public Address Book settings, 77
server naming guidelines, 73–74
server setup process overview, 70–73
Notes client software, 147–150, 152–153
IntelliWatch program, 555
international encryption type, 129
Internet. *See also* Lotus Notes Domino server; Lotus Notes Web Navigator
Internet enhancements to Notes, 10–11
mail addresses, 349
newsgroups about Lotus Notes, 565
World Wide Web
Certified Lotus Professional program Web site, 485
Lotus Web sites, 561–562
Internet Browser and Servers section, Location document, 423–424, *424*, 440
Internet Explorer. *See also* Lotus Notes Web Navigator
importing bookmarks from, 448
selecting as default browser, 440
versus Web Navigator, 418–419
Internet Options profile, 433–438. *See also* Lotus Notes Web Navigator; profiles
Collaborations Options section, 437, *437*
Database Purge Options section, 436–437
Network Preferences section, 438
Page Minder Agent Preferences section, 435–436, *436*
Presentation Preferences section, 437–438
Search Options section, 435
Setup Options section, 434
Web Ahead Agent Preferences section, 435
InterNotes server, 423–424, *424*
Invitations. *See also* calendaring and scheduling
autoaddressing feature, 402–403
broadcasting, 405
creating, **398–405**, *399*
defined, **389**, *390*
Free Time Manager and, 403–404, *404*
not responding to, 414, *414*
reserving rooms for meetings, 405, 415
responding to, 410–413, *410*, *411*, *413*
sending meeting confirmations to invitees, 414, *414*
troubleshooting, **415**
Invitee Responses dialog box, 412, *413*

J

Java Applet Security section, Location document, 441–442, *442*

K

KeyFilename NOTES.INI setting, 525
KillProcess NOTES.INI setting, 526
KitType NOTES.INI setting, 526

L

LAN[number] NOTES.INI setting, 526
LBPs (Lotus Business Partners), 32–33, 482
licenses
  selecting in individual user registration, 131
  selecting in multiple user registration, 143
limiting agent access on Notes servers, 119–121
List Server for Lotus Notes, 562–565. *See also* administration resources
  overview of, 562
  retrieving messages from a specific day, 564–565
  searching for a specific topic, 565
  sending messages to, 563
  subscribing to, 563
  temporarily shutting off, 564
  unsubscribing to, 563
Load HTTP console command, 463
Load Object Collect console command, 364, 365
Load Object Create console command, 363
Load Object Set -Never console command, 363
Load Object Unlink console command, 365
Load Replica console command, 297, *298*
Load Web console command, 425, *425*
loading
  Events server task, 103–104
  replica tasks, 297, *298*
  Report server task, 110
  Web server task, 425, *425*
Location documents, 423–424, 438–442, 491. *See also* documents; Lotus Notes Web Navigator
  Basics section, 439–440, *440*
  defined, **491**
  Internet Browser and Servers section, 423–424, *424*, 440
  Java Applet Security section, 441–442, *442*
  overview of, 438, *438*
  for workstation-to-server replication, 291–292
Location NOTES.INI setting, 526
logs. *See also* Events Monitoring; monitoring; Notes Logs; Statistics Reporting
  Domino server activity logs, **472–474**
    ASCII text logs, 473
    Notes database logs, 473–474, *473*
    setting up, 472
  Log section in Access Control List dialog box, 246–247, *247*
  Logging subsection in Server document HTTP Server section, *460*, 461–462
  NOTES.INI settings, **527–530**
    Log, 527
    Log_AgentManager, 527
    Log_MailRouting, 527–528
    Log_Replication, 528
    Log_Sessions, 529
    Log_Tasks, 529
    Log_Update, 529
    Log_View_Events, 530
  Notes Logs
    database size and, 170
    defined, **99–101**, *99*, *101*
    versus Events Monitoring, 102–103
    monitoring database activity, 207–208
    monitoring replication, 308–309
    troubleshooting replication problems, 316–317
Lotus Authorized Education Centers, 480–481
Lotus Business Partners (LBPs), 32–33, 482
Lotus certification programs. *See* Certified Lotus Professional (CLP) program
Lotus Notes
  add-on products, **552–557**. *See also* applications; utilities
    DocWatch program, 555
    IntelliWatch program, 555
    Notes Fax Server software, 554
    Open File Manager program, 557

ReCor network-based computer training courses, 40, *552–553*
Registration/Exchange program, *553*
Remark! MessageCenter program, *554*
RemoteWare Essentials software, *556*
V-Bridge NT for Notes software, *556*
administration, **5–7**
books about, **566**
defined, **2–3**
future of, **9–11**
history of, 9–11
Internet enhancements, 10–11
magazines about, **567**
as a multi-user platform, 2–3
new features in Release 4.5, **7–9**
problems with, 9–10
technical support, 560–561
Lotus Notes 3 to 4 migration, 44–67
migration plan implementation, **50–66**
database and application migration, 65–66
mail database migration, 59–65, *65*
migration rehearsal, 51
overview of, 50–51
Public Address Book conversion form, 62–65, *65*
Public Address Book replication settings, 55, 56
Public Address Book upgrades, 53–56
replica mail database upgrades, 65
server migration, 52–56
user training, 57
workstation migration, 57–58
planning, **44–50**
creating a current environment inventory, 47
creating a migration plan, 50
creating a migration team, 47–48
creating a test environment, 48–49
evaluating the new release, 45–47
hardware upgrades and, 47
overview of, 44–45
training technical support organizations, 49
post migration activities, **66–67**
migration team debriefing, 66
updating Notes standards document, 67
Lotus Notes administration, 5–7
Lotus Notes administration resources, 560–567
books, *566*
on CompuServe, *566*
Lotus technical support, *560–561*
magazines, *567*
Notes List Server, **562–565**
overview of, *562*
retrieving messages from a specific day, *564–565*
searching for a specific topic, *565*
sending messages to, *563*
subscribing to, *563*
temporarily shutting off, *564*
unsubscribing to, *563*
Usenet newsgroups, *565*
on the World Wide Web, *561–562*
The Lotus Notes Advisor magazine, *567*
Lotus Notes applications. *See also* add-on products; utilities
application development, 2–3
defined, **4**
migrating from Notes Release 3 to 4, 65–66
Lotus Notes clients. *See also* NOTES.INI file; users; workstation-based Web Navigator setup
defined, **3–4**
entering server console commands from, **498–501**, *499*, *500*
license types, **131**
migrating workstations from Notes Release 3 to 4, **57–58**
Remote Server Console screen, 198, *198*, **498–501**, *499*, *500*
replication between workstations and servers, **272**
selecting client platforms, **34–36**
setting up, **147–153**
adding icons to the desktop, 151–152
configuring Notes clients for Notes networks, 150–151, *151*
installation tips, 152–153
installing Notes client software, 147–150
workstations
Execution Control Lists (ECLs) and workstation security, **232–239**, *237*
migrating from Notes Release 3 to 4, 57–58

Notes license types, 131
replication between servers and, 272
signatures, **234–237**
Lotus Notes communications, 4
Lotus Notes Desktop license, 131
Lotus Notes Domino server, 452–474. *See also* Lotus Notes servers
activity logs, **472–474**
ASCII text logs, 473
Notes database logs, 473–474, *473*
setting up, 472
defined, **452**
Directory Mapping documents and, 466–467, *466*
hosting multiple Web sites, **463–467**
how the Domino server works, **453**
HTTP server task and, 452, 453
overview of, 452–453, 474
running, **463**
security, **467–472**
anonymous access option, 468, *468*
database access control, 469
overview of, 467–468
Secure Sockets Layer (SSL) security, 469–472, *471*, *472*
user registration options, 468–469
Server document HTTP Server section, **455–463**
Basics subsection, 456–458, *456*
Character Set Mapping subsection, *460*, 463
Logging subsection, *460*, 461–462
Mapping subsection, 459–461, *460*
Operational Information subsection, *456*, 458–459
overview of, 455, *456*
Timeouts subsection, *460*, 462
setting up, **454–463**. *See also* Server documents, HTTP Server section
Access Control List settings, 454–455, *455*
configuring, 455–463
system requirements, 454
URL Mapping documents and, 466–467, *466*
URL Redirection documents and, 466–467, *466*
URLs (Uniform Resource Locators) and, 453
Virtual Server documents and, 464–467, *465*
Lotus Notes Fax Server software, *554*
Lotus Notes licenses, 131, 143
Lotus Notes List Server, 562–565
overview of, *562*
retrieving messages from a specific day, *564–565*
searching for a specific topic, *565*
sending messages to, *563*
subscribing to, *563*
temporarily shutting off, *564*
unsubscribing to, *563*
Lotus Notes Mail, 324–370
addresses, 349
components of, **325–326**
creating Mail-In Database documents, 182–183, *183*
distributing encryption keys by e-mail, 177–179, *179*
Email Access section in Delegation Profile documents, **385–387**, *386*
e-mail conversion utility, *59–62*
hop counts, **332**
how mail gets delivered, **326–329**, *327*, *328*
Mail Address dialog box, 326, *328*
Mail administration, 6
MAIL.BOX database, **325**
Mail license, **131**
Mail Router server task, **326**
mail routing, **339–358**
between adjacent domains, 346–349, *347*, *348*
cc:Mail, SMTP, and X.400 Message Transfer Agents, 356
connecting with foreign domains, 354–357, *355*
creating Server Connection documents for, 344–346
multi-threaded mail routing, 357–358
between non-adjacent domains, 349–353, *350*, *351*, *353*
between Notes named networks, 340–346, *342*, *343*
POP3 mail support, 357
within Notes named networks, 339–340, *340*, *341*

mail routing control, **358–361**
  message priority levels, 360–361
  options to prevent mail routing, 359–360
  overview of, 358–359
migrating mail databases from Notes Release 3 to 4, **59–65**
  with mail conversion utility, 59–62
  with Public Address Book forms, 62–65, *65*
moving mail databases to new servers, **159–161**, *160*
NOTES.INI settings
  MailClusterFailover, 530
  MailCompactDisabled, 530
  MailDisablePriority, 531
  MailDynamicCostReset, 531
  MailEncryptIncoming, 531
  Mail_Log_To_MiscEvents, 533
  MailLowPriorityTime, 531
  MailMaxThreads, 532
  Mail_Retry_Delay, 533
  MailServer, 532
  MailSystem, 532
  MailTimeout, 532
  MailTimeoutMinutes, 532
  NewMailInterval, 534
  NewMailTune, 534
  NoMailMenu, 535
  SecureMail, 540
  Shared_Mail, 546
Notes List Server, **562–565**
  overview of, 562
  retrieving messages from a specific day, 564–565
  searching for a specific topic, 565
  sending messages to, 563
  subscribing to, 563
  temporarily shutting off, 564
  unsubscribing to, 563
overview of, **2**, 324
Personal Address Book
  inviting people to meetings with, 402–403
  Location document, 291–292
Public Address Book
  access roles for, 262–264
  assigning administrative servers to, 113–114
  autoaddressing feature, 402–403
  defined, **325**
  inviting people to meetings with, 402–403
  mail database migration using Public Address Book conversion form, 62–65, *65*
  replication settings, 55, 56
  settings for first Notes server installation, 77
  updating design of, 53
  upgrading, 53–56
  upgrading mail databases with Public Address Book forms, 62–65, *65*
selecting mail type
  in individual user registration, 132–133, *132*
  in multiple user registration, 143–144
Server Connection documents
  creating or editing for Notes Mail setup, 337–339, *338*
  creating for mail routing, 344–346
  and mail routing between adjacent domains, 346–349, *347*
  and mail routing between Notes networks, 340–346, *342*
  and mail routing within Notes networks, 339
setting up, **330–339**
  creating or editing Server Connection documents, 337–339, *338*
  dedicated Mail servers, 336–337
  End-to-End topology and, 333–335, *333*, *334*
  Hub and Spoke topology and, 332–333, *332*
  planning and, 335
  in simple versus complex Notes networks, 330–331
shared mail, **361–366**
  creating shared mail databases, 363–364
  deleting mail, 364–365
  deleting shared mail database, 365
  enabling, 361–362
  purging old mail, 364
  security considerations, 362–363
  Shared_Mail NOTES.INI setting, 546
  when to use, 366
troubleshooting mail problems, **366–370**
  delivery problems, 366–367

sending a trace for delivery problems, 367–370, *368*, *369*
upgrading replica mail database, 65
user mail database, **326**
V-Bridge NT for Notes e-mail gateway software, 556

Lotus Notes networks, 14–42
configuring Notes clients for, **150–151**, *151*
creating hierarchical naming schemes, 25–26
creating Notes standards documents, **24–26**
creating a roll-out plan, **37–42**
allocating time for the roll-out, 37–38
creating Notes infrastructure, 39–40
determining who gets Notes first, 40
selecting a Notes feature to focus on, 41
supporting the infrastructure and users, 41–42
training users, 40–41
defining business purpose for, **15–17**
example, 16–17, 23, *24*
LAN[number] NOTES.INI setting, 526
overview of, 14
routing mail, **339–346**
between named networks, 340–346, *342*, *343*
within named networks, 339–340, *340*, *341*
selecting Notes client platforms, **34–36**
selecting Notes server platforms, **26–34**
NetWare NLM, 28
with NotesBench utility, 32–34
OS/2 Warp and Warp Server, 30
overview of, 26
UNIX, 29
Windows 95, 27
Windows NT, 31–32
setting up Notes Mail in simple versus complex Notes networks, **330–331**
topologies, **17–24**
End-to-End (or peer-to-peer) topologies, 19, *20*, 333–335, *333*, *334*
example, 23, *24*
Hub and Spoke topologies, 18–19, *18*, *19*, *20*, 332–333, *332*
importance of, 22–23
Mesh topologies, 21–22, *22*
overview of, 17–18
Ring topologies, 21, *21*

Lotus Notes servers, 4–5, 26–34, 52–56, 70–121. *See also* Lotus Notes Domino server; NOTES.INI file; Server Connection documents; Server documents
Administration Process, **112–118**
assigning administrative servers to Public Address Book, 113–114
configuring Notes servers for, 114–115
console commands for, 117–118
creating Certification Logs, 78–79
defined, **112–113**
monitoring, 115–116
settings, 116–117, *117*
Agent Manager, **118–121**
defined, **118–119**
limiting agent access on Notes servers, 119–121
backing up, **79**, **94–95**
copying databases to, **167–170**, *168*, *169*
creating organizational unit certifiers, **84–86**
dedicated Mail server setup, **336–337**
defined, **4–5**
disaster planning, **93–98**, **306–307**
database failures, 93–94
disabling replication to prevent disasters, 306–307
documenting disaster plans, 97–98
double-site synchronization disaster plans, 98
external power failures, 96
hard drive crashes, 94–95
motherboard and other computer card failures, 95–96
Notes clusters, 97
disaster prevention, **98–112**
Events Monitoring, 102–108
Notes Logs, 99–101, *99*, *101*, 170, 207–208
overview of, 98–99
Statistics Reporting, 109–112
Events Monitoring, **102–108**
creating Events Monitoring documents, 104–108, *108*
loading Events server task, 103–104
monitoring replication with, 310

versus Notes Logs, 102–103
installing additional servers, **87–92**
installing server software, 90
registering new servers, 87–89
server setup, 90–92, *92*
installing the first server, **70–79**
Advanced Server Setup Options dialog box, 74–77, *74*, 92, *92*
creating Certification Logs, 78–79
optional server setup steps, 77–79
Public Address Book settings, 77
server naming guidelines, 73–74
server setup process overview, 70–73
InterNotes server, 423–424, *424*
migrating from Notes Release 3 to 4, **52–56**
moving mail databases to new servers, **159–161**, *160*
naming, **73–74**
NOTES.INI settings
Server_Availability_Threshold, 543
Server_Cluster_Default_Port, 543
Server_Console_Password, 544
ServerKeyFileName, 541
Server_MaxSessions, 544
Server_MaxUsers, 544
ServerName, 541
ServerNoReplRequests, 541
ServerPullReplication, 541–542
ServerPushReplication, 542
Server_Restricted, 544–545
Server_Session_Timeout, 545
ServerSetup, 542
Server_Show_Performance, 545
ServerTasks, 542
ServerTasksAt[Time], 543
versus operating systems, 4–5
replicating database design templates to all servers, 177
replicating databases to all servers, 176–177
replication between servers, **269–272**
Pull Only replication, 271–272, *272*
Pull-Pull replication, 269–270, *269*
Pull-Push replication, 270, *270*
Push Only replication, 271, *271*
replication between workstations and servers, **272**
selecting registration server in individual user registration, 128, *128*
selecting registration server in multiple user registration, 141
selecting server platforms, **26–34**
NetWare NLM, 28
with NotesBench utility, 32–34
OS/2 Warp and Warp Server, 30
overview of, 26
UNIX, 29
Windows 95, 27
Windows NT, 31–32
server access control, **223–232**
forcing password changes, 231
physical security, 224
port access control, 232
with Server Document fields, 226–232, *227*, *230*
validation and authentication, 224–226
Server Configuration documents, 494, *494*
server console
defined, **6**, *6*
entering server console commands from, 501–503, *502*
Remote Server Console screen, 198, *198*, 498–501, *499*, *500*
server console commands, **498–506**
for Administration Process, 117–118
entering from Notes clients, **498–501**, *499*, *500*
entering from the server console, **501–503**, *502*
listed, **503–506**
Load HTTP, 463
Load Object Collect, 364, 365
Load Object Create, 363
Load Object Set -Never, 363
Load Object Unlink, 365
Load Replica, 297, *298*
Load Web, 425, *425*
Remote Server Console screen, 198, *198*, **498–501**, *499*, *500*
Show Time, 374, *374*
Tell Router Exit, 326
Tell Router Use, 361, 364

troubleshooting replication problems, 317–318, *318*
Updall, 214–215
server tasks
Events server task, 103–104
HTTP server task, 452, 453
Mail Router server task, 326
Report server task, 110
Web server task, 425, *425*
server-based Web Navigator setup, **419–425**
loading Web server task, 424–425, *425*
in Server document, 419–423, *419*, 424, *425*
specifying InterNotes server location, 423–424, *424*
starting, **80–84**
NetWare servers, 82–83
OS/2 servers, 81–82
UNIX servers, 83–84
Windows NT servers, 80–81
Statistics Reporting, **109–112**
configuring statistics reporting, 111–112
loading Report server task, 110
monitoring replication, 310
setting up, 109

Lotus Notes Web Navigator, 418–450. *See also* Lotus Notes Domino server
Netscape Navigator or Internet Explorer
importing bookmarks from, 448
selecting as default browser, 440
versus Web Navigator, 418–419
overview of, 418–419, 450
Personal Web Navigator database, **433, 442–448**
creating, 433
creating Web Tours, 448
forwarding Web pages, 444
importing bookmarks from Netscape Navigator or Internet Explorer, 448
opening Web pages, 443, *443*
Page Minder agent and, 435–436, *436*, 446–447
saving Web pages, 443–444
searching in, 444–445, *445*
searching View pane, 445, *445*
viewing HTML document source code, 445–446
Web Ahead agent and, 435, 447–448
protocols and, 418–419
server-based Web Navigator setup, **419–425**
loading Web server task, 424–425, *425*
in Server document, 419–423, *419*, 424, *425*
specifying InterNotes server location, 423–424, *424*
troubleshooting, **449–450**
Web Retriever database (WEB.NSF), **425–432**
Access Control List settings, 426–427, *426*
activating Purge Agent, 431–432
and loading Web server task, 425
Refresh Agent setup, 432
Web Navigator Administration document, **427–432**, *428*
Web Navigator Administration document HTML Preferences section, 429
Web Navigator Administration document Purge Agent Settings section, 430–431
Web Navigator Administration document Server Basics section, 428–429
workstation-based Web Navigator setup, **433–442**
creating Personal Web Navigator database, 433
Internet Options profile, **433–438**
Internet Options profile Collaborations Options section, 437, *437*
Internet Options profile Database Purge Options section, 436–437
Internet Options profile Network Preferences section, 438
Internet Options profile Page Minder Agent Preferences section, 435–436, *436*
Internet Options profile Presentation Preferences section, 437–438
Internet Options profile Search Options section, 435
Internet Options profile Setup Options section, 434
Internet Options profile Web Ahead Agent Preferences section, 435
Location document, **423–424, 438–442**, *438*

Location document Basics section, 439–440, *440*
Location document Internet Browser and Servers section, 423–424, *424*, 440
Location document Java Applet Security section, 441–442, *442*
Proxy Server Configuration dialog box, 439–440, *440*
Lotus NotesBench utility, 32–34
Lotus Organizer. *See* calendaring and scheduling
Lotus Premium Business Partners, 32–33, 482
Lotus Web sites, 485, 561–562

M

Macintosh computers as Notes client platforms, 34, 36
macros. *See* Agent Manager
magazines about Lotus Notes, 567
mail. *See* Lotus Notes Mail
Mail Address Encryption Key dialog box, 178, *179*
Mail Transfer Agents (MTAs) for cc:Mail, SMTP, and X.400, 356
MailClusterFailover NOTES.INI setting, 530
MailCompactDisabled NOTES.INI setting, 530
MailDisablePriority NOTES.INI setting, 531
MailDynamicCostReset NOTES.INI setting, 531
MailEncryptIncoming NOTES.INI setting, 531
Mail-In Database documents, 182–183, *183*, 491, *491*
mailing list for Lotus Notes, 562–565. *See also* administration resources
overview of, 562
retrieving messages from a specific day, 564–565
searching for a specific topic, 565
sending messages to, 563
subscribing to, 563
temporarily shutting off, 564
unsubscribing to, 563
Mail_Log_To_MiscEvents NOTES.INI setting, 533
MailLowPriorityTime NOTES.INI setting, 531
MailMaxThreads NOTES.INI setting, 532
Mail_Retry_Delay NOTES.INI setting, 533
MailServer NOTES.INI setting, 532
MailSystem NOTES.INI setting, 532
MailTimeout NOTES.INI setting, 532
MailTimeoutMinutes NOTES.INI setting, 532
main documents in databases, 205
Manager database access level, 174, 240–241
manually initiating replication, 289–290, *290*, *291*
Mapping subsection, Server document HTTP Server section, 459–461, *460*
Mastering Lotus Notes 4, 566
maximum database size, 170–173, *170*, *172*
Medium encryption, 265
Meetings view, 395, *395*. *See also* calendaring and scheduling
Memory_Quota NOTES.INI setting, 533
merging encryption keys with user IDs, 181–182, *182*
Mesh network topology, 21–22, *22*
Mesh replication topology, 279
messages. *See also* Lotus Notes Mail
message priority levels for mail, 360–361
for replication errors, 314–315
sending to Notes List Server, 563
Microsoft Internet Explorer. *See also* Lotus Notes Web Navigator
importing bookmarks from, 448
selecting as default browser, 440
versus Web Navigator, 418–419
Microsoft Windows 3.1x Notes clients, 34
Microsoft Windows 95
as a Notes client platform, 34
as a Notes server platform, 27
Microsoft Windows NT Notes clients, 35
Microsoft Windows NT Notes servers. *See also* Lotus Notes servers
creating NT accounts with Notes users, 129
overview of, 31–32
starting, 80–81
migrating from Notes Release 3 to 4, 44–67
migration plan implementation, **50–66**
database and application migration, 65–66
mail database migration, 59–65, *65*
migration rehearsal, 51
overview of, 50–51
Public Address Book conversion form, 62–65, *65*

Public Address Book replication settings, 55, *56*
Public Address Book upgrades, 53–56
replica mail database upgrades, 65
server migration, 52–56
user training, 57
workstation migration, 57–58
planning, **44–50**
creating a current environment inventory, 47
creating a migration plan, 50
creating a migration team, 47–48
creating a test environment, 48–49
evaluating the new release, 45–47
hardware upgrades and, 47
overview of, 44–45
training technical support organizations, 49
post migration activities, **66–67**
migration team debriefing, 66
updating Notes standards document, 67
missing database response documents, finding, 205–206
ModemFileDirectory NOTES.INI setting, 533
monitoring. *See also* Events Monitoring; logs; Statistics Reporting
database activity, 206–208, *207*
replication, **307–313**
creating a monitoring routine, 312–313
with Event tasks, 310
with Notes Logs, 308–309
with Replication History dialog box, 311, *311*, *312*
with Reporter tasks, 310
motherboard failures, 95–96
moving
databases, 209–211, *210*
mail databases to new servers, 159–161, *160*
users in the organizational hierarchy, 156–159
MTAs (Mail Transfer Agents) for cc:Mail, SMTP, and X.400, 356
multiple replicators, enabling, 295–297, *296*, *297*, *298*
multiple Web site hosting with Domino server, 463–467
multiprotocol environments, controlling what gets replicated in, 306
multi-threaded mail routing, 357–358
multi-user platform, Notes as a, 2–3

N

Name_Change_Expiration_Days NOTES.INI setting, 534
Names dialog box, 402–403
Names NOTES.INI setting, 533–534
naming
hierarchical naming schemes
creating, 25–26
moving users in, 156–159
Notes servers, 73–74
renaming users, 153–156, *154*, *156*
navigating Calendar view, 396–398, *397*, *398*
Netscape Navigator. *See also* Lotus Notes Web Navigator
importing bookmarks from, 448
selecting as default browser, 440
versus Web Navigator, 418–419
NetWare Notes servers. *See also* Lotus Notes servers
overview of, 28
starting, 82–83
Network Preferences section, Internet Options profile, 438
networks. *See* Lotus Notes networks
New Copy command, File menu Database submenu, 169, 210
New Database dialog box, 376, *376*
new features in Notes Release 4.5, 7–9
New Replica dialog box, 167–168, *168*
NewMailInterval NOTES.INI setting, 534
NewMailTune NOTES.INI setting, 534
newsgroups about Lotus Notes, 565
No Access database access level, 173, 239
NoDesignMenu NOTES.INI setting, 534
NoExternalApps NOTES.INI setting, 535

No_Force_Activity_Logging NOTES.INI setting, *535–536*
NoMailMenu NOTES.INI setting, *535*
North American encryption type, 129
Not for Public Viewing option, Calendar Entry form, 401, 407
not responding to meeting Invitations, 414, *414*
Notes. *See* Lotus Notes
NOTES.INI file, 508–550
  editing, **508–511**, *509*
  enabling multiple replicators in, 296
  loading Web server task, 425, *425*
  location of on various Notes platforms, **511**
  multi-threaded mail routing settings, 358
  replication settings, 318–321
  settings, **511–550**
    ActionPaneEnabled, 512
    Admin, 512
    Admin_Access, 513
    AdminPInterval, 512
    AdminPModifyPersonDocumentsAt, 512
    Allow_Access, 513
    Allow_Access_[Portname], 513
    Allow_Passthru_Access, 513
    Allow_Passthru_Callers, 514
    Allow_Passthru_Clients, 514
    Allow_Passthru_Targets, 514
    AMgr_DisableMailLookup, 514
    AMgr_DocUpdateAgentMinInterval, 515
    AMgr_DocUpdateEventDelay, 515
    AMgr_NewMailEventDelay, 515
    AMgr_WeekendDays, 515
    AppleTalkNameServer, 516
    AutoLogoffMinutes, 516
    BillingAddinOutput, 516
    BillingAddinRuntime, 516
    BillingAddinWakeup, 517
    BillingClass, 517
    BillingSuppressTime, 517
    CertificateExpChecked, 518
    CertifierIDFile, 518
    COM[number], 518–519
    Config_DB, 519
    Console_Loglevel, 519
    Create_File_Access, 519
    Create_Replica_Access, 520
    CTF, 520
    DDE_Timeout, 520
    Default_Index_Lifetime_Days, 520
    Deny_Access, 520–521
    Deny_Access_[Portname], 521
    Desktop, 521
    Directory, 521
    Domain, 521
    DST, 522
    DST_Begin_Date, 522
    DST_End_Date, 522
    DSTlaw, 522
    EditExpnumber, 523
    EditImp, 523
    EmptyTrash, 524
    ExtMgr_AddIn, 524
    FileDlgDirectory, 524
    Fixup_Tasks, 524
    FT_Intl_Settings, 525
    FT_Max_Instances, 525
    FTV_Fields_[database], 524–525
    FTV_Max_Fields, 525
    KeyFilename, 525
    KillProcess, 526
    KitType, 526
    LAN[number], 526
    Location, 526
    Log, 527
    Log_AgentManager, 527
    Log_MailRouting, 527–528
    Log_Replication, 528
    Log_Sessions, 529
    Log_Tasks, 529
    Log_Update, 529
    Log_View_Events, 530
    MailClusterFailover, 530
    MailCompactDisabled, 530

MailDisablePriority, 531
MailDynamicCostReset, 531
MailEncryptIncoming, 531
Mail_Log_To_MiscEvents, 533
MailLowPriorityTime, 531
MailMaxThreads, 532
Mail_Retry_Delay, 533
MailServer, 532
MailSystem, 532
MailTimeout, 532
MailTimeoutMinutes, 532
Memory_Quota, 533
ModemFileDirectory, 533
Name_Change_Expiration_Days, 534
Names, 533–534
NewMailInterval, 534
NewMailTune, 534
NoDesignMenu, 534
NoExternalApps, 535
No_Force_Activity_Logging, 535–536
NoMailMenu, 535
NSF_Buffer_Pool_Size, 536
NSF_DbCache_Disable, 536
NSF_DbCache_Maxentries, 536
OS2DDE_[Command], 536–537
Passthru_Hangup_Delay, 537
Passthru_Loglevel, 537
PhoneLog, 537
POP3Domain, 538
POP3Port, 538
POP3_Enable_SSL, 538
Ports, 538
ProgramMode, 538–539
Repl_Error_Tolerance, 539
ReplicationTimeLimit, 539
Replicators, 539
Repl_Push_Retries, 539
ReportUseMail, 539–540
RTR_Cached_Handle_Disable, 540
RTR_Logging, 540
SecureMail, 540
Server_Availability_Threshold, 543
Server_Cluster_Default_Port, 543
Server_Console_Password, 544
ServerKeyFileName, 541
Server_MaxSessions, 544
Server_MaxUsers, 544
ServerName, 541
ServerNoReplRequests, 541
ServerPullReplication, 541–542
ServerPushReplication, 542
Server_Restricted, 544–545
Server_Session_Timeout, 545
ServerSetup, 542
Server_Show_Performance, 545
ServerTasks, 542
ServerTasksAt[Time], 543
Setup, 545
Shared_Mail, 546
SwapPath, 546
TCPIP_PortMapping*NN*, 546–547
TCPIP_TCPIPAddress, 547
TimeZone, 547
Update_No_BRP_Files, 547–548
Updaters, 547
Update_Suppression_Limit, 548
Update_Suppression_Time, 548
UseFontMapper, 548
ViewExpnumber, 548–549
ViewImpnumber, 549
Window_Title, 549
WinInfoboxPos, 549
XPC_Console, 550

Notes Logs. *See also* disaster prevention; logs
database size and, 170
defined, **99–101**, *99*, *101*
versus Events Monitoring, 102–103
monitoring database activity, 207–208
monitoring replication, 308–309
troubleshooting replication problems, 316–317

The Notes Report, 567

NotesBench utility, 32–34

notifying users about the new database, 185–186, *187*
.NSF file extension, 191
NSF_Buffer_Pool_Size NOTES.INI setting, 536
NSF_DbCache_Disable NOTES.INI setting, 536
NSF_DbCache_Maxentries NOTES.INI setting, 536

O

Open Database dialog box, 169, 197, 210
Open File Manager program, 557
Open URL dialog box, 443, *443*
opening Web pages, 443, *443*
operating systems versus Notes servers, 4–5
Operational Information subsection, Server document HTTP Server section, *456*, 458–459
organizational unit certifiers, creating, 84–86
Organizer. *See* calendaring and scheduling
orphan documents in databases, 205–206
OS2DDE_[Command] NOTES.INI setting, 536–537
OS/2 Notes clients, 35
OS/2 Notes servers. *See also* Lotus Notes servers
  overview of, 30
  starting, 81–82
Other options, Replication Settings dialog box, 303, *304*

P

Page Minder agent, 435–436, *436*, 446–447
parent documents in databases, 205–206
Passthru_Hangup_Delay NOTES.INI setting, 537
Passthru_Loglevel NOTES.INI setting, 537
passwords. *See also* security
  forcing password changes for server access, 231
  selecting in individual user registration, 130–131
  selecting in multiple user registration, 143
  Server_Console_Password NOTES.INI setting, 544
peer-to-peer network topology
  defined, **19**, *20*
  and setting up Notes Mail, 333–335, *333*, *334*
peer-to-peer replication topology, 279
Pencil In option, Calendar Entry form, 400, 406, 409, 412
Person documents, 492, *492*
Personal Address Book. *See also* Public Address Book
  inviting people to meetings with, 402–403
  Location documents, **423–424, 438–442, 491**
    Basics section, 439–440, *440*
    defined, **491**
    Internet Browser and Servers section, 423–424, *424*, 440
    Java Applet Security section, 441–442, *442*
    overview of, 438, *438*
    for workstation-to-server replication, 291–292
Personal Web Navigator database, 433, 442–448. *See also* Lotus Notes Web Navigator
  creating, 433
  creating Web Tours, 448
  forwarding Web pages, 444
  importing bookmarks from Netscape Navigator or Internet Explorer, 448
  opening Web pages, 443, *443*
  Page Minder agent and, 435–436, *436*, 446–447
  saving Web pages, 443–444
  searching in, 444–445, *445*
  searching View pane, 445, *445*
  viewing HTML document source code, 445–446
  Web Ahead agent and, 435, 447–448
phone numbers for Certified Lotus Professional program, 485
PhoneLog NOTES.INI setting, 537
physical security for Notes servers, 224
planning Notes 3 to 4 migration, 44–50
  creating a current environment inventory, 47
  creating a migration plan, 50
  creating a migration team, 47–48
  creating a test environment, 48–49
  evaluating the new release, 45–47
  hardware upgrades and, 47
  overview of, 44–45
  training technical support organizations, 49
planning Notes Mail setup, 335

planning Notes networks, 14–42
creating hierarchical naming schemes, 25–26
creating Notes standards documents, **24–26**
creating a roll-out plan, **37–42**
allocating time for the roll-out, 37–38
creating Notes infrastructure, 39–40
determining who gets Notes first, 40
selecting a Notes feature to focus on, 41
supporting the infrastructure and users, 41–42
training users, 40–41
defining business purpose for, **15–17**
example, 16–17
overview of, 14
selecting Notes client platforms, **34–36**
selecting Notes server platforms, **26–34**
NetWare NLM, 28
with NotesBench utility, 32–34
OS/2 Warp and Warp Server, 30
overview of, 26
UNIX, 29
Windows 95, 27
Windows NT, 31–32
topologies, **17–24**
End-to-End (or peer-to-peer) topologies, 19, *20*, 333–335, *333*, *334*
example, 23, *24*
Hub and Spoke topologies, 18–19, *18*, *19*, *20*, 332–333, *332*
importance of, 22–23
Mesh topologies, 21–22, *22*
overview of, 17–18
Ring topologies, 21, *21*
planning replication, 276–280
determining which databases to replicate, 276–277
End-to-End replication topology, 279
Hub and Spoke replication topology, 278–279, *278*
Mesh replication topology, 279
Ring replication topology, 279
selecting replication topologies, 280
POP3 (Post Office Protocol) protocol. *See also* protocols
POP3 mail support, 357
POP3Domain NOTES.INI setting, 538
POP3Port NOTES.INI setting, 538
POP3_Enable_SSL NOTES.INI setting, 538
ports
controlling port access, 232
Ports NOTES.INI setting, 538
post migration activities, 66–67. *See also* Lotus Notes 3 to 4 migration
migration team debriefing, 66
updating Notes standards document, 67
power failures, 96
preparing for Certified Lotus Professional exams, 480–481
Presentation Preferences section, Internet Options profile, 437–438
preventing
mail routing, 359–360
replication and save conflicts, 275, *275*
Principal Application Developer certification, 479
priority levels for mail messages, 360–361
private key encryption, 264–265
profiles. *See also* users
Calendar Profile documents, **379–383**
Advanced Calendar Options section, 382–383, *382*
Allow Other Users to View Your Calendar option, 384
Autoprocessing Options section, 382–383, *382*
Calendar Entry Options section, *382*, 383
defined, **379**, *380*
Freetime Options section, 381, *381*
Scheduling Options section, 380
Delegation Profile documents, **384–387**
Calendar Access section, 385
defined, **384–385**, *384*
Email Access section, 385–387, *386*
Internet Options profile, **433–438**
Collaborations Options section, 437, *437*
Database Purge Options section, 436–437
Network Preferences section, 438
Page Minder Agent Preferences section, 435–436, *436*

Presentation Preferences section, 437–438
Search Options section, 435
Setup Options section, 434
Web Ahead Agent Preferences section, 435
Site Profiles in calendaring and scheduling, 376–377
user profiles
selecting in individual user registration, 132
selecting in multiple user registration, 143
User Setup Profile documents, 495, *495*
Program documents, 492, *492*
ProgramMode NOTES.INI setting, 538–539
programs. *See* applications; utilities
programs for Lotus certification. *See* Certified Lotus Professional (CLP) program
Properties dialog box
Database section, 185, *185*, 192–193, *193*, 196, 206, *206*, 208–209, *209*
Field section, 258–259, *259*
Folder section, 256–257, *257*, *258*
Form section, 251–254, *252*, *253*, 275, *275*
Section section, 258
View section, 254–256, *255*
protocols
controlling what gets replicated in multiprotocol environments, 306
HTTP (Hypertext Transfer Protocol)
HTTP server task, 452, 453
Load HTTP console command, 463
POP3 (Post Office Protocol)
POP3 mail support, 357
POP3Domain NOTES.INI setting, 538
POP3Port NOTES.INI setting, 538
POP3_Enable_SSL NOTES.INI setting, 538
Secure Sockets Layer (SSL), **469–472**, *471*, *472*
TCP/IP
TCPIP_PortMapping*NN* NOTES.INI setting, 546–547
TCPIP_TCPIPAddress NOTES.INI setting, 547
Web Navigator and, 418–419
Web Navigator and, 418–419
Proxy Configuration section, Server Connection document, 419–421, *419*
Proxy Server Configuration dialog box, 439–440, *440*
Public Address Book. *See also* Lotus Notes Mail; Personal Address Book
access roles for, 262–264
assigning administrative servers to, 113–114
autoaddressing feature, 402–403
defined, **325**
inviting people to meetings with, 402–403
mail database migration using Public Address Book conversion form, 62–65, *65*
replication settings, *55*, *56*
Server document, server-based Web Navigator setup, 419–423, *419*, 424, *425*
settings for first Notes server installation, 77
updating design of, 53
upgrading, 53–56
upgrading mail databases with Public Address Book forms, 62–65, *65*
public key encryption, 264–265
Pull Only replication, 271–272, *272*
Pull-Pull replication, 269–270, *269*
Pull-Push replication, 270, *270*
Purge Agent in Web Navigator, 430–432
purging shared mail, 364
Push Only replication, 271, *271*

Q

Quick Search dialog box, 445, *445*
Qxcom Registration/Exchange program, 553

R

Reader database access level, 173, 240
recertification for Notes 3 professionals, 482–485
ReCor network-based computer training courses, 40, 552–553
Refresh Agent in Web Navigator, 432
refreshing database designs, 195–199, *198*

ServerPullReplication, 541–542
ServerPushReplication, 542
planning, **276–280**
determining which databases to replicate, 276–277
End-to-End replication topology, 279
Hub and Spoke replication topology, 278–279, *278*
Mesh replication topology, 279
Ring replication topology, 279
selecting replication topologies, 280
replica tasks
defined, **268**, *269*
loading, 297, *298*
replicating
database design templates to all servers, 177
databases to all servers, 176–177
replication conflicts and save conflicts, 274–275, *275*
Replication Settings dialog box, **300–307**
Advanced options, 303–305, *304*
Other options, 303, *304*
overview of, 300–301
Public Address Book settings, 55, *56*
scenarios, 305–307
Send options, 302–303, *302*
Space Savers options, 301–302, *301*
Replication submenu, File menu
Replicate command, 281
Settings command, 301
Replicator workspace, 292–295, *292*
between servers, **269–272**
Pull Only replication, 271–272, *272*
Pull-Pull replication, 269–270, *269*
Pull-Push replication, 270, *270*
Push Only replication, 271, *271*
troubleshooting, **313–321**
Access Control List problems, 316, 317–318, *318*
console command problems, 317–318, *318*
error messages, 314–315
examples, 315–318, *318*
NOTES.INI replication settings, 318–321
Notes Log problems, 316–317
when replication isn't happening, 313–314
upgrading replica mail database, 65
what gets replicated, **272–274**
between workstations and servers, **272**
ReplicationTimeLimit NOTES.INI setting, 539
Replicators NOTES.INI setting, 539
Repl_Push_Retries NOTES.INI setting, 539
ReportUseMail NOTES.INI setting, 539–540
reservations, creating in calendaring and scheduling, 377–378
reserving rooms for meetings, 405, 415
Resource documents, 492, *492*
Resource Reservations database, 375–376, *376*
resources for administrators, 560–567
books, 566
on CompuServe, 566
Lotus technical support, 560–561
magazines, 567
Notes List Server, **562–565**
overview of, 562
retrieving messages from a specific day, 564–565
searching for a specific topic, 565
sending messages to, 563
subscribing to, 563
temporarily shutting off, 564
unsubscribing to, 563
Usenet newsgroups, 565
on the World Wide Web, 561–562
resources in calendaring and scheduling
changing or deleting, 378
creating, 377
creating resource reservations, 377–378
reserving rooms for meetings, 405, 415
responding to Invitations, 410–414, *410*, *411*, *413*, *414*
response documents in databases, 205–206
RESRC45.NTF file (Resource Reservations template), 375–376
Results Database dialog box, 201–202, *202*
retrieving Notes List Server messages from a specific day, 564–565

Ring network topology, 21, *21*
Ring replication topology, 279
roles. *See also* Access Control Lists (ACLs)
overview of, **249–250**
for Public Address Book, 262–264
Roles section of Access Control List dialog box, 244–246, *246*
rolling out
creating Notes roll-out plans, **37–42**. *See also* Lotus Notes networks
allocating time for the roll-out, 37–38
creating Notes infrastructure, 39–40
determining who gets Notes first, 40
selecting a Notes feature to focus on, 41
supporting the infrastructure and users, 41–42
training users, 40–41
databases, **166–187**
copying new databases to Notes servers, 167–170, *168*, *169*
creating Database catalogs, 183–184, *184*
creating Mail-In Database documents, 182–183, *183*
distributing encryption keys, 177–182, *178*, *179*, *181*
including databases in the Database Catalog, 183–185, *185*
merging encryption keys with user IDs, 181–182, *182*
notifying users about the new database, 185–186, *187*
overview of, 166–167
replicating database design templates to all servers, 177
replicating databases to all servers, 176–177
setting Access Control Lists (ACLs), 173–176, *175*, *176*, 216
setting maximum database size, 170–173, *170*, *172*
rooms. *See* resources in calendaring and scheduling
routing mail, 339–358. *See also* Lotus Notes Mail
between adjacent domains, 346–349, *347*, *348*
cc:Mail, SMTP, and X.400 Message Transfer Agents, 356
connecting with foreign domains, 354–357, *355*
controlling mail routing, **358–361**
message priority levels, 360–361
options to prevent mail routing, 359–360
overview of, 358–359
creating Server Connection documents for, 344–346
Mail Router server task, **326**
multi-threaded mail routing, 357–358
between non-adjacent domains, 349–353, *350*, *351*, *353*
between Notes named networks, 340–346, *342*, *343*
POP3 mail support, 357
within Notes named networks, 339–340, *340*, *341*
RSA Cryptosystem, 264
RTR_Cached_Handle_Disable NOTES.INI setting, 540
RTR_Logging NOTES.INI setting, 540
running
database analyses, 199–204, *202*, *203*
Domino server, 463

S

Saint Bernard Software Open File Manager program, 557
save conflicts, 274–275, *275*
saving Web pages, 443–444
Schedule Manager (SCHED.EXE), 373–374, *374*
scheduling. *See also* calendaring and scheduling
replication with Server Connection document, 285–289, *286*
Scheduling Options section, Calendar Profile documents, 380
Search Options section, Internet Options profile, 435
searching
in Personal Web Navigator database, 444–445, *445*
for a specific Notes List Server topic, 565
section access control, 258
Secure Sockets Layer (SSL) protocol, 469–472, *471*, *472*
security, 222–266. *See also* disaster planning; disaster prevention

Access Control Lists (ACLs), **173–176**, **216**, **239–259**, **262–264**
access control levels, 173–174, 239–241, 298–299
Access Control List dialog box Advanced section, 247–251, *248*
Access Control List dialog box Basics section, 241–244, *241*
Access Control List dialog box Log section, 246–247, *247*
Access Control List dialog box overview, 77, 115, 175–176, *175*, 241, *241*
Access Control List dialog box Roles section, 244–246, *246*, 249–250
access roles for Public Address Book, 262–264
and controlling database replication, **298–300**
Domino server settings, 454–455, *455*
setting for databases, 173–176, *175*, *176*, 216
troubleshooting replication problems, 316, 317–318, *318*
user types and, 245
Web Retriever database settings, 426–427, *426*
Domino server security, **467–472**
anonymous access option, 468, *468*
database access control, 469
overview of, 467–468
Secure Sockets Layer (SSL) security, 469–472, *471*, *472*
user registration options, 468–469
encryption
defined, **264**
indexing encrypted fields in databases, 191
North American versus international encryption, **129**
overview of, **264–265**
private and public keys and, 264–265
RSA Cryptosystem, 264
encryption keys
distributing by e-mail, 177–179, *179*
distributing by exporting to files, 177, 179–181, *181*
ID files and, 265
merging with user IDs, 181–182, *182*
passwords and, 265
Execution Control Lists (ECLs) for workstation security, **232–239**, *237*
field access control, **258–259**, *259*
folder access control, **256–257**, *257*, *258*
form access control, **251–254**, *252*, *253*, *275*, *275*
Location document Java Applet Security section, 441–442, *442*
North American versus international encryption types, 129
overview of, 222–223, *223*, 259–260, *260*
passwords
forcing password changes for server access, 231
selecting in individual user registration, 130–131
selecting in multiple user registration, 143
Server_Console_Password NOTES.INI setting, 544
Properties dialog box
Field section, 258–259, *259*
Folder section, 256–257, *257*, *258*
Form section, 251–254, *252*, *253*, *275*, *275*
Section section, 258
View section, 254–256, *255*
section access control, **258**
Secure Sockets Layer (SSL) protocol, **469–472**, *471*, *472*
SecureMail NOTES.INI setting, 540
security quiz, **260–262**
server access, **223–232**
controlling port access, 232
controlling with Server Document fields, 226–232, *227*, *230*
forcing password changes, 231
physical security, 224
validation and authentication, 224–226
for shared mail, **362–363**
signatures, **234–237**
view access control, **254–256**, *255*
selecting
certifier IDs in individual user registration, 128–129

mail type in individual user registration, 132–133, *132*
mail type in multiple user registration, 143–144
Netscape Navigator or Internet Explorer as default browser, 440
North American versus international security types, 129
Notes client platforms, 34–36
Notes server platforms, **26–34**
NetWare NLM, 28
with NotesBench utility, 32–34
OS/2 Warp and Warp Server, 30
overview of, 26
UNIX, 29
Windows 95, 27
Windows NT, 31–32
passwords, license type, and user profiles in multiple user registration, 143
registration server in individual user registration, 128, *128*
registration server in multiple user registration, 141
replication topologies, 280
user profiles in individual user registration, 132
user profiles in multiple user registration, 143
self-certified key rings, 471–472, *472*
self-study programs for Certified Lotus Professional program, 480–481
Send options, Replication Settings dialog box, 302–303, *302*
sending
meeting confirmations to invitees, 414, *414*
messages to Notes List Server, 563
a trace for mail delivery problems, 367–370, *368*, *369*
Sentor Communications DocWatch program, *555*
Server Basics section, Web Navigator Administration document, 428–429
Server Configuration documents, 494, *494*
Server Connection documents. *See also* documents
defined, **489**, *489*
for Notes Mail
creating or editing for Notes Mail setup, 337–339, *338*
creating for mail routing, 344–346
and mail routing between adjacent domains, 346–349, *347*
and mail routing between Notes networks, 340–346, *342*
and mail routing within Notes networks, 339
scheduled replication with, 285–289, *286*
for server-based Web Navigator setup, **419–424**
Proxy Configuration section, 419–421, *419*
Server Location Information section, 424, *425*
Web Retriever Administration section, 421–423, *421*
server console
defined, **6**, *6*
entering server console commands from, 501–503, *502*
Remote Server Console screen, 198, *198*, 498–501, *499*, *500*
server console commands, 498–506
for Administration Process, 117–118
entering, **498–503**
from Notes clients, 498–501, *499*, *500*
from the server console, 501–503, *502*
listed, **503–506**
Load HTTP, 463
Load Object Collect, 364, 365
Load Object Create, 363
Load Object Set -Never, 363
Load Object Unlink, 365
Load Replica, 297, *298*
Load Web, 425, *425*
Remote Server Console screen, 198, *198*, **498–501**, *499*, *500*
Show Time, 374, *374*
Tell Router Exit, 326
Tell Router Use, 361, 364
troubleshooting replication problems, 317–318, *318*
Updall, 214–215

Server documents. *See also* documents
defined, **493–494**, *494*
HTTP Server section, **455–463**
Basics subsection, 456–458, *456*
Character Set Mapping subsection, *460*, 463
Logging subsection, *460*, 461–462
Mapping subsection, 459–461, *460*
Operational Information subsection, *456*, 458–459
overview of, 455, *456*
Timeouts subsection, *460*, 462
Security section for Domino server, 468, *468*
server-based Web Navigator setup, 419–423, *419*, 424, *425*
server tasks. *See also* Lotus Notes servers
Events server task, 103–104
HTTP server task, 452, 453
Mail Router server task, 326
Report server task, 110
Web server task, 425, *425*
Server_Availability_Threshold NOTES.INI setting, 543
Server_Cluster_Default_Port NOTES.INI setting, 543
Server_Console_Password NOTES.INI setting, 544
ServerKeyFileName NOTES.INI setting, 541
Server_MaxSessions NOTES.INI setting, 544
Server_MaxUsers NOTES.INI setting, 544
ServerName NOTES.INI setting, 541
ServerNoReplRequests NOTES.INI setting, 541
ServerPullReplication NOTES.INI setting, 541–542
ServerPushReplication NOTES.INI setting, 542
Server_Restricted NOTES.INI setting, 544–545
servers. *See* Lotus Notes Domino server; Lotus Notes servers
Server_Session_Timeout NOTES.INI setting, 545
ServerSetup NOTES.INI setting, 542
Server_Show_Performance NOTES.INI setting, 545
ServerTasks NOTES.INI setting, 542
ServerTasksAt[Time] NOTES.INI setting, 543
setting
Access Control Lists (ACLs) for databases, 173–176, *175*, *176*, 216
maximum database size, 170–173, *170*, *172*
setting up. *See also* configuring; installing; NOTES.INI file
activity logs for Domino server, 472
calendaring and scheduling, **375–378**
changing or deleting resources, 378
creating reservations, 377–378
creating Resource Reservations database, 375–376, *376*
creating resources, 377
creating Site Profiles, 376–377
calendaring and scheduling for users, **379–387**
creating Calendar Profile documents, 379–383, *380*
creating Delegation Profile documents, 384–387, *384*
training users to configure their own profiles, 387
Domino server, **454–463**. *See also* Server documents, HTTP Server section
Access Control List settings, 454–455, *455*
configuring, 455–463
system requirements, 454
Notes clients, **147–153**
adding icons to the desktop, 151–152
configuring Notes clients for Notes networks, 150–151, *151*
installation tips, 152–153
installing Notes client software, 147–150
Notes Mail, **330–339**
creating or editing Server Connection documents, 337–339, *338*
dedicated Mail servers, 336–337
End-to-End topology and, 333–335, *333*, *334*
Hub and Spoke topology and, 332–333, *332*
Notes network topology and, 331–335, *332*, *333*, *334*, *335*
planning and, 335
in simple versus complex Notes networks, 330–331
Notes servers, 70–73, 77–79, 90–92, *92*
Purge Agent in Web Navigator, 431–432
Refresh Agent in Web Navigator, 432
Statistics Reporting, 109
Setup NOTES.INI setting, 545
Setup Options section, Internet Options profile, 434

shared mail, 361–366. *See also* Lotus Notes Mail
creating shared mail databases, 363–364
deleting mail, 364–365
deleting shared mail databases, 365
enabling, 361–362
purging old mail, 364
security considerations, 362–363
Shared_Mail NOTES.INI setting, 546
when to use, 366
Show Time console command, 374, *374*
shutting off Notes List Server temporarily, 564
signatures, 234–237
Simple encryption, 265
Site Profiles in calendaring and scheduling, 376–377
SMTP Mail Transfer Agents (MTAs), 356
Space Savers options, Replication Settings dialog box, 301–302, *301*
specifying InterNotes server location, 423–424, *424*
SSL (Secure Sockets Layer) protocol, 469–472, *471*, *472*
standards documents
creating, 24–26
and naming servers, 73–74
updating, 67
starting Notes servers, 80–84
NetWare-based servers, 82–83
OS/2-based servers, 81–82
UNIX-based servers, 83–84
Windows NT-based servers, 80–81
Statistics & Events database, 103, 104–105, 109
Statistics Reporting, 109–112. *See also* disaster prevention; Lotus Notes servers
configuring statistics reporting, 111–112
loading Report server task, 110
monitoring replication, 310
setting up, 109
storing user ID files
in individual user registration, 133–134
in multiple user registration, 144
Strong encryption, 265
subscribing to Notes List Server, 563
supporting users, 41–42
SwapPath NOTES.INI setting, 546
Sylvan Prometric Testing Centers, 481–482
synchronizing database sites, 98
System Administrator certification, 479
system crashes, 94–95
system requirements for Domino server, 454

T

taking Certified Lotus Professional (CLP) examinations, 481–482, 483–484
tasks. *See also* calendaring and scheduling
defined, **392–393,** *393*, *394*
viewing tasks in Calendar view, 393
TCP/IP protocol. *See also* protocols
TCPIP_PortMapping*NN* NOTES.INI setting, 546–547
TCPIP_TCPIPAddress NOTES.INI setting, 547
Web Navigator and, 418–419
technical certification programs. *See* Certified Lotus Professional (CLP) program
technical support
for Notes 3 to 4 migration, 49
for Notes, **560–561**
telephone numbers for Certified Lotus Professional program, 485
Tell Router Exit console command, 326
Tell Router Use console command, 361, 364
templates
Domino Log template, 473, *473*
RESRC45.NTF (Resource Reservations template), 375–376
temporarily shutting off Notes List Server, 564
test environment for Notes 3 to 4 migration, 48–49
tests for Lotus certification. *See* Certified Lotus Professional (CLP) program
text logs for Domino server, 473
third-party programs. *See* add-on products
Timeouts subsection, Server document HTTP Server section, *460*, 462
TimeZone NOTES.INI setting, 547
To Do view. *See also* calendaring and scheduling
defined, **392–393,** *393*, *394*
viewing tasks in Calendar view, 393

Tools submenu, File menu, User ID command, 178
Tools to Manage Notes Databases dialog box, 171, *172*, 200–201, *200*, 211
topologies
network topologies, **17–24**. *See also* Lotus Notes networks
End-to-End (or peer-to-peer) topologies, 19, *20*, 333–335, *333*, *334*
example, 23, *24*
Hub and Spoke topology, 18–19, *18*, *19*, *20*, 332–333, *332*
importance of, 22–23
Mesh topology, 21–22, *22*
overview of, 17–18
Ring topology, 21, *21*
replication topologies
End-to-End topology, 279
Hub and Spoke topology, 278–279, *278*
Mesh topology, 279
Ring topology, 279
selecting, 280
tracing mail delivery problems, 367–370, *368*, *369*
training. *See also* Certified Lotus Professional (CLP) program
ReCor network-based computer training courses, 40, 552–553
technical support organization for Notes 3 to 4 migration, 49
users
deciding who will train users, 40–41
for Notes Release 3 to 4 migration, 57
users to configure their own calendaring and scheduling profiles, 387
troubleshooting
calendaring and scheduling, **415**
database performance problems, **215–217**
mail problems, **366–370**
delivery problems, 366–367
sending a trace for delivery problems, 367–370, *368*, *369*
meeting Invitations, **415**
replication, **313–321**
Access Control List problems, 316, 317–318, *318*
console command problems, 317–318, *318*
error messages, 314–315
examples, 315–318, *318*
NOTES.INI replication settings, 318–321
Notes Log problems, 316–317
when replication isn't happening, 313–314
Web Navigator, **449–450**

U

uninterruptible power supplies (UPSs), *96*
UNIX Notes clients, 35
UNIX Notes servers. *See also* Lotus Notes servers
overview of, 29
starting, 83–84
unsubscribing to Notes List Server, 563
Updall console command, 214–215
Update_No_BRP_Files NOTES.INI setting, 547–548
Updaters NOTES.INI setting, 547
Update_Suppression_Limit NOTES.INI setting, 548
Update_Suppression_Time NOTES.INI setting, 548
updating
database designs, 195–199, *198*
full text indexes, 192–194, *193*, *194*
standards documents, 67
upgrading. *See also* migrating from Notes Release 3 to 4
hardware for Notes 3 to 4 migration, 47
Public Address Book, 53–56
replica mail database, 65
URLs (Uniform Resource Locators)
Domino server and, 453
URL Mapping documents, 466–467, *466*
URL Redirection documents, 466–467, *466*
UseFontMapper NOTES.INI setting, 548
Usenet newsgroups about Lotus Notes, 565
User Activity dialog box, 206–208, *207*
User ID dialog box, 178, *178*
user ID files
encryption keys and, 265
merging encryption keys with user IDs, 181–182, *182*

storing in individual user registration, 133–134
storing in multiple user registration, 144
User Preferences dialog box, 328
user profiles. *See also* profiles
selecting in individual user registration, 132
selecting in multiple user registration, 143
User Setup Profile documents, 495, *495*
users, 124–164. *See also* Lotus Notes clients; workstations
Access Control Lists (ACLs) and user types, 245
creating multiple users from a file, **135–147**
creating user information files, 136–138
information you will need, 135–136
registering users from a file, 140–145, *140*
selecting mail type, 143–144
selecting passwords, license type, and user profiles, 143
selecting registration server, 141
storing user ID files, 144
user information file examples, 138–140
verifying user setup, 145–146, *146*, *147*
creating users one at a time, **125–135**
canceling user registration, 135
entering passwords, 130–131
information you will need, 125–126
selecting certifier IDs, 128–129
selecting mail type, 132–133, *132*
selecting North American versus international security types, 129
selecting Notes license types, 131
selecting registration server, 128, *128*
selecting user profiles, 132
storing user ID files, 130, 133–134
deleting, **161–163**
moving mail databases to new servers, **159–161**, *160*
moving users in the organizational hierarchy, **156–159**
Notes as a multi-user platform, 2–3
notifying about the new database, **185–186**, *187*
overview of, 124
renaming, **153–156**, *154*, *156*
setting up Notes clients, **147–153**
adding icons to the desktop, 151–152
configuring Notes clients for Notes networks, 150–151, *151*
installation tips, 152–153
installing Notes client software, 147–150
supporting, **41–42**
training
deciding who will train users, 40–41
for Notes Release 3 to 4 migration, 57
training to configure their own calendaring and scheduling profiles, 387
user mail database, **326**
user registration options in Domino server, 468–469
utilities. *See also* add-on products
e-mail conversion utility, 59–62
Fixup, 212–215, *214*
NotesBench, 32–34

validation, 224–226
V-Bridge NT for Notes software, 556
verifying multiple user setup, 145–146, *146*, *147*
view access control, 254–256, *255*
The View Notes magazine, 567
View pane, Personal Web Navigator database, 445, *445*
ViewExpnumber NOTES.INI setting, 548–549
ViewImpnumber NOTES.INI setting, 549
viewing
HTML document source code, 445–446
tasks in Calendar view, 393
Virtual Server documents, 464–467, *465*

Web Ahead agent, 435, 447–448
Web features. *See* Lotus Notes Domino server; Lotus Notes Web Navigator
Web Retriever Administration section, Server Connection document, 421–423, *421*

Web Retriever database (WEB.NSF), 425–432. *See also* Lotus Notes Web Navigator
- Access Control List settings, 426–427, *426*
- and loading Web server task, 425
- Purge Agent setup, 431–432
- Refresh Agent setup, 432
- Web Navigator Administration document, **427–432**
  - creating, 427–428, *428*
  - HTML Preferences section, 429
  - Purge Agent Settings section, 430–431
  - Server Basics section, 428–429

Web Tours, creating, 448
Window_Title NOTES.INI setting, 549
WinInfoboxPos NOTES.INI setting, 549
workspaces, Replicator workspace, 292–295, *292*
workstation-based Web Navigator setup, 433–442. *See also* Lotus Notes clients
- creating Personal Web Navigator database, 433
- Internet Options profile, **433–438**
  - Collaborations Options section, 437, *437*
  - Database Purge Options section, 436–437
  - Network Preferences section, 438
  - Page Minder Agent Preferences section, 435–436, *436*
  - Presentation Preferences section, 437–438
  - Search Options section, 435
  - Setup Options section, 434
  - Web Ahead Agent Preferences section, 435
- Location document, **423–424, 438–442,** *438*
  - Basics section, 439–440, *440*
  - Internet Browser and Servers section, 423–424, *424*, 440
  - Java Applet Security section, 441–442, *442*
- Proxy Server Configuration dialog box, 439–440, *440*

workstations. *See also* Lotus Notes clients
- Execution Control Lists (ECLs) and workstation security, **232–239,** *237*
- migrating from Notes Release 3 to 4, 57–58
- Notes license types, 131
- replication between servers and, 272
- signatures, **234–237**

World Wide Web. *See also* Lotus Notes Domino server; Lotus Notes Web Navigator
- Certified Lotus Professional program Web site, 485
- Lotus Web sites, 561–562

X.400 Mail Transfer Agents (MTAs), 356
XcelleNet RemoteWare Essentials software, 556
XPC_Console NOTES.INI setting, 550